MAPPING IN MICHIGAN
& THE GREAT LAKES REGION

MAPPING IN MICHIGAN
& THE GREAT LAKES REGION

Edited by David I. Macleod

Michigan State University Press • *East Lansing*

⊗ The paper used in this publication meets the minimum requirements
of ANSI/NISO Z39.48-1992 (R 1997) (Permanence of Paper).

 Michigan State University Press
East Lansing, Michigan 48823-5245

 1947· CELEBRATING 60 YEARS *of* ·2007
SCHOLARLY PUBLISHING

This project was funded in part by the Michigan Humanities Council,
an affiliate of the National Endowment for the Humanities, and by
the Clements Library at the University of Michigan.

Printed and bound in the United States of America.
ISBN: 978-0-87013-807-2

13 12 11 10 09 08 07   1 2 3 4 5 6 7 8 9 10

LIBRARY OF CONGRESS CATALOGING-IN-PUBLICATION DATA
Mapping in Michigan and the Great Lakes region / edited by David I. Macleod.
p. cm.
Papers originally presented at a conference held June 11–12, 2004, at Central Michigan
University.
Includes bibliographical references.
ISBN 978-0-87013-807-2 (cloth : alk. paper)
1. Cartography—Michigan—History—Congresses. 2. Cartography—Great Lakes
Region—History—Congresses. I. Macleod, David I.
GA431.M37 2007
526.09774—dc22
2007025209

Cover and book design by Sharp Des!gns, Inc., Lansing, MI

Ꮆ green Michigan State University Press is a member of the Green Press Initiative
press and is committed to developing and encouraging ecologically responsible
INITIATIVE publishing practices. For more information about the Green Press Initiative and the use
of recycled paper in book publishing, please visit *www.greenpressinitiative.org.*

Visit Michigan State University Press on the World Wide Web at *www.msupress.msu.edu*

Dedicated to George Kish

(1914–1989), distinguished professor of geography at the University of Michigan, whose enthusiasm for the history of cartography was infectious and unlimited.

Contents

ix   Acknowledgments

3   Introduction, *David Buisseret*

13   Louis Charles Karpinski and the Cartography of the Great Lakes, *Mary Sponberg Pedley*

39   First Nations Mapmaking in the Great Lakes Region in Intercultural Contexts:
A Historical Review, *G. Malcolm Lewis*

63   The 1767 Maps of Robert Rogers and Jonathan Carver: A Proposal for the Establishment
of the Colony of Michilimackinac, *Keith R. Widder*

91   Motives for Mapping the Great Lakes: Upper Canada, 1782–1827, *J. P. D. Dunbabin*

123   The Search for the Canadian-American Boundary along the Michigan Frontier, 1819–1827: The
Boundary Commissions under Articles Six and Seven of the Treaty of Ghent, *Francis M. Carroll*

145   The Holes in the Grid: Reservation Surveys in Lower Michigan, *Margaret Wickens Pearce*

173   Mapping the Grand Traverse Indian Country: The Contributions of Peter Dougherty,
Helen Hornbeck Tanner

209   Picturing Progress: Assessing the Nineteenth-Century Atlas-Map Bonanza, *Cheryl Lyon-Jenness*

241   An Evaluation of Plat, Sanborn, and Panoramic Maps of Cities and Towns in Michigan,
David K. Patton, Amy K. Lobben, and Bruce M. C. Pape

263   Tracing Euro-American Settlement Expansion in Southern Lower Michigan, *Kenneth E. Lewis*

287   The Shifting Agendas of Midwestern Official State Highway Maps, *James R. Akerman
and Daniel Block*

319   Michigan: Cartographic Perspectives on the Great Lakes State, *Gerald A. Danzer*

355   About the Contributors

357   Index

Acknowledgments

THIS PROJECT BEGAN IN MAY OF 2001 AS AN IDEA DEVELOPED BY MEMBERS OF THE board of editors of the *Michigan Historical Review*. Their enthusiasm and support have been vital over the years. As we developed the idea, we decided to emphasize the purposes or intentions that underlay mapping and cartography as a political, social, and cultural process. Indeed, the working title as I made contacts was "Motives for Mapping Michigan and the Great Lakes Region." And as readers of this volume will see, this has remained a central focus. The authors have emphasized both *why* and *how* people made maps. (See index, especially the entry for maps, purposes of.)

How did we find the appropriate scholars? For expert guidance, I met with John Dann, Mary Pedley, and Brian Dunnigan and began contacting other prominent researchers. I would like to thank the late David Woodward, David Bosse, Mark Monmonier, William Goetzmann, Edward Dahl, Robert Rundstrom, Robert Karrow, Mark Warhus, Michael Libbee, and a number of the eventual conference participants for advice and contacts. LeRoy Barnett's extensive research and publications form the foundation for almost any recent work on the history of cartography in Michigan. His influence will be evident throughout this volume, and he generously advised a number of the authors during their research.

The kickoff event was a public conference at Central Michigan University in June 2004, after which revised versions of these chapters appeared in the *Michigan Historical Review*. David Buisseret's introductory essay is, however, new to this volume. In preparing for the conference, Frank Boles took charge of important arrangements and secured a substantial grant from the Michigan Humanities Council. Chris Clare ably managed finances and conference day arrangements. Mary Graham handled registration, participants' travel plans, distribution of papers, and numberless other tasks. Then Mary skillfully copyedited all the revised articles for publication in the *MHR*.

Without the generosity of the Michigan Humanities Council, an affiliate of the National Endowment for the Humanities, the conference and this volume would have been impossible. Another major sponsor whose backing was vital is the William L. Clements Library of the University of Michigan. John Dann, the library's director, supplied valuable help and enthusiasm. And both the conference and the book project received significant support from the George Kish Fund of the Clements Library. Professor Kish was a noted expert in the history of cartography whose memory this volume honors. Generous assistance also came from Michigan State University Press, the Historical Society of Michigan, the Michigan Geographic Alliance, and the Michigan Map Society.

MAPPING IN MICHIGAN
& THE GREAT LAKES REGION

Introduction

David Buisseret

THERE ARE MANY DIFFERENT APPROACHES TO UNDERSTANDING HOW A GIVEN GEO-graphical area has been mapped. The simplest approach is also the oldest and consists of listing, and sometimes reproducing, the sequence of printed maps of the region. Enumerations of this kind have been made for many areas, including countries such as Spain,[1] islands such as those of the Caribbean,[2] or states such as Texas.[3] Sometimes the sequence of printed maps can be expanded to include a greater variety of maps, as in the case of a list of maps of Scotland, which includes many different kinds of thematic maps.[4]

A more subtle approach would include not only printed maps but also their manuscript precursors. Here the earliest example seems to be Carl I. Wheat's great five-volume analysis of the *Mapping the Transmississippi West, 1540–1861*,[5] which with its reproductions and extensive commentary remains a wonderful tool for understanding the mapping of a huge geographical area during more than four centuries. Another example of this approach would be William P. Cumming's *The Southeast in Early Maps* or two recent works on Louisiana and Virginia,[6] which also make exemplary use of a wide range of maps, both manuscript and printed. In Michigan, the nearest equivalent would be Louis Karpinski's *Bibliography of the Printed Maps of Michigan, 1804–1860*,[7] which in spite of its title also included considerable analysis of the earlier manuscript maps. Indeed, in this as in many other respects, the mathematician Karpinski was far ahead of his time, as Mary Pedley shows here in the chapter called "Louis Charles Karpinski and the Cartography of the Great Lakes." Perhaps because he lived before the days of excessive specialization, Karpinski demonstrated an astonishing range of talent and interest. Scholars have been interested not only in his major published work but also in his remarkable collection of map reproductions made from the European archives in the period between the world wars. Many of the great research libraries of North America contain collections of these photostats, even if they are not very well or uniformly catalogued. Their value lies partly in the fact that they contain material that has now been lost, misplaced, or destroyed, so that they are now the unique record for some important maps. Their significance was recently well demonstrated by the work of Texas scholar Jack Jackson, whose *Manuscript Maps Concerning the Gulf Coast, Texas and the Southwest (1519–1836)*[8] tellingly set out their sequence for a large part of the country, relating them to a variety of other maps. Jackson also grappled with the problem of the present location of the originals, though he did not go so far as to establish any sort of union listing of the holdings of the various North American repositories; this would form a useful and interesting research project.

So far we have been considering assessments of various geographical regions as a whole, taking account of what are generally nonthematic maps. But recent years have seen still more sophisticated surveys, which attempt to cover the whole variety of maps generated within a given region. An example of this would be the history of English mapping by Catherine Delano-Smith and Roger Kain, *English Maps: A History.*[9] Although this survey leaves out some kinds of maps—maritime charts and military surveys, for example—it does take a very wide range of cartographic activity into account. More recently, Rinaldo Comba and Paola Sereno have edited the same kind of wide survey of the early mapping of the state of Savoy.[10]

The collection of papers in this volume tries to offer a similarly inclusive coverage. Indeed, it has an advantage over the surveys of England and of Savoy in that it is able to start with indigenous mapping. G. Malcolm Lewis, who has written widely on this theme,[11] offers an overview of "First Nations maps" of the Great Lakes region. He is careful not to assert that such maps existed in written form before the coming of the Europeans, though he makes it clear that in words and models, much European information was generated from existing Indian cartographic knowledge; indeed, this dependence of early European explorers on indigenous informants has been one of the major new perceptions of the past few decades in the history of cartography. Maps eventually solicited from the Indians were hard for European eyes to decipher, since they relied on an unfamiliar spatial perception and did not, for instance, place much emphasis on the delineation of shorelines. The heritage of Indian mapping was thus a subtle one. But its existence has long been known to western scholars, and Lewis made the remarkable observation that as early as 1856, the German-born geographer Johann Kohl had been pressing for the preservation of what he called "aboriginal productions." It has taken a great many years for the importance of this observation to reach the general public, if indeed it has yet done so, even after the publication of several recent volumes.[12] Kohl, like Karpinski, was also remarkable for collecting copies of manuscript maps made by the Europeans—and usually conserved in Europe—of the New World. But whereas Karpinski was able to use the new photographic methods of copying, Kohl had to rely on scribes in order to assemble his five hundred copies of maps of America.[13]

The very complicated, not to say improbable, shape of the Great Lakes meant that European cartographers had a great deal of trouble in mastering even their approximate outline. From the early sketches of Champlain in the 1630s, to the more precise maps of the Jesuits in the 1670s and Coronelli around 1690, it was a long process, marked moreover by frequent loss of what had previously been accurately observed. By the middle of the eighteenth century, though, Jacques-Nicholas Bellin was able to provide a convincing general impression of the outline of all five lakes. At this point, local cartographers began to offer particular versions of smaller parts of the region, often in order to advance their political agendas.

The position on the Great Lakes in the late 1760s was rather like that on the Franco-Spanish frontier west of the Mississippi River in the eighteenth century, when adventurers did their best to turn national policies, decided upon in distant European capitals, to their own advantage. In the area of what would become Michigan, among the chief of these adventurers was Robert Rogers. Keith Widder describes how Rogers, in Michilimackinac, did his best to circumvent his superior, Thomas Gage, in New York, in an attempt to establish Michilimackinac as the center of a new British empire in North America. Drawing on the ideas of J. B. Harley, Widder explains how Rogers used cartography to advance the argument he made—over Gage's head—to London. Rogers's map thus showed a great deal of empty space (in reality filled with Indian groups) around Michilimackinac, which thus seemed poised to become the new British headquarters, leaving Gage on the eastern seaboard in a position of reduced importance. Rogers's map compares interestingly with that of Jonathan Carver, who took pains on his map, compiled at the same time, to set out the lands of various Indian groups, which he identified as "kingdoms." Here again, nomenclature was pressed into service for political aims, for on the printed version of Carver's map the significance of the Indian units was much reduced. The outcome of the Revolutionary War eventually put an end to the dreams of Rogers and other frontier adventurers.

The emergence of the United States gave rise to a new set of cartographic problems. Relying largely on maps found in Joan Winearls's *Mapping Upper Canada, 1780–1867*,[14] John Dunbabin explains how numerous maps were generated after the peace of 1783. Some were designed to elucidate a boundary agreed upon only verbally; others aimed to delineate lands on which both Indian allies and a flood of northbound Loyalists might be settled. The boundary was so long, and its geography so complex, that many problems remained after the 1790s. The peace of 1814 engendered a fresh crop of surveys, including those of a binational commission, which ran a line from the Bay of Fundy in the east to the Lake of the Woods in the west. Considerable progress was made, particularly when the Royal Navy's Hydrographic Office took a hand in reviewing existing charts and generating new ones. The work of Henry Bayfield, in particular, set out the shoreline parts of the Great Lakes with a new precision; indeed, it was not until his surveys that the distinctive shape of the glacier-formed Lake Huron and Georgian Bay came to be understood. Still, the continent was huge, and even after the eastern half of the U.S.-Canadian border had been more or less understood, the western half long remained stubborn. So it was that as late as 1846, the boundary in what is now British Columbia had been defined only verbally; actual identification of the border on the ground was eventually confided to the emissaries of the German emperor in 1871.

In "The Search for the Canadian-American Boundary," Francis Carroll looks in detail at the work of the commissioners charged with identifying the boundary agreed upon at the Treaty of Ghent in 1814. The work was not entirely completed until 1842, but Carroll's account makes it clear that the commissioners succeeded in collaborating very effectively. These surveyors and their work are reminiscent of the U.S.-Mexican commission that determined the two countries' boundary after the peace of Guadalupe Hidalgo in 1848. Recently analyzed by Paula Rebert in *La Gran Línea: Mapping the United States-Mexico Boundary, 1849–1857*,[15] the work of these commissioners offers striking comparisons with that of their counterparts along the line of the St. Lawrence River and the Great Lakes. In the southerly case, it was the line of the Rio Grande that needed to be determined, and then the precise orientation of the boundary that cut away across the desert to the Pacific Ocean just south of San Diego. In a further development of her work, Rebert also has shown how the U.S.-Mexican commissioners published what amounted to a survey of the natural history of the area they had delineated;[16] no such extension of geographical duties took place on the northern boundary. In general, both these commissions seem to have worked remarkably efficiently and with little dissension. Indeed, disagreements were generally solved more easily than internal U.S. quarrels would be, between states on each side of problematic rivers such as the Mississippi and the Savannah, with their frequent and unpredictable changes of channel.

Once the external boundaries of Michigan had been identified, it remained to decide precisely how the township-and-range system, spreading westward out of Ohio after 1785, would divide up the country. There was, to start with, the problem caused by imposing a quadrilateral system upon a spherical earth; this was resolved by allowing those offsets that can still puzzle motorists in Michigan, when a north-south road suddenly, and apparently without reason, makes a right-angle turn before soon reverting to its former course.

More problematic was the way in which the surveyors might be expected to deal with preexisting land claims. The most extensive of these consisted of concessions made to various Indian groups, often involving diagonal and otherwise irregular holdings along river courses.

Margaret Pearce explains that when surveyors came up against these holdings, they were instructed to make them conform as far as possible to the cardinally oriented townships of the new system. Indian representatives often accompanied the surveyors, who generally succeeded in bringing the grants into rough conformity with the quadrilateral system. These Indian grants were regarded as temporary (and indeed proved to be so), unlike the long lots held by the French settlers near Detroit and along the Wabash River. Whereas most of the Indian grants have left little trace, except a red line on the map, the French grants—though Pearce does not pursue this line of thought—have deeply marked the modern landscape, not only in Michigan but even more strikingly in states such as Illinois and Louisiana.[17]

Another line of thought that emerges from a reading of Pearce's chapter involves the profound political significance of the activities of the township-and-range surveyors. When there were long-established settlers, they naturally viewed the approach of the surveyors with apprehension; such, for instance, was the case with the Mormons of Utah. Indeed, when the Canadian counterparts of the U.S. surveyors approached the holdings of the Métis around Winnipeg in the 1860s, the latter's foreboding was such that they were easily persuaded to join the (eventually abortive) rebellion of Louis Riel in 1869–70. In general, the progress of the township-and-range survey offers a great deal of neglected historical information not only in the maps, which often show early roads and settlements, but also in the accompanying field notes, particularly useful for establishing presettlement vegetation patterns.[18]

The specific historical circumstances of nineteenth-century Michigan gave rise to some remarkable maps. Helen Tanner explains in her chapter that most of the printed maps of the 1830s, on which immigrants relied, were conspicuously erroneous for Michigan north of the Grand River. She maintains that in the 1840s and 1850s, the best map of the Grand Traverse area was the work of Peter Dougherty, a missionary and teacher who established himself there in the late 1830s. Cartographers such as Dougherty and Henry Schoolcraft were primarily concerned to set out the settlement patterns of local Indian groups, in the largely abortive attempt to safeguard their hunting grounds.

Immigrants' maps were often designed to put the best face on things,[19] and as Cheryl Lyon-Jenness explains, this was also one of the major functions of the nineteenth-century county atlases, which enjoyed a brief popularity in the 1870s. This seems to have been a decade when everything came together in the midwestern states to encourage the appearance of this particular map type. Farmers were now often prosperous enough to wish to record their holdings, which had been in Indian hands not so long before. Printing presses able to handle large engraved sheets were now commonplace, and a dynamic urban economy produced entrepreneurs with the ideas and capital to put these favorable circumstances into action. Each county could be subjected to a regular campaign, with representatives offering space in the proposed atlas and surveyors and printers ready to produce it. A remarkable percentage of farmers responded to the solicitations, and the result was a cartographic form that leads the historian deep into an understanding of the nineteenth-century landscape.

According to Lyon-Jenness, the individual farm views were generally accurate, though some other commentators have claimed that there was a good deal of standardization in the portrayal of farms and animals.[20] This rural map type had had a precursor in the form of the estate map, common in England from the 1590s onward and eventually found as well in states such as South Carolina. But the estate map was very different from the county atlas, in that it always portrayed the holdings of a single individual or corporation and was always manuscript; it was the product of a completely different economic and social structure, with larger estates and often with absentee owners. It shared with the maps of the county atlases, though, the common feature that both used a planimetric approach to mapping, and both were intended in part to celebrate the landowners' possessions.[21]

Quite soon, the fashion for county atlases passed. In this, they were perhaps like the aerial farm photographs of the 1930s. In each case, a new technique allowed a new form of imaging; representatives were sent out to seek commissions from farmers, and in some cases the resultant images were collected into albums (which, it might be added, are curiously uninformative and boring to the modern reader). But like the county atlas, the collection of aerial maps was essentially a passing fashion, in essence nonfunctional; thus, aerial maps differed sharply from estate maps, which were essential instruments for making the most of agricultural properties and were often used year after year in order to decide on agricultural tactics. County atlases were often succeeded by another transient form—the county history—which offered another way to commemorate the leading figures of the early phase of European settlement.

The urban bird's-eye view, classically described by John W. Reps in *Views and Viewmakers of Urban America . . . 1825–1925*,[22] was another fashionable cartographic form. In western Europe, such views had become abundant in the late sixteenth century, when increasing urban prosperity and rising literacy combined with advances in printing technology to make such imagery possible.[23] During the nineteenth century, most towns and cities in the United States generated similar images, sometimes in multiple versions. Often, the views were rather optimistic, showing towns not only basking in fine weather but also prospering from intensive economic activity; those were the days when belching smokestacks did not connote pollution. The views also might show streets that lay still in the minds of developers who had contributed to the subscriptions of the image makers. In general, then, the accuracy of bird's-eye views has been much criticized, but they were remarkable testimonies to local pride, and they often can give the historian a condensed view of the nineteenth-century urban landscape that is matched by no other source.[24]

Much more sober were the plats and fire insurance maps, described here in the chapter by David Patton, Amy Lobben, and Bruce Pape. *Plat* is a curious word, used in sixteenth-century English to mean a survey of some small area of ground, generally to establish legal ownership. Like many other such words, it has passed out of this use in England but continues in the United States to describe the great mass of local surveys; sixty-six thousand such plats are now on file for Michigan alone. Plats vary widely in their scale and degree of elaboration. Many are extremely simple, showing only "locative points," the boundary of the land held, and the scale and orientation. Others, particularly the ones in the eastern states, are quite elaborate, showing natural features, roads, house sites, and even architectural sketches. Plat maps are often the sources of first recourse for a wide variety of studies by specialists such as genealogists, historians, and archaeologists.[25]

The Sanborn fire insurance maps, which eventually covered a large number of urban sites in North America,[26] were equally utilitarian. Sometimes based on the outlines offered by plat maps, they aimed to show for each town site everything that would be useful for the purpose of fire insurance: the shape and composition of all structures, their economic uses, their firefighting provisions, and so forth. Often, these detailed, large-scale maps were kept up-to-date by the insertion of errata slips, designed to be glued near the structure that had undergone change. For the most part, they appear very accurate and allow the full reconstruction of the economic activities of whole areas of nineteenth-century towns. They are in this respect a remarkable resource; economic development has often meant that it is impossible to effect such a reconstruction by any other means.

The authors not only insist on the importance for historians of the fire insurance maps, but they also suggest that such images have their full effect only when combined with the information found on plat maps and, particularly, on bird's-eye views. Such panoramic views and fire insurance maps are indeed competing ways of viewing a city, the one more or less subjective in character and the other objective. As Richard Kagan has put it, this is the distinction between, respectively, "communicentric" and "chorographic" ways of looking at any given urban area.[27] It would be an interesting exercise to make a study for a particular city.

It was the latticework provided by the township-and-range system that allowed many plat maps to be precisely situated. That system also was used in determining how post offices should be distributed in newly settled territories, as described here in the chapter by Kenneth Lewis. The chapter begins by explaining that in assessing antebellum (European) settlement in southern lower Michigan, the spread of the county system is a rather gross tool, incapable of capturing the actual presence on the ground of small and often fluctuating settlements.[28] Lewis turns instead to the process by which post offices were established, which offers a much clearer reflection of the actual situation in the areas of new European settlement.

Sometimes the post offices were established in response to a clear new need, but sometimes—though Lewis does not go into this—the postmaster general sent out pro formas to be filled in by those hoping to establish post offices. These forms required applicants to fill in the geographical location of their proposed post offices, on a background made up of the divisions of the township-and-range system. Outside this system, though, there could be problems. One of these arose in northern Texas, which was not covered by the system and relied on a variety of other means of land identification. One aspiring postmistress noted on the document that it was a "Yankee map" and superimposed her own map on it. Her sketch was convincing, and the post office was duly established in her locality.

Related to the postal system was the network of roads, traveled in antebellum days not only by horsemen but also by stagecoaches. The National Road, passing through Indiana on its way from Washington to St. Louis, formed an important part of this. It is notoriously difficult to use maps to reconstruct the stagecoach route system, but it would be an interesting research project to relate the many contemporary advertisements from coach services to contemporary maps, some of which show what purport to be coach routes. Eventually, the stagecoaches were supplanted by the railroads, for which a great many maps survive.[29] In their turn, the railroads were largely replaced for passenger traffic by highways and automobiles, and it is the cartographic aspect of this development that concerns James Akerman and Daniel Block in their chapter.

They leave aside the maps generated by oil companies,[30] concentrating instead on the state highway maps produced by midwestern states bordering the Great Lakes. These maps began as rather humdrum accounts of the state of the roads, generally produced by in-house mapmakers. But as time went by, this desire to show the state of the roads—which in the 1920s often might be precarious—was joined by the urge to promote and celebrate a state's touristic possibilities. Eventually, too, the maps were used to advance the idea that a state was powerful and well governed. Today, with the total effacement of the oil-company map, they have become the means by which most motorists navigate the roads of all the states of the Union.

Increasingly, motorists now make use of electronic maps as well, not considered in this volume. More and more cars are now equipped with such imaging devices, which sometimes rely on data gathered from satellite transmissions. Increasingly, too, cities are run by the use of electronic maps, which generally take the form of a base map, upon which can be added at choice such features as sewer lines, electric conduits, computer networks, crime-incidence points, and so forth. It thus becomes possible to make decisions about structural changes that can be much better informed and speedier than they were in the past. Electronic maps also have become indispensable as navigation tools in the air and on the sea. Air passengers are familiar with the bulkhead maps that show the progress of an aircraft; this is a rather crude but strangely compelling form of map. Much more sophisticated ones are used not only in the cockpits of aircraft but also on the navigation bridges of ships. Here again, there will be a base map, on which, for ships, such transient phenomena as other vessels, tides, temporary obstructions, and winds can be displayed. It would now be difficult to imagine how crowded areas such as the English Channel or the Houston Ship Channel could be navigated safely without such electronic aids.

Satellite transmissions are often parts of such systems, an extension of the massive development of aerial imagery since the end of World War II. Maps were sometimes generated before that from aerial photographs, but it was after 1945 that such imagery came into its own. Whole countries now could be mapped with an economy and speed hitherto unimaginable, and in states such as Michigan, aerial photography provided a kind of mapping that was central in planning both agricultural development and urban expansion. Often, such photographs could be combined with historic maps to provide extraordinarily effective analyses of particular problems. A good example of this is Michael Chrzastowski and Molly E. Read, *Inventory of Federal and State Historical Maps, Charts, and Vertical Aerial Photographs Applicable to Erosion-Rate Studies along the Illinois Coast of Lake Michigan.*[31] Cartographers have been rather slow to take advantage of the large-scale possibilities of satellite imagery, but this could be remarkably effective in studies of the landforms of a state like Michigan.

The last chapter in this book is also the most general one; it attempts to view the mapping of Michigan over a long duration and in its midwestern context. Gerald Danzer begins with the French intruders, for whom the area was a sort of hinge between their twin axes of penetration, along the St. Lawrence River valley and up the valley of the Mississippi River. He mentions the great complexity of manuscript map sources that track this development. These French map sources are still not very well known, particularly since the losses and adjustments of the Parisian archives during and after World War II. To trace the development of French knowledge of the early Midwest would be a remarkable, though very difficult, research project.

Proceeding to the era of widespread printed maps, Danzer points out the important role played by school atlases in imprinting state shapes on the minds of the populace. The mitten of Michigan's Lower Peninsula is memorable among some merely quadrilateral states, though its iconic status may not quite rival that of the boundaries of Texas, whose outline is so deeply embedded in the psyche of Texans that it has even inspired a book on the theme.[32] In the end, Michigan turns out to have been a state that was privileged not only in the variety of its cartography but also in the range of those who tabulated and interpreted the maps. Preeminent among them, to judge only by the notes in this book, was Louis Karpinski. He surely would have been proud, if surprised, to see how his pioneering work has borne fruit.

NOTES

1. Carmen Liter and Francisca Sanchis, *Tesoros de la Cartografía Española* (Madrid: Biblioteca Nacional, 2001).

2. See the many publications of Kit Kapp, for the Map Collectors' Circle (London, c. 1970).

3. Enumerated by James C. Martin and Robert Sydney Martin in *Maps of Texas and the Southwest, 1513–1900* (1984; reprint, Albuquerque: University of New Mexico Press, 1999).

4. D. G. Moir, ed., *The Early Maps of Scotland to 1850*, 2 vols. (Edinburgh: Royal Scottish Geographical Society, 1973 and 1983).

5. Carl I. Wheat, *Mapping the Transmississippi West, 1540–1861*, 5 vols. (San Francisco: Institute of Historical Cartography, 1957–63).

6. William Patterson Cumming, *The Southeast in Early Maps*, 3rd ed., rev. and enl. by Louis De Vorsey Jr. (Chapel Hill: University of North Carolina Press, 1998). See also Alfred Lemmon, John Magill, and Jason Wiese, eds., *Charting Louisiana: Five Hundred Years of Maps* (New Orleans: Historic New Orleans Collection, 2003); and Richard Stephenson and Marianne M. McKee, eds., *Virginia in Maps: Four Centuries of Settlement, Growth, and Development* (Richmond: Library of Virginia, 2000).

7. Louis Karpinski, *Bibliography of the Printed Maps of Michigan, 1804–1860* (Lansing: Michigan Historical Commission, 1931).

8. Jack Jackson, *Manuscript Maps Concerning the Gulf Coast, Texas and the Southwest (1519–1836)* (Chicago: Newberry Library, 1995).

9. Catherine Delano-Smith and Roger Kain, *English Maps: A History* (Toronto: University of Toronto Press, 1999).

10. Rinaldo Comba and Paola Sereno, *Rappresentare uno Stato: Carte e Cartografi degli Stati Sabaudi dal XVI al XVIII Secolo* (Turin: Umberto Allemandi, 2002).

11. See his *Cartographic Encounters: Perspectives on Native American Mapmaking and Map Use* (Chicago: University of Chicago Press, 1998) and the volume he edited with David Woodward, *Cartography in the Traditional African, American, Arctic, Australian, and Pacific Societies* (Chicago: University of Chicago Press, 1998).

12. These include Mark Warhus, *Another America: Native American Maps and the History of Our Land* (New York: St. Martin's Press, 1998).

13. This is interestingly explained in the G. Malcolm Lewis chapter, n. 55.

14. Joan Winearls, *Mapping Upper Canada, 1780–1867* (Toronto: University of Toronto Press, 1991).

15. Paula Rebert, *La Gran Línea: Mapping the United States-Mexico Boundary, 1849–1857* (Austin: University of Texas Press, 2001).

16. See Paula Rebert, "Views of the Borderlands: *The Report on the United States and Mexican Boundary Survey, 1857–1859,*" *Terrae Incognitae* 37 (2005): 75–90.

17. See, e.g., Cole Harris on "French Landscapes in North America," in *The Making of the American Landscape*, ed. Michael Conzen (Chicago: University of Chicago Press, 1990), 63–79.

18. See P. J. Comer et al., *Michigan's Presettlement Vegetation, as Interpreted from the General Land Office Surveys, 1815–1856* (Lansing: Department of Natural Resources, 1995).

19. For a recent account of these maps, see Brian McFarland, "From Publisher to Pocket: Interpreting Early Nineteenth-century American History through the Pocket Maps of Samuel Augustus Mitchell" (master's thesis, University of Texas at Arlington, 2002).

20. See, e.g., "The County Atlas," in *American Maps and Mapmakers: Commercial Cartography in the Nineteenth Century,* Walter W. Ristow (Detroit: Wayne State University Press, 1985), 403–25.

21. See David Buisseret, ed., *Rural Images: Estate Maps in the Old and New Worlds* (Chicago: University of Chicago Press, 1996).

22. John W. Reps, *Views and Viewmakers of Urban America . . . 1825–1925* (Columbia: University of Missouri Press, 1984).

23. On this development, see David Buisseret, ed., *The Mapmakers' Quest: Depicting New Worlds in Renaissance Europe* (Oxford: Oxford University Press, 2003), 165–69.

24. For an interesting analysis of one such view, see Frank Passic et al., eds., *A Comprehensive Guide and Key to Artist Albert Ruger's 1866 Bird's-Eye View of the City of Albion, Calhoun Co., Michigan* (Albion, Mich.: Albion Historical Society, 1988).

25. See, e.g., Marjorie Clark, ed., *Oakland County, Michigan: 1857 Plat Map Transcription* (Birmingham, Mich.: Oakland County Genealogical Society, 1993).

26. See the bibliography for the chapter by Patton, Lobben, and Pape.

27. See Richard Kagan, "Urbs and Civitas in Sixteenth- and Seventeenth-Century Spain," in *Envisioning the City: Six Studies in Urban Cartography,* ed. David Buisseret (Chicago: University of Chicago Press, 1998), 75–108.

28. For many years, John Long has been publishing at The Newberry Library in Chicago the successive volumes of the County Boundary Project, which aims to bring precision into our knowledge of these divisions.

29. See Andrew M. Modelski, *Railroad Maps of North America: The First Hundred Years* (Washington, D.C.: Library of Congress, 1984).

30. See Walter W. Ristow, "A Half-Century of Oil-Company Road Maps," *Surveying and Mapping* 24, no. 4 (1964): 617–37.

31. Michael Chrzastowski and Molly E. Read, *Inventory of Federal and State Historical Maps, Charts, and Vertical Aerial Photographs Applicable to Erosion-Rate Studies along the Illinois Coast of Lake Michigan* (Champaign: Illinois State Geological Society, 1993).

32. Richard Francaviglia, *The Shape of Texas: Maps as Metaphors* (College Station: Texas A&M University Press, 1995).

Louis Charles Karpinski and the Cartography of the Great Lakes

Mary Sponberg Pedley

FOR GREAT LAKES MAP ENTHUSIASTS AND MICHIGAN HISTORIANS, THE NAME "KARpinski" evokes two related phrases: "Karpinski number" and "not in Karpinski." These phrases refer, of course, to the 1931 *Bibliography of the Printed Maps of Michigan*, by Louis Karpinski, with its accompanying *Historical Atlas of the Great Lakes and Michigan*. But these are not the only works that deserve the appellation "Karpinski." Even more famous is his *Bibliography of Mathematical Works Printed in America through 1850*, which has served collectors of American imprints so well. The work *Early Military Books in the University of Michigan Libraries*, written with Thomas Spaulding, may also claim "Karpinski" status.[1]

These titles represent only a small portion of Karpinski's written opus. His work in the form of monographs and articles concerning the history of mathematics and the history of science fills a foot of shelf space. The most recent bibliography of Karpinski articles, reviews, and speeches in the history of cartography numbered 166 items.[2]

Besides bibliographies and monographs, the label "Karpinski" also refers to collections. For the cartographically inclined, the "Karpinski collection" signifies the more than seven hundred photostats of manuscript maps in European collections relating to American history.

But this is not the only "Karpinski collection." Yale University houses the Karpinski–von Wieser collection of maps and atlases; another Karpinski map collection resides at the University of Miami in Coral Gables, Florida; and yet another finds its home in the library of the Polish Institute of Arts and Sciences of America in New York City.

Nor are "Karpinski collections" just maps. There is a Karpinski collection of Lutheriana and early Protestant books in the Colgate Rochester Crozer Divinity School.[3] And Karpinski sold a collection of children's literature to the Detroit Public Library.[4] The one hundred slides concerning the history of mathematics that Karpinski produced from the illustrations in his *Bibliography of Mathematical Works* and sold in sets could also be called a "Karpinski collection."

In addition to the books he wrote and the maps he collected, Karpinski also sold books, maps, and atlases to many libraries throughout North America, from Yale in the East to The Newberry Library in the Midwest. He also gave away books: to college libraries, like that of St. Olaf in Minnesota; to individuals, such as prisoner number 54578 in Jackson Prison; and to worthy causes, such as the "Committee for the Rehabilitation of Polish Science and Culture" after World War II.[5]

Louis Charles Karpinski (1878–1956) was a professor of mathematics on the faculty of the University of Michigan from 1904 to 1948 (fig. 1). His scholarly expertise was twofold. First, he specialized in mathematical education and wrote about the quality of teaching, curriculum, and textbooks in America's schools. Second, he was a historian of mathematics. His research on early mathematical texts led to several jointly authored monographs on the history of numbers, on the numerical notation for zero, and on the manuscripts of early works of algebra. He was a collector of manuscripts, maps, and books. He was a campus gadfly who did not hesitate to write directly and often to the board of regents of the university, nudging them to raise faculty salaries, encouraging faculty representation on the board, and deploring the decline of academic standards. Karpinski also raised intellectual and ethical questions on the national level. He was one of the first people in academe to warn of the mushrooming connection between money and science, as the link between private business interests and "scientific experts" grew ever stronger. And he was a dealer who plied his wares of books and maps to numerous libraries during the 1930s, 1940s, and 1950s. The focus for this chapter is on Karpinski's *Bibliography of the Printed Maps of Michigan* and his contributions to the history of cartography of the state. But widening the lens to include Karpinski's other interests and aspects of his character provides a context for assessing and appreciating his work on Michigan maps.

Karpinski was born on August 5, 1878, in Rochester, New York. His father, Henry Karpinski, had emigrated from Warsaw, Poland, and his mother, Mary Louise Engesser, from Gebweiler in the Alsace. Henry Karpinski worked for the very young Eastman Company (founded in 1884) in Rochester before moving his family to Oswego, New York, to start his own cleaning and dyeing business. Louis's later letters to his parents from Europe, written in English, French, and German (though, surprisingly, not Polish—a lack he himself regretted), reflect this immigrant background. He graduated from the English and German curriculum of Oswego High School, where he exhibited his mental gifts as a chess player, challenging older players in high-level matches sponsored by the New York State Chess Association and becoming state champion in 1896.[6] After receiving a teacher's diploma from Oswego State Normal School in 1897, Karpinski taught for two years—in Southold, Long Island, and then at Berea College in Kentucky. This Appalachian experience of training teachers to serve in poor mountain communities taught Karpinski about the large demands made on public school teachers and convinced him of the need for a practical approach to teaching mathematics in order to educate a numerate population. These ideas would be incorporated in his later writing.

In 1899, Karpinski entered Cornell University, where he earned a B.A. in mathematics in 1901. He received high recommendations from his professors at Cornell, one of whom described him as an "excellent student, clear in thought, thorough in his work, good looking with fine manners, making a favorable impression," adding that "he is human and takes a living active interest in the affairs of the day."[7]

Figure 1. Louis Charles Karpinski (1878–1956), professor of mathematics at the University of Michigan, 1904–1948. Faculty Portraits Collection, Courtesy of the Bentley Historical Library, University of Michigan.

Yet when Karpinski sought posts teaching math at universities west of the Appalachians, he was disappointed to learn that a Ph.D. was required. Since few institutions in America offered Ph.D. programs in mathematics in the early twentieth century, Karpinski went to Europe to complete his training.

In September 1901, he entered the University of Strasbourg in his mother's native Alsace, which was then part of Germany. His only financial support came from his parents and his salary from teaching young men at the American College in Strasbourg, a prep school for American boys from wealthy families.[8] Karpinski wrote his thesis on number theory with Professor Hans Weber and received his Ph.D. in 1903. During his two years in Strasbourg, he visited paternal relatives in Poland and traveled to Italy, Austria, and Germany, whetting an appetite for European travel that would only increase in his later years. Returning to the United States in 1903, Karpinski married his sweetheart from Cornell, Grace Woods, with whom he would have six children. He taught at his alma mater, Oswego State Normal School, for a year and in 1904 arrived at the University of Michigan's Department of Mathematics, where he remained until his retirement in 1948.

At Michigan, he deepened his commitment to the teaching of mathematics in public schools. From 1905 to 1907, he worked with schoolteachers in the summer schools of the Chautauqua Institution in New York. In 1909 and 1910, he was invited to participate in the summer school for teachers at Columbia University. There he met and collaborated with the founder of Columbia's mathematics education program, David Eugene Smith, who fueled Karpinski's interest in the history of mathematics through his own writings and collections. Together, he and Karpinski wrote *The Hindu-Arabic Numerals,* which explored the transmission of Hindu numerals to the Arabs.[9] Smith collected rare mathematical works and introduced Karpinski to his fellow collector and enthusiast, George A. Plimpton, the founder of Ginn and Company.[10] Back in Ann Arbor, Professor Alexander Ziwet, who taught mathematics in the engineering college, encouraged Karpinski's historical enthusiasms and was a model of the collecting spirit. Eventually, Ziwet's collection of early mathematical works became part of the collections of the University of Michigan.[11]

Karpinski's scholarly work in the history of mathematics focused on the transmission of ideas, especially from the East to the West and particularly on primary manuscript sources, such as the translation of algebraic texts from Arabic into Latin in the twelfth and thirteenth centuries.[12] Whether exploring the origins of "algorithm" and "algebra" or unraveling the history of numbers and the use of the zero, Karpinski identified and reiterated in numerous publications the importance of Arabic and Hindu contributions to math and science. Although this debt to the East was not new to mathematical audiences, Karpinski brought it to the attention of a more general audience, particularly teachers. His scholarly prestige was rewarded in 1937, when President Franklin Roosevelt appointed him as one of three United States representatives to the celebration in Paris of the René Descartes tercentary.

Karpinski wrote widely for both learned audiences and the popular press. One finds him discoursing on "The 'Quadripartitum Numerorum' of John of Meurs" in *Bibliotheca Mathematica* or on "The Decimal Point" in *Science* or on "Notes on the Word 'Algebra'" in *Modern Language Notes.*[13] He contributed more than one hundred articles to Henry Ford's weekly, *The Dearborn Independent,* ranging from the historical ("How the Great Lakes Were Placed on the Map") to the topical ("France and America—an Industrial Contrast").[14] Taking advantage of the University of Michigan's recently acquired papyrus collection, Karpinski published articles on the mathematical papyri that introduced algebraic equations into Greece.[15] He contributed to mathematics teaching with his textbook *Unified Mathematics.*[16] He also wrote many short articles and pamphlets dealing with the practical applications of mathematics, such as "Arithmetic for the Lumberman" and "Arithmetic for the Farm."[17] Such articles not only provided pedagogical examples and instructions for the teacher but also lambasted contemporary textbooks for offering no useful help in employing arithmetic for everyday purposes.[18]

Karpinski had a finely tuned sense of the importance of public education and the accessibility of knowledge; he viewed college professors as stewards of the public trust. He sharply criticized those who abused their university status or quasi-intellectual qualifications. He blasted the "textbook racket" run by "educational quacks" whose students, when they arrived at positions of power and influence in school systems, ensured that the textbooks written by their former professors were adopted by their schools. "At one teachers' college enjoying an international reputation," he railed, "there was [*sic*] at one time no less [*sic*] than 12 faculty members writing textbooks on arithmetic.... Yet I would testify, under oath if necessary, that at least 10 of these men are incompetent." Though such writers knew nothing about their subjects, complained Karpinski, they were richly rewarded when school districts adopted their books.[19]

Karpinski's idealism and intellectual honesty were not always appreciated. In 1943, he was elected president of the History of Science Society for his work on the history of mathematics. Ex officio, he addressed the American Council of Learned Societies (ACLS) on the universities' involvement with private industry in developing resources that could be used for the public good but were used instead for private gain. He offered a resolution urging the ACLS to deplore the support of university professors and researchers by private industry and to encourage those professors who did receive support to declare their private interests before they offered "expert" testimony as scientists.[20] His position on this issue was so controversial that Karpinski was asked to resign as president of the History of Science Society, which he did in December 1943.[21]

Describing himself as a "Democrat, reformed Republican," Karpinski was never slow to stir the political pot. Such headlines as "Karpinski Says GOP Tax Cut Would Be 'Gift' for the Wealthy" reflect both his interest in current affairs and his detailed response to statistical issues.[22] As a concerned citizen, Karpinski wrote several articles questioning the setting of utility rates by private companies and the methods used to assess fees, pointing out that shifting rate scales could manipulate the costs passed on to the consumer. He was fiercely opposed to the privatization of energy and water resources, commodities necessary for human existence. His uninhibited directness earned him a reputation of "always making speeches" and provoking sharp discussion in the faculty club.[23] He did not hesitate to approach the regents of the university on a variety of issues. For example, he urged them to appoint a faculty member to the governing board, as was the case at Cornell, and questioned private practice and fees charged by professors in the university's medical school. He was the driving force behind the petition of 1917 asking for a study of faculty salaries, a survey completed in 1918.[24] He was an early promoter of the Teachers Insurance and Annuity Association, holding life insurance policy number one.[25]

His concern for equitable faculty stipends appears in his scholarly work. Describing the life of the sixteenth-century mathematician and scholar Johann Scheybl, professor of Euclid and arithmetic at the University of Tübingen, Karpinski could not forbear remarking, "How little some aspects of university life have changed during four centuries is shown by the fact that Scheybl twice, in 1551 and 1562, requested of the university authorities an increase of salary in order that he might pay his debts and obtain the necessaries of life."[26]

New technology captured Karpinski's imagination. He saw great potential in the photograph, the slide, and the photostat as tools for teaching and research. He appreciated the potential of the photostat for allowing scholars access to rare materials, and his early book reviews reveal his faith in illustrations as a boon to abstract subjects such as mathematics. He himself used the slide projector as a pedagogical device at an early moment in its history by presenting an *illustrated* lecture on the history of algebra at the first meeting of the Mathematical Association of America in 1915. In 1931, Karpinski designed four sets of slides depicting the history of arithmetic, algebra, geometry, and higher mathematics that were projected on the four sides of a column devoted to mathematics in the Hall of Science, for the Century of Progress Exposition at the 1932 World's Fair in Chicago.[27] They were advertised as "The History of Mathematics in 100 slides . . . as run continuously every day on four screens in the Mathematics Exhibit, Century of Progress Exposition." He later offered the slide sets for sale: twenty-five slides for $22. Each slide had text on the left (two hundred words, with a finely calibrated reading time of one minute) and an illustration on the right.

The practical mathematics of Karpinski's growing family of six children no doubt drew him to buy and sell slides, photostats, books, and maps. His 1947 tax return describes his secondary business as selling books to libraries.[28] It is not clear when Karpinski's business interests in the book and map trade began, though his New York mentors and fellow collectors, David Eugene Smith and George Plimpton, perhaps offered opportunities to him. By 1925, he had amassed a collection of 297 American imprints that he offered to the William L. Clements Library for $1,000.[29] Karpinski had clearly entered the trade by 1932, when he made a remarkable sale to Yale University. He had acquired (or was the agent for) the collection of Franz von Wieser, a geographer who had been one of the scholars who drew attention to the extraordinary Waldseemüller world map of 1507, known for first using the name America. On his travels in Austria and Germany, Karpinski met von Wieser's son, Hans, who introduced him to his father's student and Waldseemüller map scholar, Father Josef Fischer, S.J. Fischer introduced Karpinski to the owner of the map, Prince Max Waldburg-Wolfegg. For a brief time, Karpinski claimed to have procured the right to sell the map in the United States for one million Reichsmarks. The prince, however, ultimately proved reluctant to sell, noting that a time of economic depression with extensive unemployment was not a propitious moment for a national treasure to leave Germany.[30]

Karpinski combined Franz von Wieser's maps and atlases with a complete collection of the works of the Americanist Henry Harrisse and enough other titles to make up a collection of 625 atlases, more than 3,000 maps, in excess of 1,300 geographical works, and a pair of twenty-four-inch Blaeu globes. Karpinski sold this collection to Yale for $25,000, a sum so large in the early years of the Great Depression that the Yale officials negotiated an installment plan to pay the debt.[31]

Over the years, Karpinski sold maps, atlases, and books to many other institutions, including The Newberry Library, the New York Public Library, Ohio State University, Indiana University, Purdue University, the State University of New York at Albany, and Michigan State College. Many of these sales were under the aegis of the McGregor Plan, with which the Clements Library at the University of Michigan was associated.[32] Karpinski also donated books and maps to the law library of Berea College, where he had taught as a young man, to the American Book Center for War Devastated Libraries, and to the Rebuilders of Poland.[33] In the manner of many dealers, when he sold maps and books to libraries, he often left several others as gifts.[34] He sometimes offered his services as a lecturer in addition to the sale of maps. To the Cleveland Public Library, he wrote: "I have an interesting group of twenty separate maps

. . . of great value as a permanent exhibition. . . . I offer them to you for $1,000. . . . I would be glad to lecture on the subject. . . . I would bring this group as well as slides of other maps. The lecture fee would be one hundred dollars."[35] In his retirement years, Karpinski continued his trade in maps and atlases and expanded his interests to include the American Civil War, English literature, and early American history.

Karpinski's connection with the history of cartography can be traced to the expansion years at the University of Michigan. When Karpinski arrived in 1904, the university's third president, James B. Angell (who was eighty and had been president for thirty-eight years), was near retiring. The "golden years" of the Angell presidency were noted for the growth and increasing prestige of the school. Harry B. Hutchins succeeded Angell as the university's fourth president, and by 1910, Michigan's fifty-six hundred students made it the third-largest university in the United States, after Columbia and the University of Chicago. Hutchins was supported by a board of regents that included three members especially interested in curriculum, buildings, and libraries: Junius Beal, a local Ann Arbor editor and book collector; Lucius L. Hubbard, a geology professor at Michigan Technical University in Houghton, a Harvard graduate with a Ph.D. from Bonn and a law degree from Boston University, and a collector of rare books; and William L. Clements, an industrialist from Bay City, whose collection of rare books on early America derived from a literature course he had taken as an undergraduate at the university.[36] Clements would leave his collection, which included many maps and atlases, to the university along with the money to build the library that now bears his name. His energy and commitment to acquiring original source material would attract and engage Karpinski in the pursuit of maps.

President Hutchins enlarged the scope of the university by adding courses in journalism, an extension service, the departments of fine arts and political science, and a "tough" graduate school.[37] The building of the university's collections and its library kept pace with these efforts. Francis Kelsey, professor of classics and archaeology, was given a two-year leave from 1919 to 1921 to travel in Europe and the Near East to acquire antiquities and papyri for the university. William Warner Bishop was lured away from the Library of Congress in 1915 to direct and build the collections of the university library. Bishop traveled to France in 1921, where he acquired the large library of the Americanist Henri Vignaud, with William Clements paying a share of the cost.[38] The Vignaud collection contained a large number of atlases and antiquarian maps, many of which entered the collections of the Clements Library. Throughout the 1920s, Clements continued to collect materials for his library, aided by antiquarian book dealers and his librarian, Randolph G. Adams.

Figure 2. *Amerique Septentrionale* (1685–1686). J. B. L. Franquelin, Karpinski photostat 641. Courtesy of the William L. Clements Library, University of Michigan.

In this atmosphere of growth at the university, Karpinski was able to give full rein to his own collecting instincts, particularly in the history of mathematics. With the support of the university librarians, Theodore Koch and William Bishop, as well as Randolph Adams, Karpinski traveled regularly to Europe to collect books for the university's history of mathematics collection.[39] His acquisitions included volumes about applied geometry and trigonometry, navigation, surveying, and geodesy. Thus, the history of cartography was an easy leap for Karpinski. Ann Arbor was becoming a congenial center for this subject, with the Clements Library pushing the University of Michigan to the forefront of research institutions for American history and the acquisition of the Vignaud maps and atlases adding to its stature.

In this same period, immediately following the First World War, the work of the Carnegie Institution in Europe attracted Clements's attention. The Carnegie Institution was supporting the American historian Waldo G. Leland, who was assembling the *Guide to Materials for American History in the Libraries*

Figure 3. Detail of *Amerique Septentrionale,* J. B. L. Franquelin, Karpinski photostat 641, showing Karpinski's handwritten label for the map with location, size, and collection identified. Courtesy of the William L. Clements Library, University of Michigan.

and Archives of Paris. Leland had been at one time an assistant to University of Michigan history professor Claude Van Tyne, one of Clements's advisors on acquisitions. Leland also directed the foreign copying program of the Library of Congress for French manuscripts relating to the United States and initiated work on the *Calendar of Manuscripts in Paris Archives and Libraries Relating to the History of the Mississippi Valley to 1803.*[40] His right-hand man in Paris was Abel Doysié, a historian and poet, who oversaw the copying of documents for the Library of Congress. Clements saw an opportunity in the Carnegie–Library of Congress project to add important manuscript material to his growing collection. In 1921–22, Clements hired Doysié to work for him in the evening to copy more materials and to make photostats of manuscript maps in the archives, procuring in this way more than one hundred fifty map reproductions for the Clements collection. When Doysié's work was complete, Clements knew that more material remained to be photographed pertaining to the Great Lakes and upper Mississippi Valley. He engaged Karpinski, who was planning to be in France during his sabbatical year of 1926–27, to identify and procure photostats of manuscript maps and documents relative to the American Revolution and the United States and Alaska not already included in the Wisconsin Historical, Michigan Historical, and Mississippi Valley Historical Documents programs.[41]

This project resulted in the Karpinski collection of nearly eight hundred photostats of manuscript maps of America in European archives. Five libraries in addition to the Clements Library subscribed to the project and received the complete set of photostats.[42] Though these photostat maps have been widely used by scholars and remain an invaluable resource, the collection itself has not been thoroughly studied. The index to the maps in the collection varies from institution to institution, and a concordance to the archives in which the maps were photographed is not easily available.[43] The photostats themselves are of exceptionally high quality, and the provenance of most of the maps can be determined from the name of the institution and the call number or shelf mark that is usually visible in the photostat. Karpinski provided measurements of both the original and the photostat, but any additional information about the map—such as author, date, and context—is not always clear from these minimal labels (figs. 2 and 3).

Karpinski's analysis of the manuscript maps of the Great Lakes in the photostat collection formed the springboard for his work on the history of the cartography of Michigan. His assessment of the manuscript material may be found in the first three chapters of the *Bibliography of the Printed Maps of Michigan, 1804–1880,* which is discussed below. Paralleling his efforts on the history of mathematics, this work illustrates Karpinski's primary interest, which was the transmission of knowledge. He understood the manuscript map as a link between the observed geographical phenomenon and the public conception of it. He gathered photostats of cartographic riches from the archives of three of the most powerful European nations involved in mapping the Americas—France, Portugal, and Spain. The French archives and repositories were intimately linked to the European discovery and exploration of the Great Lakes, especially the records of the Ministry of the Marine, where reports and maps were deposited in the Dépôt des Cartes, Plans, et Journaux de la Marine (later called the Service Hydrographique de la Marine). Karpinski also searched in the archives of the Ministry of War (Dépôt de la Guerre) and of the Ministry of Foreign Affairs (Affaires Étrangères). He looked for any map showing the area of the Great Lakes, the land between the Appalachians and the Mississippi River, and the eastern seaboard of North America in general.

Karpinski's reputation as a scholar in the history of mathematics, his successful work for Clements in Europe in assembling the photostat collection, and his prodigious energy made him an excellent candidate for assembling a new bibliography of Michigan maps, which was finally published in 1931. This project was conceived and sponsored by the Michigan Historical Commission, whose board included at least three members who knew Karpinski well: William Clements, University of Michigan history professor Claude Van Tyne, and William Lee Jenks, a lawyer and map collector from Port Huron, Michigan.[44] Already in 1921, the commission had published a two-volume *Michigan Bibliography,* assembled by Floyd Benjamin Streeter, which included maps and atlases and to which Jenks had made a significant contribution.[45] By 1927, enough additional maps had come to the attention of the commission that a revised bibliography seemed to be in order, and Clements, who appreciated Karpinski's recent work for him in Europe, chaired the commission in 1927. Accordingly, the commission's report for 1928 recorded that Karpinski "continued in the service of the commission for the compiling and editing of a bibliography of maps of Michigan and the Great Lakes region."[46] Jenks was also acutely interested in the new project, contributing three supplementary essays to the 1931 *Bibliography:* "A Michigan Family of Mapmakers" (on John Farmer and his descendants), "The Hutchins Map" (regarding the 1762 manuscript map of Michigan by Thomas Hutchins housed in the collection of the Huntington Library), and "Michigan Copyrights."[47]

What models existed for Karpinski's study of the bibliographical history of the cartography of a particular region? As a collector and researcher on the history of mathematics and mathematical texts, he understood the value of a thorough bibliography, but he needed a conceptual framework for organizing it as well as an accessible layout design. He found Joseph Sabin's *Bibliotheca Americana* an indispensable resource for atlas titles, but it did not list individual maps.[48] For an example of a map bibliography, Karpinski could look to the Library of Congress, where, from 1909 onward, Philip Lee Phillips had supervised the publication of a multivolume bibliography and finding tool for the geographical atlases in the national collection. Phillips included collated contents lists for each atlas. Karpinski may also have known the work of Sir Herbert Fordham, a map collector in Cambridge, England, who was publishing cartobibliographies throughout the first decades of the twentieth century on English and French mapmakers.[49]

The absence of any discipline that might be called the history of cartography hampered such bibliographical work, however. There was neither a standard text nor a scholarly journal devoted to maps. Leo Bagrow would not found *Imago Mundi,* the international journal of the history of cartography, until 1935, and he did not publish his own history of cartography until 1951.[50] (Karpinski contributed a brief article on cartographic collections in America to the first volume of *Imago Mundi.*)[51]

Although the idea of a bibliography of printed maps of a region was not entirely new, Karpinski's work was in the forefront of such efforts to assemble thorough catalogues of cartographic resources for regions of North America. Karpinski had helped Boston collector Henry P. Kendall by editing the publication of his collection of *Early Maps of Carolina and Adjoining Regions* (first edition 1930, second edition 1937). This work became the basis of William P. Cumming's magisterial *The Southeast in Early Maps.*[52] Close on the heels of Karpinski's *Bibliography of the Printed Maps of Michigan* came Henry Wagner's book, *The Cartography of the Northwest Coast of America to the Year 1800,* which was published in 1937.[53]

Karpinski did not assemble his bibliography de novo. His introduction credits the many works that preceded his, of course, including particularly the preliminary list assembled by Streeter and published by the Michigan Historical Commission in 1921.[54] Streeter's bibliography differs from Karpinski's in a number of ways, however. It is less numerous, with 973 titles, and it includes maps printed as recently as 1917, four years before its publication. Karpinski's bibliography, though a richer selection of 1,120 maps, stops with the year 1880 for reasons he never revealed. Streeter organized his work chronologically under the following thematic headings: "A. Great Lakes Region and Old Northwest; B. State; C. Sections; D. Counties; E. Cities, Towns, and Villages; F. Geology and Topographical; G. Mines and Mineral Regions; H. Lands; I. Islands; J. Lakes and Bays; K. Harbors; L. Rivers, Straits, and Canals; M. Railroads and Roads; and N. Miscellaneous."[55] Streeter's work is essentially an annotated list: each entry consists of the map title, author, publication place and date, current location, and brief description. No measurements are given. By contrast, Karpinski discusses in his work the background of European conceptions of the region in chapter three, "Fundamental Maps of Michigan and the Great Lakes." Thereafter he divides his bibliography into large chronologically organized chapters that concentrate on the development of the state map: "Maps of the United States and Great Lakes Area, 1804–1825"; "Maps of the State of Michigan, 1822–1880"; "Maps of Michigan in School Atlases and Geographies"; "County, Township, Village, and City Maps of Michigan to 1880"; and "Official Maps Including Public Surveys, Geological, Mines and Minerals, Lakes, Bays, Rivers, Harbors, and Miscellaneous Maps of Michigan Regions."

Karpinski was always interested in visual presentation, so he did not continue the Streeter layout but emulated that used by Philip Lee Phillips in his *List of Geographical Atlases in the Library of Congress* (fig. 4). The publication year in bold type is centered above the entries for a given year. Individual titles are in quotes, a number is assigned to each entry and appears on the left, and measurements and collection locations are given beneath the title on the right. Further notes in smaller type might include the scale, the area covered, any significant features, and cross-references to related maps elsewhere in the bibliography (fig. 5).

With his customary eye for fine detail, Karpinski used his system for numbering entries to distinguish two phases in the cartographic history of Michigan. His *Bibliography of Printed Maps* really begins in

325

1732?

Moll, H.

Atlas minor: or a set of sixty-two new and correct maps, of all the parts of the world. 2d ed. 1 p. l., 62 maps. obl. 8°. London, printed for T. Bowles and J. Bowles [1732?] 578

NOTE.—First edition published 1729. See titles 574, 585, 602 and 635.
In this edition dates have been erased from the plates and many maps changed and supplemented.
Map no. 32, "Great Tartary," dated 1732, substituted for "Great or Asiatick Tartary," undated, in 1st ed.
Map no. 41, "The west part of Barbary," date changed from 1729 to 1732.
Changes noted in American maps nos. 1, 2, 47, 48, 56, 57, 58, 59.
The following maps relate to America:

no. 1. A new map of the whole world with the trade winds . . . Printed for Thos. Bowles . . . and John Bowles . . . London. [Imprint first appears in this ed.]
" 2. A map of the North Pole . . . Printed for Tho. Bowles . . . & John Bowles . . .
" 40. Africa . . . [Shows] C. St Augustine [Brazil]
" 45. America . . .
" 46. A new map of ye north parts of America claimed by France under ye names of Louisiana, Mississipi, Canada & New France, with the adjoyning territories of England & Spain . . .
" 47. New Found Land St Laurence bay, the fishing banks, Acadia and part of New Scotland . . . [Differs from 1st ed. "Point Raye" omitted, "C. Ray" and "C. Sud" added]
" 48. A description of the bay of Fundy . . .—The harbour of Annapolis Royal by Nathaniel Blackmore esqr. Printed and sold by Tho: Bowles . . . & Ino Bowles . . .
" 49. New England, New York, New Jersey and Pensilvania . . .
" 50. Virginia and Maryland . . .
" 51. Carolina.
" 52. A plan of Port Royal harbour in Carolina . . .
" 53. The island of Bermudos . . .
" 54. Florida called by ye french Louisiana &c . . .
" 55. A map of the West-Indies &c. Mexico or New Spain . . .
" 56. The island of Jamaica . . . [Legend added]
" 57. The island of St Christophers alias St Kitts . . . [Legend added]
" 58. The island of Antego . . . Sold by T. Bowles . . . and I. Bowles.
" 59. The island of Barbadoes . . . Printed and sold by Tho: Bowles . . . & I. Bowles . . . [Legend added and notes changed]
" 60. The Scots settlement in America calle'd [!] New Caledonia . . .
" 61. A map of Terra Firma Peru, Amazone-land, Brasil & the north p. of La Plata . . .
" 62. A map of Chili, Patagonia, La Plata and ye south part of Brasil . . .

1732–1739

Châtelain, H. A.

Atlas historique; ou, nouvelle introduction à l'histoire, à la chronologie & à la géographie ancienne & moderne . . . par m. C. * * * [anon.] Avec des dissertations fur l'histoire de chaque état, par m.

Figure 4. One page from Philip Lee Phillips's *A List of Geographical Atlases in the Library of Congress,* showing his layout. Philip Lee Phillips, *A List of Geographical Atlases in the Library of Congress: With Bibliographical Notes,* vol. 1 (Washington, D.C.: Government Printing Office, 1909). Courtesy of the William L. Clements Library, University of Michigan.

chapter four, "Fundamental Maps of the Great Lakes Area." These are numbered with roman numerals, from I to CXX. Karpinski explains that fundamental maps are those "issued before the year 1805 which may properly be called fundamental in the historical determination of the cartography of Michigan."[56] In other words, these are maps that cover a larger area than Michigan and the Great Lakes but that influenced the cartographic rendering of what would become the state of Michigan. They are fundamental but preliminary maps; roman numerals indicate their prefatory nature. For the remainder of the maps from chapter five ("Maps of the United States or Parts of the United States Naming Michigan, 1804–1825") to chapter nine ("Official Maps"), Karpinski used arabic numerals, from 1 to 1,000. These printed maps depict Michigan as a distinct political entity and as such deserve the more conventional arabic numerals.

The full title of the *Bibliography* is somewhat misleading, for the entries are not limited to nineteenth-century maps of Michigan. In fact, the core of Karpinski's contribution is found in the first four chapters, which are essays exploring the historical context for the early discovery and mapping of the Great Lakes region in general and the peninsulas of Michigan in particular. Chapter one provides an overview of the printed maps of Michigan. Chapter two discusses the earliest European manuscript maps (most dating from the seventeenth century) that include Michigan. Chapter three analyzes the fundamental maps of the Great Lakes region. Chapter four lists the fundamental maps in bibliographic detail. Karpinski's research in European archives and his photostat collection refine and focus his discussion of maps.

Karpinski understood that unpublished manuscript representations illustrated knowledge closer to the original observations than did the printed maps. Although he did not examine the connection between the manuscript maps and the derivative printed maps, he pointed the way: "Further study of these maps by competent students of American cartography will doubtless make clear the part of many of these maps in the evolution of the printed delineation of America."[57] He was wary of using printed maps to draw conclusions about the state of contemporary geographic knowledge. Karpinski's perceptions were particularly acute concerning the time lag between the gathering of geographical information and its dissemination in print. He knew that French explorers, missionaries, voyageurs, and soldiers were primary sources of geographical knowledge of the upper lakes but that their work was slow to appear in print. As an example, he pointed to the masterful mapping of the Great Lakes region performed by Jesuit missionaries in the seventeenth century but its sluggish entry into the European printed-map market. Similarly, he emphasized the cartographic work of the French hydrographer and cartographer Jean-Baptiste-Louis Franquelin (c. 1651–c. 1712) and its equally hesitant debut on the maps of commercial mapmakers. He outlined the important survey work performed in the eighteenth century by the French-Canadian engineers Gaspard-Joseph Chaussegros de Léry and his son of the same name, nudging the reader to inquire more closely into the relationship of their manuscript work to the printed French maps of the period.[58] Such publishing time lags occurred even when distance and the Atlantic Ocean were not the obstacles. Though Michigan received official status as a territory in 1805, the first separate map of Michigan Territory did not appear, as Karpinski points out, until 1822 (fig. 6).[59]

When he turned to the evolution of the printed map of the Great Lakes, Karpinski's focus was typical of his historiographic era. He used the "accuracy" of the shape of Michigan and the Great Lakes as the litmus test for a map's value. He stressed elimination of error as the chronological marker of the evolution of Michigan's cartography. In this regard, he looked for three particular "mistakes." The first was the representation of the mittenlike Lower Peninsula. He pointed out the wide variance from the pointed

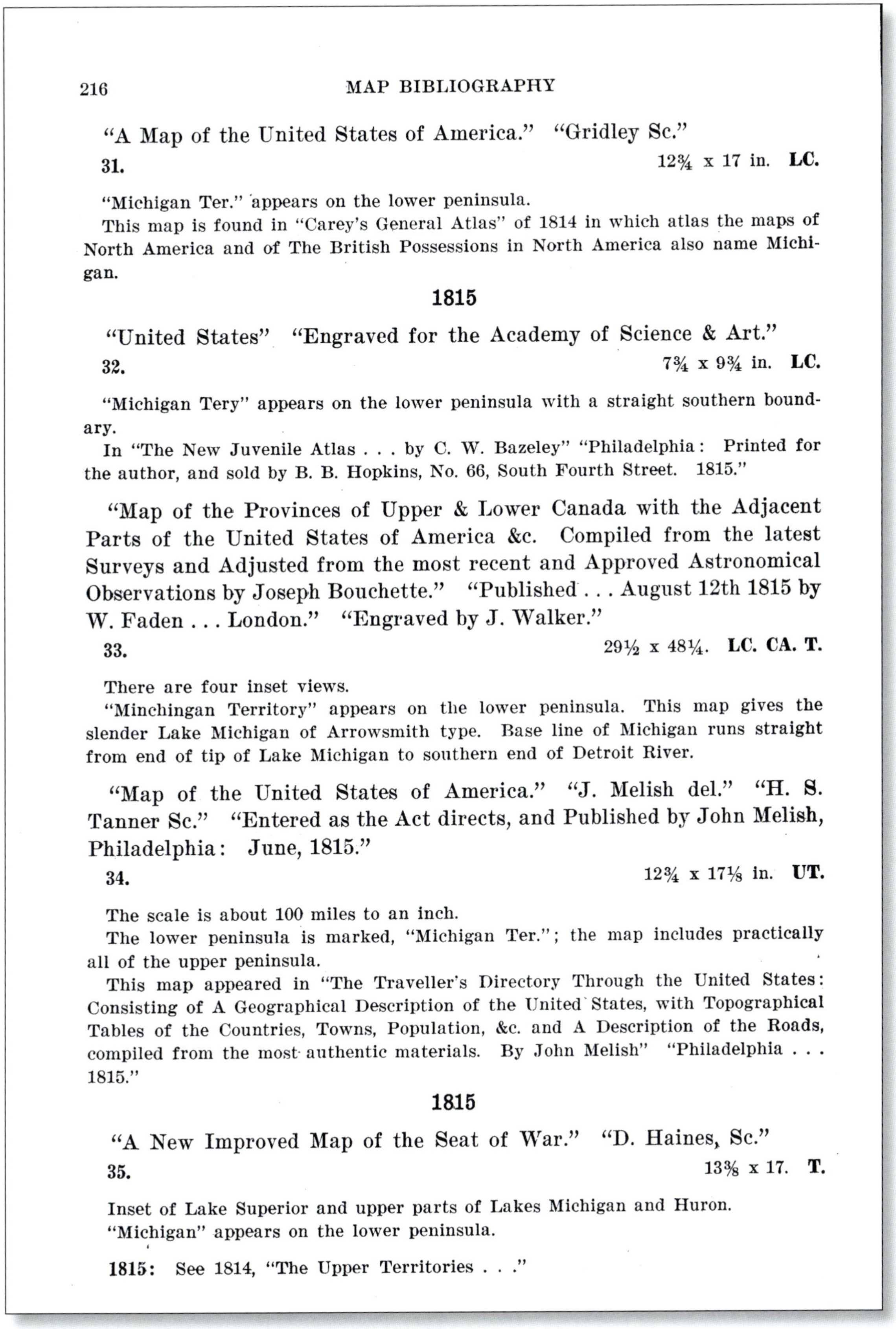

216   MAP BIBLIOGRAPHY

"A Map of the United States of America." "Gridley Sc."
31.   12¾ x 17 in. **LC.**

"Michigan Ter." appears on the lower peninsula.
This map is found in "Carey's General Atlas" of 1814 in which atlas the maps of
North America and of The British Possessions in North America also name Michi-
gan.

1815

"United States" "Engraved for the Academy of Science & Art."
32.   7¾ x 9¾ in. **LC.**

"Michigan Tery" appears on the lower peninsula with a straight southern boundary.
In "The New Juvenile Atlas . . . by C. W. Bazeley" "Philadelphia: Printed for
the author, and sold by B. B. Hopkins, No. 66, South Fourth Street. 1815."

"Map of the Provinces of Upper & Lower Canada with the Adjacent
Parts of the United States of America &c. Compiled from the latest
Surveys and Adjusted from the most recent and Approved Astronomical
Observations by Joseph Bouchette." "Published . . . August 12th 1815 by
W. Faden . . . London." "Engraved by J. Walker."
33.   29½ x 48¼. **LC. CA. T.**

There are four inset views.
"Minchingan Territory" appears on the lower peninsula. This map gives the
slender Lake Michigan of Arrowsmith type. Base line of Michigan runs straight
from end of tip of Lake Michigan to southern end of Detroit River.

"Map of the United States of America." "J. Melish del." "H. S.
Tanner Sc." "Entered as the Act directs, and Published by John Melish,
Philadelphia: June, 1815."
34.   12¾ x 17⅛ in. **UT.**

The scale is about 100 miles to an inch.
The lower peninsula is marked, "Michigan Ter."; the map includes practically
all of the upper peninsula.
This map appeared in "The Traveller's Directory Through the United States:
Consisting of A Geographical Description of the United States, with Topographical
Tables of the Countries, Towns, Population, &c. and A Description of the Roads,
compiled from the most authentic materials. By John Melish" "Philadelphia . . .
1815."

1815

"A New Improved Map of the Seat of War." "D. Haines, Sc."
35.   13⅜ x 17. **T.**

Inset of Lake Superior and upper parts of Lakes Michigan and Huron.
"Michigan" appears on the lower peninsula.

1815: See 1814, "The Upper Territories . . ."

Figure 5. One page from Louis C. Karpinski's *Bibliography*, showing his layout. Louis C. Karpinski, *Bibliography of the Printed Maps of Michigan, 1804–1880* (Lansing: Michigan Historical Commission, 1931). Courtesy of the William L. Clements Library, University of Michigan.

Lower Peninsula of Sanson (1656, the first printed map to show the five Great Lakes) (fig. 7) and Lahontan (1703)[60] to Hennepin's southern-dipping Lake Erie (1683–1688) and Aaron Arrowsmith's slender, sloping shape of Lake Michigan, which distorts the state's western shore (1796).[61] The second "error" is the shape of Lake Superior, admirably and accurately rendered in 1672 in a map published in the *Jesuit Relations* (fig. 8),[62] but which deteriorated when it was distorted in subsequent renditions by Hennepin (1683), Lahontan (1703), and Moll (1701–1720). Fictitious islands appeared in Lake Superior on the map prepared by J. N. Bellin (fig. 9), published in the Jesuit Father Charlevoix's *Journal* and reproduced by many mapmakers who followed.[63] The third "mistake" was the chain of hills running along the central north-south spine of the Lower Peninsula, the so-called Mountains of Michigan that first appeared on Guillaume Delisle's *Carte de la Louisiane et du Cours du Mississipi [sic]* (1718) (fig. 10), followed by Henry Popple (1733) and Cadwallader Colden (1747).[64] This error was perpetuated well into the nineteenth century by mapmakers such as Matthew Carey of Philadelphia (1814).

Because of the distinctive shapes of Michigan's peninsulas and the surrounding Great Lakes, it would have been difficult for Karpinski to resist the temptation to use accuracy as the litmus test for his cartographic analysis, praising those maps that got it right and castigating those that got it wrong. He slanted his descriptions in favor of the accurate rendering of the area. "Arrowsmith's unfortunate slender representation of Lake Michigan in 1802 exerted a pernicious influence over a long period of time, making this a noteworthy map for Michigan" (fig. 11).[65] Karpinski did not reflect deeply upon the phenomenon of the uncritical transmission of geographical shapes in printed maps over a long period of time. However, he did note the problems inherent in the "erroneous ideas which received wide circulation" resulting from some cartographers who gave "two distinctly different conceptions of the Great Lakes in the same work" and from other authors who "gave quite different treatment[s] in two maps involving the Great Lakes Area, circulated simultaneously although not so issued."[66] Karpinski gives as an example Alexis-Hubert Jaillot's "Partie de la Nouvelle France" of 1685, the content of which relies on the manuscript work of French explorers such as Joliet and Franquelin and the Jesuit map of Lake Superior (Lac Tracy) published in 1672. Jaillot published a map with "a remarkably correct Superior and northern portions of Michigan and Huron."[67] Yet five years later, in 1690, Jaillot published maps of North America based on the "old open lakes of Sanson, apparently without a thought about the fine correct map that he had published five years before."[68] This disjunction between what appeared to be certain knowledge based on observation, as delineated in the manuscripts, and the printed map, with its out-of-date information, caused Karpinski some bewilderment, but it encouraged him to caution the researcher not to rely on the printed map.

By raising questions about the transmission of knowledge and the accessibility of information in the public sphere, Karpinski was well ahead of his time. However, in striking contrast to his contributions to the history of mathematics, his work in the history of cartography makes little attempt to answer these thoughtful queries. As a hunter-gatherer of maps, Karpinski did not linger long in the garden of analysis.[69] The tendency of the printed-map market to sustain differing and sometimes opposing ideas about far-away lands was a common feature of early modern map production. Karpinski noted the phenomenon and pointed to the archives for explanations. More recent studies of commercial map firms reveal how market forces often exerted a more powerful influence than the force of "accuracy," especially on regions of the world where "accuracy" simply could not be determined. Jaillot, a sculptor by training, had come into the business of engraving and publishing through his first marriage; he was

GEOGRAPHICAL, STATISTICAL, AND HISTORICAL MAP OF MICHIGAN TERRITORY.

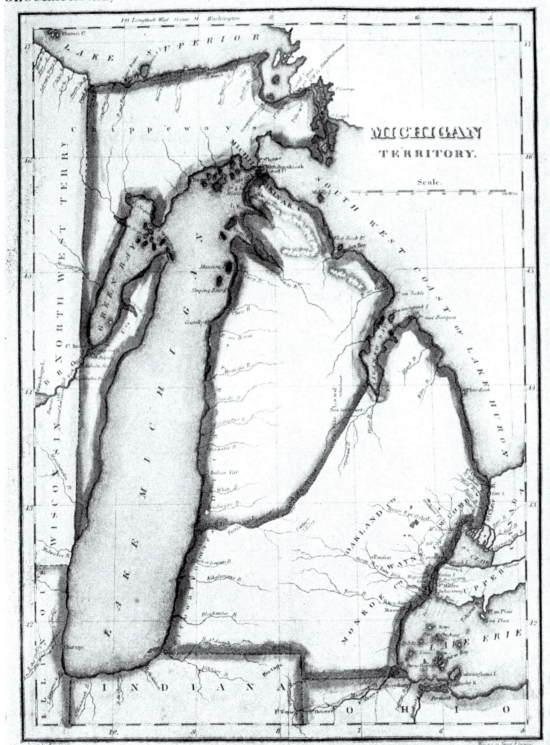

Figure 6. Karpinski claimed this map of Michigan Territory as the first separately printed map of Michigan (Karpinski, *Bibliography*, 91). J. Finlayson, *Michigan Territory* (Philadelphia: H. C. Carey and I. Lea, 1822). Courtesy of the William L. Clements Library, University of Michigan.

Figure 7. *Le Canada ou Nouvelle France*, the first printed map to show the five Great Lakes, exhibits the pointed Lower Peninsula (Karpinski, *Bibliography*, VIII). Nicolas Sanson, *Le Canada ou Nouvelle France* (Paris: Chez Pierre Mariette, 1656). Courtesy of the William L. Clements Library, University of Michigan.

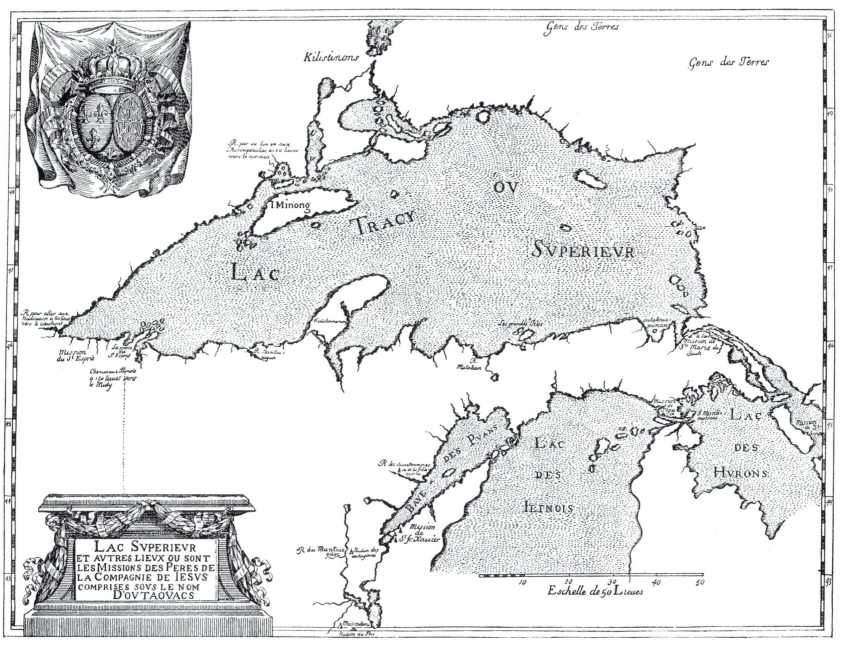

Figure 8. *Lac Superieur*, based on the reconnaissance of Jesuit missionaries, shows remarkable similarity to the lake's actual geographic shape (Karpinski, *Bibliography*, XIII). Claude Dablon, S. J., *Relation de ce Qui s'est Passé de Plus Remarquable aux Missions des Pères de la Compagnie de Jesus en la Nouvelle France, les Années 1670 & 1671* (Paris: Sebastien Mabre-Cramoisy, 1672). Courtesy of the William L. Clements Library, University of Michigan.

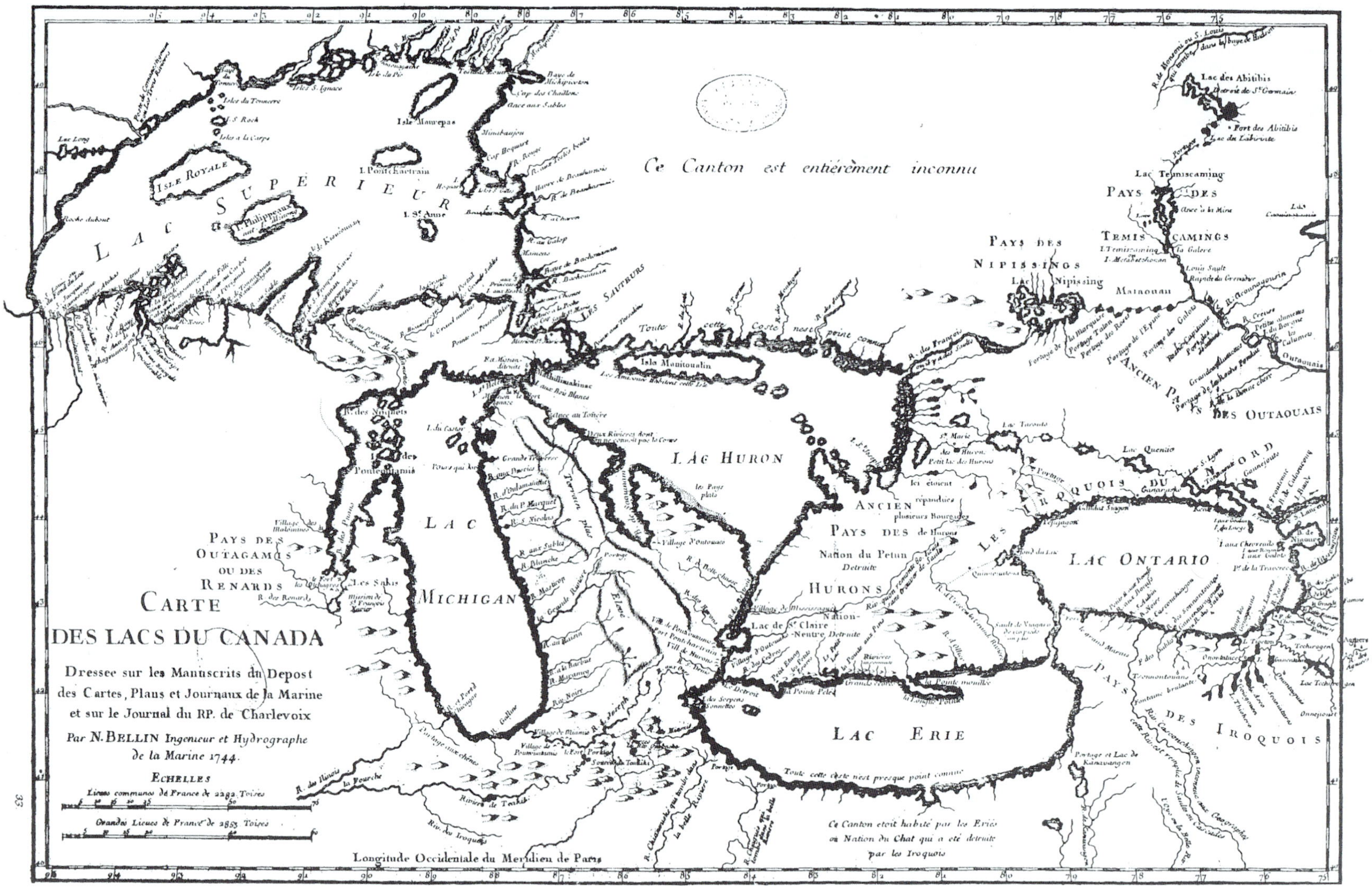

Figure 9. *Carte des Lacs du Canada*, showing fictitious islands in Lake Superior (Karpinski, *Bibliography*, LV). Jacques Nicolas Bellin, *Carte des Lacs du Canada* (Paris: n.p., 1744). Courtesy of the William L. Clements Library, University of Michigan.

not a geographer. He joined the sons of Nicolas Sanson in a contract to engrave and print their maps; this arrangement initially provided Jaillot with commercial success. But when the partnership faltered, Jaillot turned to other sources of maps to edit and publish.[70] At the same time, he continued to print and sell maps that he had acquired through his earlier contracts with the Sansons, thus providing later historians of cartography with a rich array of conflicting geographic representations. Jaillot's purpose was to sell maps and profit from them, not to elucidate a new and changing cartography.

Karpinski himself was aware of the role of the marketplace in the dissemination of knowledge. His inclusion of school atlases and school geographies in his bibliography paralleled his interest in the teaching of mathematics and the history of the mathematical textbook. These works were often overlooked as a means of understanding how the ordinary citizen viewed his or her state or nation, but Karpinski stressed their importance. Though their fragile nature rendered them scarce ("In large measure the books were destroyed by the pupils in use"), Karpinski noted that "the school atlas or geography has

Figure 10. *Carte de la Louisiane et du Cours du Mississipi* [sic] shows an elevated plain running north to south in Michigan's Lower Peninsula, an "error" perpetuated on maps well into the nineteenth century (Karpinski, *Bibliography*, L). Guillaume Delisle, *Carte de la Louisiane et du Cours du Mississipi* [sic] (Paris: n.p., 1718). Courtesy of the William L. Clements Library, University of Michigan.

Figure 11. Detail of *A Map of the United States of North America,* showing the slender, sloping Lake Michigan and the tapering point of the Lower Peninsula, which distorted the state's western shore (Karpinski, *Bibliography*, CXVa). Aaron Arrowsmith, *A Map of the United States of North America* (London: A. Arrowsmith, 1802). Courtesy of the William L. Clements Library, University of Michigan.

been the one book almost certain to be found in every home where there is a child of school age. Doubtless in the early days when citizens of the Eastern States were considering migration to the Middle West these works were the ones most frequently consulted. . . . These school text-books deserve most careful attention in any study of the spread of ideas by the printed page."[71]

If we ask what Karpinski's bibliography lacks or where it falls short, we are asking the wrong questions. These are the same questions we pose when we look only at a map's inaccuracies and judge it by its mistakes. If instead we ask how Karpinski's bibliography fits into the historiography of the history of cartography, we find it was among the first of its kind. As a dealer and collector, Karpinski appreciated the need for a comprehensive list, a cohesive catalogue that would provide a chronological order and bibliographic framework for printed and manuscript materials. He also understood the need for historical context, though it is in this regard that his *Bibliography of the Printed Maps of Michigan* does not stand up well against his work in the history of mathematics. He did not pursue the answers to his queries, rarely exploring the larger issues of how, for whom, on whose orders, and for what purpose maps were created and printed. Such questions were not the primary purpose of a bibliographer. Karpinski listed, measured, compared, and offered tentative conclusions. If his bibliography has a fault at all, it is that it does not give the complete information we now have come to expect of map descriptions, with full measurements of borders, plate marks, descriptions of insets, expressions of scale, and the precise features of variants and later editions. His introductory essays do little more than outline many of the tantalizing problems inherent in a study of the transmission of geographic knowledge. Yet Karpinski raised questions that still need to be answered, and his *Bibliography of the Printed Maps of Michigan* will be the starting point for the history of cartography of the state that remains to be written.

NOTES

1. Louis C. Karpinski, *Bibliography of the Printed Maps of Michigan, 1804–1880: With a Series of Over One Hundred Reproductions of Maps Constituting an Historical Atlas of the Great Lakes and Michigan* (Lansing: Michigan Historical Commission, 1931); reprinted as *Maps of Famous Cartographers Depicting North America: An Historical Atlas of the Great Lakes and Michigan, with Bibliography of the Printed Maps of Michigan to 1880* (Amsterdam: Meridian Publishing, 1977). Louis C. Karpinski, *Bibliography of Mathematical Works Printed in America through 1850* (Ann Arbor: University of Michigan Press, 1940). Thomas M. Spaulding and Louis C. Karpinski, *Early Military Books in the University of Michigan Libraries* (Ann Arbor: University of Michigan Press, 1941).

2. Phillip S. Jones, "Louis Charles Karpinski, Historian of Mathematics and Cartography," *Historia Mathematica* 3 (May 1976): 185–202. This brief biography and bibliography of Karpinski's work was written by his former student and colleague in the Department of Mathematics at the University of Michigan. It is the source of most of the biographical information in this article.

3. "The Ambrose Swasey Library," *Catalogue of Fine Books and Manuscripts Including Americana* (New York: Sotheby's, 2003), 9. The collection of Lutheriana and early Protestant books was added to the library of the Colgate Rochester Crozer Divinity School in 1924.

4. Note of L. C. Karpinski, October 13, 1947, regarding the Karpinski collection of children's books sold to the Detroit Public Library for $1,200, folder 9, box 1, Louis Charles Karpinski Papers (hereafter Karpinski Papers), Bentley Historical Library, University of Michigan, Ann Arbor.

5. Melvin Mills to L. C. Karpinski, October 9, 1945; Bohdan Azwadski to L. C. Karpinski, February 8, 1946, both in folder 8, box 1, Karpinski Papers. Karpinski also donated books to the American Book Center for War Devastated Libraries and to the Rebuilders of Poland Association, May 5, 14, 1941, folder 9, box 1, in ibid.

6. John S. Hilbert, "Louis Charles Karpinski: Polish-American Chess Player and Historian of Mathematics," 1998, http://www.astercity.net/~vistula/karpinsk.htm. Hilbert details Karpinski's performance in state chess competitions, citing the *Daily Standard-Union* of Brooklyn, New York, August 26, 1893. For the midsummer congress of the New York State Chess Association, held at Skaneateles, New York, he quotes from the *Daily Standard-Union*, August 10, 1895. He also cites the *Albany*

Evening Journal of October 30, 1897, and the *New-Yorker Staats-Zeitung* of September 15, 1901. Hilbert notes that "Karpinski also played successfully for Cornell University, where by 1901 he was first board on the school's championship team. He was instrumental in organizing the Triangular Chess League, with teams from Cornell, Brown, and the University of Pennsylvania, a league that continued for many years after Karpinski had graduated."

7. D. A. Murray to the president of the University of Oregon, May 11, 1901, folder 1, box 1, Karpinski Papers.

8. L. C. Karpinski to his parents, 1901–1903, folder 1, box 1, Karpinski Papers. The school was run by a Mr. and Mrs. Goss.

9. Louis C. Karpinski and David Eugene Smith, *The Hindu-Arabic Numerals* (Boston: Ginn and Co., 1911).

10. The collections of both Smith and Plimpton are now found in the rare books and manuscript division of the library of Columbia University.

11. Jones, "Louis Charles Karpinski," 187. Jones cites Karpinski, "The Ziwet Collection," *American Mathematical Monthly* 28 (1921): 484.

12. An important example of this type of inquiry is Karpinski's *Robert of Chester's Latin Translation of the Algebra of Al-Khowarizmi* (Ann Arbor: University of Michigan Press, 1930). In the preface (p. ix), Karpinski makes special mention of his indebtedness to Professor David Eugene Smith "for having suggested the work; to Mr. George A. Plimpton for the generous use of his unique mathematical library."

13. *Bibliotheca Mathematica* (3) 13 (1913): 99–114; *Science* 45 (1917): 663–65; *Modern Language Notes* 28 (1913): 93.

14. *Dearborn Independent,* July 19, 1924; September 24, 1927.

15. Louis C. Karpinski and Frank E. Robbins, "Michigan Papyrus 620: The Introduction of Algebraic Equations in Greece," *Science* 70 (September 27, 1929): 311–14; L. C. Karpinski, "Michigan Mathematical Papyrus 621," *Isis* 5, no. 1 (1923): 20–25.

16. Louis C. Karpinski, with Harry Y. Benedict and John W. Calhoun, *Unified Mathematics* (Boston: D. C. Heath, 1918), 1922.

17. *American Lumberman* 16 (April 25, 1914): 52–53; *The Education Journal* 16 (1915): 132–35. These are cited in Jones, "Louis Charles Karpinski."

18. In "Arithmetic for the Farm" (p. 132), Karpinski disparaged the typical "story problems" found in contemporary textbooks, such as the following: "How many sacks, holding 2 bushels, 3 pecks and 2 quarts each can be filled from a bin containing 366 bushels, 3 pecks, 4 quarts of wheat?" Karpinski comments: "How carefully would you have to fill a sack to make it hold 3 pecks 2 quarts of anything? And who filled the bin so marvelously that the capacity is known with an accuracy of one-25th of 1% of the total?" He recommended an easier, more practical means of doing such problems, noting that a bushel is about 1¼ or ⁵⁄₄ cubic feet. Therefore, the number of bushels in the bin is the length times width times ⅘; the easiest way to get ⅘ of anything is to take away one-fifth of it.

19. "Textbook Racket Blasted by Teacher: Prof. Karpinski, U. of M., Urges Inquiry into Practices of Educational Quacks," *Detroit News,* November 3, n.d., clipping in folder 7, box 1, Karpinski Papers. "Prof. Karpinski charged that many of the primary readers and arithmetics used in the grade schools of the United States are compiled by persons ignorant of textbook preparation, without actual experience in presenting the subject to children and without regard for the manner in which the book will appeal—or fail to appeal—to children. . . . It is because the authors have the power to name complacent and obliging superintendents to important committees of national educational organizations, because they can recommend the compliant for promotion or because they have found other crass means of rewarding the faithful."

20. Louis C. Karpinski, "National Learned Society Groups and the Public Interest," *Science* 97 (May 7, 1943): 422–23.

21. Chauncey Leake to Louis Karpinski, August 13, 1943, requesting Karpinski's resignation; Alexander Pogo to Louis Karpinski, December 22, 1943, accepting Karpinski's resignation, both in folder 7, box 1, Karpinski Papers.

22. *Michigan Daily,* March 23, 1947. According to Karpinski, a Republican-sponsored bill proposing a $4 billion tax cut would result in a rebate of $12,000 to each of 65,000 men and $34 on average to 25 million people, with 9 million receiving nothing at all. Folder 46, box 3, Karpinski Papers.

23. Professor George Hay, emeritus member of the Department of Mathematics, University of Michigan, January 19, 2003, conversation with author. Hay arrived at the University of Michigan in 1940, six years before Karpinski retired. Phillip Jones's biographical article also stresses Karpinski's acerbic character.

24. Forty-three married instructors in the literary department supported the petition, declaring that a married couple in Ann Arbor could not live reasonably on less than twelve hundred dollars a year. Karpinski's notes and some of the raw data from this survey are in folder 4, box 1, Karpinski Papers. The survey noted that someone who worked in the factory for Henry Ford made more money than did a junior faculty member at the university. Howard H. Peckham, Margaret L. Steneck, and Nicholas H. Steneck, *The Making of the University of Michigan, 1817–1992* (Ann Arbor: University of Michigan, 1994), 131.

25. R. McAllister Lloyd, president, TIAA, to L. C. Karpinski, March 3, 1949, folder, 9, box 1, Karpinski Papers.

26. Louis C. Karpinski, *Robert of Chester's Latin Translation of the Algebra of Al-Khowarizmi* (with an introduction, critical notes, and an English version) (New York: Macmillan, 1915), 41. Karpinski used Scheybl's edition of a Robert of Chester manuscript as a guide for his own translation.

27. He had been thinking about such a set since 1913, when he wrote to John Burnam of the University of Cincinnati with a proposal. Folder 3, box 1, Karpinski Papers.

28. 1947 tax return, folder 9, box 1, Karpinski Papers. According to the obituary in *Science* 124 (July 6, 1956): 19, Karpinski "died in his sleep early in the morning of 25 January 1956 at his home in Winter Haven, Florida, from which since his retirement he had continued as a book dealer to exercise his bibliophilistic urge."

29. Randolph Adams to William Clements, July 8, 1925, RG Adams folder, W. L. Clements box, manuscript division, William L. Clements Library, University of Michigan, Ann Arbor.

30. Prince Max Waldburg-Wolfegg to Louis Karpinski, June 8, 1932, folder 6, box 1, Karpinski Papers. Accompanying this letter is a copy of the agreement between the prince and Karpinski, written in Karpinski's hand, dated August 14, 1931. This map was sold to the Library of Congress for $10 million in 2003. See *Library of Congress Information Bulletin* 62 (September 2003): 187–93.

31. The American Association of Geographers had met in Ypsilanti, Michigan, for their 28th annual meeting in December 1931. Karpinski presented a paper on significant maps of Michigan during the first day of the meetings. In his copy of the program, he noted, "When I really sold the maps and atlases to Yale." Folder 46, box 3, Karpinski Papers.

32. The McGregor Plan was administered by the Committee on Americana for College Libraries of the American Historical Association, headed at that time by Dr. Randolph G. Adams of the William L. Clements Library. The object of the plan was to help college and small university libraries acquire rare Americana, which they otherwise would not have been able to obtain. Randolph G. Adams, *The McGregor Plan for the Encouragement of Book Collecting by American College Libraries* (Ann Arbor: American Historical Association, 1937).

33. See records in folder 9, box 1, Karpinski Papers.

34. Karpinski's list of items sold to Florida State University at Tallahassee leaves four additional titles as gifts, April 21, 1949, folder 11, box 1; Karpinski's three-page list of items sold to the Library of Congress ends with fifteen items included without charge, December 14, 1938, folder 42, box 3, both in Karpinski Papers.

35. "Draft," Louis Karpinski to Linda Eastman, Cleveland Public Library, n.d., folder 33, box 2, Karpinski Papers.

36. Clements's professor was Moses Coit Tyler, professor of rhetoric and English literature. His monumental *History of American Literature, 1607–1765* (New York: G. Putnam, 1878) "inaugurated the heroic age of scholarship in American literary history." Peckham, Steneck, and Steneck, *Making of the University of Michigan*, 62–63 (quotation), 128.

37. Peckham, Steneck, and Steneck, *Making of the University of Michigan*, 129.

38. Ibid., 162.

39. "In [my] search for books I made six trips to Europe and Asia Minor, two on sabbatical leaves. . . . I searched the libraries of

France, England, Italy, Austria & Czechoslovakia . . . Egypt, Turkey, and Palestine. I secured through the collaboration of Dr. Max Meyerhof a fairly large collection of Arabic books and manuscripts, financed by the McGregor Foundation." "Prefatory Remarks Regarding the Arithmetic in Provençal," folder 31, box 2, Karpinski Papers.

40. Waldo G. Leland, *Guide to Materials for American History in the Libraries and Archives of Paris* (Washington, D.C.: Carnegie Institution, 1932); Nancy Maria Miller Surrey, ed., *Calendar of Manuscripts in Paris Archives and Libraries Relating to the History of the Mississippi Valley to 1803* (Washington, D.C.: Carnegie Institution, 1926).

41. Louis C. Karpinski, "Manuscript Maps of American [*sic*] in European Archives," *Michigan History Magazine* 14 (1930): 5–14. See also idem, "Manuscript Maps Relating to American History in French, Spanish, and Portuguese Archives," *American Historical Review* 33 (January 1928): 328–30. The use of photostats for research purposes was relatively new. The New York Public Library had installed a photostat copying camera in 1912 for reproduction, and it added a second machine in 1917. Charles Flowers McCombs, *The Photostat in Reference Work* (New York: New York Public Library, 1920), 3–4.

42. Complete sets of these photostats were initially bought by the William L. Clements Library; The Newberry Library in Chicago; the Henry E. Huntington Library in San Marino, Calif.; the New York Public Library; Harvard College Library; and the Library of Congress. Other institutions bought reduced or partial sets, as noted in Karpinski, "Manuscript Maps," 14.

43. The Huntington Library maintains a short title list of its Karpinski photostat collection on its Web site, http://www.oac.cdlib.org/findaid/ark:/13030/tf3m3n99sf. My thanks to William Frank for providing this information. The Library of Congress preserves a typescript list of the maps in the Karpinski photostat collection organized by original archive. My thanks to Ronald Grim for providing the Clements Library with a copy of this typescript.

44. On the evolution of the map project, see "Annual Reports of the Michigan Historical Commission," *Michigan History* 7 (1923): 119–20; 12 (1928): 127–29; 13 (1929): 327–28; 14 (1930): 317; 16 (1932): 233–34. Reports were published the year following each reporting year, and there is no report for 1930.

45. Floyd Benjamin Streeter, *Michigan Bibliography: A Partial Catalogue of Books, Maps, Manuscripts, and Miscellaneous Materials Relating to the Resources, Development, and History of Michigan from Earliest Times to July 1, 1917; together With Citation of Libraries in Which the Materials May Be Consulted, and a Complete Analytical Index by Subject and Author* (Lansing: Michigan Historical Commission, 1921), vol. 2.

46. "Sixteenth Annual Report of the Michigan Historical Commission," *Michigan History* 13 (1929): 327.

47. The Michigan Historical Commission was not the first to envision a history of the cartography of the Great Lakes. Henry N. Stevens, a map dealer and frequent writer on American topics, had corresponded in 1911 with University of Michigan Regent Lucius Hubbard, sending him a long report on the "cartography of the District of the Great Lakes." Henry N. Stevens to L. L. Hubbard, typescript letter, March 8, 1911, Discovery of the Great Lakes folder, vertical file, map division, Clements Library. Stevens attached to his letter a descriptive list of fifty-five maps showing the region of the Great Lakes, ranging from a Sanson map of North America, published by Jaillot in 1696, to the 1819 edition of Aaron Arrowsmith's "Map of the United States." However, Stevens's work, though comprehensive, was a list of maps for sale rather than an exhaustive catalogue. Karpinski himself left an undated typescript for a history of cartography in five chapters, and he had planned to compile a bibliography of all maps printed before 1600. Folder 32, box 2, Karpinski Papers.

48. Joseph Sabin and Wilberforce Eames, *Bibliotheca Americana: A Dictionary of Books Relating to America, from Its Discovery to the Present Time,* 29 vols. (New York: Sabin and the Bibliographical Society of America, 1868–1936). Karpinski expressed his gratitude to Sabin's successor, Wilberforce Eames, as "my constant counselor, an inspiration always to greater effort," in the preface to his *Bibliography of Mathematical Works,* vii.

49. A list of the cartographic works of Herbert George Fordham (1854–1929), the English map collector, may be found in M. J. Freeman and J. Longbotham, "The Fordham Collection at the RGS: An Introduction," *Geographical Journal* 146 (July 1980): 218–31. Fordham concentrated on county maps of Hertfordshire and Cambridgeshire, road maps and itineraries published

in England and France, and the works of John Cary. However, this brief description does not do justice to the more than fifty books and articles he published between 1901 and 1929, many of them catalogues and cartobibliographies, the latter a term Fordham may have coined. Fordham, *Studies in Carto-Bibliography, British and French, and in the Bibliography of Itineraries and Road-Books* (Oxford: Clarendon Press, 1914).

50. Bagrow, a Russian scholar who fled to Germany following the Russian Revolution, had completed his history of cartography in 1943, but wartime bombing in Berlin destroyed the illustration material. Leo Bagrow, *Geschichte der Kartographie* (Berlin: Safari-Verlag, 1951); J. B. Harley, "The Map and the Development of the History of Cartography," in *The History of Cartography*, vol. 1, *Cartography in Prehistoric, Ancient, and Medieval Europe and the Mediterranean*, ed. J. B. Harley and David Woodward (Chicago: University of Chicago Press, 1987), 25.

51. Louis C. Karpinski, "Cartographical Collections in America," *Imago Mundi* 1 (1935): 62–64. In this short piece, he pointed out the cartobibliographical work being done in North America in various collections, the catalogues available, and the curators responsible for valuable compilations and reproductions of resources. He particularly highlighted the collections in the Clements Library and his own bibliographical work on the printed maps of Michigan.

52. Louis C. Karpinski, ed., *Early Maps of Carolina and Adjoining Regions: Together with Early Prints of Charleston from the Collection of Henry P. Kendall* (Columbia, S.C.: Library of the University of South Carolina, 1930); William P. Cumming, *The Southeast in Early Maps* (Princeton: Princeton University Press, 1958), preface. Cumming dedicated a later work, *British Maps of Colonial America* (Chicago: University of Chicago Press, 1974), to three "valued mentors and well-remembered friends," of whom Louis C. Karpinski heads the list.

53. Wagner expressed his "appreciation of much help from Dr. Louis C. Karpinski." Henry Wagner, *The Cartography of the Northwest Coast of America to the Year 1800* (Berkeley: University of California Press, 1937), vi.

54. Streeter, *Michigan Bibliography*, vol. 2.

55. The final "Miscellaneous" category includes such maps as "Isolation and Disinfection, restricted scarlet fever and diphtheria in Michigan, ten years, 1887–96."

56. Karpinski, *Bibliography*, 81.

57. Ibid., 24.

58. Ibid., 26–79.

59. J. Finlayson, *Michigan Territory* (Philadelphia: H. C. Carey and I. Lea, 1822).

60. Karpinski, *Bibliography*, VIII, XXXIX–XLIII.

61. Ibid., XVIII; Arrowsmith's 1802 edition: ibid., CXVa.

62. Karpinski, *Bibliography*, XIII: Claude Dablon, S.J., *Relation de ce Qui s'est Passé de Plus Remarquable aux Mission des Pères de la Compagnie de Jesus en la Nouvelle France, les Années 1670 & 1671* (Paris: Sebastien Mabre-Cramoisy, 1672).

63. Karpinski, *Bibliography*, LV–LVIa. More recent study of the fictitious islands of Lake Superior may be found in Robert Karrow, "Lake Superior's Mythic Isles: A Cautionary Tale for Users of Old Maps," *Michigan History* 69 (Spring 1985): 24–31. See also Pierre-François-Xavier de Charlevoix, *Journal d'un Voyage Fait par Ordre du Roi dans l'Amérique Septentrionale* (Paris: Didot, 1744); Karpinski, *Bibliography*, L, LIII, LX, 27.

64. Guillaume Delisle, *Carte de la Louisiane et du Cours du Mississipi* [sic] (Paris: n.p., 1718).

65. Karpinski, *Bibliography*, 81.

66. Ibid.

67. Karpinski, *Bibliography*, 109. In fact, in 1700, Jaillot purchased manuscripts from Franquelin to use for his mapmaking. Mireille Pastoureau, *Les Atlas Français, XVIe–XVIIe Siècles: Repertoire Bibliographique et Étude* (Paris: Bibliothèque Nationale, 1984), 232–33.

68. Karpinski, *Bibliography*, 109, maps XX and XXI.

69. Karpinski seems not to have consulted the work of three-well known cartographic historians who wrote about North America and New France: Gabriel Marcel, Henry Harrisse, and Henri Vignaud. For Guillaume Delisle and his use of Jesuit and other missionary sources for his maps, see Nelson-Martin Dawson and Charles Vincent, *L'Atelier Delisle: L'Amérique du Nord sur la Table à Dessin* (Sillery, Quebec: Septentrion, 2000), 145–78. For the relationship between Louis XIV and the geography of New France, see Monique Pelletier, *Tours et Contours de la Terre: Itinéraires d'une Femme au Coeur de la Cartographie* (Paris: Presses de l'École Nationale des Ponts et Chaussées, 1999), 199–240.

70. Pastoureau, *Les Atlas Français,* 262.

71. Karpinski, *Bibliography,* 330.

First Nations Mapmaking in the Great Lakes Region in Intercultural Contexts: A Historical Review

G. Malcolm Lewis

AT THEIR FIRST CONTACT WITH EUROPEANS, FIRST NATIONS PEOPLES THROUGHOUT North America were making what Europeans intuitively categorized as terrestrial maps. Because mapmaking presupposes an ability to organize knowledge spatially, understanding First Nations cartographic expressions involves recognizing something of their spatial awareness. This was a complex product of travel and migrations within their own region, contacts with peoples beyond it, belief systems (including cosmographic), and the modes whereby they received, organized, shared, and perceived information about their world.

The Great Lakes catchment (the focus area for this chapter) covers some three hundred thousand square miles, of which the five Great Lakes themselves occupy almost one-third. On the eve of European contact the region's approximately one hundred fifty thousand people were unequally distributed. Half were Iroquoian-speaking, primarily horticultural village dwellers to the south and west of Lake Ontario. Those to the south (the League of the Iroquois) were becoming great travelers, using an extensive network of forest trails. Conversely, their elm-bark canoes were unsuitable for long voyages, dangerous on large lakes, and useless in white water. In contrast, the Huron, to the northwest of Lake Ontario, were to become skilled in the use of ever-larger birch-bark canoes and would be the region's most important long-distance traders. To the far west, around the three upper lakes, were scattered groups of Algonquian speakers. Their economies were mixtures of hunting, fishing, vegetable collecting, and, to the south, horticulture, which involved seasonal movements, sometimes over considerable distances.

Long-distance trade from outside the region was already well established. Bison skins arrived from the west, marine shells from the south, furs from the north, and so forth. Outward trade sent corn and tobacco to the north. Increasingly, European goods were traded within the region. The primary watershed was rarely more than one hundred miles from a shore of one of the five lakes. Many streams rose in relatively easy portages. To the south, these afforded natural routes into the Allegheny-Ohio drainage system. On the rocky shield to the north, rapids necessitated more frequent and difficult portaging. Following the easiest river routes when going upstream involved knowing which fork to take at each bifurcation.

The emergence of long-distance forest trails in the south of the region reflected a knowledge of easy river crossings and easily traversed former lake floors. Conversely, these trails also indicated awareness of difficult-to-traverse wetlands and rough morainic terrains.

Though important, the Great Lakes themselves were dangerous. Wherever possible, canoe routes followed the coasts. Two routes were particularly important: from Georgian Bay via the sheltered North Channel of Lake Huron either to Lake Superior via Sault Ste. Marie, or to Lake Michigan via the Straits of Mackinac. Lake Erie was probably the least used of the five lakes. Although oriented approximately east-west, it did not lead to a water route west.

Geographical information could be communicated orally. All the languages were richly endowed with locative suffixes and locative directional markers. Several languages were spoken, but Ojibwe was the lingua franca around the northern edge of the region. Many individuals were conversant in several languages. At council meetings, interpreters were almost always present. There were, of course, no scripts. Hence, there were no equivalents of written geographies. But pictography was well developed, and mapmaking was an undifferentiated part of it.

During the postcontact period, the population of the region became even more dynamic. Wars, alliances, involvements in frontier diplomacy, displacements within, incursions from without, European-initiated trade in furs and imported goods, and the influx of Europeans themselves together served to increase the quantity, quality, and spatial range of information about the region. First Nations peoples had superb memories. Inevitably, however, contact with Europeans resulted in acculturation, not least of their maps.

Unlike the First Nations peoples of the Great Plains and the Southwest, those of the Great Lakes region did not make celestial charts. Though not always expressed graphically, their cosmologies did, however, have strong spatial components. For example, Iroquois League tradition was permeated by the concept of path, and this was manifested as a behavioral map in several of its rituals. The concept of spatial overview was central to the Iroquois myth of a large bird that flew high and watched over all the world. The linked concepts of node, network, and distance decay were embodied in the league's symbolism of the central hearth, by the side of which was a great tree with roots spreading to the north, east, south, and west.

From earliest contact and in every part of North America, Europeans and Euro-Americans observed First Nations peoples representing spatial arrangements graphically. Then and until very recently at least, these representations were categorized by European appellatives derived from either of the late Latin words *mappa* or *carta*.[1] But there is no evidence that any of the First Nations languages contained equivalents, certainly not among the Algonquian and Iroquoian peoples who occupied the Great Lakes region.[2]

In September 1541, Jacques Cartier met four young St. Lawrence Iroquoian men at the second of what were later to be named the La Chine Rapids on the St. Lawrence River near Mont Royal. Having reached the second of the *saults* by portaging around the first, Cartier was given to understand by these men "that there was but one more to passe . . . and that [it] was but a third part farther than we had travailed, shewing us the same with certaine little stickes, which they layd upon the ground in a certaine distance, and afterwards layde other small branches betweene both, representing the Saults. And by the sayde marke, if their saying be true, it can be but six leagues by land to passe the sayd Saults."[3] Richard Hakluyt, who collected and translated this account, ended it with "Here after followeth the figure of the three Saults." He either failed to supply it, or the printer omitted it. Textual omissions and ambiguities are even more unfortunate when we try to reconstruct Cartier's perceptions of the event and to infer something of the St. Lawrence Iroquoians' actions and intents. Yet, in the history-of-cartography field, the circumstances, cultural contexts, and techniques of mapmaking are now considered to be as important as the maps themselves.

Cartier's account of the events at the La Chine Rapids has been instanced by historians of cartography as an early-contact example of First Nations mapmaking. Yet he did not use the word *carte* or any of its European equivalents. However, on the basis of the distance he had already portaged around the first of the three *saults* and the Iroquoians' model of all of them, Cartier's conclusion that the series could be passed in "sixe leagues by land" implied an assumption that he had seen a map and, furthermore, that the "little stickes" and "small branches" had been selected and arranged to achieve something approaching a constant linear scale in one direction.

The St. Lawrence Iroquoians' three *saults* were to become known as the Deuxième Sault. Cartier had seen the Première Sault only a few miles downstream on his earlier expedition of 1535, and it appeared as an engraved inscription on the Americas map in the first edition (1570) of Abraham Ortelius, *Theatrum Orbis Terrarum*.[4] But not so the Deuxième Sault. Yet, acknowledged or otherwise, First Nations spatial representations were soon to be incorporated on maps made by Europeans. Samuel de Champlain's 1612 map of Novvelle Franse (fig. 1) shows Lake Ontario ("Lac Contenant"), Niagara Falls ("sault de au"), and the easternmost part of Lake Erie ("grand lac contenant"). At that date, however, neither Champlain nor any other European had seen any of these places. There is no acknowledgment of the information source on the map itself, but in 1603, near the site of what would be Montreal, Algonkins (the easternmost division of the Chippewa) had given Champlain a "sketch" representing each of these features.[5] His account makes it clear that this sketch was solicited in the course of verifying another one that he had got other First Nations peoples to "draw by hand" only a few days earlier but at a location some two hundred miles downstream.[6] This, too, had represented the same two large lakes and a waterfall on the river between them that was said to be "somewhat high." Neither the originals nor transcripts of these sketches have survived, but they were almost certainly important parts of the evidence upon which the easternmost approximately ten percent of the Great Lakes' surface area was represented for the first time on a printed map.[7] In modern terminology, Champlain's evidence was obtained by remote sensing at locations approximately four hundred miles and two hundred miles below the nearest point on the Great Lakes—the outlet of Lake Ontario near what is now Kingston, Ontario.

Sometimes, First Nations sources were acknowledged on European maps but ambiguously so. Almost 10 percent of the four-color linework on a manuscript map of northeastern North America believed to have been compiled in 1611 in London for Philip III of Spain is blue. This includes the eastern end of the unnamed Lake Ontario.[8] A legend below the lake explains that "All the blue is done by the relations of the Indians." Although it was a map compiled from several unacknowledged sources, the compiler evidently felt it important to indicate aboriginal inputs but did not or was not in a position

Figure 1. "Carte Géographique de la Novvelle Franse . . . faict len 1612," by Samuel de Champlain. Image courtesy of the William L. Clements Library, University of Michigan.

to acknowledge either which First Nations peoples had supplied the information or the nature of their inputs.[9] In the early seventeenth century, "relation" implied words, but did it exclude models, gestures, and graphics?

Unacknowledged First Nations sources can frequently be inferred on European maps.[10] But sometimes incorporations gave rise to serious errors and gross omissions. The western part of Champlain's printed map of 1616 is a good example (fig. 2).[11] It represents, albeit very schematically, Lake Huron ("Mer douce"), probably the eastern part of Lake Superior, and, arguably, a diminutive Lake Michigan. Yet Champlain had been no farther west than Georgian Bay at the eastern end of Lake Huron, which he had reached in January 1616—the beginning of the year in which the map was engraved in Paris. We know that Champlain had collected geographical intelligence from the Huron and the Ottawa. In June 1611, near Mont Royal, he had won the admiration of a visiting group of Huron by shooting rapids in a canoe. They remained with him for several days, "showing . . . by drawings all the places they had visited, taking pleasure in telling [him] about them."[12] In 1615 and early 1616, Champlain traveled with Huron, Petun, and Ottawa peoples around the eastern end of Georgian Bay. One can imagine him in his cabin aboard ship on his return voyage to France later in 1616, incorporating First Nations intelligence on the draft of the map he would hand to the engraver Gabriel Tavernier soon after his arrival in Paris.[13] Remarkable though the printed map is, there are surprising omissions, unprovable possibilities, and gross errors. Most of these arose from Champlain's misinterpretations and misincorporations of First Nations graphical and oral intelligence that was doubtless valid according to their geographical epistemology. There is no hint of Lake Erie, perhaps because it was off these peoples' axes of trade and warfare.[14] Given his preoccupation with finding feasible ways west and northwest, Champlain, of course, may not have asked them what lay to the south. The representation of Lake Michigan is a possibility about which one could debate inconclusively forever. Such was the slow progress of European cartography in the seventeenth century that the linework Champlain had so urgently had engraved in 1616 was still being published in 1688, though with many additional names.[15] These additions make retrospective interpretation even harder, and it is not clear who was responsible for adding them. Without ever leaving Europe, commercial map publishers and their assistants were reading the writings of later explorers with an eye to engraving additional content on existing copperplates but avoiding the technical difficulties of correcting what was already there. Sometimes serious mistakes were made. For example, on the updated plate of 1653, "Lake Erie" is placed on a body of water represented as being much smaller than "lac de Champlain," whereas its actual surface area is now known to be more than twenty times greater.[16]

Very occasionally, one finds maps of large areas that, although unacknowledged, appear to be entirely First Nations in origin. One such is included in the collection of papers left by Robert Livingston, the late-seventeenth-century, Albany-based frontier entrepreneur.[17] Done in ink over cruder red crayon, it has the stylistic characteristics of First Nations mapmaking: straight-line rivers with angular bends and confluences, each rising in a small, pear-shaped lake; larger oval lakes; no attempt to conserve linear scale, direction, or shape; and extreme distortion toward the edges arising from the "squeezing in" of peripheral features. The long axis of Lake Erie, for example, is almost at right angles to that of Lake Ontario. Endorsed on the verso "alb^y 2 m[arch] 1696/7 Drafft of this Countrey," it is, as one would expect of a First Nations map of this period, devoid of place names. But features are given letters or numerals, and these are explained in an inked key done in a hastily written but bold longhand. This was clearly added after the red-crayon linework as it overlaps it in several places. The whole represents the main rivers and lakes in an area of approximately 150,000 square miles, extending from the Connecticut Valley and Quebec in the east to the Hudson and Susquehanna Rivers in the south and Lake Erie in the west. By 1696, Livingston could have purchased printed maps representing all five of the Great Lakes in ways we can now recognize easily with or without names.[18] But these did not represent the spatial relationships among the commercially important interconnecting waterways, carrying places, and First Nations villages in a manner easily interpretable when traveling on the waterways as well as this (presumably) Iroquois map did.

Sometimes, First Nations peoples communicated geographical intelligence together with cosmographies of their cosmological beliefs. This confused Europeans in their attempts to establish something about their own terrae incognitae. Their confusion was often compounded by wishful thinking, especially when they were trying to establish distances from and routes to a supposed western sea. In 1607, for example, on the banks of the York River not far upstream from Chesapeake Bay, seven Virginia Algonquians involved John Smith in a three-day event intended to divine his intentions toward their people. It involved modeling on the ground their cosmography of the universe. A small circle signifying "their Country" was surrounded by a second circle signifying "the bounds of the Sea." They imagined

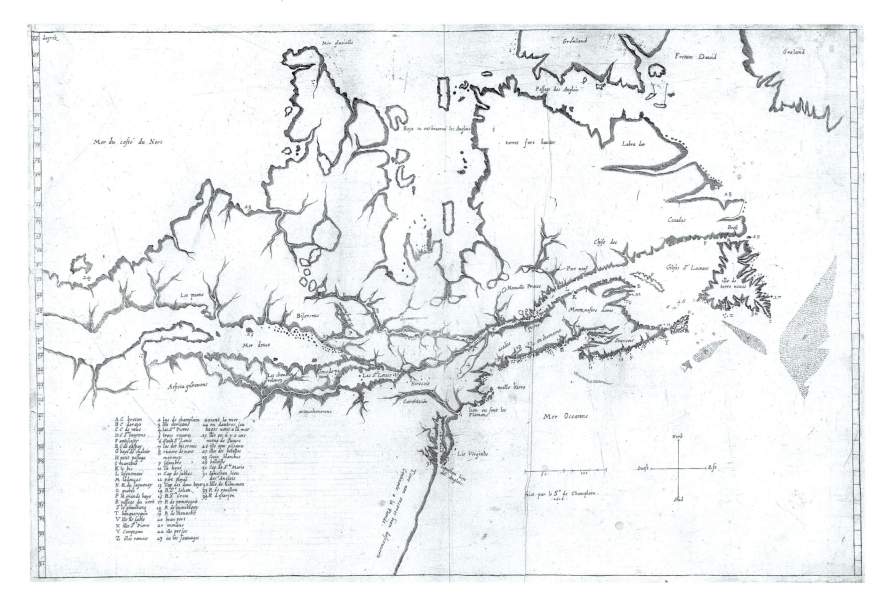

Figure 2. Proof map of northeastern North America, "faict par le Sr de Champlain, [Paris,] 1616," in the John Carter Brown Library, Providence, R.I. Image courtesy of the John Carter Brown Library at Brown University.

their "world to be flat and round like a trencher, and they in the middest." That world was enclosed by an outer circle representing the outer limits of the all-encompassing "Sea." To the east, that "Sea" was a geographical reality. Smith had crossed it en route from England, and the Virginia Algonquians recognized the essence of this by placing a pile of "stickes" in the "Sea" to represent "his Country."[19] However, in the other cardinal directions, their "Sea" was conjectural. Smith must have hoped that, to the west at least, it was a geographical reality and not too far distant. But in the following year, Powhatan, the Virginia Algonquian chief, cautioned him concerning "any salt water beyond the [Appalachian] mountains," adding that "the relations [accounts] you have had from my people are false." He then "began to draw plots upon the ground (according to his discourse) of all those regions."[20] A recently discovered but unauthenticated manuscript map may have originated as an attempt to combine Powhatan's "plots." It represents the central Appalachians as a single ridge and, in greater detail, the rivers draining east to Chesapeake Bay. Rivers also flow from the ridge westward, but to the sheet edge, with no suggestion of a coast in that direction. Yet John Smith's printed map of 1612 represents by stipple a body of water beyond the hill symbols of the Appalachians. Small Tuscan crosses on the upper parts of the Atlantic-flowing rivers indicate the limits of what "hath bin discovered" and the beginning of that learned about "by relation."[21] Neither the map nor Smith's account of it makes clear the mode in which the "relations" were transmitted: orally, gesturally, graphically, or by a mixture of these methods. But the source of these relations could only have been First Nations peoples. Smith's stippled body of water may have originated as a representation either of their cosmographic "Sea" or of the south shore of Lake Erie, though if it were the latter, the absence of any hint of the intervening Ohio drainage system seems strange. Notwithstanding long-distance trade in valuable materials and goods, it is doubtful that the Virginia Algonquians knew of the Pacific coastline almost three thousand miles to their west. In a bit of wishful thinking, Smith may have been implying that they did know about the Pacific but stopped short of indicating this by extending the stipple all the way to the sheetline. By so doing, he left the reader to decide whether it was an enclosed lake or a more extensive body of open water.

Not so John Farrer, a long-serving officer of the Virginia Company in London, whose 1651 map derived much information from Smith's work. Immediately beyond the straight row of hill symbols representing the Appalachians on Farrer's map is "The Sea of China and the Indies" on the coast of which "Sir Francis Drake . . . landed An.° 1577 . . . Calling it new Albion." These "happy shores" were stated to be but "ten days march . . . from the Ieames [James] River." The "Sea" could be reached via either the "Canada flu" (St. Lawrence River) or "Hudsons River," both of which led to "A Mighty great Lake," represented, however, as a deep embayment of the "Sea" coast.[22] A bar scale, when applied to distances between estuaries and bays on the Atlantic coast, gives distances that, although not correct, are of the right order of magnitude. This is not true for the distance between the Appalachian ridge and the coast of the "Sea" to the west, which, according to the bar scale, is a mere twenty to thirty-five miles. In producing what was a promotional map, Farrer had drawn on First Nations intelligence but probably without knowing he did so because he was several times removed from the source. Furthermore, he either failed to realize or did not wish to acknowledge that the intelligence was in part cosmographic.

John Farrer's error reflected a problem that first the Dutch and then the English were to try to solve: Where were the Great Lakes in relation to the middle Atlantic seaboard they were then in the process of colonizing? The Dutch and English knew of the lakes' existence because they were appearing in greater and greater detail on printed maps of French origin. Notwithstanding *saults* and the obstructive policies adopted from time to time by some First Nations peoples, from their base in Quebec, the French had natural access to the Great Lakes either via the St. Lawrence River route to the lower lakes or by taking the Ottawa River–Lake Nipissing–Georgian Bay route to the three upper lakes. The French were to monopolize information about the Great Lakes almost until the end of their regime in 1760. In contrast to the St. Lawrence, the Hudson and Susquehanna, which were major rivers draining to the middle-Atlantic seaboard, did not lead directly to the lakes. Some of their headstreams, however, did lead to carrying places into the southern catchment of Lake Ontario, and these were well known to the Iroquois and Susquehanna peoples. The earliest known European map to have represented the "New [i.e., Susquehanna] River" may well have incorporated intelligence received from some of these peoples.

Cornelis Hendricksen's manuscript map of 1616 incorporated a representation of the Susquehanna River and its north-bank tributaries that had been given to him by two members of the New Netherland Company. They had traveled some way down the river from its source before they were captured by Susquehanna peoples. Hendricksen himself had ransomed them in exchange for kettles and other goods. The men apparently gave him "two sketches of small maps partly finished," which, with some uncertainty on his part, Hendricksen incorporated on his map.[23] Whether the incorporated intelligence was based on the company men's own observations or given to them by their Susquehanna captors is not known, but Hendricksen's map represents the Susquehanna River as rising in a large "Water," the other end of which is left suggestively open. Whatever Hendricksen might have intended to imply, it was not Lake Ontario or even one of the Finger Lakes but the very small Otsego Lake that formed the source of the Susquehanna River, some thirty miles southeast of what is now Utica, New York. This representation of the upper Susquehanna was to appear on maps printed in Holland by eminent cartographers from 1635 to about 1729, in every case without any indication of the existence of Lake Ontario.[24] Yet, in 1656, with his access to original French sources, Nicolas Sanson published in Paris a map of the three lower Great Lakes in their entirety and parts of Lakes Michigan and Superior.[25] Contemporary inability to establish longitude on land was, in large measure, the cause of Dutch failure to relate their intelligence to that of the French.[26]

A representation of the Susquehanna River not dissimilar to Hendricksen's, made in 1683 by two Cayuga and one Susquehanna, went one stage further.[27] It marked the carrying places and journey times from the tributaries of the upper Susquehanna River to the Iroquois villages south of Lake Ontario. However, it, too, gave no hint of that lake or of how to reach it.

In 1634, at the Oneida village some fifty miles from the southeastern corner of Lake Ontario, near what is now Munnsville, New York, villagers were questioned by three members of the Dutch West India Company "concerning the situation in their [Iroquois] castle[s] and their names, and how far they were from each other. They showed us with stones and maize grains and Jeronimus [de la Croix—one of the three] then made a chart of it."[28] As with the St. Lawrence Iroquoians at La Chine Rapids in 1541, almost one hundred years later, the Oneida were still modeling maps on the ground. Remarkably, La Croix's "chart," or an early transcript of it, has survived. It may have incorporated information given at the same time by the Oneida chief Arenias, who had just returned from the "French savages," probably the Huron to the north of Lake Ontario but possibly the Algonquian in the Ottawa Valley. Essentially, the "chart" is of the Mohawk River to its source in Oneida Lake. A short, apparently northwest-flowing river just beyond and to the north of that lake leads to the sheet edge. An inscription alongside indicates that it was the "river along which the French come."[29] This was what is now named the Salmon River, flowing a mere thirty miles to Port Ontario at the southeast corner of Lake Ontario. But once again, a First Nations map shows nothing of that lake.

Exactly one hundred twenty-five years after the Oneida modeled the basis of what became La Croix's "chart" at Oswego, a mere twenty miles to the west of what was to be Port Ontario, General Thomas Gage was presented by Sir William Johnson with a "rough draft of the River St. Lawrence from Frontinac [at the outflow of Lake Ontario] to the island below La Galette, drawn by the Red Head, an Onondaga Indian" (fig. 3).[30] In 1759, Gage had been ordered to attack the French fort at La Galette. Sailing there from Oswego would involve navigating the complex and dangerous Thousand Islands reach of the St. Lawrence River immediately downstream from its outflow from Lake Ontario. Even the French maps of the period represented that reach badly, and it was even less well known to the English. The Red Head's "draft," therefore, was valuable intelligence not least for its relatively detailed representation of Chaumont and Black River Bays at the eastern extremity of Lake Ontario and possible routes from there

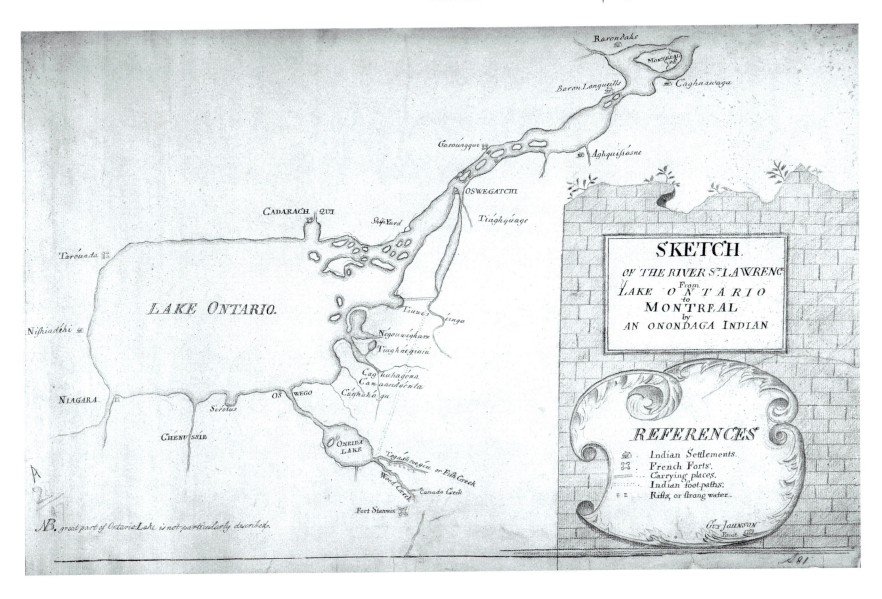

The map contains the following labels and text:

Rarondaks
MONTREAL
Baron Longueuils Caghnawaga
Garoungqui Aghquifsasne
OSWEGATCHI
CADARACH. QUI Ship Yard Tiaghquage
Tarounda SKETCH.
OF THE RIVER St. LAWRENC
from
LAKE ONTARIO
to
MONTREAL
by
AN ONONDAGA INDIAN
Nishiadthi
LAKE ONTARIO.
Tiuwe singa
Negouweghary
Tiaghneginiu
Cag huhagona
Cax aandoonta
Caghuhaga
NIAGARA OS WEGO
Serotus
CHENUSSIE REFERENCES
ONEIDA Indian Settlements.
LAKE French Forts.
Tegash megiu or Fish Creek Carrying places.
Indian foot-paths.
Wood Creek Riffs, or ftrong water.
Canada Creek
Fort Stanwix Guy Johnson
NB. great part of Ontario Lake is not particularly described.

Figure 3. "Sketch of the River St. Lawrence from Lake Ontario to Montreal by an Onondaga Indian [the Red Head]." Image courtesy of the British Library, London, UK.

to La Galette ("Oswegatchie" on the "draft") that avoided the treacherous Thousand Islands reach of the main river. Perhaps it is for these reasons that it has survived, though as a contemporary transcript with an artistically elaborate frame or cartouche containing the title and key to symbols and occupying approximately one-quarter of the sheet area.[31] Like La Croix's "chart," the Red Head's "sketch" represents but leaves unnamed the Salmon River, though it does show it, albeit diminutively, as flowing into Lake Ontario. However, the Salmon River was of no significance in relation to the "sketch's" purpose. Like almost all maps made by First Nations peoples, it was made for a specific purpose and focused almost exclusively on features pertinent to that purpose. Lake Ontario is represented—but schematically as a rectangle—and done with a thinner ink line, much smaller than it should be in relation to the Thousand Islands reach, and it is not mentioned in the title. Perhaps it was added by Sir William Johnson to help the newly arrived General Gage obtain a clearer regional perspective on the task before him. If so, the Red Head's original "sketch" was the fourth Iroquois and Susquehanna map in one hundred forty-three

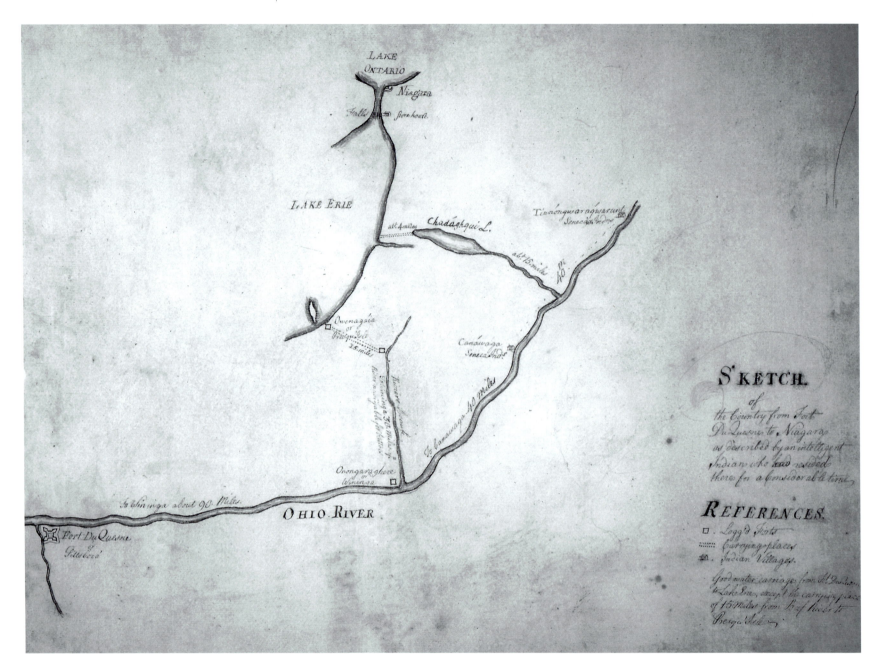

Figure 4. "Sketch of the county from Fort Du Quesne to Niagara," c. 1759. Image courtesy of the William L. Clements Library, University of Michigan.

years to stop short of representing even the southern shore of Lake Ontario. This could, of course, have been an accident of survival. There were doubtless other maps that are no longer extant. But to these peoples, large lakes were barriers or edges, whereas rivers and transwatershed portages were the channels of trade, warfare, and migration. Except for brief periods, Lake Ontario was certainly a barrier between north and south.[32]

During the period after 1750, when Great Britain was increasingly involved in the Ohio Valley, the geographical position of the Ohio River vis-à-vis the Great Lakes was still very uncertain. Longitude was particularly difficult to determine on land (including rivers), as were distances.[33] In the course of his journey down the Ohio River in 1766, the British military engineer Thomas Hutchins, in an attempt to measure distances, could do no more than make detailed records of the direction and state of the water: "swift, Midling, slow." Although observing the latitude of a few places, he did not establish any longitudes.[34] In the same year, in preparation for a journey that was to follow approximately one-third of the shoreline of the Great Lakes, Jonathan Carver decided to estimate all of his distances to the nearest half-mile. In preparation for this, he "practised several times the pacing out of lengths of a mile by land and then would go the same distance in a battou or canoe by water."[35] Such were the survey methods being used by the British at the beginning of their brief rule in the Ohio Valley and the Great Lakes region. Not surprisingly, they made gross errors. Inevitably, it would still be necessary to solicit maps from First Nations peoples.

The vast region between the Ohio River and the Great Lakes was an information vacuum as far as the British were concerned. The Erie peoples, whose tribal area had been to the south of Lake Erie, had abandoned their lands after epidemics and defeat at the hands of the Iroquois in 1656. For similar reasons, the Shawnee of the Ohio Valley proper were soon to do likewise.[36] Although the area was used for seasonal hunting, permanent repopulation did not begin until the 1730s. Great Britain was anxious to learn something of the geography of what was, for its officials, this vast terra incognita, and in the course of doing so it solicited maps from First Nations peoples. Given the fact that those Native Americans living to the north of the Ohio River had done so for only a few years, or at the most for one or two decades, their mapmaking would seem to have been surprisingly good. "Sketch of the Country from Fort Du Quesne to Niagara as described by an intelligent Indian . . ." (fig. 4) was one of the first of these and was sufficiently valued to merit neat redrafting and preservation for posterity in the papers of General Thomas Gage.[37] Apparently made soon after the French abandoned Fort Duquesne in 1758, this map represents two river routes, each involving one clearly marked portage, between "Pittsboro" (later Pittsburgh) and the southeast shore of Lake Erie. Unlike truly indigenous First Nations maps, it would have been eminently usable by the British. It is not explained how the "intelligent Indian" communicated his intelligence, but so soon after the British had captured Montreal and while Gage was its governor, this map must have been invaluable in linking the formerly French world of the lower Great Lakes with the increasingly British world of the upper Ohio Valley.

British and French interests had also been in conflict in the lower Ohio Valley. Proposals intended to strengthen Britain's position in the interior involved planting English colonies within the region. James Glen, the governor of South Carolina, made one such proposal in a letter of 1754 to the secretary of state for the Southern Department of the Board of Trade in London and leader of the House of Commons Glen summarized descriptions of the region given to him by the Cherokee, mentioning in particular "the great Rivers, Ohio, Quabash and Tenessie." But he had not, he wrote, "rested satisfied with a verbal description of the Country from the Indians" but had "often made them trace the Rivers on the Floor wth Chalk, and also on Paper, and it is surprising how near they approach to our best Maps."[38]

It is unlikely that any of Glen's Cherokee maps traced the Wabash River to its headwaters, let alone to Lake Michigan just beyond. It is improbable that his concerns extended so far north, and his Cherokee mapmakers would be unlikely to have traveled the full course of the river. However, one First Nations map of the Ohio River–Great Lakes region has survived from that period. Acquired by the Library of Congress in 1867 from the collector Peter Force, it was part of a large collection of maps, many of which were "original military maps and plans in manuscript, covering the period of the French war [French and Indian War, 1750–1763] . . . many of them . . . the work of officers of the British Army stationed in America. . . ."[39] "Map of the Country about the Mississippi [Verso] Drawn by Chegeree (the Indian) who Says he has Travell'd through the Country [Recto]" has all the hallmarks of one of these maps.[40] It has much in common with "A Draft of the Ohio from an Indian Account," which supposedly dates from the same year. But it covers a larger area and associated documents reveal more about its purpose. Covering approximately one hundred seventy-five thousand square miles, Chegeree's map extends from the Allegheny River in the east to the middle Mississippi River in the west and from Lake Erie in the north to the south-bank tributaries of the Ohio River. The river systems and settlement locations were almost certainly transcribed from Chegeree's original. These form the matrix on which is plotted a great deal of intelligence supplied by him, much of it in response to a list of questions preserved on one of two explanatory sheets. This includes place names (mainly phonemic transcriptions of First Nations names for features and settlements), distances in miles along dotted routes, and numbered sites, which in some cases are described on the explanatory sheets. A simple compass rose was presumably added by the transcriber. Given the topological geometry of the matrix, this directional marking is meaningless and was potentially very misleading.

The significance of Chegeree's map to the British authorities was that it contained much information on the locations and strengths of the French and their "French Indian" allies at a time when both European powers were competing for what was still Indian territory. It has been suggested that Chegeree may have been a Miami, and the strategic information content is particularly rich for the Wabash, Illinois, and middle Mississippi Valleys, each of which was then well beyond the sphere of British influence.[41]

Recognizing the historical context of Chegeree's map should not detract from what it does and does not reveal about the Great Lakes. The Illinois River is represented to its source but without a hint of the nearby Lake Michigan shoreline. Lake Erie is represented schematically and almost in its entirety but with some interesting details that appear to have been overlooked hitherto. Lewis Evans's work, *A General Map of the Middle British Colonies in America,* first published in Philadelphia in the probable year of Chegeree's map, places three unnamed, approximately equally spaced islands at the western end of Lake Erie. They are arranged like uniformly spaced stepping-stones between Fort Sandusky and the outflow of the Detroit River.[42] These symbolize five actual but unequally spaced islands, of which Pelee is the largest. A legend alongside the three islands states, "The Indians cross the Lake here in Canoes from Isle to Isle." Presumably this was a preferable alternative to the longer route via the marshy coast between what are now Toledo and Detroit. Chegeree's map represents the same straight line of islands and implies their communicational significance. Like Evans, Chegeree just included at the top of his map the southern tip of Lake Huron and a recognizable Lake St. Clair. Unnamed, perhaps because their significance was not made clear to the British transcriber, are two protuberances facing each other and at right angles to the otherwise undifferentiated north and south shores of Lake Erie. Undoubtedly these represent Long Point and Presque Isle, respectively. Chegeree may well have been implying the existence of another canoe crossing at what is the narrow waist of the lake, between rare natural harbors, one on each shore.

Other, perhaps many, maps of this region were made by First Nations peoples during this period. The Gage Papers contain another supplemented transcript of the strategically critical area between Oniagara (Fort Niagara) and a symbolized but unnamed Fort Duquesne, in all probability done by the same copyist who drew the "Sketch" of c. 1755.[43] Once again, only those parts of the Great Lakes are shown that were essential for the map's purpose: to show the routes between Fort Duquesne and Niagara.

We know very little about the individuals who made these maps for British military intelligence purposes, under what circumstances they were made, or the extent to which the extant pen-and-ink versions differ from the originals. But from our perspective, they are more intelligible than the truly indigenous maps would have been. It is increasingly apparent that acculturation in the zone of contact between First Nations peoples and Europeans was more rapid than formerly supposed, and it was doubtless even faster for some individuals than for others. However, at the time of the creation of military intelligence maps, other maps were still being made for Europeans that were closer in style to indigenous ones. In 1767, for example, at the site of what became Toronto, a Mississauga gave the Montreal-based trader James Morrison a "plan of the Country [at] the Back of Toranto." A transcript has survived in Morrison's journal of a trading trip to Michilimackinac via Niagara and Detroit.[44] But the Mississauga's "plan" is of the rivers, portages, lakes, and trading posts along a route parallel to but to the north of the one Morrison was about to take. It had been pioneered by Étienne Brûlé between 1615 and 1621: Lake Simcoe, Georgian Bay, and the North Channel to Michilimackinac. Though not straight, the structure of the "plan" is linear. Lake shapes are extremely schematic, each emphasizing one or two distinctive headlands or bays. Even so, the "plan" would now verge on the unintelligible if Morrison had not named the three main lakes. An itinerary of travel times on the facing page of the journal suggests that the Mississauga had probably traveled from Curot's trading post on Georgian Bay. Certainly the "plan" was made for a specific purpose and, Morrison's annotations and place names apart, was in the indigenous tradition. Evidently it offered him an alternative route to Michilimackinac that he rejected for unknown reasons.

Although Hudson's Bay Company men solicited many maps from First Nations peoples, company territory by definition only extended as far south as the northern watersheds of the basins of Lakes Huron and Superior. Hence, prior to the Hudson's Bay Company's merger with the North West Company in 1821, these lakes were beyond the southern limits of the company's trading hinterland. In part for this reason the northern and western fringes of these two lakes do not appear to have been a focus of First Nations peoples' mapmaking—not, at least, in the context of their contact with Europeans. There were, of course, exceptions. One linear map (fig. 5) in the same tradition as the Mississauga-Morrison "plan" was made by a Métis, Joseph la France, with chalk, on the floor of the dining room at the Golden Fleece in London.[45] It linked two areas of which the British had some awareness—the upper Great Lakes and York Factory on Hudson Bay—via a waterway system that was virtually unknown to Britons. This was potentially an intelligence map, which would have been valuable to the Hudson's Bay Company in its inland rivalry for trade with the Montreal-based independent fur traders operating via Lakes Huron and Superior to and beyond Lake Winnipeg. Ironically, what we know of this map's form as it was chalked on the floor is through its incorporation on a printed map in a publication criticizing company policy.[46] The five Great Lakes are represented in their entirety but badly so by the standards of the best printed maps then available. As the two northern lakes were on the first part of the Canadian traders' route from Montreal, this is surprising. Equally surprising is the poor representation of the river-portage route between Lake Superior and the Lake of the Woods. A possible explanation for these unexpected weaknesses is that Joseph la France was not from the Great Lakes region but from Cree or Chipewyan territory well to the north.

La France's effort was not the first non-European map of the drainage system to the northwest of Lake Superior. I have explained elsewhere how in 1729 or 1730, Pierre Gaultier de Varennes et de la

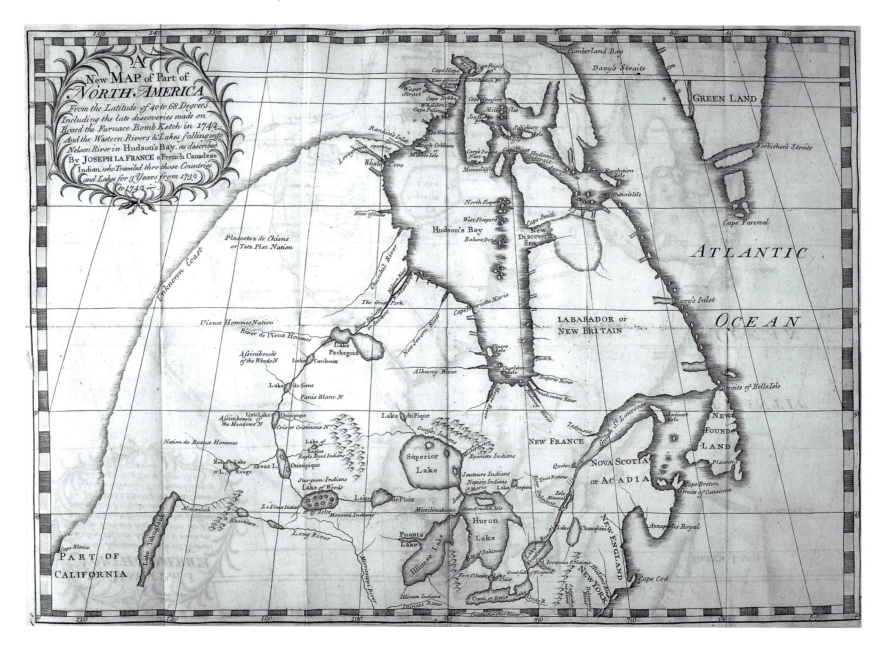

Figure 5. Joseph la France's linear map linking the upper Great Lakes and York Factory. Image courtesy of the William L. Clements Library, University of Michigan.

Vérendrye composited three separate Cree maps to produce one of the most influential eighteenth-century representations of the drainage system beyond Lake Superior and how this influenced important published maps until the end of the eighteenth century.[47] Like John Smith more than one hundred years before, la Vérendrye, too, failed to recognize the mythical elements on primarily geographical maps. These gave rise to some of the most serious of all cartographic errors concerning the western interior, including a little red river, a mountain of stone that shone night and day, and a place where the water in a river began to ebb and flow.

First Nations maps were still being solicited during the nineteenth century, many for journeys through forests and off the main canoe routes and well-established paths. In March 1804, for example, the Canadian fur trader George Nelson, at a camp near Lac Courte Oreilles in what is now northern Wisconsin, "had occasion to send to Lake Superior for liquor," a journey of perhaps seventy-five miles. No guide was available, but "the Indians made [Jean Baptiste Brunet, Nelson's Canadian assistant] a map [and] Brunet found [his way] exactly as he was told, & he reached the house, I believe it was the 5th day as straight as if he had been travelling upon a well beaten road."[48] Writing retrospectively and after twenty years' experience as a fur trader, Nelson summarized his opinion of this kind of map as follows: "A man must be very stupid indeed who cannot go by their charts. They are so clear, concise and expressive. I have myself frequently gone upon these maps [i.e., navigated on the basis of them] drawn on my floor or hearth, or a piece of bark & yet, strange to say, sometimes [been] at a loss to find my way back!"[49]

The last clause could be significant. Nelson's father was a schoolmaster, from whom he had received "an excellent education for the time"; and by that period, because of the increasing use of instrumental surveys, educated Canadians might make unwarranted assumptions about the reliability of maps of small areas.[50] Was Nelson, therefore, being confused by trying to read in the reverse direction linear route maps that had been made for unidirectional use, emphasizing critical features and conditions as confronted from the direction in which they were intended to be used? Similar reports and observations of this kind doubtless occur in the journals of others trading for furs within the region, but for every such instance there must have been thousands that went unreported.

By the middle of the nineteenth century, First Nations maps of the Great Lakes region were of decreasing interest among Americans and Canadians for their information content but of increasing intrinsic interest. For example, in 1869, the Canadian geologist Robert Bell persuaded several Ojibwe at Fort William (near Thunder Bay, Ontario) to make a map of Lake Nipigon, the nearest part of which was approximately seventy-five miles to the northeast and just within the Lake Superior catchment (fig. 6). They did so on paper, using the cook's baking board as a work surface.[51] The map is extant, as is Bell's account of its making, both having been used within the following few months in the course of a lecture he delivered under the auspices of the Natural History Society of Montreal.[52] Thumbtack holes at each corner of the sheet presumably date from that occasion. The map itself is of interest in that it is a good example of the influence of paper proportions on overall map shape. What might have been a surprisingly good representation of the outline of the nineteen-hundred-square-mile lake was "squeezed" in a north-south direction as a consequence of the long axis of the paper sheet having been adopted for the east-west axis of the map.[53] One wonders if the shape and handling of the baking board influenced this unfortunate choice.

A few years before Bell's visit to Fort William, the geographer Johann Kohl visited an area then being settled by fellow Germans in the upper valley of the Cannon River, some fifty miles south of Minneapolis. While he was there, Kohl "started a conversation with a Sioux sitting next to me [somewhere near the newly settled Faribault] about the various lakes and tributaries of the headwater regions of the Cannon River. He named for me numerous lakes . . . of which there was no trace on my American maps. I asked him if he could put this on paper and he got hold of my pencil straight away and designed for me a detailed map of the whole region."[54]

The unnamed Sioux's map is not extant, and its mention would not be appropriate here but for the significance of its solicitor. Before visiting North America, Kohl had made manuscript copies of many of the rare maps of the continent held in European archives and libraries.[55] One of these was "An Indian Map of the Upper-Missouri, 1801," which he had copied in the archives of the Hudson's Bay Company,

Figure 6. "Sketch Plan of Lake Neepigon," 1869.

Manuscript, 1869, NMC 21734, Bell Papers, National Archives

of Canada, Ottawa, Ontario.

which were then in London.[56] In the winter of 1856, soon after his visit to Minnesota, Kohl gave a lecture at the Smithsonian Institution in Washington, D.C., which was published almost immediately. It was an informed, lengthy, and detailed plea for the establishment of a federal map library. Doubtless remembering his experiences in Faribault and London, in his discussion of categories of maps to be collected, Kohl made a strong case for collecting and preserving "all those rude sketches of interior parts of America, which on different occasions, have been drawn by the Indians on skin or the bark of trees, and which sometimes were the first guides, by the help of which Europeans were enabled to find their way. . . . It is evident, then, that we cannot neglect the study of these aboriginal productions, but must give them also a place in our collection."[57]

This part of Kohl's lecture mirrored an interest among German geographers in maps and mapmaking in traditional cultures worldwide.[58] It also coincided with an escalation in the collecting of artifacts from these cultures. In the Great Lakes region, this included Mide migration charts (religiously significant representations of Ojibwe migration westward to their eighteenth-century home territory) and also wampum belts, though at the time their map content was barely perceived. One consequence of the vogue for collecting was that many artifacts left the region, some being taken abroad. Another was that maps and map artifacts found their way into different kinds of collections: museums, map libraries, archives, and private holdings.

First Nations peoples did continue to make maps but increasingly in styles that were closer to those of Euro-Americans. "The chiefs Esquamady & Koosays plan for their town or village consisting of 40 lots. 1839" on Traverse Bay, Michigan, is a good example.[59] Included in the Henry R. Schoolcraft Papers, it is almost certainly a consequence of the treaty made with the Ottawa and Chippewa in Washington, D.C., three years earlier. Schoolcraft had been the U.S. commissioner on that occasion, and Aishquagonabee (i.e., Esquamady?) and Akosa (i.e., Koosays?), both of Grand Traverse, were among the signatories.[60] The map was done in pencil on paper, in traditional First Nations style, and there was no attempt to conserve scale. The proposed "town or village," which was to be on the lands reserved for the Chippewa on the north shore of Grand Traverse Bay, is enormous on the "plan" when compared with "Grand Traverse Peninsula & Harbour." But the "plan" of the "town or village" is evidence of the chiefs' adept use of pencil and ruler.

By this date, some Chippewa were being trained to make maps according to scale. In 1826, for example, Catitugegwonhale (also known as George Whitefield), a twelve-year-old Chippewa from somewhere in the western Great Lakes region and then at the Foreign Mission School in Cornwall, Connecticut, made a remarkable ink-and-watercolor plan of the roads, field boundaries, and buildings of the school's agricultural surroundings. It was at a scale of 1:4,000 and distinguished, for example, between stone walls and split-rail fences and among pastures, cultivated fields, and orchards.[61] It is not known whether Catitugegwonhale participated in the ground survey or, indeed, whether he merely copied from an extant plan of which nothing is now known. Whatever the circumstances of its making, it is clear evidence that by the 1820s some First Nations children from the Great Lakes region were receiving training in large-scale cartography as part of their formal education.

Particularly in the remoter parts of the Great Lakes region, for immediate local purposes but in contact contexts, First Nations peoples did continue to make maps structured according to traditional geometry, albeit on paper. These may have been numerous, but most were only of immediate significance, and very few have survived. The Schoolcraft Papers contain several of these maps, a good example of which dates from July 30, 1832. On the St. Croix River, near the point at which State Highway 70 now crosses from Wisconsin to Minnesota, Lieutenant James Allen was following Schoolcraft in their search for the source of the Mississippi River when he met three Chippewa men who had a written message from Schoolcraft directing him to follow Schoolcraft up the St. Croix. Eventually Allen persuaded one of the men, Tatausay, to guide him up the river for the next two days. In return, Tatausay was promised a "liberal offer" plus the "calico shirt" Allen himself was then wearing. When he refused to go farther, Tatausay's final duty was to "sketch me a map of the river above." This "he did very badly."[62] Even so, the map merits attention and is extant.[63] The representation of the St. Croix River approximates its true shape, but its lateral tributaries are drawn for the most part straight and approximately of equal length. There are, however, a few exceptions. The Yellow River is particularly well represented, as are the Rice River and Rice Lake in the rice-gathering region near its source. This was an important Chippewa resource region, but it is not clear why it merited precise representation on this map. The gable ends of two Euro-American style cabins on the lower Yellow River almost certainly represent a post or posts of the North West and XY fur-trading companies, which by 1832 were probably being operated by the American Fur Company.[64] The only other symbol on the map is for rapids and falls on the St. Croix River: pairs of small circles, one on each side of the river. One pair differs from all the others in that the circles are connected by parallel straight lines transverse to the river, giving the appearance of a cylinder or short tube. One can only speculate that the "Falls" with which it was associated were of a different order from the others.[65] Crude, empty, and problematic though maps of this kind may at first appear, they can be revealing if they can be placed in the cultural context in which they were made.

First Nations peoples made maps in the course of negotiating and contesting treaties, though probably more so in Canada than in the United States. In 1892, for example, the Mississagi River band of Ojibwe on the north shore of Lake Huron's North Channel made a retrospective protest about the northern boundary of reserve number 8. Two maps were enclosed with a letter of June 25, which was addressed to the acting deputy minister of Indian affairs in Ottawa. One map was of the boundary as it had been surveyed after the Robinson Treaty of 1850, and the other was a "true map" drawn by the chief as evidence of how the tribe had been "wronged." Though done on paper, the latter has many of the characteristics of a birchbark map.[66] Indeed, in the course of negotiating the Shawanaga Reserve on the east coast of Georgian Bay, the Ojibwe band there had indicated its desire for areas other than those that had been proposed in the schedule of reservations with the aid of "their own 'Indian plan' on birchbark."[67]

In the decades immediately after World War II, some First Nations peoples were coopted to make maps in connection with recreation, conservation, and historical research. During 1972–73, for example, Craig Macdonald, a recreation specialist based at Dorset, Ontario, was "in charge of a canoe route study for all of Southern Ontario, covering a system of some five thousand miles." He realized that unlike "many of the current geographical names, the Anishinabi [the Ojibwe's preferred name for themselves] names often served as important navigational tools." They were "the names that would be given to the traveller verbally to help ascertain his position en route." It was obviously important to retrieve these. By this date, 1:50,000 topographic maps were available for much of the area. However, they did not necessarily show all the detail "required to navigate with on the ground." Hence, Anishinabi informants were encouraged to make their own maps of the drainage networks in pencil on paper, onto which their Ojibwe names were then written.[68]

During the second half of the twentieth century, some First Nations individuals from within the region doubtless trained in and practiced topographical surveying (including the use of aerial photographs to obtain accurate measurements) and cartography. However, those who did would have worked in the white American and Canadian worlds, contributing to the production of maps over the styles and contents of which they had negligible influence. But as the twentieth century ended, some First Nations peoples were beginning to use Geographical Information Systems (GIS) technology for tribal, band, or community purposes. In so doing, they were moving in a matter of a few years from modified traditional mapmaking to state-of-the-art technology that was intended to serve their own interests. However, some well-disposed observers of these developments have expressed serious reservations about them. Robert Rundstrom, for example, was skeptical "about motivations for inscribing indigenous geographical knowledge into GIS" and concluded his critique of these developments with the opinion that "the institutions of assimilation that have silenced indigenous peoples throughout history have been those of the state, education, and religion. Clearly, GIS has been promoted by agents of the first two."[69] Within the Great Lakes region, these institutions of assimilation had virtually extinguished cosmographical mapping by the end of the nineteenth century. However, though the contexts and styles varied somewhat, traditional mapmaking on riverine matrices continued until the recent past, particularly in the northern and western parts of the region. It may, however, now be at risk.

Indigenous mapmaking was quickly adapted by First Nations peoples in the course of communicating with Europeans and Euro-Americans. The aliens were particularly interested in obtaining spatially arranged information about the terra incognita; and in communicating this to them, First Nations peoples often found that graphics were more effective than speech. Either proffered or solicited, geographical maps were made of larger areas than would normally have been necessary intraculturally. Such maps afforded both valuable intelligence for the French in their explorations of the Great Lakes and sources for the earliest printed maps of the region. They provided the British with equally valuable intelligence in their approach to the Great Lakes via the Ohio Valley. Later, in both Canada and to a lesser extent the United States, these maps were made and used in the course of negotiating and disputing treaties.

Most of the geographical maps made in contact contexts emphasized drainage networks. Indeed, in the absence of lines of latitude and longitude, these functioned as the matrices in relation to which other information was positioned. Conversely, Great Lakes shorelines were rarely represented. Perhaps because they were solicited for logistic purposes rather than for economic reasons, very few of the maps plotted resources.

There is no doubt that, hitherto, the variety and significance of former First Nations mapmaking in intercultural contexts have been grossly underestimated.

NOTES

1. Paul D. A. Harvey, *The History of Topographical Maps: Symbols, Pictures, and Surveys* (London: Thames and Hudson, 1980), 10.
2. Early word lists contained very few words, and *map* was never included. Whether this was because First Nations languages had no equivalents or because they were not sought is unclear. The evidence of modern dictionaries suggests that there may

not have been any. The majority of these dictionaries, many of which verge on the exhaustive, do not include *map*. When *map* is included, there is almost always a root for *land, earth,* or *country*. These were doubtless indigenous concepts, but the second root usually suggests a European influence, e.g., *paper* and *toy*.

3. Richard Hakluyt, *The Principal Navigations, Voyages, Traffiques & Discoveries of the English Nation* (London: George Bishop, Ralfe Newberie, and Robert Barker, 1600), 3: 235.

4. Abraham Ortelius, "Americae Sive Novi Orbis Nova Descriptio," in *Theatrum Orbis Terrarum*, 1570 (Antwerp: Standaard Uitgeverij, 1570).

5. On June 9, 1603, according to the text, but almost certainly during July of that year, on the Ile d'Orléans near Quebec. Henry P. Biggar et al., eds., *The Works of Samuel de Champlain* (Toronto: Champlain Society, 1922), 1: 159–61.

6. In early July 1603, at the La Chine Rapids near Mont Royal. Ibid., 1: 153–55, n. 5.

7. Samuel de Champlain, "Carte Géographique de la Novvelle Franse . . . faict len 1612 . . . ," in *Les Voyages du Sievr de Champlain* (Paris: Chez Jean Berjon, 1613).

8. Untitled manuscript map in colored inks of northeastern North America, probably dated 1611, *legajo* 2588, folio 22, Estado, Archivo General de Simancas, Simancas, Spain.

9. As a Spanish diplomat communicating with his king, Don Alonso de Velasco may have distinguished lakes, rivers, and coasts based on First Nations "relations" as a way of indicating areas where neither the French nor the English had formally taken possession.

10. I have considered this elsewhere, though at the time I was insufficiently aware of the transformation into cartographic form of orally received intelligence. G. Malcolm Lewis, "Indications of Unacknowledged Assimilations from Amerindian Maps on Maps of North America: Some General Principles Arising from a Study of La Vérendrye's Composite Map, 1728–29," *Imago Mundi* 38 (1986): 9–34.

11. Untitled, unfinished, engraved, unpublished proof map of northeastern North America, "faict par le Sr de Champlain, [Paris,] 1616," John Carter Brown Library, Providence, R.I.

12. The "drawings," which were doubtless maplike, appear to have been done by Ochateguin, Iroquet, and Tregouaroti, three Charioquois (Huron) chiefs. Biggar et al., eds., *Works of Samuel de Champlain*, 1: 192, n. 5.

13. Philip D. Burden, *The Mapping of North America: A List of Printed Maps, 1511–1670* (Rickmansworth, U.K.: Raleigh Publications, 1996), 231.

14. Conrad E. Heidenreich, "The Great Lakes Basin, 1600–1653," in *Historical Atlas of Canada*, ed. R. Cole Harris (Toronto: University of Toronto Press, 1987), 1: plate 35.

15. "Le Canada faict par le Sr de Champlain . . . Paris . . . 1653," state 6 (one of a sequence of printings made from a plate that has been modified one or more times), in Pierre Duval, *Cartes Géographiques* (Paris: n.p., 1677). According to Burden, the last-known edition of this atlas was published in 1688. Burden, *Mapping of North America*, 396.

16. Lake Erie, 9,910 square miles; Lake Champlain, 420 square miles.

17. A probable First Nations map of parts of five drainage systems: the lower Great Lakes Basin and the St. Lawrence, Connecticut, Hudson, and Susquehanna Rivers. Ink over red crayon on paper. Endorsed on verso: "alb^y 2 m[arch] 1696/7 Drafft of this Countrey," GLC 3107, Livingston Collection, Pierpont Morgan Library, New York.

18. E.g., Pierre Mortier, *Le Canada ou Partie de la Nouvelle France, Contenant la Terre de Labrador, la Nouvelle France, les Isles de Terre Neuve, de Notre Dame &c.* (Amsterdam: Chez Pierre Mortier, 1693).

19. John Smith, *The Generall Historie of Virginia, New England, & the Summer Isles* (London: Michael Sparkes, 1624), 48. For a graphical reconstruction of the described cosmographic model, see David Woodward and G. Malcolm Lewis, eds., *The History of Cartography*, vol. 2, book 3, *Cartography in the Traditional African, American, Arctic, Australian, and Pacific Societies* (Chicago: University of Chicago Press, 1998), fig. 4.11.

20. Philip L. Barbour, comp., *The Jamestown Voyages under the First Charter, 1606–1609* (Cambridge: Cambridge University Press, 1969), 2: 413–14.

21. John Smith, *Virginia Discovered and Discribed by Captayn John Smith, Graven by William Hole* (London: n.p., 1612). The untitled manuscript map, which could be a composite of the "plots" Powhatan made on the ground, is often referred to as the "Krauss Virginia Map." Harry Ranson Humanities Research Center, University of Texas at Austin. Purchased from H. P. Kraus and described in his catalogue, *Monumenta Cartographica*, 43–46, where it is dated c. 1610.

22. John Farrer and John Goddard, *A mapp of Virginia discovered to yᵉ Falls and in it's Latt* (London: I. Stephenson, 1651).

23. Cornelis Hendricksen, untitled Dutch manuscript map of 1616 showing the courses of the Hudson, Delaware, and Susquehanna Rivers, found in the Municipal Archives of the Hague, Netherlands. A full-size transcript is reproduced in E. B. O'Callaghan, ed. and trans., *Documents Relative to the Colonial History of the State of New York* (Albany: Weed and Parsons, 1856), 1: 1.

24. William Jansz Blaeu, "Nova Belgica et Anglia Nova," in *Theatrum Orbis Terrarum, Sive, Atlas Novus*, by William Jansz Blaeu and Joan Blaeu (Amsterdam: Apud Guijelmum and Iohannem Blaeu, 1635); Nicolaas Jansz Visscher, *Novi Belgii Novaeque Angliae* (Amsterdam: N. Visscher, c. 1655). A fifth state with the additional imprint "Nune apud Petr: Schenk Iun" dates from c. 1729, more than 110 years after Hendricksen's map on which its representation of the Susquehanna headwaters was based.

25. Nicholas Sanson, *Le Canada, ou Nouvelle France &c.* (Paris: Chez Pierre Mariette, 1656).

26. The gross errors made by William Blaeu, Nicolaas Visscher, and others might not have occurred if Hendricksen had revised his map according to his own best judgment. In a somewhat ambiguous inscription on the map concerning his sources, he admitted that the upper Susquehanna River and villages "ought to be marked down considerably further west into the Country." There was, however, an urgency to his mapmaking. Referred to as the "Figurative Map," it was annexed to a petition first read on August 18, 1616, requesting a southward extension of the charter to trade in New Netherlands that had been granted to an Amsterdam-based company in October 1614. O'Callaghan, ed., *Documents Relative to . . . New York*, 1: 11–13, n. 23.

27. "Draught of Ye Susquehannes River" by two Cayugas (Ackentjaekon and Kaejaegoehe) and one unnamed Susquehannock, September 7, 1683, contemporary transcript, GLC 3107, Livingston Collection, Pierpont Morgan Library, New York.

28. Harmen M. van den Bogaert, "Narrative of a Journey into the Mohawk and Oneida Country, 1634–1635," in *Narratives of New Netherland, 1609–1664*, ed. J. Franklin Jameson (New York: Charles Scribner's Sons, 1909), 149–50.

29. Probably Jeronimus de la Croix, untitled manuscript "chart" on paper of the Mohawk River and adjacent areas, 1634, reproduced in L. G. van Loon, "Letter from Jeronimus de la Croix," *Yearbook—The Dutch Settlers Society of Albany* (Albany: The Society, 1939–40), 15: between pages 9 and 10.

30. Milton W. Hamilton, ed., *The Papers of Sir William Johnson* (Albany: University of the State of New York, 1962), 13: 124–25.

31. "Sketch of the River St. Lawrence from Lake Ontario to Montreal by an Onondaga Indian [the Red Head]," manuscript transcript endorsed "Guy Johnson," 1759, Add. Ms. 57,707.1, Manuscript Division, British Library, London.

32. The main exceptions were 1640–1651, when the Iroquois Confederacy crossed Lake Ontario in the course of dispersing the Huron, Petun, and Nipissing far to the northwest, and again in 1667–1670, when some of them crossed the lake to settle sites on the north shore, by then only seasonally occupied. Conrad E. Heidenreich, "The Great Lakes Basin, 1600–1653"; idem, "Expansion of French Trade, 1667–1696," both in *Historical Atlas of Canada*, ed. Harris, 1: plates 35, 38, n. 14. In contrast, after La Salle's first expedition of 1679, French traders moved seasonally and more or less freely via the long axis of Lake Ontario.

33. G. Malcolm Lewis, "Changing National Perspectives and the Mapping of the Great Lakes between 1755 and 1795," *Cartographica* 17 (Fall 1980): 12–16.

34. Beverley W. Bond, Jr., ed., *The Courses of the Ohio River taken by Lt. T. Hutchins, Anno. 1766, and Two Accompanying Maps* (Cincinnati: Historical and Philosophical Society of Ohio, 1942), 19–44.

35. John Parker, ed., *The Journals of Jonathan Carver and Related Documents, 1766–1770* (St. Paul: Minnesota Historical Society, 1976), 59.

36. Helen Hornbeck Tanner, ed., *Atlas of Great Lakes Indian History* (Norman: University of Oklahoma Press, 1987), 31.

37. "Sketch of the Country from Fort Du Quesne to Niagara as described by an intelligent Indian who had resided there for a considerable time," manuscript c. 1759, Thomas Gage Papers (hereafter Gage Papers), William L. Clements Library, University of Michigan, Ann Arbor.

38. Governor James Glen, South Carolina, to Sir Thomas Robinson, secretary of state for the Southern Department of the Board of Trade and leader of the House of Commons, London, August 15, 1754, vol. 26, British Public Record Office Transcripts, South Carolina Department of Archives and History, Columbia.

39. Richard W. Stephenson, "Maps from the Peter Force Collection," *Quarterly Journal of the Library of Congress* 30 (July 1973): 187.

40. "Map of the Country about the Mississippi [Verso] Drawn By Chegeree (the Indian) who Says he has Travell'd through the Country [Recto]," manuscript c. 1755, Force Map no. 8, Geography and Map Division, Library of Congress, Washington, D.C.

41. Mark Warhus, *Another America: Native American Maps and the History of Our Land* (New York: St. Martin's Press, 1997), 109–13.

42. Lewis Evans, *A General Map of the Middle British Colonies in America* (Philadelphia: Jas. Turner, engraver, 1755).

43. "A Draft of the Ohio from an Indian Account," manuscript c. 1755, Gage Papers.

44. "Journal of a voyage in a large Cannoe by Jas. Morrison from Montreal to Toranto. Set out on a Monday the 13th of Apr. [1767]" (the entries for May 22 and 23, 1767, were made at Toronto), MG 23 GIII 5, folio 123, James Morrison Papers, National Archives of Canada, Ottawa.

45. Walter Bowman's manuscript foreword to his bound collection of three pamphlets published in the dispute between Captain Christopher Middleton and Arthur Dobbs concerning the Northwest Passage. William L. Clements Library, University of Michigan, Ann Arbor. Published in part in Christian Brun, "Dobbs and the Passage," *The Beaver* (Fall 1958): 29.

46. "A New Map of Part of North America From the Latitude of 40 to 68 Degrees, Including . . . the Western Rivers & Lakes falling into Nelson River in Hudson's Bay as described by Joseph La France a French Canadese Indian who Travaled thro those Countries and Lakes in 3 Years from 1739 to 1742," in *An Account of the Countries Adjoining to Hudson's Bay*, by Arthur Dobbs (London: printed for J. Robinson, 1744).

47. G. Malcolm Lewis, "La Grande Rivière et Fleuve de l'Ouest: Realities and Reasons behind a Major Mistake in the Eighteenth Century Geography of North America," *Cartographica* 28 (Spring 1991): 54–88.

48. George Nelson, *My First Years in the Fur Trade: The Journals of 1802–1804*, ed. Laura Peers and Theresa Schenck (St. Paul: Minnesota Historical Society Press, 2002), 150.

49. Ibid., 121.

50. Ibid., 5.

51. "Sketch Plan of Lake Neepigon," manuscript, 1869, NMC 21734, Robert Bell Papers (hereafter Bell Papers), National Archives of Canada, Ottawa. Figure 6 can be found at the Web site of the National Archives: http://www.collectionscanada.ca/archivianet/020154_e.html. Search the database for "Lake Neepigon."

52. "Lecture on 'Exploration in the Nipigon Country,' by R. Bell, Delivered under the Auspices of the Nat. Hist. Socy. of Montreal, Feby. 10th 1870. Being the First of the Sommerville Course," manuscript, MG 29 B15, vol. 36, Bell Papers.

53. Woodward and Lewis, eds., *History of Cartography*, vol. 2, book 3, fig. 4.86, n. 19.

54. Translated from Johann G. Kohl, *Reisen im Nordwestern der Vereinigten Staaten* (New York: D. Appleton, 1857), 268.

55. Kohl's collection of nearly five hundred hand-drawn copies of maps of America was assembled in Dresden before 1854. It preceded by three-quarters of a century Louis C. Karpinski's photographic collection of similar maps in European libraries and archives. Kohl's collection and one set of Karpinski's are preserved in the Geography and Map Division, Library of Congress, Washington, D.C.

56. "An Indian Map of the Upper-Missouri, 1801," Johann Georg Kohl Collection, Geography and Map Division, Library of Congress, Washington, D.C.

57. Johann G. Kohl, "Substance of a Lecture Delivered at the Smithsonian Institution on a Collection of the Charts and Maps of America," *Annual Report of the Board of Regents of the Smithsonian Institution, 1856* (Washington, D.C.: Smithsonian Institution, 1857), 127.

58. G. Malcolm Lewis, ed., *Cartographic Encounters: Perspectives on Native American Mapmaking and Map Use* (Chicago: University of Chicago Press, 1998), 38–40.

59. "The chiefs Esquamady & Koosays plan for their town or village consisting of 40 lots. 1839," container 91, no. 22, Henry R. Schoolcraft Papers (hereafter Schoolcraft Papers), Manuscript Division, Library of Congress, Washington, D.C.

60. "Articles of a treaty made and concluded at the City of Washington . . . between Henry R. Schoolcraft, commissioner on the part of the United States, and the Ottawa and Chippewa nations," March 28, 1836, in *Indian Affairs: Laws and Treaties,* comp. and ed. Charles J. Kappler (Washington, D.C.: Government Printing Office, 1903), 2: 450–56.

61. "Sketch of Cornwall Valley Done by George Whitefield [Catitugegwonhale] of the Chippeway Nation Aged 12 yrs.," manuscript ink and watercolor, 1826, scale 1:4,000, Litchfield Historical Society, Litchfield, Conn. Described and reproduced in part in Peter Benes, *New England Prospect: A Loan Exhibition of Maps at the Currier Gallery of Art, Manchester, New Hampshire* (Boston: Boston University for the Dublin Seminar of New England Folklife, 1981), 111–12.

62. James Allen, Official Report, 23rd Cong., 1st sess., 1833–1834, Doc. 323. Reprinted in Henry R. Schoolcraft, *Schoolcraft's Expedition to Lake Itasca: The Discovery of the Source of the Mississippi,* ed. Philip P. Mason (East Lansing: Michigan State University Press, 1958), 321–22.

63. Untitled sketch map of the St. Croix River and tributaries, Wisconsin-Minnesota, linework in pencil with place names in ink, probably July 31, 1832, on verso, "Tatausay, elder son of Peegheeka," container 91, no. 28, Schoolcraft Papers.

64. Probably Forts Folle Avoine as identified at site BU3. See David Woodward et al., *Cultural Map of Wisconsin: A Cartographic Portrait of the State* (Madison: University of Wisconsin Press, 1996).

65. In 1975, a Northern Ojibwe, whose ancestors would have been called Chippewa, at Weagamow Lake, Ontario, approximately five hundred miles to the north of this part of Wisconsin, distinguished by symbols on a map among eight types of rapids and falls on the basis of a mix of characteristics: length, water speed, the presence or absence of rocks, suitability for the construction of fish traps, and degree of accessibility for predatory mammals. Edward S. Rogers and Mary B. Black, "Subsistence Strategy in the Fish and Hare Period, Northern Ontario: The Weagamow Ojibwa, 1880–1920," *Journal of Anthropological Research* 32 (spring 1976): 8, fig. 2.

66. Untitled manuscript map in ink by Chief Michael Sahgatchewaikezhis of the lower Mississauga and Blind Rivers, Ontario, accompanying a letter of June 25, 1892, from himself and fifteen other members of his band, addressed to R. Sinclair, acting deputy minister of Indian affairs, Dominion of Canada, file 27013–6, pt. 1, vol. 7751, RG 10, National Archives of Canada, Ottawa.

67. David T. McNab, "Research Report: The Location of the Northern Boundary, Mississagi River Reserve #8, at Blind River," typed report, Office of Indian Resource Policy, Ministry of Natural Resources, Province of Ontario, November 17, 1980, revised March 8, 1984, 11.

68. Craig Macdonald, Recreation Specialist, Leslie M. Frost Natural Resources Centre, Dorset, Ontario, to G. Malcolm Lewis, September 8 and October 3, 1978.

69. Robert A. Rundstrom, "GIS, Indigenous Peoples, and Epistemological Diversity," *Cartography and Geographic Information Systems* 22 (Spring 1995): 56.

The 1767 Maps of Robert Rogers and Jonathan Carver: A Proposal for the Establishment of the Colony of Michilimackinac

Keith R. Widder

IN 1767, WHILE MAJOR ROBERT ROGERS AND CAPTAIN JONATHAN CARVER WERE AT MICHilimackinac, each man prepared a manuscript map of the region bordering on the western Great Lakes. These two cartographic images are important snapshots of part of Great Britain's expanded North American empire soon after its conquest of Canada. The maps and related documents evince the growing strength of British imperial authority and commerce in the region since the arrival of British traders and troops at Michilimackinac in 1761, the Chippewa's capture of the fort in 1763, and its reoccupation by the British in 1764. More important, the maps also show how the initiatives of one person, Robert Rogers, furthered Britain's imperial objective to extend its influence, if not its sovereignty,[1] throughout the western Great Lakes—even though at the same time, he was pursuing a personal agenda that had dubious authorization at best. The first map, called the Rogers map in this article, was drawn before May 24, 1767 (fig. 1).[2] It was a sketch of most of eastern North America that identified very few places. Carver drew the second map after he returned to Michilimackinac on August 29, 1767, from his travels into the interior (fig. 2).[3] When the maps are read and interpreted in sequence, their purposes become clear.

Kenneth Roberts's novel *Northwest Passage* and the 1940 movie of the same name grafted Robert Rogers's persona and his passion to find the Northwest Passage onto the historical consciousness of generations of Americans.[4] Roberts characterized Rogers as a fearless leader and Indian fighter—he saw him as a man driven by ambition who was not easily deterred by other people, including his superiors, or the environment. Rogers's biographer, John Cuneo, gives a detailed account of Rogers's military career during the French and Indian War, as well as his efforts to locate the Northwest Passage. Roberts's fictional account presents Rogers as being appointed "Governor of Michilimackinac," when in fact the

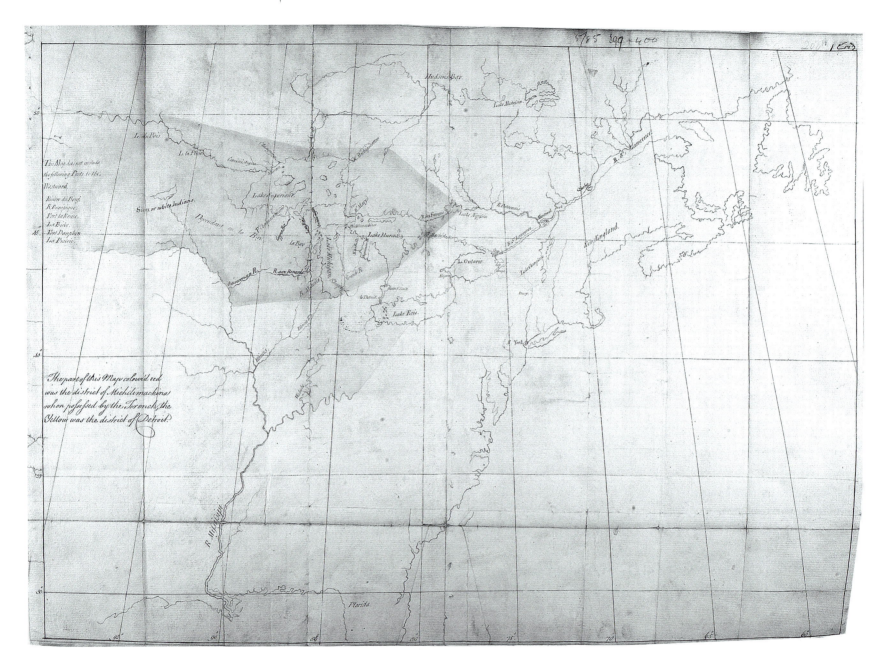

Figure 1. Map of eastern North America accompanying Robert Rogers's 1767 memorial to the Board of Trade. Image courtesy of the National Archives, Kew, Richmond, Surrey, UK, MPG 1/18.

king ordered General Thomas Gage, commander in chief of the British Army in North America, to make him the commandant. Cuneo recognized that Rogers hoped to make Michilimackinac into "the shining capital of a separate government,"[5] but he did not fully interpret the significance of Rogers's tour of duty at the Straits of Mackinac. Rogers's desire to find the Northwest Passage was only part of his larger vision for Michilimackinac and its surrounding territory—a fact that has not been accorded sufficient attention by historians.

The maps, when read in the context of other documents, reveal that Rogers's most important goal at Michilimackinac in 1766 and 1767 was to persuade the British government to create a new colony out of the "District of Michilimackinac" and name him its governor. Finding the Northwest Passage, though important, was for the moment a distinctly secondary goal. The huge costs incurred by the treasury during the wars of the previous decade and unsettled conditions in the American colonies made it very unlikely that the British government would enact Rogers's proposal. But his plan was a serious one that had an internal logic. Before he could hope to fulfill his dream, Rogers needed to do two things that ran counter to the policies of the British government that were then being administered by General Gage and Sir William Johnson, superintendent of Indian affairs for the Northern Department. First, Rogers had to complete the restoration, begun by his predecessor Captain William Howard, of the French system for the fur trade that depended upon traders wintering among the Indians who harvested the furs. (The alternative, mandated by Gage and Johnson, was to confine trade to Michilimackinac, forcing Indians to make a long and burdensome trip to the fort with their furs.) Rogers also had to negotiate a peace between the British and the Native peoples and among different groups of Indians living in the western Great Lakes region. To accomplish this, he would be required to hand out large quantities of presents in council with his Native counterparts—anathema to the pound-pinching Gage and Johnson. Only if Rogers succeeded in both of these endeavors could the Canadian traders compete successfully against French traders coming from west of the Mississippi River and from New Orleans. When Rogers was relieved of his command at Michilimackinac on December 6, 1767, he had allowed the traders to winter in the interior and had brought a relative peace to the region. The Canadian fur trade was flourishing again.

Rogers's accomplishments displeased some powerful people, as did his disregard for orders. Gage had him arrested and brought to Montreal to face court-martial in October 1768.[6] The maps and documentation of Rogers's activities at Michilimackinac cleared him of treason but would have convicted him of insubordination. It is beyond the scope of this article to examine the testimony given at Rogers's trial (where he was found not guilty of all charges), but the evidence presented here leaves little doubt that Major Rogers never contemplated deserting to either the French or the Spanish. Rogers *was* guilty, however, of working closely with French-Canadian traders (who were now British subjects), Indians, and Métis as he put the French system of trade back into practice for the benefit of Great Britain and himself.

Robert Rogers was no stranger to the western Great Lakes when he and his wife, Elizabeth Browne Rogers, arrived at Michilimackinac on August 10, 1766. Rogers had first come to Detroit in late 1760 to receive the French surrender of the settlement to the British after the French defeat at Montreal on September 8, 1760. The onset of winter prevented him from proceeding to Michilimackinac, which was finally garrisoned by Captain Henry Balfour of the 80th Regiment of Foot on September 28, 1761. Rogers appeared again at Detroit in 1763 to help defend the fort during the Indian siege led by the Ottawa chief Pontiac. Through negotiation and conflict, Rogers had become well acquainted with Native peoples around the western lakes, and he clearly understood the role they played in the fur trade. He believed that amicable relations with leaders such as Pontiac and Indian harvesters and sellers of furs were essential if British traders hoped to establish and maintain a profitable fur trade in the western Great Lakes.[7] Rogers, deeply in debt, had gone to England in 1765 to try to get his finances in order and to seek authorization to search for the Northwest Passage. On August 12, 1765, he presented a proposal "to the Wisdom of the Kings most Excellent Majesty and his Ministers" calling for a force of two hundred men plus officers to go on a three-year expedition at a cost of more than thirty-two thousand pounds. Rogers also laid the groundwork for his future plan to establish a colony in the western Great Lakes:

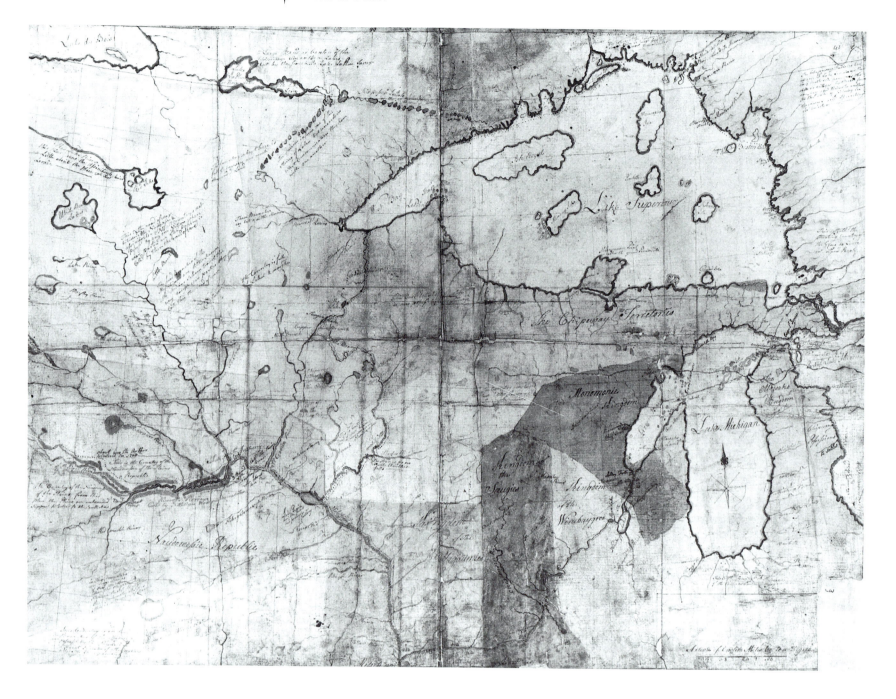

Figure 2. Jonathan Carver's 1767 map of the western Great Lakes. By permission of the British Library, Add. 8949 f. 41.

Should this Design be patronized, Major Rogers thinks it would be Expedient and absolutely necessary, to Subserve this proposal, that he should be Appointed Governor Commandant of His Majesty's Garrison of Michlimakana and its Dependancies on the Great Lakes, & that he has a Deputy-Governor Commandant who is well acquainted with the Manners of the Indians, to remain constantly at the said Garrison, on whose Diligence, Steadiness and Integrity he can rely, and from whom at his Setting out, & while on his Journey, as well as at his Return, he may depend upon receiving what Assistance shall be requisite; And that the General Commanding in Chief in North America, & Sir William Johnson have Orders to give him their Assistance in their respective Departments as Occasion may require.[8]

Rogers was appointed commandant, however, not governor commandant, and he would be under Gage's command, not independent of him, while at Michilimackinac. Although the king and the Board of Trade never approved Rogers's proposal to find the Northwest Passage, he had acquainted them with his ambitious agenda for Michilimackinac.

Rogers enlisted the support of prominent people for his scheme, including Charles Townshend, who became chancellor of the exchequer in 1766. Rogers later claimed to have received letters at Michilimackinac in the summer of 1766 from "Sundry Gentlemen in England," including Townshend, backing his plan. The major also referred to the Act of Parliament in 1745 that offered a twenty-thousand-pound payment for "the Discovery of the North West passage."[9] Such a sum would have eased Rogers's financial pains. After returning to America in early 1766, he engaged Captain James Tute, who had served with Rogers' Rangers during the French and Indian War, to lead a small expedition from Michilimackinac in quest of the Northwest Passage. Jonathan Carver, a self-taught cartographer and a veteran of the French and Indian War from Massachusetts, met Rogers in Boston, where he agreed to be the mapmaker for Tute's party.[10]

The purpose and content of Rogers's and Carver's maps differed significantly from the first British manuscript maps of the western Great Lakes made by Lieutenant Dietrich Brehm and Ensign Thomas Hutchins in 1761 and 1762. Brehm's work had been commissioned by General Jeffery Amherst, commander in chief of the British Army in North America, and Hutchins's by Sir William Johnson. Amherst and Johnson wanted cartographic and descriptive information that would help them create policies and practices needed to incorporate Britain's newly acquired territory into its empire.[11] The 1767 maps, however, were produced as a result of Robert Rogers acting against the wishes of General Gage, Amherst's successor, and Johnson. Rogers needed, in the first instance, a cartographic sketch to explain the geography of his proposed colony and the western fur trade to the Board of Trade and, in the second, a representation of the lands explored by Carver and Tute.

The circumstances of Major Rogers's appointment as commandant at Michilimackinac created confusion and mistrust between Rogers and Gage, leading Rogers to pursue his quest for the Northwest Passage without the authorization or even the knowledge of the general. Following George III's directive, Gage reluctantly placed Rogers in command at Michilimackinac on January 10, 1766.[12] Gage did not appreciate Rogers's machinations in London, where he went over Gage's head to secure the post at Michilimackinac. Consequently, Gage framed his instructions to the major in such a way that he was accountable to three superiors: Gage, Johnson, and the commandant at Detroit. Gage admonished Rogers to practice "the strictest Oeconomy" in expenditures, to follow Johnson's orders regarding "intercourse with the Savages," and to send frequent reports "to the Officer Commanding at Detroit, under whose immediate Command You are."[13] Gage, who neither liked nor trusted Rogers, conveyed his feelings to Johnson, asking him to instruct his interpreters and commissaries at Michilimackinac to watch the major's "Transactions with the Indians" carefully.[14] Gage made no mention of the Northwest Passage in his communications with Rogers or Johnson—and for good reason—since he did not know about Rogers's intention to commission a party to go from Michilimackinac in search of the elusive way to the Orient.[15] Rogers, however, justified outfitting and sending Carver and Tute to explore on the basis of his dealings with Charles Townshend and others in London.

Rogers's ambitions suggest several interrelated motivations for the preparation of the two maps. In all likelihood, Rogers was trying to increase the value of land given to him when he was in Detroit by chiefs representing the Lake Superior Chippewa. This took place on December 23, 1760. The grant was located between the Ontonagon and Copper Rivers along the southern coastline of Lake Superior.[16] For Rogers to profit from this property, the Native peoples had to be at peace with each other and with the British. Even more important, peace, or at least the absence of war, in the western Great Lakes was necessary for a prosperous fur trade. Both maps reflected Rogers's efforts to bring about a viable, stable trade.[17] The Rogers map incorporated and promoted his ambition to be appointed governor over a new colony, which he hoped would be created in the western Great Lakes region.[18] Carver's map is a cartographic record of his travels through parts of present-day Michigan, Wisconsin, and Minnesota. Rogers ordered Carver to draw plans of the region as he searched it by himself and then as a member of James Tute's party while it looked for a route to China.[19] In order to understand Rogers's and Carver's maps beyond their drawn features, a number of questions must be asked. J. B. Harley argues that we should try "to tease out new meanings, hidden agendas, and contrasting views from between the lines on the image."[20] He also says that all maps "strive to frame their message in the context of an audience." They "state an argument about the world and they are propositional in nature."[21] From Harley's perspective, it is also important to look for what "is absent from maps" as well as what is included.[22] Addressing these issues will help scholars examine Rogers's and Carver's maps critically and discern the impressions that these men wished to convey to their audiences.

Native peoples helped Europeans create maps of North America, since the Europeans knew little or nothing of vast regions of this continent that they intended to explore, exploit, and settle. For the most part, Indians kept the cartographic images of their world in their minds and transmitted them to others orally, through sketches on bark or the ground, or via messages put on trees or other places. Europeans had plugged into the Indian trade network and relied on Native cartography long before either Rogers or Carver set foot in the western Great Lakes.[23] Relationships created through trade helped to shape the human and cultural geography that Carver and Rogers reported.

Rogers's instructions to Jonathan Carver and to James Tute reveal his goals for their missions. Rogers spelled out clearly in the first paragraph of his commission to Carver why the two maps under discussion needed to be drawn: "Whereas it will be to the honour and dignity of the nation as well as for the good of His Majesty's service to have some good survaies of the interiour parts of North America espeeseely to the west and north west from this garrison [Michilimackinac]." He asked Carver to proceed along the north coast of Lake Michigan to Green Bay and on to the Falls of St. Anthony, "taking an exact plans of the country by the way marking down all Indian towns with their numbers, as also to take survaies of the diffrant posts, lakes, and rivers as also the mountains." Rogers ordered Carver to explore, during the winter, the area surrounding the Falls of St. Anthony and to send him reports "early in the spring." If Carver received further instructions to join another detachment, Rogers wanted him to proceed with that party and to send his journal to Rogers by way of a trusted person. If no such orders came, Carver should return to Michilimackinac by way of the Illinois River, Fort St. Joseph, and the eastern shore of Lake Michigan.[24] There was no mention in the directive to Carver of searching for the Northwest Passage—that task fell to Captain Tute, who would integrate Carver into his own exploration party.

Rogers left little doubt that he expected Tute and his party to find a way to the Pacific Ocean and to make a cartographic record of their discoveries. The opening words in his directive to Tute were: "Instructions to Captn. James Tute Esqr. commanding a party for the discovery of the North West Passage from the Atlantick into the Passifick Occian, if any such passage there be or for the discovery of the great Reriver Ourigan that fall into the Passifick Occian about the latitude fifty." To assist Tute, Rogers enlisted the services of James Stanley Goddard, a trader familiar with the region, to function as the secretary for Indian affairs during the mission, and Joseph Reaume to serve as interpreter. Rogers ordered Tute to proceed to the Falls of St. Anthony "to take Captn. Johnathan Carver under your command who is to be draftsman for the detachment." The instructions contained a number of specific details to guide Tute on his journey as well as levels of compensation, chain of command, and the authority to purchase goods from traders along the way. Rogers also specified: "From the above description you will do your utmost endeavor to find out and discover the said cuntry and take all possable means to obtain a draft of it as well as by the way reporting from time to time to me all your proceedings, at every oppertunity sending such scetches or plans as your draftsman has taken, and you are further desired to make all the interest you possibly can with the diffrent nations that others may pass after your return to open a trade a cross the continent to those people equaly advantageous to them selves as to us."[25]

Rogers's interest in finding the elusive Northwest Passage and the efforts he expended in his search need to be understood as but another try in a long series of attempts by European explorers to find a short and quick way to the Orient through North America. English exploration and commercial ventures into Hudson Bay in the seventeenth century led to the establishment of the Hudson's Bay Company in 1671. In the eighteenth century, the company made exploratory voyages that reconfirmed the hazards posed by ice, tides, snow, fog, and cold temperatures in this area. They discovered no outlet to the sea that would allow them to sail to China. The historian Glyn Williams summed it up: "The story of the search for a passage in the eighteenth century is one of credulity and some duplicity, of hopes raised and dashed, of the misdirection of practical seamen by those 'closet navigators' or armchair geographers much reviled in the explorers' journals."[26] James Knight, Christopher Middleton, Arthur Dobbs, William Moor, and Francis Smith, among others, all contributed to a sequence of complicated endeavors that brought together the Crown and Parliament, English commercial and navigational interests, scientists, and adventurers to ensure that the route, upon discovery, would be English rather than French.

Rogers's plans also depended on French initiatives to probe for the Western Sea, or the Mer de l'Ouest, and, perhaps more important, to build fur-trading posts to compete with the Hudson's Bay Company. West and northwest of Lake Superior, many groups of Indians and French-speaking Métis, who were the offspring of unions between Native women and French men, had lived and worked together for a century before Rogers assumed command at Michilimackinac. Like many of his fellow British officers, Rogers condemned the French as "a very bad set of Poeple"[27] but discovered that he was able to bring peace and order to the western Great Lakes only when he followed the French example and established good relations with the Native peoples.

When Rogers arrived at Michilimackinac in August 1766, he entered a world where the Chippewa, Odawa, Menominee, Ho-Chunk (Winnebago), Fox, Sac, Sioux, and Cree along with French Canadians had created a society unlike any other in North America. French traders began to integrate themselves into Native American trade networks in the second half of the seventeenth century, and in 1717, they renewed their push into the extensive system of rivers, streams, and lakes west of Lake Superior.[28] Settlements at Michilimackinac, La Baye (Green Bay, Wisconsin), La Pointe (Madeline Island, Wisconsin), and Kaministiquia (Thunder Bay, Ontario) all stood as evidence that a permanent and influential French presence existed in the western Great Lakes region.

Furthermore, the French had established a line of fur-trading posts west from Lake Superior to the Saskatchewan River. In succession, Zacharie Robutel de la Noue, Pierre Gaultier de Varennes et de la

Vérendrye and his sons, Nicolas-Joseph de Noyelles de Fleurimont, Jacques Legardeur de Saint-Pierre, and Louis de la Corne endured great hardships as they negotiated with Native peoples to receive permission to build forts and to carry on trade.[29] As a result, by 1760, French outposts stood near Rainy Lake (Fort Saint-Pierre, 1731), the Lake of the Woods (Fort Saint-Charles, 1732), Lake Winnipeg (Fort Maurepas, 1734, 1739), the Assiniboine River (Fort La Reine [Portage La Prairie, Manitoba], 1738), Lake Winnipegosis (Fort Dauphin, 1741), Cedar Lake (Fort Bourbon, 1743), the Saskatchewan River (Fort Paskoya, c. 1750), and the forks of the Saskatchewan River (Fort des Prairies [Fort la Corne], 1753).[30] French exploration and settlement prepared the way for Rogers's plan for the western Great Lakes.

Robert Rogers created his sketch of eastern North America to accompany a lengthy memorial to a very specific audience—the Earl of Dartmouth and the Board of Trade. The purpose of the map can be ascertained only when viewed as part of Rogers's entire communication with the board, which included copies of his orders and instructions from General Gage and Sir William Johnson.[31] In his memorandum, Rogers explained Michilimackinac's place in the western fur trade, primarily as it had existed under the French regime, and what was required for it to operate most efficiently. Rogers then laid out a scheme for the creation of a separate civil government for Michilimackinac, asking to become its governor. The following analysis of Rogers's plans and activities at Michilimackinac unlocks the meaning of his map.

In one year, Robert Rogers had completed the reconstruction of the French fur trade system that had been thrown into disarray by the violence of Pontiac's War in 1763. After the fall of Canada in 1760, British arrogance toward the western nations led to a policy that considered the Indians a conquered people (which they were not), a significant reduction in presents (including gunpowder) given to Indians by British officers, and general mistrust of the British by Native peoples, all of which fueled resentment and anger. As a result, Indians throughout the West warred against the British intruders and captured a number of garrisons, including Michilimackinac on June 2, 1763. The fur trade collapsed. British authority disappeared at Michilimackinac and was weakened at Detroit by Pontiac's siege of the fort there from May through October. After hostilities melted away, Captain William Howard and a contingent of the 17th Regiment of Foot regarrisoned Michilimackinac in September 1764.[32] In response to demands from both Indians and traders, Howard began to put the trade back together in accordance with the French system. In 1765, he allowed some traders to winter in the interior away from the fort in defiance of Sir William Johnson's policy, which confined the trade to the post.[33] Howard was roundly criticized by those traders who were forced to remain at the fort and by his superiors for violating orders.[34] Howard let even more traders go into the interior for the winter of 1766–67. Rogers claimed that "the People of Michilimackinac were all gone a wintering before His arrivall" in the summer of 1766.[35]

It had not taken long for Howard to recognize that in order to negotiate peace with and among the western nations, he had to allow traders to go into the interior to carry on transactions with their Native trading partners. The French system had put the responsibility for transporting both trade goods and furs between Michilimackinac and Native villages upon the French Canadians and Métis. Indian men and women who harvested furs, which were coveted by Europeans, saw no need to travel great distances to Michilimackinac to do business with traders just because a British officer now commanded the garrison there. More was at stake than inconvenience, however. Traders who treated their customers fairly promoted peace in the region and provided intelligence to Howard regarding relationships between Native groups and the passage of war belts among them. Such information enabled the commandant to try to negotiate understandings between groups who were at war or threatened war against each other.[36]

Howard also acknowledged a second element of an effective Indian trade policy at Michilimacki-nac. The commandant met with Indian leaders and parties whenever they came to the post, and he gave them enough presents to satisfy their minimal expectations from their British "father." Howard's predecessors and other British officers in the West had struggled to do likewise before Pontiac's War in 1763. But these efforts had been undercut by General Amherst's orders that British officers must treat Indians as a conquered people; the Native peoples soon came to believe, with good reason, that the British intended to take their land and enslave them.[37] Howard, and Rogers after him, were both fully aware that if they hoped to get along with the Indians, they had to recognize them as equal partners in diplomacy and trade. Only through the liberal distribution of gifts in council could British officials earn the trust of the western nations. Once trust had been established, the British could maintain it only by giving more presents and actively working to settle disputes between the Indian nations living in the region surrounding Michilimackinac.

Howard lost no time in requesting that goods for Indian presents be forwarded to him. In his first letter from Michilimackinac, he asked Colonel John Bradstreet in Detroit "to prevail on the Gen[l] [Gage] to send me some presents for the Indians, without which it will be difficult for me, to keep the Indians in temper." Howard barely had time to unpack his trunks in late September 1764 before French-Canadian residents of the fort and visiting Indians brought to his attention a host of thorny issues. One inhabitant had received a pipe "dyd with Green" from a Sioux chief and presented it to Howard with a message that if he wished the Sioux "to strike against the Chippeways," he should paint it red and return it to them. The Sioux also begged Howard to send traders into their country. Before Howard could allow traders to go, he had to arrange a peace between the Sioux and the Chippewa. It did not take the Indians very long to teach Howard the relationship between trade and war and peace in their country. Remembering the deaths of British soldiers during the attack in 1763, the Odawa from L'Arbre Croche came to Howard presenting him with "6 Strings and two belts" of wampum welcoming him and "to whipe away the blood that was spilt of their Brothers the English." Although Howard had no wampum to give them in return, he dispensed "some presents" as he spoke to them.[38] By giving sufficient presents during his conference with the Odawa, Howard had followed the French manner of gift giving and had put the Brit-ish at Michilimackinac on a track, continued by Robert Rogers, that enabled their successors to become effective brokers of diplomacy among the western nations for at least the next twenty years.[39]

Robert Rogers elevated British diplomacy with the Indians of the western Great Lakes to a level approximating the way the French had formerly carried on negotiations with them at Michilimackinac. Sir William Johnson had held extensive councils with the Chippewa, Odawa, and other western na-tions at Detroit, Niagara, and Oswego, but he never got to Michilimackinac. So the Indians in the West welcomed the attention Rogers—who understood their worldview—gave to them at their traditional gathering place at the Straits of Mackinac. It is striking how closely Rogers's way of relating to Native leaders and their people fulfilled the Chevalier de Raymond's account of the prerequisites for successful diplomacy by French officers when treating with their Indian counterparts. In 1754, Raymond, a thirty-two-year veteran of service in New France, wrote:

The diplomacy and care that are necessary to keep them faithful are incredible, because they are dis-trustful, vindictive, traitorous, perfidious, changeable, suspicious. That is why every care that a com-mandant must employ in order to serve usefully should attract the confidence of the Indians where he is in command. In order to succeed, he must be affable; appear to share their feelings; be generous without prodigality; always give them something, especially to their children; give them precisely the presents that are sent to him to be given to them; distribute them appropriately, as upon the occasions when they are needed for the service or to prevent them from going to the English. In giving them these presents, let it always be in the name of the Great Onontio, chief of all the French whom they call their father.[40]

Robert Rogers's French-style Indian diplomacy angered his immediate supervisors. Sir William Johnson, who was a master at Indian negotiations, would have had little quarrel with many of Raymond's prescriptions for dealing with the Indians.[41] Johnson asked Rogers to get to know the Indians at Michilimackinac, be attentive to their concerns, and protect them from abuse by traders and soldiers. But Johnson made no mention of presents in his instructions, and this was not an oversight. General Gage's orders to all post commandants forbade giving presents to Indians except "on Occasions which shall render such measures unavoidable." Furthermore, if one of Johnson's subordinates was at a post during an Indian council, he was to "be employed in delivering the Presents."[42] Johnson had no deputy at Michilimackinac when Rogers arrived in August 1766. In March 1767, Johnson appointed Lieutenant Benjamin Roberts commissary at Michilimackinac with the responsibility for Indian relations. Rogers refused to recognize his authority. Roberts, who appeared in late June, quarreled incessantly with Rogers, and his complaints to Gage played a role in Rogers's removal from command and his arrest later in the year.[43] Roberts's charges that Rogers intended to desert to the French only confirmed Johnson and Gage's suspicions (or wishful thinking) that Rogers was a traitor. Roberts's accusations also reinforced Johnson and Gage's disapproval of the expenses Rogers had incurred for Indian presents. The first account submitted by Rogers for expenditures of nearly four hundred thirty pounds exceeded the cost for presents for the preceding year.[44]

Following a path similar to that laid out by the Chevalier de Raymond, Rogers spent much time and money communicating to Indian leaders the good intentions of the "Great King of England Your Father" in order to establish understandings predicated on mutual trust. Eight days after Rogers had assumed command at Michilimackinac, he entertained the Odawa and Chippewa at councils for four days. Amid the proper exchanges of protocol, chiefs from both nations raised the issue of letting traders winter among them.[45]

Five weeks after his initial meetings with Indian leaders, Rogers traveled twenty-five miles to L'Arbre Croche to hold a council with three hundred Odawa and their chiefs. The Odawa, who had not joined in the attack against the fort in 1763, reaffirmed their friendship for the English and told Rogers they had learned that a large French army was coming from New Orleans to drive the English out of the Great Lakes before moving on to join another French force, which would land at New York. The Odawa wanted to know if the report was true, and if it was, they pledged to fight the French. Rogers's pointed response to the chiefs was attentive to Native peoples' protocol, attitudes, and sensitivities. He gave a ratteen (thick woolen cloth) coat and a shirt to each of the two principal chiefs and twenty gallons of rum to the village before chastising them for giving "credit" to rumors regarding a French army coming to wage war against the English. The major then made the requisite reference to their "sturdiness," which he had "lately recommended" to Sir William Johnson. Next, Rogers gave the Odawa a wampum belt, following this presentation with a speech condemning both the French and the Spanish. The French had ceded their lands west of the Mississippi River to the Spanish—a people who had poured melted gold and silver "like water, by hot fire down thier [*sic*] Throat," when they first came to America. He asked the Odawa how they could believe anything that the deceitful Spanish might say. There were no French troops in America, and no French troops were coming: "Our Ships are much superior to the French & Spaniards shou'd they join together & on the other hand all the English in America and the French in Canada are subjects to the Great King of England Your Father." Rogers gave them another wampum belt, exhorting the Odawa to find out more about the French threat and bring this information to Rogers, who would "acquaint" Johnson and the king of the Odawa's allegiance to their English father. Wishing them well, Rogers concluded the council by giving them one more string of wampum and twenty stroud (coarse woolen) blankets.[46]

During the year that followed, Rogers met with Native chiefs and men from many villages and bands, fulfilling their ceremonial and material needs as he strengthened and broadened British influence throughout the western Great Lakes. On October 10, 1766, a party of one hundred Odawa, who lived along the Grand River in southern Michigan, gave Rogers a beaver blanket as they pleaded poverty. The major replied with a cache of presents, answering their need for hunting supplies and clothing: "8 stroud blankets, 8 stroud leggings, 8 breechcloths, 12 ratteen coats, 12 calamanco gowns, 4 linen shirts, 60 pounds of gunpowder, 150 pounds of salt, 400 gunflints, 78 pounds of tobacco, 3 pounds of vermilion, 24 gallons of rum, 14 laced hats, [and a] wampum belt." Before the Odawa departed, Rogers reminded them that traders who had gone to their winter grounds could supply them with more goods. Others who called at Michilimackinac during the fall of 1766 and the winter of 1767 included Chippewa from the St. Marys River, Cheboygan, and La Cloche and Mississauga from Thunder Bay.[47]

Rogers's efforts to negotiate peace among the western nations reached a climax at a general council held at Michilimackinac on July 2 and 3, 1767. At a series of conferences leading up to the "Grand and General Council," leaders of the Odawa, Potawatomi, Chippewa, Mississauga, Menominee, Winnebago or Ho-Chunk, Sac, Fox, and Sioux all told the commandant of their grievances with one another and their efforts to maintain a fragile peace. Chippewa attacks on members of tribes living west of Lake Michigan had led to calls, particularly by young men, for revenge. Tribal leaders had expended considerable energy restraining their young warriors from inflaming a volatile situation. Now the chiefs called upon Rogers to calm the waters and resolve their differences.

Rogers understood that his credibility among the western Indians as well as the future of the British fur trade depended on the outcome of the grand council. Before the conference commenced, Rogers assessed the situation west of Lakes Michigan and Superior: "I could not but observe a pretty Hostile Temper to prevail & most of them upon the Point of an open war & rupture to the Westward, there had been Injuries Provocatons and Bloodshed on both sides which joined to yᵉ natural inclination of those Savages to Frequent Wars, and the perfidious Conduct of the French and Spanish Traders from the other side of the Misisipi by instilling false notions into their Minds and Stiring them up to war among themselves and into a bad opinion of us and our Traders made matters look very unfavorable to our Trade in that part of the Country at present."[48]

Undaunted, Rogers met with the chiefs of each nation outside the fort walls, where they expressed their concerns. Seizing on a "general disposition to peace and Amity," Rogers "lighted the Calumet or Pipe of Peace." As each chief smoked the pipe, he gave assurances of friendship and asked that traders be

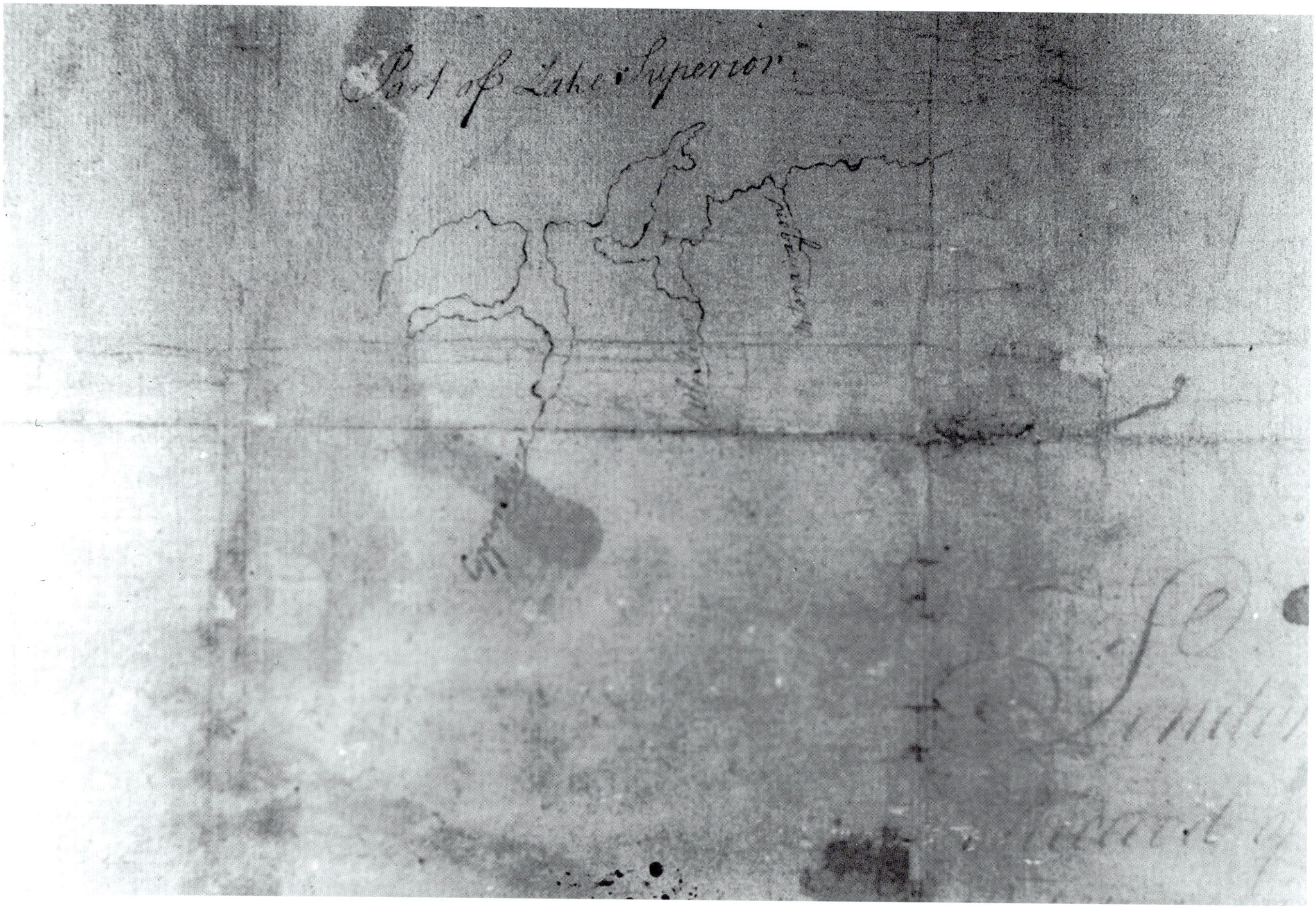

Figure 3. Sketch of "Parts of Lake Superior" showing "Copper River," "little River," and "Ontonawagon [River]." Image courtesy of the Burton Historical Collection, Detroit Public Library.

allowed to come to their "distant Villages and Hunting grounds." Rogers assured the chiefs that traders would soon be on their way. On the second day of the grand council, Rogers passed out presents and rum to seal the peace.[49]

Rogers allowed for the full return of traders to their interior posts, in essence restoring the French system of trade under British authority and supervision. Although British merchants such as Alexander Henry, Benjamin Frobisher, Stephen Groesbeck, Forrest Oakes, and Isaac Todd provided much of the capital and security for the trade, French Canadians were in charge of nearly all of the one hundred twenty-one canoes sent out during the summer of 1767. Most traders went to winter among groups of Native peoples who had sent representatives to the council. Most of the French-Canadian traders and voyageurs were men who had worked in the trade at the time of the British conquest; they now considered themselves loyal subjects of George III, not Louis XV.[50]

Chippewa chiefs coming from the St. Marys River, La Pointe, the Kaministiquia River, Rainy Lake, and the Lake of the Woods were pleased that traders accompanied them back to their homelands in the Lake Superior country and beyond. Other canoes found their way to the Odawa along the Grand River, the Potawatomi at Fort St. Joseph, and the Potawatomi, Odawa, and Sac at Milwaukee. Traders also carried on transactions with the Menominee near Green Bay, the Ho-Chunk along the upper Fox River, the Sioux and Chippewa living in the area surrounding the upper Mississippi River, and the Chippewa and Mississauga who wintered near Lake Huron. The Canadian traders were back in business as a breakdown of the destinations for the canoes in 1767 demonstrates: eighteen to Lake Superior, fourteen via Lake Superior to the northwest, five to Lake Huron, twenty-four into Lake Michigan, forty-three by Lake Michigan to Green Bay, and seventeen by Green Bay into the Mississippi.[51]

The map that Robert Rogers sent to the Board of Trade on May 24, 1767, can be understood only as being part of, not a mere attachment to, his lengthy memorial to the board. As Rogers's plan for Michilimackinac unfolds in his memorial, much of the map's empty space fills up. On first glance, the proposals put forth by Rogers seem to have been the work of a person whose ambitions had trumped reality, leading to the formulation of a grandiose scheme that no one would take seriously. But this was not the case. When Rogers was in London in 1765, he engaged in discussions with high-level British officials and influential men. Lord Rockingham, the first lord of the treasury, received full accounts of Rogers's ideas, which had been worked out in conjunction with Charles Townshend.[52]

Townshend had a personal interest in the realization of Rogers's vision for the western Great Lakes. On October 10, 1765, Rogers sold an interest in the land granted to him by the Lake Superior Chippewa in 1760 to Townshend and Chase Price for two hundred pounds. On the 1760 deed appears a small sketch of "Parts of Lake Superior," showing "Copper River," "little River," and "Ontonawagon [River]" as the only details (fig. 3).[53] The Chippewa reserved the right to hunt and fish on these lands, but they gave the other uses of the land to Rogers, including mineral rights. It is not a coincidence that these rivers are identified on Rogers's 1767 map; Townshend would have been looking for them.

A wampum belt accompanying the deed created an Indian map and record of the ceded territory (fig. 4). The "Memorandum," which is not completely legible, defines the boundaries of the grant. "Three white marks" represent the Copper, Little, and Ontonagon Rivers. Three rows of purple beads at each end of the belt identify the outer limits of the grant—apparently three miles west of the Copper River and three miles east of the Ontonagon River. The purple fields between the white are lands between the rivers. The terms of the transaction required the presentation of the belt to Chippewa leaders whenever the lands were being referred to by holders of the deed.[54]

Townshend would have been expecting much more on the map than the three rivers, for he had hoped that Rogers's commission in 1765 would make the major governor of Michilimackinac. Townshend, Rogers, and others believed that the success of their "design" for Michilimackinac and the country surrounding it depended upon Rogers receiving a charge that would supersede General Gage's authority to limit Rogers's power at the Straits of Mackinac. In October 1765, Rogers and Townshend outlined for Lord Rockingham the territory for which a separate government would be created that was consistent with Rogers's petition of August 12 to the king for "Michlimakana and its Dependancies on the Great Lakes." The description of the proposed colony as envisioned by Rogers and Townshend called for "boundaries you [Townshend] *wou'd* recommend for a *govern^t* at *Michilimakana:* Rogers thinks that if it comprehended the adjacent country around *Lake Superior* and *Michigan* [with] *y^e* Lakes, Rivers &c and

Figure 4. Wampum belt presented to Robert Rogers. Image courtesy of the Detroit Historical Museum.

with part only of Lake Huron and its dependencies, half way to Detroit; or as far as *Saguinam bay* upon the south and West side of it; and upon the North and down the East Shore, as far as the *little Islands of Sᵗ Joseph*, it wou'd consider all his [Rogers's] purposes, and be fully sufficient." Townshend and Rogers recognized that a separate jurisdiction centered at Detroit was also needed, for the West was "too extensive to be plac'd under the Jurisdiction of one officer."[55]

Rogers and his audience had similar views about the need to find the Northwest Passage and his plan of government for the western Great Lakes, which explains why he drew his sketch and wrote his memorial. Rogers, the king, and the king's ministers assumed that the Northwest Passage to the Pacific Ocean existed, and Rogers seemed a suitable person to direct the effort to find it. They also believed that the discovery of such a passage would be of enormous economic and political benefit to Great Britain and would increase the value of its recent addition to its North American empire. Expeditions to find the passage would be expensive, and approval for Rogers's scheme in 1765 had been withheld, in part, because of its high cost. So the question of who would pay for an expedition remained unanswered. The documents Rogers sent to London on May 24, 1767, were intended to provide information gathered on the scene for top-level decision makers, who would be expecting such a communication from him. Silence relative to Rogers's desire to find the Northwest Passage should not obscure the fact that some in his audience probably believed that Rogers had already sent off a party to look for it. The plan for the creation of a civil government for Michilimackinac was presented as the best way to reestablish, maintain, and protect both a flourishing fur trade and peace in the region. A strong trade was a valuable asset to England and the proposed Michilimackinac colony. Rogers put forth a plan of government freeing the commandant at Michilimackinac from the authority of General Gage and Superintendent Johnson by making the governor of the District of Michilimackinac answerable directly to the "King and Council." The governor would command the troops and deal with matters relating to the Indians. The lieutenant governor, who should be experienced in Indian negotiations, would stand in for the governor during his absences. The traders and leading civilians would choose a "council of twelve" to "enact such Laws as may be necessary" subject to the king's "approbation." Critical of regular troops and their "inferior officers," Rogers argued that several companies of rangers, under the governor's command, would make a more effective fighting force than the existing small garrison. In addition, the British government would need to provide an annual allowance for Indian presents, which were absolutely essential "to keep them peacable and well disposed towards his Majesty's Just & Mild Government." Payment for these bills would be drawn in London and would not be subject to Gage's review and approval.[56]

The proposal was much more than a design for governing a large territory, for Rogers had written a job description for the governorship—a position for which he was applying. He anticipated that Charles Townshend and others in London would expect him to seek the appointment, with its broad powers, which he had failed to secure in 1765.[57] Writing from Michilimackinac, Rogers now made his case from firsthand observation and experience. Rogers spelled out in considerable detail why the fur trade needed to operate as it had under the French regime. He described the benefits of allowing the traders to winter among the Indians and how vital giving presents to the Native peoples was to peace, the trade itself, and the well-being of British interests in the region. Even though the grand council was still six weeks in the future, he fortified his credentials by saying that he had "acquired a perfect knowledge and Confidence of the Natives."[58]

Rogers's thinking about the French and how their presence might affect his efforts to secure the western Great Lakes for the British gives further insight into the purpose and meaning of his sketch. Advocating the removal of the French, many of whom were Métis, he said: "That the French at Michilimackinac, St Joseph's, the Bay [Green Bay], St Mary's & other places in this Country where they are lurking & walking up and down are an Indolent sloothful sett of Vagabonds, ill disposed to the English and having a great influence over the Savages, are continually exerting their Territories & stirring up their hatred and revenge against us."[59]

Rogers went on to condemn the encroachments east of the Mississippi River made by French and Spanish traders coming from west of the river and up from New Orleans. There is no question that the French trading out of New Orleans threatened the livelihood of the Montreal and New York traders. If the British hoped to restore profitability to the Canadian trade, they had to prevent the New Orleans–based traders from gaining a foothold in the region. To accomplish this, Rogers and the Canadian traders (French-Canadian and British alike), depended upon French Canadians coming from Quebec to transport furs and merchandise. Even more important, the trade could not function without the French-speaking Métis, who lived throughout this region, to provide the needed personal and family connections to Native harvesters of furs.[60] Admittedly, these were the very people he had accused of causing trouble for the British. Rogers knew all this when he composed his memorial, but by presenting the French, Britain's hated rival, as a pervasive menace in the region, he strengthened his argument that the governor of Michilimackinac needed the powers called for in his plan. In practice, Rogers allowed scores of French Canadians to winter among the Indians and Métis of the interior without regret. He did little or nothing to disturb the place of the Métis in the fur-trading society. If he had done otherwise, Rogers would have had no hope of establishing a viable fur trade under British auspices.

Confident that he had support in London, Rogers sought to put himself under the direct authority of the king, the king's ministers, and the Board of Trade, even though the king had ordered Gage to appoint Rogers as only the commandant at Michilimackinac. From Rogers's perspective, direct authority gave him the right to disregard Gage's and Johnson's instructions if they kept him from doing what he thought to be either in his own best interests or useful to further British authority and influence in the western Great Lakes. Rogers made reference to the directions given him by Gage and Johnson with a startling admission that he had violated them: "By which orders & Instructions your Lordships will plainly perceive that his Majesty's Royal Pleasure and Intentions toward your Memorialist are in Some respects not all comply'd with; as he Commands & Acts here without a Commission and by Instructions only which he apprehends never was meant nor intended by His Majesty's Ministers."[61]

Rogers's dismissal of Gage's instructions as not being consistent with the intentions of "His Majesty's Ministers" does not hold up when examined against the communication of Henry Seymour Conway, secretary of state for the Southern Department, to Gage, dated October 12, 1765. Conway conveyed the king's "pleasure" to Gage that he appoint Rogers "to have the Command at the Fort of Michilimackinac." Conway went on to say: "It is recommended to give him power & instructions for that purpose [to carry on matters relating to the Indians] as far as you shall judge to be for his Majesty's service, & as shall not interfere with the superintendance with which Sʳ William Johnson is now invested, to whom if thought proper he might be made subordinate."[62] The major had willfully disobeyed his orders from Gage and Johnson, even though they derived their authority from the king.

The memorial and the map also need to be interpreted in light of James Tute and Jonathan Carver's search for the Northwest Passage, even though both documents are silent regarding the mission.[63] Rogers was in no position to pay for this search, and he certainly did not want the cost of an expedition, which might not be successful, to interfere with his larger design. Rogers's plan for a civil government for the District of Michilimackinac would make enough demands on the treasury. If Tute and Carver found the Northwest Passage, the importance of Michilimackinac to Britain's empire would be greatly enhanced and its operational costs justified more easily. Charles Townshend and others in London understood this reality and would have interpreted Rogers's plan and map with the Northwest Passage in mind.

The preceding review of Rogers's activities at Michilimackinac from August 1766 through July 1767 permits analysis of the meaning of his and Carver's sketches in terms of the issues raised by J. B. Harley. Determining each map's audience, the propositions and agendas shaping the map, its specific contents, and the features missing from it reveals that both Rogers and Carver intended to use their sketches to convey far more to their readers than just geographical information. The Rogers map (fig. 5) appears to be no more than a hurriedly drawn image (by an unknown hand) identifying important rivers and lakes, a few settlements, and little else. The most obvious feature of the drawing, which encompasses hundreds of thousands of square miles, is empty space—and this was most likely by design. Rogers wanted to be named governor of the District of Michilimackinac. His map clearly puts forth that agenda. By placing the proposed colony close to the middle of the image and coloring it red, Rogers drew it to his audience's attention. Michilimackinac became the center of North America, which appeared otherwise to be largely uninhabited. The only places labeled in the thirteen eastern colonies are "N. York," Albany, New England, and Lake Champlain. In the province of Quebec, only Montreal and Quebec are labeled. Robert Rogers had made his reputation fighting the French and Indians near many of these places. Readers of his map would not have missed the connection between Rogers's storied past during the French and Indian War and his wish for promotion.

The map makes a bold statement with its emphatic illustration of the proposed District of Michilimackinac's boundaries. Robert Rogers was challenging the Board of Trade to rethink how it viewed its new empire in North America. The district encompassed all or part of the present states of Michigan, Wisconsin, Minnesota, and North and South Dakota and the Canadian provinces of Ontario, Manitoba, and Saskatchewan. On this map, Lake Nipissing functions as a focal point, fixing the eye's attention on the farthest eastern point of a red field that marks the proposed district. Two straight lines coming

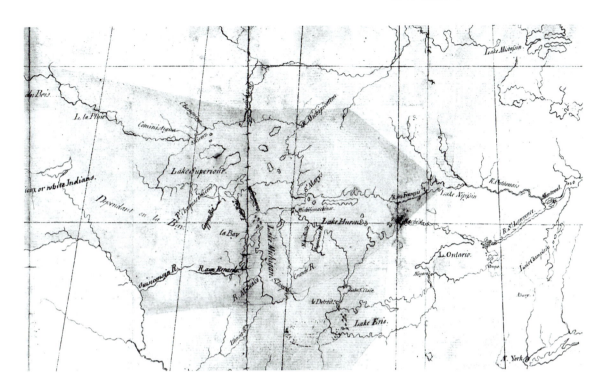

Figure 5. Detail of Robert Rogers's 1767 map. The more darkly shaded portion is red and represents the extent of the proposed District of Michilimackinac. Image courtesy of the National Archives, Kew, Richmond, Surrey, U.K., MPG 1/18.

together at almost a right angle extend to the northwest and the southwest before turning westward to form the rest of the outline of the district. The northern boundary turns west at what appears to be Lake Abitibi and runs all the way to the Winnipeg River. The southern boundary extends from Lake Nipissing through southern Lake Huron across southern Michigan to the base of Lake Michigan, west to the Mississippi River, up the Mississippi to the Minnesota River, and west to the edge of the sketch. The cartographer left no doubt about the location, size, and scope of the proposed colony.

With the Rogers map at their fingertips, men reading the memorial would have made the connections among the Northwest Passage, the strategic importance of Michilimackinac for maintaining both peace in the region and the fur trade, and Rogers's plan for civil government. In one paragraph, Rogers brought together these three elements of his proposition to the Board of Trade and at the same time served as an eloquent spokesman for Indians living in the western Great Lakes region:

It need not surely be repeated that the Case of Michilimakinac is very different, this is the outside or Frontier Brittish Post in America. It is or ought to be a Barrier to all that may come Westerly, North Westerly or South Westerly to the Pacific Ocean—It is or ought to be a Beacon from which a most extensive and hitherto unknown Territory is watched and observed. It is or ought to be a Store House fraught with all manner of Necessarys for the constant supply of Innumerrable Bands, Tribes & Nations of Savages; Savages removed from it five, Six & Eight Hundred and some a Thousand Leagues who cannot annually, nor do they ever in their lives visit it as a markett. They must loose one years Hunt to make Sale of another. They must leave their Families distressed and Starving, their Country and Substance naked and exposed to Enemies and perhaps perish themselves wth Hunger and Want on their way, Savages long acceptance to expect Traders annually, with Supplies, in their respective Country's—T'is true some Principal Persons from some of these distant Tribes + nations generally visit this Garrison once a year or rather every Two years, but it is their whole years employment—When they come they bring nothing with them except some trifling present or some small Matter to Exchange for Necessary's to carry them back again. They do not come to Markett, Their business is to renew & brighten the Chain or Path of Friendship and make solemn Declarations of their peacable Dispositions & Amiable Intentions towards us, but their principal request of the Commandant is, that Traders may come into their particular Country's that their Wives, Children, Old Men, Friends & Country Men may be supply'd with such things as having been long accustomed to the use of, they cannot with any degree of Comfort or Patience subsist without.[64]

Rogers's choice of the word "beacon" directed toward the west, northwest, and southwest from Michilimackinac impressed upon readers the need for exploration to throw light onto unknown territories. This was a graphic and powerful illustration of Michilimackinac's significance.

Another intriguing feature of the sketch is how Rogers validated his proposal and behavior by recalling the French way of organizing and operating the fur trade. Traders who were licensed for Michilimackinac or Detroit were free to trade within the district specified on their passes.[65] Under the French, trading posts existed at or near rivers or lakes depicted on the map, including "St. Marys R.," "Michipicoten," "R. Nipigon," "Coministigua" (Kaministiquia), "la Bay" (Green Bay), "Pt. Chaguacomicon" (Chagouamigon), "L. la Pluie" (Rainy Lake), and "L. du Bois" (Lake of the Woods). At the left edge of the sketch is a list of six posts farther west: "Riviere du Beuf" (Boeuf), "R. Ounipique" (Winnipeg), "Fort la Reine," "La Biche," "Fort Dauphin," and "La Prairie."[66] The only people mentioned are the "Sioux or white Indians" on either side of the uppermost reaches of the Mississippi River. Rogers's memorial makes no reference to specific Indian tribes except for "the Country of the Scioux." Otherwise, the Native peoples are referred to as "the Indians from the West of Lake Michigan or from the South and West of Lake Superior." Another reference to Native peoples calls them "the several Nations, Tribes, & Bands of Indians" trading to "the Out Posts." Indians appear throughout the memorial, but they are not identified by tribal names. Rogers's plan was to establish a structure of civil government over a territory populated primarily by people who were not British subjects.[67] Their names were not considered important.[68] What mattered was that the French had "governed" the district by successfully managing the fur trade. When British officials and policy repudiated the French system by preventing traders from wintering among the western nations and refusing to give Native leaders enough presents, Pontiac's War ensued. The French way worked, and Rogers argued the point forcefully through his memorial and his map.

In the sketch, the need to search for a route to the Pacific was unstated, but it was implied for an audience in London acquainted with Rogers's aspirations. British agents who respected Indian ways and could make competent cartographic images would need to travel through the map's empty space in the West. They could locate Native villages, hunting grounds, and territories in dispute with neighboring bands or nations in addition to streams, paths, lakes, and other significant geographic features and enter them on maps. The exploration party could assure the Native peoples that their "English father" intended to treat them well through his representative, Robert Rogers, the commandant (perhaps soon to be governor) at Michilimackinac. Looking east, it is astonishing to observe that just beyond the beginning point of the District of Michilimackinac at the eastern end of Lake Nipissing, the map depicts the waterway between Lake Nipissing and the St. Lawrence River as substantially wider than it was in reality. Although everyone knew that nothing larger than a freight canoe could pass from Montreal to Georgian Bay, the sketch generates the impression that a skilled navigator could sail from Bristol or Liverpool to the western end of Lake Superior! When the Northwest Passage was found, Great Britain would have, at long last, its route through North America to the Pacific Ocean. Even though Rogers made no such explicit claim, his sketch creates the appearance of an easy east-to-west passage through Canada, uninhibited by such obstacles as rapids and shallow water.

As the government officials in Whitehall looked at North America on Rogers's map, they saw no sign of any existing authority on the continent except for a fort symbol at Michilimackinac. The map-maker wanted to form the impression that creation of the District of Michilimackinac and Rogers's appointment as governor would pose no problem for people already holding high-level positions of military or civil authority. Rogers simply dismissed General Gage, his commander in chief, by ignoring him when he petitioned higher authorities to be appointed as governor. Likewise, Sir William Johnson's relevance to Indian affairs merited no mention. Rogers consulted neither of his superiors regarding his plans, and his map gives no evidence of their existence. Although New York, the location of Gage's headquarters, appears on the sketch, there is no indication that even one British soldier was stationed in North America except at Michilimackinac. The absence of Indians (except for the Sioux) blots out the presence or the need for Johnson's office of superintendent of Indian affairs for the Northern Department. The king's ministers were fully aware of the responsibilities assigned to Gage and Johnson and had ordered Rogers to be subordinate to them, but Rogers's sketch and plan were skillful attempts to persuade Whitehall to ignore the two men most responsible for integrating the western Great Lakes into the empire.

Without regard for Gage or Johnson, Rogers hired his own employees to help him incorporate the western Great Lakes into the British Empire. Jonathan Carver, James Tute, James Stanley Goddard, and Joseph Reaume were authorized to hold councils with Native peoples to win their loyalty to Britain, to maintain peace among the nations, and to promote the Canadian fur trade and drive away rival traders. By giving presents and wampum to village and band leaders, Rogers's agents won the allegiance and trust—often tenuous—of the western nations. If Carver and Tute failed in their negotiations, they would have no chance to find the Northwest Passage, for Indians at war threatened their lives. These explorers also depended on Indian and Métis guides to provide them with essential geographic information about the region and the vast territory that lay farther west.

Upon his return to Michilimackinac on August 29, 1767, Carver's immediate audience was Robert Rogers. Carver's cartographic information helped Rogers fulfill the "King's Minister's" request in London that he "correct any of the Maps of the Country" while at Michilimackinac.[69] Although Carver's map formed the basis for the printed map he included in his published accounts of his travels in 1778, that use is beyond the scope of this chapter. Carver was Rogers's eyes and ears, observing the region's waterways, forests, plains, and wildlife. If Rogers were to serve as governor of the District of Michilimackinac, he needed to learn as much as possible about its cultural and physical geography, and this knowledge had to be passed on to London. Of course, Rogers hoped that Tute's and Carver's trek through the West would produce information revealing the fabled passage to the Pacific Ocean, which could then be shown on future maps.

Carver shared his findings with Rogers even before he returned to Michilimackinac. He sent Rogers plans, journals, and reports "concerning the situation of the country" with Indians going to the fort to see the commandant. Rogers gave Carver's documents to Alexander Baxter, requesting him to take them to London and present them to the Board of Trade.[70] Baxter had been at Michilimackinac to promote a scheme for mining copper and other minerals on land in the grant Rogers had received from the Chippewa along the southern shore of Lake Superior.[71]

After Carver got back to the fort, he drew maps documenting his travels, filling in some of the spaces left in the sketch Rogers had sent to London earlier in the year. Carver found his commander displeased that Tute had incurred huge expenses for Indian presents and had failed to continue his search for the Northwest Passage because of a lack of provisions.[72] But Rogers valued new information—especially cartographic details—that were relevant to his proposed district. Carver gave copies of his journals to Rogers, and he drew "Different Maps" for him.[73] Unfortunately, these maps have been lost as a result of Rogers's arrest on charges of "High Treason or being a Traitor to his King and Country."[74]

Acting on orders from General Gage, Captain Frederick Spiesmaker of the 2nd Battalion, 60th Regiment of Foot placed Major Robert Rogers under arrest on December 6, 1767. On that same day, Spiesmaker seized Rogers's "Papers, Plans, Pocket Book & ca"; upon examining them, he commented that he "found nothing of Consequence, but his Plan of Lake Huron, St Clear, Superior, and part of the River Mississippi; The Journal of the Detachment he sent from this [Michilimackinac] to find out the Northwest Passage, with their Orders, and a few Indian speeches."[75] Spiesmaker sent the map, possibly made by Carver, to Gage, but it and the other documents never found their way back to Rogers, who wanted to use them at his trial in Montreal during October 1768.[76] The Carver map under discussion could be his original from which he made copies, or it might be a rendition made after Rogers's papers were confiscated. It is not known whether they included Carver's original drawing.

Carver's map brings life to the barren sketch produced by Rogers and gives us a picture of the western Great Lakes region populated by people who moved about to trade, to wage war, and to follow traditional seasonal migrations. Using a dotted line, Carver showed his route, which took him from Michilimackinac along the north shore of Lake Michigan to Green Bay, up the Fox River to the Wisconsin River, and then on to the Mississippi. After passing through Prairie du Chien, Carver paddled up the Mississippi to the mouth of the Minnesota River (St. Paul, Minnesota), whence he followed the river west to his winter quarters in the country of the "Nauduwesse or Sioux of the Plains." Once the ice broke up in the spring of 1767, Carver returned to Prairie du Chien, where he joined Tute and went with him to Lake Superior by way of the Chippewa, Namekagon, and Brule Rivers. Entering Lake Superior, they headed west, then northeast to Grand Portage. Lacking enough provisions to continue their quest, Tute and Carver decided to return to Michilimackinac. Leaving Grand Portage, their canoes hugged the north shore of Lake Superior until they reached the St. Marys River. After descending into Lake Huron, the party arrived at Michilimackinac on August 29, 1767, bringing an end to yet another unsuccessful attempt to find the Northwest Passage. Carver spent the winter at the fort producing the first cartographic images of parts of Wisconsin and Minnesota made by a British mapmaker from his own observations and surveys.

The most prominent features of Carver's map are the delineations of lands inhabited by the Native peoples and his notations giving information about numerous places throughout the region (fig. 2). The map reveals that its maker viewed the western nations as distinct sovereign entities. When the map is laid alongside his accounts of negotiating with Indian leaders and giving them presents, it is clear that Carver viewed them and their people as requiring much attention if they were to be persuaded to give allegiance to the king.[77] Carver located seven nations on his map, coloring each homeland a different shade:

1. "The Chipeway Terretories"—around Lake Superior, red, and "Chipeway Possessions"—eastern half of Lower Michigan, also red.
2. "Menomonie Kingdom"—along Green Bay, brown.
3. "Ottawahs Land"—Door Peninsula, tan, and "The Ottawahs Kingdom"—western half of Lower Michigan, also tan.
4. "Kingdom of the Winebaygoes"—along the upper Fox River, light blue.
5. "Kingdom of Saugies"—west of the Winnebago, blue.
6. "Kingdom of Ottigaumies"—west of Sac to the Mississippi River, gray-blue.
7. "Naudowessie Republic"—west of the Mississippi River, along the Minnesota River up to the "Chipeway Territories," light brown.

Carver's references to kingdoms and a republic reflect the Indians' assumption that they, not the British or the French, were sovereign over their lands and people. It is worth noting that in 1778, when Carver published his map in his *Travels,* "kingdom" became "Land," and "Republic" became "Country." In 1767, British officials could not afford to offend people living in the western Great Lakes by refusing to acknowledge their sovereignty.

Notations on the map demonstrate Carver's dependence on Indians and others for information, particularly for places he did not visit. Several comments about the geography west of Grand Portage serve as examples of how Carver relied on informants to extend the reaches of his map beyond his travels. Starting with the Pigeon River (which is not named on the map), Carver drew a series of small lakes and streams, which today form the boundary waters between Minnesota and Ontario, leading west to Rainy Lake. He called attention to these features by saying, "This Passage leads to Lake Wenepeck [Winnipeg] and Hudsons Bay or the North West." His comment about a string of lakes going southwest from a small lake near the entrance to Rainy Lake offers little useful information: "The Indians inform me of this String of Lakes but uncertain what Communication they have with one another." Above Rainy Lake, readers learn that "A Large Band or Canton of the Chipeways Live on these Lakes Call'd by the French the Lake La Plue Savage." At other points on the map, readers find marshes, Indian paths, and the location of Native villages.

Carver enlarged much of the District of Michilimackinac that appeared on Rogers's sketch and drew his map to give credence to Rogers's plan for civil government, while leaving only an inkling of the failed search for the Northwest Passage. Carver's comment on the upper left corner beneath the "Red Lake River," which flows west-northwest out of Red Lake (eventually running into the Red River at East Grand Forks, Minnesota), hints at exploration deeper into the continent than appears on the map. He wrote: "This River [Red] Joyns the Assinibouls [Assiniboine] River Little above the Place Call[d] Fort Lorain [La Reine]."[78] But even this observation and the sketch of Red Lake and Red Lake River fill in details missing on the Rogers map. The strongest reference to a quest for the Northwest Passage is a note written beneath the "S[t] Pierre [Minnesota] River" near Carver's winter camp: "The Country of the Naudowessie of the Plains from this place the Plains are unbounded suppos[d] to extend to the South Sea." This citation taken together with other notes about the Sioux brought to the reader's attention a valuable body of information about an important group of people, living within the District of Michilimackinac, who were virtually unknown to the British in 1767. Whether or not a passage was ever found, the commandant or a future governor at Michilimackinac could use Carver's findings to conduct negotiations with the western nations and to oversee the fur trade with them.

Rogers's removal from command at Michilimackinac thwarted his use of Carver's map and journals to promote his schemes to create a colony and to find the Northwest Passage. But Carver's manuscript map demonstrates how cartography and the motivations for its production can serve to advance an agenda that may not be readily apparent. Carver and Rogers played a role in the search for the Northwest Passage that is well known. Carver's publication of his *Travels* in 1778, which included the map with revisions, presented an account that differed from what he recorded in his manuscript journal.[79]

The quest for the Northwest Passage and the actions of Robert Rogers have fascinated many people over the years. This fascination, coupled with the inevitable romanticizing of such a quest, has overshadowed Rogers's serious, although unrealistic, proposal to create a colony out of the District of Michilimackinac. The maps prepared by Rogers and Jonathan Carver in 1767 enable us to look beyond the myth and legend associated with Rogers's, Carver's, and Tute's search for the Northwest Passage and to see how Rogers used maps and mapmaking to further his own political agenda. Unrest in the colonies along the eastern seaboard, the high cost of maintaining Britain's North American empire, and Rogers's personal troubles rendered his plan "dead on arrival" at the Board of Trade. But he had recognized that a civil government needed to be created for the region surrounding Michilimackinac if the Crown hoped to incorporate this territory into the empire. Rogers's personal ambition must not obscure the validity of his perception. The Quebec Act of 1774 and the later inclusion of different parts of the District of Michilimackinac into state, provincial, and federal governments of the United States and Canada bore out the truth of Rogers's objective. On the other hand, the Northwest Passage, as Rogers envisioned it, still awaits discovery.

NOTES

The author would like to thank Robert Andrews, Brian Leigh Dunnigan, John Fierst, G. Malcolm Lewis, David Macleod, and Agnes Haigh Widder for their comments on earlier drafts of this chapter.

1. Gregory Evans Dowd offers a fascinating analysis of the status within the British system of government of Indians living in territory ceded to the British by the French after the French and Indian War. Writing about the Royal Proclamation of 1763, Dowd identifies a critical distinction between the status of French inhabitants and that of Indians living in the western Great Lakes region: "Unlike the former French subjects in the newly conquered regions, Indians would be treated as separate peoples, not as newly minted subjects of the king." Dowd, *War under Heaven: Pontiac, the Indian Nations, and the British Empire* (Baltimore: Johns Hopkins University Press, 2002), 178. This distinction is important when assessing Rogers's diplomacy with the western nations at Michilimackinac. For a discussion of the cartographic record for Rogers and Carver, see David Bosse, "The Maps of Robert Rogers and Jonathan Carver," *American Magazine and Historical Chronicle* 2 (Spring–Summer 1986): 45–61.

2. Robert Rogers, 1767 map of eastern North America, MPG 1/18, National Archives, Kew, Richmond, Surrey, U.K. (hereafter National Archives, U.K.).

3. Jonathan Carver, 1767 map of the western Great Lakes, Add. 8949 f. 41, British Library, London.

4. Kenneth Roberts, *Northwest Passage* (Garden City, N.Y.: Doubleday, 1937); *Northwest Passage,* directed by King Vidor, MGM Studios, 1940.

5. John R. Cuneo, *Robert Rogers of the Rangers* (Ticonderoga, N.Y.: Fort Ticonderoga Museum, 1988), 205.

6. David A. Armour, ed., *Treason? At Michilimackinac: The Proceedings of a General Court Martial Held at Montreal in October 1768 for the Trial of Major Robert Rogers* (Mackinac Island, Mich.: Mackinac Island State Park Commission, 1972), 9–10.

7. Robert Rogers, *A Concise Account of North America* (1765; reprint, New York: Johnson Reprint, 1966), 244. Rogers's attitude toward Pontiac coincided with his views about the western nations generally.

8. "A Proposal by Robert Rogers . . . ," August 12, 1765, in T. C. Elliott, "The Origin of the Name Oregon," *Quarterly of the Oregon Historical Society* 22 (June 1921): 102. In 1772, Rogers made another proposal to undertake a much less expensive expedition to find the Northwest Passage, which made reference to his 1765 scheme: "To the King's Most Excellent Majesty in Council," the Petition of Major Robert Rogers, February 11, 1772, Robert Rogers–Jonathan Carver Papers, William L. Clements Library (hereafter Clements Library), University of Michigan, Ann Arbor; Hillsborough et al., "To the Right Hon'ble the Lords of the Committee of His Majesty's most Hon'ble Privy Council for Plantation affairs," March 17, 1772, C.O. 324/18, 409–13, National Archives, U.K.

9. Robert Rogers's testimony, October 27, 1768, in Armour, ed., *Treason?* 63–64.

10. John Parker, ed., *The Journals of Jonathan Carver and Related Documents, 1766–1770* (St. Paul: Minnesota Historical Society Press, 1976), 1–15; "Some Account of Captain J. Carver," in *Travels throughout the Interior Parts of North America, in the Years 1766, 1767, and 1768,* by Jonathan Carver, 3d ed. (1781; reprint, Minneapolis: Ross and Haines, 1956), 1–3; C. P. Stacey, "Rogers, Robert," *Dictionary of Canadian Biography* (Toronto: University of Toronto Press, 1966), 4: 679–83; Cuneo, *Robert Rogers,* 185–93.

11. Keith R. Widder, "The Cartography of Dietrich Brehm and Thomas Hutchins and the Establishment of British Authority in the Western Great Lakes Region, 1760–1763," *Cartographica* 36 (Spring 1999): 1–23. For an excellent overview of both seventeenth-century and eighteenth-century mapping of the Great Lakes, see Conrad E. Heidenreich, "Mapping the Great Lakes: The Period of Exploration, 1603–1700," *Cartographica* 17 (Autumn 1980): 32–64; idem, "Mapping the Great Lakes: The Period of Imperial Rivalries, 1700–1760," *Cartographica* 18 (Autumn 1981): 74–109; G. Malcolm Lewis, "Changing National Perspectives and the Mapping of the Great Lakes between 1755 and 1795," *Cartographica* 17 (Autumn 1980): 1–31; and Conrad E. Heidenreich, "Measures of Distance Employed on 17th and Early 18th Century Maps of Canada," *Canadian Cartographer* 12 (December 1975): 121–37.

12. H. S. Conway to Thomas Gage, October 12, 1765, vol. 5, Papers of Thomas Gage, English Series, Clements Library; Cuneo, *Robert Rogers,* 179–80.

13. Thomas Gage to Robert Rogers, January 10, 1766, 47, Papers of Thomas Gage, American Series (hereafter Gage Papers, American Series), Clements Library. Amherst had misgivings about giving Rogers too much authority over a territory as large as that proposed for Michilimackinac. Amherst, according to Chase Price, wished "to fix Col. [John] Bradstreet at Detroit" and to make the governor or commandant at Michilimackinac subject to the authority of the governor or commandant at Detroit. Price believed that "by narrowing the elbow room of Rogers," Amherst would thwart Rogers's and Townshend's "schemes" for Michilimackinac. Both the king's and Gage's orders reflected Amherst's views. Chase Price to [Charles Townshend], October 2, 1765, Charles Townshend Papers, 296/1/49, Clements Library.

14. Thomas Gage to William Johnson, June 2, 1766, in *The Papers of Sir William Johnson,* ed. James Sullivan and Alexander C. Flick (Albany: University of the State of New York, 1960), 12: 100–101.

15. Thomas Gage to James Tute, May 2, 1768; Thomas Gage to Jonathan Carver, May 2, 1768, Gage Papers, American Series, 76.

16. Grant of land to Robert Rogers, "on the South Side of Lake Superieur," Detroit, December 23, 1760, LMS/Detroit Histori-cal Society, 1760, Dec. 23, Burton Historical Collection (hereafter Burton Collection), Detroit Public Library, Detroit. The Chippewa also gave a grant of land at Sault Ste. Marie to Robert Rogers, Alexander Henry, and Jean Baptiste Cadot on the same day. "Grant of land to Robert Rogers, Jean Baptiste Cadot, and Alexander Henry 'on the North and South Side of the falls of St. Marys,'" Detroit, LMS/Detroit Historical Society, 1760, Dec. 23, Burton Collection. For an interesting analy-sis of this claim, see Theresa Schenck, "Who Owns Sault Ste. Marie?" *Michigan Historical Review* 28 (Spring 2002): 109–20. There is some question about the authenticity of these grants. Several things are known, however, that strongly suggest that these grants were actually made as claimed by Rogers. Rogers was in Detroit on December 23, 1760. He left on this date, and Donald Campbell reported that "two of the Tribes that depends [*sic*] on Michillimakinac" were represented at Detroit on that day. Donald Campbell to Henry Bouquet, December 23, 1760, in *The Papers of Col. Henry Bouquet*, ed. Louis M. Waddell, John L. Tottenham, and Donald H. Kent (Harrisburg: Pennsylvania Historical and Museum Commission, 1984), 5: 196.

17. Robert Rogers's Memorial to the Board of Trade, May 24, 1767, C.O. 5/85, 178–94, National Archives, U.K.

18. Memorial of Robert Rogers to the Earl of Dartmouth and the Board of Trade, May 24, 1767, C.O. 5/85, 172–74, National Archives, U.K.

19. Robert Rogers to Jonathan Carver, August 12, 1766, in *Journals of Jonathan Carver*, ed. Parker, 192.

20. J. B. Harley, "Text and Contexts in the Interpretation of Early Maps," in *From Sea Charts to Satellite Images: Interpreting North American History through Maps*, ed. David Buisseret (Chicago: University of Chicago Press, 1990), 4.

21. J. B. Harley, "Deconstructing the Map," in *The New Nature of Maps: Essays in the History of Cartography*, ed. Paul Laxton (Balti-more: Johns Hopkins University Press, 2001), 163.

22. J. B. Harley, "Silences and Secrecy: The Hidden Agenda of Cartography in Early Modern Europe," in ibid., 86.

23. G. Malcolm Lewis, "Indian Maps," in *Old Trails and New Directions: Papers of the Third North American Fur Trade Conference*, ed. Carol M. Judd and Arthur J. Ray (Toronto: University of Toronto Press, 1980), 18–19. For an in-depth account of Native North American cartography, see G. Malcolm Lewis, "Maps, Mapmaking, and Map Use by Native North Americans," in *The History of Cartography*, vol. 2, book 3, *Cartography in the Traditional African, American, Arctic, Australian, and Pacific Societies*, ed. David Woodward and G. Malcolm Lewis (Chicago: University of Chicago Press, 1998), 51–182. Lewis has analyzed in great depth the contributions of Native peoples to the cartographic work of Pierre Gaultier de Varennes et de La Vérendrye and the subsequent significance of his maps. See G. Malcolm Lewis, "Indicators of Unacknowledged Assimilations from Amer-indian Maps on Euro-American Maps of North America: Some General Principles Arising from a Study of La Vérendrye's Composite Map, 1728–29," *Imago Mundi* 38 (1986): 9–34; idem, "Misinterpretation of Amerindian Information as a Source of Error on Euro-American Maps," *Annals of the Association of American Geographers* 77 (December 1987): 542–63; and idem, "La Grande Rivière et Fleuve de l'Ouest: The Realities and Reasons behind a Major Mistake in the 18th-Century Geography of North America," *Cartographica* 28 (Spring 1991): 54–87.

24. "Jonathan Carver's Commission from 'Robert Rogers Esqr. Agent to the Western Indians and Governor Commandant of His Majesty's Garrison of Michillmakinac and its Dependances,' dated at Michilimackinac, August 12, 1766," in *Journals of Jonathan Carver*, ed. Parker, 192–93.

25. "Robert Rogers' Instructions to James Tute, dated at Michilimackinac, September 12, 1766," in *Journals of Jonathan Carver*, ed. Parker, 193–96.

26. Glyn Williams, *Voyages of Delusion: The Quest for the Northwest Passage* (New Haven: Yale University Press, 2001), xviii. A help-ful cartographic record of British attempts to find the Northwest Passage appears in Derek Hayes, *Historical Atlas of Canada: Canada's History Illustrated with Original Maps* (Seattle: University of Washington Press, 2002), 77–84.

27. Robert Rogers to Thomas Gage, February 12, 1767, Gage Papers, American Series, 62; Keith R. Widder, "The French Con-

nection: The Interior French and Their Role in French-British Relations in the Western Great Lakes Region, 1760–1775," in *The Sixty Years' War for the Great Lakes, 1754–1814*, ed. David Curtis Skaggs and Larry L. Nelson (East Lansing: Michigan State University Press, 2001), 125–44.

28. Richard White, *The Middle Ground: Indians, Empires, and Republics in the Great Lakes Region, 1650–1815* (New York: Cambridge University Press, 1991), ix–185.

29. See Lawrence J. Burpee, ed., *Journals and Letters of Pierre Gaultier de Varennes de La Vérendrye and His Sons* (Toronto: Champlain Society, 1927); Joseph L. Peyser, ed. and trans., *Jacques Legardeur de Saint-Pierre: Officer, Gentleman, Entrepreneur* (East Lansing: Michigan State University Press, 1996), 129–200; Marcel Trudel, *Atlas de la Nouvelle-France* (Quebec: Les Presses de l'Université Laval, 1968), 128–29; Hayes, *Historical Atlas of Canada*, 85–87.

30. R. Cole Harris, ed., *Historical Atlas of Canada*, vol. 1, *From the Beginning to 1800* (Toronto: University of Toronto Press, 1987), plates 37, 38, 39, 40; Gerald Friesen, *The Canadian Prairies: A History* (Lincoln: University of Nebraska Press, 1984), 45–65.

31. Robert Rogers to the Earl of Dartmouth and the Board of Trade, May 24, 1767, C.O. 5/85, 172–74; Robert Rogers to the Board of Trade, May 24, 1767, C.O. 5/85, 178–94; H. S. Conway to Thomas Gage, October 12, 1765, C.O. 5/85, 195; Thomas Gage to Robert Rogers, January 10, 1766, C.O. 5/85, 174; Extracts of orders given by Thomas Gage to officers commanding posts relative to their treatment of Indians, C.O. 5/85, 175; William Johnson to Robert Rogers, June 3, 1766, C.O. 5/85, 176, all in National Archives, U.K.

32. William Howard to John Bradstreet, October 15, 1764, enclosed in John Bradstreet to Thomas Gage, December 7, 1764, Gage Papers, American Series, 28.

33. John Campbell to Thomas Gage, September 11, 1765, Gage Papers, American Series, 42. Johnson's policy was predicated upon the so-called Plan of 1764. The full text of this plan is: "Copy of a Plan for the future management of Indian Affairs, prepared by the Lords Commissioners for Trade and Plantation in the Year, 1764," Indian Records, RG 10, series 2, vol. 15 (Six Nations, Niagara & Upper Canada, 1763–1819), 35–60, microfilm, reel C-1224, National Archives of Canada, Ottawa; Thomas Gage to William Johnson, June 24, 1764; William Howard to William Johnson, June 24, 1765; William Johnson to William Howard, July 2, 1765, all in *Papers of Sir William Johnson*, ed. Sullivan and Flick, 11: 242–44, 804–09, 814–16.

34. Montreal merchants to Thomas Gage, January 22, 1766; Eyre Massey to Thomas Gage, note appended after contents of William Howard to Eyre Massey, July 4, 1766; William Howard to Eyre Massey, July 18, 1766, enclosed in Eyre Massey to Thomas Gage, August 6, 1766, all in Gage Papers, American Series, 47, 55.

35. George Turnbull to Thomas Gage, October 19, 1766, Gage Papers, American Series, 58.

36. William Howard to Ralph Burton, September 24, 1765, in ibid., 43.

37. Dowd, *War under Heaven*, 78.

38. William Howard to John Bradstreet, October 15, 1764, in John Bradstreet to Thomas Gage, December 7, 1764, Gage Papers, American Series, 28.

39. The effectiveness of British Indian and trade policy at Michilimackinac is discussed in depth in David A. Armour and Keith R. Widder, *At the Crossroads: Michilimackinac during the American Revolution* (Mackinac Island, Mich.: Mackinac Island State Park Commission, 1986); and Keith R. Widder, "Effects of the American Revolution on Fur-Trade Society at Michilimackinac," in *The Fur Trade Revisited: Selected Papers of the Sixth North American Fur Trade Conference*, ed. Jennifer S. H. Brown, W. J. Eccles, and Donald P. Heldman (East Lansing: Michigan State University Press, 1994), 299–316.

40. Joseph L. Peyser, ed. and trans., *On the Eve of the Conquest: The Chevalier de Raymond's Critique of New France in 1754* (East Lansing: Michigan State University Press, 1997), 55–58. Testimony at Rogers's trial revealed that he was following Raymond's formula. Jean Baptiste Bernard dit Jolicoeur, testimony, October 28, 1768, in *Treason?* ed. Armour, 79.

41. William Johnson's instructions to Robert Rogers, June 3, 1766, C.O. 5/85, 176, National Archives, U.K.

42. Extracts of orders given by Thomas Gage to officers commanding the posts, C.O. 5/85, 175, National Archives, U.K.

43. For a lively discussion of Roberts's stay at Michilimackinac, see Peter Marshall, "The Michilimackinac Misfortunes of Commissary Roberts," in *Fur Trade Revisited*, ed. Brown, Eccles, and Heldman, 285–98.

44. Thomas Gage to Benjamin Roberts, September 14, 1767, Gage Papers, American Series, 69; "An Account of Goods Given to the Several Nations in the District of Michilimackinac . . . by Order of Robert Rogers . . . from the 21st of September 1766 to the 1st of February, 1767," T.1/478:36, National Archives, U.K.

45. Major Rogers's speech to Several Chiefs of the Ottawa, . . . 18th Augt 1766; Ottawas Answer, 19th August; Major Rogers's speech to the Chiefs of the Souties or Chippeways, 20th of August 1766; The Souties or Chippeways Answer, Aug. 21, MS/ Rogers, Robert, 1:1, correspondence, 1760–1771, Burton Collection.

46. William L. Clements, ed., "Rogers' Michilimackinac Journal," *Proceedings: American Antiquarian Society* 28 (October 16, 1918): 231–34; "An Account of Goods Given . . . from the 21st of September 1766."

47. Clements, ed., "Rogers' Michilimackinac Journal," 234–53; "An Account of Goods Given . . . from the 21st of September 1766."

48. Clements, ed., "Rogers' Michilimackinac Journal," 256.

49. Ibid., 257–58.

50. Guy Carleton to William Johnson, March 27, 1767, in Guy Carleton to the Board of Trade, March 28, 1767, C.O. 323/25, 68–71, National Archives, U.K.

51. "An Account of the Number of Canoes Gone Out Wintering from the Post of Michilimackinac," 1767, C.O. 42/14, 98A, National Archives, U.K.; Helen Hornbeck Tanner, ed., *Atlas of Great Lakes Indian History* (Norman: University of Oklahoma Press, 1987), 58–59.

52. Price to [Townshend], October 2, 1765.

53. Sketch of "Parts of Lake Superior" showing "Copper River," "little River," and "Ontonawagon [River]," from Grant of land to Robert Rogers . . . Dec. 23, 1760 (see note 16 above).

54. Grant of land to Robert Rogers . . . Dec. 23, 1760. The wampum belt is in the collection of the Detroit Historical Museum. I am grateful to John Gibson, curator of manuscripts, Burton Historical Collection, for his painstaking transcription of the text of the deed; to David Poremba, manager, Burton Historical Collection, for allowing me to photograph the deed; and to Patience Nauta, registrar, Detroit Historical Museum, for making an image of the wampum belt available to me.

55. Price to [Townshend], October 2, 1765, italics in original.

56. Rogers to the Board of Trade, May 24, 1767.

57. Price to [Townshend], October 2, 1765.

58. Rogers to the Earl of Dartmouth and the Board of Trade; Rogers to the Board of Trade, both May 24, 1767.

59. Rogers to the Earl of Dartmouth and the Board of Trade, May 24, 1767.

60. See Widder, "French Connection"; and Susan Sleeper-Smith, "'Ignorant bigots and busy rebels': The American Revolution in the Western Great Lakes," in *Sixty Years' War*, ed. Skaggs and Nelson, 145–66.

61. Rogers to the Earl of Dartmouth and the Board of Trade, May 24, 1767; Thomas Gage to Robert Rogers, September 21, 1767, Gage Papers, American Series, 70.

62. Conway to Gage, October 12, 1765.

63. Gage was outraged when Tute and Carver informed him in December 1767 that Rogers had employed them "to make Discoverys to the Westward of the Head of the Mississippi." Gage told them that he knew of "no authority Major Rogers, or any other person had, to Employ You, or any body else on such business." Gage to Tute; Gage to Carver, both May 2, 1768.

64. Rogers to the Board of Trade, May 24, 1767.

65. Guy Carleton to the Earl of Shelburne, March 2, 1768, C.O. 42/28, 159–62, National Archives, U.K.; "Répertoire des Engage-

ments pour l'Ouest Conservés dans les Archives Judiciares de Montréal (1670–1788)," *Rapport de L'Archiviste de la Province de Québec pour 1931–1932* (Quebec: Rédempti Paradis, Imprimeur de sa Majesté le Roi, 1932), 243–365.

66. An interesting manuscript map that locates places and posts as a result of La Vérendrye's work is "Cartes des Decouvertes qui ont eté faites dans la Partie Occidentale du Canada," drawn by Jacques-Nicolas Bellin in 1752, in Hayes, *Historical Atlas of Canada*, 87.

67. Dowd, *War under Heaven*, 174–212.

68. The memorial sent to the Board of Trade by Rogers on May 24, 1767, was the second half of a larger document, which also contained his journal of "Proceedings with the Indians in yᵉ district of Michilimackinac." The journal included accounts of Indian councils through July 3, 1767, six weeks after Rogers had sent his memorial and sketch to the Board of Trade. Rogers's complete journal has been published in "Rogers' Michilimackinac Journal," ed. Clements, 224–73. The original is in the collections of the American Antiquarian Society.

69. Robert Rogers to Thomas Gage, December 11, 1767, Gage Papers, American Series, 72.

70. Jonathan Carver to Abigail Carver, September 24, 1767, in *Journals of Jonathan Carver*, ed. Parker, 199–202.

71. For a discussion of this affair, see Louise Phelps Kellogg, *The British Régime in Wisconsin and the Northwest* (New York: Da Capo, 1971), 107–14.

72. Parker, ed., *Journals of Jonathan Carver*, 132; Robert Rogers to James Tute, July 20, 1767, in ibid., 198.

73. Robert Rogers to Thomas Gage, July 3, 1768, Gage Papers, American Series, 78.

74. Frederick Spiesmaker to Thomas Gage, December 9, 1767, Gage Papers, American Series, 72.

75. Ibid.

76. Rogers's statement at court-martial, October 27, 1768, in *Treason?* ed. Armour, 63–64.

77. For example, when Carver met his first band of Naudowessee on November 10, 1766, he held a council and "delivered a belt, and a kegg of rum, and a prick of tobacco, with a speech from Major Rogers." Parker, ed., *Journals of Jonathan Carver*, 90.

78. "Cartes des Decouvertes," c. 1740, shows these features. It is possible that Carver may have had access to copies of some of La Vérendrye's maps at Michilimackinac.

79. In his introduction to the *Journals of Jonathan Carver*, John Parker discusses at some length Carver's efforts to publish his journals and how they were transformed into a book that would appeal to a large audience. *Travels* included material from accounts written by Father Louis Hennepin, Pierre François Xavier de Charlevois, and Baron Lahontan. *Travels* also placed greater emphasis on the search for the Northwest Passage than the fur trade, and it gave Carver a more prominent role in the expedition than is found in the manuscript journals. Parker, ed., *Journals of Jonathan Carver*, 21–56.

Motives for Mapping the Great Lakes: Upper Canada, 1782–1827

J. P. D. Dunbabin

"WHAT ARE MAPS FOR?" AN OBVIOUS REPLY WOULD BE "TO FIND THE WAY." Tourists carry maps; locals do not need them. But it is easier to be taken to a new destination by someone who knows it; and most, though certainly not all, European exploration of the North American Midwest was done this way. Thus, in 1784, the North West Company of fur traders detailed Edward Umfreville to "explore another passage into the interior country independant [*sic*] of the old one" by the "Grand Portage" from Lake Superior, which the 1783 Treaty of Paris appeared to have ceded to the United States. Umfreville started with "an Indian guide to pilot us to Lake Nipigon," and then a Canadian who knew "the way very well from Pais Plat to Sturgeon Lake" but not beyond. Fortunately the party had been joined by an Indian, without whom "the fruits of our voyage must have been lost, and we probably perished." While Umfreville was being conducted toward the Winnipeg River, a passing group of Indians "inadvertently let fall" that there was a shortcut: "Luckily our trusty guide was acquainted with the way," though his family preferred not to take it.[1]

En route, Umfreville encountered the canoes of both Indians and other fur traders, sometimes traveling over considerable distances. These people could not always answer his inquiries, but they knew their own way, without maps. And when, in answer to European inquiries, Indians did draw maps, these were commonly route maps, noting features that a traveler would encounter (such as lakes and portages) but little else. The sketches given to La Vérendrye of the alternative passages from Lake Superior to the Lake of the Woods are examples.[2] Nor indeed did Umfreville himself produce a map of his journey, but rather a detailed itinerary emphasizing the directions in which one should turn: "From the bottom of the mountain across a small bay S.S.W. ¾ mile; S.W. by W. 1 mile across another; W. by S. 1½ miles three islands on left S.W. by W. across a small bay to portage la Prairie." Sometimes he also included the signs to look out

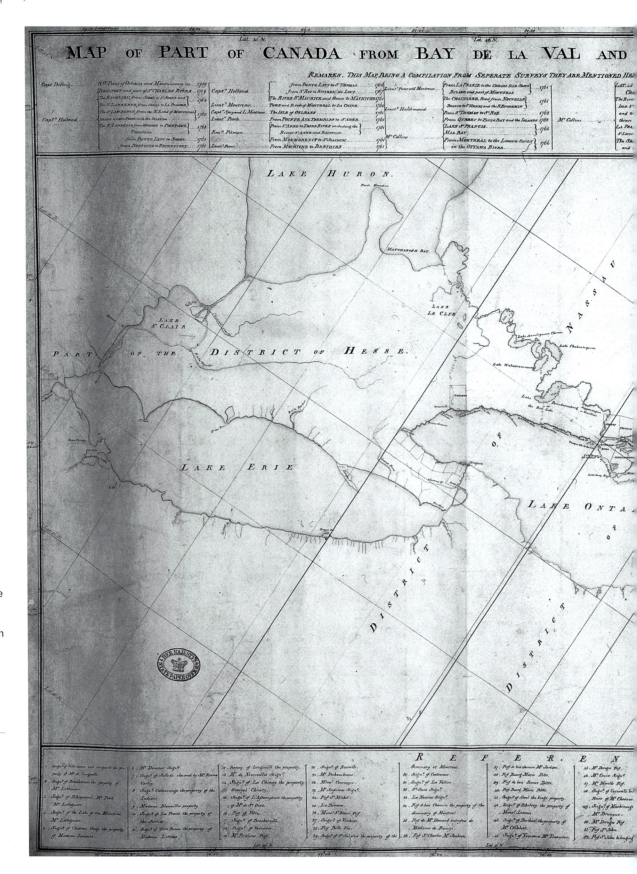

Figure 1. "Map of Part of Canada from Bay de la Val and Island of Barnaby in the River St. Lawrence to the Lakes Huron and Erie." The map notes that "this map is a reduction from the Map of Six British Statute Miles to an Inch, compiled for the Use of His Majesty's Secretary of State at Quebec 1st Octr. 1790" [W.10 (3)]. Public Record Office, National Archives, U.K.

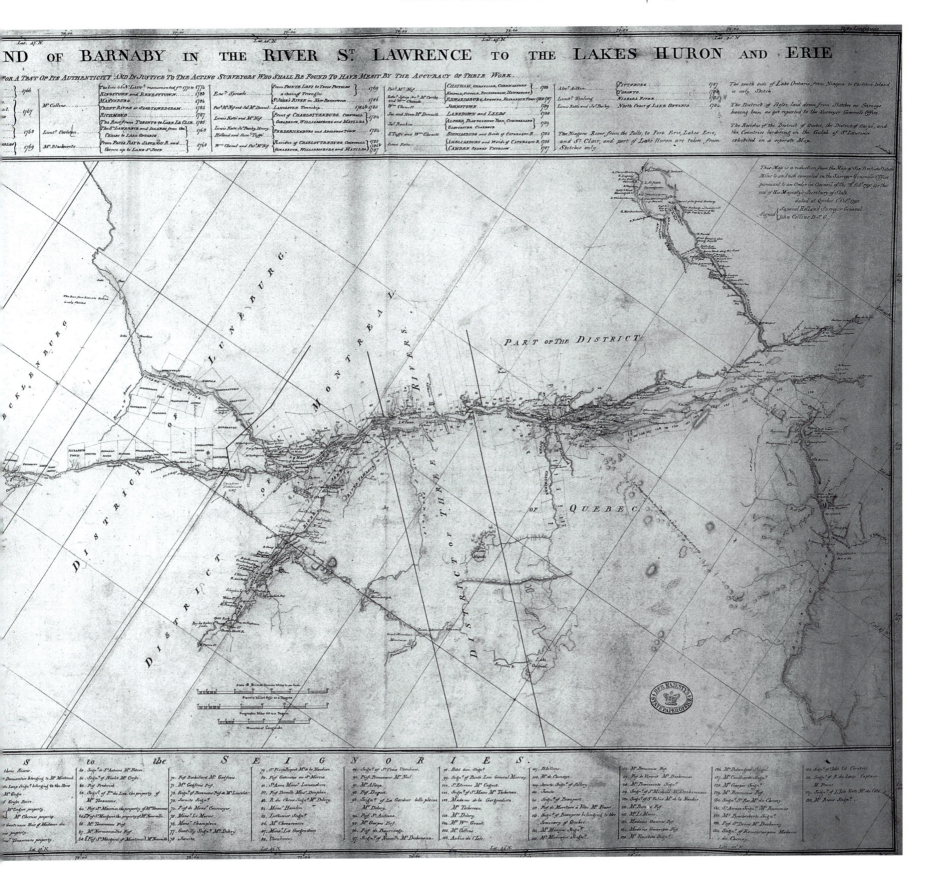

for: "As this portage is not very easy for a stranger to find, . . . it is necessary to mention that at the beginning several trees are barked and on the right is a small run of water, with large stones at its mouth."[3]

This sort of folk-memory-cum-gazetteer approach had disadvantages; for example, routes could simply be overlooked. This happened with the Kaministiquia route to the Lake of the Woods; it was an alternative to the Grand Portage that had been known to and occasionally used by the French. Unlike Umfreville's roundabout passage via Lake Nipigon, the Kaministiquia route did constitute the coveted viable alternative to the Grand Portage. But its rediscovery was fortuitous: Roderick Mackenzie learned accidentally of the route's existence from a family of Indians and, thus encouraged, secured a guide at a North West Company post that happened already to be located on it.[4] Even then, this Kaministiquia route was not mapped in the modern sense of the word. True, it was depicted on David Thompson's celebrated "Map of the North-West Territory of the Province of Canada," displayed at the North West Company's Fort William compound. But people could not carry this with them on their journeys; and the map's scale was far too small to provide the sort of detailed information given in the previous paragraph. In fact, travelers found their own routes; and when a boundary commission came to survey the "direct water communication" in 1823, it found that travelers had instead "opened the easiest route, and wherever the little lakes . . . could be readily approached by portages, . . . [avoiding] the more circuitous line of direct water communication, . . . they have done so . . . (a fact not heretofore of my knowledge, nor known to most of the traders familiar with the country)."[5]

Eighteenth-century maps of the lakes were, therefore, not created primarily for travelers. So we must look to other uses and "audiences." Many of these maps, especially those that were published, were small-scale depictions of the Great Lakes or indeed of eastern North America as a whole. A surprisingly common feature is their lack of concern about accurate detail. Thus, as Karpinski writes, "The earliest American gazetteers and atlases followed the pernicious practice of their European predecessors in presenting . . . two variant forms of the Great Lakes area."[6] Doubtless the practice sometimes reflected genuine uncertainty—as admitted by Joshua Fry and Peter Jefferson in their 1751 "Map of the Inhabited Part of Virginia," where they observe that "Maps differ much in the Longitude and Latitude of the Lakes and wether [sic] Lake Erie in this Map is in its proper situation or not must be left to further Discoveries."[7] But this approach could also be the product of a relative unconcern about the truth.[8] A picturesque example is Father Charlevoix's insertion into Lake Superior (which his Jesuit predecessors had mapped remarkably well) of four apocryphal islands, named after the family, estate, and saint of his patron, Jean Frederic Phelippeaux, Count of Maurepas. His "Isle Philippeaux" "continued to appear for nearly a century upon subsequent maps," including that of John Mitchell. Thus, it came to figure in the 1783 peace treaty, which ran the British-American border "through Lake Superior, northward of the isles Royal and Phelipeaux."[9]

Mitchell's 1755 "Map of the British and French Dominions in North America" had been sponsored by the Board of Trade with the clear purpose of checking French advances and was praised by another cartographer for "almost wholly restoring to us our just Rights and Possessions, as far as Paper will admit of it."[10] Ironically, Mitchell's map was chiefly influential through its use by the 1782 peace negotiators to determine the borders of the new United States. But it was, in fact, ill fitted both to determine what is now the Maine–New Brunswick border and to plot a boundary through Lake Superior and points west. Indeed, the space on Mitchell's map west of the Lake of the Woods is covered by another inset map. The peace negotiators simply accepted Mitchell's assumption that the Mississippi River could be projected into that space and ordained a border running due west to it from the Lake of the Woods, which was an impossibility. On this and other geographical points relating to British interests, Montreal fur traders and their London associates knew better.[11] But peace was negotiated on the basis of a relatively small-scale map, not uncodified local knowledge.

Following the British conquest of Canada, the country significantly upstream from Montreal had (apart from an enclave around Detroit) been closed to European agricultural settlement. Boats sailed the lakes, and this resulted in a limited sounding of navigable channels[12] and a more general knowledge of the coastline. In 1779, Walter Butler recorded creeks at the northwestern end of Lake Ontario, named by their distances from Niagara or Burlington (thus, the "12 and 16 Mile Creeks[s]" and the "20 mile Creek"). But his information about these creeks' sources and interior portages was defective, and Butler journeyed along a wilderness in which the former French forts at Toronto and Frontenac (Kingston) had been abandoned.[13] In cartographic terms, this lack of official interest in the area is illustrated by the early "Surveys" used to create the 1790 "Map of Part of Canada for the Use of His Majesty's Secretary of State" (fig. 1). Of the thirty-one surveys antedating the War of Independence, only two clearly related to access to the lakes.[14]

In 1782, General Haldimand, commanding in Quebec, was already considering where to place the prospective flood of Loyalist refugees. His first thoughts, influenced by Surveyor General Samuel Holland, were of Cape Breton Island (Nova Scotia). But he also contemplated "an Establishment" for New York and New England frontiersmen "at, or near Detroit." He noted that "the lands there are fertile," and the new settlers "will be a great Support to our Indian Allies, who have everything to fear from the Encroachment of the Americans." They would also soon be capable of provisioning "the Garrisons which it will be necessary to keep in the Upper Countries." In February 1783, the London government approved, mechanically asking for "as accurate an Account as you can obtain of the Quantity" of land in question and of its likely produce.[15] However, by that point, the November 1782 Preliminaries of Peace had negotiated boundaries that would entail the surrender to the United States of Detroit and the other "Upper Country" posts.

On hearing this, Haldimand had Holland examine "the north side of Lake Ontario and the . . . Outawa River, so that I may make the most of these Places for the advantage of Commerce in case the Limits of the Province should be the same in the definitive Treaty as in the Preliminaries."[16] "Commerce" in this context meant fur trade with the Indians, and it meshed with Haldimand's fear that, feeling betrayed by the peace, the Indians would take indiscriminate revenge. So when a delegation from the Six Nations arrived asking what "measures [the] Government intended to take for their Security and Welfare," Haldimand invited its leaders, Joseph Brant (Thayendanegea) and Captain John (Deserontyon), to accompany Holland on his explorations, with the idea of settling the Mohawks there "provided the Country . . . should be found propitious." Holland was back within a month, reporting that, although he had not had time for an "Actual Survey of the ungranted Lands on the North Side of the River St. Lawrence," he had collected information about their suitability for settlement. The Indians had "made excursions into the Woods: They seemed . . . well satisfied with the Country . . . but [only] told me that as soon as they have examined the North Side of the Lake, they will inform your Excellency of the Spot they'll chuse to fix their abode."[17] Accordingly, some Indians joined the party of "Capt. Laforce, Mr. Cotte, & Mr. Peachey," who "proceeded [from the Bay of Quinte] to survey the North Shore of Lake Ontario all the way to Niagara." This survey resulted in the 1784–85 "Plan of the North Side of Lake Ontario from Cateraque to Niagara as surveyed . . . by Mrss. Kotte and Peachey . . . with Niagara River surveyed by Lieut. Tinling."[18]

Interest concentrated on the area north and east of Cataraqui (near Kingston). The superintendent general, Sir John Johnson, had suggested securing a "report of the Quantity and Quality of the Lands" along the Rideau River. Haldimand agreed, observing, "Our Plans of this Country are very imperfect, according to them I should conjecture that due North from [Cataraqui the Ottawa] River lies about 150 miles distant . . . but have no doubt, but that the Savages are much better acquainted with the Distance than we are." Accordingly, Lieutenant French went, with eight soldiers, "two Canadians, and an Indian as a Guide," to Cataraqui via the Ottawa, the Rideau, and the Gananoque Rivers, estimating the distances traveled and observing the country. French accompanied his expedition journal with a detailed sketch of the Rideau and Gananoque Rivers, commenting on their navigability, as well as a more general sketch of the area between the Ottawa and the St. Lawrence Rivers.[19] That fall, other inspections were made of land on the Ottawa up to the Chaudière Falls and of the country between de Longueuil's *seigneurie* and the Isle aux Gallots.[20]

By then, preparations for settlement were well advanced. By July, encouraged by Holland's report, Haldimand was disposed to settle white as well as Indian Loyalists at Cataraqui, "where the Land is fertile and the climate rather better than at Montreal." It was soon established that the local Mississaugas had no objection to this plan and that the Mohawks even desired it. In October, an indeterminate land purchase ("from the Lake as far back as a man may travel in a day") was made from the Mississaugas,[21] and on October 27, 1783, Deputy Surveyor John Collins laid out "A Township or Tract of Land of Six Miles Square . . . near the Ancient Fort of Frontenac."[22] In November, Haldimand enthused to London about the "advantages from this Settlement," and he contested Lord North's suggestion that the Loyalists be chiefly resettled east of the St. Lawrence, along the U.S. border. Haldimand saw this as a recipe for dangerous frontier incidents—hence "the great advantage which the Land between the River St. Lawrence and the Ottawa River toward Cataraqui possesses for making useful and happy Settlements for the Loyalists." By the next spring, London had accepted his arguments.[23]

At this point, Haldimand was seeking to round out his settlements through purchases near Niagara, for Joseph Brant had become convinced that a settlement near Cataraqui would attract fewer Mohawks from the United States and that it would be cut off from his budding Indian confederation farther west. "After examining the situation of the Country upon the Map," Haldimand was persuaded to fall in with Brant's new preference for the Grand River (running into eastern Lake Erie). Conveniently, land purchased from the Mississaugas for this purpose could also help to complete the settlement of men demobilized from Butler's Rangers at Niagara, where they had been stationed during the Revolutionary War.[24]

These Indian purchases and grants generated many sketches.[25] Accordingly, "some of the earliest maps . . . are those relating to Indian treaties," but "many . . . are sketchy." Thus, the map of c. 1799 shows areas "conjectured to be the extent of cessions from the Indians" on the north shore of Lake Ontario. Although there were exceptions to this, such as the 1795 purchase from the Chippewas near Chenail Ecarté, in the formal transactions boundaries were usually described in words alone.[26] In this regard, however, these Indian treaties were in good company: the borders of the United States itself were so defined in the 1783 peace treaty, leaving it quite unnecessarily doubtful, for instance, precisely which river was the true St. Croix separating what are now Maine and New Brunswick. Indeed, as late as 1846, the treaty resolving the Oregon dispute was still drawn in words only, with no map to indicate how the new border should divide the Gulf Islands in the Strait of Georgia.

In the 1780s, Canadian surveys switched from their prewar focus to service this new settlement around Lake Ontario. Of the eighteen surveys between 1783 and 1789 listed on the 1790 map (see fig. 1), all but one were of what became "Upper Canada."[27] Few, however, extended much beyond Kingston: the map admits that the Ottawa River above the Rideau, the south side of Lake Ontario, and the "Niagara River from the Falls to Fort Erie, Lakes Erie and St. Clair and part of Lake Huron are taken from Sketches only."[28] In addition, the map claims—surprisingly—that "no Surveys" of the "District of Hesse" (north of Lake Erie) had been "as yet reported to the Surveyor General's Office."[29] Holland later told the new lieutenant governor of Upper Canada that past surveys had been "altogether local and confined to a small tract of that valuable country now under your . . . Government [and] still far from accurately delineated on any plan or map . . . owing to want of a general survey being made and latitudes and longitude taken to ascertain the true position of the most principal places situated on the several Upper Lakes."[30]

Official attention to such areas beyond the reach of current settlement owed much to strategic concerns. In 1783–84, fearing that the Indians would turn on the Canadian fur traders, Haldimand refused to transfer to the United States the forts controlling the southern side of the lakes, as the peace treaty required. But, despite one odd flicker of renewed interest in settlement north of Detroit, he clearly anticipated their surrender. So, "to shun everything which might bring on a rupture with bad neighbours, which surround us," he sought to keep "the upper Country" uninhabited as long as possible and refused applications for land grants there. Indeed, one of the attractions Haldimand saw in Brant's scheme for Mohawk settlement along the Grand River was that it would be "a Frontier to our other Settlements in that Quarter."[31] His successor, acting Governor Henry Hamilton, had previously commanded in Detroit and may have been more sympathetic toward the fur traders, who had been lobbying vigorously in the winter of 1784–85. And in March 1785, we find Hamilton reporting to London on a project "for establishing a carrying place on the communication between Cateraquoui and Lake Huron" that would "be secure from the jealous interference of our [U.S.] neighbours." It would also reduce the time and costs of using the traditional Ottawa River route to Lake Huron (with its thirty-six portages); and, by thus supplying the Indians more cheaply than could be done from the United States, it would keep open their "intercourse with any posts it may be thought proper to establish in the upper Country." By way of explanation, Hamilton forwarded "A Plan of [that proposed] communication," made inquiries of the merchant Benjamin Frobisher, and undertook to "order the survey of the remainder to be proceeded upon this Spring."[32]

Frobisher agreed that the route from Kingston would be worth investigating "as there is no Man . . . capable of giving any certain information about it," and in July, John Collins left Kingston to do so.[33] But Frobisher had always doubted whether there was enough water on that route for "a Communication for Boats or Large Canoes," and he suggested that Lake Simcoe should instead be approached from Toronto. On June 6, 1785, Hamilton therefore sent London a revised plan emphasizing this communication.[34] Its attractiveness was sufficient to induce the purchase of a tract including the site of Toronto from the Mississaugas in 1787.[35] This was followed the next year by a "Plan of the Harbour of Toronto with a proposed Town and Settlement 1788." However, nothing was done on the ground, and the precise topography remained obscure.[36]

Directly military considerations generated further, and more systematic, official examination of the Great Lakes. On returning to Quebec as governor general, Guy Carleton, Lord Dorchester, requested a decision on the "upper country" posts: "the most injudicious [course] of all is a *no resolution*"; so should they be surrendered or repaired? Whitehall equivocated: they should be put "into a temporary state of defence."[37] Dorchester therefore instructed Captain Gother Mann, "Commanding Engineer," to visit "the fortifications at Ontario, Niagara, Erie, Detroit and Michilimackinac" and to "thoroughly . . . survey and report their condition," recommending appropriate repairs and defense measures. He should also consider alternatives in the event that they might have to be given up, investigating "the best communication from the upper part of Lake Ontario to the lower end of Lake Erie on this [Canadian] side of the Water." While so engaged, he should also examine

> the entrance leading to Lake Superior, as far as the Falls of St. Mary, . . . to give an opinion whether there is any place near the foot of the Falls fit for a post or settlement, for the convenience of Trade to Lake Superior, or whether Thessalon the place formerly in contemplation will better answer those purposes.
>
> You will examine the mouth of French river, and that of the River Matchadosh upon Lake Huron, likewise Torrento [sic] upon Lake Ontario, . . . how far they will answer for shipping and of what size, whether the Country adjacent is propitious for settlements, and if these . . . can at a small expence [sic] be defended.
>
> Besides these observations you will inquire what other posts there may be on this side of the different Lakes offering similar advantages, what sort of vessels are best calculated for trade as well as for war on these waters, and to what posts . . . each may navigate, and enter on both sides of the Lakes.[38]

Mann's report answered the specific queries. Thus, Carleton Island would be better than Kingston as a naval station, though not for civilian trade, while the works at Michilimackinac were overly elaborate "as a defence against Musquetry or Indians only," but "if against Cannon by far too little." Thessalon's utility was limited by its shallow harbor bar. Nor was Mann much taken with either French River or Matchadosh Bay and its "communication (sometimes used) to Toronto," remarking that "if, as I am informed, it is impossible to pass with large Canoes on account of the Rapids and difficult carrying places; and if to this is added the great length of Portage from Toronto to Lake La Clie [Simcoe], and the being obliged to keep Canoes upon that Lake, there seem altogether at first view to be very serious obstacles to any business being carried on this way upon the great scale of trade."[39]

Other recommendations were more positive: Mann suggested either specific improvements to the existing transshipment arrangements on the south side of Niagara or the construction of a new road from Navy Hall (Niagara-on-the-Lake) to Chippewa to the south just above the Niagara Falls (this was undertaken in the 1790s). Although he thought the construction of a ship channel with locks at Sault Ste. Marie would be too expensive, Mann proposed blasting one through the rocks for canoes.

Mann also gave verbal descriptions of the harbors on Lake Erie (better on the south side), of the passage and shores from Detroit to Lake Huron, and of the latter's northern and (in more detail) eastern sides. This eastern shore of Lake Huron from Matchadosh Bay southward, "which has hitherto been little known or frequented except by some few Indians," was of mixed soil but contained "several considerable tracts of Land, which I make no doubt may be hereafter settled to advantage; but for more distinct knowledge . . . I beg leave to refer to the annexed general sketch of Lake Huron."[40]

As this passage suggests, the report was illustrated by numerous maps; some are small-scale sketches covering large areas, others far more precise.[41] Detailed investigation underlay the depiction of the "communication from Lake Erie to Detroit." "Assisted by Captain Grant of the Naval Department," Mann took careful soundings to establish "whether there was a good ship channel between Grosse Isle

and the West Shore," before concluding that the best route lay east of Bois Blanc Island and suggesting a post to command it. The report concludes by observing that since vessels involved in lake shipping were seldom out of sight of land for long, "the Navigation must be considered chiefly as Pilotage, to which the use of good Nautical Charts are essential, and are therefore much wanted."[42] (Maps of specific harbors often gave soundings,[43] and general maps sometimes provided a rough guide to the depth of water along the coasts; but full nautical charts were not forthcoming for at least another generation.)

Figure 2. "A Survey of Lake Ontario done by H. Laforce of the Naval Department & Lewis Kotté, Assistant Engineer, the North Shore in 1783 and the East and South Shores in 1789" [W.9]. Public Record Office, National Archives, U.K.

Latitude of Fort Erie being the mean of a number of observations of the Stars N. & S. of the Zenith taken in the winter of 1789-1790 by Lt. Campbell 60th Regt. and Mr. Ellicot Geographer to the American States
N.B. The Lat. of Fort Erie in the Journal annex'd is 42°:20', but this and the other Latitudes on this Plan have been corrected by the above Observation.
Fort Erie
Buffalo Cr.
HARBOUR
Catfish Creek
Large flats of excellent cleard land on both sides of the Creek
A good harbour for Boats
This Creek is the Western boundary of the Six Nations
No harbour for Boats
From X to X a high rocky bank very dangerous to approach in a Storm, there being no Landg. Place
From the entrance of this Creek there is an open Cart-Road of 12 miles leading to a small Lake which empties itself into a branch of the Allegheny River call'd Canawagy Creek. On which about 10 miles from the Lake is a settlement call'd Mary's Town
Reduced and Copied from the original Survey in the Drawing-Room of the Engineer's Departmt. at Quebec by Wm. Hall Draughtsman
Examined
Gother Mann
HER MAJESTY'S STATE PAPER OFFICE
A SURVEY of the SOUTH SHORE of LAKE ERIE, commencing at the Narrows at Fort Erie, and ending at the entrance of Detroit River: taken in 1789 by Hy. Ford Naval Offr. Pr. McNiff Asst. Surv. by order of His Excellency The Rt. Honble. Lord Dorchester Governor & Commander in Chief &c. &c.
Scale, two miles to an Inch
28 miles

Dorchester complemented Mann's report in 1789 by having René Hippolyte Pepin dit Laforce and Lewis Kotté complete their survey of Lake Ontario (fig. 2) and Commander Henry Ford and Assistant Surveyor Patrick McNiff undertake one of the southern and western shores of Lake Erie.[44] Ford and McNiff's measurements of latitude were corrected in the light of observations taken, during the 1789-90 winter, by Lieutenant Campbell and by Andrew Ellicott, "Geographer to the American States,"[45] before the final production of maps (fig. 3) for dispatch to London.

In the 1780s, it is clear that many people had begun to show an interest in potential shortcuts between the lakes; but there had been little official observation beyond their coasts. This changed with the appointment of John Graves Simcoe as the lieutenant governor of Upper Canada. Simcoe approached his new responsibilities with a vision shaped by classical learning and the "armchair" study of maps. His father had seen Montreal as so situated "that with the assistance of a few Sluices it will become the centre of Communication between the Gulf of Mexico and Hudson's Bay, by an interior navigation: formed for drawing to itself the wealth and strength of the vast adjacent countries, so advantageously placed, if not destined to lay the foundation of the most potent and best connected Empire that ever awed the World."[46] Simcoe, too, had early in life "formed an opinion of the immense importance which the Possession of the Isthmus between the Lakes Ontario, Erie and Huron must be to the King and British Nation in the growing population and consequence of North America, and . . . been confirmed in this Opinion by the revolt of the Atlantic Colonies."[47] Shortly after his appointment, and while he was still in England, Simcoe pictured himself as the "Romulus" of a new imperial province, which he would develop largely from scratch, using a corps of soldiers who would open up the country, then retire to settle on land grants very much on the Roman model: "For the purpose of Commerce, Union and Power, I propose that the Site of the Colony should be in that Great Peninsula between the Lakes Huron, Erie, and Ontario, a Spot destined by Nature, sooner or later, to govern the interior World. I mean to establish a Capital in the very heart of the Country, upon the River La Tranche [Thames], which is navigable for batteaux for 150 miles, and near to where the Grand River which falls into Erie, and others that communicate with Huron and Ontario, almost interlock."[48]

Encouraged by discovering in the Quebec "Surveyor's Office an actual Survey of the River La Tranche [which] answers my most sanguine Expectations," Simcoe ordered further exploration and then proceeded in person to locate what he wanted to find.[49] In March 1793, a day's inspection of the forks of the Thames demonstrated it "to be a capital situation, eminently calculated for the metropolis of all Canada."[50] Even his critics praised his "indefatigable industry." They noted that "last winter he went to Detroit on snow shoes; early this spring he coasted the Lake from Niagara to Toronto; he has now gone to look into Lake Huron by way of Lake La Claye [Simcoe], and next winter we expect a visit from him here [Kingston] by way of the Bay of [Quinte]."[51] On these journeys, Simcoe was accompanied by surveyors, who were later sent back to conduct "actual Surveys."[52] However, the resulting maps could be somewhat Potemkin affairs, drawn meticulously to scale but showing little detail or, worse, what was desired rather than what was. Thus, William Chewett's October 23, 1794, map[53] of the communication from Lake St. Clair via the Thames River and Dundas Street to Burlington Bay and York (Toronto), and thence by Yonge Street to Lake Simcoe, implies that these military roads were already fully operational and that there really were towns at York, Oxford, Dorchester, London, and Chatham. In fact, despite plans like "Birds eye view . . . of the Forks with a project for a town [including] Mrs. Simcoe's intended villa," the site for London was not finally chosen until 1826.[54]

Figure 3. "A Survey of the South Shore of Lake Erie commencing at the Narrows at Fort Erie, and ending at the entrance fo Detroit River: taken in 1789 by Hy. Ford Naval Offr., Pk. McNiff Asst. Survr." The map notes, by Fort Erie, that its (and other) latitudes had been corrected from that originally given in the survey Journal, following observations in the 1789–90 winter by Lt. Campbell and "Mr. Ellicot Geographer to the American States." Andrew Ellicot had been commissioned by the federal government to survey the New York–Pennsylvania state boundary on Lake Erie, which required him to ascertain the longitude of the western end of Lake Ontario. While so engaged, Ellicot "made the first accurate measurement of the length of the [Niagara] river and height of the falls and rapids." John A. Garraty and Mark C. Carnes, eds., *American National Biography*, vol. vii (New York: Oxford University Press, 1999), 416. Public Record Office, National Archives, U.K.

Simcoe's enthusiasms prompted a blizzard of maps—some, including a presentation sketch of Upper Canada on birch bark for the prince regent, drawn by his wife.[55] The intention was probably always that these should lead on to the production of a major map. During the winter of 1792–93, William Chewett had drawn what was sent to the home secretary in 1795 as a "Plan of the Province of Upper Canada divided into Counties; by Order of His Excellency John Graves Simcoe."[56] In October 1794, McNiff contributed to the project "A Sketch of the North Shore of Lake Superior collected from a Journal of a Coasting Survey" and another of "the River St. Mary's." The eventual outcome was the 1800 publication in London of *A Map of the Province of Upper Canada*.[57] In its general outlines, this map was, for its time, quite good. As it was published (unlike its official predecessors), it could be reissued with minor updates—and was, twelve times before 1862. But though Simcoe had left Upper Canada some years earlier, the map was still attuned to promoting his vision of the province. Thus, Olsen observes that many of the settlements depicted derive from Simcoe's plans, with his "major places . . . tinted red" on at least one copy, while the subsequent neglect of "many of his proposals . . . is not apparent." Although they were never built, "proposed canals," which were "another of Simcoe's ideas, are shown [inter alia] to join the Welland to the Grand River and then to the Thames." Simcoe's military roads, Yonge and Dundas Streets, are drawn, but other roads are only represented by dotted lines. "Dundas Street is shown connecting the planned [but nonexistent] capital, London, with Lower Canada," although "the part east of York [Toronto] was never built along the inland route shown on the map."[58]

Richard Cartwright saw Simcoe's fixation on "another and a second London" as "a little wild," observing how much more usefully his Rangers might have been employed "in opening roads and building bridges in the more settled parts of the country" (chiefly downriver from Kingston) instead of "cutting a road from the head of Lake Ontario to the river La Tranche, where there is not a single inhabitant." In the same vein, Joseph Brant observed dismissively that Simcoe had "done a great deal for this province, he has changed the name of every place in it."[59] The real impact of Simcoe's vision is therefore debatable. But he did direct political development to the head of Lake Ontario. At the outset, he chose Newark (Niagara-on-the-Lake) for the seat of government instead of Kingston, which was located in the most settled area. From Newark, he would have liked to move to London; but in the absence of British ministerial approval, he pitched instead on Toronto (renamed York), from which his roads were to radiate. In the next century, Toronto came into its own. But for some time, it was hard to reach except by water, and the choice was initially eccentric. "The Officers of Govt. were obliged [in 1796] to move from comfortable houses at Niagara into an absolute wood where people were sometimes losing themselves between one hut and another."[60]

Securing the move to Toronto was one of Simcoe's last official acts. The close of his governorship was marked by disputes with his commander in chief, Lord Dorchester, who insisted on most troops withdrawing to Lower Canada following Jay's Treaty and the 1796 surrender to the United States of the "upper country" posts. These arrangements generated more maps; to illustrate his proposed military dispositions, and also to round off his service in Quebec, Dorchester sent London "a sketch of the Rapids of St. Mary, comprehending Cariboux [St. Joseph's] Island and Michilimackinac, together with one of part of the entrance of [the] Detroit River and two of the River Niagara, which (with a map delivered into the Secretary of State's office in 1791, of the Province of Quebec, extending from the Sea to the Mississippi) will elucidate all the arrangements for Upper Canada."[61]

Strategic considerations were, naturally, even more prominent during the War of 1812, which generated the next major burst of mapmaking. The U.S. Army realized that it was ill informed about objectives in Canada and sought to remedy this, even reworking obsolete British plans.[62] Two 1813 sketches of Kingston, giving a "Route by which to avoid pickets," are indeed rightly marked "incorrect," while Winearls comments on the "Sketch of the Entrance into Lake Ontario Upper Canada Oct 15 1813" that it was "obviously not made from a reconnaissance survey."[63] Years later, General Peter Porter was to write that if the information now contained in his boundary commission maps had been "possessed by our government during the late war it would probably have saved many times their cost to the treasury, and perhaps something to its reputation."[64] Once military operations got under way, they generated sketch maps of the opposing forces and positions, to accompany reports sent back to superior officers. Also, an attentive public in both countries was, as in earlier wars, regaled with maps of the "Seat of the War" that were "intended to Illustrate the Operations of the British and American Armies." One map was even "Done in part, from a sketch of the [war hero] the late Major General Isaac Brock." These sketches were followed up in retrospective apologias such as James Wilkinson's *Memoirs of My Own Times*.[65]

More was contributed to geographical knowledge by the British hydrographic surveying that followed the war. The course of military operations had been greatly influenced by the fluctuating naval fortunes on the lakes. So in the spring of 1815, Captain William Owen was sent over, "charged" as his brother Edward, the senior local naval officer, put it, "with the duty of Surveying such parts on the lake Frontier as may enable me to report ... upon the Naval defence thereof."[66] June to October 1815 saw a crash reconnaissance, based on a combination of existing maps and reports and new surveys by William Owen and others. Thus, "Chart 30 is a survey of the new Settlement on Drummond Island [in northern Lake Huron] with a statement made respecting it in 1796 by Lieutenant Bryce R.E."[67] The schematic map of the road from Lake Simcoe to Penetanguishene explains that it is partly "traced in from Mr Wilmot's Survey of 1812."[68] Sir Edward Owen digested all this information into a succession of reports to the Admiralty. These are heavily map-dependent. Owen explains that "Chart no. 5 is a hasty Survey made by Captain William Owen of the ... entrance to the Bay of Quinte east of Amherst Island. This Channel is near two miles wide and it would be difficult to prevent a Vessel's entering with a strong fair wind, but Batteries at the situations marked P, Q, R, S would impose a risk of doing it which the object of cutting off a coaster would not justify."[69]

Overall, some forty-six maps and plans were attached to these reports. But Owen records surprising lacunae: "The River Humber is one of the most considerable on Lake Ontario but has not been examined, and very little information could be gained of it. There is a good Salmon Fishery at its entrance. ... From York to Burlington Bay the distance is about eight leagues. The coast has not been much examined, but is free from danger." And while there were uncertainties in relation even to Lake Ontario, "Of the navigation of Lake Huron scarcely anything is known. To the southward of the Manitoulin Islands it is said to be clear of dangers, and to the northward to be intricate and full of them."

Unsurprisingly, we find William Owen writing of the need for a "more particular survey." The Admiralty's hydrography office had seen the end of the Napoleonic Wars as a "favourable moment" for remedying "the great deficiency of our Nautical knowledge in almost every part of the World, but more particularly on the coastline of our own Dominions." Nautical knowledge was presumably more easily expanded in America than in British home waters, but the period's uncertainties about the Great Lakes are set in context by the fact that there were still important discoveries to be made off the English coast. Indeed, between 1815 and 1829 approximately equal numbers of surveys were devoted to the United Kingdom and to the rest of the world.[70]

In November 1815, Owen was instructed to make "a compleat Survey . . . as far as you shall have power to do so, of every part of the River, and Lake of the Thousand Islands, as well as of the three Lakes, Ontario, Erie and Huron, [together with their tributary] Waters and Rivers . . . as far as may be necessary to obtain a knowledge of them, where they can be usefully employed in facilitating the communications."[71] The years 1815 and 1816 saw a start made on Lake Ontario. But in June 1817, as the survey was moving on to Lake Erie, Captain Owen and all but one of his assistants were ordered home—money was tight, and the Admiralty's secretary, J. W. Croker, saw its hydrographic office as inessential (since it had not existed before 1795) and sought to curb its rising costs. So Lieutenant Bayfield was left to continue on a much reduced basis. Nevertheless, in 1817, he completed work on Lake Erie and began surveying Lake Huron, which took five more seasons. Bayfield later claimed, "There has perhaps been no Survey made of greater labor of detail than that of the 20,000 Islands, Islets, & rocks of Lake Huron." His superior, Commissioner Barrie, was sometimes impatient with the delays; but he urged the Admiralty to extend the exercise to Lake Superior, observing that although there were no naval vessels on the lake "at present, yet it is possible that at some future period they may be required; and of the Navigation . . . we are extremely ignorant—even the North West Traders pretend to little knowledge of the lake beyond the Coast." A schooner was chartered from the Hudson's Bay Company, and Bayfield indented for new instruments.[72] He received the standard instructions not to antagonize either the Americans or the Indians, but to "recollect that from [the latter] you may obtain correct information of the productions of the Country, Course and extent of the Rivers, the best Fishing Stations &c."[73] Bayfield was not only to report on timber, like most earlier explorers, but also to collect specimens of ores and minerals. He later claimed that his survey had been the first to point out "the exact locality"[74] of the region's copper deposits. Lake Superior took three seasons, 1823 to 1825, to survey.

Bayfield then spent two years in London in the Admiralty's hydrographic office reducing his findings to charts. Most military maps (hence a high proportion of all exploring surveys) had heretofore been tightly held,[75] but from 1823 onward, Admiralty charts were made available to the public—with a first catalogue published in 1825. So for a mere £3.675, one could, beginning in 1828, purchase twenty-eight sheets covering most of the Canadian Great Lakes, with soundings, coastal reliefs, and notes on the nature of the shore.[76] These Bayfield charts were not impeccable—calls for a resurvey mounted after 1877 as new deep-draft steamers struck rocks in Georgian Bay that Bayfield had not noticed.[77] But the Admiralty charts antedated their U.S. counterparts by some thirty years; and in 1845, Bayfield was delighted by an American comment that "the only correct chart of the entire [Lake Superior] coast is that made by the British Government . . . the only map used by the Ordnance department at Washington and by the superintendent of the mineral lands at Porter's Island, is that of Bayfield."[78]

By establishing the coastline of the lakes, the postwar naval surveys markedly improved general maps of Upper Canada. According to Olsen's analysis of these, "The greatest advance in accuracy occurs between the Chewett 1813 map and the [1826] Chewett/Ridout map. . . . The real credit . . . must go to the hydrographic surveyors who did so much to change the outline of the province between these years."[79]

The Treaty of Ghent that ended the War of 1812 provided for commissions to demarcate the United States–British border from the Bay of Fundy to the Lake of the Woods. Among Sir Edward Owen's November 1815 instructions had been that the naval surveyors of the lakes should furnish the commissioners "with Information, if they call upon you for it." This was not so much an altruistic response as an attempt to alert the British participants in the commissions to presumed security needs.[80] But mention of these commissions brings us to other motives for mapping: decision and record. The Ghent treaty states this clearly. The 1783 peace treaty, it explains, had run the boundary "along the middle" of the St. Lawrence, the lakes, and the "water communications" between them and the "most North Western point of the Lake of the Woods." But doubts had "arisen [about] what was the middle . . . and whether certain islands . . . were within the [British or American territories]. In order therefore finally to decide these doubts, they shall be referred to two Commissioners [who shall] designate the boundary . . . and decide to which of the two Contracting parties the several Islands . . . do respectively belong in conformity with the true intent of said Treaty."[81]

To accomplish this, the commission first surveyed the islands and waterways in question, with a thoroughness that in 1818 led the House of Representatives to call for "some mode of designating the boundary line . . . which shall require less time and expense."[82] The relevant coasts, shores, and islands were laid down by theodolite observation and meticulous triangulation, and twenty-five maps were drafted (extending from St. Regis to just short of the Neebish Channels in the St. Marys River). Using these maps, the commissioners assigned islands to one country or the other, mostly on a commonsense basis, but with some horse trading and one goodwill concession by the British Foreign Secretary. The U.S. commissioner, General Porter, could then correctly report that they had "designated the line with a certainty and precision which will preclude all future disputes and doubts" and had "ascertained the precise location and the several areas of more than two thousand islands." But if the maps fully answered this purpose, they did not fulfill Porter's earlier hopes that they would contain "all the information necessary to the safe navigation of these extensive waters" and so benefit "the commerce of the western people." For though soundings were sometimes taken, they were not entered; and the maps accordingly gave little guidance about navigation channels, shoals, and so forth. Nor were the complete expanses of Lakes Erie and Huron covered, since some parts were clearly irrelevant to the border.[83]

In theory there should have been more scope for exploration in the next stretch, from St. Marys River to the Lake of the Woods, since the 1783 description of the boundary was—as Porter put it— "not applicable to the localities, as they have since been found to exist." Hence it would "be necessary to explore not only the points referred to in the Treaty, but also other parts of the adjacent country." However, because the territory in question was "remote and comparatively unimportant," the commission's agents were told to relax their standards and abandon "trigonometrical survey." "Great care and accuracy must be observed" in locating "the most northwestern point of the Lake of the Woods," but "the other geographical points" needed only to be determined "with ordinary certainty." As for the shores and islands of the Lake of the Woods, only "such rapid surveys . . . as upon examination thereof you may deem necessary to a fair designation of the boundary" were to be taken.[84] In fact, national disagreements, and the use of territorial claims as bargaining chips, led to more exploration and maps than had originally been intended. But this had its limits: the British devoted considerable efforts to locating a "most northwesternmost point of the Lake of the Woods" that kept the border from cutting off their important Rat Portage (Kenora) route to Lake Winnipeg. However, more thorough exploration would have revealed a yet more northwesterly (and equally advantageous) point.[85] Exploration and mapmaking were not ends in themselves; they were means to determine and record the border, and so prevent possible future trouble.

What the commission's surveyors did at the international level, others did domestically, the laying out of townships and registration of land claims being their bread and butter. In 1788, the new districts west of Montreal were equipped with land boards. In 1792, the board for the District of Hesse was meeting one day a week.[86] The incoming lieutenant governor, John Graves Simcoe, was very scornful of the administration he inherited: "There are great errors in the Surveyor General's Department; I greatly fear thro' the incompetence of the persons whom Major Holland, that able [but infirm] Servant of the Crown, has been formerly obliged to employ in Upper Canada, I shall have considerable difficulty . . . in . . . preventing . . . the most mischievous litigations."[87]

When Whitehall denied him an established post of surveyor general, Simcoe fell back on David Smith, who had caught his attention as the "Efficient Person" of the Hesse Land Board and who, as a serving officer, could afford to act without pay until London changed its mind, which was not until 1798. Smith was an administrator, not a practicing surveyor, and during the next decade, "the township surveys, conducted by 17 different deputies, were of varying quality, but they were systematically conceived and regularly executed."[88] Over time, such township surveys also improved the quality of more general maps, since—unsurprisingly—these tended to be better for areas thus measured and settled than for those covered only by sketches or what are technically known as exploring surveys. However, township surveys were essentially two-dimensional—the mechanical laying out of squares.[89] This concentration led nineteenth-century Canadian mapmakers to ignore relief, sometimes with unfortunate consequences. For example, the first railway (bypassing Niagara) proved too steep for steam engines and had to be worked by horses.[90]

Map production, then, was stimulated by both strategic thinking and bureaucracy. Both could also be encountered outside government, notably in the North West Company. As its name implies, this trading group depended on the fur-producing regions it was opening up beyond Lake Winnipeg, access to which could potentially be disrupted by the United States if American authority were to be firmly ensconced on the 1783 border. In the late eighteenth century, the fur production of these regions was still less than that of the lands south and west of Michilimackinac. But these latter lands did not generate comparable mapping activity, probably for three reasons: they were already reasonably known, at least in outline, unlike the Canadian northwest and the routes to the Pacific; the enterprises trading there were smaller and so less able to devote resources to exploration; and although they were even more exposed to pressure by the United States (which ultimately led to a takeover by Astor's American Fur Company), this was not concentrated at specific choke points that might be bypassed if only alternative routes could be found.

The wish to bypass such a choke point at Grand Portage led, as we have seen, to Umfreville's 1784 explorations. These were cited in a North West Company petition that October to General Haldimand for a ten-year monopoly on trade over both the Grand Portage and the alternative "passage they may discover from the north side of Lake Superior to the River Ouinipique." Such a grant would "give them the opportunity of making the [further] discoveries they propose . . . exploring at their own Expence, between the latitudes of 55 and 65, all that tract of Country extending west of Hudsons Bay to the North Pacific Ocean," making surveys "so far as it is practicable," and communicating them to the governor general. Next spring (1785), after acting Governor Hamilton had exhibited an interest in the idea of a westward route via Lake Simcoe that would be safe from American interference on the lower lakes, the North West Company returned to the charge. On its behalf the traveler Peter Pond showed Hamilton his map of his explorations, convinced him that these "discoveries may prove of infinite utility to this Country [Quebec], consequently of great importance to the parent state," and warned him of American preparations "for the carrying on of discoveries in those regions." Pond submitted a memorial "on behalf of [and drafted by] the North West Company in which he is a Partner," again petitioning for a ten-year monopoly of "the trade to the North West of Lake Superior." In return, the company would "pursue the work already begun until the whole extent of that unknown Country between the latitudes Fifty Four and Sixty Seven to the north Pacific Ocean is thoroughly explored," supplying the governor with "correct Maps of those Countries, and exact accounts of their Nature and production, with remarks upon every thing useful or curious, that may be met with."[91]

The North West Company never got its monopoly. But this did not end the process of exploration. Pond went back to the wilderness, and although he never tested his more ambitious ideas, these led to Alexander Mackenzie's "Voyage performed by Order of the N.W. Company . . . in search of a Passage by Water through the N. W. Continent of America from Athabasca to the Pacific Ocean in Summer 1789."[92] Disappointingly, the Mackenzie River took him instead to the Arctic Ocean. But in 1793, after an interlude in London improving his surveying skills and buying better instruments, Mackenzie did cross to the Pacific (albeit not by a practically useful route). These journeys eventually resulted in improved maps, though not of the Great Lakes.

North West Company exploration on the Great Lakes resumed when the 1796 surrender of the northern posts revived fears of U.S. harassment. Lord Dorchester sent Lieutenant Bryce, R.E., to find an alternative to the post at Michilimackinac, and then "view the Rapids of St. Mary, and . . . give his advice to the Gentlemen of the North West Trade who purpose making a Road within the [British] Frontier for the convenience of transporting their Goods over the Carrying Place."[93] Perhaps to ensure access to any resultant maps, the North West Company hired Deputy Surveyor Theodore de Pincier to accompany him. In 1797, de Pincier produced, with Bryce's authentication, a "Plan of the Falls of St. Mary . . . Surveyed by Order of the North West Company." This shows, on the Canadian side, buildings, a lock, a short canal and "Drag Road for Canoes and Boats" around the falls, and a "Carriage Road" for the transshipment of goods between larger vessels.[94] Following a subsequent corporate split, the North West Company sought to deny its rivals (the XY Company, which Mackenzie had joined) the use of these facilities, on which it claimed to have spent four thousand pounds (Halifax currency), and also of land nearby for the erection of alternative portage facilities. Lieutenant Governor Hunter sent Captain de Bruyères, R.E., to arbitrate on the spot. In July 1802, de Bruyères produced a "Sketch [deriving from de Pincier's] of the North Shore contiguous to the Falls of St. Mary shewing the improvements made by the North West Company," but both he and Hunter failed to broker a solution. Mackenzie then visited the area in 1803, unilaterally appropriated plots for his "New Company," constructed a second portage road, and in December sent Hunter a "Copy of the Plan of part of the ground at the Sault of St. Mary's, and note thereon what we now pray for."[95] Much of this activity proved unnecessary, because both banks of the St. Marys River in fact remained under British control until the War of 1812. During this war, an American raiding party burned the facilities on the north bank. This was noted on "A Sketch of the passage from Drummond Island . . . to the Falls of St. Mary & to Lake Superior taken by [U.S.] Maj. Gl. Macombe in 1818," while he was on a prospecting mission prior to the establishment of Fort Brady on the American side in 1822.[96]

Meanwhile, David Thompson, who had been trained in surveying by the Hudson's Bay Company, was induced to transfer to the North West Company in 1797. He was then sent, Alexander Mackenzie tells us, "expressly" to ascertain the precise geographical correlates of "the North-West part of the Lake [of the Woods]" and of "the Northernmost branch of the source of the Mississippi." For it seemed that the border might be set (as indeed it was in the abortive King-Hawkesbury treaty of 1803) to run directly from the one to the other. On this expedition, Thompson established the correlates of all the North West Company posts in the area as well as of the northern bend of the Missouri River, and returned to Grand Portage by circling the southern and eastern sides of Lake Superior.[97] Thompson produced a plan of the route from Lake Superior to the Lake of the Woods, "Sketched from my Survey in 1798," that was probably used by J. L. Tiarks on his 1825 mission to locate an acceptable northwest angle on the Lake of the Woods. There followed an outline plan of Lake Superior "Surveyed by Mr. Thompson, Astronomer & Surveyor employed by the N. W. Company, 1802," though a penciled note on it describes the project as "very ill drawn." Lake Superior also featured as the departure point in his "Map of the North-West Territory of the Province of Canada . . . made for the North West Company in 1813 and 1814 and delivered to the Honourable William McGillivray then Agent."[98]

In 1798, as we have seen, Sir Alexander's cousin Roderick Mackenzie had rediscovered the Kaministiquia route from Lake Superior into the interior, and the next year, the North West Company decided to switch to using this route. A new depot, later called Fort William, was opened on Lake Superior in 1803 and completed in 1807, supposedly at a cost of fifty thousand pounds. Later in 1807, we find the company bragging about its accomplishments at Sault Ste. Marie and along the Kaministiquia River route, "by which His Majesty's subjects might be enabled to carry on their trade to the interior, or Indian country, without passing through the possessions of the United States," and asking (unsuccessfully) to be granted land north of Sault Ste. Marie as a reward.[99]

Lastly, the company continued to interest itself in the route via Lake Simcoe to Georgian Bay, devoting (at the turn of the nineteenth century) twelve hundred pounds "towards making Yonge Street a better road"—"for the double purpose of shortening the distance to the Upper Lakes, and of avoiding any contact with the American frontiers," as Bouchette put it in 1815.[100] In 1810, the company heard that the governor intended, as a further step, to open a road from Lake Simcoe to Penetanguishene on Georgian Bay. It indicated enthusiastic readiness to use the new road to transport stores and provisions hitherto sent via the lakes, but asked for extensive land grants along the road to defray the costs of the switch. Although these were refused, Lieutenant Governor Gore "directed a Survey of a tract of Land belonging to the Indians . . . to be made, with a view to meeting the wishes of the gentlemen engaged in the fur trade."[101] Gore's successor, General Brock, added that "the Merchants are particularly anxious in the present uncertain state of our relations to obtain a route for their goods unconnected with the American territory." Their interest is further evident in the plan (fig. 4), dated August 12, 1812 (that is, shortly after news had arrived of the U.S. declaration of war), "by actual survey of the Street of Communication between Kempenfeldt Bay . . . and Penetangushene Harbour . . . made out [by Samuel Wilmot, Surveyor] at the particular request of Angus Shaw, Esq., Agent to the North West Company."[102] The line of the road was traced at the company's expense, but that amounted at most to blazing trees along its path. The actual construction was rushed through by the military in the winter of 1814–15 in order to permit the building at Penetanguishene of a warship large enough to dominate Lakes Huron and Erie.[103]

We have seen that reasons for mapping could be quite varied. Sometimes they could be idiosyncratic, like Charlevoix's flattery of his patron. Quite often, maps stated their purposes explicitly in lengthy titles. For example, see the 1790 "Sketch of Lake Erie . . . & Part of Lakes Huron & Ontario Intended to show the Extravagant Claims to Lands in the District of Hesse."[104] In very broad terms, maps were tools enabling people at a distance to understand and control events on the ground. Beyond this, most maps served more than one purpose. Generally, their aims can be seen as either strategic or practical. But we should note, too, the further motives of profit, professionalism, and enjoyment.

Profit could be looked for only from that small number of maps that were actually published. Policy fluctuated, but individual surveyors were sometimes allowed, or, in the case of such senior figures as Captain W. F. Owen, even assisted by the Admiralty, to work up some of their surveys for publication.[105] Surveyors General Smith and Bouchette, probably also Senior Surveyor Chewett, sought a mixture of patronage, renown (for themselves and their provinces), and profit by publishing general maps—though Bouchette actually lost £1,702 on his 1815 map and *Topographical Description*, since most of the support promised by the Lower Canada Assembly did not come through.[106] Publication itself was by specialized businesses in London. It was also accepted that these firms might continue to reissue such maps, often with very limited updating. For example, Smith's 1800 map of Upper Canada went through thirteen editions (to 1862), while Chewett's 1813 map went through six.[107] But the most obvious instances of commercialism were war maps, in this context those of the War of 1812. These were presumably aimed at a larger market and were correspondingly priced. Smith's map and *Topographical Description* was priced at £0.525 (compare Jane Austen's 1811 *Sense and Sensibility* at £0.75), but *A Map of the American Lakes and Adjoining Country: The Present Seat of War between Great Britain and the United States*, which was issued in January 1813, cost only £0.075.[108]

Many of the mapmakers discussed here were serving officers who could be sent (though they might also volunteer) to conduct surveys. Some surveyors, both civilian and military, sought to make a living out of mapmaking. In 1792, Holland listed for Simcoe nine deputy surveyors "under your Excellency's Command," although at least four were described as "not employed."[109] Their abilities no doubt varied. But regulations had been put in place in 1785, requiring that all surveyors be examined before their initial appointment,[110] that they should keep field notes, and that survey instruments should be tested before use. In 1792, Simcoe further directed (for Upper Canada) that surveys should "in general" be drawn on a scale of twenty chains to an inch and transmitted to the surveyor general's office with an explanatory report and a copy of the field notes.[111] Surveyors usually used their own tools, "compasses and, at least, horizontal theodelites."[112] Earnings depended on employment. In June 1793, the three assistant surveyors in Upper Canada were paid £0.20 a day when they were not employed, £0.375 when they were.[113] It is probable that the burst of land settlement after 1783 constituted a bonanza for surveyors, which must have been especially welcome to half-pay officers in the lean years of peace. In 1791, with the year's surveys budgeted at £1,351, Lord Dorchester sought to cut back: "As soon as the business of settling the Loyalists . . . should be brought to a conclusion, there could be no further occasion for the employment of extraordinary Surveyors . . . at stated daily allowances." The practice was to be phased out by the end of 1792.[114] This order prompted Chewett to protest to Collins, "I now find I have been serving my whole life for nothing . . . there is no surveyor in the same line as myself, that has the same right to expect continuation from having been always on service. . . . I trust you will be able to find me some employment either in our department or in some other before the expiration."[115]

Ultimately, Simcoe's activism prolonged the need for surveyors in Upper Canada, and Chewett continued in senior employment. In 1803, even the critical Lord Selkirk conceded, "The papers in the Surveyor Genl's Office are in very good arrangement."[116] Admittedly, efficiency here did not prevent serious

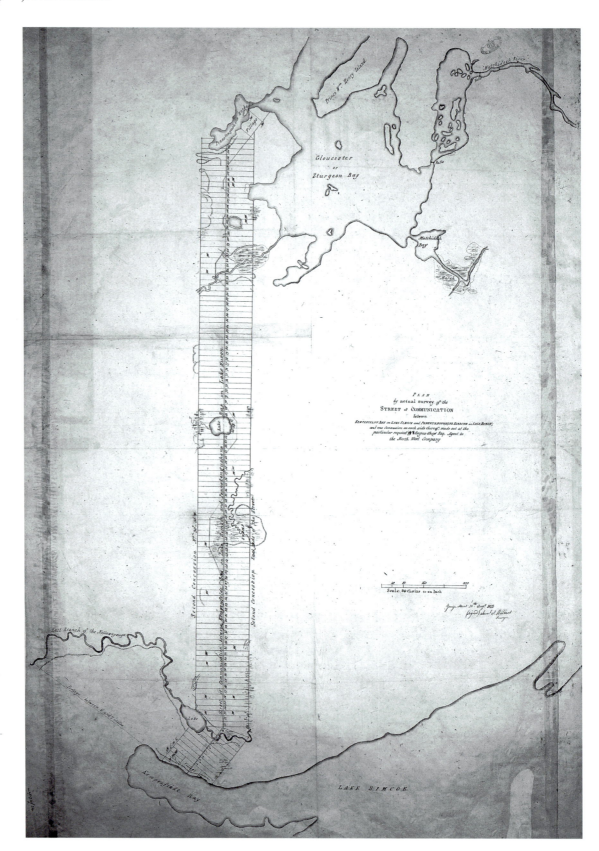

Figure 4. "Plan by Actual Survey of the Street of Communication between Kempenfeldt Bay on Lake Simcoe and Pennetengushene Harbour on Lake Huron and one Concession on each side thereof made out at the particular request of Angus Shaw, Esq., Agent to the North West Company" [W. C41 and also 334.3]. Public Record Office, National Archives, U.K.

difficulties over land grants from arising elsewhere. But the value of the professionals in the surveyor general's office was highlighted when C. B. Wyatt (who had succeeded David Smith as surveyor general) tried to get rid of the office's chief clerk, Thomas Ridout. The Upper Canada Executive Council took the line that Ridout was indispensable and that Wyatt was "very young, without experience." In 1807, Wyatt was suspended, and the office was left under the charge of Ridout and Chewett, who between them ran it until 1832.[117]

As in any profession, some surveyors and mapmakers fared well, others badly. Two famous explorers, Peter Pond and David Thompson, both died in poverty, although in Thompson's case this was due to misfortunes after his retirement. Nor did Thompson secure, in his lifetime, the full recognition he sought for his explorations. The North West Company supported him generously for three years on his return from the wilderness, so that he might produce his 1814 "Map of the North-West Territory . . . Comprising the Surveys and Discoveries of 20 years." William McGillivray hung this map in the great hall of Fort William on Lake Superior, but he did not publish it.[118] Thompson tried to have an updated version published in London in 1820, but he failed to secure backers. The map remained in Canada, largely unconsulted until the late 1850s, when new interest in the West prompted its issue (with little acknowledgment) by the Canadian government.[119] Alexander Mackenzie was more fortunate. His ghostwritten *Voyages from Montreal . . . to the Frozen and Pacific Oceans* appeared in London in 1801 and helped secure Mackenzie a knighthood. In 1802, it came out in the United States—where it contributed to the dispatch of the Lewis and Clark expedition—and also in French and German translations. A Russian translation followed in 1808.[120] Mackenzie, but not Thompson, gained both fame and fortune from his explorations.

As for more conventional surveyors, Patrick McNiff, after ten years' work in Canada, had acquired the reputation of being immobilized by even the "shadow of a difficulty," and by 1795 he was unemployed. He chose to stay in Detroit after its surrender to the United States, keeping a number of surveys, which he sold to General Wayne for one hundred dollars. He also secured several posts—including the surveyorship of Wayne County, and a forty-dollar-a-month post supervising military stores—only to be sacked in 1798.[121] On the other hand, Gother Mann (whose finances had been distinctly tight in the 1780s) died a very senior general, and William Owen and Henry Bayfield became admirals, all three having made their careers through surveying.[122] Similarly, Lieutenant Bryce became Major General Sir James Bryce, while Bouchette went from a lowly position in the Provincial Marine to surveyor general of Lower Canada, initially at £600 per annum (although in 1818 his salary was cut to £400 as an economy).[123] Bouchette speculated in land, as did David Smith, the first surveyor general of Upper Canada. Lord Selkirk remarked that "his [Smith's] inspection of the Field notes shows him every good and bad lot in any surveyed Township—which he has taken advantage of, for in all the Plans the lots marked D.W.S. are sure to be the choice spots—& next to these [acting Governor] P. Russell's & other persons into whose hands the S. Gl. found it proper to play."[124] For his services in Canada, Smith secured fees of £2,210, a pension of £200 per annum, and more than twenty thousand acres of land for his family (although these proved far less profitable than Selkirk implied). He spent the second half of his career in England as estate manager to the duke of Northumberland, in comfortable, but not striking, affluence.[125]

Surveying could be dangerous: the first day William Owen surveyed on the ice, four horses fell through, and he was nearly drowned; and in 1819, Commissioner Ogilvie and two other members of the British party died of malaria contracted in the Lake Erie marshes during the Treaty of Ghent boundary survey.[126] When it was not dangerous, surveying was often unpleasant. Bayfield cited the following drawbacks: soakings; scurvy deriving from putrid meat; "the Intermittent Fever, with which we were all at one time or other attacked far away from medical aid—under these circumstances we continued to work for weeks lying down on the bottom of our boat, having the paroxysms of the disease"; "being cut off from society, . . . particularly female society, for six years"; and "perhaps the greatest of all, . . . the myriads of mosskittoes [*sic*] and other Flies, . . . a pest which actually drives the wild animals from the forest."[127]

But for some, the exploring life held powerful attractions. When he was offended by the financial reconstruction of the North West Company in 1784, Peter Pond took his map of the interior off to the United States. On March 1, 1785, he submitted it to Congress, with a memorial claiming to have discovered a passage to the Arctic Ocean and suggesting that a Northwest Passage could fairly readily be found.[128] (He was perhaps strengthened in this hope by placing Lake Athabasca distinctly too far west, hence too close to Cook's discoveries on the Pacific coast.) Since Pond could generate no interest in the United States, he returned to Montreal, now voicing patriotic British sentiments. As acting Governor Hamilton noted, "Encouragement may attach him to the British interest, a want of it to court employment elsewhere."[129] Pond's heart was set on exploration and, no doubt, the glory it might produce. He went back to the wilderness, where he became increasingly optimistic about finding a route to the Pacific. Such a route would have proved valuable to Russia, which was then moving up the Aleutians toward Alaska. Pond talked of going from Great Slave Lake to Cook's "River" (Inlet) on the coast and returning via Russia. He was said to be "preparing a fine map to lay before the Empress of Russia." However, something, probably suspicion of his involvement in murder, interrupted this, and Pond returned east (as it proved, forever), leaving Alexander Mackenzie to attempt the journey he had himself contemplated.[130]

Others shared similar hopes. In 1789, Samuel Holland's rather wild son John (also a surveyor) interested Lord Grenville in such an expedition, but "the disagreement with the Spaniards relative to Nootka Sound then prevented my proceeding." In 1792, Samuel Holland had advocated ascertaining not only "the true position" of the "principal places" on the upper lakes, but also the length of Lake Superior and the distance from its western end to Captain Cook's "line of coast, discovered in the Western Ocean." In 1793–94, both Hollands discussed with Simcoe "proposals for exploring the passage overland to Nootka" and submitted costings.[131] Their ideas do not inspire confidence, and perhaps it is fortunate that nothing came of them.

No account of the attractions of surveying would be complete without reference to David Thompson, who left the Hudson's Bay Company's service rather precipitately in order to concentrate on it, and whose subsequent wedding present from his North West Company employers was a specially ordered set of drawing instruments and reams of mapping paper.[132] Thereafter he spent another dozen years in the interior, exploring and surveying. "Nothing less," he claimed (admittedly in his 1820 prospectus), "than an unremitting perseverance bordering on enthusiasm could have enabled him to have brought these maps to their present state; in early life he conceived the idea of this work, and Providence has given him to complete, amidst various dangers, all that one man could hope to perform."[133]

NOTES

The major annotated bibliography is Joan Winearls, *Mapping Upper Canada, 1780–1867: An Annotated Bibliography of Manuscript and Printed Maps* (Toronto: University of Toronto Press, 1991). In this chapter, maps described are identified by her numbers, prefaced by a W: thus, W.10 for "A Map of Part of Canada for the use of His Majesty's Secretary of State," 1790. As its title indicates, this map (like many others) was sent to the government in London; such maps are now in the Public Record Office (now National Archives) at Kew and listed in P. A. Penfold, ed., *Maps and Plans in the Public Record Office, II, America and West Indies* (London: Her Majesty's Stationery Office, 1974). Hereafter the Public Record Office is referred to as PRO; PRO citations give document classes, e.g., CO (Colonial Office), FO (Foreign Office), ADM (Admiralty), and MPG and MR (Map Collections).

1. Edward Umfreville, *The Present State of Hudson's Bay*, ed. W. Stewart Wallace (Toronto: Ryerson Press, 1954), 72; R. Douglas, ed., *Nipigon to Winnipeg: A Canoe Voyage through Western Ontario by Edward Umfreville in 1784* (Ottawa: R. Douglas, 1929), 15–16, 22, 33–34, 48, 338–39. In 1800, the North West Company hired "several men we did not want" to stop their rivals "getting any one who could guide them into the Churchill River or Athabasca." Marjorie Wilkins Campbell, *McGillivray, Lord of the Northwest* (Toronto: Clarke, Irwin, 1962), 108. In 1814, U.S. naval operations in Georgian Bay were effectively stymied by the "want of pilots acquainted with that unfrequented part of the lake." Claire Campbell, "'Behold me a sojourner in the wilderness': Early Encounters with the Georgian Bay," *Michigan Historical Review* 28 (Spring 2002): 47.

2. G. Malcolm Lewis, "Indicators of Unacknowledged Assimilations from Amerindian Maps on Maps of North America: Some General Principles Arising from a Study of La Vérendrye's Composite Map, 1728–29," *Imago Mundi* 38 (1986): esp. 10–15. In using straight lines to depict "linkages between points . . . Indian maps had . . . more in common with modern transport-users' guides than with topographic maps." Also see G. Malcolm Lewis, "First Nations Mapmaking in the Great Lakes Region in Intercultural Contexts: A Historical Review," *Michigan Historical Review* 30 (Fall 2004): 1–34. [Reprinted in this volume, see page 39.]

3. Douglas, ed., *Nipigon to Winnipeg*, 23, 25.

4. Roderick Mackenzie, "Reminiscences," in *Les Bourgeois de la Compagnie du Nord-Ouest*, ed. L. R. Masson (Quebec: A. Coté, 1889), 46–47.

5. Major Delafield to Secretary of State John Quincy Adams, October 9, 1823, in *The Unfortified Boundary: A Diary of the First Survey of the Canadian Boundary Line from St. Regis to the Lake of the Woods by Major Joseph Delafield*, ed. Robert McElroy and Thomas Riggs (New York: privately printed, 1943), 74–75. The phrase "direct water communication," in the context of Delafield's letter to Adams about the boundary commission, recalls the 1783 treaty provision that the border should run along the direct water communication through the lakes to the Lake of the Woods. Delafield is saying that, at points, the rivers, etc., were too circuitous for convenience, and travelers had simply cut across them using portages.

6. Louis C. Karpinski, *Historical Atlas of the Great Lakes and Michigan* (Lansing: Michigan Historical Commission, 1931), 73, with specific reference to Joseph Scott, *The United States Gazetteer* (Philadelphia: F. Bailey and R. Bailey, 1795).

7. Joshua Fry and Peter Jefferson, *The [Joshua] Fry and [Peter] Jefferson Map of Virginia and Maryland: A Facsimile of the First Edition in the Tracy W. McGregor Library* [printed c. 1752–1754] (Princeton: Princeton University Press, 1950). Contemporaries were aware of the imperfections even of good maps: cf. Thomas Penn's comment that Lewis Evans's 1755 "General Map of the Middle British Colonies . . . of the Lakes Erie, Ontario and Champlain," though "by much the best thing of its kind," had the Ohio "much straiter [*sic*] than an intelligent Indian laid it down . . . from his own observations," and Penn's earlier commendation of a map for Lord Halifax's use "with this observation, that Lake Erie is not of the shape laid down and is placed rather too far North (being copied from other Draughts)." Lawrence Henry Gipson, *Lewis Evans* (Philadelphia: Historical Society of Pennsylvania, 1939), 58, 61.

8. Pedley notes the "complete absence of critical criteria for the maps ordered." Mary S. Pedley, *The Map Trade in the Late Eighteenth Century: Letters to the London Map Sellers Jefferys and Faden* (Oxford: Voltaire Foundation, 2000), 24.

9. Spellings of *Phelippeaux* varied. Seymour I. Schwartz and Ralph E. Ehrenberg, *The Mapping of America* (New York: H. N. Abrams, 1980), 162, plate 97 (Nicholas Bellin's 1744 "Carte des Lacs du Canada"); Louis C. Karpinski, *Bibliography of the Printed Maps of Michigan, 1804–1880* (Lansing: Michigan Historical Commission, 1931), 43; "Treaty of Paris, Article 2," in *The Consolidated Treaty Series, 1781–1783*, ed. Clive Parry (Dobbs Ferry, N.Y.: Oceana Publications, 1969), 48: 491. Ironically, Charlevoix is commended, in other contexts, for his "historiographical concern for documentation of all kinds." When he passed through the lakes on a mission of exploration, he estimated distances and verified latitudes in calculations used by Bellin for his maps. "Charlevoix, Pierre-François-Xavier de," *Dictionary of Canadian Biography* (Toronto: University of Toronto Press, 1966), 3: 104–5, 107.

10. Edmund Berkeley and Dorothy Smith Berkeley, *Dr. John Mitchell: The Man Who Made the Map of North America* (Chapel Hill: University of North Carolina Press, 1974), 176–78; Ellis Huske, *The Present State of North America* (London: R. Dodsley and J. Dodsley, 1755), 27.

11. For a warning that the line to the Mississippi "probably should go south" not west, see Benjamin Vaughan to Lord Shelburne, February 21, 1783, British Library, Add. MS.42,397 fols. 256–57; for a demonstration that "there is no such thing as a Long Lake as expressed in the Treaty," see Benjamin Frobisher to Adam Mabane, April 19, 1784, in *Documents Relating to the North West Company*, ed. W. Stewart Wallace (Toronto: Champlain Society, 1934), 67.

12. In 1760 to 1764, effort was devoted to locating a safe passage over the sandbar at the north end of Lake St. Clair; one survey party was wiped out by Indians in 1763. Work was also done on the exit from Lake Erie into the Niagara River. More generally, Lieutenant Brehm and Ensign Hutchins were instructed, while visiting the surrendered French forts west of Lake Erie, "to explore the country in the best manner you can, taking Plans or Sketches . . . as much as time will permit you." Brehm also updated a French plan of Detroit and produced one of Lake Ontario. Keith R. Widder, "The Cartography of Dietrich Brehm and Thomas Hutchins and the Establishment of British Authority in the Western Great Lakes Region, 1760–1763," *Cartographica* 36 (1999): esp. 3, 8, 10, 14–15, 17; Don W. Thomson, *Men and Meridians: The History of Surveying and Mapping in Canada* (Ottawa: R. Duhamel, 1966), 84–85. In 1790, the Engineers' Drawing Room in Quebec also held an "Actual Survey of the South Side of Lake Erie by Capt. Montresor, 1764," Gother Mann's "Index" of the plans there, forwarded by Lord Dorchester to William Grenville, November 10, 1790, PRO: CO 42/72 fols. 120–23.

13. James F. Kenney, ed., "Journal of Walter Butler," *Canadian Historical Review* 1, no. 4 (1920): 381–91.

14. W.10; PRO: CO 700 Canada40. This lists the surveys on which the map was based. The two mentioned were "From Montreal to the Long Sault in the Ottawa River" (Collins, 1766); and "The St. Lawrence and Islands from the Cedars to Lake Ontario" (Lieutenant Carleton, 1768). The latter survey had been curtailed by Indians, who stopped Carleton from going beyond Ogdensburg. Marilyn B. M. Olsen, "Aspects of the Mapping of Southern Ontario, 1783–1867" (M. Phil. dissertation, University of London, July 1968), 46.

15. General Haldimand to Thomas Townshend, October 25, 1782, PRO: CO 42/43 fols. 209–10; Thomas Townshend to General Haldimand, February 28, 1783, PRO: CO 42/44 fols. 47–48.

16. General Haldimand to Thomas Townshend, May 7, 1783, PRO: CO 42/44 fol. 120.

17. There survives a sketch, delivered in December 1783, saying, "The Mohawks from Lachine have pitched upon this Tract of Land and Wish Government to give them a grant for it in lieu of their lands . . . usurped by the [American] Rebels." W.409.

18. General Haldimand to Lord North, June 2, 1783, PRO: CO 42/44 fol. 126; Samuel Holland to General Haldimand, June 26, 1783, in E. A. Cruikshank, *The Settlement of the United Empire Loyalists on the Upper St. Lawrence and the Bay of Quinte in 1784: A Documentary Record* (Toronto: Ontario Historical Society, 1934), 2–3. The north-shore survey was completed in 1784; the survey of the Niagara River was undertaken in 1785. The resulting plan is W.4.

19. Sir John Johnson to General Haldimand, August 18, 1783; General Haldimand to Major Ross, September 15, 1783; "A Journal of Lieut. French's Proceedings from September 29 to October 13," all in Cruikshank, *Settlement*, 5, 11, 14–18. Lieutenant French found good land along the Ottawa and Rideau Rivers, but along the Gananoque not as much "as would serve one Farmer." The sketches are W.411.

20. Cruikshank, *Settlement*, 18–21, 25–29; see also the "Plan which was received with Captain Sherwood's Journal" ("Journal from Montreal to Lake Ontario," September–October 1783), estimating—optimistically—that 3,415 families could be settled on the north side of the Bay of Quinte, 1,857 on the south side, and at least 250 on "the Isle Tonte." W.410.

21. General Haldimand to Lord North, July 21, 1783, PRO: CO 42/44 fol. 181; General Haldimand to Lord North, August 27, 1783, PRO: CO 42/45 fol. 1; Sir John Johnson to General Haldimand, August 11, 1783; General Haldimand to Major Ross, September 15, 1783; and General Haldimand's instructions of September 11, 1783, to John Collins as to the laying out of Loyalist townships, all in Cruikshank, *Settlement*, 4, 8–9, 12, 21–22. Also see Thomson, *Men and Meridians*, 219ff.

22. W.412.

23. General Haldimand to Lord North, November 6, 27, 1783, PRO: CO 42/46 fols. 7, 41–43; Lord North to General Haldimand, August 8, 1783, PRO: CO 42/44 fol. 159; Thomas Townshend, Baron Sydney to General Haldimand, April 8, 1784, PRO: CO 42/46 fol. 55.

24. General Haldimand to Sir John Johnson, March 15, 23, 1784; General Haldimand to Colonel A. S. de Peyster, March 29, 1784, in *Records of Niagara, 1784–7*, ed. E. A. Cruikshank (Niagara-on-the-Lake, Ont.: Niagara Historical Society, 1928), 12, 14, 15–16, 28–32 (May 22, 1784 purchase of some 2.8 million acres from the Mississaugas), 55. Indians who had settled near Kingston were encouraged, but not compelled, to remove to the Grand River.

25. E.g., W.665 (copy of a "Sketch of a Tract of Land purchased of the Mississaugas for His Majesty by Col. Guy Johnson at Niagara 9th May 1781"); W.673 2 ("Plan of a Tract of Land situate in the District of Nassau reserved for the Mohawk Indians . . . agreeable to an Order of . . . 4th January 1791—Taken from Mr. Jones Plan of the settled part of that District"); W.15 (a sketch of Upper Canada colored to show "Lands purchased from the Indians," "The settlement proposed on Lake Huron," and "Brant's Grant," with "The Huron Reserve at Detroit & the Indian lands white"); John Graves Simcoe to Henry Dundas, March 10, 1792, in *The Correspondence of Lieut. Governor John Graves Simcoe*, ed. E. A. Cruikshank (Toronto: Ontario Historical Society, 1923), 1: 118–19; W.722 ("Plan [probably of the early 1800s but with information to 1819] shewing the Lands granted to the Six Nation Indians situated on each side of the Grand River," marked "To be kept to copy from [signed] W. C." [William Chewett]).

26. Quotation: Winearls, *Mapping Upper Canada*, ix; "conjectured to be . . .," W.328; 1795 purchase, W.918 2.

27. Admittedly, the list does not cover all known surveys; in 1787 Gother Mann was laying out Sorel below Montreal and exploring "a variety of situations at present but little known" on the Lake Champlain border. Hilda Maud Thorold and Violet Mary Mann, *The Mann Family . . . Compiled from Old Letters* (n.p.: privately printed, 1950), 27–28.

28. Governor Simcoe's mapmaking wife found "our Maps to be little better than Sketches, little of the country being surveyed. The Surveyors draw slowly & I am told when they want to suit their map to the Paper do not scruple cutting off a few miles of a River or adding to it." Mary Quayle Innis, ed., *Mrs. Simcoe's Diary, with Illustrations from the Original Manuscript* (Toronto: Macmillan, 1965), 54.

29. In fact Philip, Frey had worked between Detroit and Niagara in 1784 to 1789. When he left for the United States, his Niagara work was completed by his former assistant Augustus Jones, while Patrick McNiff succeeded him in Hesse. McNiff's maps have been criticized, but they were partly "delineated from my own Surveys, made in the Years, 1784, 1785, 1786, 1787, 1788, 1789," W.11. In 1789, Commander Henry Ford and McNiff conducted what the latter called a "Coasting Survey" of the St. Clair River and one of the "South Shore of Lake Erie." PRO: MR 1/1099. A sketch of the river from Fort Niagara to the landing above the falls "may date from the 1770s"; and Allan Macdonell had mapped "New Settlement Niagara" in 1783. Olsen, "Aspects of the Mapping," 14–15; Winearls, *Mapping Upper Canada*, 11, 12, 315, 418, 664, 666, 668, 670, 908, 910.

30. Samuel Holland to Governor Simcoe, October 4, 1792, in Thomson, *Men and Meridians*, 227–28. In 1790, the Quebec Council had rejected John Collins's proposal for determining the latitudes and longitudes of salient points "between the entrance of Lake Superior and the town of Montreal." John L. Ladell, *They Left Their Mark: Surveyors and Their Role in the Settlement of Ontario* (Toronto: Dundurn Press, 1993), 83. Sebert claims that "in 1793 the position of Norway House [Manitoba] was known to much greater precision" than that of Detroit. "In Upper Canada land settlement was the order of the day—fancy maps could come later. On the prairies . . . small-scale maps were needed so that trading routes could be planned . . . back at headquarters." L. M. Sebert, "The Land Surveys of Ontario," *Cartographica* 17, no. 3 (1980): 96.

31. General Haldimand to Lord North, November 6 (Detroit), 27, 1783; General Haldimand to Lord Sydney, July 16, 1784, PRO: CO 42/46 fols. 8, 42, 212.

32. Henry Hamilton to Lord Sydney, March 10, April 7, June 6, 1785, PRO: CO 42/47, esp. 385–87, 396–97, 633, forwarding John Collins's April 7 "Plan of part of a projected communication from Cateraquoui to Lake Huron," PRO: MPG 1/1153, described in W.6.

33. Benjamin Frobisher to Henry Hamilton (in response to an inquiry of March 10, 1785), May 2, 1785, PRO: CO 42/47, 659–73. Winearls states that "no map of the full route from [Collins's] 1785 survey has been found." Winearls, *Mapping Upper Canada*, 6. However, it is cited on subsequent plans. See W.315, W.315 2. In 1792, Simcoe extracted and sent to London the section describing a salt spring, Collins's "Proceedings on my route from Kingston to Lake Huron." W.6 2; PRO: MPG 1/91. Cited in *Simcoe*, ed. Cruikshank, 1: 159.

34. The plan was largely derived from "information . . . from Mr. Curot, who resided several years at Toronto." PRO: MPG 1/426; see also W.5; Cruikshank, ed., *Simcoe*, 1: facing p. 8. Captain Hare had been sent in 1780 by General Haldimand to explore routes between Toronto and Lake Huron, but his journey seems to have had little impact. Ladell, *They Left Their Mark*, 59–60.

35. W.313, endorsed "Toronto Purchase in 1787. A. Aitken did the surveying for the purchase boundaries in 1788."

36. One version of this plan carries a later comment, "does not agree with the Survey made by L. Kotté in 1783. Kotté's Survey agrees with one taken in 1793 by J. Bouchette." W.2010; see also Penfold, ed., *Maps and Plans in the Public Record Office*, nos. 1599, 1601.

37. Lord Dorchester to Lord Sydney, January 16, 1787; Lord Sydney to Lord Dorchester, September 14, 1787, in *Records of Niagara*, ed. Cruikshank, 101, 120.

38. Dorchester's instructions (of May 29, 1788) and Mann's report were copied as "Plans with Lord Dorchester's Instructions to Capt. Gother Mann—in Ld. Dorchester's no. 58 of 26 Oct. 1790," PRO: CO 700 Canada38 fols. 20–32 (plans), 2–3 (instructions). Mann's report is dated December 6, 1788.

39. Ibid.

40. W.7.

41. A, "Harbour at Kingston"; B, "Plan of Toronto" [*sic*]; C, "Niagara to Lake Erie"; D, "Lake Erie to Detroit"; E, "Falls of St. Mary"; also "Matchadosh Bay, Lake Huron." Winearls, W.7 4, reproduces Mann's "Sketch of Lake Huron 1788," which was long used "as a source for general maps." See also NMC 18558, Public Archives of Canada (hereafter PAC), Ottawa.

42. PRO: CO 700 Canada38, esp. fols. 2–3, 5, 10–11, 15–19, 21–23, 24, 25–32.

43. E.g., "Plan of Toronto Harbor with the Rocks, Shoals & Soundings Thereof Surveyed . . . by Joseph Bouchette, 15th Nov. 1792," W.2013. Bouchette later waxed lyrical about the bay's then "untamed beauty." Thomson, *Men and Meridians*, 265.

44. W.9; La Force and Kotté, "Survey of Lake Ontario," PRO: CO 700 Canada44; the accompanying journal, PRO: CO 42/70, 75ff.; "Survey of the South Shore of Lake Erie . . .," PRO: MR 1/1099; the accompanying journal, PRO: CO 42/70, 101–13. Dorchester rounded this off by sending the "Map of the Part of Canada," which is described in the introductory passage at the start of the notes and in note 14, as well as lists of the 101 plans held in the surveyor general's office and of the numerous

maps in the office of the commanding engineer in Quebec. Lord Dorchester to William Grenville, November 10, 1790, PRO: CO 42/72 fols. 92, 94–95, 98–136.

45. Andrew Ellicott had secured British permission to visit the area in order to ascertain the longitude of the western end of Lake Ontario, on which depended the Lake Erie section of the New York–Pennsylvania border that the U.S. federal government had commissioned him to survey. While there, out of personal interest he also "made the first accurate measurement of the length of the [Niagara River] and height of the falls and rapids." *American National Biography*, ed. John A. Garraty and Mark C. Carnes (New York: Oxford University Press, 1999), 7: 416; Catharine Van Cortland Mathews, *Andrew Ellicott: His Life and Letters* (New York: Grafton Press, 1908).

46. Captain Simcoe to Lord Barrington, June 1, 1755, as recalled in John Graves Simcoe to Evan Nepean, December 3, 1789, in *Simcoe*, ed. Cruikshank, 1: 8.

47. John Simcoe to Henry Dundas, October 19, 1793, in ibid., 2: 91.

48. John Simcoe to Sir Joseph Banks, January 8, 1791, in ibid., 1:18; Romulus was the founder of Rome.

49. John Simcoe to Henry Dundas, December 7, 1791, in ibid., 1: 90; the reproduction opposite that page of the "Survey," W.911. On November 12, 1792, McNiff and Jones were instructed to survey the Thames (and a site for a town at its forks) and to look for a connection with the Grand River. On December 19, Jones was further instructed "to explore for a route from Thames R to Burlington Bay." W.912 and W.913 (both dated 1793) were the results.

50. Littlehales expands further on the site's advantages. See Major E. B. Littlehales, "Journal from Niagara to Detroit," in *Simcoe*, ed. Cruikshank, 1: 293.

51. Richard Cartwright to Isaac Todd, October 14, 1793, in ibid., 2: 89. Simcoe's February 4–March 10, 1793, journey from Niagara to Detroit and back is chronicled by Major Littlehales in ibid., 1: 288–93; the journey from Humber Bay via Lake Simcoe to Matchedash Bay and back is told by Alexander Macdonell in ibid., 2: 70–79. Then from March 26 to April 27, 1794, Simcoe again went overland to Detroit. He traveled on to the Miami River, returning by ship. Ibid., 2: 219.

52. On September 20, 1793, Simcoe sent London "an actual survey of the [River] Thames, as far as it serves to communicate between Lakes Ontario and [St. Clair] together with the Military Road leading thereto, and which is now opening by the Queen's Rangers." Ibid., 2: 56. His optimistic account on October 19 of the journey via Lake Simcoe was accompanied by two charts and the statement that he had "directed the Surveyor early in the next Spring to ascertain the precise distance of the several Routs [*sic*] which I have done myself the honor of detailing to you." Ibid., 2: 90–91.

53. W.21; PRO: MPG 1/98.

54. Landmann records "passing through Chatham and London without knowing it" in a winter journey in 1800; in the wilderness, he had to bridge streams by felling trees across them. George Landmann, *Adventures and Recollections of Colonel Landmann, Late of the Corps of Royal Engineers* (London: Colburn, 1852), 2: 136. For the final choice of a site for London, Ontario, see Winearls, *Mapping Upper Canada*, xxv, and map descriptions nos. 1568–71.

55. W.18; reproduced in *Mrs. Simcoe's Diary*, ed. Innis, 92–93.

56. W.16.

57. David W. Smith (Smyth), *A Map of the Province of Upper Canada . . . Compiled at the Request of . . . John G. Simcoe* (London: W. Faden, 1800); W.843; W.844; W.30.

58. Olsen, "Mapping of Southern Ontario," 95, 105–6, 110–11. Ibid., 82–112, analyzes both Chewett's 1792–1793 and Smith's 1800 maps, W.16, W.30.

59. Cartwright to Todd, October 14, 1793, also October 21, 1792, in *Simcoe*, ed. Cruikshank, 1: 239–40. For Brant, see Patrick C. T. White, *Lord Selkirk's Diary, 1803–1804: A Journal of His Travels in British North America and the Northeastern United States* (Toronto: Champlain Society, 1958), 153.

60. White, *Selkirk's Diary*, 145–46. In 1797, council members were compensated for the rigors of the move by land grants of

six thousand acres each. Gerald M. Craig, *Upper Canada: The Formative Years, 1784–1841* (Toronto: McClelland and Stewart, 1963), 69.

61. Lord Dorchester to the Duke of Portland, April 16, 1796, PRO: CO 42/105 fol. 154, enclosing maps MPG 1/33–41.

62. E.g., "General Survey of the River St. Lawrence . . . from Quebec to Montreal—From Original British Documents," with "Montreal to Ontario . . . added from an original [possibly of 1768] in Genl. Montresor's public collection by order of the Hon. J. Armstrong, Secy at War," February 1813, W.454.

63. W.507; W.455.

64. Peter Porter to John Quincy Adams, February 12, 1822, RG 76 E 141, no. 50, U.S. National Archives, College Park, Md.

65. Winearls, *Mapping Upper Canada*, xxi, nos. 39–41, 462; James Wilkinson, *Memoirs of My Own Times* (Philadelphia: Abraham Small, 1816).

66. Ruth McKenzie, *The St. Lawrence Survey Journals of Captain Henry Wolsey Bayfield, 1829–1853* (Toronto: Champlain Society, 1984), 1: xvi.

67. "It seems in many respects preferable to Mackinac which has been given back to the Americans, and the latter has apparently no further advantages over it in situation except that arising from the prejudices of the Indians." PRO: CO 42/171 fols. 126–27.

68. PRO: MPG 1/175 (schematic map of the road from Lake Simcoe to Penetanguishene), recalling Wilmot's survey, W.C41, for which see the discussion on pg. 108.

69. Sir Edward Owen's reports can be found in "Appendix, Mr. Croker's Letter of the 6th July 1816, State of the Naval Establishment in Canada & Survey of the Lakes by Sr. E. Owen," PRO: CO 42/171 fols. 4ff.

70. See Thomas Hurd's letter of May 7, 1814, setting out these deficiencies "of our knowledge" worldwide. Archibald Day, *The Admiralty Hydrographic Service, 1795–1919* (London: H.M.S.O., 1967), 27–29. In 1818, nine surveys were in progress (four in home waters, three in North America [including the lakes], one in Sicily, and one in Australia). In 1823, there were twelve (the locations of the surveys were much as before, but with an extra survey in Newfoundland and a new one in West Africa, also an extra survey in U.K. waters). In 1829, there were fifteen (seven in home waters, two in North America, three in South America, and one each in West Africa, the Mediterranean, and "Particular Service"). L. S. Dawson, *Memoirs of Hydrography, Including Brief Biographies of the Principal Officers . . . between the Years 1758 and 1885* (Eastbourne, U.K.: H. W. Keay, 1885), 47–48, 101–2.

71. For a good general description of the initial instructions and of the surveys, see McKenzie, *St. Lawrence Survey Journals*, xvi–xvii. Also see PRO: CO 42/171 fols. 94–95, 99, 127, 258–61, esp. fol. 259, "Instructions . . . 1815." After finishing the Great Lakes, Owen was supposed to survey the Richelieu River and Lake Champlain.

72. A Troughton's or Jones's "Sextant cut to 10ths," a "Troughtons Theodelite cut to Minutes Horizontal," a "Dollands Telescope" (one of the two instruments he had had in each category had been worn out on Lake Huron), an "Arnolds 2020 timekeeper," two "Masseys Patent Logs," a "Caters Compass" and "a good small boat compass," a set of magnetic bars "to touch the Compass needles," and for drafting his maps a pentagraph, a pair of proportional compasses, and two steel pens. List forwarded in Commissioner Barrie's letter no. 18 to J. W. Croker, November 16, 1822, PRO: ADM 1/3445 (also available on microfilm, reel B 3710, PAC).

73. Commissioner Barrie to Henry Bayfield, April 20, 1823; Barrie's 1820 instructions to Midshipman Grant, who was further enjoined never to send his crew to work ashore without their breakfasts. Commissioner Barrie's Letter-book, F 66, vol. 3, 37, 192, MG 24, PAC.

74. Henry Bayfield to Captain Beaufort, November 26, 1845, microfilm, reel A 424 PAC (quoted in McKenzie, *St. Lawrence Survey Journals*, xxvi).

75. One exception was the appearance in William James, *A Full and Correct Account of the Military Occurrences of the Late War between*

Great Britain and the United States of America (London: privately printed, 1818), facing p. 131, of "A Map of Part of Lake Ontario ... from an actual Survey by Captn. W. F. Owen, R.N. 1816"; W.468.

76. Six sheets related to Lake Superior, three to the St. Marys River and the exit by the Neebish Islands, seven to Lake Huron, two to the St. Clair River and the Detroit River, four to Lake Erie and the exit to Niagara, one to York (Toronto) harbor, and five to the St. Lawrence River from Kingston to the Galop Rapids. Winearls, *Mapping Upper Canada*, W.C 96–W.C 123, with their individual prices.

77. McKenzie, *St. Lawrence Survey Journals*, xxvii; Stanley Fillmore and R. W. Sandilands, *The Chartmakers: The History of Nautical Surveying in Canada* (Toronto: NC Press, 1983), 57–58.

78. McKenzie, *St. Lawrence Survey Journals*, xxvi; comment enclosed in Bayfield to Beaufort, November 26, 1845.

79. Olsen, "Mapping of Southern Ontario," 215–16, 220. The maps mentioned are W.43 and W.69 2. Still, some surprising distortions continued. Before 1826, most depictions of the St. Lawrence and St. Clair Rivers were too long; thereafter, they were too short.

80. Owen's Instructions, PRO: CO 42/171 fol. 258; J. W. Croker to Henry Goulburn, July 6, 1816, calling attention to the Admiralty's desiderata in this connection, in ibid., fols. 4, 6–8. See also Commissioner Anthony Barclay's (largely unconvinced) comments to Stratford Canning on Sir Edward Owen's views, December 13, 1821, PRO: FO 5/170 fols. 188–92. Security concerns were, of course, equally in evidence on the American side.

81. Parry, ed., *Consolidated Treaty Series, 1813–1815*, 63: 426–28, Articles 6, 7.

82. *New York Evening Post*, April 23, 1818, 2.

83. Peter Porter to Secretary of State Adams, November 3, 1817, cited in Francis M. Carroll, *A Good and Wise Measure: The Search for the Canadian-American Boundary, 1783–1842* (Toronto: University of Toronto Press, 2001), 101–2; and Porter to Adams, February 12, 1822, portion in McElroy and Riggs, *Unfortified Border*, 64. The maps for Article 6 (St. Regis River to St. Marys River) and Article 7 (thence to the Lake of the Woods) are listed by Winearls, *Mapping Upper Canada* (W. D5-D6, W. D14-D16). They are also mostly reproduced in John Bassett Moore, *History and Digest of the International Arbitrations to Which the United States Has Been a Party* (Washington, D.C.: Government Printing Office, 1898), vol. 6.

84. Porter to Adams, February 12, 1822; "Commissioners' Instructions in Respect of Article 7," in McElroy and Riggs, *Unfortified Boundary*, 64–65.

85. Carroll, *Good and Wise Measure*, 134–38, n. 345; see also idem, "The Search for the Canadian-American Boundary along the Michigan Frontier, 1819–1827: The Boundary Commissions under Articles Six and Seven of the Treaty of Ghent," *Michigan Historical Review* 30 (Fall 2004): 77–104. [Reprinted in this volume, see p. 123.]

86. Col. R. G. England to John Simcoe, July 30, 1792; John Simcoe to Henry Dundas, November 4, 1792, in *Simcoe*, ed. Cruikshank, 1: 185, 249.

87. John Simcoe to Evan Nepean, April 28, 1792 ("greatly fear thro' the incompetence ..."); John Simcoe to Henry Dundas, June 21, 1792, both in ibid., 1: 146–47, 172–73.

88. "Smith (Smyth), Sir David William," *Dictionary of Canadian Biography*, 7: 812.

89. In 1783, Haldimand formulated a design for the rapid laying out of township lots in squares; in 1792, surveyors estimated the time required to lay out such a township at fifty-seven days. At least thirteen variations of such approved plans were used between then and 1799, W.3, 1–13. The most important one was D. W. Smith's 1792–93 "Chequered Plan" discriminating "the Reserves of the Crown from those of the Clergy"; W.3 12. For a discussion of this topic (with reproductions of plans), see Ladell, *They Left Their Mark*, 64, 68–69, 80–82, 89, 93.

90. Sebert, "Land Surveys of Ontario," 99–101; Olsen, "Mapping of Southern Ontario," 221.

91. Benjamin Frobisher and Joseph Frobisher to General Haldimand, October 4, 1784; Governor Hamilton to Baron Sydney, April 9, 1785; Peter Pond's Memorial, April 18, 1785, all in PRO: CO 42/47, 637–39, 649–51, 667. On June 6, 1785, Hamilton

forwarded to London a map of North America from Lake Huron to the Pacific (PRO: MPG 1/425), of which Penfold writes that it "may be based on information supplied by Peter Pond but is not his work." Penfold, ed., *Maps and Plans*, no. 80.

92. Mackenzie's diary was titled "Journal of a Voyage performed . . . ," *Dictionary of Canadian Biography*, 5: 538. Campbell claims that Mackenzie's two great expeditions each cost the company more than fifteen hundred pounds. Marjorie Wilkins Campbell, *The North West Company* (Toronto: Macmillan, 1957), 87.

93. Lord Dorchester to the Duke of Portland, April 16, 1796, in *Simcoe*, ed. Cruikshank, 4: 246.

94. Hiring de Pincier was expensive, probably costing forty-five pounds though perhaps as much as two hundred seventy pounds. The relevant sentence is ambiguous in McTavish, Frobisher & Co.'s April 1802 petition, C series, vol. 363, reel C-2930, 8–19, microfilm, PAC. An 1852 copy of his "Plan of the Falls of St. Mary . . . Surveyed by Order of the North West Company by Theodore de Pincier 1797" is described in W.845 2; a microfiche can be found at H2/410 St. Mary's R/1797, microfilm, PAC.

95. De Bruyères's report, September 10, 1802, on the situation on the north shore of the St. Marys, C series, vol. 382, reel C-2395, 215–18, microfilm, PAC, and that at the "Entrance of the Kaministiqua River" from Lake Superior (where, however, no problems arose), ibid., 221–25. He enclosed maps of both (W.852, W.853). In March 1803, Forsyth Richardson (acting for the XY Company) was sent a copy of the "Plan of St. Marys" on which Lt. Governor Hunter's compromise proposals were shown. On December 23, 1803, they sent Hunter's aide, Major Green, an account of Mackenzie's unilateral actions, with a "Sketch" illustrating both the North West Company's "pickets" obstructing the portage and the bypass and other facilities Mackenzie had constructed or commenced. Ibid., 29, 37–41 (the file is out of chronological order on the microfilm).

96. Joseph Bayliss, Estelle Bayliss, and Milo Quaife, *River of Destiny: The St. Marys* (Detroit: Wayne University Press, 1955), esp., 56, 60, 63–64, 74–77; also see W.856.

97. Alexander Mackenzie, *A General History of the Fur Trade from Canada to the North-West* (1801; facsimile ed., Ann Arbor, Mich.: University Microfilms, 1968), lviii. There is a misapprehension, based on Thompson's retrospective 1840s account, *David Thompson's Narrative, 1784–1812*, ed. Richard Glover (Toronto: Champlain Society, 1962), 186, that his mission was to trace the 49th parallel and the North West Company's trading posts' relationship to it. But his contemporary journals provide no support for this, and the 49th parallel was only picked as a possible United States–Canadian border when President Jefferson needed grounds for withdrawing his support for the King-Hawkesbury treaty, in view of Senate opposition.

98. "Sketched," W.850; "surveyed," W.851; "map," reproduced in many sheets at the end of *David Thompson's Narrative of His Explorations in Western America*, ed. J. B. Tyrrell (Toronto: Champlain Society, 1916); also produced in reduced format in *David Thompson's Narrative*, ed. Glover.

99. Campbell, *North West Company*, 112–13, 138, 160–61; George C. Patterson, *Land Settlement in Upper Canada, 1783–1840*, Sixteenth Report of the Department of Archives for the Province of Ontario (Toronto: C. W. James, 1921), 109 (quotation).

100. Joseph Bouchette, *A Topographical Description of the Province of Lower Canada, with Remarks upon Upper Canada* (London: W. Faden, 1815), 609. Yonge Street, now Toronto's leading north-south artery, ran north from what was then called York to Lake Simcoe. Campbell, *North West Company*, puts the figure at twelve thousand pounds. Campbell's later work, *McGillivray*, 97, cites the more persuasive amount of twelve hundred pounds (plus improvements to the Niagara ox-cart road, a road at Detroit for transporting locally purchased provisions, and, of course, the Sault Ste. Marie canoe lock).

101. North West Company's petition of November 5, 1810, to Lt. Governor Gore, and his reply rejecting said petition on November 29, 1810, PRO: CO 42/351 fols. 123–24, 125. Sir Isaac Brock forwarded the correspondence to Lord Liverpool on November 23, 1811, mentioning that Gore had directed the making of a survey, and enclosing the resulting "Plan of a Tract of Land intended to be purchased from the Chippewa Indians . . . Containing about 250,000 acres for £4000 Halfx Currency," and related documents. Ibid., fols. 121, 128, 130. This plan shows both the currently proposed purchase (whose boundaries were also verbally defined) and the two previous ones it consolidated. W.333 2; PRO: CO 42/351 fols. 127–28, 130.

102. W.C41; Campbell, *North West Company*, 114, 189.

103. Bouchette, *Topographical Description*, 609; William Dunlop, *Recollections of the War of 1812* (Toronto: Historical Publishing Co., 1908), 90–100; Ladell, *They Left Their Mark*, 108–9; Percy J. Robinson, "Yonge Street and the North West Company," *Canadian Historical Review* 24 (1943): esp. 259–64.

104. W.12. "Probably the map Henry Motz instructed the Land Board of Hesse to make 19 Jan. 1790."

105. Dawson, *Memoirs of Hydrography*, 46, 48, 100.

106. "Bouchette, Joseph," *Dictionary of Canadian Biography*, 7: 95–98.

107. Winearls, *Mapping Upper Canada*, xxii.

108. Claire Tomalin, *Jane Austen: A Life* (London: Penguin, 2000), 221; Bouchette, *Topographical Description*, W.30; Bouchette, *Map of the American Lakes*, W.42.

109. Samuel Holland to John Simcoe, June 7, 1792, in *Simcoe*, ed. Cruikshank, 5: 13–14. In October 1792, the Lower Canada Surveyor General's office employed, besides Holland and Deputy Surveyor Collins, sixteen surveyors; in 1793, it employed twenty-seven. Claude Boudreau, *La Cartographie au Québec, 1760–1840* (Sainte Foy, Quebec: Presses de l'Université Laval, 1994), 71.

110. Chewett's 1792 examination of Lewis Grant involved arithmetic, trigonometry, and surveying (a field, a small and a large river, laying out a township), fixing the meridian and finding the latitude, finding the variation of a compass, and "levelling, for the purpose of making aqueducts." Ladell, *They Left Their Mark*, 94–95. In 1798, Chewett noted Wilmot's lack of knowledge of trigonometry, the theodolite, and the fixing of a meridian; he could only run a line on a given course, and further study was recommended. In 1820, Chewett sent out "detailed instructions" on "ascertaining latitude and correcting for magnetic variation." Olsen, "Mapping of Southern Ontario," 33–36.

111. Thomson, *Men and Meridians*, 223, 227.

112. Olsen, "Mapping of Southern Ontario," 35–36. In 1791, Collins owned "A Theodelite, by Rowley," a "3' 8" Acre master Telescope" with "magnifying Powers . . . for Land Objects about 50 times, . . . for Astronomical uses 80 times," one "Hadley's Quadrant," one "Mason's level," and both an English and a French chain. "Report of the Quebec Land Committee," June 7, 1791, PRO: CO 42/85 fol. 332.

113. John Simcoe to Henry Dundas, June 21, 1792, in *Simcoe*, ed. Cruikshank, 1: 173. Simcoe also adjusted deputy surveyors' allowances for the feeding of survey parties to bring them into line with Lower Canada's rates. Thomson, *Men and Meridians*, 227. Naval surveyors were more highly skilled—and paid: £0.75 a day from 1817 for lieutenants (such as Bayfield) and £0.25 a day for officers used as assistant surveyors. Dawson, *Memoirs of Hydrography*, 47.

114. Ladell, *They Left Their Mark*, 85.

115. Ibid., 86.

116. White, *Lord Selkirk's Diary*, 151; Patterson, *Land Settlement in Upper Canada*, 89, 103–4, 107–8.

117. Patterson, *Land Settlement*, 107–8; "Chewett (Chewitt), William," *Dictionary of Canadian Biography*, 7: 175.

118. In 1831, Ross Cox observed that "this immense territory is very little known, except to those connected with the Company; and if it did not interfere with their interests, the publication of Mr. Thompson's map would be a most valuable addition to our geographical knowledge." Ross Cox, *The Columbia River; or, Scenes and Adventures during a Residence of Six Years on the Western Side of the Rocky Mountains* (1831; reprint, Norman: University of Oklahoma Press, 1957), 332.

119. Tyrrell, ed., *David Thompson's Narrative*, lxiv; Richard I. Ruggles, *A Country So Interesting: The Hudson's Bay Company and Two Centuries of Mapping, 1670–1870* (Montreal: McGill–Queen's University Press, 1991), 283, n. 3; D'Arcy Jenish, *Epic Wanderer: David Thompson and the Mapping of the Canadian West* (Toronto: Doubleday Canada, 2003), 217–18.

120. Alexander Mackenzie, *Voyages from Montreal, on the River St. Laurence, through the Continent of North America, to the Frozen and Pacific Oceans; in the Years 1789 and 1793: With a Preliminary Account of the Rise, Progress, and Present State of the Fur Trade of That*

Country; Illustrated with Maps (London: T. Cadell Jun. and W. Davies, 1801); "Mackenzie, Sir Alexander," *Dictionary of Canadian Biography*, 5: 541, 543.

121. "McNiff, Patrick," *Dictionary of Canadian Biography*, 5: 551–53.

122. However, Bayfield claimed that his career had been static while he surveyed the lakes, since (as one of his superiors had explained to him) "I had, unfortunately for myself, been employed in a remote part of the world out of view of the Admiralty, and scarcely heard of for nine years." Henry Bayfield to Capt. Beaufort, stating his case for promotion, May 8, 1832, microfilm, reel A 423, PAC.

123. "Bouchette, Joseph," 95–98. He became surveyor general through his abilities and consequent support from the acting governor, not (as is sometimes stated) because he was the nephew of Samuel Holland, the previous post holder.

124. White, *Lord Selkirk's Diary*, 151. In January 1800, Landmann happened upon "a snug sale" of three hundred thousand acres of government land at a season when, despite formal advertisement, "it would not be known beyond the limits of York, so that there would be land enough for everybody in the town to purchase without competition." He bought three thousand acres on the Thames. Landmann, *Adventures and Recollections*, 2: 132–33.

125. "Smith (Smyth), Sir David," 811–12.

126. For Owen, see "Owen, William FitzWilliam," *Dictionary of Canadian Biography*, 8: 670; for Ogilvie, see Carroll, *Good and Wise Measure*, 104–5. Ogilvie's U.S. counterpart, General Porter, wrote that "there is now in the British camp, but one Surveyor and one man fit for duty, and the condition of our own is but little better." However, this does not compare with, for instance, the rigors of the East African coast, where in 1823 two-thirds of the officers and half the seamen on Captain Owen's survey died of fever. Dawson, *Memoirs of Hydrography*, 59.

127. Bayfield to Beaufort, May 8, 1832. Nevertheless, Bayfield felt he could not be "more honorably, or more usefully employed in these peaceable times."

128. "Copy of a Map submitted to Congress by Peter Pond," reproduced in John Warkentin and Richard I. Ruggles, *Manitoba Historical Atlas* (Winnipeg: Historical and Scientific Society of Manitoba, 1970), 106; Gordon C. Davidson, *The North West Company* (Berkeley: University of California Press, 1918), 36–37; Appendix B (esp. 265–66), contains a copy of another map apparently submitted to Congress and of a French translation of the accompanying memoir.

129. Governor Hamilton to Baron Sydney, April 9, 1785, PRO: CO 42/47, 667.

130. Harold A. Innis, *Peter Pond: Fur Trader and Adventurer* (Toronto: Irwin and Gordon, 1930), 110–11; Barry M. Gough, "Peter Pond and Athabasca: Fur Trade, Discovery, and Empire," in *Britain, Canada, and the North Pacific: Maritime Enterprise and Dominion, 1778–1914*, ed. Barry M. Gough (Aldershot, U.K.: Ashgate, 2004), 11–13. Pond said he left Mackenzie instructions "to go down the River [to Cook's Inlet] and from thence to Unalaska, and so to Kamskatka, and thence to England through Russia." Isaac Ogden to David Ogden, November 7, 1789, PRO: CO 42/72 fol. 248. But Mackenzie's 1789 attempt to follow Pond's directions took him instead to the Arctic Ocean.

131. Holland to Simcoe, October 4, 1792; John Simcoe to Henry Dundas, August 23, 1793, in *Simcoe*, ed. Cruikshank, 2: 40; John Simcoe to Under-Secretary King, March 7, 1794, transmitting letters from the Hollands to Simcoe of January 20, 1794, and a copy of the proposals submitted to (and approved by) Grenville in 1789, PRO: CO 42/318 fols. 88, 94–99.

132. Thompson's departure from the Hudson's Bay Company is discussed in Glover, ed., *David Thompson's Narrative*, xxxv–xliii; for the wedding present, see Campbell, *North West Company*, 110.

133. Jenish, *Epic Wanderer*, 218.

The Search for the Canadian-American Boundary along the Michigan Frontier, 1819–1827: The Boundary Commissions under Articles Six and Seven of the Treaty of Ghent

Francis M. Carroll

THE INTERNATIONAL BOUNDARY BETWEEN THE UNITED STATES AND CANADA, OR specifically Michigan and Ontario, was a product of the negotiations in Paris in 1782 and 1783 leading to the treaty that ended the Revolutionary War. We recognize that boundary as basically the water courses between Lake Erie and Lake Huron and between Lake Huron and Lake Superior. In retrospect, that boundary using the Great Lakes and their waterways seems like the obvious and simplest solution to dividing the central part of the continent between the new United States and British North America. The reality was more complicated. The diplomats in Paris first had to agree on the nature of the boundary, and that was not an easy or straightforward task. Then it took the explorers, surveyors, and diplomats of both the United States and Britain another sixty years to agree on what the Treaty of Paris meant and where the boundary should be placed.[1]

Maps have a commanding presence. They shape our perceptions of both topography and the political landscape. In a discussion of the international boundary of Michigan, one is conscious of the outlines of the Lower Peninsula in the south and the Upper Peninsula in the north, familiar to us from countless maps. However, it would be well to keep in mind that in the negotiations in Paris in 1782, the question of how to end the American War of Independence included several propositions that would have steered this discussion away from a Great Lakes boundary and reduced the salience of the two peninsulas as an American coastline. To begin with, Benjamin Franklin, the American envoy in Paris, suggested that amicable relations between the United States and Great Britain could be most effectively restored, and countless future frictions avoided, if Britain were to turn all of its North American holdings over to the new United States. This intriguing proposition was eventually dropped in the complicated circumstances surrounding the early negotiations. If all the British holdings in North America had been retained by the United States, there would be no international boundary, whatever shape a subsequent Michigan might have taken.[2]

The allies of the United States, France and particularly Spain, also had interests in the boundaries of the new republic in its western regions. In late June 1782, John Jay, one of the American peace negotiators, began discussions in Paris with Count Pedro d'Aranda of Spain about Spanish aspirations in the war. Spain had lost both East and West Florida to the British in the Seven Years' War, although France had ceded Louisiana to Spain at the end of that conflict. In the Revolutionary War, the Spanish had retaken both East and West Florida, and they wanted to reassert themselves all along the eastern watershed of the Mississippi River to consolidate their control of the central portions of the continent. To that end, d'Aranda, while discussing Florida, claimed territory south of Lake Superior and west of a line running along the western shore of Lake Huron to Lake Erie, then south across country to the Ohio River, and then southeast to the headwaters of the Flint River, and on into the St. Marys River and East Florida. In short, this included the western Great Lakes and almost the entire eastern watershed of the Mississippi River. Jay insisted that the Mississippi River must be the western boundary of the United States and broke off the talks with d'Aranda. D'Aranda consulted with the French foreign minister's secretary, Joseph-Matthias Gérard de Reyneval, to devise a compromise boundary. Several propositions were brought forward that attempted to mediate the claims of the Spanish and the United States to territory in the Ohio River Valley. A final proposal was presented to Jay on September 6, 1782. Spanish claims on the east bank of the Mississippi River would extend only as far north as the Ohio River, east to the Cumberland River, and then south by a series of lines to the Apalachicola River in West Florida. The territory north of the Ohio River was to remain in British jurisdiction, perhaps as an Indian buffer zone. These proposals would have barred the United States from effective occupation of the Great Lakes–Ohio River–Mississippi River region. With one partial exception, the Appalachian Mountains would effectively have been the western boundary of the new United States, and under none of the four boundaries proposed by the Spanish and the French would Michigan have fallen within United States territory. It is not surprising, in these circumstances, that the American negotiators in Paris became increasingly suspicious of the intentions of the French and the Spanish and carried out their talks with the British without consulting their allies.[3]

By September 27, 1782, the credentials and powers of the British delegation in Paris had been sufficiently recast to allow negotiations with the Americans to begin in earnest, and in slightly more than one week (October 5), a first draft of the articles of peace was signed. Drafted largely by John Jay, the terms included a Canadian boundary that followed the instructions given in 1779 to John Adams, another American delegate. This boundary line began in the east by following the St. John River to the origin of the Connecticut River and then south to the 45th degree of north latitude and west to the St. Lawrence River, then by a line to Lake Nipissing, northeast of Lake Huron, and by a second line to the source of the Mississippi River (not yet discovered). The western boundary of the United States would then have extended down the Mississippi River. This "Nipissing line" would have included within the United States much of southern Ontario and, of course, all of modern Michigan, except the Keweenaw Peninsula and Isle Royale. This would have given Michigan an international boundary, but a peculiar one.[4]

When this draft of the peace terms reached London, a number of objections were raised. Among other things, the 1774 Quebec Act boundary line in the west was urged upon the British negotiators—that is to say, a line from the St. Lawrence River to Lake Ontario to the Ohio River and west to the Mississippi. The

Americans, recognizing in this line something of the Franco-Spanish boundary suggested earlier in the summer, objected that they could not sign a peace treaty that denied the United States a western boundary on the Mississippi River. The Americans made two counterproposals. The first was to extend the 45th degree of north latitude (the Quebec–New York boundary) due west to the Mississippi River. This line would also have placed much of southwestern Ontario in the United States, but it would have cut across the northern part of the Lower Peninsula of Michigan and extended into central Wisconsin before reaching the Mississippi River. The second proposal was to extend the 45th degree of north latitude to the St. Lawrence River and to proceed through the main channels of the Great Lakes and by the main watercourse to the Lake of the Woods and then west to the Mississippi. A British government led by Lord Shelburne accepted the second western boundary proposal, along with a number of changes dealing with other matters in the peace process.[5] On November 30, 1782, the preliminary treaty was signed in Paris. The passages dealing with what would be the Michigan boundary with Canada read as follows: "[The boundary would run] through the middle of said Lake [Erie], untill it arrives at the Water Communication between that Lake and Lake Huron; thence along the middle of said water communication into the Lake Huron; thence through the middle of said Lake to the Water Communication between that Lake and Lake Superior; thence through Lake Superior northward of the Isles Royal & Phelipeaux, to the Long Lake; thence through the middle of said Long Lake, and the water Communication between it and the Lake of the Woods, to the said Lake of the Woods, thence through the said Lake to the most Northwestern point thereof, and from thence on a due west Course to the River Mississippi."[6] The definitive Treaty of Paris ending the war, in which the boundary provisions remained unchanged, was signed on September 3, 1783.

On the face of it, and in comparison to many of the other parts of the treaty dealing with boundaries, the terms affecting the future state of Michigan were fairly clear. Although not specifically mentioned in the treaty, the water communications between Lake Erie and Lake Huron were, of course, the Detroit River, Lake St. Clair, and the St. Clair River. The water communication between Lake Huron and Lake Superior was the St. Marys River at Sault Ste. Marie. The line was to extend north of Isle Royale, which was plain enough, but there was no Isle Phelipeaux and no agreement about the Long Lake and the subsequent water communication between it and the Lake of the Woods. The Mississippi River proved to be south and east of the northwesternmost point of the Lake of the Woods, not due west as indicated in the treaty. Some of these problems grew out of the errors contained in John Mitchell's 1755 "Map of British and French Dominions in North America," which had been used by the negotiators. Most important, however, what became Michigan Territory and eventually the State of Michigan fell within the lands ceded to the United States.

Of course, there were still problems that barred the United States from occupying and asserting its sovereignty in Michigan. British forces continued to hold seven forts along the frontier from Lake Champlain in the east to Detroit and Michilimackinac in the west, and from those forts the Crown was able to protect the fur trade operating out of Montreal and to consolidate its relations with the Native peoples. Not until the Jay-Grenville Treaty of 1794 did the British government agree to withdraw its troops, an act that did not take place until 1796. Even then, the situation was so unstable, and relations between the American government and the Native peoples so volatile, that the resumption of hostilities in 1810 and 1811 contributed directly to the causes of the War of 1812.

That conflict proved to be a disaster for almost everyone concerned. The attempted invasion of Upper Canada by United States troops from Detroit resulted in a counterinvasion by British and Native forces that led to the surrender of Detroit and eventually the collapse of the American position in all of Michigan and much of the Northwest Territory. Despite Commodore Oliver Hazard Perry's September 1813 victory at Put-in-Bay on Lake Erie and General William Henry Harrison's recapture of Detroit, reinvasion of Upper Canada, and defeat of British forces at the Battle of the Thames in October 1813, American possession of the Northwest Territory in general and Michigan in particular remained precarious. At the peace talks in Ghent in 1814, the British demand for an Indian buffer state north of the Ohio River and the outright cession of territory in Maine and Minnesota threatened to terminate the negotiations. Only skillful tactics by the American diplomats and a growing impatience on the part of the British public to end the war moved the British government to accept a settlement that returned the boundary to the status quo antebellum—the 1783 Treaty of Paris boundary. For Michigan, this boundary ran along the Detroit and St. Clair Rivers, the St. Marys River, and north of Isle Royale. Nevertheless, the British and American diplomats at Ghent recognized that the 1783 boundary had contained numerous errors and had been a source of endless problems. Therefore, the Treaty of Ghent authorized the creation of four joint commissions to explore, survey, map, and decide where the boundary described in 1783 was actually to be found.

The first two eastern boundary commissions met in Halifax, Nova Scotia, in October 1816. One commission would decide the boundary between the islands in Passamaquoddy Bay, and the other commission would find and trace out the boundary between New Brunswick and Quebec (or Lower Canada as it was then) and Maine, New Hampshire, Vermont, and New York. The Boundary Commission under the Sixth Article of the Treaty of Ghent, the first of the two western commissions, met on November 18, 1816, in Albany, New York. The task of this commission was to determine the boundary from where the 45th parallel intersects with the St. Lawrence River, through the river and Lakes Ontario, Erie, and Huron to Sault Ste. Marie. The Boundary Commission under the Seventh Article of the Treaty of Ghent was to be made up of the same commissioners and crews and was to determine the boundary from the Sault through Lake Superior and along the watercourses to the northwesternmost point of the Lake of the Woods. In the event that any of the four boundary commissions was unable to reach an agreement, the Treaty of Ghent provided for arbitration of the dispute by a "friendly sovereign or State," that is to say, a single arbitrator or umpire.[7]

The American commissioner under Articles Six and Seven of the Treaty of Ghent was General Peter B. Porter. Porter was born in Connecticut in 1773, educated at Yale, and trained in the law by Judge Tapping Reeve. He moved to Black Rock, New York, in the 1790s, where he practiced law and conducted several businesses, including one that was involved in building the Erie Canal. During the War of 1812, he raised a number of troops, campaigned in Upper Canada, and was promoted to major general. Porter also served several terms in Congress and later was secretary of war under John Quincy Adams. He was an able manager and, although willing to compromise, was determined to represent American interests. The British commissioner was Colonel John Ogilvy. Born in Scotland in 1769, he came to Montreal in 1790 and within six years was a partner in Parker, Gerrard, and Ogilvy, which dealt in furs and shipping. Ogilvy worked for the merger of his and several other firms into the larger North West Company in 1804, and within a decade he was able to retire a very wealthy man. Ogilvy had also earned a colonelcy in the militia during the War of 1812. As a former fur trader, Ogilvy was familiar with the Great Lakes region and was in many ways an ideal head of the commission for the British. Unfortunately, Colonel Ogilvy died at Amherstburg of a "bilious" fever while working with the survey crews on the lower Detroit River in September 1819. He was replaced by Anthony Barclay, the youngest son of Colonel Thomas Barclay, a distinguished New York Loyalist and the British boundary commissioner under Articles Four and Five of the Treaty of Ghent. Young Barclay had been born in Nova Scotia in 1792, but he was raised largely in New York City, where his father represented the British government in several capacities. Anthony Barclay was trained in the law at the Inns of Court in London and had served as secretary of the commission under the Fourth Article of the Treaty of Ghent. Here was a young man who had literally grown up with the boundary question and the tangle of Anglo-Canadian-American relations. It is fair to say that General Porter and Colonel Ogilvy had more cordial relations than did Porter and Barclay. The latter was of a younger generation, and he had more difficult decisions to make. The position of boundary commissioner carried both status and material rewards: the men were paid £1,000 sterling, or $4,444 U.S.[8]

Agents for the western boundary commission were John Hale, a Quebec lawyer, for the British, and Colonel Samuel Hawkins, a lawyer, for the United States. Hawkins quarreled with General Porter about his role as agent and eventually quit in 1819. He was replaced by another former soldier, Major Joseph Delafield of New York, a Yale graduate and lawyer who was also an amateur geologist. The leading British surveyor was David Thompson, the well-known explorer and mapmaker for the fur trade. Thompson had joined the Hudson's Bay Company as a boy in 1784, had learned surveying in the field, and had undertaken extensive explorations in western Canada; but in 1794, he switched to the North West Company in order to expand his explorations. He retired from the fur trade in 1811. As a surveyor for the boundary commission, he brought to the task an unsurpassed knowledge of the country to be explored and a well-developed ability to work with the French-Canadian boat crews and the Native peoples whose cooperation would be needed. The Americans employed several people as surveyor: David P. Adams, on leave from the Navy, served from 1817 to 1819; William A. Bird, born in Salisbury, Connecticut, but living in Buffalo, New York, served from 1819 to 1822; James Ferguson from Scotland, who had worked as an engineer on the Erie Canal, served from 1822 to 1827.

The operating procedure of what was in fact a joint commission was flexible, but in general the commissioners acted as representatives of their respective governments in something of a judicial capacity. The commissioners decided what the survey parties would attempt to examine each summer; agents were then responsible for seeing that the crews were supplied and able to carry out their work. The agents looked after financial matters for the surveys and eventually took on the role of lawyers, presenting their cases before the board of commissioners. In practice, the commissioners also went into the field to oversee the work, but not on a regular basis. The surveyors in fact managed much of the actual work in the field; indeed, as the survey and exploration work proceeded farther west and the commissioners and agents were less able to travel with the crews, the surveyors took on a still larger managerial role. Although the Treaty of 1783 stipulated that the boundary was to run along the middle of the lakes and rivers, the commissioners decided that as a practical procedure they would attempt to place the boundary in the main channels of the rivers, that they would not divide islands, and that they would attempt to balance the number of large islands allotted to each country. After the new season's work was determined by the commissioners, the crews of boatmen, axmen, chainmen, and cooks (paid between $15 and $20 a month) and draftsmen and surveyor's assistants (paid between $106 and $110) would be sent out again. At the end of each season, the surveyors converted their data into maps and tables that would be presented by the agents the following spring to the commissioners sitting as a board. Once maps and data had been accumulated for the entire section of the border, the board of commissioners had to decide whether it could agree upon a boundary line that conformed to the terms of the Treaty of 1783 and report its results to the members' respective governments. If the board of commissioners agreed, the boundary was recognized and accepted by both governments.[9]

Work began in the spring of 1817. The first steps required locating the 45th degree of north latitude by astronomical sightings and surveying the St. Lawrence River by a process of triangulation. The St. Lawrence River and the Thousand Islands occupied the surveyors for most of two summers, but by the end of the 1818 season, the survey parties had reached the Niagara River. A year later, they were at the western end of Lake Erie, with the expectation that the survey of Lake Huron could be completed by the end of 1820. However, in the late summer of 1819, with no wind, high temperatures, and low water, while mapping the marshy western end of Lake Erie and the mouth of the Detroit River, both the British and American parties suffered from fever, probably malaria. Commissioner Ogilvy and two members of the British crews died, and all were incapacitated for some period of time. General Porter, arriving from Black Rock in late September, recognized the danger of the situation and sent both survey parties back east for the winter. Concern over the perils of working in marshy areas in the summer heat prompted several changes. The British appointed a physician, Dr. John Bigsby, as assistant secretary to the commission the following year, so that there would be someone who could minister to any members of the survey parties who might fall ill. It was also decided that the marshy regions of Lake Erie and Lake St. Clair would be surveyed early in the season and that Lake Huron would be examined in the summer.[10]

General Porter and Anthony Barclay, the new British commissioner, traveled by steamboat from Buffalo, New York, to Grosse Ile in the Detroit River for their first board meeting on June 3, 1820, to instruct the survey crews. Work began charting the Detroit River (fig. 1) and Lake St. Clair (fig. 2). A measured baseline would be established by a link chain along a stretch of one shore, sightings were then taken on a marker on the opposite side of the river or on an island to form a triangle, the angles were calculated with a sextant or a theodolite, and the distance was computed by simple geometry. By creating a series of triangles, as well as taking astronomical sightings to determine latitude and longitude, the river and its islands could be accurately surveyed and mapped. The crews camped on Fighting Island and worked on the river until June 28, when they made their way onto Lake St. Clair.[11]

Meanwhile, Major Delafield, the American agent, recorded in his diary a very active social life for senior members of the commission staff, with regular dinners in Detroit. The high point was the celebration of the Fourth of July. At ten A.M., a large party of gentlemen and ladies, including Governor Lewis Cass, Mrs. Cass, and General Alexander Macomb, boarded the steamboat *Walk-in-the-Water* for an excursion down the river. Salutes were fired, a military band played, dances were held, and a festive dinner was provided. "The day was passed with great mirth, and with entire satisfaction to every person," Delafield observed. The Detroit community numbered about fourteen hundred people, and there was a lively traffic in people passing through the area. One of the British party recounted meeting the Reverend Jedidiah Morse (later famous as both a geographer and the father of Samuel F. B. Morse), dressed in a long black coat, black knee breeches, silk stockings, a white neck cloth, and a broad-brimmed hat. Rural life was stirring, too. One member of the commission observed, "The Rivers Detroit and St. Clair have a lively fringe of comfortable and even pretty dwellings, embowered in pear, apple, and peach orchards, with here and there a church-tower or a clump of wych-elms shadowing an advanced bank of the river. Productive farms stretch out of sight into the woods behind." Although Detroit still had something of the atmosphere of a fur-trading post and garrison town, it was poised for rapid growth. The appearance

Figure 1. The Detroit River. Boundary commission map, map collection, RG 76, National Archives of the United States, College Park, Maryland.

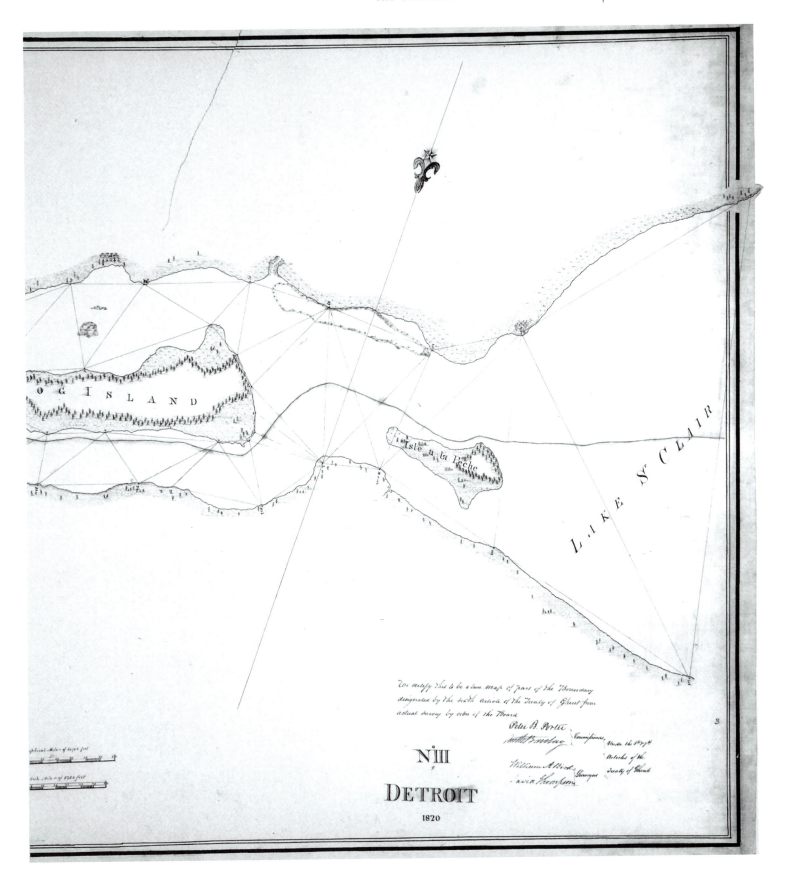

OG ISLAND

Isle a la Peche

LAKE St CLAIR

We certify this to be a true map of part of the Boundary
designated by the sixth article of the Treaty of Ghent from
actual survey by order of the Board.

Peter B. Porter
Anthy Barclay ⎬ Commissioners Under the 6ᵗʰ & 7ᵗʰ
⎱ Articles of the
William A. Bird ⎬ Surveyors Treaty of Ghent
David Thompson

N° III

DETROIT

1820

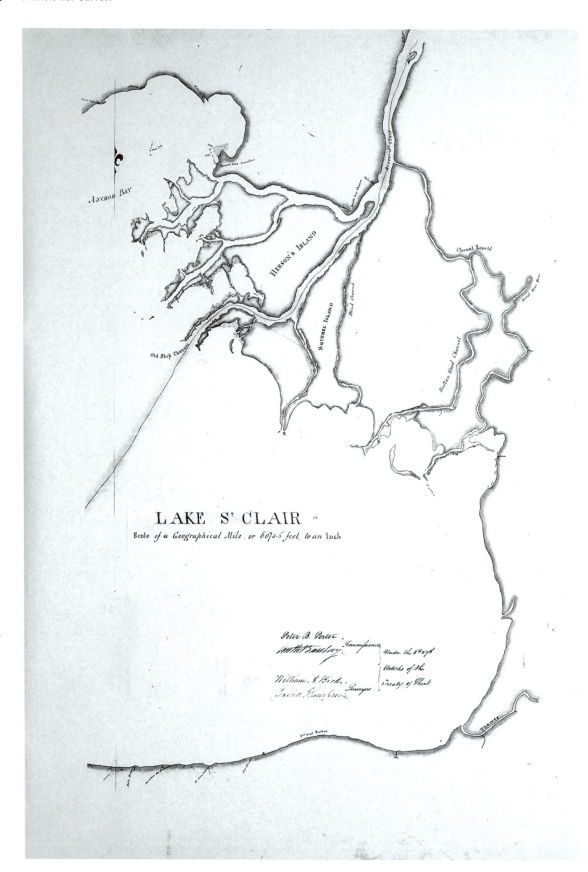

Figure 2. Lake St. Clair. Boundary commission map, map collection, RG 76, National Archives of the United States, College Park, Maryland.

in 1818 of *Walk-in-the-Water*, the first steamboat on Lake Erie, together with the opening of the Erie Canal in 1825, made Michigan, Wisconsin, and Illinois accessible in a dramatic fashion.[12]

Having moved north, Major Delafield commented on Lake St. Clair, its shallow depth, the flatness of the surrounding shore, the several outlets of the St. Clair River, and the growing concern about fever. Dr. Bigsby noted that "we found the scenery here very pretty, the borders of the lake, for miles inland, being a savannah of long, bright green grass, with woods in the rear disposed in capes, islands, and devious avenues."[13] However, he found when he stepped off the boat into the grass that his feet sank into six inches of water. In the following year, 1821, the surveyors built platforms on poles in the shallow water, a half-mile from shore, from which to take their sightings with theodolites and sextants. "The Base Line is measured and the gentlemen proceed to take angles in the neighborhood of the points and at their stations of the mouth of the Huron River," Delafield recorded. Gradually the shape of Lake St. Clair came into focus on the maps, and the merits of Eagle Channel, Old Ship Channel, Middle Channel, and Chenail Écarté as possible borders were debated. (Old Ship Channel was finally agreed upon.) The crews also surveyed and mapped the St. Clair River from its entrance at the south end of Lake Huron (fig. 3). Delafield noted that the St. Clair was about nine hundred feet across at the head of the river opposite Fort Gratiot.[14]

By July 21, 1820, the advanced survey parties left their work on Lake St. Clair and headed north across Lake Huron. The Americans were bound for Mackinac Island on board the newly built schooner *Red Jacket*. The survey work resumed about a week later among St. Joseph Island, Drummond Island, what is now Cockburn Island, and Manitoulin Island. Of the region near St. Joseph Island, Bigsby wrote, "From the summit of the adjoining main[land] is presented a truly scenic and striking combination of high and somber rocks, scantily clad with pine, and overshadowing a labyrinth of waters."[15] St. Joseph Island had a high ridge, some fourteen hundred feet above sea level, that dominated the area. This island had been occupied by a British garrison before the War of 1812, and Drummond Island, although it had a community of American citizens, still had two companies of British troops. Neither island had been particularly well fortified, and in their book, Joseph E. Bayliss, Estelle M. Bayliss, and Milo Quaife conclude that both were unsuitable for military establishments. The waters surrounding these islands, as far up the St. Marys River as the Neebish Rapids, were regarded as the northern extremity of Lake Huron and the extent of the territory covered under Article Six of the Treaty of Ghent. The survey, therefore, required careful mapping of all the islands as far as the western end of Manitoulin Island and the shoreline as far as the Mississagi River. The Americans formed two parties: one, led by James Ferguson, surveyed the mouth of the St. Marys River; the other, led by Delafield, worked among the islands from the *Red Jacket*. Delafield concluded, "No map that I have seen has any truth as it respects the position of Drummond's or the other islands about St. Marys. We entered this bay without a pilot, but are told that we cannot proceed up the river without one."[16] In fact, the island, which was about one mile from the American mainland, dominated direct access to the St. Marys River by the De Tour Passage and the False De Tour Channel on either side of it.

In these waters, the American surveyors met David Thompson, John Bigsby, and the British survey party, working from their own ship, HMS *Confiance*, a vessel that had been captured from the Americans during the recent war. Several members of the British party were sick with fevers, although none died in 1820. The work, moreover, was difficult. Thompson complained of many obstacles, and the Americans worried that the survey would be as vast as that of the Thousand Islands in the St. Lawrence River. The

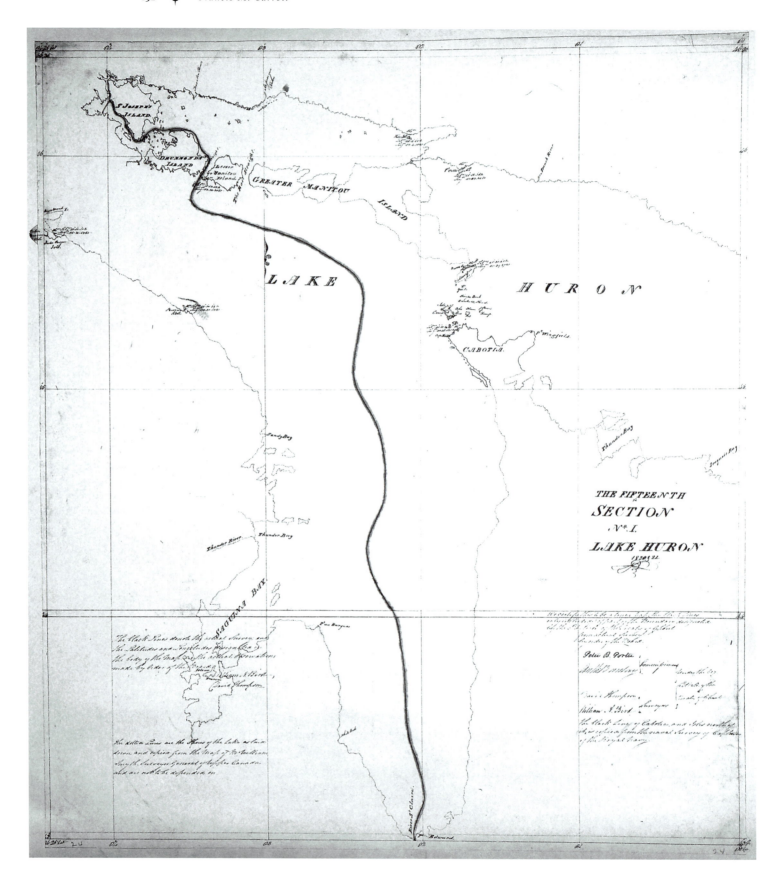

channels between the islands were quite unknown, so large vessels like the *Red Jacket* had to proceed with extreme caution. Both the shore and the bottom were rocky and dangerous. The unpredictable winds, both calm and storm, made things all the more stressful. Skies filled with smoke from forest fires obscured navigational sightings, Thompson grumbled, and mosquitoes made everyone uncomfortable. Nevertheless, the work proceeded through August and September until October 4, when the season was deemed over, the crews discharged, and the *Red Jacket* sailed for Detroit. Sailing on the *Lady of the Lakes,* Delafield was back in Black Rock, New York, by October 20, able to report to General Porter.[17]

The 1821 season opened early for the boundary commission surveyors. David Thompson took midwinter sightings off Point Pelee in Lake Erie and on the Detroit River. Parts of Lake St. Clair and the several channels of the St. Clair River entering the lake were surveyed in May and June, before the heat of summer made the marshy regions dangerous. By the end of June, the survey parties returned to the northern parts of Lake Huron; ice remained on parts of the lake in May. Surveys were undertaken along the northern shoreline of Lake Huron from the Straits of Mackinac in the west to the French River in Georgian Bay to the east. This work occupied the rest of the summer, but by the end of the season, crews had completed the survey of the boundary from roughly St. Regis, New York, on the St. Lawrence River, to Sault Ste. Marie in Michigan Territory.[18]

On November 12, 1821, the board of commissioners met to examine the twenty-two official maps prepared and all of the accumulated data to make a final decision about the allotment of islands and channels in the placement of the boundary. It took almost four weeks, even though there was substantial agreement among the participants. No major disagreement emerged over the placement of the boundary in the St. Lawrence River or the channels in the Niagara River. At the north end of Lake Huron, St. Joseph Island went to Canada and Drummond Island to the United States (necessitating the removal of the British garrison once again). However, it was the islands in the Detroit River that caused a problem, not, as it turned out, the major islands but, ironically, several of the smaller ones. Grosse Ile (fig. 4) on the Michigan side of the river was ceded to the United States, but General Porter also claimed Bois Blanc (Boblo) Island opposite Amherstburg and Fort Malden. At that time the navigable channel ran between Bois Blanc Island and the Canadian shore, and the island had also been fortified by the Americans at the end of the War of 1812. However, Anthony Barclay claimed Sugar, Fox, and Stoney Islands, just a few yards off Grosse Ile, as well as Bois Blanc Island. Barclay said he would concede Sugar, Fox, and Stoney Islands to the United States if Porter could guarantee that they would not be fortified. Porter was willing to give up the claim to Bois Blanc in exchange for Sugar, Fox, and Stoney Islands, but he replied that under the terms of his commission, his powers were limited to deciding the boundary, not matters of defense. A commitment not to arm the islands would require a special treaty. Despite the Rush-Bagot Agreement in 1817 to limit naval vessels on the Great Lakes, the shadow of the War of 1812 hung heavily over these talks. The result was that the two commissioners wrote to Secretary of State John Quincy Adams and British Minister of Foreign Affairs Stratford Canning for advice.[19]

In the uneasy circumstances of postwar British-American relations, the status of the three small islands raised a vexing problem. Canning replied to Barclay that he did not consider the rest of the boundary settlement favorable enough to British interests to empower him to offer the islands to the Americans without the guarantee. Canning in turn wrote to the foreign secretary, Lord Castlereagh, or Lord Londonderry as he had become, for advice. Adams wrote to the American minister in England, Richard Rush, to say that he could not support a special treaty guaranteeing that the United States

Figure 3. Lake Huron. Boundary commission map, map collection, RG 76, National Archives of the United States, College Park, Maryland.

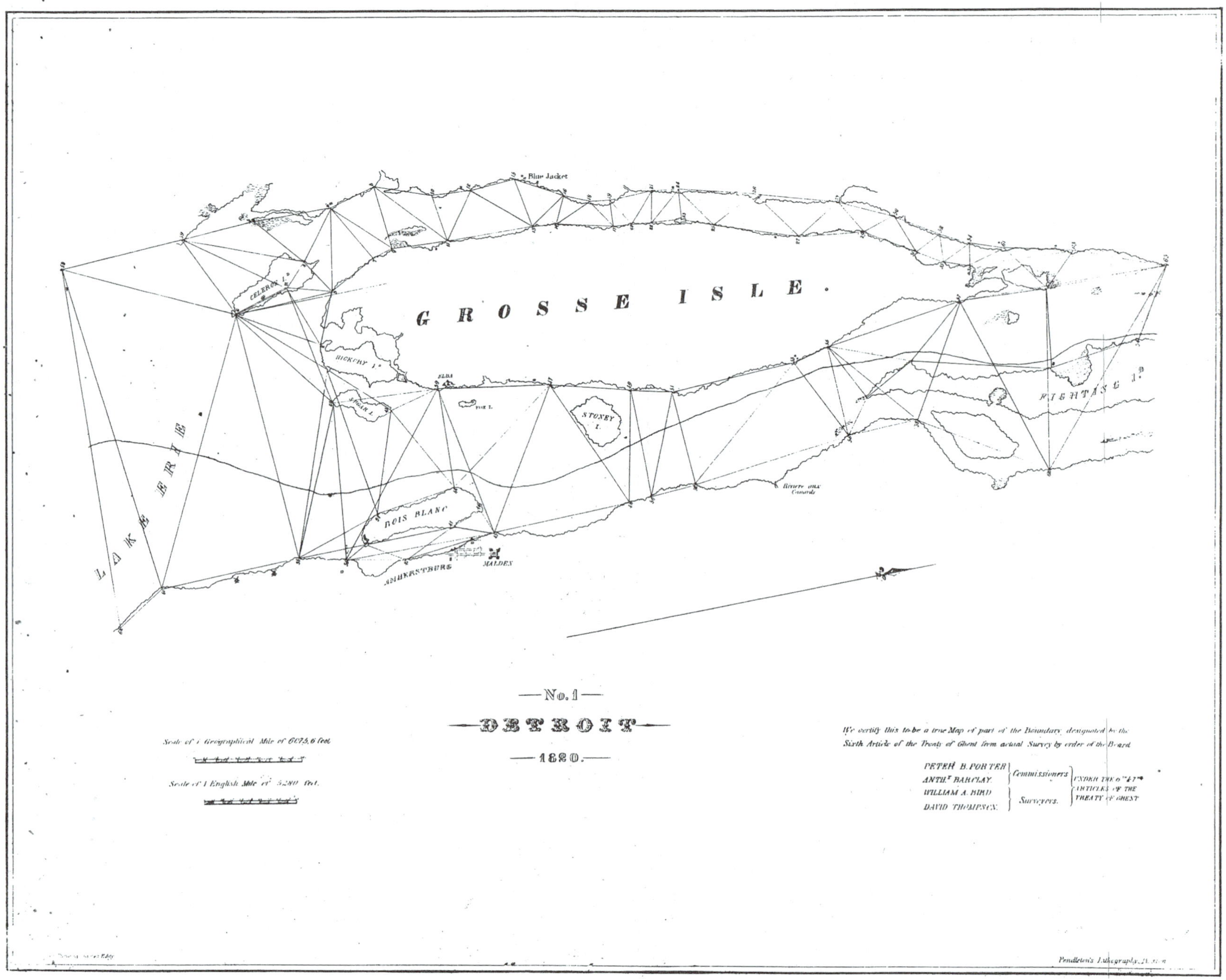

Figure 4. Grosse Isle [today Grosse Ile]. Boundary commission map, map collection, RG 76, National Archives of the United States, College Park, Maryland.

would never fortify the islands. However, he asked Rush to inquire whether the British would consider a treaty disarming all of the islands in the mouth of the Detroit River.[20] The situation did not seem very promising, but Castlereagh stepped forward to break the impasse. The foreign secretary wrote to Canning on March 9, 1822, to say that His Majesty's government agreed "to concede to the U. States the possession of the three small islands which at present appear to constitute the only point of difference between the two Commissioners," with the only condition being that the rest of the boundary be ratified immediately. Canning replied that Adams appreciated the generosity of Castlereagh's gesture.[21] In fact,

the United States never did fortify the islands, nor did Britain ever build a naval base at Amherstburg, although it did have a shipyard at nearby Fort Malden.

The Board of Commissioners under Article Six met in Utica, New York, on June 18, 1822, and the terms of the agreement were written out and signed. Even at this point a few problems arose. Canning thought that the delays in convening the board undercut the condition of immediate ratification. General Porter, when the time came for signing, objected to the demand that the signature of the British commissioner be placed above that of the American commissioner. A compromise was worked out whereby the signature of each commissioner appeared first on the copy of the agreement to be kept by his government.[22] With the signing of this agreement, the boundary was established between the United States and British North America, from the point where the 45th degree of latitude crossed the St. Lawrence River through the Great Lakes to the mouth of the St. Marys River at the Sault. For Michigan, the crucial boundary along the Detroit River, Lake St. Clair, and the St. Clair River was surveyed, mapped, and settled, and not to Michigan's disadvantage, either. To the north, the boundary ran through Lake Huron midway between the eastern shore of Michigan and the Bruce Peninsula of Upper Canada. Drummond Island, the gateway to the St. Marys River and the Sault, was given to Michigan.

This settlement under Article Six of the Treaty of Ghent was of great importance for Michigan in determining a part of the international boundary in the most settled part of the territory; it did, however, leave extensive reaches of the northern international boundary yet to be determined by the work of the Boundary Commission under Article Seven. The region extended from the St. Marys River at the Sault to Isle Royale and then by the "water communication" to the northwesternmost point of the Lake of the Woods. Although only the Sault and Isle Royale fall within the boundaries of Michigan today, from 1818 to 1834, Michigan Territory extended to the Lake of the Woods and the Mississippi River, and briefly, from 1834 to 1836, as far west as the Missouri River in what is now North and South Dakota. Thus, the work of the boundary commission in the 1820s would have been of great importance to Michigan Territory. The Boundary Commission under Article Seven consisted of very much the same personnel as the Boundary Commission under Article Six: General Porter and Anthony Barclay were the commissioners, and Major Delafield and John Hale were the agents. James Ferguson had become the American surveyor and had recruited as his assistant a young army officer named George W. Whistler, later the father of the famous painter. Work actually had begun in the St. Marys River while the decisions were still pending about results under Article Six. Some members of David Thompson's crews had started mapping the St. Marys River the year before. Lake Superior, however, lay beyond and presented a formidable task.

The Sault Ste. Marie was one of those crucial water passages in the world before railways and practical surface roads became common. Like Detroit and Michilimackinac, the Sault was a key gateway, controlling travel to the west and influencing the fur trade and Indian affairs. The North West Company had a fur-trading post on the Canadian side of the St. Marys River, and the American Fur Company enjoyed the services of John Johnston, an Anglo-Irish trader, on the Michigan side. The settlement was not large, but it had several houses, including Johnston's large house and famous library, as well as an Indian village. Governor Lewis Cass, passing through the Sault in 1820 on his way to find the source of the Mississippi River, had clashed with the Ojibwe chiefs over the acquisition of land for the building of an army fort; this dispute was settled by the timely intervention of Johnston's Native wife, Susan. In addition to building Fort Brady, the United States government had also established an Indian agency at the Sault in 1821, headed by Henry Rowe Schoolcraft.[23] A simple and obvious decision about the boundary in the St. Marys River was made difficult by the large obstruction posed by St. George's (or Sugar) Island, which was some twenty miles long. The island could be reached from the open water of the St. Marys River on the north side and through Lake George and the three Neebish Rapids on the east side. This was the only practical ship channel. To the west of the island was another body of water, but it was shallow and unsuitable for vessels other than canoes. Control of the island, therefore, would give access to the best, or least difficult, channel connecting Lake Superior with Lake Huron. Farther upstream, as Bigsby observed, "The [St. Marys] river itself (seventeen miles long by half a mile to a mile and a quarter wide) is deep, silent, broad: massive woods overhang its banks," together with, he noted, "the boiling rapids, called St. Mary's Falls."[24]

After passing through Sault Ste. Marie in June 1822, the surveying parties headed onto Lake Superior. The Americans traveled along the east and north shores of Lake Superior, stopping at Fort William, the fur-trading post at what is now Thunder Bay. Then they proceeded southwest to the Pigeon River, the location of the abandoned fur-trading post of Grand Portage. At that point, they followed the old canoe route west as far as Lake Saganaga. Thompson's surveyors headed west along the south shore of the lake to Fond du Lac, near the present cities of Duluth and Superior. Fond du Lac was then an American Fur Company post, and the site had been visited by Governor Cass on his expedition to explore Michigan Territory and search for the source of the Mississippi River in 1820. He had returned there to negotiate the Treaty of Fond du Lac with the Native peoples in 1826. Meanwhile, Thompson, who was now traveling in country he had traversed in 1798, turned northeast along the north shore of Lake Superior until he, too, came to the Pigeon River. He ascended the river and then made his way as far west as Lake Namakan before turning back. In the course of the 1822 season, the American and British survey parties had managed to work their way around the entire shoreline of Lake Superior and also penetrate the historic canoe route up the Pigeon River. Delafield wrote confidently to Secretary of State Adams that the Pigeon River route would be agreed to without difficulty and that the work should be completed the next season.[25] He could not have been more wrong.

Because of the vast distances now involved in getting from the cities of the east to the frontier being mapped, the American surveying party wintered at Fort William. Although the fort was somewhat diminished in importance since the 1821 merger of the North West Company with the Hudson's Bay Company, it was still a substantial establishment, with palisades and block houses. It had numerous shops and buildings, not the least being dining facilities for one hundred people or more. Wintering there enabled the crews to work much longer in the autumn and actually do the triangulation necessary to plot the location of Isle Royale from the surface of the ice in the winter. Getting an early start in 1823, the American surveyors once again made their way up the Grand Portage route through a chain of lakes that led to Lac la Pluie (Rainy Lake) and all the way to the Lake of the Woods. Working his way among the many islands and bays in the Lake of the Woods, Ferguson concluded from the sightings he took with his sextant that the northwesternmost point of the lake was near Rat Portage (now Keewatin, Ontario). Major Delafield, who left New York City on May 3, 1823, joined Ferguson at the Lake of the Woods on July 31, after traveling for three months. On their return trip, Delafield took the current fur-trading route to Fort William, along the Kamanistiquia River, and Ferguson took the historic route to the Pigeon River.[26]

Thompson and the British crew started from Lower Canada, passing through Georgian Bay and the Sault, and they reached Grand Portage by June 29. They, too, worked toward Lac la Pluie, although they

did not encounter Ferguson and the Americans. Both parties had abandoned the meticulous and time-consuming process of triangulation in favor of astronomical sightings at regular intervals. Thompson was able to use a new invention, Massey's Patent Log. When it was pulled through the water from a canoe, this device rotated and allowed for a surprisingly accurate measure of distance. Thompson and several others in his crew fell ill, and they also ran out of food. Thus, by August 23, they were back in Fort William, and after some more work on the St. Marys River, they were ready to head home.[27] At the board of commissioners meeting in Albany, New York, in February 1824, just as both General Porter and Major Delafield had begun to suspect, David Thompson asserted that Fond du Lac should be considered as possibly the "Long Lake" of the Treaty of 1783 and that the St. Louis River was the largest stream entering Lake Superior. The British agent, John Hale, insisted that the St. Louis River route to Lac la Pluie be explored and considered, which would mean at least another season of work before the board could reach a decision.[28]

During the 1824 season, the Americans, reacting to the British interest in the Fond du Lac route, began a survey of the chain of lakes from Fort William to Lac la Pluie, the route developed by the North West Company after the closure of the Grand Portage in 1803. The British themselves made a major effort to survey the Lake of the Woods. Thompson took numerous astronomical observations and established several possible sites for the northwesternmost point of the Lake of the Woods. However, in the end, he agreed with Ferguson's calculation of the previous year that the northwesternmost point was near Rat Portage, where the Winnipeg River flowed out of the Lake of the Woods and on toward Lake Winnipeg. When the board of commissioners met in Montreal in October 1824, the Americans felt that the commissioners had all the relevant information they needed to make a decision, but John Hale, the British agent, now argued firmly for a full survey of the Fond du Lac–St. Louis River route from Lake Superior to Lac la Pluie. General Porter acquiesced to yet another season of work in the field, fearing that his refusal would lead to the breakup of the commission.[29]

Cordial relations at the board meetings were beginning to break down. Another controversy quietly began to unfold in late 1824, when the Foreign Office sent officials of the Hudson's Bay Company maps of the Lake of the Woods with the northwesternmost point identified by both Ferguson and Thompson as Rat Portage. Nicholas Garry, the deputy governor of the company, replied that a boundary line that so interfered with the fur-trading routes "ought not, under any circumstances, be admitted to by His Majesty's Government." As a result, the Foreign Office sent a scientist from London, Dr. Johann Ludwig Tiarks, whose services had been used to help determine the New York–Quebec boundary in 1817 to 1820. Tiarks and Anthony Barclay himself made their way to the Lake of the Woods by July 24, 1825. Tiarks calculated that the northwesternmost point of the Lake of the Woods was in a narrow finger of water that is now called Angle Inlet—in fact, it was one of the several markers Thompson had set the year before and rejected. Angle Inlet, rather than Rat Portage, was accepted by the Americans as the northwesternmost point of the Lake of the Woods. David Thompson's son Samuel, meanwhile, surveyed and mapped the Fond du Lac–St. Louis River route from Lake Superior to Lac la Pluie. Numerous elements of unfinished map work on the St. Marys River were completed by the end of the season, ending the surveys required under Article Seven.[30]

The board of commissioners met in Albany, New York, in November 1825, but the maps and astronomical data were by no means ready to be presented, thereby making another meeting necessary. Deferred several times, it did not take place until October 4, 1826, in New York City. The agents made their arguments and presented their claims, while the surveyors submitted their maps (Thompson himself had completed four sets of eight maps) and books of notes. Although the northwesternmost point of the Lake of the Woods as determined by Tiarks was accepted by Porter, two other problems loomed. Which of the three "water communications" between Lake Superior and the Lake of the Woods had been intended in the Treaty of 1783: the Fond du Lac–St. Louis River route in the south, the Fort William–Kamanistiquia River route in the north, or the Grand Portage–Pigeon River route in the middle? The second problem concerned the claims of both agents to Sugar, or St. George's, Island in the St. Marys River at the Sault. After three weeks of talks, there was some movement on both sides. Both Porter and Barclay were willing to abandon their maximum claims on the "water communication" and accept the Pigeon River route as the border, but Barclay would do so only if the eight-mile portage on the south bank of the river was made British territory. Porter concluded that this suggestion violated the precise terms of the Treaty of 1783 that described the boundary as running through a water system. Barclay claimed Sugar Island but agreed to allow the Americans to use the east Neebish Channel around it in exchange for American agreement to allow British subjects to use the south channel around Barnhart's Island in the St. Lawrence River. But matters concerning Barnhart's Island had already been decided, despite much protest in Upper Canada, with the conclusion of the work under Article Six of the Treaty of Ghent. And as a commissioner, Porter was not authorized to negotiate a new, separate treaty.[31]

When the board of commissioners adjourned, matters stood at an apparent impasse. Barclay, however, was aware that neither the eight-mile portage on the Pigeon River nor Sugar Island in the St. Marys River was of great strategic or economic importance to British North America. He wrote to the Foreign Office saying as much, pointing out that if these issues were sent to arbitration, the result would not likely be a significant improvement over what the Americans actually claimed.[32] In effect, he requested authority to make the kind of compromise that had been made in the settlement of the Sixth Article. The British government, however, was in turmoil during 1827. Lord Liverpool, the prime minister, suffered a stroke on February 17, was incapacitated for some time, and eventually resigned. George Canning, the foreign secretary, formed a government on April 12, but it was very unpopular and split the Tory Party. Canning's own health was also failing, and he died on August 8. Lord Goderich formed a government next, but it fell in January 1828, at which time the duke of Wellington was able to put together a more long-lasting government. Not surprisingly in these circumstances, no one in the Foreign Office was prepared to authorize Barclay to make any compromises, as Lord Castlereagh had done in 1822. Instead he was instructed to "close your Commission with as little delay as possible, & make your Report in the manner provided by Treaty, on the points of disagreement." The board of commissioners met on October 26, 1827, in New York to exchange maps and reports and again on December 24 to discharge its financial obligations.[33] Unfortunately, the boundary questions on the St. Marys River and between Lake Superior and the Lake of the Woods remained undecided. As it turned out, nothing was done for another fifteen years.[34]

When Michigan entered the Union as a state in 1837, it gave up claims to the unsettled boundary region beyond Isle Royale, but its boundary with British North America at the Sault was still undecided. Not until 1842 and the negotiations between British special envoy Lord Ashburton and American Secretary of State Daniel Webster was the St. Marys River boundary settled. Ashburton and Webster represented governments newly formed in 1840 and 1841; there had been a shift away from the more chauvinistic Whigs in England and the Jacksonian Democrats in the United States. The

looming problem at these negotiations was the Maine–New Brunswick boundary question that had threatened to erupt into a general conflict over the rivalry of lumbermen and militias in the so-called Aroostook War. Nevertheless, once agreement had been reached on the northeast-boundary question, Webster and Ashburton turned to the unresolved matters of the northwest boundary. As talks progressed during the summer of 1842, Ashburton had advice from Anthony Barclay, the former British commissioner, and Webster met with Major Joseph Delafield, the former American agent, and James Ferguson, the former American surveyor. In their deliberations, Webster and Ashburton relied on the maps produced by the boundary commissions. Ashburton supported a variation of the claim that Barclay had put forward in 1826—abandoning Sugar Island in the St. Marys River and claiming the Pigeon River with its eight-mile portage. He also asked for the right of British subjects to use water channels on the United States side of the St. Clair River, the St. Lawrence River around Barnhart's Island, and the Long Sault rapids. Webster agreed to these terms with several exceptions. Although Webster refused to give up the territory of the eight-mile portage on the Pigeon River, he would allow British subjects the right to use the portage. Similarly, Webster granted British subjects the right to use the channels on the American side of the St. Clair, Detroit, and St. Lawrence Rivers in exchange for the right of Americans to use channels on the Canadian side of those same waters. With the signing of the Webster-Ashburton Treaty on August 9, 1842, the last of Michigan's international boundaries (and indeed all of the 1783 boundaries) was completed.[35]

In subsequent years, minor parts of the boundary were straightened or simplified, as was done by the International Waterways Commission of 1908, but in all important matters, the boundaries of Michigan and Canada have remained unchanged. It is a testimonial to the skillful work of the boundary commissions arising out of the Treaty of Ghent, exploring, surveying, and mapping the vast countryside from the Bay of Fundy to the Lake of the Woods, that such a workable and lasting boundary was devised. It is a particular tribute, however, considering how many boundary problems were created by the errors in Mitchell's map and the ambiguous language of the Treaty of 1783.

NOTES

1. There is almost no monographic literature on the making of the Canadian-American boundary in the Great Lakes region. John J. Bigsby's classic memoir, *The Shoe and Canoe; or, Pictures of Travel in the Canadas,* 2 vols. (London: Chapman and Hall, 1850); and Robert McElroy and Thomas Riggs, eds., *The Unfortified Boundary: A Diary of the First Survey of the Canadian Boundary Line from St. Regis to the Lake of the Woods, by Major Joseph Delafield* (New York: privately printed, 1943), are both primary material and the fullest account of the boundary commissions in the West. Fred Landon, *Lake Huron* (Indianapolis: Bobbs-Merrill, 1944), has about five pages on the commissions, drawn largely from Bigsby; Grace Lee Nute, *Lake Superior* (Indianapolis: Bobbs-Merrill, 1944), has four pages, drawn from Bigsby and the journals of Joseph Delafield and David Thompson; Chase S. Osborn and Stella Brunt Osborn, *The Conquest of a Continent* (Lancaster, Pa.: Science Press, 1939), has two pages; and H. George Classen, *Thrust and Counterthrust: The Genesis of the Canada-United States Boundary* (Chicago: Rand McNally, 1967), has six pages. Don W. Thomson, *Men and Meridians: The History of Surveying and Mapping in Canada* (Ottawa: Roger Duhamel, 1966), vol. 1, has a chapter on the "International Boundary Surveys," which includes two well-researched pages on the Great

Lakes survey. Francis M. Carroll, *A Good and Wise Measure: The Search for the Canadian-American Boundary, 1783–1842* (Toronto: University of Toronto Press, 2001), provides as much detail as any on the surveys in the Michigan region.

2. Samuel Flagg Bemis, *The Diplomacy of the American Revolution* (New York: D. Appleton-Century, 1935), 175, 196; Richard B. Morris, *The Peacemakers: The Great Powers and American Independence* (New York: Harper & Row, 1965), 262–63. Also see Jonathan R. Dull, *A Diplomatic History of the American Revolution* (New Haven: Yale University Press, 1985), 137–51. For a discussion of how the various boundary proposals would have affected Michigan, see Clarence Monroe Burton, "The Boundary of the United States in 1782," in his *When Detroit Was Young: Historical Studies* (Detroit: Burton Abstract and Title, 1951), 181–91.

3. Conde d'Aranda to Conde de Floridablanca, Memorandum on Boundary Discussions, August 3, 1782, in *The Emerging Nation: A Documentary History of the Foreign Relations of the United States under the Articles of Confederation, 1780–1789*, vol. 1, *Recognition of Independence, 1780–1784*, ed. Mary A. Giunta, J. Dane Hartgrove, and Mary-Jane M. Dowd (Washington, D.C.: National Historical Publications and Records Commission, 1996), 490–501; Richard B. Morris, ed., *John Jay: The Winning of the Peace: Unpublished Papers, 1780–1784* (New York: Harper & Row, 1980), 2: 268–84; Bemis, *Diplomacy of the American Revolution*, 215–20; Morris, *Peacemakers*, 305–10, 320–27.

4. "Preliminary Articles of Peace: First Draft Treaty, October 5–8, 1782," in *Emerging Nation*, ed. Giunta, Hartgrove, and Dowd, 1: 597–600; Morris, ed., *John Jay*, 2: 368–436; Bemis, *Diplomacy of the American Revolution*, 228–31; Morris, *Peacemakers*, 335–37, 346–50.

5. "Preliminary Articles of Peace: Second Draft Treaty, November 4–7, 1782," in *Emerging Nation*, ed. Giunta, Hartgrove, and Dowd, 1: 634–37; "First Proposition: Alternative Boundaries Proposed by the American Commissioners, November 7, 1782," in *John Jay*, ed. Morris, 2: 415–16; Bemis, *Diplomacy of the American Revolution*, 232–38; Morris, *Peacemakers*, 357–77; Charles R. Ritcheson, "The Earl of Shelburne and Peace with America, 1782–1783: Vision and Reality," *International History Review* 5 (August 1983): 322–45.

6. David Hunter Miller, ed., *Treaties and Other International Acts of the United States of America* (Washington, D.C.: Government Printing Office, 1931), 2: 97.

7. Ibid., 574–83.

8. The senior Barclay (Thomas) had studied law under John Jay and served with distinction in the War of Independence. After moving to Annapolis, Nova Scotia, he was elected to the legislature and eventually became the speaker. He was made British commissioner to locate the St. Croix River boundary from 1796 to 1798, the British consul in New York, and the commissioner for prisoners during the War of 1812. For more about these figures, see Carroll, *Good and Wise Measure*, 95–97, 105–6; and Michael F. Scheuer, "Peter Buell Porter and the Development of the Joint Commission Approach to Diplomacy in the North Atlantic Triangle," *American Review of Canadian Studies* 12 (Spring 1982): 65–73.

9. Carroll, *Good and Wise Measure*, 51–52, 107.

10. Ibid., 95–105.

11. Ibid., 107–11.

12. McElroy and Riggs, eds., *Unfortified Boundary*, 277 (first quotation); Bigsby, *Shoe and Canoe*, 1: 261 (second quotation). Also see Harlan Hatcher, *Lake Erie* (Indianapolis: Bobbs-Merrill, 1945), 107–10; and Alec R. Gilpin, *The Territory of Michigan, 1805–1837* (East Lansing: Michigan State University Press, 1970), 69–138.

13. Bigsby, *Shoe and Canoe*, 1: 297.

14. McElroy and Riggs, eds., *Unfortified Boundary*, 282, 337 (quotation), 348–49.

15. Bigsby, *Shoe and Canoe*, 2: 120. Cockburn and Manitoulin Islands were known as the Lesser and Greater Manitou Islands, although Manitoulin was sometimes used.

16. McElroy and Riggs, eds., *Unfortified Boundary*, 288; Joseph E. Bayliss, Estelle M. Bayliss, and Milo Quaife, *River of Destiny: The Saint Marys* (Detroit: Wayne University Press, 1955), 120–21. Bigsby gives a dismal account of British garrison life on Drum-

mond Island; it was seriously deficient in either provisions or useful activity. The results, he concluded, were drunkenness, poor morale, and frequent desertion. He related a macabre story of several deserters who fled to Michilimackinac. A party of Native peoples was sent to find them and returned with their heads in a bag. Bigsby, *Shoe and Canoe,* 2: 140–43.

17. McElroy and Riggs, eds., *Unfortified Boundary,* 266–330.

18. David Thompson Journals, 1821, vols. 17–19, Joseph B. Tyrrell Papers, MG 30 D 49, National Archives of Canada, Ottawa; Joseph Delafield to Peter B. Porter, May 31, 1821, E-117–4; and Peter B. Porter to Anthony Barclay, July 30, 1821, E-120–1, both in Peter B. Porter Papers (hereafter Porter Papers), Buffalo and Erie County Historical Society, Buffalo, N.Y.; McElroy and Riggs, eds., *Unfortified Boundary,* 335–58.

19. See Peter B. Porter to John Quincy Adams, December 17, 1821, box 1, Northern Boundary, RG 76, National Archives, Washington, D.C. See Anthony Barclay to Stratford Canning, December 18, 1821, FO 5/170; and Journal of the Commission under Articles 6 and 7, January 3, 1822, FO 303/29, both in Public Record Office, London. See John Hale to the Board of Commissioners, December 12, 1821, E-125–11; and Major Joseph Delafield to the Board of Commissioners, December 13, 1821, E-125–12, both in Porter Papers. Delafield thought that Barclay's demand for a guarantee that the islands would not be fortified arose from a British intention to build a naval base at Amherstburg. If they were fortified, the three small islands would control access to such a base. Major Joseph Delafield to John Quincy Adams, December 18, 1821, box 1, Northern Boundary, RG 76, National Archives, Washington, D.C. As for Bois Blanc Island, which went to Canada, Delafield wrote in his diary discounting its military importance, concluding that "in time of war the strongest will possess it." He noted that American settlers wanted it because of its navigable channel, but he held that there were other channels nearly as good. McElroy and Riggs, eds., *Unfortified Boundary,* 340–41. United States troops had occupied Bois Blanc Island at the end of the War of 1812 and had been reluctant to give it up until Mackinac Island, held by the British, was returned. See Anthony Butler to the Acting Secretary of War, May 8, 31, 1815, in *The Territorial Papers of the United States,* vol. 10, *The Territory of Michigan, 1805–1820,* comp. Clarence Edwin Carter (Washington, D.C.: Government Printing Office, 1942), 532–35, 543–44. Also see Albert B. Corey, *Canadian-American Relations along the Detroit River* (Detroit: Wayne State University Press, 1957), 8–10. Bayliss, Bayliss, and Quaife relate a local tale that St. Joseph Island went to the British and Drummond Island went to the United States because the British commissioner was persuaded to agree to this while he was drunk, although there is no evidence for this. The authors argue with some justification that the ownership of the two islands could have been reversed. Bayliss, Bayliss, and Quaife, *River of Destiny,* 129–30.

20. Stratford Canning to Lord Londonderry, January 1, February 8, 1822, FO 5/166, Public Record Office; Stratford Canning to Anthony Barclay, January 1, February 2, 1822, box 8, Anthony Barclay Papers (hereafter Barclay Papers), Maine Historical Society, Portland; John Quincy Adams to Richard Rush, January 5, 1822, diplomatic instructions, all countries, M 77, microfilm, roll 4, RG 59, National Archives, Washington, D.C.

21. Lord Londonderry to Anthony Barclay, March 9, 1822, FO 5/170; the Foreign Office to Stratford Canning, March 9, 1822, FO 5/165; and Stratford Canning to Lord Londonderry, April 29, 1822, FO 5/167, all in Public Record Office; Stratford Canning to Anthony Barclay, April 22, 1822, box 8, Barclay Papers. For a useful analysis of this problem, see Michael F. Scheuer, "Deadlock: Charting the Canadian-American Boundary on the Detroit River," *Michigan History* 67 (March–April 1983): 24–31.

22. Anthony Barclay to Lord Londonderry, June 19, 1822, FO 5/170, Public Record Office; Peter B. Porter to John Quincy Adams, June 21, 1822, box 1, Northern Boundary, RG 76, National Archives, Washington, D.C.; Journal of the Commission under Articles 6 and 7, June 18, 1822, FO 303/29, Public Record Office. For the text of the decision and the report of the commissioners, see "Proceedings of the Commissioners under the Sixth and Seventh Articles of the Treaty of Ghent with Great Britain," in *American State Papers, Foreign Relations* (Washington, D.C.: Gale & Seaton, 1858), 5: 241–44; and "Declaration of the Commissioners under Article 6 of the Treaty of Ghent (Document 33), signed at Utica, New York, June 18, 1822," in *Treaties and Other International Acts,* ed. Miller, 3: 65–69. Although the three small islands in the Detroit River were never again the

source of great controversy, a large protest was registered by many people in eastern Upper Canada about the cession to the United States of Barnhart's Island in the St. Lawrence River. Although this could be justified in terms of the distribution of islands in the St. Lawrence, it was not welcomed by the local population.

23. For more details of conditions at the Sault in the 1820s, see Carroll, *Good and Wise Measure*, 124–26; and Bayliss, Bayliss, and Quaife, *River of Destiny*, 54–72. Also see McElroy and Riggs, eds., *Unfortified Boundary*, 370; Bigsby, *Shoe and Canoe*, 2: 124–28; and Henry R. Schoolcraft, *Personal Memoirs of a Residence of Thirty Years with the Indian Tribes on the American Frontiers: With Brief Notices of Passing Events, Facts, and Opinions* (Philadelphia: Lippincott, Grambo, 1851), 87–93.

24. Bigsby, *Shoe and Canoe*, 2: 122; Bayliss, Bayliss, and Quaife, *River of Destiny*, 70–71.

25. Joseph Delafield to John Quincy Adams, September 24, 1822, box 1, Northern Boundary, RG 76, National Archives, Washington, D.C. For more details of the first year of work in Lake Superior, see Carroll, *Good and Wise Measure*, 117–23. Thompson told Barclay that they would not be able to complete the work until at least the end of the season in 1825—in other words, it was going to take three years instead of two. Even that forecast was optimistic. John Hale to Anthony Barclay, April 7, 1823, box 8, Barclay Papers; Anthony Barclay to George Canning, May 19, 1823, FO 5/187, Public Record Office.

26. McElroy and Riggs, eds., *Unfortified Boundary*, 375–461; William A. Bird, "Reminiscences of the Boundary Survey between the United States and British Provinces," in *Publications of the Buffalo Historical Society*, ed. Frank H. Severance (Buffalo, N.Y.: Peter Paul Book Co., 1896), 4: 4–7.

27. Bigsby, *Shoe and Canoe*, 2: 132–307; John Bigsby to Anthony Barclay, July 28, 1823, box 8, Barclay Papers.

28. Report of Mr. Thompson, February 20, 1824, "Journal of the Commission under Article 7," February 21, 1824; and Peter B. Porter to John Quincy Adams, February 26, 1824, both in box 1, Northern Boundary, RG 76, National Archives, Washington, D.C.

29. Memorial by Joseph Delafield, October 25, 1824; and Peter B. Porter to John Quincy Adams, November 10, 1824, both in box 1, Northern Boundary, RG 76, National Archives, Washington, D.C. Anthony Barclay to George Canning, October 28, 1824, FO 5/187; and "Journal of the Commission under Article 7," October 28, 1824, FO 303/29, both in Public Record Office.

30. Nicholas Garry to Lord Bathurst, October 30, 1824, FO 5/187, Public Record Office; John H. Pelly to George Canning, November 25, 1824, "London Correspondence with All Government Departments, 1813–1825," A 8/1, Hudson's Bay Company Archives, Winnipeg, Manitoba; "Diary of Nicholas Garry," *Proceedings and Transactions of the Royal Society of Canada*, series 3 (Ottawa: The Society, 1912), 6: 128; "The Report of J. L. Tiarks, Astronomer on the part of His Britannic Majesty under the Sixth and Seventh Articles of the Treaty of Ghent, on his Astronomical Observations for ascertaining the north-western point of the Lake of the Woods, November 18, 1825," sent to Donald Fraser, E-161, Porter Papers.

31. Peter B. Porter to Henry Clay, November 16, 1825, October 16, 1826, box 1, Northern Boundary, RG 76, National Archives, Washington, D.C.; Peter B. Porter to Henry Clay, October 8, 1826, in *The Papers of Henry Clay*, vol. 5, *Secretary of State, 1826*, ed. James F. Hopkins and Mary W. V. Hargreaves (Lexington: University Press of Kentucky, 1973), 395–96; "Journal of the Commission under Article 7," November 1, 2, 1825, October 5–11, 1826, FO 303/29; Anthony Barclay to George Canning, February 27, 1826, FO 5/215; Joseph Planta to Anthony Barclay, March 8, 1826, FO 5/215; George Canning to Anthony Barclay, June 17, 1826, FO 5/215, all in Public Record Office. Also see Bayliss, Bayliss, and Quaife, *River of Destiny*, 70–72.

32. Anthony Barclay to Joseph Planta, October 28, 1826, April 4, 1827, FO 5/240, Public Record Office.

33. Foreign Office to Anthony Barclay, July 5, 1827 (quotation); Anthony Barclay to Peter B. Porter, September 13, 1827, FO 5/240; "Journal of the Commission under Article 7," October 23–27, 1827, FO 303/29, all in Public Record Office. Peter B. Porter to Henry Clay, October 26, 30, 1827, in *Papers of Henry Clay*, vol. 6, *Secretary of State, 1827*, ed. Hopkins and Hargreaves, 1189, 1208–9, 1238–39. For a brief description of the English political crisis, see Carroll, *Good and Wise Measure*, 141–42.

34. In the summer of 1839, Secretary of State John Forsyth proposed to the British minister to the United States, Henry S. Fox, that the undecided boundary under Article Seven of the Treaty of Ghent be submitted to the arbitration of a friendly

sovereign, as provided for in the Treaty of Ghent. Lord Palmerston, the British foreign secretary, did not respond to this suggestion.

35. Lord Ashburton to Daniel Webster, July 16, 1842; Daniel Webster to Lord Ashburton, July 27, 1842, in *The Papers of Daniel Webster*, series 3, *Diplomatic Papers, 1841–1843*, ed. Kenneth Shewmaker (Hanover, N.H.: University Press of New England, 1983), 1: 624–27, 645–49; Daniel Webster to Lord Ashburton, July 25, 1842; Lord Ashburton to Daniel Webster, July 29, 1842, both in *Diplomatic Correspondence of the United States: Canadian Relations, 1784–1860*, ed. William R. Manning (Washington, D.C.: Carnegie Endowment for International Peace, 1942), 3: 182, 772. For a full discussion of the Webster-Ashburton negotiations, see Carroll, *Good and Wise Measure*, 243–306; and Howard Jones, *To the Webster-Ashburton Treaty: A Study in Anglo-American Relations, 1783–1843* (Chapel Hill: University of North Carolina Press, 1977), 87–180.

The Holes in the Grid: Reservation Surveys in Lower Michigan

Margaret Wickens Pearce

ON MANY OF THE TOPOGRAPHICAL MAPS PRODUCED BY THE U.S. GEOLOGICAL SURVEY for Michigan, you will see a feature represented by a thin red line, curiously labeled "Old Indian Treaty Boundary" or "Old Indian Boundary." Sometimes this line follows visible landscape features, such as roads, railroads, or property boundaries, but sometimes it is an abstract line on the quad sheet, referencing only itself. These lines are the reminder of a nineteenth-century mapping process—the mapping of treaty reservations in Michigan Territory by public land surveyors. The treaty reservations were lands set aside for Native villages as part of the provisions of the treaties negotiated between the United States and Native peoples. Between 1795 and 1855, forty such treaties dispossessed Native peoples of the upper Great Lakes region. Eight of these treaties were used by the United States to obtain the Neshnabe and Wyandot territories of Michigan's Lower Peninsula.[1]

Controversial and often coercive, treaties of the upper Great Lakes were secured by the use of threats, annuity payments, alcohol, and deception. Each treaty contained different provisions concerning how the land would be ceded, the nature of the annuities and other services to be distributed, the extent of land-use rights to be preserved for Native peoples on that territory, and the list of the parcels that would be set aside for Native villages or individuals within the land cessions. These reservations were a key factor in the terms and success of treaty negotiations.[2]

For Native peoples, the reservation boundaries signified where dispossession began and ended—the space through which the Public Land Survey would not run and thus where Euro-American settlement could not penetrate. For the United States, the reservation boundaries signified temporary placeholders for a group of people perceived to be incompatible with white civilization and the settlement of the Old

Figure 1. Treaty boundaries of lower Michigan. Data from Charles E. Cleland, *Rites of Conquest: The History and Culture of Michigan's Native Americans* (Ann Arbor: University of Michigan Press, 1992). Map by author.

Northwest. These temporary reservations would serve as the first step toward relocation and removal of Native peoples to lands west of the Mississippi.

Despite their significance, the logistics of how and where these reservations would be located were vaguely expressed in the treaty agreements and left to be worked out at a later date. Although the governments of both the United States and the different Neshnabe communities all had their own views about where the reserves should be located, ultimately the decision making fell on the shoulders of the deputy surveyors of the General Land Office, the Indian agents, and the Neshnabe *ogemak* (chiefs) who monitored the surveys.

Deputy surveyors were given separate contracts to survey the Indian reservations within their districts. These surveyors used many of the same techniques to map the reservations that they used to map the township and range lines. They worked in crews of five to seven men, including an axman, a chainman, a packer, and a cook. Measuring their angles by vernier compass and Gunter's chain, they recorded bearings in degrees, and bounds in miles, chains, and links. These surveyors marked corners using witness trees if they were available and, if not, using posts. They recorded the descriptions of these corners in their field books.[3]

In many other ways, however, the surveys of the reservations were very different. Deputy surveyors received their instructions for how to proceed not from the surveyor general but from the governor of Michigan Territory. Their field notes were kept separately from their regular township and range field books. Section lines were not to be run through the reservations, nor were interior corners to be marked. The result was a township grid punctured by large "holes" ranging from a few acres to tens of thousands of acres in size.

This chapter explores the mapping of the reservations from three treaties in lower Michigan: the 1807 Treaty of Detroit, the 1819 Treaty of Saginaw, and the 1821 Treaty of Chicago (fig. 1). These three treaties can help us understand the strategies employed by Native and non-Native peoples to ensure that the reservations would be mapped in their own interests, the ways in which these strategies changed over time, and their impact on the map of lower Michigan.[4]

When Lewis Cass became the governor of Michigan Territory in 1813, he inherited the additional responsibility of directing the Michigan Superintendency of Indian Affairs. As superintendent, Cass served as a liaison among the federal government, Indian agents and traders, and Native peoples. Cass's sphere of influence soon expanded from Michigan Territory to include most of the Old Northwest.[5] As both governor and Indian superintendent ex officio, his primary tasks were to acquire as much Native territory as possible and to supervise the conversion of these dispossessed territories into a grid of marketable public lands through the Public Land Survey.

To begin these tasks, Cass already had the territories in the southeast part of the Lower Peninsula that had been acquired through the 1795 Treaty of Greenville and the 1807 Treaty of Detroit. The lands conveyed by these treaties had not yet been legally brought onto the market because the Public Land Survey had not been implemented in the territory and the reservations from the Treaty of Detroit had not been mapped. By 1815, however, parts of the baseline and the principal meridian were in place, enough to start a grid in southeast Michigan. In 1817, the survey of township and range lines began, with several deputy surveyors leading crews to the north and south of Detroit.[6] Confusion about how to survey the *reservations,* however, remained unresolved.

The text of the 1807 Treaty of Detroit listed nine reservations in what is now Michigan and Ohio. They were defined first in terms of square miles or sections and second in terms of their general location. The treaty included a note that the reservations should be constrained in shape as follows: "It is further understood and agreed, that whenever the reservations cannot conveniently be laid out in squares, they shall be laid out in paralelograms [*sic*] or other figures, as found most practicable and convenient, so as to contain the area specified in miles, and in all cases they are to be located in such manner, and in such situations, as not to interfere with any improvements of the French or other white people, or any former cessions."[7]

When Cass started working on the problem of reservation location, he wrote to Josiah Meigs, the commissioner of public lands, in May 1817: "In the surveys, which [we] are now making, I am informed that no respect has been paid to these reservations, and a formal application has been made to me by the Indians, to secure to them the rights guaranteed by Treaty. These tracts embraced the scites [*sic*] of ancient villages, and it is therefore necessary, they should be surveyed with references to these villages

Figure 2. Reservations as described in the 1807 Treaty of Detroit.

1. three miles square on lake St. Clair, above the river Huron, to include Machonces village;

2. two sections of one mile square each, on the river Rouge, at Seginsiwin village;

3. two sections of one mile square each, at Tonquishs village, near the river Rouge;

4. three miles square on the river Raisin, at a place called Macon, and where the river Macon falls into the river Raizin . . .

5. four miles square on the Miami bay, including the villages where Meshkemau and Wau-gau now live;

A. six sections, each containing one mile square, within the cession aforesaid. [2 of these sections located at "A"]

B. [Wyantoe reserve relocated from the Treaty of Brownstown.]

Data from Charles C. Royce, comp., *Indian Land Cessions in the United States: 18th Annual Report of the Bureau of American Ethnology for the Years 1896–1897* (Washington, D.C.: Government Printing Office, 1899). Map by author.

& not with reference to the artificial lines of the general survey—[t]he thing should no[t] only be done in conformity with the stipulations of the treaty, but if possible in a manner satisfactory to the Indians themselves."[8]

In this letter to Meigs, Cass seems to have been stating that demarcating the reservations as part of the general survey would not work because each reservation had to conform to the siting of a particular village. Meigs replied that the reservations should be measured "conformably to the Treaty,

& if practicable, in a manner satisfactory to the Indians."[9] In his letter, Meigs shifted from Cass's idea of making surveys satisfying to the Indians "if possible" to one of producing surveys satisfying to the Indians "if practicable." In other words, the reservations must be mapped in conformity with the general survey.

At Meigs's urging, Cass worked with Surveyor General Edward Tiffin to determine how to locate the reservations, and Cass also held a council of Native leaders to discuss the surveys. As part of that council, an additional reservation was added along the Huron River for the Wyandot to resolve claims from a smaller treaty granting a right-of-way for the Chicago Road, the Treaty of Brownstown.[10] The contracts for the work were given to the men working in the districts where the reservations would be located: William Preston for the reservations on Lake St. Clair and the St. Clair River and James McCloskey for the Huron and Rouge Rivers and the River Raisin (fig. 2).

Preston apparently began his reservation surveys (the reservations at 1 and A in fig. 2) in 1817, along with his regular township and range survey tasks. Although Tiffin reported to Meigs that Preston had completed his survey responsibilities, the field notes for his reservation surveys appear to be incomplete.[11] In the State Archives of Michigan, there is a map done in watercolor showing Preston's reservations in red and the existing private claims in black (fig. 3). In this figure, the map is turned sideways to align north at the top. The two reservation surveys assigned to Preston appear as the darker gray parcels at Port Huron in the north and on Lake St. Clair in the south. The figure illustrates how the surveys fit the preexisting property boundary protocol of French long lots in that region. When we compare this early watercolor to Preston's survey plat of the township (fig. 4), we see the first evidence of the holes in the grid—the slanting tracts of the reservations make awkward angles across the section lines. As these reservations were mapped the same year that Cass wrote to Meigs stating that the reservations should fit the Native villages and not the general survey, Preston's work may have been completed before he received Meigs's orders that reservations should be made to fit the township grid.

James McCloskey's surveys were completed in 1818. He was a Maryland native who had been surveying in Detroit for about ten years; he had only recently been promoted to deputy surveyor.[12] To prepare him for the work, Cass wrote to McCloskey: "I am not aware that any more specifick [sic] are necessary than are contained in the Treaty itself. The tracts should be run so as to preserve a due regard to the Interest of the United States, and to a faithful execution of their obligations to the Indians. I know of no reason why they cannot be run in a square form. But if you discover any from the nature of the Country, or from the existence of other claims, you are at liberty to run them in such form, as will best attain the objects to be answered." Cass also wrote that he would send the Indian agent Colonel Godfroy to serve as an interpreter. And then he added an additional tract to be surveyed, the Wyandot reservation from the Treaty of Brownstown. For the Wyandot reservation, he was more specific:

> It would be very desirable that it should be laid out in a square form upon one side of the River. If the Indians evince too much repugnance to this mode, you will then propose that the Tract should be laid out in a Square form, but extending equally on each side of the River. But if no other arrangement will satisfy them, you may finally agree to survey the Tract upon both side [sic] of the River, with its lines up and down the River twice as long as those which cross it.
>
> I am informed that there are falls upon the River near the Wyandot improvements which will hereafter furnish valuable sites for mills. If you will run the lines, if possible, in such manner as to exclude

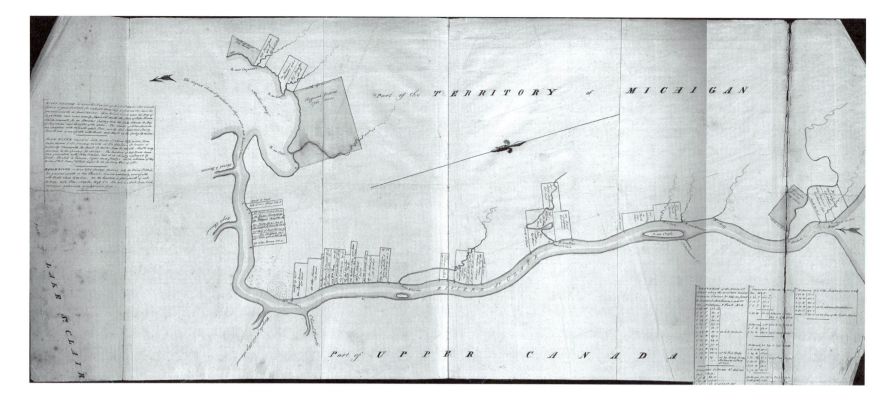

Figure 3. Untitled manuscript map of claims on the St. Clair River. Department of Conservation, Lands Division, RG 62-16, series 1, County Plats, State Archives of Michigan.

Figure 4 (opposite). Plat of T3N R14E, by William Preston, 1817. Department of Conservation, Lands Division, RG 62-16, series 1, County Plats, State Archives of Michigan.

these falls from the Indian reservations. The place of beginning for these tracts can only be determined by you upon an Inspection of the Country. They must of course include the Indian improvements.[13]

McCloskey worked on the surveys through the winter and spring, presumably with Godfroy assisting the crew, although no interpreter is named in the field notes.[14] By February, they had finished surveying the reservation on the River Raisin (4 in fig. 2), and although it was square (fig. 5), it did not ultimately match the section lines. Joseph Fletcher subdivided the township the following year, and it can be seen in the plat that the reservation overlaps slightly into adjacent townships to the west and north (fig. 6).

By spring, McCloskey's crew had mapped two additional reservations from the Treaty of Detroit, as well as the resituated Wyandot reservation (2, 3, and B in fig. 2). In contrast to the River Raisin survey (4 in fig. 2), these surveys were run on land already divided into townships and laid out to run on section lines. In addition, McCloskey's plats indicate that he was successful in keeping the valuable falls site outside the reservation line in accordance with Cass's request. In his report to Surveyor General Edward Tiffin, McCloskey wrote that he had completed the work according to Cass's wishes. "The reservations on rivers Huron & rouge [*sic*] has been made agreeably to the lines of the public surveys. [I]t was with some difficulty I could persuade the Indians to ascent [*sic*] to the reservations being located in that way, [i]t will save much [t]rouble in calculating the [f]ractions adjoining the reservations which would have been necessary had the lines been run otherwise."[15]

These latter reservations were the only surveys that McCloskey described as conforming to the township grid. He did not make the same claim for his earlier survey at the River Raisin. Was the offset

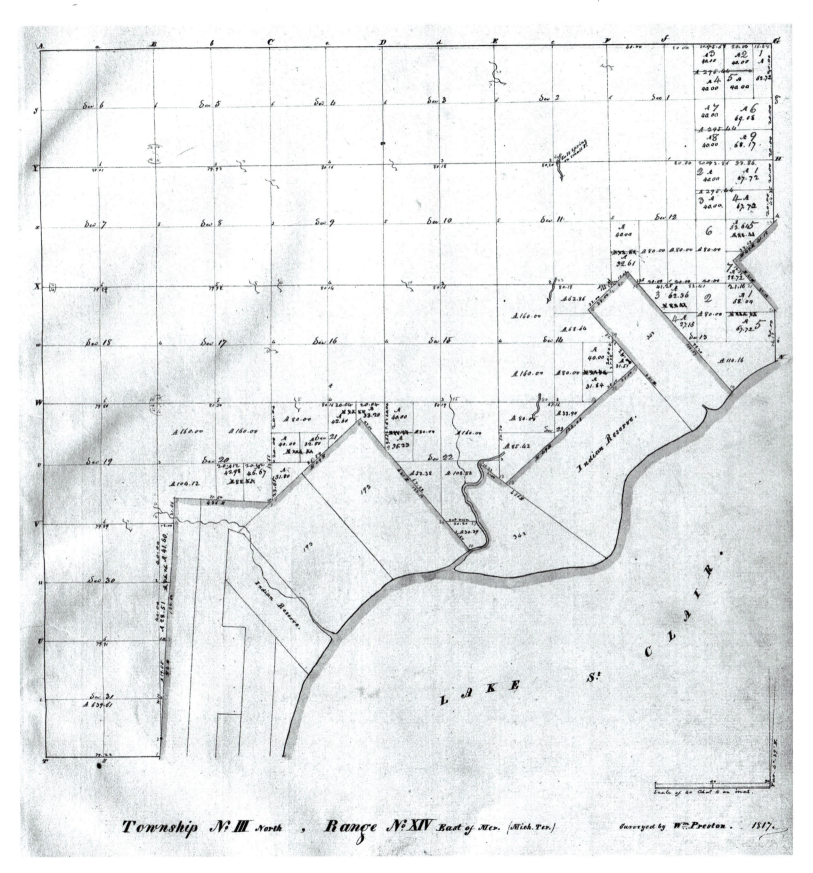

Township Nº III North , Range Nº XIV East of Mer. (Mich. Ter.)   Surveyed by Wm. Preston. 1817.

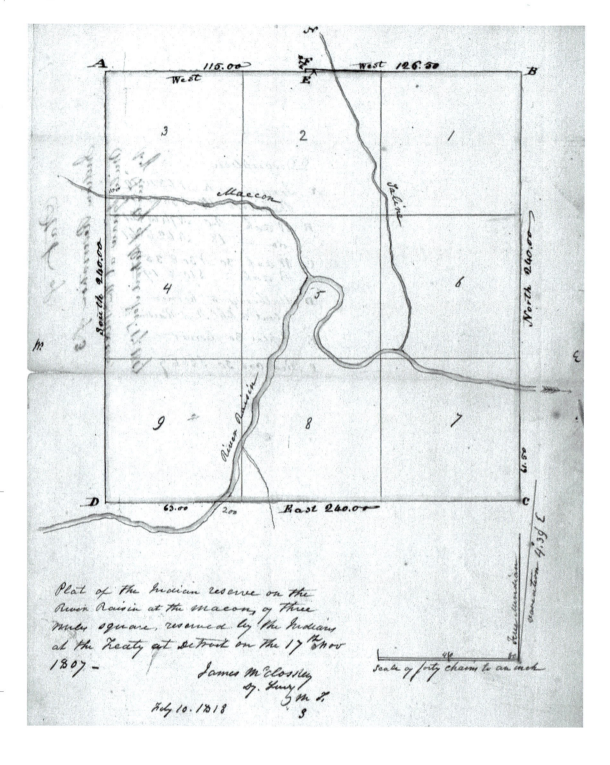

Figure 5. Plat of the Indian Reserve on the River Raisin, by James McCloskey, 1818. Department of Conservation, Lands Division, RG 62-16, series 1, County Plats, State Archives of Michigan.

Figure 6 (opposite). Detail of plat of T6S R7E, by Joseph Fletcher, 1819. Department of Conservation, Lands Division, RG 62-16, series 1, County Plats, State Archives of Michigan.

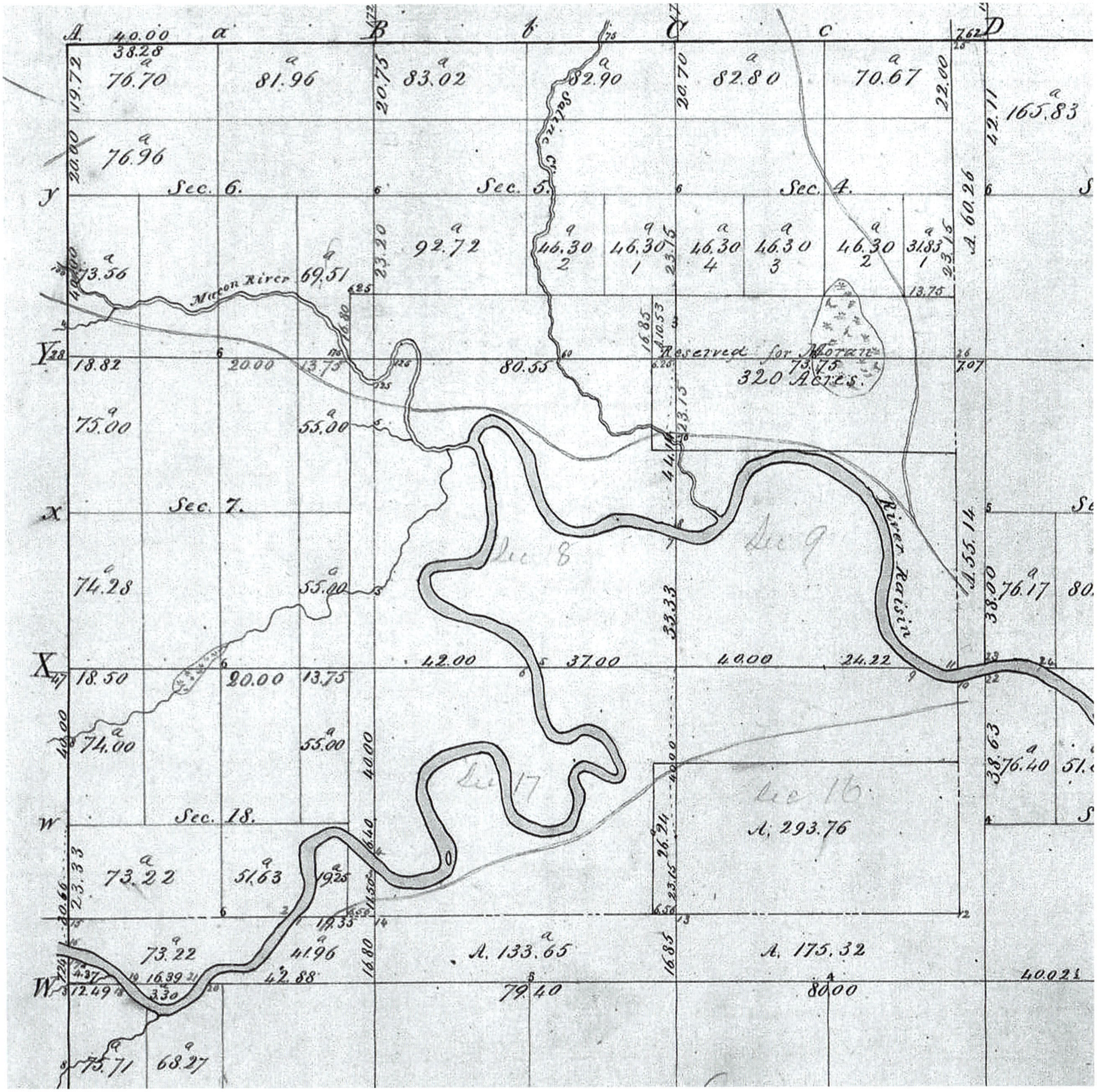
Sec. 6.
Sec. 5.
Sec. 4.
Sec. 7.
Sec. 18.
Macon River
Saline Cr.
Reserved for Moran
320 Acres.
River Raisin

of the square on the River Raisin a surveyor's error or the outcome of a compromise with the *ogema* (chief) at that village site? McCloskey left no answer to this question.

A year after the Detroit surveys, Cass and the treaty commissioners laid plans for the next treaty to obtain lands to the north of the Detroit cession. The 1819 Treaty of Saginaw resulted in sixteen reservations clustered on the major rivers between Detroit and Saginaw Bay (fig. 7). (One reservation, on the Au Sable River, was never located and so does not appear in the map.)

The contract to survey the region of the ceded lands was initially extended in August 1820 to Deputy Surveyor John Hassler.[16] Cass instructed Hassler:

> The views of the Indians should be consulted, and that their wishes should be complied with, as far as may be compatible with the interest of the United States.... The gradual progress of our settlements will soon render it necessary for these Indians to recede further west, and these reservations will then become as part of the great mass of public property. The particular mode therefore in which they shall be surveyed is comparatively unimportant to the United States but justice & sound policy equally require that any choice which the nature of the subject admits should be offered to the considerations of the Indians....
>
> You will therefore conform your surveys generally to the wishes expressed by them. And I think all the discretion that be exercised by the Indians should be limited to these parts of the Survey. You will allow them to choose either side or both sides of a River where the reservation is described as being upon a River. And you will run the lines upon such courses as they may wish without regard to the cardinal points.
>
> But you will in all cases lay out the tracts as near as circumstances will permit either into squares or parallelograms. If they are bounded by streams, exceptions to this rule must occur....
>
> It is scarcely probable, that the Indians will request, that you should survey any of their reservations in such a manner as to make the length greatly disproportionate to the breadth. Should a demand of this nature be made so that a compliance with it would be very injurious to the United States, you must refuse it & exercise your own discretion. I think it would not be politick [sic] to refuse a proportion of two, three, & over four to one, but I would recommend that you should endeavour by argument and persuasion to induce them to agree to such Surveys, as will have the different sides of each part not greatly disproportionate to each other.[17]

Hassler was not able to follow through with these instructions, however. Another surveyor, Horatio Ball, found Hassler injured and wandering in the Detroit vicinity that winter, far from the region of his contract and obligations. As Hassler had been missing for some time, his contract had already been turned over to Deputy Surveyor Joseph Wampler, and Cass forwarded the same instructions to Wampler that he had previously sent to Hassler.[18]

Joseph Wampler was a resident of Ohio and had previously surveyed areas in McCloskey's district before he was assigned to Saginaw.[19] For his surveys of Indian reservations near Saginaw, Wampler left two chaotic field books, each lacking specific dates for his surveys or notes regarding interpreters or Indians in attendance.[20] Many of the details of his surveys can be reconstructed, however, from his long and animated letters to his superiors.

In the summer of 1821, Wampler and his assistants started the survey of the reservation at Kishkawbawee (14 in fig. 7), and three additional reservations along the Cass River (10–12 in fig. 7). They

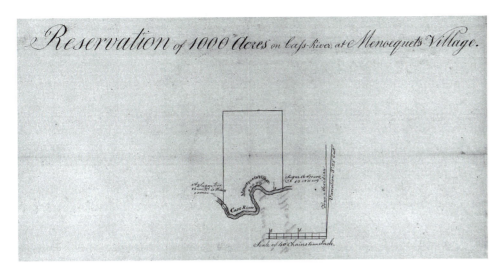

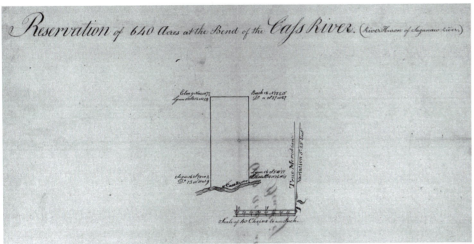

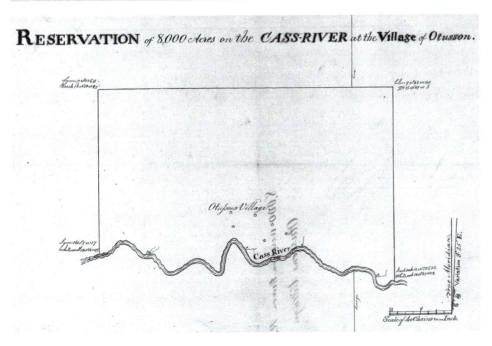

Figure 8. "Reservation of 1,000 acres," "Reservation of 640 acres," and "Reservation of 8,000 acres," by Joseph Wampler, 1821. Department of Conservation, Lands Division, RG 62-16, series 1, County Plats, State Archives of Michigan.

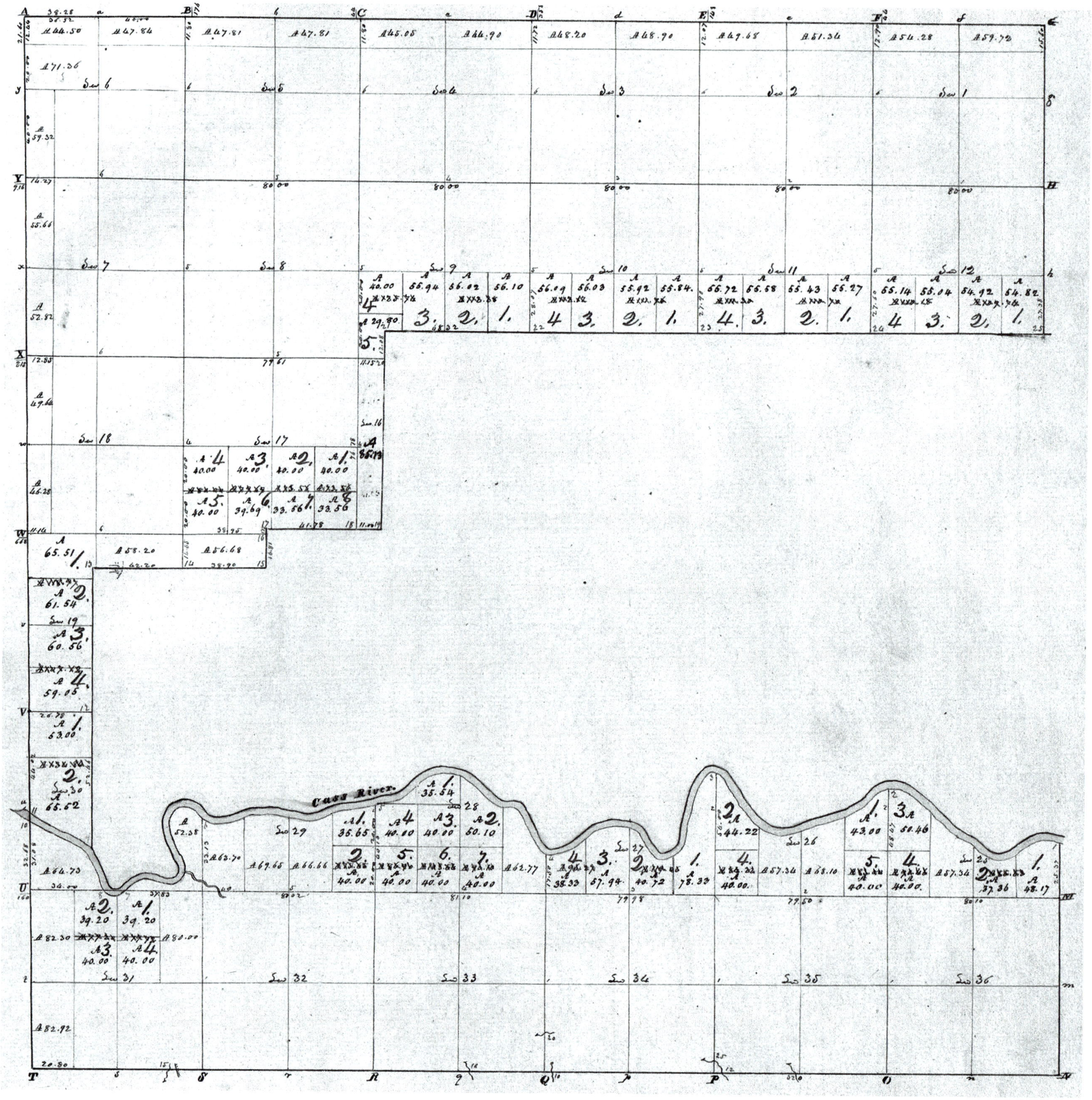
Cass River

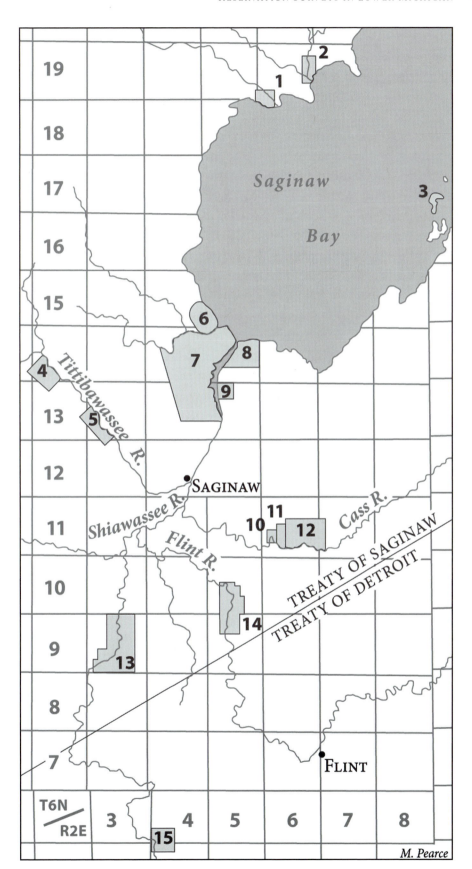

Figure 7. Reservations as described by the 1819 Treaty of Saginaw.

1 two thousand acres on the river Mesagwisk

2 two thousand acres, at the mouth of Point Augrais River

3 one island in the Saginaw Bay

4 six thousand acres at the Little Forks on the Tetabawasink River

5 six thousand acres at the Black Bird's town on the Tetabawasink River

6 six thousand acres on the north side of the river Kawkawling, at the Indian village

7 forty thousand acres on the west side of Saginaw River

8 two thousand acres where Nabobask formerly lived

9 one thousand acres near the island in the Saginaw River

10 six hundred and forty acres at the bend of the river Huron

11 one thousand acres on the river Huron at Menoequet's village

12 eight thousand acres on the head of the river Juron which empties into the Saginaw river at the village of Otusson

13 ten thousand acres on the Shawassee River at a place called the Big Rock

14 five thousand seven hundred and sixty acres upon the Flint River to include Reaum's village and a place called Kishkawbawee

15 three thousand acres on the Shawassee River at Ketchewaundaugenink

Data from Charles C. Royce, comp., *Indian Land Cessions in the United States: 18th Annual Report of the Bureau of American Ethnology for the Years 1896–1897* (Washington, D.C.: Government Printing Office, 1899). Map by author.

were instructed to survey "no more of the reserves for Indians . . . than are necessary for connecting the said reservations with the said thirty Townships."[21] Earlier in the summer, Wampler reported that his surveys remained only partially complete because "as my Interpreter (who is sent by the Governor) had fixed upon the time when I must meet him at the places where the Reservations were to be laid out I was obliged to leave part of some of the west lines without running out all the way on account of which my notes in the same book are part full & part blank." He concluded, "So far I have had no trouble nor difficulty with the Indians."[22] From the sketchy quality of his notes and plats, however, it may be more accurate to conclude that there had been little (if any) interaction with the Indians (fig. 8).

All four surveys that came in were offset from the grid. For the three reservations along the Cass River, the section lines were run the following year by Ball and Fletcher. An examination of the plat indicates that the reservations were all slightly misaligned with the township lines (fig. 9).

By the autumn, Wampler and his crew were working on the reservations to the north, on the south side of Saginaw Bay, assisted by the Indian agent Joseph Smith. There they were stopped by the Saginaw *ogema* Kishkako leading a blockade of other Neshnabek. Kishkako demanded that the annuity payments from the 1819 treaty be paid before they would allow the surveyors to continue their work, in keeping with the text of the treaty agreement. As Wampler later related to Cass, "the whole Complaint of the chiefs is (as they say) that you have not fulfilled your Contract, or they should not be stubborn."[23]

Wampler sent word to Detroit that they needed assistance, and Colonel Louis Beaufait, who had served as the interpreter for the original treaty agreement, arrived with the outstanding annuity payments. A council was held with Wampler, Beaufait, Smith, Kishkako, and forty other *ogemuk*, to discuss the reservations. In December, they finally reached a compromise on reservation location.[24] Wampler credited Smith with the ultimate resolution of the dispute: "Mr. Smith made haste to Assemble them, and he endeavoured all the while to persuade them to abandon their old Saganaw [*sic*] village, and to take their large Reserve along the mouth of Kawkawling, & Saganaw Rivers & the Bay. I now think we shall in all probability gain this point if so Smith has accomplished a great thing for Government. [The] difference in the value of the Soil of the different places is many thousand dollars."[25]

Cass praised the men's success at Saginaw: "I never supposed that there would be anything serious in the opposition of the Indians."[26] But to the Indians, he wrote, in a characteristically duplicitous fashion, "I am happy to learn that you are determined to do what is right and to permit the surveyor to go on with his work. Any opposition would have made difficulties, of which no man could see the end. . . . Rely with confidence on the justice of the United States, and you will not find yourselves deceived."[27]

In the spring of 1822, Wampler reported that he had "just returned from my long & tedious Surveying-tour in the Saganaw Country."[28] He submitted completed plats for seven more reservations (4–9 and 13 in fig. 7).

Comparing Wampler's reservations north of Saginaw to his earlier surveys south of Saginaw (as shown in fig. 7) presents a striking contrast. The reservations at Little Forks and Blackbird's Town (4 and 5 in fig. 7) are laid out in similar fashion to Preston's surveys of five years earlier on the St. Clair River: long-lot style, around the village. The reservations on the west side of the river (6 and 7 in fig. 7) are also independent pieces, enclosing Native communities on the river and bay without township and range definition. Those on the east side (8 and 9 in fig. 7) are indeed parallelograms in keeping with Cass's wishes, but with the exception of the northern border of the reserve at 9, they do not follow section lines, even though Wampler was running these lines simultaneously.

Meanwhile, a reservation to be located at a place called Ketchewaundaugenink was found to be located south of the treaty boundary on the Shiawassee River (15 in fig. 7). Ketchewaundaugenink fell into the district of another deputy surveyor, John Mullett, a resident of Detroit who had switched careers from tailor to surveyor earlier in the year.[29] In a letter to Cass, Mullett wrote, "I do not know how to obtain the wishes of the Indians unless there be an officer whose duty it is to attent [sic] to on such occasions."[30] Cass honored Mullett's request by sending Colonel Beaufait. On the topic of how exactly to reconcile the Indians' interests with the Public Land Survey, Cass was not helpful: "I should be glad to have it laid out in such a manner as to satisfy the Indians, with the least possible injury to the settlement of that part of the Country. This I consider an important object and I beg you not to lose sight of it."[31] The outcome of this collaboration between Mullett and Beaufait fit the grid at two sections wide, without any offsets. Mullett's survey was thus the only one of the Saginaw reservations to fit the grid.

While the Saginaw reservation surveys were under way, Cass was preparing to obtain all Native lands west and south of the Saginaw cession at a treaty negotiation in Chicago. In June 1821, Cass wrote to the Chicago Indian agent Alexander Wolcott that "there are no definite boundaries within which we are limited. The primary object is to extinguish as much of their title to land in this peninsula as possible."[32] Ultimately, the territory that would be obtained included most of the lands south of the Grand River.

The terms of this controversial treaty included five reservations (fig. 10). (The fifth reservation, at a place called Mangachqua, was never located and so does not appear in the map.) Again, surveys of the ceded territory began before any annuities had been received. That the United States had not changed its behavior on this issue angered the Neshnabek in the St. Joseph Valley, in particular Ashkebe, who

Figure 9 (opposite). Detail of plat T11N R6E, by Joseph Fletcher, 1822. Department of Conservation, Lands Division, RG 62-16, series 1, County Plats, State Archives of Michigan.

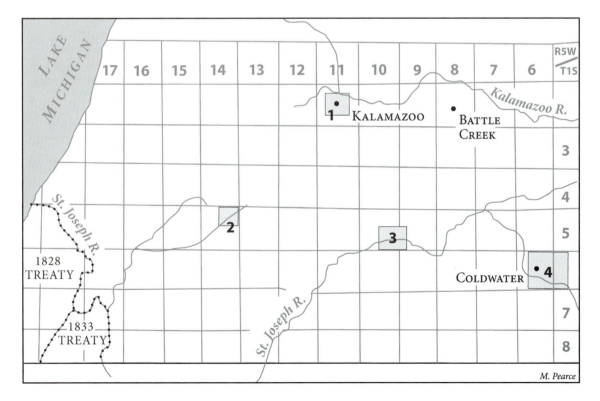

Figure 10. Reservations as described in the 1821 Treaty of Chicago.

1 One tract at the village of Match-be-barh-she-wish, at the head of the Kekalamazoo river

2 One tract at the village of Prairie Ronde, of three miles square

3 One tract at the village of Na-to-wa-se-pe, of four miles square

4 One tract at Mick-ke-saw-be, of six miles square

Data from Charles C. Royce, comp., *Indian Land Cessions in the United States: 18th Annual Report of the Bureau of American Ethnology for the Years 1896–1897* (Washington, D.C.: Government Printing Office, 1899). Map by author.

had signed the treaty, and Mickesawbe, an earlier signer of the Treaty of Saginaw.[33] On March 10, 1824, Mickesawbe and Ashkebe wrote to Cass through their Indian agent James Godfroy to express their indignation:

> When we went to pay you a visit in the [first] part of the present winter &, that we talked together on different subjects, you did not advertise us that you had sent your young men to survey our lands, we were very much surprised that when on our return from visiting you, we perceived that your young men had began to mark the trees, we thought then & still think so that you should have told us of it. . . . [I]f your young men will come & survey amongst us & survey our villages, let us know it. . . . [Y]ou know it is the custum [*sic*] with the whites that when you buy any thing, you pay for it before you take it away, Now we think you ought to act the same way with us, not to take possession of our lands before you have paid for them.[34]

To their letter, Godfroy attached a postscript which clearly articulates his own position on assisting the *ogemuk* with their treaty rights:

> I having been called upon by the foregoing named Indians to write you their harrangue, I plainly perceived in the course of their talk, that their reasons of writing you the present about the Survey of their lands is owing to the fear that they apprehend that their villages are to be settled with Americans, . . . as they have had it said to them, by some worthless fellows who had nothing else to do but to put these poor ignorant people in great apprehension of being expelled from their abodes, and that was to be soon. I assured them that they [should] not apprehend any such things, that it was not in the least the intention of our Government to injure them but to promote their welfare as much as possible, and I told them they might rest in safety, and they told me if they had an answer on this subject from you then they would rest easy. So sir I think if you would condescend to give them an answer to this, & assure them that no such things as that they were to be expelled from their villages would happen it would very much satisfy them and ease their fears so groundless; [p]oor wretches they are so credulous, that they will believe any thing said to them even were it said by a crazy person they would still believe it.[35]

Figure 11. "Indian Reservation of Six Miles square, at Mickesawbe (Mic. Ter.)," by John Mullett, 1825. Department of Conservation, Lands Division, RG 62-16, series 1, County Plats, State Archives of Michigan.

But Cass did not send the annuity payments, and when Mullett and his crew began surveying in the sugar camps along the St. Joseph River a year later, the Neshnabek were determined to stop them. As Mullett later reported, "I frequently met with small parties all of whom evinced a determination not to permit my surveying in some instances they would follow me, pull up the posts and efface the marks at other times would peremtoraly [*sic*] order me to leave the country, and with threats and menances [*sic*] step in before me lay hold of my compass &c." When one of Mullett's crew attempted to dispel the anger through explanation, the Neshnabek replied "that the land was theirs and we had no right to hack the trees," and continued to ask the crew to leave.[36] Finally, on one notorious day, two Neshnabe men walked into the surveyors' camp on the baseline with guns drawn for what would later be immortalized as the battle of Battle Creek.[37] Although no one was killed, the cumulative effect of Native resistance to their survey forced Mullett and his crew back to Detroit.

In the fall of 1825, however, Mullett was back to run the treaty reservation lines (1, 3, and 4 in fig. 10), bringing with him the interpreter William Knaggs. In September, they arrived at Mickesawbe's village

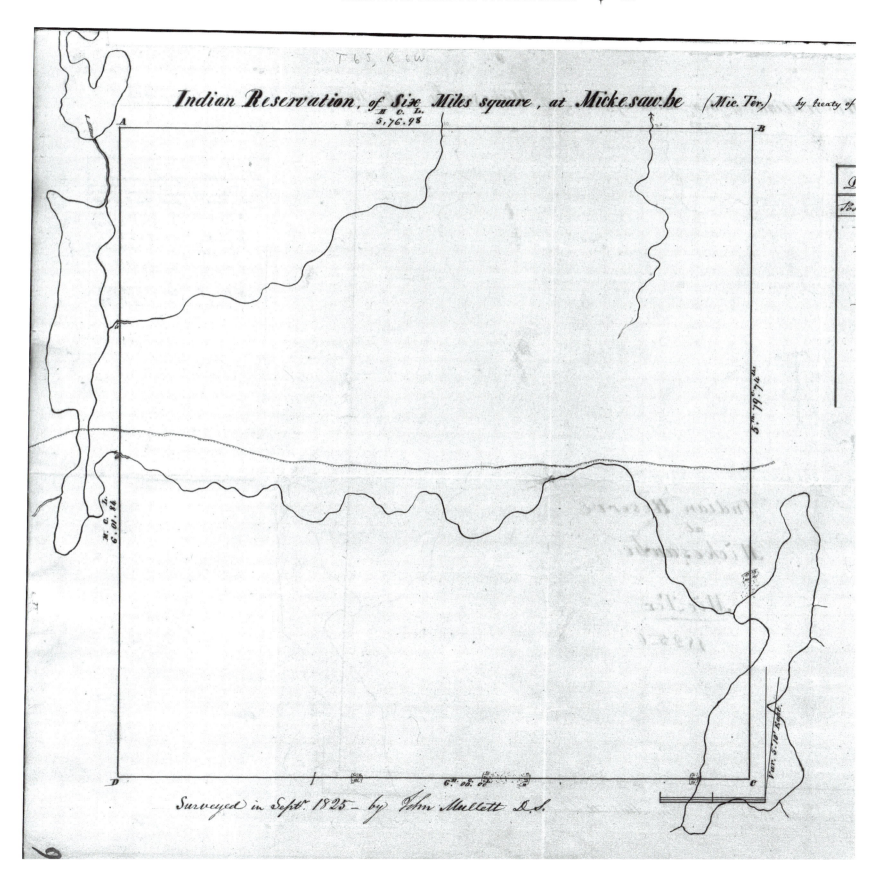

T 6 S, R 6 W

Indian Reservation, of Six Miles square, at Mickesaw.be (Mic. Ter.) by treaty of

Surveyed in Sept. 1825 – by John Mullett D.S.

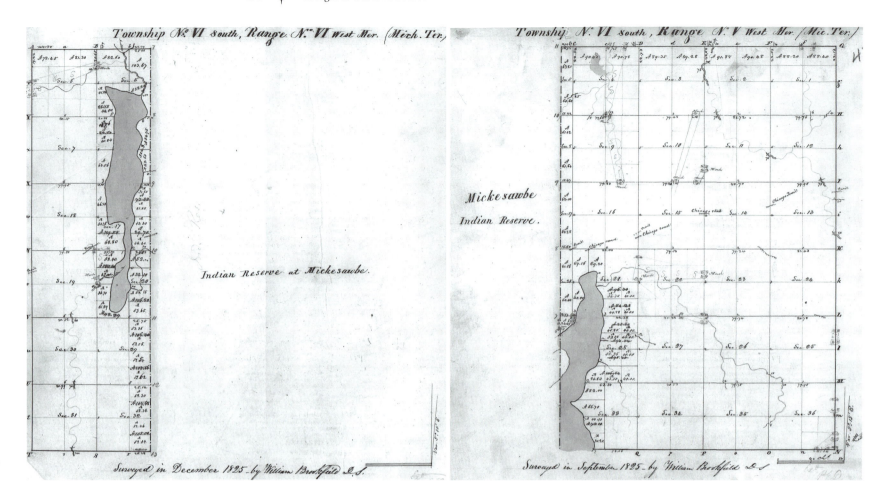

Township N.° VI South, Range N.° VI West Mer. (Mich.Ter.)

Indian Reserve at Mickesawbe.

Surveyed in December 1825 by William Brookfield D.S.

Township N.° VI South, Range N.° V West Mer. (Mic.Ter.)

Mickesawbe Indian Reserve.

Surveyed in September 1825 by William Brookfield D.S.

Figure 12. Plat of T6S R6W and plat R6S R5W, by William Brookfield, 1825. Department of Conservation, Lands Division, RG 62-16, series 1, County Plats, State Archives of Michigan.

Figure 13 (opposite). "Indian Reserve of three miles square, at the Village of Matchebenashewish (Mic.Ter.)," by John Mullett, 1825. Department of Conservation, Lands Division, RG 62-16, series 1, County Plats, State Archives of Michigan.

on the St. Joseph River to survey the reservation (4 in fig. 10). Both Ashkebe and Mickesawbe were there to meet them. Over the next three days, this group of men surveyed the bounds of the reservation together (fig. 11).[38] Mickesawbe and Ashkebe not only accompanied the crew, but according to Johnson's *History of Branch County,* they also set the east and west bounds. Mullett's orders were to run the reserve on section lines. Mickesawbe and Ashkebe wanted the reserve sixty rods west of those lines, and Mullett was forced to acquiesce.[39] The offset of this survey from the township and section lines can be seen clearly in the township plat (fig. 12). Why did Mickesawbe and Ashkebe seek to locate the boundaries in this way? Johnson suggests that the east and west lines maximized the amount of land within the reservation and minimized the amount of water.

A month later, the crew arrived at the borders of the four-miles-square Nottawasepe reserve (3 in fig. 10). On this two-day survey, a Native person, Kosheshawa (the *ogema* at Nottawasepe), again accompanied the crew, and Mullett recorded his presence in the field book.[40] In this survey, the northern and southern reservation boundaries were located neatly along section lines, with the east and west reserve lines following the half sections. This reservation, unlike the previous one at Mickesawbe's village, was laid out in harmony with the grid, which was a success for Mullett.

In November, Mullett's men reached their last boundary survey, the three-miles-square survey of the Matchebenashewish reserve. Matchebenashewish had signed the 1795 Treaty of Greenville and was

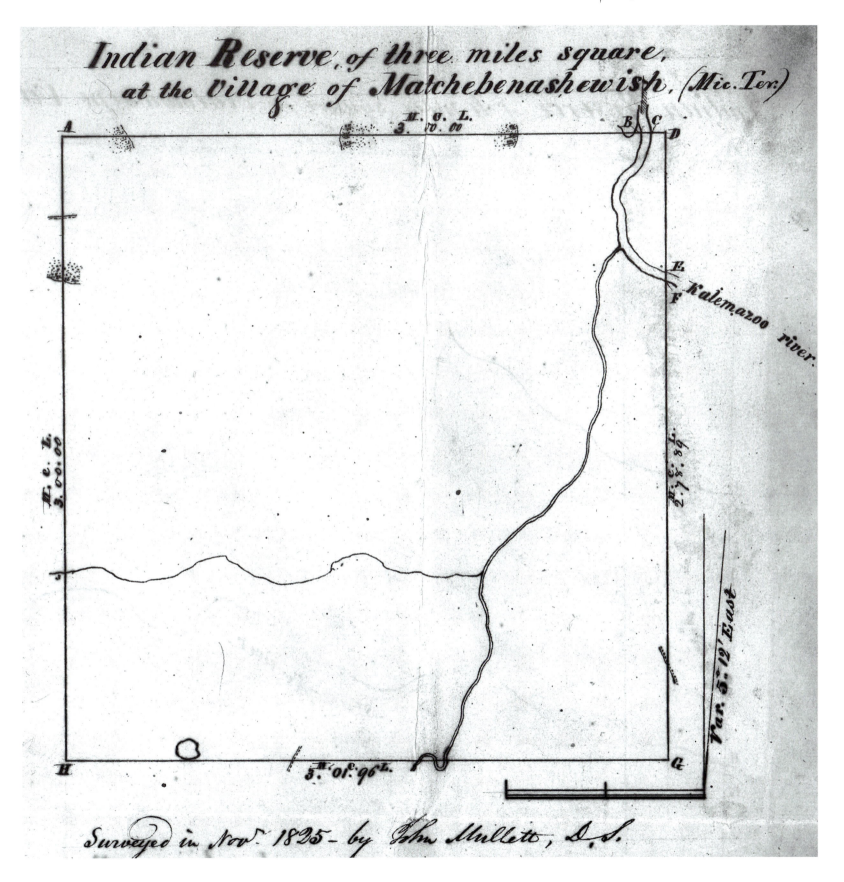

Indian Reserve, of three miles square, at the Village of Matchebenashewish, (Mic. Ter.)

Surveyed in Nov. 1825 by John Mullett, D. S.

a key leader in the St. Joseph Valley. He did not escort the surveyors, however; it was a Neshnabe by the name of Goselah who would be recorded as present on the survey in Mullett's field notebook. In his notes, Mullett writes that the place where they began at the northeast corner of the reserve was "near Goselahs house."[41] Although the reserve was small, the party proceeded extremely slowly; ultimately, it took four days to survey the bounds, about one side, or three miles, a day (fig. 13). The outcome was a reserve again offset from the Public Land Survey. In the plat, it can be seen that the square does not follow the section grid on any side; the whole is offset slightly north and east, but not by the same distance (fig. 14). Again, the offset is a mystery. Was it a compromise with Goselah? Or Mullett's mistake? The field book does not provide an answer.

Prairie Ronde, the fourth and westernmost reserve in the treaty (2 in fig. 10), was surveyed by a different deputy surveyor, William Brookfield. Brookfield had been recommended for the position of deputy surveyor by James McCloskey, the surveyor of the Detroit reservations.[42] In October 1826, Tiffin contracted with Brookfield to run the northern townships in the St. Joseph district. He included a description of the western boundary of the Treaty of Chicago, noting that Brookfield should not run the lines beyond the line of cession. It is evident from Tiffin's instructions that the perimeter of the treaty had never been surveyed; he writes that he has drawn the treaty boundary "represented from imagination, on the diagram."[43]

At that time, Prairie Ronde (along with Mickesawbe, Matchebenashewish, and the fifth, unlocated reservation) was slated to be ceded at a treaty in September. Thus, when Brookfield's crew of five surveyed Prairie Ronde in a single day, April 4, 1827, they mapped a definition that would exist in the landscape for five short months. They employed no interpreter, nor were they accompanied by any Native people.[44] Prairie Ronde reservation fit the grid perfectly, three sections by three sections in T5S/R14W (fig. 10).

In keeping with federal removal policy, treaty reservations were temporary holes in the Public Land Survey. The 1827 Treaty at St. Joseph eliminated three of the reservations from the Treaty of Detroit and all of the Chicago reservations except Nottawasepe. In return, the Nottawasepe reserve was increased in size as a consolidation of Neshnabe holdings and then ceded entirely in 1833. All sixteen Saginaw reservations were lost to the treaty of 1837.[45] Removing the Neshnabe people in lower Michigan first from their territory to scattered reservations and then to a single reservation in the southwest corner of the territory, Cass and the other commissioners used treaty reservations to situate Native peoples gradually on smaller and smaller areas. From these consolidated reservations, U.S. officials thought that a policy of removal could be more easily applied and enforced.[46]

Where is the evidence of these reservations today? Do the holes persist, or have they been filled in? If the landscape is a palimpsest, storing spatial history in layers for anyone who stops to look, then it is incomplete. Where there was a seamless fit between reservation and grid, as in McCloskey's section surveys and Brookfield's survey of Prairie Ronde, there is no visible evidence today of this map history. It is where the surveys do not fit the grid, where the boundary between reservation and township left awkward pieces, section fragments, and unmarketable corners, that this map history becomes visible.

Today, some of these surveys break into visibility only on the map. These are the ghosts of the treaty agreements, the lines residing in the in-between spaces as the conventional landscape adheres to township and range lines.[47] The reserves west of the Saginaw River are such ghosts; they figure prominently on the U.S. Geological Survey topographic map for Bay City, and yet no road or utility so much as references a corner of these surveys (fig. 15).

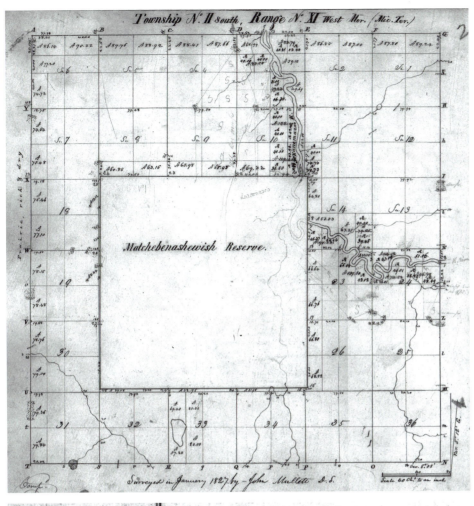

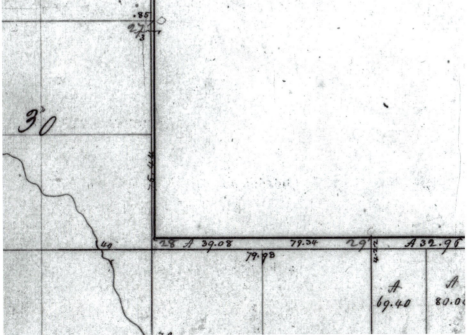

Figure 14. Plat of T2S R11W, top and detail of southwest corner, bottom, by John Mullett, 1827. Department of Conservation, Lands Division, RG 62-16, series 1, County Plats, State Archives of Michigan.

Figure 15. "Reservation of 40,000 acres," by Joseph Wampler, 1822, and detail of Bay City, Mich., 1:24,000. Department of Conservation, Lands Division, RG 62-16, series 1, County Plats, State Archives of Michigan; U.S. Geological Survey, 1973.

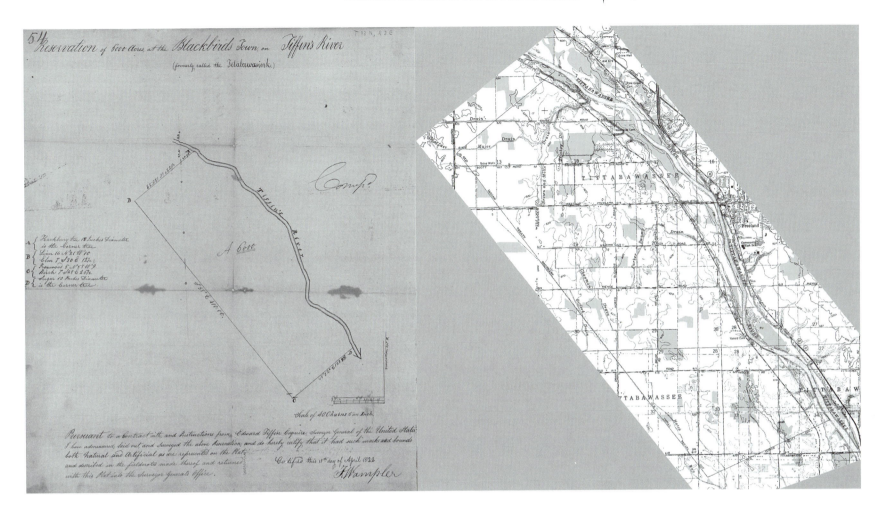

Other surveys were influential enough to have an impact on the arrangement of built features or cadastral boundaries, and they have left their imprints in both the map and the visible landscape. For example, in figure 16, Wampler's survey of Blackbird's Town from the Treaty of Saginaw is shown on the left. On the right, the U.S. Geological Survey map of this area shows that the reservation boundaries exist in the built landscape. The long boundary of the southwest edge of the former reservation exists today in property boundaries, a utility line, and a drainage. Preston's early survey along Lake St. Clair is embedded in the road and property boundaries, like the boundaries of the private claims that surround it (fig. 17). McCloskey's offset survey on the River Raisin also erupts into the landscape. The section road north of the town of Dundee shifts to follow the western reservation boundary instead of following the township line, which runs north and south just to the east of Dundee Azalia Road on the map (fig. 18).[48]

These examples are among the imprints on the built landscape that remain from the mapping of the treaty reserves. The holes in the grid may have long since been subdivided into sections, but their boundaries remain a solid, if stealthy, presence in the topographic map. Where their edges are rough, these boundaries persist visibly in the physical landscape.

In his study of the bureaucratic apparatus of colonial dispossession, R. Cole Harris wrote that the survey of reservations was a critical step in the colonization and resettlement of Native territory by

Figure 16. "Reservation of 6,000 acres," by Joseph Wampler, 1822, and detail of Midland South, Mich., 1:24,000. Department of Conservation, Lands Division, RG 62-16, series 1, County Plats, State Archives of Michigan; U.S. Geological Survey, 1973.

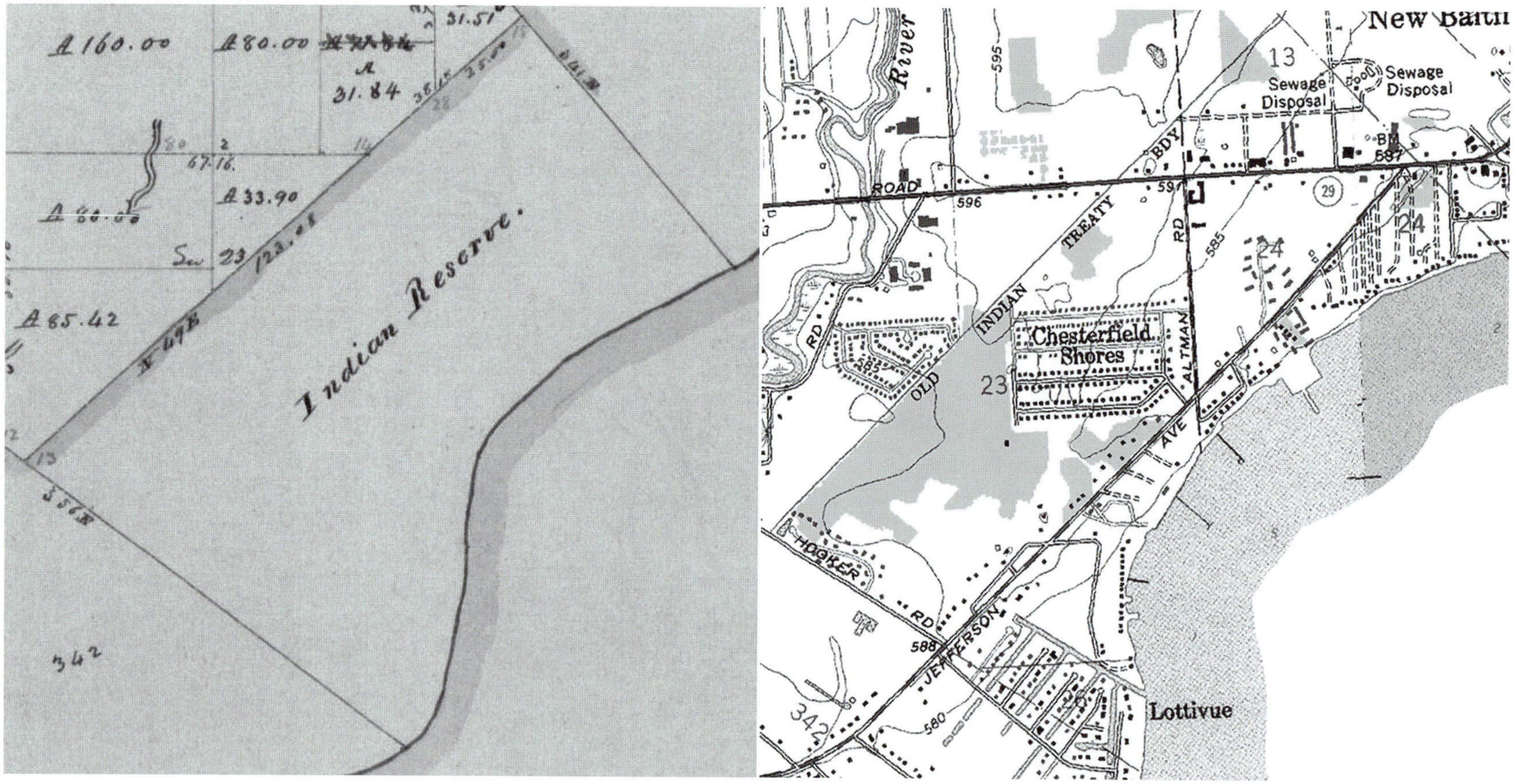

Figure 17. Detail of plat of T3N R14E, by William Preston, 1817, and detail of USGS Quadrant New Haven, Mich., 1:24,000. Department of Conservation, Lands Division, RG 62-16, series 1, County Plats, State Archives of Michigan; U.S. Geological Survey, 1983. (The modern municipality illustrated is New Baltimore, which lies within the New Haven USGS quadrant.)

white settler society.[49] Reservation surveys created the divided spaces that colonialism requires, what Frantz Fanon described as "a world divided into compartments."[50]

The dispossession of Native lands in the upper Great Lakes created two compartments: one large compartment for white settler society on the townships of the Public Land Survey and one smaller compartment for Native peoples on the treaty reservations. These reservations were used by the United States as a device to control and limit Native rights to territory as a necessary step in the progress toward statehood and Indian removal.

There was no compromise on the way the townships of the Public Land Survey were mapped in Michigan. But there was compromise, between Americans and Neshnabek, on the survey of the reservations. In lower Michigan, the policy of creating and controlling reservations was put into effect under the direction of Lewis Cass. As both the governor and the Indian superintendent, Cass put federal reservation policy onto the map of Michigan by working with Tiffin, the Indian agents, and the deputy surveyors. For the Neshnabe people, responsibility for monitoring the reservation surveys fell primarily on the shoulders of the *ogemak* who signed the treaties, as well as on those in the community who participated in blockades, planned confrontations, and exercised diplomacy. Although most of the treaty reservations were ultimately temporary, they interrupted the Public Land Survey long enough to leave irregular holes in the cadastral grid. These holes indicated the spaces where there was a rupture between the two surveys—the edges where the two compartments conflicted. Today, these holes remain imprinted on our visible landscape and on our maps, as well as on our memories.

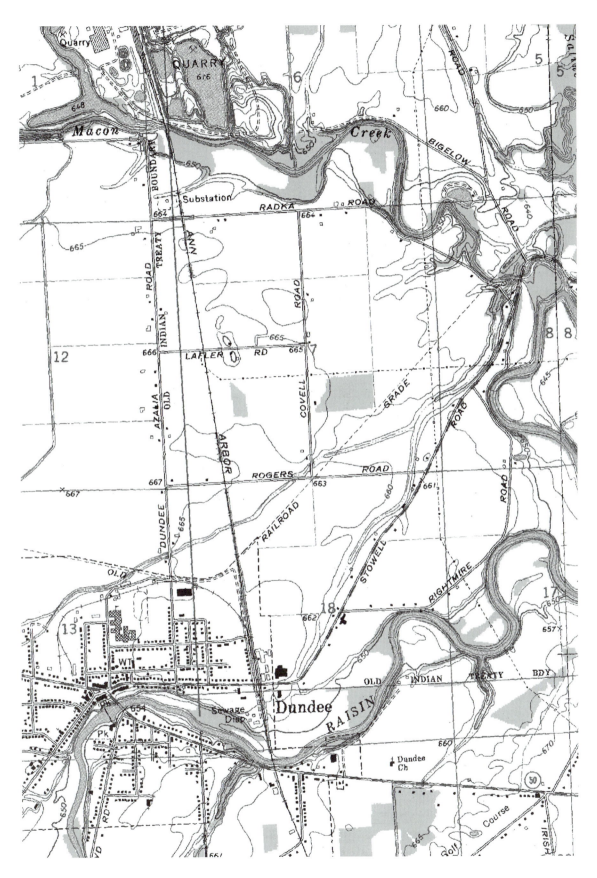

Figure 18. Detail of Ann Arbor East, Mich., 1:24,000.

U.S. Geological Survey, 1983.

NOTES

I would like to thank especially Mark Harvey and the staff of the State Archives of Michigan for all of their help with the surveyors' field notes and plats. In addition, I would also like to thank LeRoy Barnett, Norman C. Caldwell, William Cremin, James McClurken, Michael McDonnell, D. K. Sprague, and John Shagonaby, as well as the librarians and staffs of the Clarke Historical Library, the William L. Clements Library, and the State Library of Michigan, for guiding me on my way. Any shortcomings that remain are entirely my own.

1. For a full discussion of Michigan treaty history, see Charles E. Cleland, *Rites of Conquest: The History and Culture of Michigan's Native Americans* (Ann Arbor: University of Michigan Press, 1992); and an electronic exhibit of the Clarke Historical Library titled "Native American Treaties: Their Ongoing Importance to Michigan Residents," at http://clarke.cmich. edu/nativeamericans/treatyrights/treatyintro.htm. For the treaty history and geography of the upper Midwest, see Helen Hornbeck Tanner, *Atlas of Great Lakes Indian History* (Norman: University of Oklahoma Press, 1987), 162–68; and Charles C. Royce, comp., *Indian Land Cessions in the United States: 18th Annual Report of the Bureau of American Ethnology for the Years 1896–1897* (Washington, D.C.: Government Printing Office, 1899).

2. In this chapter, I focus on the general reservations granted to Native villages. For scholarship on the reservations granted to individuals, see LeRoy Barnett, "Land for Family and Friends: The Saginaw Treaty of 1819," *Michigan History* 87 (September–October 2003): 28–35; idem, "Private Land Grants in Michigan Awarded by the Treaty of 1821," *Chronicle & Newsletter of the Historical Society of Michigan* 26 (Winter 2004): 16–18; and idem, "Private Land Grants Awarded by the Treaty of Saginaw in 1819," in ibid., 19.

3. For an overview of the Public Land Survey in Michigan, see LeRoy Barnett, "Getting Southern Michigan into Line," *Michigan History* 87 (January–February 2003): 210–17.

4. Little attention has been paid to reservation surveys as part of Great Lakes map history, except when the boundary of a single reservation has had an impact on the map history of a particular township. For example, see Ronald E. Grim's analysis of the Billy Caldwell reservation boundary in Skokie, Illinois. Ronald E. Grim, "Maps of the Township and Range System," in *From Sea Charts to Satellite Images: Interpreting North American History through Maps*, ed. David Buisseret (Chicago: University of Chicago Press, 1990), 101.

5. Cleland, *Rites of Conquest*, 204.

6. For the story of the Michigan baseline and meridian, see C. Albert White, *Initial Points of the Rectangular Survey System* (Westminster, Colo.: Publishing House, 1996), 90–113.

7. Charles J. Kappler, ed. and comp., *Indian Treaties, 1778–1883* (New York: Interland Publishing, 1972), 94.

8. Lewis Cass to Josiah Meigs, May 24, 1817, in *The Territorial Papers of the United States*, comp. Clarence E. Carter (Washington, D.C.: Government Printing Office, 1942), 10: 699–700.

9. Josiah Meigs to Governor Cass, June 11, 1817, in ibid., 702.

10. Meigs to Cass, June 11, 1817; Josiah Meigs to Edward Tiffin, June 11, 1817, 702; Governor Cass to Edward Tiffin, July 4, 1817, 704; Edward Tiffin to Josiah Meigs, October 4, 1817, 706–7, all in ibid.

11. Edward Tiffin to Josiah Meigs, June 22, 1817, M511, microfilm, roll 3, Indian Office, Letter Books, Michigan Superintendency of Indian Affairs, National Archives, Washington, D.C. (hereafter MSIA, NA); William Preston Field Notebooks, 1817, Department of Natural Resources, Real Estate Division, 87–153, series 2, folders 4 and 5, box 4, State Archives of Michigan, Lansing. Preston's field books contain notes for the reservation boundaries but no plats, and the areas he surveyed were resurveyed in 1836. See Ralph Moore Berry, *Special Instructions to Deputy Surveyors in Michigan, 1808–1854*, ed. Norman C. Caldwell (Lansing: Michigan Museum of Surveying, 1990), 229.

12. Norman C. Caldwell, comp., *Surveyors of the Public Lands in Michigan, 1808–2000* (Auburn Hills, Mich.: Data Reproductions, 2001), 246–47.

13. Lewis Cass to James McCloskey, January 22, 1818, M511, microfilm, roll 3, Indian Office, Letter Books, MSIA, NA.

14. James McCloskey Field Notebook, 1818, Department of Conservation, Lands Division, 60–8-A, series 65, Surveys of Indian Reservations, folder 10, box 53, State Archives of Michigan, Lansing.

15. James McCloskey to Edward Tiffin, June 25, 1818, in *Territorial Papers,* comp. Carter, 10: 766.

16. Berry, *Special Instructions,* 64–65.

17. Lewis Cass to Deputy Surveyor Hassler, December 20, 1820, M511, microfilm, roll 4, Indian Office, Letter Books, MSIA, NA.

18. Horatio Ball to Edward Tiffin, May 2, 1821, in *Territorial Papers of the United States,* comp. Clarence E. Carter (Washington, D.C.: Government Printing Office, 1943), 11: 117–18; Lewis Cass to Joseph Wampler, May 4, 1821, M511, microfilm, roll 4, Indian Office, Letter Books, MSIA, NA.

19. Carter, comp., *Territorial Papers,* 10: 530, n. 42; Caldwell, comp., *Surveyors of the Public Lands,* 347.

20. Joseph Wampler Field Notebooks, Department of Conservation, Lands Division, 60–8-A, series 65, Surveys of Indian Reservations, folder 10, box 53, State Archives of Michigan, Lansing.

21. Josiah Meigs to Edward Tiffin, July 7, 1820, in *Territorial Papers,* comp. Carter, 11: 46.

22. Joseph Wampler to Edward Tiffin, July 16, 1821, in ibid., 138–39.

23. Joseph Wampler to Lewis Cass, December 13, 1821, M511, microfilm, roll 9, Indian Office, Letters Received, MSIA, NA.

24. Ibid.

25. Ibid.

26. Lewis Cass to Joseph Wampler, December 24, 1821, M511, microfilm, roll 4, Indian Office, Letter Books, MSIA, NA.

27. Lewis Cass to the Chippewas of Saginaw, December 24, 1821, in ibid.

28. Joseph Wampler to Edward Tiffin, March 20, 1822, in *Territorial Papers,* comp. Carter, 11: 230–32.

29. Caldwell, comp., *Surveyors of the Public Lands,* 265.

30. John Mullett to Lewis Cass, May 30, 1823, M511, microfilm, roll 12, Indian Office, Letters Received, MSIA, NA.

31. Lewis Cass to John Mullett, June 8, 1823, M511, microfilm, roll 5, Indian Office, Letter Books, MSIA, NA.

32. Lewis Cass to Alexander Wolcott, June 2, 1821, in ibid.

33. Kappler, ed. and comp., *Indian Treaties,* 187, 201.

34. Ashkebe and Mickesawbe to Lewis Cass, March 10, 1824, M511, microfilm, roll 14, Indian Office, Letters Received, MSIA, NA.

35. James Godfroy to Lewis Cass, March 10, 1824, in ibid.

36. John Mullett to Lewis Cass, March 21, 1825, in *Territorial Papers,* comp. Carter, 11: 667–69.

37. Mullett's account has been gradually distorted into a pioneer ghost story; for example, see the evolution of the story in *Pioneer Collections: Report of the Pioneer Society of the State of Michigan* (Lansing: The Society, 1903), 3: 581; and *Pioneer Collections* (Lansing: The Society, 1907), 6: 248–51.

38. John Mullett Field Notebook, September 15, 1825, Department of Conservation, Lands Division, 60–8-A, series 65, Surveys of Indian Reservations, folder 10, box 53, State Archives of Michigan, Lansing.

39. Crisfield Johnson, *History of Branch County, Michigan* (Philadelphia: Everts and Abbott, 1879), 34.

40. John Mullett Field Notebook, October 14, 1825, Department of Conservation, Lands Division, 60–8-A, series 65, Surveys of Indian Reservations, folder 10, box 53, State Archives of Michigan, Lansing; Harry G. Cutler, *History of St. Joseph County, Michigan* (Chicago: Lewis Publishing, 1911), 1: 20.

41. John Mullett Field Notebook, November 27, 1825, Department of Conservation, Lands Division, 60–8-A, series 65, Surveys of Indian Reservations, folder 10, box 53, State Archives of Michigan, Lansing.

42. Caldwell, comp., *Surveyors of the Public Lands,* 247.

43. Berry, *Special Instructions,* 108–9.

44. Alfred Mathews, *History of Cass County, Michigan* (Chicago: Waterman and Watkins, 1882), 31; William Brookfield Field Notebook, November 27, 1825, Department of Conservation, Lands Division, 60–8-A, series 65, Surveys of Indian Reservations, folder 10, box 53, State Archives of Michigan, Lansing.

45. Kappler, ed. and comp., *Indian Treaties,* 283–84, 402–15, 482–86.

46. The actual outcome of the Indian Removal Act in southern Michigan was complex. For example, see Susan Sleeper-Smith, *Indian Women and French Men: Rethinking Cultural Encounter in the Western Great Lakes* (Amherst: University of Massachusetts Press, 2001), esp. 96–115.

47. The idea of the reservation surveys as ghostly presences is from Jay Johnson, personal communication with author, March 16, 2004.

48. Compare figure 18 to the southwest corner of James McCloskey's survey in figure 5 and Joseph Fletcher's plat in figure 6.

49. R. Cole Harris, "How Did Colonialism Dispossess? Comments from an Edge of Empire," *Annals of the Association of American Geographers* 94, no. 1 (2004): 165–82.

50. Frantz Fanon, *The Wretched of the Earth* (New York: Grove Press, 1963), 37–38; R. Cole Harris, *Making Native Space: Colonialism, Resistance, and Reserves in British Columbia* (Vancouver: University of British Columbia Press, 2002), xxiv.

Mapping the Grand Traverse Indian Country: The Contributions of Peter Dougherty

Helen Hornbeck Tanner

THE REVEREND PETER DOUGHERTY (1805–1894) CAME TO NORTHWESTERN MICHIGAN in 1838 as a missionary sent out by the Board of Foreign Missions of the Presbyterian Church. He has not been known as a cartographer, but his sketch maps of the Grand Traverse region in letters sent back to his superiors in Philadelphia are the earliest reasonably accurate record of the contours of Grand Traverse Bay and the distribution of the Indian population in the vicinity. For this coastal region, as well as interior lower Michigan, the age of discovery, exploration, and accurate mapping was delayed until the mid-nineteenth century. Previous travelers who informed mapmakers about their journeys clearly had followed the outer coastline of the east shore of Lake Michigan and never entered Grand Traverse Bay.

Dougherty came to northwestern Michigan a year ahead of the initial surveys of this little-known section of the new state, which had been admitted to the Union in January 1837. He returned in 1839, the year after his initial visit, to establish a school and mission. He met the first survey teams to reach Grand Traverse Bay and remained vitally interested in their progress toward opening up the region for land sales. Dougherty's particular concern was to see that reservations or public lands be secured for his neighbors, the Ottawas and Ojibwes (called Chippewas at the time), as well as for the Presbyterian Church's mission site.

A review of the maps of Michigan available in the 1830s indicates general ignorance of the northwestern Lower Peninsula in contemporary cartographic representations of the region. A typical example is James Finlayson's map "Michigan Territory," published at Philadelphia in 1822 in an atlas brought out by the well-known firm Carey and Lea (fig. 1).[1] In this characteristic map of the era, Grand Traverse Bay is tilted to the southeast and lacks the identifying peninsula dividing the bay into two separate arms.

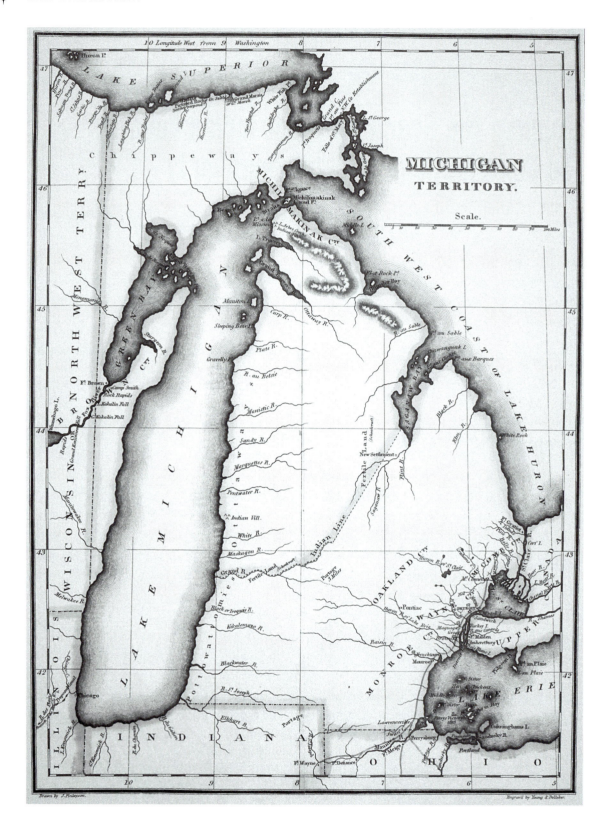

Figure 1. Michigan Territory. James Finlayson, 1822. James Finlayson, "Michigan Territory," in *A Complete Historical, Chronological, and Geographical American Atlas* (Philadelphia: H. C. Carey and I. Lea, 1822), plate 36. Courtesy of The Newberry Library, Chicago.

A main purpose of this particular map was to give some idea of the land southeast of the Grand River and Saginaw Bay ceded to the federal government by the resident Ottawas, Ojibwes, and Potawatomis in 1819 and 1821 treaties.[2] The coastal outlines of Lower Michigan in maps of the 1820s are all similar to their eighteenth-century predecessors.

A reasonably accurate map of lower Michigan was not published until 1841, following the completion of basic surveying in 1840. But when Peter Dougherty arrived at Mackinac Island in 1838, surveying was just beginning northwest of the Grand River. The first survey map of Michigan land, appearing in 1825 (fig. 2), covered only the southeastern section of the territory.[3] In 1830, John Farmer began publishing an annual map indicating the progress of government surveys in southern Michigan. His ambitious map of the Michigan and Wisconsin Territories, included in a Colton atlas of 1836 (fig. 3), exaggerates the area actually surveyed by featuring projected counties in color, as well as those in which surveys had been completed.[4] More realistic is Farmer's map of Michigan published by Colton a year later (1837), showing no land surveyed north of the Grand River in western Michigan but an extension of surveys southwest of Saginaw Bay. Yet the inset in the 1837 edition of Farmer's map (fig. 4) portrays the same general outline of northwestern Michigan seen in maps printed fifteen years earlier.[5] None of the early-nineteenth-century maps of Michigan by Farmer, or any other cartographer, shows the established Indian towns, with one exception, a Farmer map included in a volume for prospective German immigrants published in Baltimore in 1834.[6] This map identifies twenty-two Indian villages in southern Michigan. Present-day Michigan northwest of the Grand River was still an unknown area except to Indians and fur traders.

In contrast to the professionally produced maps of the early nineteenth century—maps that are conspicuously erroneous in their representation of Michigan north of the Grand River—the hand-drawn maps of Henry R. Schoolcraft and Peter Dougherty provide significant information because they had personal knowledge of the area. Slight progress in mapping northern Michigan began with the map drawn by Schoolcraft, who was acting superintendent of Indian affairs, to accompany his 1837 report to the commissioner of Indian affairs. Although the delineation of the Lower Peninsula follows the distortion typical of the 1820s, this hand-colored manuscript map for the first time draws the little peninsula dividing Grand Traverse Bay (fig 5).[7] Schoolcraft had received firsthand information about the bay and the peninsula from his brother-in-law, John Johnston, who traded at Grand Traverse during the winter of 1834–35. The main purpose of the Schoolcraft map was to portray approximate locations of Indian reservations created by treaties within the Michigan superintendency.

Far more accurate and complete for the Grand Traverse region are two small sketch maps drawn by Peter Dougherty after he set up a school and mission on the bay in the spring of 1839. In a letter sent to Philadelphia in June, Dougherty draws for the first time a recognizable outline of Grand Traverse Bay including the peninsula. He also presents for the first time the human geography of the region, showing the location of contemporary Indian settlements (fig. 6).[8] More complete is a second map, with additional Indian villages, which he constructed after he had talked with government surveyors later in 1839 (fig. 7).[9] In fact, Dougherty represents the link between informal exploratory cartography and the organized government surveys that led to the sale of lands in the public domain. In the Grand Traverse region this procedure made halting progress over a period of twenty years, from 1839 to 1859. Dougherty's correspondence throughout this period reveals the effects of the surveying and mapping process on the lives of the resident Indian population.

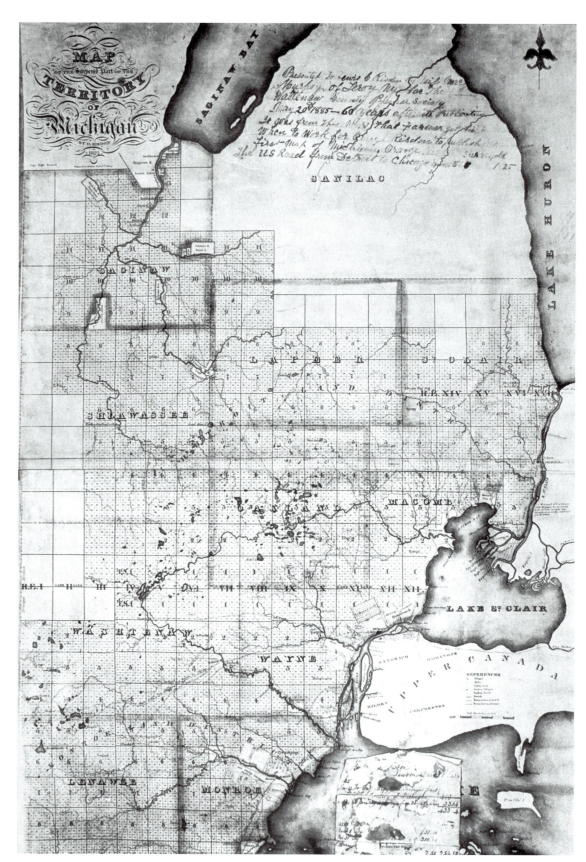

Figure 2. Map of the Surveyed Part of the Territory of Michigan. Orange Risdon, 1825. Orange Risdon, *Map of the Surveyed Part of the Territory of Michigan* (Albany: Rawdon, Clark, 1825). Courtesy of The Newberry Library, Chicago.

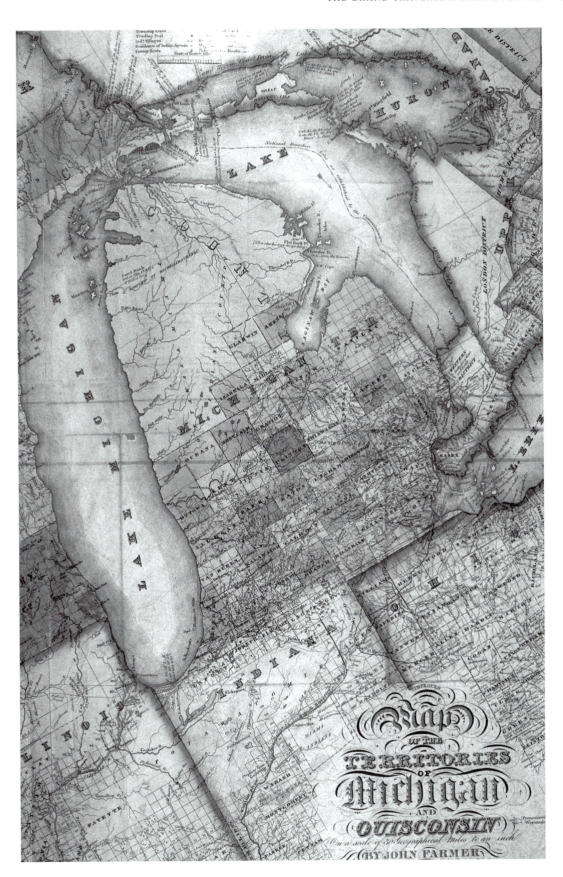

Figure 3. Improved Map of the Territories of Michigan and Ouisconsin (Pronounced Wisconsin). John Farmer, 1836. John Farmer, *Improved Map of the Territories of Michigan and Ouisconsin (Pronounced Wisconsin)* (New York: J. H. Colton, 1836). Courtesy of The Newberry Library, Chicago.

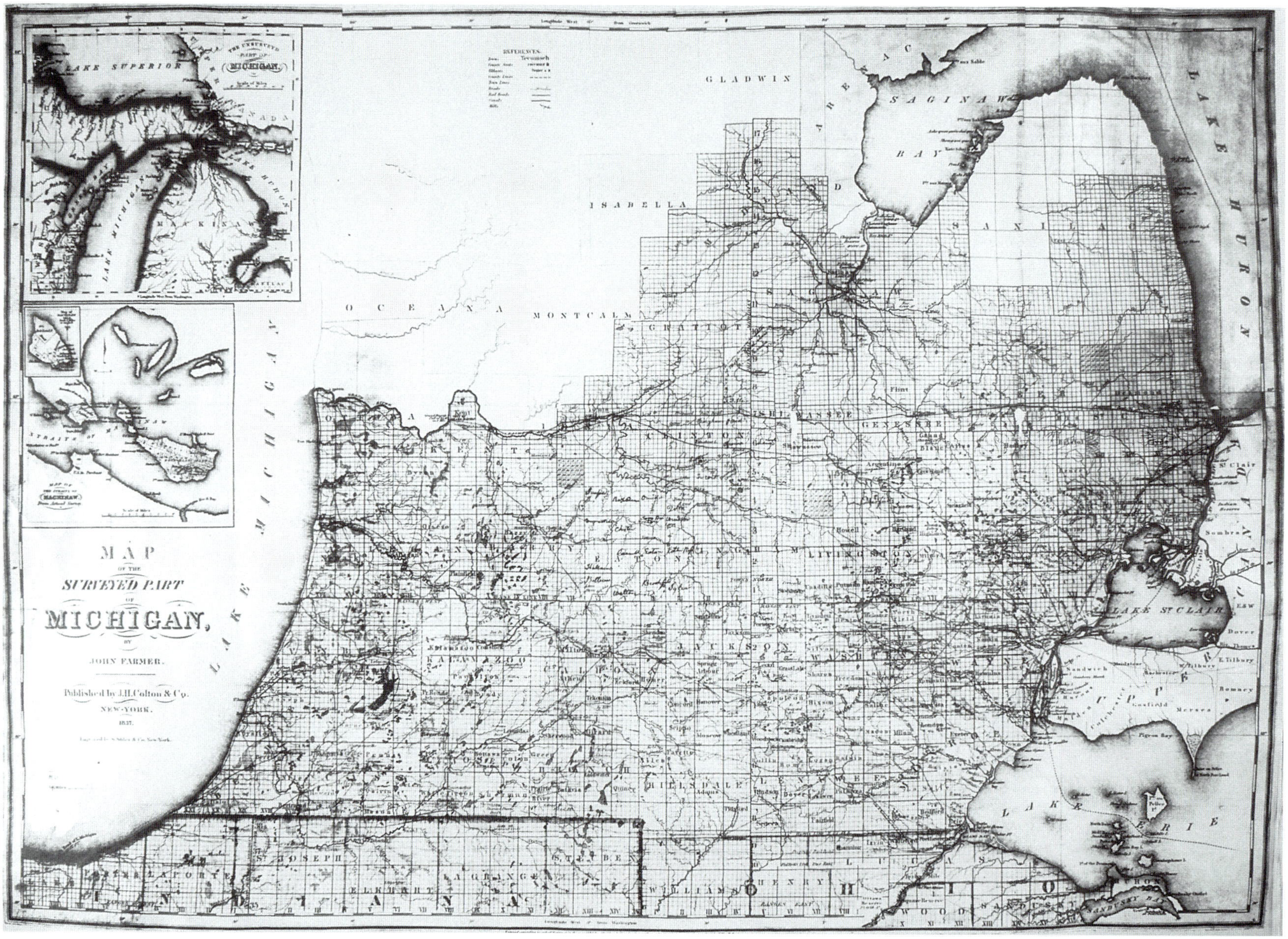

Figure 4. Map of the Surveyed Part of Michigan. John Farmer, 1837. John Farmer, *Map of the Surveyed Part of Michigan* (New York: J. H. Colton, 1837). Courtesy of The Newberry Library, Chicago.

From a historical point of view, the same course of events was responsible for the creation of the Schoolcraft reservation map and Dougherty's sketch maps and for the arrival of surveyors in northwestern Michigan. This sequence of events began with the negotiation of a treaty in March 1836 by which Indians ceded homelands in northwestern Michigan and the Upper Peninsula to the federal government, followed by the achievement of Michigan statehood in January 1837, and culminating with organized surveys and mapping in the years 1838 to 1852. Progress toward the first two goals, land acquisition and statehood, proceeded simultaneously, during a complex interval in Michigan history. It is important to understand the human as well as the cartographic consequences of this course of events. With that emphasis in mind, this story of surveying and mapping now turns to the Indian residents of the Grand

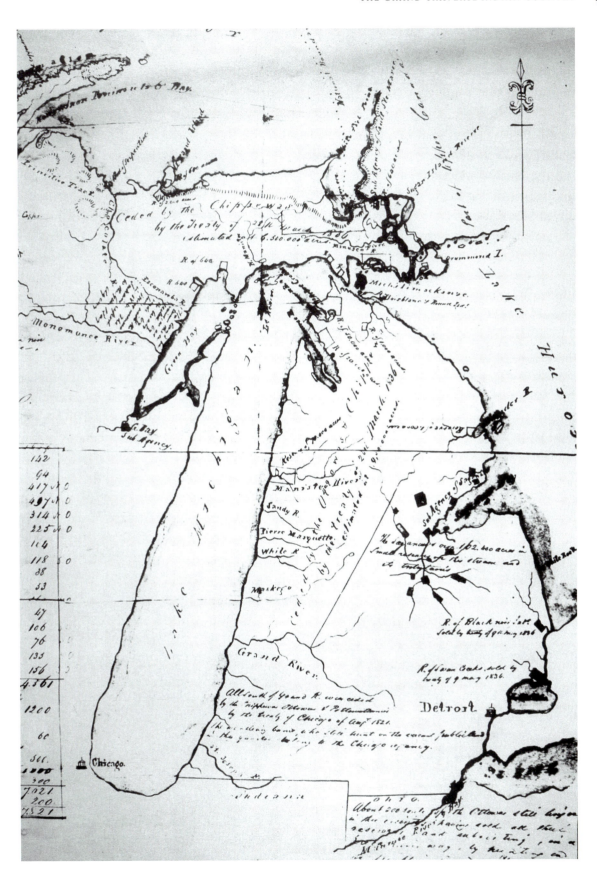

Figure 5. Map of the Acting Superintendency of Michigan. Henry R. Schoolcraft, 1837. Henry R. Schoolcraft, "Map of the Acting Superintendency of Michigan, 1837," RG 75, National Archives, Washington, D.C. Courtesy of The Newberry Library, Chicago.

Traverse region and the changes that treaty making, statehood, and surveying brought to their lives and to their local advocate, Peter Dougherty.

The Indian people whom Peter Dougherty came to know in 1839 were Ojibwes and Ottawas who were reported to be mid-eighteenth-century arrivals in the Grand Traverse region.[10] Recent archaeological evidence indicates two significant periods of much earlier occupation, and intervening eras of hunting activity in the bay area, beginning perhaps as early as 400 C.E. with the latest occupancy ending about 1420, long before the appearance of the Ottawas and Ojibwes[11]

The Ottawas originally came from Manitoulin Island in northern Lake Huron and from territory on the Bruce Peninsula and the shores of Georgian Bay in present-day Ontario. Their name means "trader," and they were allies of the more numerous Wendats (called Hurons and Petuns by the French and Wyandots by the British) who lived in large agricultural villages between the southern end of Georgian Bay and Lake Simcoe. Ottawas carried surplus corn and tobacco to western tribes by way of well-known transcontinental canoe routes.[12] The principal Great Lakes travel route from Georgian Bay went through the Straits of Mackinac, across northern Lake Michigan to Green Bay, then up the Fox River portaging to the Wisconsin River, which entered the Mississippi River at present-day Prairie du Chien, Wisconsin. On war expeditions, Ottawas followed this route to the western plains to bring back captives.[13] Ottawas had long been familiar with the Straits of Mackinac, but the Grand Traverse region and eastern side of Lake Michigan were infrequently traveled in comparison with the constant canoe traffic along the northern and western shorelines.

The Ottawas took over the northwestern part of Michigan's Lower Peninsula by expansionist warfare. According to the traditional historian Andrew J. Blackbird, lands in what are now Emmet, Charlevoix, and Cheboygan Counties were earlier occupied by the "Prairie Tribe," whom he identified as the "Mush-co-desh," in modern terminology Mascoutins. The Ottawas were allies of these people until they received an insulting reception at the Mascoutin village at Seven Mile Point north of Little Traverse Bay when they were returning from a western war expedition. In retribution, the Ottawas organized their forces at Manitoulin Island and proceeded to destroy or drive southward the entire population of the Mascoutin villages scattered in the northern part of the Lower Peninsula. Blackbird claimed that vestiges of the abandoned Mascoutin village at Seven Mile Point could still be seen at the time that he was writing in the 1880s.[14]

The westward shift of the Ottawa people to Michigan in the seventeenth century was not only a consequence of war and trading expeditions but also a reaction to aggressive campaigns of the Iroquois living in northern New York against the Wendats, which began in 1649 and continued for a half-century.[15] As a consequence, the Ottawas temporarily abandoned Manitoulin Island and joined the main Wendat refugee band from the Lake Simcoe area in an odyssey that took them to Green Bay, Wisconsin, the upper Mississippi River in Minnesota, and back to the present-day Upper Peninsula of Michigan. In 1671, the two groups established neighboring villages, with a Catholic mission at what is now St. Ignace on the protected harbor facing Mackinac Island. Some of the Ottawas returned to their traditional base on Manitoulin Island at this time.[16] Others moved to Detroit, where a French fort was established in 1701 immediately following the peace treaty signed at Montreal to end widespread Iroquois warfare.

The main center for Ottawa leadership in Michigan became the northwestern part of the Lower Peninsula after they constructed a village near the new Fort Michilimackinac, built by the French in 1715 at present-day Mackinaw City. By this time, the Ottawas had guns and needed the services of the fort's

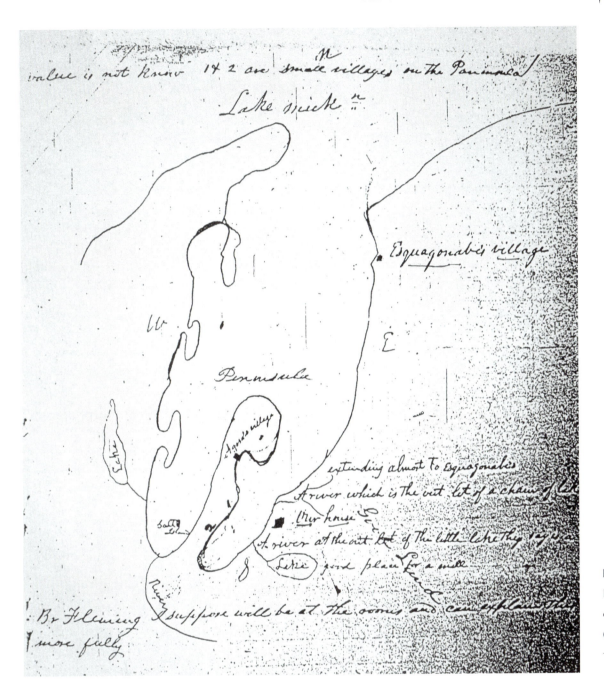

Figure 6. Sketch of Grand Traverse Bay. Peter Dougherty, 1839. Sketch by Peter Dougherty. Courtesy of the Presbyterian Historical Society, Presbyterian Church (U.S.A.).

blacksmith to repair their weapons and sharpen the metal tools they had acquired by trading. In 1742, the Ottawa leaders shifted their headquarters about twenty-four miles southwest to L'Arbre Croche, a district identified by a particular crooked tree that marked the Lake Michigan bluffs near present-day Good Hart.[17] The previous year, they were reported to have shown interest in settling at Grand River and had made clearings at Grand Traverse.[18] Expanding southward along the Lake Michigan shoreline, Ottawas established settlements with fields and orchards in the Grand River valley, and they often wintered in the interior among the Potawatomis living throughout southern Michigan. The Grand Traverse Ottawas, who

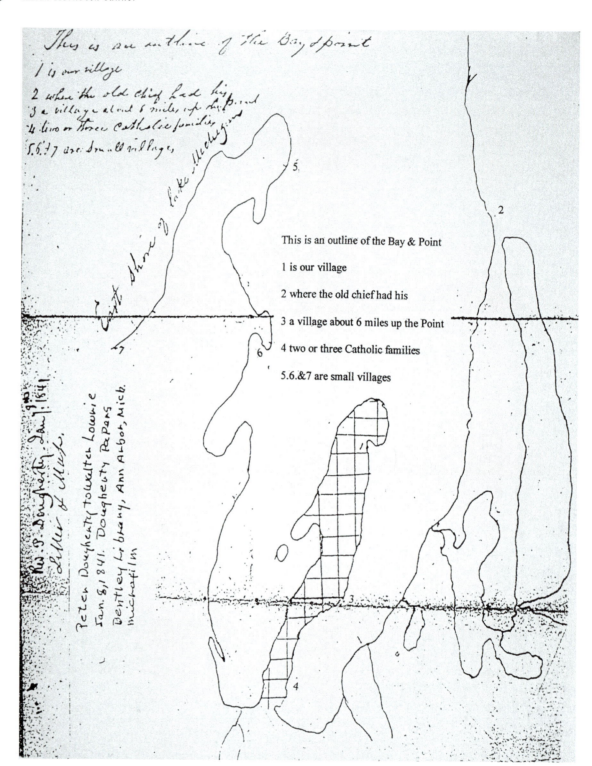

Figure 7. Sketch of Grand Traverse Bay. Peter Dougherty, drawn 1840. Sketch by Peter Dougherty. Courtesy of the Presbyterian Historical Society, Presbyterian Church (U.S.A.).

were in a less favored agricultural region, remained on the southern fringe of the more densely settled Little Traverse Bay communities. At one time there were fifteen miles of Ottawa habitations along the Lake Michigan shore north of Little Traverse Bay, according to Andrew Blackbird.[19] But the population diminished markedly following a smallpox epidemic attributed to the British, who took over Fort Michilimackinac along with the rest of French Canada as a consequence of the Treaty of Paris in 1763.

When Peter Dougherty arrived as the first outsider to settle in the Grand Traverse region, Ottawa communities were spread around what is now the Leelanau Peninsula on the west side of Grand Traverse Bay. Ojibwes distant from the main body of their people lived on the east side of the bay. The leading communities of Ojibwes in the upper Great Lakes were at Baweting, named Sault Ste. Marie by the French, and at Chequamegon, also called La Pointe or Madeline Island, in present-day Wisconsin.[20] In the eighteenth century, Sault Ste. Marie Ojibwes began hunting in the Lower Peninsula east of what is now Mackinaw City, where the line between Ottawa and Ojibwe country was well respected. The Ojibwes claimed both Mackinac Island and Bois Blanc Island, which their representatives gave to the United States government in 1795 at Greenville during treaty proceedings there.

There are two explanations for the presence of Ojibwes among the Ottawas on Grand Traverse Bay. The first account, given by Andrew J. Blackbird, states that following a quarrel over fishing in the Straits resulting in the death of an Ojibwe, and after many subsequent councils, the Ottawas granted the Ojibwes a strip of land extending from the Sleeping Bear sand dunes southeastward to the headwaters of the Muskegon River.[21] An alternative explanation was given to Indian Agent Henry R. Schoolcraft by Aishquagonabee, an Ojibwe who was the leading chief of the Grand Traverse Indians in the 1830s. Aishquagonabee stated that the Ojibwes had assisted the Ottawas in the warfare that drove the Mascoutins from northwestern Michigan and thus had gained the right to establish their own settlements in the conquered territory.[22]

For whatever explanation, Peter Dougherty found two Ojibwe communities on the east arm of Grand Traverse Bay, Aishquagonabee's at or near present-day Eastport on the east shore of the bay and Agosa's on the harbor at the western tip of what is now known as Old Mission Peninsula. Aishquagonabee, "Feather of Honor," is described as a veteran fighter who had taken scalps in the British-Indian action regaining Mackinac Island during the War of 1812.[23] His village included about sixty men, implying a total population of two hundred fifty or three hundred persons.[24] According to local reports, Agosa had been born in the St. Clair River district of southeastern Michigan and lived on an island near Mackinac (probably one of the Les Cheneaux Islands east of present-day St. Ignace) before coming to the Lower Peninsula. He lived near what are now Charlevoix and Norwood before moving to the peninsula in Grand Traverse Bay.[25] After establishing a school and a mission on the peninsula in 1839, Dougherty received the impression that occupation of the location was fairly recent. Writing in November 1850, he stated: "The son of the Chief who first settled here is still living and has built a house near the spot where his father had his lodge and on the ground where he had his first garden."[26]

The principal Ottawa leader on Grand Traverse Bay in the 1830s was Shabwasson, who was well established on the west shore of the bay at present-day Omena Point, about five miles south of modern Northport. The other long-standing Ottawa village, Chemogobing, was located at the river mouth site, called Carp River, that has become modern-day Leland. Other small Ottawa communities were noted at Cat Head Bay on the tip of the Leelanau Peninsula, at what is now Sutton's Bay, at Good Harbor on the Lake Michigan coast, and also farther south in the Platte River valley.[27] In the 1830s, the Indian population of the

Grand Traverse region was probably at least six hundred people.[28] Chiefs of the two major Ojibwe villages were principal representatives of the Grand Traverse band at negotiations for the land-cession treaty signed March 28, 1836, in Washington, D.C. They were also the leaders Dougherty dealt with when he founded a school and mission on the peninsula, carrying out provisions of the treaty. In the Grand Traverse region, the Ojibwes and Ottawas were directly affected by the mapping process brought about by the cession of territory in northern and western Michigan, providing land for the state in the process of formation.

Political leaders in Michigan Territory, aspiring for statehood, realized that they needed to acquire the land making up the entire Lower Peninsula in order to have an adequate geographical base. This would require a cession of the land north of the Grand River by the Ojibwes and Ottawas living in that region. From the preliminary proposal for a small land sale in the summer of 1835 until the final approval by Ottawa and Ojibwe leaders of the United States Senate's treaty alterations in July 1836, negotiations for the major Michigan land-cession Treaty of Washington, March 28, 1836, involved the interrelated objectives of many interested parties. People involved in the treaty making included Indian factions, individual federal and state officials, the U.S. Senate, Protestant missionaries, land developers, and American Fur Company personnel. It would be an oversimplification to think that the provisions of this treaty were determined by the treaty commissioner, Indian Agent Henry R. Schoolcraft, and the twenty-four Indian representatives who assembled in Washington, D.C., that winter of 1835–36 to discuss a treaty. They were, however, the principal figures at the final treaty "signing."

Although preliminary suggestions for small land cessions had been circulated, Ottawas from Manitoulin Island, or the "Ottawa Island," in British territory made the first proposal, setting in motion the chain of events leading to the large-scale cession of land in Michigan. In the summer of 1835, a delegation came to Schoolcraft at Mackinac Island with an offer to sell Drummond Island, situated adjacent to the eastern tip of the present-day Upper Peninsula.[29] With this odd proposition as a start, Schoolcraft began an exchange of correspondence with federal officials concerning the possibility of an extensive land cession and sent out inquiries about lands that regional Indians might be willing to sell.

By this time in his career, Schoolcraft had been the Indian agent in Michigan since 1822, stationed first at Sault Ste. Marie and then at Mackinac Island in 1834 when the office at the Sault was closed as part of a reorganization of the federal Indian administration. His wife, Jane, was the daughter of an Irish trader at Sault Ste. Marie who had married the daughter of an influential Ojibwe leader at La Pointe. Jane's three brothers were among the eight Schoolcraft relatives who held posts on the staff of Schoolcraft's Indian agency.[30] With considerable treaty-making experience, Schoolcraft in 1835 began the steps that he expected would lead to a treaty conference in Michigan in 1836. His personal contacts were closest to the Indian bands near Sault Ste. Marie; he had never visited Grand Traverse Bay.[31]

After notifying the Indian Office late in October 1835 that an unauthorized Ottawa delegation from L'Arbre Croche had taken off from Michigan to talk about a treaty, Schoolcraft himself left for Washington in November, stopping en route at New York, where he talked with the president of the American Fur Company, Ramsey Crooks.[32] The American Fur Company had a major interest in the outcome of treaty negotiations since the Ottawas and Ojibwes were heavily in debt to the company's traders, and prospects were poor for collecting from the Indians since there was every evidence that hunting was declining in their home country. Traders counted on a treaty to include provisions for paying the outstanding Ottawa and Ojibwe debts. Through their Indian wives and extended kinship networks, traders exerted considerable influence among their Indian clientele.[33] The Indians themselves had diverse views.

One contingent of Little Traverse Bay Ottawas was most eager for a land sale but wanted to sell land south of Manistee away from their home territory. The Grand River Ottawas were generally opposed to a land sale, but ultimately their missionary escort, Reverend Leonard Slater, succumbed to pressure when offered a grant of land for a mission. The Grand Traverse representatives do not appear to have played any role in these negotiations.

When Schoolcraft finally reached Washington in mid-December, he found that Secretary of War Lewis Cass was already planning for a large-scale treaty. Schoolcraft arranged for a "power of sale" to be sent from Fort Mackinac, where all visiting Indians had been urged to add their signatures, creating an important document that arrived in the middle of the treaty negotiations.[34] Charles C. Trowbridge in Detroit took charge of organizing additional delegations so that the entire area northwest of the Grand River would be represented. Since Robert Stuart, the American Fur Company's agent at Detroit, told him a treaty would be doubtful without the influential presence of Rix Robinson, the firm's representative on the Grand River, and John Drew, company agent at Mackinac, Trowbridge arranged for these men to escort regional delegates to Washington. Lucius Lyon, the senator-elect from Michigan, also sent letters to Robinson and Drew urging them to bring Indian leaders to Washington for a land-cession treaty, and he closely followed the progress of the subsequent negotiations.[35] Robinson brought the Ottawa and Ojibwe delegates from the area between the Grand River and Grand Traverse Bay, so he was responsible for recruiting in the Traverse Bay region. To represent the Grand Traverse bands, Robinson brought the Ojibwe leaders Aishquagonabee and Agosa and an Ottawa identified in the record of the proceedings as "Chawaneenesse," whose name was more accurately written "Oshawan Epenaysee" ("South Bird") at the end of the list of treaty signers.[36]

As a preliminary to the treaty negotiations, Indian delegates were invited to the White House on March 14, 1836, to meet President Andrew Jackson, veteran Indian fighter and supporter of the Indian Removal Act of 1830, which instituted the program to transfer all eastern Indians to territory west of the Mississippi River. The same day, Henry Schoolcraft received from Lewis Cass a formal appointment as sole commissioner to arrange a land sale with the Ottawa and Ojibwe delegates, allowing considerable latitude in arranging the specific provisions of the treaty.

On March 15, 1836, the opening session of treaty negotiations between the Ottawas and Ojibwes of Michigan and the federal government convened at the Masonic Hall in Washington, with an address to "My Children" by Henry R. Schoolcraft, speaking on behalf of the president and by authority of the secretary of war. In the course of his remarks, Schoolcraft set forth the dimensions of a vast land cession, which would extend south to Washtenong on the Grand River and north to the Chocolate River on Lake Superior, near present-day Marquette in the Upper Peninsula. He urged the delegates to take time in making up their minds concerning the quantity of land they would cede. Furthermore, a commissioner would visit them next summer to pay the amount of all just debts. On the subject of reservations, Schoolcraft explained: "No objection will be made, if you deem it imperative, to your fixing on proper and limited reservations to be held in common; but the President judges it best that no reservations should be made to individuals. . . . The usual privilege of residing and hunting on the lands sold till they are wanted will be granted."[37]

The formalities of treaty signing proceeded smoothly on Monday, March 28, 1836, in the presence of the delegates and escorts who had attended the opening session on March 15, with the addition of Army and Navy representatives and Michigan's senator-elect, Lucius Lyon. The final treaty bore evidence of the personal dealings that had gone on outside the formal meetings. The arrangement for reservations in the final treaty was much different from the initial proposal for one hundred thousand acres in two locations that had been discussed in the treaty proceedings. By contrast, the final treaty provided for five separate reservations on the mainland of the Lower Peninsula, plus all of the Beaver Islands and a dozen other locations north of the Straits from Bay de Noc to the lower St. Marys River.[38] The Grand Traverse reservation of twenty thousand acres was allocated to "the north shore of Grand Traverse Bay," a designation that not only reveals the contemporary geographical perceptions of the terrain but also indicates that Schoolcraft was aware of the location of Aishquagonabee's village in that area.

The final treaty, revised and ratified by the Senate in May 1836, also included reference to possible removal of Michigan Indians, a subject that had not been mentioned in any correspondence prior to the treaty. Neither was it mentioned in the instructions that Cass gave to Schoolcraft, nor in the official records of the public sessions. Indicating that any removal was optional, Article Eighth stated clearly that "as soon as the said Indians desire it," arrangements would be made to look at sites either between Lake Superior and the Mississippi River or someplace west of the Mississippi, later adding, "When the Indians wish it," the United States would remove them and provide a year's subsistence.[39]

The thirteen articles of the lengthy original treaty brought about some discussion following the formal signing.[40] The reservations described in the treaty seem to have been satisfactory to the delegates, for the subject brought forth no reported comment or controversy. Schoolcraft's jubilation at the conclusion of the treaty was only temporary, however; for in ratifying the document, the Senate made significant and troublesome changes. Most critical were those in Articles Second and Third, canceling the permanent reservations and reducing their existence to five years "unless the United States grant them permission to remain on said lands for a longer period." Furthermore, if the Indians should choose to remove, the revised treaty (proclaimed on May 27, 1836) eliminated the option of going to Ojibwe country west of Lake Superior. The only possible removal destination was land "southwest of the Missouri River."[41] The payment of an additional two hundred thousand dollars in return for giving up the permanent reservations was expected to be a persuasive measure in gaining the Indians' acceptance of the altered treaty.

The Ottawas and Ojibwes did not find out about these changes until July 1836, when their leaders were summoned to Mackinac Island for a council that concluded with their signed assent to the changes, which was only achieved with considerable difficulty. As Schoolcraft explained, it was only his emphasis on the continued use of ceded territory specified in Article Thirteenth, which had no time limit and therefore was considered permanent, that brought the Indians' acquiescence to these changes. Reservations with a five-year legal restriction had little utility for the Grand Traverse Indians and the rest of the Ottawas and Ojibwes. They wanted assurance of permanent land assignments, either through a presidential order or through purchase of land when it became available for sale. They planned to use their annuities created by the land-cession treaty to purchase their own homesites.

The Treaty of March 28, 1836, as a whole took on increasing significance for people in Michigan during the period when the treaty was progressing from the planning stages to final approval, from November 1835 to the summer of 1836. Concurrently, the state government was in the process of formation, despite a heated controversy with Ohio about the southeastern boundary that delayed Michigan's admission to the Union. In November 1835, Michigan voters, at the time assuming that the state would include just the Lower Peninsula, elected a governor and representatives to Congress, although they were not seated.[42] Since the opening of the Erie Canal in 1825 and the subsequent increase in passenger traffic on Lake Erie, the population of southern Michigan had risen rapidly to 175,000, and more land was needed for expansion. The first road across southern Michigan, begun in 1825, was completed by 1835, and stagecoaches made the trip from Detroit to Chicago twice a week.

More land for settlement in Michigan was a personal interest of the senator in waiting, Lucius Lyon, a surveyor and land developer who had attended the signing of the treaty in 1836. He was involved with the American Land Company, a group of investors from upstate New York with ties to Vice President Martin Van Buren that had an interest in Grand River Valley land. (Henry R. Schoolcraft had an interest in the same speculative venture.) Lyon's long effort to have another government land office in Michigan aside from the one in Monroe finally became a reality in 1836 with the opening of the office at Ionia, about thirty miles east of Grand Rapids and close to the eastern boundary of the new land cession.[43] In 1836, land sales in Michigan, where speculation reached a temporary peak, were the highest in the nation, with the greatest excitement over lands in the Grand Rapids area.

In June 1836, Congress voted to admit Michigan as a state whenever the territory agreed to give up its claim to the "Toledo Strip" and accept instead land north of the Straits of Mackinac that had long been considered part of Wisconsin. The land north of the Straits, which is now the Upper Peninsula of Michigan, had been acquired by the treaty signed three months earlier. Although the proposition to accept Upper Peninsula land and relinquish Toledo was initially rejected by Michigan voters in September 1836, it was finally accepted on a second vote in December, enabling Michigan to join the Union in January 1837. Approximately three-eighths of the new state's total territory was acquired from the Ottawas and Ojibwes in the Treaty of Washington that had been signed on March 28, 1836. The state government as well as the federal government began to take an interest in the development of the hitherto remote "Indian Country" in the northern part of "The Peninsula," as the region south of the Straits had always been identified. This now became "The Lower Peninsula," while the old "mainland" of the era of French exploration and trading became Michigan's "Upper Peninsula."

In the spring of 1837, Henry Schoolcraft was eager to have all the reservations in the Lower Peninsula surveyed promptly. He wrote to John Mullett, a Detroit surveyor who was put in charge of the assignment, specifically requesting that surveys be made during the current season of the reservations at Little Traverse and Grand Traverse, on the Manistee River (for Grand River bands), and at Cheboygan. He hoped that Mullett would do these surveys even if there was not yet an appropriation to pay for the work.[44] Nothing happened, however, until two years later, after surveyors had worked their way north of the Grand River and arrived at Grand Traverse Bay. The intervening territory, with its forests and swamps, was formidable to survey. In 1837, a team tried to carry the United States mail overland from Detroit to Mackinac but became lost northwest of Saginaw for ten days. Members of the team were rescued by a group of Indians and led to their destination, but thereafter they returned to their customary mail route following the shoreline of Lake Huron.

Peter Dougherty became personally involved in establishing the reservation on Grand Traverse Bay. In Article Fourth, the 1836 treaty provided three thousand dollars a year for missions and five thousand dollars for "education, teachers, school-houses, and books in their own language, to be continued twenty years, and as long thereafter as Congress may appropriate for the object." The prospect of government support provided added motivation for the missionary programs of religious organizations. The Presbyterian Board of Foreign Missions contacted Schoolcraft after the 1836 treaty was ratified, inquiring about establishing a mission in the Mackinac area. With Schoolcraft's approval, the board sent Dougherty out in the spring of 1838.[45]

Schoolcraft, who had gone through a conversion experience in 1831 and again in 1835, was an active member of the Presbyterian Church and consequently was personally interested in promoting schools and missions. When Dougherty arrived at Mackinac Island in the summer of 1838, Schoolcraft was absent. Invited to stay at the Schoolcraft home, Dougherty began learning about the Indian people of the region and received language instruction through conversations with Jane Schoolcraft and her brother John Johnston, an interpreter at the Mackinac Agency. In a report sent later to Presbyterian headquarters in Philadelphia, Dougherty wrote: "Mr. Johnston informed me that the Grand Traverse Bay, in point of numbers, of character, as well as freedom from Catholic influences, was the most promising place to commence operation. The Indians are beginning to gather on that reservation. The soil on the Bay is the best in that part of Michigan. . . . He advised [me] to visit the village of Aischquagonabe and, if I could, to go as far as the Manistee."[46]

Dougherty set out on a reconnaissance of the Lake Michigan coast on July 28, 1838, in the company of a mechanic employed at the government reservation at Manistee, a man headed for the Grand River who agreed to act as an interpreter, and an Indian whose destination was Muskegon. En route, Dougherty was able to see the prospering Catholic community at Little Traverse Bay, where the priest was absent.

Dougherty's report of his investigation of the Grand Traverse area in the summer of 1838, beginning with a description of the principal village of Aishquagonabee, states:

> When I came to the principal village on the Grand Traverse, which is situated up the bay about twelve miles, on the north bank; I found the chief was absent, and could do nothing more than see the situation of the village and the country around it. His absence, however was not a thing that very much interfered with my object in visiting the place, which was to see, as Mr. Schoolcraft advised not to say much about the object of my visit further than to say that according to their treaty the President had promised them teachers, that it was one of their privileges to which they had a right and I had been sent to select a place and build a school house and wished him to point out to me the best location, and that Mr. S would explain the whole matter when he went to Mackinac. . . .
>
> On the bay there are about four hundred living in three or four villages, at different points, but they are gathering Mr. Johnston says on the reservation which will bring them all within the sphere of a missionary stationed at the village of Esquagonabe [sic]. Mr. Johnston stated further that several of the Indians are laying by from their yearly receipts money to purchase lands there when they come in market.[47]

After leaving Aishquagonabee's village, Dougherty's single-canoe expedition crossed to the tip of the Leelanau Peninsula and continued down the Lake Michigan shoreline, stopping to investigate another village, which from his description was most likely at the site of present-day Leland. He wrote:

> About twenty five miles further up the Lake [i.e., going south] there is a village at the mouth of a fine stream of water. It is not quite as large as the one mentioned on the bay [i.e., Aishquagonabee's], but the situation, the appearance of the soil, the aspect of the village, made a very favourable impression. The chief felt favourable toward the establishment of a school and said they were at home all the time except

when absent on their hunting excursions or in the sugar bush. This place is more easy of access to vessels going up and down the lake as they pass directly in sight and the water is deep so that almost any vessel could run close to the shore. . . . There is less probability of white men settling near this village. There are men, several, at Mackinack who are talking of going in to the Bay to take up lands, out of the limits of the reservation, however, most of them are men of good morals. One is a carpenter, and one a blacksmith.[48]

In gathering information about potential mission sites and reservations, Dougherty continued south to Manistee, a twelve-day trip from Mackinac. Here he found Mr. and Mrs. Geary at the seventy-thousand-acre government reservation designated for the Grand River Valley Indians by the 1836 treaty. The chief was absent on an expedition to examine land southwest of the Missouri River in case any of the Michigan Indians ever considered removing. Mrs. Geary was expecting that a missionary would be sent to them. Dougherty commented: "This place was selected as a reservation on the advice of Mr. Geary but many of the Indians were not pleased with it and refuse to settle on it. The soil is not very good. The country is well timbered with Pine."[49]

Plagued by mosquitoes, Dougherty and his remaining companions went on to the mouth of the Grand River, where he boarded a larger vessel destined for Chicago and then returned to Mackinac Island. He had seen a selection of potential mission and reservation sites in the more remote parts of Michigan.

On the basis of his reconnaissance in 1838 and advice from Mackinac Islanders, Dougherty decided to establish a mission on Grand Traverse Bay. First he went back to New York, however, and when he returned in the fall to Mackinac Island, it was too late in the season to begin his new venture. Mackinac was still the hub of all activity in the north country, the halfway point between fledgling Chicago and century-old Detroit. As soon as the ice melted in the spring of 1839, Dougherty organized a small expedition to Grand Traverse Bay. He found the Indian residents of the east arm of the bay at a new site by the river entering Grand Traverse Bay at present-day Elk Rapids. Arriving with an assistant minister, an interpreter, a crew of four workmen, and a heavy boatload of supplies, Dougherty set up a house and a school building in a few weeks' time. In his correspondence, he reported that "the chief" (Aishquago-nabee) had "pitched his tent near the new house" and brought almost daily gifts of fish and meat, while Dougherty in turn gave samples of his cooking and invited the whole family to his home to eat. The heads of families were favorably inclined toward a school, and they wondered if Dougherty would keep their children and teach them while they were off hunting in the winter. It seemed like a good location, even if it was not one of the "old villages." The river mouth was an entrance to the routes to hunting grounds, a favorite fishing site, and near the Indians' sugar groves. The two local Ojibwe leaders, Aishquagonabee and Agosa, had talked of forming a single village at this new site.[50]

A change of location for the entire community was precipitated by the unexpected arrival on June 13, 1839, of Indian Agent Henry R. Schoolcraft, who brought along a blacksmith as the first member of the government staff for a reservation. He also announced plans to bring the government farmer and cattle from the unsuccessful Manistee operation to Grand Traverse Bay. At first, Schoolcraft wanted the mission enterprise to move to a little bay (present-day Bower's Harbor) on the west side of the small peninsula dividing the two arms of Grand Traverse Bay. But after Agosa issued a warm and sincere invitation to move the mission to his village located on the harbor at the tip of the peninsula, Dougherty persuaded Schoolcraft to select this site for the government staff provided by terms of the 1836 treaty.

The well-protected harbor at Agosa's village was an important factor in the relocation, for the shallow beach near the mouth of the Elk River made a poor landing place for any boat or vessel bringing supplies or trade goods.[51] Furthermore, Agosa did not really want to move from his existing base. American Fur Company traders at Mackinac also favored a reservation headquarters placed at the harbor on the peninsula.

As a consequence, around June 20, 1839, Dougherty found himself living in a fourteen-foot-square Indian cabin out on the peninsula near Agosa's village at a site Agosa selected. Here he had two boarders: the government blacksmith, Isaac George, and an assistant farmer, the Reverend Alvin Coe, who had been transferred from Manistee. They were awaiting the arrival of a boat with supplies to construct the government buildings where they would work. Dougherty had established a school immediately upon his arrival, teaching the alphabet and reading to Indians of all ages. Peter Greensky, the interpreter, took over the teaching responsibilities while Dougherty supervised the collecting of logs to build another house.[52] His Indian neighbors offered to help with this task at no charge and formally welcomed him as a brother. The community on the peninsula showed immediate signs of growth. As the logs were being collected, Aishquagonabee arrived with three or four families and announced he expected to move there permanently. Most of his people were already there. Two men from L'Arbre Croche (near present-day Goodhart) called on Dougherty to inform him that a group of their people was considering a move south to Grand Traverse. The school was the attraction, for they wanted their children to learn English.[53] The Catholic priests at Little Traverse Bay were all foreign, for the most part trained in Austria, and although they were teaching their students to be literate in the Ottawa language, they were not English speakers.

Indian settlements on the Grand Traverse Bay and the two sites of the mission constructions are shown on maps drawn by Dougherty in 1839 and 1840 (see figs. 6 and 7). For his 1839 map, he was able to use information from government surveyors who first appeared on the east shore of the bay in early June while workers were building the house and school at the river's mouth. A local story recounts the fear expressed at that time by the Indian who first saw the imprint of a horse's hoof bearing the marks of a horseshoe. Indian horses were all unshod. The hoofprint indicated the presence of white men. The newcomer proved to be a lost packman, who was guided back to his survey team. Dougherty had the opportunity to talk with the surveyors and get their views on the low market value of this country, where swamps and thickets made surveying a real hardship.[54] Dougherty was also told that Grand Traverse Bay was about thirty or thirty-one miles long, and "the point" or dividing peninsula was about twelve miles long.[55] For the information of the Presbyterian Board in New York, Dougherty sent his first map, drawn before the move to the peninsula, indicating the following locations: "Our House" located south of "a river which is the outlet of a chain of lakes" (Elk River), "Esquagonabe's village" on the northeast shore near the mouth of the bay (present-day Eastport), "Agosa's village" on the harbor near the tip of the dividing peninsula (Old Mission Peninsula), and two small villages on the peninsula to the south of Agosa.[56] In his correspondence, Dougherty sometimes referred to the "middle village" on the peninsula, and on the subsequent map, he noted the most southern community as a place where a few Catholic families lived. The later map indicated the sites: "1. Is our village," and "2. where the old chief had his," a recognition of the fact that by 1840, Aishquagonabee no longer lived in the Eastport vicinity.[57] On the Leelanau Peninsula, number 5 is north of present-day Northport Point; number 6 is Shabwasson's village at present-day Omena Point; and number 7 is probably meant to indicate the community at modern-day Leland. Aishquagonabee's village on the peninsula was about six miles from the mission. Dougherty's first report to Schoolcraft ended with the plea: "In conclusion I would say it would be an act of great generosity and kindness on the part of the Government if it would give that little point to those people."[58]

During the 1839 season, surveys were completed for the tier of townships in the Grand Traverse Bay area, including the dividing peninsula called "the point."[59] In 1840, surveys were finished for all but twenty-three of the townships in the Lower Peninsula.[60] The completion of the land surveys achieved two milestones in Great Lakes cartography: the outline of the northwest border of the Lower Peninsula was at last accurately portrayed, and, simultaneously, Lake Michigan was completely outlined thanks to the land survey of the northeast shoreline.

Noting the survey's progress, Schoolcraft considered it was an appropriate time to delineate the reservations in the Lower Peninsula established by Article Second of the 1836 treaty. After directing his brother James to learn the wishes of the Grand Traverse Ojibwes and Ottawas, Schoolcraft wrote Commissioner of Indian Affairs T. Hartley Crawford on May 18, 1840: "Sir: The Indians at Grand Traverse bay, have selected their reservation of 20,000 acres under the 2nd Article of the treaty, on the point of land extending North into that bay, being parts of fractional Townships No. 28, 29, 30 in Range 10 West of the principal meridian, which they request may be exempted from sale."[61] The exterior boundaries of the reservation did not require surveying, since "the point" was a distinct geographical feature.

When Schoolcraft's report of the selection for the Grand Traverse reservation reached the General Land Office in Washington, D.C., the staff calculated that the area of parts of the three fractional townships on "the point" was only 16,206.93 acres.[62] To make up the twenty-thousand acres specified for the reservation in Article Second of the 1836 treaty, the staff decided to add the rest of Township 28 North, Range 10 West, to the reservation. The additional parcel was a disconnected triangle of land on the southeast shore across the bay from "the point" selected by the Indians.[63] A report of this modification, originating in the General Land Office, was sent to the commissioner of Indian affairs as part of a formal statement describing the land to be withheld from a sale that was to be held the following October. Writing on August 10, Commissioner Whitcomb of the General Land Office stated: "I have to inform you that by order of the President the whole of fractional Townships twenty eight, twenty nine and thirty North of Range ten West of the Michigan Mer. [i.e., meridian] in the Ionia district have been withdrawn from the public sale advertised to take place on the 26th of October next, as reserved for the reservation of 20,000 acres on the north side of Grand Traverse Bay, under the second article of the Ottawa and Chippewa Treaty of the 28th of March 1836 and that the Register and Receiver have this day been instructed accordingly."[64] The difference between Schoolcraft's request and this final decision was simply replacing "parts" with "whole" in the land description referring to the three fractional townships.

The decision, made in Washington, D.C., by top-level administrators, concerning the additional land for the Grand Traverse reservation apparently was never conveyed back to Schoolcraft. Consequently, he did not learn that officially this reservation extended beyond the Grand Traverse band's original request. No further discussion concerning the dimensions of the Grand Traverse band reservation has been found in Schoolcraft's official correspondence, nor was any mention made of this in his "Personal Memoirs." In October 1840, he wrote the Commissioner of Indian Affairs on the subject of the reservations for the Little Traverse and Cheboygan bands. In this case Schoolcraft did not think that they needed to be marked off and withheld from sale. His reasoning was based on information from the district surveyor that the public surveys could not be completed in time for the land to be brought into sale earlier than June 1841 and the 1836 treaty provision that the five-year reservation status expired for all reservations in May.[65]

The surveyors' and Schoolcraft's view of the imminent end of the 1836 treaty reservations was not shared by Commissioner of Indian Affairs T. Hartley Crawford. The commissioner responded to Schoolcraft, specifically referring to the language of Article Second of the treaty, which stated that the reservations were limited to a five-year existence "unless the United States shall grant them permission to remain on said lands for a longer period." Crawford's response showed that although he had not abandoned the idea of ultimate removal, he had some sympathy for the situation faced by about five thousand Indians living in northern Michigan. He wrote on November 4, 1840:

> No measures have yet been adopted to remove these Indians from the lands now occupied by them, and it is not probable that any arrangement can be effected by which they can be migrated within the period referred to by you, May 1841. As you indicate in your Annual Report that all the land south of the Straits of Michilimackinac has been surveyed and subdivided into sections, with a view to it being reported to the General land Office as ready for sale, and that the enterprise of our industrious agriculturalists is pressing up to that point, motives of public policy and of humanity would seem to dictate that the Indians should be furnished with a place to which they can resort, and from which they may be enabled to procure the means of subsistence, until provision can be made for their final removal, without being considered and treated by the settlers as intruders in the public domain. As it may be the pleasure of the United States to permit them to remain for a longer period than five years from the date of the ratification of the treaty, it is the opinion of this office that the reservation should be made and marked, in accordance with the request of the Indians communicated to you, and be exempted from sale. The same course ought I think to be pursued in regard to the remaining unlocated reservations under the same treaty, and I suggest that the proper surveyor be requested to respect them in his surveys.[66]

At the end of 1840, the only 1836 treaty reservations that had been surveyed were those at Manistee and Grand Traverse. All the others were included in the "List of Reserves still required to be made in Michigan for the Ottawas and Chippewas under the treaty of 28th of March 1836 with their location" sent to the surveyor general in Cincinnati, Ohio, on November 22.[67] The fifty-thousand-acre reserve intended for Little Traverse Bay, the thousand acres at Cheboygan and Thunder Bay, and all of the islands (including the Beaver Islands) and other locations in the Upper Peninsula listed in the 1836 treaty never achieved cartographic expression beyond Schoolcraft's sketch map.

The records of field surveys are complete for the Manistee reservation but only fragmentary for Grand Traverse. In issuing a contract in 1839 to John Brink to survey the area around the Manistee River, the surveyor general included directions to also survey the seventy-thousand-acre reservation intended for the Grand River bands. Brink's small, handwritten volume describing the survey of that reservation, with a copy dated 1898, is in the State Archives of Michigan.[68] The Grand Traverse reservation had not yet been selected in 1839, and no special orders have been found for a survey in 1840. Usually, contracts and instructions for surveys were issued early in the season, in January or February, but the selection of the townships for the Grand Traverse reservation on "the point" was not reported until May 1840.

The only reference to a survey of "the point," the area selected for the Grand Traverse reservation in 1840, comes from the correspondence of the missionary Peter Dougherty, who had been absent from the area during that summer. He returned to the mission on September 11, 1840, bringing with him his new wife, Maria. In his first letter sent back to Philadelphia on September 14, 1840, he referred to copying a map from a recent survey in two separate passages: "As soon as I get time I will send you a sectional map of this point so that you can see just where we are and the part of [the] section on which the mission house stands. We copied it from the corrected survey which has recently been made. . . . I have copied the survey of this point with the outlines of the Bay from a corrected map of Mr. Douglass." Since no record of a surveyor by that name has been found in the correspondence dealing with federal government survey activities in northwestern Michigan at that time, the identity of "Mr. Douglass" has not been established. In the same letter, Dougherty noted that the Indians "were excited" about the sale of their land scheduled for the fall but knew that the reservation had been withheld from sale. They had also heard that it could be offered for sale the following May (1841), but only by a special order of the president.[69]

Dougherty had a very busy fall and did not manage to send his second map, containing much pertinent information, to his regular correspondents at the Presbyterian Board, David Wells and Walter Lowrie, until early January 1841. He reported the mission's location in section 35 of Township 30 North, Range 10 West.[70] Dougherty believed that the peninsula where the mission was located covered twenty-five to thirty thousand acres, more than enough land for the twenty-thousand-acre reservation specified in Article Second of the 1836 treaty.[71]

A map displaying the official dimensions of the Grand Traverse Band's 1836 treaty reservation did not appear until 1899, with the publication of Charles C. Royce's comprehensive compilation of maps and Indian treaty boundaries titled *Indian Land Cessions in the United States.*[72] Of the five locations designated by Henry Schoolcraft in the treaty ceding the land in northwestern Michigan, only the Manistee site had an official survey, but the Indians refused to move there, and these seventy thousand acres were sold in 1848. Despite the lack of a separate survey, the Grand Traverse site became the only functioning reservation in the entire area of both the Lower and Upper Peninsulas ceded by the Ojibwes and Ottawas in 1836.

The Grand Traverse reservation was in full operation by the fall of 1840, with headquarters on the bay near Agosa's village. The government staff included two of Henry Schoolcraft's brothers-in-law, John Johnston as farmer and George Johnston as carpenter, although Schoolcraft soon had to end their assignments because of criticism of the number of relatives he had on the payroll. The blacksmith, Isaac George, had a new assistant, the eighteen-year-old future historian "Jackson" Blackbird, who began a five-year term as apprentice blacksmith.[73] Although the school was in operation and religious services were being held, construction of a mission church was not completed until 1843.[74]

The official determination of their reservation in 1840 under terms of the 1836 treaty brought little security to members of the Grand Traverse Band—and anxiety was not limited to the Grand Traverse Bay region. All of the bands wanted firm title to land, where they could live with the confidence that their children would have the land as well. In the atmosphere of conflicting rumors, fears, and occasional encouraging news, Indian leaders found it difficult to face the future with confidence. The year 1840 was particularly traumatic for Michigan Indians, for that year, General Hugh Brady used army troops to seek out and collect Potawatomis scheduled for removal from the southern section of the state, implementing the controversial 1833 Treaty of Chicago. Some Potawatomis fled to Canada; others who were able to evade the soldiers fled northward in both Wisconsin and Michigan, bringing with them accounts of the pursuit and capture of their neighbors.[75]

In this disquieting situation, the Ottawas and Ojibwes of northwestern Michigan sought advice and assistance from government officials, traders, and missionaries. Among the earliest appeals was a long and sincere "talk" dated July 2, 1839, sent by a committee at L'Arbre Croche (north of Little Traverse Bay) to the young governor of Michigan, Stevens T. Mason. Summarizing the concerns expressed at a general council, the speech was written out in the flourishing hand of European-educated Augustin Hamelin, Jr., who had escorted a delegation to the Treaty of Washington, March 28, 1836. It concluded: "In sending this talk to you, it is our desire and prayer that you will give us information respecting the following points—1st Whether these Indians will have the right to buy lands from the Government. 2nd Whether the same Indians at least those who wish to conform to the Laws will be allowed by the State to remain in it. 3rd Whether they will be acknowledged as citizens. 4th Supposing the answer to the foregoing queries be the affirmative, whether it will be possible for us to buy this very place the Little Traverse bay where we are at present, and where our missionary priest is stationed."[76]

Governor Mason's response to the committee at L'Arbre Croche, directed to Hamelin in Mackinac, was encouraging. His principal message stated: "In answer to their enquiries you will communicate to them, that the Indians have a right to purchase lands from the Government; that those who conform to the laws are allowed by the constitution to remain in the State; that they will have secured all the privileges of citizens, except the right of voting, and that that right can only be secured by an amendment of the constitution; and that they will also have the same right with any citizen to purchase the lands at Little Traverse Bay when those lands are brought into market. An application to Congress might secure those lands at its next session if a representation is made shewing their desire to become citizens. The state has no control over the public lands."[77] Although encouraging in tone, the letter's most important piece of information was the last sentence.

Anxiety had affected the Little Traverse community two years before similar unrest became widespread at Grand Traverse Bay. In 1840, surveyors in the northernmost sections of the Lower Peninsula brought back reports that all the Indians were moving to Canada; this was a great exaggeration, but there was a considerable exodus from that region.[78]

By midwinter of 1841, Chief Agosa asked Peter Dougherty to write a letter to the Mackinac Island traders John Drew and William Biddle in an effort to "know the truth" about the best course of action for his people. Agosa and others had been greatly disturbed by a report that they might be removed from their land. This inaccurate report came from the reservation's former carpenter, George Johnston, whom Dougherty regarded as a troublemaker. Biddle wrote back assuring Agosa that Schoolcraft's latest report said nothing about a need to remove, adding that "the Indians had better not listen to what Mr. Johnston had to say, and that he thought that the best thing for them would be to buy land and come under the laws of the white man or of the State. And in order to [do] this they must have a petition drawn up and signed and forwarded to the State authorities next summer."[79]

Dougherty remained concerned but patient. The surveyors who talked to him in the spring of 1839, when he was temporarily camped at the mouth of the Elk River, convinced him that it would be a long time before settlers reached Grand Traverse Bay. Dougherty estimated the arrival of settlers would occur in about ten or fifteen years, which was a remarkably accurate forecast. He reasoned that there was better and more accessible land in Wisconsin and Iowa. Furthermore, the surveyors did not think that the land in the Grand Traverse region would ever pay for the cost of the surveys, since it was barren and swampy. The surveyors' descriptions were confirmed by one of the local Indian leaders who explained that he crossed desolate prairie land for a day and a half or more to get to his hunting grounds on the upper Manistee River.[80]

Keeping close track of the land status of the 1836 treaty reservations, the surveyor general in Cincinnati wrote the commissioner of the Land Office in Washington, D.C., on April 1, 1841, recommending that reservation lines be ignored in any further surveying in Michigan. He pointed out that the Indian inhabitants would soon be "tenants at will," and he expected that "they will probably not remain long in the land."[81] Although their status was precarious, the Ottawas and Ojibwes continued their efforts to remain in their Michigan homes, while the federal government gave no sign that it had removal plans. Indeed, there was no land less valuable to which the several thousand Michigan Indians could be removed. Schoolcraft had suggested removal to the Rum River country of Minnesota, but that area was ceded in 1837 by Minnesota and Wisconsin Ojibwes.[82]

In 1841, settlers and developers had not yet arrived in northwestern Michigan. The big land boom of 1836 had been largely speculative, and it was followed by a severe depression in 1837. Furthermore, a high percentage of the land surveys made between 1837 and 1840 were rejected. The area of rejected surveys included the land on both sides of Grand Traverse Bay, Range 9 West and Range 11 West of the principal meridian in Michigan. The only land in that area where the original survey had been accepted was Range 10 West, Townships 28, 29, and 30, the three townships designated for the Grand Traverse reservation. No instructions for surveys in Michigan were issued in the spring of 1841, and the surveying and promoting of Michigan lands halted for five years, except in the Saginaw area.[83]

On May 27, 1841, the day the five-year reservation status ended for the 1836 treaty lands, tribal representatives gathered at Mackinac Island to formulate a petition requesting an extension of the privilege of holding their reservations.[84] Dougherty was also at Mackinac. This spring council took place at the beginning of the term of a new Michigan Indian Superintendent, Robert Stuart, Schoolcraft's replacement. Schoolcraft had been accused of political activity and removed from office. As regional representative of the American Fur Company, Stuart had been in Washington, D.C., at the time of the 1836 treaty and had signed the Supplementary Article. In October 1841, Dougherty sent a personal appeal to Stuart at the request of the Grand Traverse chiefs, asking his support for their petition to Congress for an end to their uncertain land status.[85]

Seeking alternatives, Aishquagonabee led a substantial group of Grand Traverse Indians to Canada in July 1842 to receive presents and look over the situation on Manitoulin Island. In preparation, they built a special large canoe on the east shore of the bay. Although they urged him to join the canoe brigade, Agosa refused to accompany the travelers.[86] The number of Grand Traverse Indians who moved permanently to Canada does not seem to have been large. Following a long-established custom, the Ottawas and Ojibwes (and many other midwestern Indians) went to Manitoulin Island and Fort Malden (near Windsor) to receive presents from the British government, an annual event recognizing their support of the British during the War of 1812. Although the British tried to restrict the gift distribution to Indians residing in Canada, gifts to Indians from the United States continued, though somewhat curtailed, until the 1850s.

With the future status of their reservation unresolved, buying land seemed the best solution to the individual problems of the Grand Traverse families. Dougherty was equally eager that the Presbyterian

Church be able to purchase the land on "the point" (i.e., the reservation) where a church was built in 1842, along with other structures. But the Grand Traverse residents could not be sure that news of a prospective land sale would reach them before the land was actually put on the market. In 1844, at the time of the fall payment of annuities at Mackinac Island, a spurious rumor circulated that the land on the peninsula was "in market." The rumor was reinforced by a further report that "a canoe from a village at the head of the bay went to the land office at Ionia and [the occupants] had purchased [the land] where they lived." Further investigation revealed that they had "deposited their money at the office with a promise from the land agent that he would write to Washington stating the application they have made and hereafter inform them if the purchase can now be made."[87] Such an incident increased the anxiety pervading Indian homes.

In a state of perpetual uncertainty, members of the Grand Traverse Indian community turned to buying land where they could as the best solution to their problem. Writing on Christmas Day in 1848, Dougherty reported on local land purchases: "One band of six or eight families have made a small purchase on the west side of the Bay and are making arrangements to move next year. Another band of six or eight, most of them members of our church, made a purchase this fall on the east side of the Bay." The purchase on the east shore of the bay marked the establishment of the first Indian village on the east side of Grand Traverse Bay since Aishquagonabee left the Eastport area in 1839. In his long Christmas letter, Dougherty went on to explain that forty or fifty families or more would remain on their lands on the peninsula if their ownership would be secure. They had made considerable progress with farming and wanted to have lands to enclose for cattle pasture and fruit raising. Dougherty had already purchased fruit trees for the mission grounds.[88] Two months later, he reported that there was talk about "getting up a petition here praying the government to bring this point into market that the Indians may purchase if they wish. . . . Persons are beginning to look about here for locations. All is uncertainty at present with regard to this land whether it is regarded still by the government as a reservation to which the laws relating to Indian territory apply or not. If a reservation, preemption cannot hold here, hence all improvements are made at considerable hazard."[89]

In the spring of 1849, the owner of the sawmill at the head of Grand Traverse Bay returned from the Ionia land office with the false rumor that the reservation might be on the market during the summer.[90] By fall, people living on "the point" were aware that stories were circulating about white persons who wanted its reservation status terminated so that they could purchase land. Dougherty hoped that by whatever strategy it could, the Presbyterian Board might be able to buy the developed land including the mission property and the Indian village on the harbor.[91]

The year 1850 marked a new era in the historical development and mapping of the Grand Traverse region. The bay area no longer was an isolated and relatively unknown region of Michigan. Visitors and prospective settlers were talking about locating at the attractive harbor, where a government post office named "Grand Traverse" was established that year. On May 16, 1850, former senator and land promoter Lucius Lyon disembarked at the harbor to begin the resurvey of the Grand Traverse region, starting on the east side of the bay.[92] Survey teams worked in the area for the next seven years, from 1850 through 1856.

Lyon brought high standards to the surveying of northern Michigan. He had just completed a five-year term (1845–1850), as surveyor general for the district northwest of the Ohio River, which had its headquarters in Detroit. Earlier in his career, Lyon had surveyed the northern boundary of Illinois. Lyon remeasured the township lines for the tier of Townships 28, 29, and 30 North in Range 9 West during the summer and fall of 1850, but the subdivisions were not made until two years later. Lyon died in September 1851, and though the subdividing of Township 28 took place early in 1852, the map for the township was not approved by Charles Noble, surveyor general in Detroit, until April 11, 1853.[93] The subdivision of the two townships to the north took much longer. Township 29, including Elk Rapids and land on the east side of Elk Lake, presented a particular challenge since the original drawing was so erroneous, but it was finally approved in December 1856.[94] On the west side of Grand Traverse Bay, veteran surveyor Orange Risdon began the corrective township surveys and subdividing in the fall of 1851. Risdon had produced the very first survey map of southeastern Michigan in 1825. After completing work on the Leelanau Peninsula, Risdon moved to the east side of the bay to subdivide Township 30 in the fall of 1855. That survey was approved in November 1856.[95]

The survey teams working in the Grand Traverse Bay area in the 1850s recorded illuminating information in their maps and survey notes about population, land use, and natural resources. This information has been assembled and reproduced, enhanced by color coding, in maps by J. William Trygg, which were published in 1964.[96] The Trygg maps provide a graphic display of the Grand Traverse area (fig. 8), making it possible to discern changes in the cultural landscape that had occurred between the area's earlier portrayal by Peter Dougherty in 1840 and the 1850s surveys. Comparing the maps is a cartographic exposition of local history.

The Trygg map reveals the concentration of Ottawa and Ojibwe population in the northern half of the Leelanau Peninsula, where five Indian villages are identified, the largest an "Old Indian village of 10 Lodges" at present-day Leland, with adjacent "Indian Fields" and a "clearing." Farther north, surveyors recorded Indian trails, a wood-chopping site, and an Indian village with "improvements" a mile or so from Cat Head Bay at the tip of the peninsula. To the east, on the bay side, the Indian village is marked at present-day Northport along with the mission station of George N. Smith, who had moved from the Holland region in 1849. A trail southward leads to the next small peninsula, long the home of Shabwasson, who lived near the well-known "Indian Apple Orchard," which probably dated from the pre-1760 French era. Part of the orchard was included in Peter Dougherty's land purchase for a new mission site, but the information for this section of the map, noting the sugar camp and field, was collected before the establishment of the "New Mission" in 1852. Farther south along the bay shore is the final Indian village with a note about "extensive cultivation."[97]

Since the Old Mission Peninsula was not subject to resurvey, except for the west side of the lower part that fell into Range 11 West, the basic information here is from the original 1839 survey that noted the village on the harbor where Agosa lived. The 1851 survey at the base of the bay recorded a portion of the recently constructed wagon road from Traverse City to Old Mission. For this part of the bay area, local history already recounted fills in the picture, supplementing the cartographic record. On the east side of the bay, the Indian field with a path to the shore is of particular interest, since the manuscript map records "Indian graves" where the path strikes the shore. This site, about three miles north of present-day Eastport, is in the vicinity of Aishquagonabee's old village. The mouth of Elk River is marked as a sawmill site; however, the manuscript map provides a place name, "Elk Rapids," and shows four triangles indicating a local community where Indians were reported to have moved by 1850. In the interior, around the southern end of Torch Lake and Elk Lake, ten locations are noted as sugar camps or sugar bush or grove. These are the places where Indians living on "the point" went in early spring to make sugar, fish, and secure materials for constructing canoes.

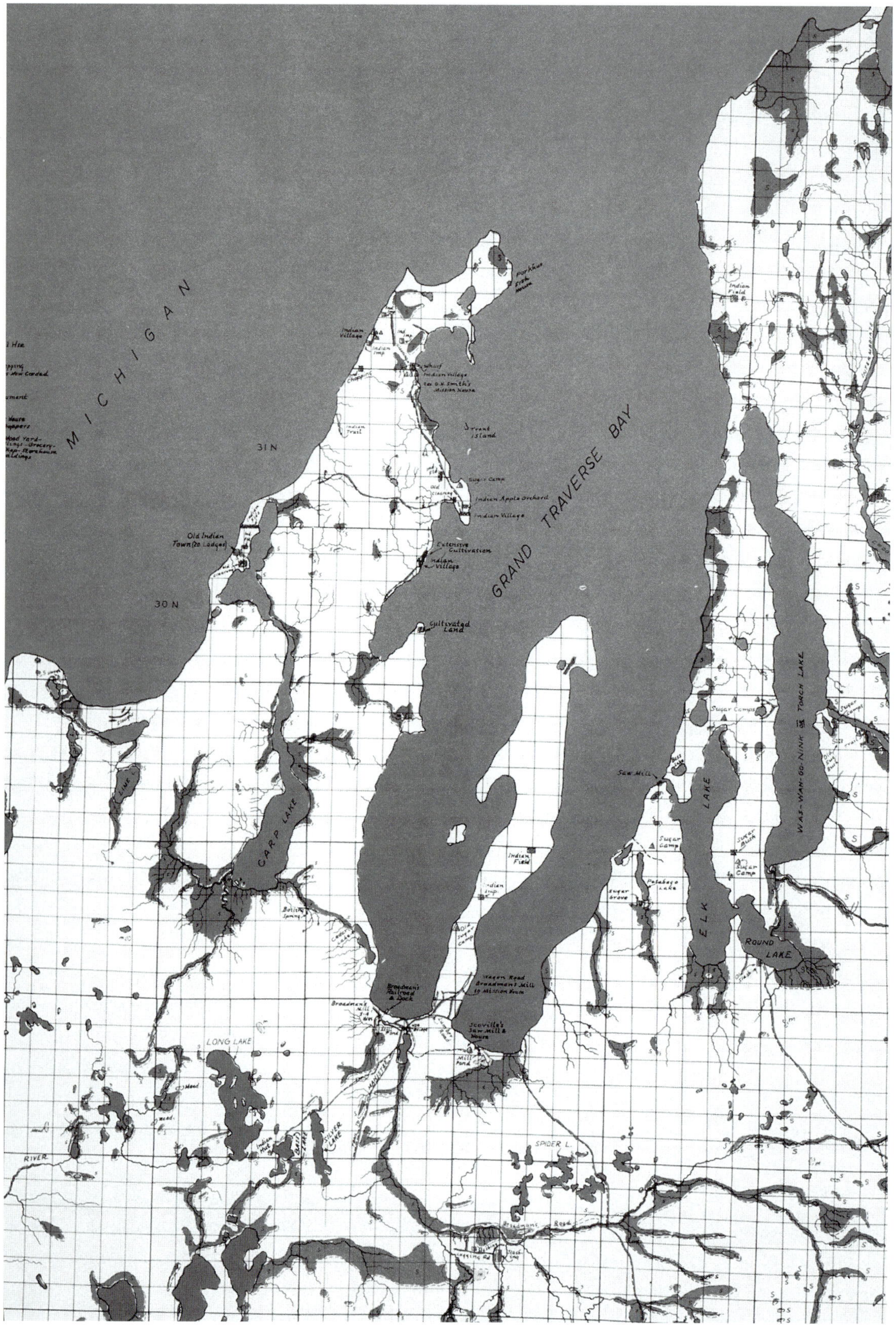

Figure 8. Old Mission Peninsula, 1840, surrounding Grand Traverse Bay area, 1850s. Courtesy of J. W. Trygg, Ely, MN.

At the base of Grand Traverse Bay, the map notes Boardman's mill on the west arm and the more recently established Scoville's mill on the east arm, each with a millpond. To the south, the legends "Boardman's Road" and "logging road" indicate the location of early lumbering operations. Three main trails show overland communication routes. From the west arm, the beginning of the trail southwest to Manistee is marked. To the east are two trails toward the upper Manistee River, one from the east arm of Traverse Bay and a second from "Round Lake" (Lake Skegemog).

The surveying and mapping of the early 1850s recorded recent changes in the population picture and forecast questionable future developments. In the larger political sphere, 1850 was significant for Michigan Indians because the new state constitution enfranchised Indian men who were considered civilized and not just members of a tribe.[98] This change facilitated Indians' ability to purchase land. At the national level, the Bureau of Indian Affairs was transferred from the War Department and incorporated into the new Department of the Interior, which was established in 1849. Thereafter, Indian matters became more influenced by party politics.

The year also saw the decrease and further dispersion of the Indian population living on the Grand Traverse reservation. Even at their peak, communities on "the point" probably included less than half of the total Grand Traverse region's Ottawa and Ojibwe population. Indian families who decided to move away from the village near the harbor sold their homes to white men, who could not yet purchase the land on which the homes were built.[99] Further population decrease on "the point" was forecast when eight or ten Catholic families living there indicated that they were moving to the west shore where they could buy land. The Catholic community represented a substantial population. They had their own mission school, which reported twenty-eight students for the academic year 1850–51. By comparison, the Presbyterian school counted forty-three enrolled students, but attendance averaged twenty. As part of their widespread interest in securing land, the Indians discussed a request to the government for land in exchange for the two hundred thousand dollars due to them by the terms of the 1836 treaty when they gave up their reservations. Much discouraged, Dougherty decided that the reservation on "the point" no longer was of any use to the Indians and should be sold as soon as possible.[100] All of these incidents and reports indicate that a movement to abandon the Grand Traverse reservation was well under way five years before the Ottawas and Ojibwes of northwestern Michigan officially ceded their reservation lands in a new treaty signed in July 1855.

At the foot of the west arm of the bay, signs of development were unmistakable by 1850. Horace Boardman had begun limited lumbering in 1847, and he built a wharf the following year. Boardman also hired local Indians to strip bark from hemlock trees, which was to be shipped to Chicago for use in tanning leather. In 1850, however, three Chicago businessmen organized the firm Hannah, Lay, and Co., whose operations really led to the settlement of the future Traverse City area. These men came in the spring of 1851, took over the Boardman property, and began expanded lumbering operations. By wintertime, the small community counted about a dozen families and an equal number of single residents, mostly men.[101]

With the local non-Indian population obviously increasing, leading residents of the reservation on "the point" made two major land purchases in 1851. In August, Peter Dougherty embarked on a weeklong trip to the land office in Ionia, going by water along the coast of Lake Michigan to the Grand River and then upriver to Grand Rapids, where he completed the journey by stagecoach. In the name of Walter Lowrie, secretary of the Presbyterian Board, Dougherty purchased three hundred thirty-three acres of land on the west side of Grand Traverse Bay, near present-day Omena, acreage that actually included some of the agricultural land of Shabwasson's village.[102] Since the Indians were fearful of disease and the temptations offered by liquor-selling traders at Mackinac Island, seventy heads of families asked Dougherty to attend the fall payment and bring back their annuities.[103] This is very likely a principal source of the fund of twelve hundred dollars that Chief Agosa took with him when he went through the woods to the Ionia land office in November to purchase forty-acre plots for members of his band. Overland travel was facilitated in 1851 by a new trail cut through the forests from Croton on the Muskegon River to Traverse City, a distance of about one hundred miles.[104] Construction of the new Presbyterian mission on the west shore of Grand Traverse Bay began in the early spring of 1852 using lumber brought across Lake Michigan from Green Bay, Wisconsin. The residential school opened in the fall with approximately twenty-five girls and twenty-five boys in attendance.[105] The church, "New Mission," was completed in 1858, and it continued in operation until 1870. Cherry trees that Dougherty planted are credited with starting the agricultural enterprise that eventually made Traverse City the "National Cherry Capital."

The New Mission under Presbyterian auspices was just one of the additions to the Ottawa and Ojibwe communities on the Leelanau Peninsula within the period 1849 to 1852. In 1849, George N. Smith, a Congregationalist, brought his "Ottawa Colony" under the leadership of Waukazoo from the Black River, near modern Holland, to establish Waukazooville at present-day Northport. At the new location, Smith soon dealt with three other groups in the northern Leelanau Peninsula: the Shabwasson, Nagonabe, and Onomunese bands. According to some local accounts, Onomunese's band arrived on the northwest shore of the Leelanau Peninsula about this time, fleeing intertribal strife in Wisconsin. The new Catholic community on the west shore of Grand Traverse Bay increased with the arrival of Ottawas from Cross Village with their priest, marking the beginning of Eagletown, later Peshawbestown.[106] In 1842, Peshawbe was still living at the base of "the point."[107] In another population shift, several families from the original mission community on "the point" on Grand Traverse Bay bought land and moved to Bear River on the south shore of Little Traverse Bay (present-day Petoskey). This location also attracted Catholic families from the north shore who were eager to have a school for their children with English-language instruction, which the foreign-trained priests at Harbor Springs would not provide.[108]

In all of the communities around Grand Traverse Bay, as well as among other Ottawas and Ojibwes living in the area ceded in the Treaty of March 28, 1836, people raised questions not only about their homes and lands but also about payments due under various treaty provisions. Claiming to represent "Chiefs of the Ottawa and Chippewa Tribes of Indians, residing in Michigan," William Johnston wrote directly to the commissioner of Indian affairs in 1850, asking for a new treaty to be made in Washington, D.C., to "adjust existing matters appertaining to the Two tribes; which are now unsettled and cannot be adjusted otherwise."[109] Matters continued to be "unsettled" for another five years.

In the meantime, Michigan political leaders exerted pressure in Washington through the Committee on Indian Affairs in the United States Senate. On April 6, 1852, the Senate "Resolved, That the Committee on Indian Affairs be instructed to inquire into the expediency of making provisions for the amicable arrangement with the Ottawa and Chippewa Indians of all questions arising under the treaty with them of 1836, relative to the continued occupancy of the lands reserved to them and the consideration to be paid for such cession; and also, as to the expediency of making an appropriation to enable the proper Department to consummate such measures as may be necessary for their permanent settlement in the country where they now reside." The resolution, promptly forwarded to the commissioner of Indian affairs, was introduced by Michigan Senator Alpheus Felch, who had previously been a justice of the Michigan Supreme Court and served a term as the state's governor.[110] The matter did not move forward until August, when George Manypenny, the new Commissioner of Indian Affairs, finally sent a long explanatory letter to the Secretary of the Interior requesting a twenty-thousand-dollar appropriation to hold a treaty council with the "Ottawa and Chippewa" with a view to arranging for them to continue living in their own ceded lands.[111]

Progress toward a treaty was more rapid after Henry C. Gilbert became head of the Michigan Indian Agency in May 1853. Gilbert's interest was not entirely altruistic. He called attention to the fact that under the 1836 treaty, annual payments would end in 1855, with the possibility that several thousand northwest Michigan Indians might need subsistence aid from the state rather than the federal government. Pointing out the pressure of incoming population, he made the erroneous statement that all lands were "on the market."[112] The Grand Traverse band's 1836 reservation was not yet open for sale. Michigan Indians were becoming increasingly impatient to have their government-owed payments made and the status of their lands settled.

During the following winter, all of the Ottawas and Ojibwes in northwestern Michigan organized a joint presentation to take place in Washington, D.C., on February 26, 1855. In preparation, leaders from all of the bands north of Manistee first met at Grand Traverse to prepare a memorial, written in their own language with an English translation, expressing a "unanimous wish." This memorial asked the government to keep the money owed to the bands, explaining that "our request is to have the interest of that money distributed yearly amongst our children, to enable them to pay for lands and taxes." The document dated at Grand Traverse, January 16, 1855, carried forty-seven signatures, while the supplementary statement dated February 7, 1855, added thirty-four more signatures and the comment that the Grand River Ottawa "with one mind agree with our friends & connexions."[113]

A major factor in the impending crisis was the advent of Michigan's second land boom, created in large part by the passage of the Graduation Act of 1854, which reduced the price of land for ten years to one dollar an acre, with larger reductions for land that had been on the market for longer periods of time.[114] Furthermore, transportation improvements, such as the completion of a railroad across the southern part of the state, and increased immigration and ship traffic brought a new wave of settlers, as well as lumbermen, into Michigan.

Manypenny favored the allotment of individual parcels of land to each Indian family, with special provisions for single households and orphans, as a basis for permanent settlements in a new treaty. This was the arrangement agreed upon at treaty councils that met in Detroit from July 25 until July 31, 1855, when the new treaty was signed.[115] For the Grand Traverse bands, the lands set aside in the Fifth Clause of Article I were located on the Leelanau Peninsula, with a half township on the east side of Elk Rapids.[116] These were areas where the Indians had already settled and where some had already purchased land. The treaty also enabled the Board of Foreign Missions of the Presbyterian Church to acquire the approximately sixty-three acres where the school, mission, and other buildings had been constructed. A separate paragraph of Article I of the treaty stated that the land "shall be vested in the said board on payment of $1.25 per acre; and the President of the United States shall issue a patent for the same to such person as the said board shall appoint."[117]

The era of the 1836 treaty reservations effectively ended when arrangements were made for payment of the two hundred thousand dollars granted by the Senate because the reservations were limited to a five-year existence. The Grand Traverse bands gave their approval to the amended treaty at a council held at Northport on July 5, 1856, with the names of Aishquagonabee and Agosa leading the list of seven signers.[118]

After the new 1855 treaty went into effect, the old reservation on "the point" (becoming known as the Old Mission Peninsula) still retained a considerable Indian population, even though many families had resettled on the Leelanau Peninsula, along Elk River and the north end of Elk Lake, and at Bear River community on the south shore of Little Traverse Bay. An Indian village near the base of "the point" helped guide a settler safely to shore after he had become lost while crossing the ice from Traverse City to Bower's Harbor on a foggy evening in March 1858. A new Methodist Episcopal minister began preaching at the old mission church in 1857 to a varied congregation of settlers, occasional visiting sailors, and ornamented, traditionally clad Indians. Aishquagonabee, principal chief of the Grand Traverse bands, was a conspicuous member of the congregation from time to time. He had moved from the northeast shore of the bay to the peninsula in June 1839 and remained there.[119]

The land making up the Grand Traverse Indians' 1836 treaty reservation was finally placed on the market in 1859 as a result of the combined efforts of settlers, developers, and local politicians who carried their appeals to Washington, D.C. By that time, prospective buyers no longer had to make the long trek to a distant land office, as one had opened in Traverse City on August 2, 1858.[120] In 1851, land purchases still had to be made in Ionia, but a new northern office began entries in 1852 at the town of Duncan, near present-day Cheboygan. That office was transferred to Mackinac Island from March 1 to July 1, 1858, and then relocated in Traverse City in August 1858.[121]

The Indian reservation on the peninsula in Grand Traverse Bay, first drawn by Peter Dougherty in 1839, surveyed later the same year, and including the only northwestern Michigan townships that were not resurveyed, apparently became the last tract of land in the Lower Peninsula to become part of the public domain. Although the original Indian residents never were able to buy the land on the peninsula where they had homes and cultivated fields, the Presbyterian Board of Foreign Missions in Philadelphia purchased the mission and school sites when land on the peninsula at last went on sale in 1859.

NOTES

The author would like to thank the following for their assistance in gathering material for this article: the staffs at the Bentley Historical Library, the State Archives of Michigan, the Presbyterian Historical Society, and especially John Aubrey, Pat Morris, and Robert Karrow of The Newberry Library. Thanks also go to John Powell of The Newberry Library and Laurence White for map reproduction.

1. James Finlayson, "Michigan Territory," in *A Complete Historical, Chronological, and Geographical American Atlas* (Philadelphia: H. C. Carey and I. Lea, 1822), plate 36.

2. A prominent feature of the map is the "Indian Line" extending south from Saginaw Bay, an inaccurate dashed line probably intended to represent the northern boundary of land ceded by the Saginaw Chippewas in the 1819 treaty. The identical line appears in the map used as a poster and program for the conference "Mapping in Michigan and the Great Lakes Region,"

which was presented by the *Michigan Historical Review* and the Clarke Historical Library at Central Michigan University, Mount Pleasant, on June 11–12, 2004. This map is the work of Fielding Lucas, Jr., *A General Atlas, Containing Distinct Maps of All the Known Countries in the World* (Baltimore: F. Lucas, Jr., 1823), plate 75.

3. Orange Risdon, *Map of the Surveyed Part of the Territory of Michigan* (Albany: Rawdon, Clark, 1825). The mapped area extends north into the Thumb region and is restricted to land east of the Michigan meridian, a line running north and south just east of present-day Jackson.

4. John Farmer, *Improved Map of the Territories of Michigan and Ouisconsin (Pronounced Wisconsin)* (New York: J. H. Colton, 1836).

5. John Farmer, *Map of the Surveyed Part of Michigan* (New York: J. H. Colton, 1837).

6. Traugott Bromme, *Michigan* (Baltimore: C. Scheld, 1834).

7. Henry R. Schoolcraft, "Map of the Acting Superintendency of Michigan, 1837," RG 75, National Archives, Washington, D.C. (photostat in The Newberry Library).

8. Peter Dougherty to David Wells, c. June 18–20, 1839, Peter Dougherty Papers (hereafter cited as Dougherty Papers), microfilm, Bentley Historical Library, Ann Arbor, Mich. The originals can be found at the Presbyterian Historical Society, Philadelphia. See also fig. 6, which shows the location of Aishquagonabee's village (the leading chief) at present-day Eastport, Agosa's village and two other village sites on the peninsula, and the school temporarily built at present-day Elk Rapids.

9. Peter Dougherty to Walter Lowrie, January 8, 1841, Dougherty Papers. See also fig. 7, which shows the recently surveyed section lines on the peninsula that had been selected by the Ojibwes and Ottawas as their 1836 Treaty reservation. Also noted are the location of the Presbyterian mission and school near Agosa's village, established c. June 20, 1839 (1); Aishquagonabee's former village site (2); and five other Indian communities on the west side of the bay (3–7). Aishquagonabee probably lived at site 3 at this time.

10. Joanna E. Feest and Christian F. Feest, "Ottawa," in *Handbook of North American Indians*, vol. 15, *The Northeast*, ed. Bruce Trigger (Washington, D.C.: Smithsonian Institution, 1978), 772–73.

11. Michael Jay Hambacher, "The Skegemog Point Site: Continuing Studies in the Cultural Dynamics of the Carolinian-Canadian Transition Zone" (Ph.D. diss., Michigan State University, 1992), 305–8, 328–29. Lake Skegemog is a southeastern extension of Elk Lake, east of Grand Traverse Bay.

12. Conrad E. Heidenreich, "Huron," in *The Northeast*, ed. Trigger, 368–69, 384–85.

13. Andrew J. Blackbird, *History of the Ottawa and Chippewa Indians of Michigan: A Grammar on Their Language, and Personal and Family History of the Author* (Ypsilanti, Mich.: Ypsilanti Job Print, 1887), 25–26.

14. Ibid., 90–92.

15. Warfare ended with an intertribal treaty conference at Montreal in 1701. See Helen Hornbeck Tanner, ed., *Atlas of Great Lakes Indian History* (Norman: University of Oklahoma Press, 1987), 29–35.

16. Feest and Feest, "Ottawa," 772.

17. "Speech of the Outaouacs of Missilimakinac, June 16, 1742," in *The French Regime in Wisconsin, II, 1727–1748*, ed. Reuben Gold Thwaites (Madison: State Historical Society of Wisconsin, 1906), 17: 372.

18. Messeur de Celeron, Commandant at Missilimackinac, to the Marquis de Beauharnois, September 2, 1741; the Marquis de Beauharnois to the French Minister, September 26, 1741, in ibid., 359–60, 367–69.

19. Blackbird, *History*, 9–10.

20. The Upper Peninsula Chippewas are a separate western division of the Ojibwe people, different from the eastern or Mississauga Ojibwes of the north shore of Lake Huron. The Mississauga Ojibwes advanced southward across the Ontario peninsula in the later years of the Iroquois wars, reaching Lake Ontario by 1696 and establishing a base on the delta of the St. Clair River. They spread westward into the Saginaw Valley of Michigan and have remained a separate entity, with a treaty history different from that of the Sault Ste. Marie Chippewas.

21. Blackbird, *History*, 15.

22. Henry R. Schoolcraft, *Historical and Statistical Information Respecting the Indian Tribes of the United States*, vol. 6, *History of the Indian Tribes of the United States* (Philadelphia: Lippincott, Grambo, 1857), 205–6.

23. Ruth Craker, *The First Protestant Mission in the Grand Traverse Region* (Leland, Mich.: Leelanau Enterprise, 1935), 38.

24. This figure was given to Dougherty at the village in 1838. Peter Dougherty to Walter Lowrie, Report for 1838, 18, microfilm, Dougherty Papers.

25. Craker, *First Protestant Mission*, 35–36.

26. Peter Dougherty to David Wells, November 1850, Dougherty Papers.

27. Principal sites are shown in *Atlas*, ed. Tanner, map 25, 134. On this map, the site "Wequagemog" on the east shore of Grand Traverse Bay at present-day Elk Rapids should be deleted as a consequence of postpublication research in the Dougherty Papers.

28. Henry R. Schoolcraft, "Annual Report to the Commissioner of Indian Affairs for 1837," Edward E. Ayer Collection (hereafter Ayer Collection), The Newberry Library.

29. For an account of the treaty by a biographer of Schoolcraft, see Richard G. Bremer, *Indian Agent and Wilderness Scholar: The Life of Henry Rowe Schoolcraft* (Mount Pleasant, Mich.: Clarke Historical Library, 1987), 158–68.

30. Helen Hornbeck Tanner, "Henry Rowe Schoolcraft," in *American National Biography*, ed. John A. Garraty and Mark C. Carnes (New York: Oxford University Press, 1999), 19: 424–25.

31. A more detailed account of events preliminary to the 1836 treaty is included in Helen Hornbeck Tanner, "Report," *United States of America v. State of Michigan*, no. M 26–73 C.A., U.S.D.C., 1974, Exhibit P 17, 53–63.

32. Bremer, *Indian Agent*, 159.

33. Bruce A. Rubenstein and Lawrence E. Ziewacz, *Michigan: A History of the Great Lakes State* (St. Louis: Forum Press, 1981), 59–60.

34. For a journal of treaty proceedings, see John Hulbert, "Records of a Treaty Concluded with the Ottawa & Chippewa Nations at Washington, D.C., March 28, 1836" (manuscript in Henry Rowe Schoolcraft Papers, Library of Congress, Washington, D.C.), Exhibit P 17A, Appendix A-1, in Tanner, "Report."

35. Tanner, "Report," Appendix A-1, 59–61. Also see George W. Thayer, "Life of Senator Lucius Lyon," in *Michigan Historical Collections* (Lansing: Historical Society of Michigan, 1896), 27: 407–12; and Letters: Section I #24 to Rix Robinson, December 25, 1835; #25 to John A. Drew, December 26, 1835; #32 to John A. Drew, January 2, 1836; Section III #82 to George Crawford, March 12, 1836; #84 to A. E. Wing, March 19, 1836; #93 to C. C. Trowbridge, March 17, 1836, in ibid., 416ff.

36. A Grand Island (Lake Superior) chief by the same name is on the list of 157 leaders at the end of the treaty who were designated for individual financial awards.

37. Hulbert, "Records of a Treaty."

38. See Articles Second and Third of the treaty, cited in note 39 below.

39. For the complete original treaty, with the list of amendments, see Richard Peters, ed., *The Public Statutes at Large of the United States of America* (Boston: C. C. Little and J. Brown, 1848), 7: 491–97.

40. Ibid., 496.

41. The final treaty is printed in *Indian Treaties, 1778–1883*, comp. and ed. Charles J. Kappler (New York: Interland Publishing, 1972), 450–56.

42. Rubenstein and Ziewacz, *Michigan*, 60–63.

43. Dallas Lee Jones, "Survey and Sale of the Public Land in Michigan, 1815–1862" (master's thesis, Cornell University, 1952), 172–73.

44. Henry Schoolcraft to C. A. Harris, Commissioner of Indian Affairs, April 18, 1837, National Archives Microfilm, M1, Records

of the Michigan Superintendency of Indian Affairs, 1814–1851, roll 37, 201 RG 75; C. A. Harris to Henry Schoolcraft, July 1, 1837, National Archives Microfilm, M21, Letters Sent by the Office of Indian Affairs, 1824–1881, roll 22, 52, RG 75; Henry Schoolcraft to John Mullett, July 25, 1837, National Archives Microfilm, M1, roll 37, 265, RG 75, Federal Records Center, Chicago.

45. Henry Rowe Schoolcraft, *Personal Memoirs of a Residence of Thirty Years with the Indian Tribes on the American Frontiers: With Brief Notices of Passing Events, Facts, and Opinions, A.D. 1812–1842* (Philadelphia: Lippincott, Grambo, 1851), 598.

46. Peter Dougherty to Walter Lowrie, Report for 1838, 17, Dougherty Papers.

47. Ibid., 19. Dougherty's description of the village location notes that it was on the "north bank" of the bay. Similarly, Schoolcraft's description of the proposed location of a reservation for the Grand Traverse Indians in the 1836 treaty specified the "north shore" of the bay. The terminology in both cases comes from the experience of canoeing southward toward the Grand River from Mackinac Island. On that route, the big open-water crossing is the broad mouth of Grand Traverse Bay, where the geographical perception is that the route south heads to the tip of the Leelanau Peninsula. Therefore, the Charlevoix side of the mouth of Grand Traverse Bay was identified as the *north* side.

48. Ibid. Local history accounts have mistakenly identified present-day Elk Rapids as the site of this village, based on the idea that Dougherty followed the bay shore rather than continuing along the lakeshore.

49. Ibid.

50. Peter Dougherty to David Wells, June 1, 1839, Dougherty Papers.

51. Schoolcraft, *Personal Memoirs*, 650.

52. Craker, *First Protestant Mission*, 29.

53. Peter Dougherty to David Wells, July 9, 1839, Dougherty Papers.

54. Craker, *First Protestant Mission*, 28.

55. The peninsula is close to sixteen miles long.

56. Dougherty to Wells, June c. 18–20, 1839.

57. See figure 7; Peter Dougherty to Walter Lowrie, January 8, 1841, Dougherty Papers.

58. Peter Dougherty to Henry Schoolcraft, September 1839, National Archives Microfilm, M1, Records of the Michigan Superintendency of Indian Affairs, 1814–1851, roll 47, 251–56, RG 75, Federal Records Center.

59. Townships 21 through 30 in Ranges 8 through 12 were reported April 10, 1840, in E. J. Haines, Surveyor General, to James Whitcomb, Commissioner of the General land Office, National Archives Microfilm, M478, Letters Received by the Secretary of the Treasury and the Commissioner of the General Land Office from the Surveyor General of the Territory Northwest of the River Ohio, 1797–1849, roll 9, 1656, RG 49, Federal Records Center.

60. Jones, "Survey and Sale," 20, 26–27.

61. Henry Schoolcraft to T. Hartley Crawford, May 18, 1840, National Archives Microfilm, M1, Records of the Michigan Superintendency of Indian Affairs, 1814–1851, roll 38, 268, RG 75, Federal Records Center.

62. James Whitcomb to T. Hartley Crawford, June 9, 1840, National Archives Microfilm, M234, Letters Received by the Office of Indian Affairs, 1824–1881, roll 427, 567–69, RG 75, Federal Records Center.

63. See #206 on plate CXXXVI, "Michigan 1," in *Indian Land Cessions in the United States: 18th Annual Report of the Bureau of American Ethnology for the Years 1896–1897*, part 2, comp. Charles C. Royce (Washington, D.C.: Government Printing Office, 1899).

64. J. W. Whitcomb to T. Hartley Crawford, August 10, 1840, National Archives Microfilm, M234, Letters Received by the Office of Indian Affairs, 1824–1881, roll 424, 571, RG 75, Federal Records Center. The three townships totaled 20,672.74 acres. Survey maps, RG 87–155, 16–3, 6, 11, State Archives of Michigan, Lansing.

65. Henry R. Schoolcraft to T. Hartley Crawford, October 16, 1840, National Archives Microfilm, M1, Records of the Michigan Superintendency of Indian Affairs, 1814–1851, roll 38, 400, RG 75, Federal Records Center.

66. T. Hartley Crawford to Henry Schoolcraft, November 4, 1840, National Archives Microfilm, M1, Records of the Michigan Superintendency of Indian Affairs, 1814–1851, roll 29, 359–60, RG 75, Federal Records Center.

67. Henry R. Schoolcraft to Ezekiel S. Haines, November 22, 1840, National Archives Microfilm, M1, Records of the Michigan Superintendency of Indian Affairs, 1814–1851, roll 38, 433–34, RG 75, Federal Records Center. Another copy can be found in National Archives Microfilm, M479, Letters Received by the Surveyor General of the Territory Northwest of the Ohio River, 1797–1856, roll 27, 772–75, RG 49, Federal Records Center.

68. John Brink, Indian Reserve of 70,000 Acres at the Mouth of the Manistee River, 1839, Conservation, 60–8-A, B53, F2, State Archives of Michigan.

69. Peter Dougherty to David Wells, September 14, 1840, Dougherty Papers.

70. Peter Dougherty to David Wells, January 7, 1841, Dougherty Papers. See also fig. 7.

71. Ibid.

72. Royce, comp., *Indian Land Cessions,* plate CXXXVI, "Michigan 1."

73. Blackbird, *History,* 54–56; Craker, *First Protestant Mission,* 30–31.

74. Craker, *First Protestant Mission,* 32; "School Report of Peter Dougherty," in *Annual Report of the Commissioner of Indian Affairs,* Michigan Superintendency no. 19 (Washington, D.C.: A. O. P. Nicholson, 1843), 327–28, in Ayer Collection.

75. James A. Clifton, *The Prairie People: Continuity and Change in Potawatomi Indian Culture, 1665–1965* (Lawrence: Regents Press of Kansas, 1977), 299–300.

76. Committee of Little Traverse Bay to Stevens T. Mason, July 2, 1839, RG 44, B157 F6, State Archives of Michigan, Lansing.

77. Draft reply of Stevens T. Mason to Augustin Hamelin, Jr., July 15, 1839, RG 44, B182, F3, State Archives of Michigan, Lansing.

78. E. S. Haines, Surveyor General, to J. W. Whitcomb, General Land Office, November 18, 1840, National Archives Microfilm, M477, Letters Sent by the Surveyor General of the Territory Northwest of the Ohio River, 1797–1854, roll 8, 64, RG 49, Federal Records Center; Schoolcraft, *Personal Memoirs,* 648.

79. Peter Dougherty to David Wells, March 19, 1841, Dougherty Papers. Dougherty gives an account of the correspondence with Biddle.

80. Ibid.

81. E. S. Haines to J. W. Whitcomb, April 1, 1841, National Archives Microfilm, M477, Letters Sent by the Surveyor General of the Territory Northwest of the Ohio River, 1797–1854, roll 8, 485–86, RG 49, Federal Records Center.

82. See Treaty of St. Peter's, July 19, 1837 (7 Stat. 536), in *Indian Treaties,* comp. and ed. Kappler, 491–93.

83. Jones, "Survey and Sale," 20, 27, 28, fig. II, "Surveys, Southern Peninsula," fig. III, "Map showing area . . . which was defective."

84. Peter Dougherty to David Wells, May 26, 1841, Dougherty Papers.

85. Peter Dougherty to Robert Stuart, October 2, 1841, National Archives Microfilm, M234, Letters Received by the Office of Indian Affairs, 1824–1881, roll 425, 518–21, Federal Records Center.

86. "The Diary of Peter Dougherty, vol. 2," *Journal of the Presbyterian Historical Society* 30 (December 1952): 248–52 (entries for June 18, July 13, 21, 25, 1842).

87. Peter Dougherty to David Wells, November 4, 1844, Dougherty Papers.

88. Peter Dougherty to Walter Lowrie, December 25, 1848, Dougherty Papers.

89. Peter Dougherty to David Wells, February 1849, Dougherty Papers.

90. Peter Dougherty to Walter Lowrie, June 8, 1849, Dougherty Papers.

91. Peter Dougherty to Walter Lowrie, September 21, 1849; January 21, 1850, both in Dougherty Papers.

92. "Diary of Peter Dougherty, vol. 1," *Journal of the Presbyterian Historical Society* 30 (September 1952): 191.

93. "Township No. 28 N. Range No. 9 West," Map 16–12, RG 87–155, State Archives of Michigan, Lansing.

94. "Township No. 29 N. Range No. 9 West," RG 57–31, State Archives of Michigan, Lansing. The difference between the original black lines and red correction lines is conspicuous. The final correct version is Map 16–5, RG 87–155.

95. "Township No. 30 N. Range No. 11 West," Map 16–12, RG 87–155, State Archives of Michigan, Lansing.

96. J. William Trygg, *Composite Map of the United States Land Surveyors' Original Plats and Field Notes* (Ely, Minn.: J. W. Trygg, 1964), 46 sheets. See sheet 9, Michigan Series. Trygg originally compiled these maps for use as evidence in land-claims cases, based on treaties presented before the Indian Claims Commission in Washington, D.C. See fig. 8, which shows the Grand Traverse section of sheet 9. Recent development of the land is shown by the resurvey of the bay area (except for the Old Mission Peninsula) beginning in 1850.

97. Ibid.

98. "Article 7, 1850 Constitution of the State of Michigan," in *Michigan Compiled Laws, 1979* (Lansing: Michigan Legislative Council, 1981), lxxxi.

99. Peter Dougherty to David Wells, May 23, 1850, Dougherty Papers.

100. Peter Dougherty to Walter Lowrie, September 4, 1850, Dougherty Papers. See also Reports to William Sprague, Mackinac Indian Agency, from Peter Dougherty, no. 3; from George N. Smith, no. 5; and from Bishop P. P. Lefevre, no. 6, in *Annual Report of the Commissioner of Indian Affairs* (Washington, D.C.: A. O. P. Nicholson, 1851), 312–15, 320.

101. M. L. Leach, *A History of the Grand Traverse Region* (Traverse City, Mich.: Grand Traverse Herald, 1883), 45–47, 52–53.

102. Peter Dougherty to Walter Lowrie, August 19, 1851, Dougherty Papers.

103. Peter Dougherty to Walter Lowrie, September 14, 1851, Dougherty Papers.

104. Peter Dougherty to Walter Lowrie, November 22, 1851, Dougherty Papers.

105. Craker, *First Protestant Mission*, 37–38.

106. George N. Smith to Wm. Sprague, in *Annual Report . . . Indian Affairs* (1851), 315; Elvin L. Sprague and Mrs. George N. Smith, *Sprague's History of Grand Traverse and Leelanau Counties, Michigan* (Chicago: B. F. Bowen, 1903), 337.

107. "Diary of Peter Dougherty, vol. 2," 247 (entry for June 11, 1842).

108. Peter Dougherty to Walter Lowrie, October 23, 1851, Dougherty Papers.

109. W. Johnston to Orlando Brown, June 1, 1850, National Archives Microfilm, M234, Letters Received by the Office of Indian Affairs, 1824–1881, roll 426, 660–62, RG 75, The Newberry Library.

110. D. R. Atchison, Chairman of the Committee on Indian Affairs, to Luke Lee, Commissioner of Indian Affairs, April 7, 1852, enclosing Senate Resolution April 6, 1852, National Archives Microfilm, M234, Letters Received by the Office of Indian Affairs, 1824–1881, roll 403, 702–3, RG 75, The Newberry Library. See also F. Clever Bald, *Michigan in Four Centuries* (New York: Harper, 1954), 252–53.

111. George Manypenny to R. McClelland, August 30, 1852, National Archives Microfilm, M234, Letters Received by the Office of Indian Affairs, 1824–1881, roll 403, 705–7, RG 75, The Newberry Library.

112. Henry C. Gilbert to George Manypenny, March 6, 1854, National Archives Microfilm, M234, Letters Received by the Office of Indian Affairs, 1824–1881, roll 404, 369–71, 376–77, RG 75, The Newberry Library.

113. Memorial of the Chippewa and Ottawa of Michigan, January 16 and February 7, 1855, National Archives Microfilm, M234, Letters Received by the Office of Indian Affairs, 1824–1881, roll 404, 561–65, RG 75, The Newberry Library. For a report of their communications in Washington, D.C., see Delegates to the Commissioner of Indian Affairs, February 27, 28, 1855, in ibid.

114. "An Act to Graduate and Reduce the Price of the Public Lands to Actual Settlers and Cultivators," approved August 4, 1854, 33d Congress, 1st sess., chapter 244, 574.

115. Proceedings of a Council with the Chippeways & Ottawas of Michigan . . . July 25th, 1855, RG 123, file 27537, box 1537, National Archives; *United States v. Michigan*, Plaintiffs Exhibit 18, 471, F. Supp. 192 (Western District of Michigan, 1979).

116. Treaty of July 31, 1855 (22 stat. 621), in *Indian Treaties,* comp. and ed. Kappler, 725–31.

117. Ibid., 728.

118. Ibid., 731.

119. Leach, *Grand Traverse Region,* 59–61.

120. H. R. Page & Co., *The Traverse Region: Historical and Descriptive* (1884; reprint, Evansville, Ind.: Unigraphic, 1974), 26, 46; Annual Report of Thomas A. Hendricks, Commissioner of the Land Office, to Jacob Thompson, Secretary of the Interior for 1858, in Hendricks, *Report of the Commissioner of General Land Office* (Washington, D.C.: Land Office, 1858), 40. Land offices in Michigan were located in Detroit, East Saginaw, Ionia, Kalamazoo, Mackinac, and Marquette. See Joseph A. Wilson, Commissioner of General Land Office, to Jacob Thompson, Secretary of Interior, November 29, 1860, in Wilson, *Report of the Commissioner of General Land Office* (Washington, D.C.: Land Office, 1860), 54–55, for the report of sales in 1859–1860 at Michigan land offices in Detroit, East Saginaw, Ionia, Marquette, and Traverse City.

121. Page, *The Traverse Region,* 26.

Picturing Progress: Assessing the Nineteenth-Century Atlas-Map Bonanza

Cheryl Lyon-Jenness

IN DECEMBER 1873, RESIDENTS OF JACKSON COUNTY IN SOUTHEASTERN MICHIGAN LEARNED of a new countywide project. "Mr. D. J. Stewart, of the firm Everts & Stewart was in the city yesterday," the *Jackson Daily Citizen* reported, "organizing his forces for a winter campaign of hard work in preparing materials for our new county atlas." For wide-awake Jackson County citizens, the arrival of David Stewart and the proposed county atlas came as no surprise. Stewart or his partner, Louis H. Everts, had paid similar visits to newspaper offices in neighboring Lenawee and Washtenaw Counties in the late winter and early spring of 1873. Local newspapers in those counties obligingly announced their arrival and kept tabs on the firm's progress as teams of canvassers, illustrators, surveyors, and writers spread out over the region, gathering subscriptions and information for their proposed atlases.[1]

When Louis Everts and David Stewart moved their team of surveyors, illustrators, and writers into southeastern Michigan, they were counting on a long-standing interest in regional maps to promote sales, but they also had something different to offer local residents.[2] Their "new atlas" promised cadastral maps (maps showing landownership boundaries) for each township drawn on a scale of two inches to the mile, hundreds of lithographic views of farm and village homes, an accurate account of local history, biographies and portraits of local residents, and even a "business directory" listing all those citizens who had the good sense to support the project. The firm's successful canvass of the three-county area suggests that the combination concept struck a chord with local residents. More than seven hundred families, businessmen and women, and local officials agreed to support the project by purchasing lithographs of their homes or properties. Other individuals paid for their portraits or biographies to appear in the atlas maps. Perhaps most striking, nearly six thousand residents in Jackson, Lenawee, and

Washtenaw Counties clearly thought the project worthwhile and agreed to purchase a nine-dollar atlas map of their locales.[3]

Proud supporters of these new *Combination Atlas Maps* might have been surprised to learn that they were not alone in their enthusiasm for the genre. During the brief heyday of atlas-map production in the 1870s, a number of firms competed with Everts and Stewart for midwestern customers. Some, such as Alfred T. Andreas or Higgins, Belden & Company, centered their businesses in Chicago, while others, such as members of the Beers family, had strong roots in the eastern mapmaking establishment. Details of format and marketing strategy varied among competing firms, but they all produced, as geographer Michael Conzen has pointed out, "maps for the masses," and most of them enjoyed at least some measure of financial success from their venture into regional mapping. Before the genre gave way to the more text-laden, largely map-free county histories of the 1880s and 1890s, most prosperous agricultural counties in the Midwest had supported the production of at least one county atlas or atlas map.[4]

The popularity of combination atlas maps among mapmaking entrepreneurs and their midwestern customers invited commentary from proponents and critics alike. Many pundits, particularly local newspapers editors, promoted the phenomenon as a way to enhance regional interests. Newspapers such as the *Jackson Daily Citizen* routinely praised completed atlases for their beauty and accuracy and lauded citizens for supporting such a worthwhile local project. But in a far-reaching critique of the subscription-book industry, Bates Harrington, a former atlas-map company employee, offered another perspective. Atlas production, Harrington claimed, was often quickly and carelessly done, leaving behind duped customers, a flawed record of local landscapes, and greedy entrepreneurs gleefully counting the proceeds.[5] Such comments roused the ire of atlas-map publishers, and they occasionally responded in kind. To those "inclined to find fault" or who "think they can produce a superior work," publishers of the 1873 Will County, Illinois, atlas map issued the challenge: "We say in all candor, let them try it."[6]

Historians and geographers have also evaluated the atlas-map bonanza, and while some have noted the publications' efficacy in documenting material culture, the critiques have often focused on the accuracy of the maps or lithographs.[7] Using the work of Louis Everts and D. J. Stewart in Lenawee, Jackson, and Washtenaw Counties as a springboard for analysis, this chapter seeks to broaden that discussion by assessing atlas-map production and popularity within the context of midwestern rural culture. The chapter first considers the significance of atlas maps from the perspectives of those who promoted and produced them and then examines the composition and motivation of the audience that so willingly purchased these works. Finally, the chapter evaluates the meaning of combination atlas maps for these diverse players and assesses their contribution to our understanding of mid-nineteenth-century rural life.

For Louis Everts and his new partner, David Stewart, producing combination atlas maps for Jackson, Lenawee, and Washtenaw Counties posed both an opportunity and a challenge. Neither man had been at the profession long, but both had enough experience to know that the public appetite for local maps and images offered lucrative rewards if they could only devise the right format and organizational strategies. Stewart brought at least some mapmaking experience to the partnership, but it was Everts who provided the driving force and the business acumen to take on the challenge. Louis Everts was born in Cattaraugus County, New York, in 1836, and in 1851 moved with his family to Geneva Township in Kane County, Illinois, where his father, Samuel Everts, once again took up dairy farming. In his early twenties, Louis Everts and his young bride, Louisa, left the farm for the bustling town of St. Charles, Il-

linois, where he clerked in a local store. Perhaps prompted by Louisa's untimely death after barely a year of marriage, Everts soon moved to Chicago and took a "position of trust" in Potter Palmer's dry-goods store. In the fall of 1861, Everts returned to Kane County to join friends and neighbors in organizing the 52nd Illinois Infantry and eventually served as assistant adjutant general with the Fourth Division, Fifteenth Army Corps. His military colleagues apparently appreciated Everts's skills as a manager of people and goods, for the field officers of the Fourth Division successfully petitioned for his promotion to the rank of major.[8]

Everts's war experience not only underscored his administrative talents but also brought sustained contact with other Kane County residents. One of these men, Thomas Hinkley Thompson, had a profound influence on Everts's subsequent career. Like Everts, Thompson came from a Kane County farm family that had moved from New York State in the early 1830s and settled in Dundee Township just north of Geneva. Moses H. Thompson, one of the older Thompson brothers, left the family farm in the mid-1850s, studied civil engineering, and eventually worked as a government surveyor. Sensing an opportunity, Moses Thompson moved on to establish his own mapmaking business, and from the firm's headquarters in Elgin, Illinois, he set about producing wall maps for counties in northern Illinois and adjoining states. When he was about eighteen years old, Thomas H. Thompson joined his older brother in the mapmaking trade, and it was not long before the youngest of the Thompson brothers, Charles, also began to assist in map production.[9]

Thomas Thompson had little time to hone his mapmaking skills before he, like Louis Everts, joined the 52nd Illinois Infantry. The two men may have been acquainted before the war, but their military experience cemented the bond. Shortly after the war's end, Everts joined Thompson in a new mapmaking enterprise. The partners established headquarters in Anamosa, Iowa, and within a few years had published county wall maps of Jones, Jackson, Dubuque, and Linn Counties in eastern Iowa. In the late 1860s, the pair moved the company's headquarters back to Geneva, Illinois, and canvassed Blackhawk and Delaware Counties in central Iowa as well as Carroll County in northwestern Illinois for map customers.[10]

Although produced by a new firm, Thompson and Everts's wall maps employed the familiar formats long established by Moses Thompson and others. Thompson and Everts's map of Carroll County, for example, included hand-colored cadastral maps of each township and identified features such as farmhouses, churches, blacksmith shops, and railroads. Several advertisements, along with plats of five towns, were inset on the left side of the map, while lithographs depicting local institutions bordered the top of the map. In order to make this local detail legible, the map was quite large, measuring nearly three feet by five feet. Atlas-map commentator Bates Harrington estimated that Thompson and Everts's Carroll County map brought in approximately nine thousand dollars and that map sales in each of fourteen Illinois counties averaged more than fifty-seven hundred dollars. Clearly, midwesterners had a strong interest in map depictions and were willing to support mapping projects in the region.[11]

By the late 1860s, the county wall-map industry had been booming for nearly a decade and was ripe for experimentation and change. The vision for innovation came from an unexpected source. In 1867, Thompson and Everts asked another army comrade, Alfred T. Andreas, to join them for the canvass of Scott County, Iowa, and Rock Island County, Illinois. Andreas agreed, and as he studied the trade, he came up with a new format that would revolutionize the mapmaking business. Why not, Andreas reasoned, combine the popular attributes of the county wall map with the more readily handled atlas format? Emphasizing locale by publishing each township as a separate map would enable mapmakers to produce a very clear image of landownership, transportation links, and other features of interest to local residents. The book format would also mean that the amount of printed matter and the number of lithographs, severely limited by the space on one wall map, could expand exponentially. Both Everts and Thompson were dubious about this new approach, but they decided to experiment with what they dubbed a "combination atlas map." Andreas, with an eye to his own business prospects, agreed to stay on through the experiment but began calculating his chances for success as a competitor in the atlas-map trade.[12]

After Andreas agreed to join them, Thompson and Everts selected Henry County in southeastern Iowa for their first venture into atlas-map publishing. In 1870, Henry County seemed a likely prospect, with a population base of nearly twenty-two thousand residents and a productive agricultural economy. The *Combination Atlas Map of Henry County, Iowa* that emerged from their efforts established several precedents. The title page, for example, set the tone for the new genre with a lithograph showcasing Thompson and Everts's company headquarters in downtown Geneva (fig. 1). The title page boldly assured patrons that the atlas map was "Compiled, Drawn, and Published from Personal Examination and Surveys," although an observant reader might have noted that Norman Friend of Philadelphia was responsible for lithography.[13]

Although it was relatively small when compared to later ventures, the Henry County atlas map featured an Iowa state map, a map of the entire county along with a brief history, and twelve separate hand-colored landownership maps of individual townships. Each township map page also listed "Principal Products and How Stocked," included a paragraph of "Historical and Statistical Information," and noted the "Representative Views" depicting businesses, public buildings, and homes pictured on following pages. In addition, the Henry County atlas included maps of several towns and villages and a business directory of project patrons. The final pages of the Henry County atlas map provided space to record real estate transfers, a short-lived innovation that offered patrons the opportunity to keep local landownership records up-to-date.[14]

After completing the *Combination Atlas Map of Henry County*, Andreas moved on, crafting a checkered career in atlas-map, county atlas and state history production and publishing. In the early 1870s, he established headquarters in Davenport, Iowa, and with the financial support of his brother-in-law, J. M. Lyter, published at least seven atlas maps of central Illinois counties. Andreas continued to innovate as he moved into other midwestern locales, adding lists of atlas-map subscribers with each one's date of settlement, occupation, and post office address, plus portraits of family members depicted along with a lithograph of their village or farm home.[15]

Thompson and Everts, in turn, completed a combination atlas map for Johnson County, Iowa, in 1870, then published combination atlas maps for Stephenson and DeKalb Counties in Illinois in 1871 and one for their own Kane County in 1872 (fig. 2). The two men left behind a trail of increasingly thick volumes as the number of lithographs and the amount of text increased and business directories lengthened. The largest of these projects, the *Combination Atlas Map of Stephenson County, Illinois*, also signaled a growing awareness of specific atlas-map audiences. This atlas featured a map reference key in both English and German, a clear effort to draw support from the large German contingent (nearly 20 percent of the population) in this northern Illinois county.[16]

On completion of the Kane County atlas map in 1872, the partnership between Thompson and Everts fell apart. Both men moved on to new ventures and business associations, often based on family

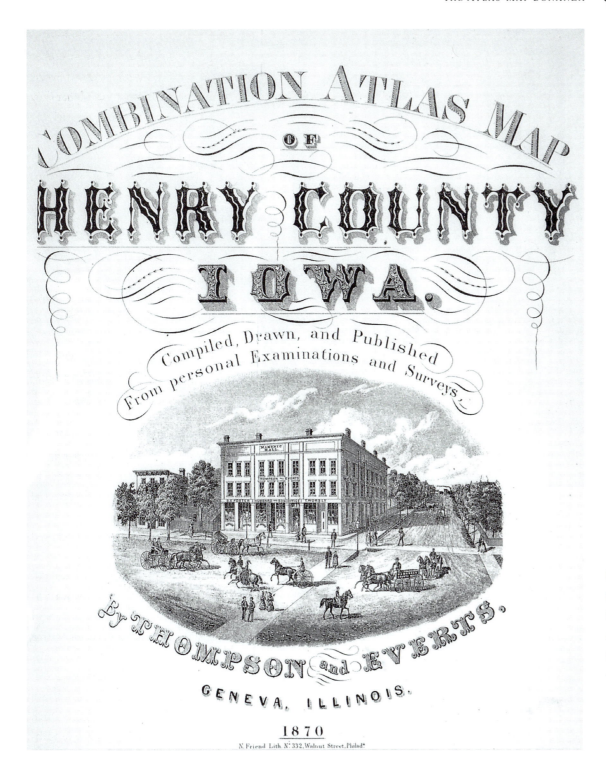

Figure 1. Company headquarters, pictured on the title page of Thompson and Everts's first combination atlas map. Source: Thompson and Everts, *Combination Atlas Map of Henry County, Iowa* (Geneva, Ill.: Thompson and Everts, 1870).

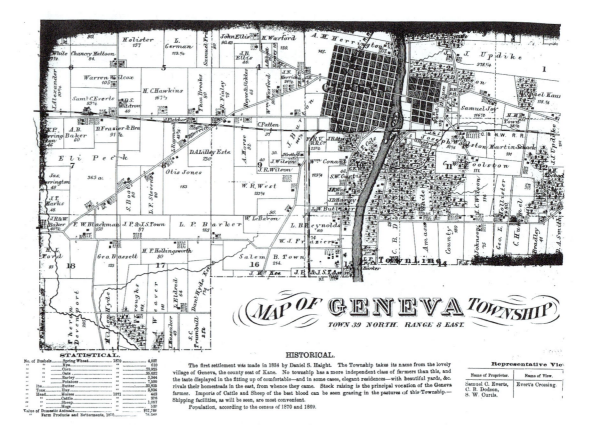

Figure 2. The Kane County atlas map featured an illustration of Samuel Everts's dairy farm and a map of Geneva Township. Source: Thompson and Everts, *Combination Atlas Map of Kane County, Illinois* (Geneva, Ill.: Thompson and Everts, 1870).

ties or local connections established in their Kane County days. Thomas H. Thompson briefly rejoined the family mapmaking firm to publish atlas maps of Will and DuPage Counties in northeastern Illinois. Moses Thompson, the eldest and perhaps most skilled of the Thompson brothers, had already turned away to other business ventures by the early 1870s, eventually becoming a prominent Kane County dairy farmer. G. S. Burr, another Kane County resident, started his adult career as a carpenter but by 1870 had joined the Thompson brothers in map canvassing. Reflecting the shifting alliances so common in this business, Burr eventually partnered with Andreas to publish an atlas of Orange County, New York. James Everts, Louis's younger brother, also worked in map production and spent at least part of his time aligned with the Thompson brothers, receiving credit for having "mounted, colored, and varnished" the Thompsons' 1870 map of LaSalle County.[17]

In yet another twist in this complex web of business associations, Thomas Thompson briefly worked for his former employee A. T. Andreas. Andreas had spotted a new and lucrative market in the production of state atlases. In 1873, while he was experimenting with this idea for Minnesota, he hired Thompson to oversee the yearlong canvass of the state. Still restless, Thompson left the Midwest in the mid-1870s for California. There, working with several partners, he eventually produced "historical atlas maps" for a number of California locales.[18]

In contrast to Thompson, Everts looked eastward for new opportunities. Although he continued to publish atlas maps for midwestern counties in the mid-1870s, he moved the company's headquarters to Philadelphia in search of a "more central point of business facilities."[19] Chicago was rapidly developing a reputation for atlas production, but the shift to Philadelphia may have been a competitive strategy, offering Everts a way to distinguish his firm from others that remained centered in the Midwest. Whatever his real motivation was for the move, it underscored Everts's broadening geographic focus, for he went on to publish histories and atlases for many counties in the Northeast.

Like others in the trade, Everts also engaged in constantly shifting partnerships with friends, family members, or former employees, many of whom went on to other joint ventures or their own enterprises. In 1872, for example, Everts partnered with employees David J. Stewart and Oliver C. Baskin to produce atlas maps for Lee, McHenry, and Ogle Counties in Illinois, and in a brief foray into Wisconsin they also published atlas maps of Rock and Walworth Counties. Although Baskin's initial role is unclear, Stewart titled himself a civil engineer and had developed both township and city plat maps for Thompson and Everts's Stephenson County atlas map. Baskin soon broke away from the firm and joined Andreas to produce more atlas maps.[20]

The relationship between Everts and Stewart persisted much longer than most such partnerships, but even it appeared to be quite fluid. Along with the atlas maps of Jackson, Lenawee, and Washtenaw Counties in Michigan published in 1874, Everts and Stewart produced at least six atlas maps for Ohio counties in the mid-1870s. In the same time period, Everts, seemingly without Stewart, published eighteen atlas maps for counties in southwestern, central, and northeastern Ohio. Stewart, in turn, produced an atlas map for Seneca County, Ohio (1874), and Macomb County, Michigan (1875), on his own. Although David Stewart joined Everts at the new company headquarters in Philadelphia, city directories from the mid-1870s document multiple business relationships, including Everts and Stewart; Everts, Ensign, and Everts; L. H. Everts and Company; and Louis H. Everts and James Holcomb, Publishers, all at the same 716 Filbert Street address. Both Everts and Stewart lived in Philadelphia, but other partners remained in Illinois. James Everts, for example, continued to live in Kane County and from there canvassed for the firm

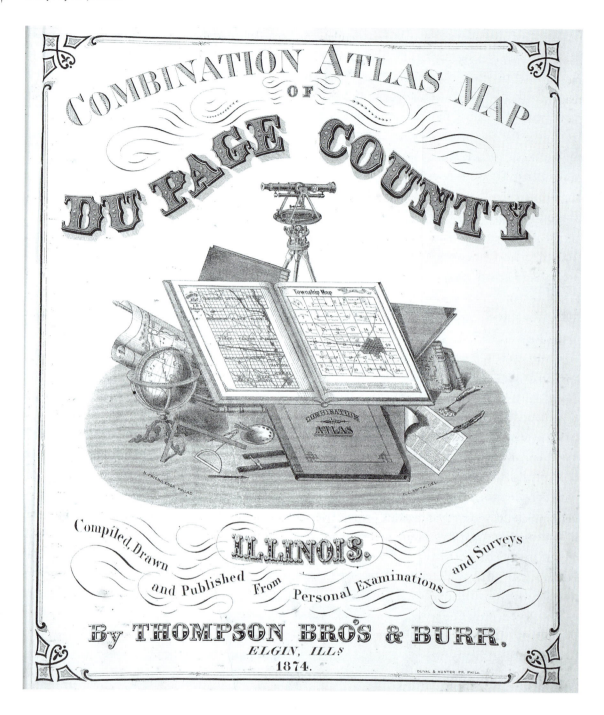

Figure 3. Even after dissolving their partnership, Thompson and Everts used the same illustration for the title pages of their atlas maps. Source: Thompson Bro's and Burr, *Combination Atlas Map of DuPage County, Illinois* (Elgin, Ill.: Thompson Bro's and Burr, 1874).

and supervised other atlas-map agents. Another partner, Dwight W. Ensign, also continued to produce maps from Illinois. Eventually, Louis Everts's youngest brother, Edward, moved to Philadelphia (reversing the pattern) in order to oversee the "publication department" in his brother's publishing business.[21]

Although atlas-map business associations shifted frequently, the evolving alliances did not appear to reflect overt conflicts among competing firms or individuals. Successful innovations by one firm quickly found their way into volumes published by competitors with seemingly little rancor from the innovators. After Thompson and Everts dissolved their partnership, for instance, both firms adopted the same new title page for their independently published atlas maps (fig. 3). The lithograph of company headquarters in Geneva was gone, replaced by an assemblage of devices underscoring the professional nature of the atlas-map enterprise. These seemingly friendly relationships may have reflected a business reality. To map counties within a circumscribed region, atlas-map firms could not afford direct competition. They needed to divide up the territory; an agreement among friends on how the state should be portioned out eased conflict and the possibility of economic failure. Subscription sales also benefited from a sound industrywide reputation, encouraging competing firms to share expertise and production policies that might boost the entire trade. On an even more basic level, the problem of fielding an adequate staff and providing it with an opportunity to piece together a reasonable livelihood might also have encouraged these interconnected business relationships.

The atlas-map business offered men like Louis Everts, David Stewart, and the Thompson brothers the opportunity to craft a potentially lucrative career, but it also provided occupation for a sizable sales force and a number of skilled craftsmen. When Everts and Stewart moved into Jackson County, the *Daily Citizen* reported that a crew of "about thirty artists, civil engineers, writers and canvassers" was fanning out across the region to get the job done quickly and efficiently.[22] Crew members' tasks were varied. Canvassers made the first foray into the targeted county, drumming up interest and securing a sufficient number of subscribers to make the proposed atlas map economically viable. The fruits of their labors appeared in the "Business Directory," a list of subscribers, with their occupations, places of birth, dates of settlement in the county, and post office addresses. Although simply assembled and produced, these directories vastly increased the number of stakeholders in the atlas-map project (fig. 4).

Along with canvassers, atlas-map companies hired writers to gather information for county, township, and village histories, and to promote and produce biographies of local residents. Skilled illustrators also roamed the county, often carrying samples of their work in hopes of persuading residents to commission lithographs of their homes or businesses. If successful, the illustrator visited the family, determined the most advantageous perspective, and set about sketching the homegrounds (the term often used for yards). When signing their work, these illustrators often designated themselves as "del," an abbreviation for *delineavit,* the person who "drew it." In most cases, these "field artists" turned their sketches over to a professional lithographer in preparation for printing.[23]

In addition to illustrators and writers, Everts and Stewart employed a team of surveyors and mapmakers. In Michigan, surveyors normally began their task by copying township plat maps housed in the state land office in Lansing. Then, with the help of local tax records, they added the current owner's name to the appropriate parcel. To give the maps additional interest, field surveyors traveled the county, noting from "personal observation" cultural features and significant landscape elements that were also incorporated into township cadastral maps. Most atlas maps also featured plat maps and an occasional bird's-eye view of towns and villages in the region produced by company mapmakers or illustrators.[24] Mapmaking firms such as Rand McNally of Chicago or H. H. Lloyd of New York often supplied the maps of the entire state and of the United States as a whole that appeared at the beginning of many atlas-map volumes.

As surveyors, illustrators, writers, and canvassers completed their work in any one county, the information was passed on to company headquarters, where another group of employees parceled out the lithography, printing, and binding processes needed to complete the project. Continuing the tradition of earlier partnerships, Everts and Stewart turned to Norman Friend for lithography and Duval and

BUSINESS DIRECTORY OF JACKSON COUNTY, MICHIGAN.

GIVING NAMES OF THE PRINCIPAL PROFESSIONAL AND BUSINESS MEN IN THE CITIES AND VILLAGES, A DESCRIPTION OF THEIR BUSINESS, AND OF THE PRINCIPAL PRODUCERS OF EACH TOWNSHIP WHO PATRONIZE THIS ATLAS.

JACKSON CITY.

NAME.	BUSINESS PLACE AND RESIDENCE.	Date of Settlement.	NATIVITY	DESCRIPTION OF BUSINESS.
Angell, A. D.	264 Main ; res. 42 Francis			Eclectic Physician and Surgeon.
Aldrich, W. E.				Farmer.
Allen, C. H.	215 Main ; res. Ing'm & Cal'n			Photographer and Dentist.
Austin, H. D.	Trail, near Blackstone			Engineer for H. A. Hayden & Co.
Avery, W. H.				Engineer of the Jackson City Water Works.
Brown, W. R.	County Jail			Sheriff and Farmer.
Bennett, W. I.	160 Greenwood [Harris			County Superintendent of Schools.
Black, H.	196 Main ; res. Ganson, near			Agent Wheeler & Wilson Sewing Machine.
Bronson, W. I.	216 Main ; res. 47 Franklin			Physician and Surgeon.
Brenk, J. J.	Cor. First and Morrell			Merchant Tailor (Brenk & Feldher, 265 Main).
Buck, W. N.	249 Main ; res. 90 Milwaukee		N. Y.	Insurance and Real Estate.
Bascom, H.	211 Main ; res. 31 N. Main			Bakery and Confectionery. [chandise.
Brown, A. H.	220 Main ; res. 66 Main			Publisher of Music and Dealer in Musical Mer-
Bullock, R. D.	Keystone Bl'k ; res. 55 Ste'rt			State Agent for Smith's American Organ and
Burnham, G. E.	Biddle, near Jackson			Butter Trade. [First-Class Pianos.
Bunnell, D. V.	113 Mason			Clothier and Merchant Tailor (Bunnell & Ever-
Bush, Harvey	Court House ; res. 43 Clinton			Register of Deeds. [ard].
Brooks, P. R.	92 Wilkins			Carpenter and Joiner.
Bauer, John	151 Main ; res. 141 Francis			Grocer (deceased).
Bader, J. C.	174 Main ; res. 90 Ford			Hardware Merchant.
Boland & Co., W. J.	148 Main			Meat Market.
Basden, H.	Blackstone, near Wilkins			Boot and Shoe Maker.
Barrett & Champlin	Cor. Cortland and Jackson			Dealers in Flour and Feed.
Brooks, C. F.	74 Mechanic			Prop'r Lumber Yard and Planing Mill.
Bennett, W. W.	Bds. Milwaukee			Clerk for C. F. Brooks, Lumber Dealer.
Bieber, J.	30 Mill			Carriage and Wagon Maker.
Bedell, H. O.	21 First			Carpenter and Builder.
Brown, H.	Cor. Cooper and Detroit			Superintendent Hayden's Flouring Mills.
Blair, Austin	272 Main ; res. 7 Lansing Av			Attorney-at-Law, Ex-Governor, and Congressman.
Bailey, G. J.	227 Main ; res. 81 Wash'ton			Boots and Shoes, Retail.
Busley, H. C.	41 Cortland			Baker and Confectioner.
Bates, L. P.	41 Cortland			Engineer. [ricultural Implements.
Bennett, F. D.	56 Luther			Foundry and Machine Works, Manufacturer Ag-
Brown & Pilcher	250 Main			Books and Stationery.
Bingham, H. H.	123 Blackstone			Real Estate Dealer.
Burkhart, N. W.	248 Ganson			Keeper, Michigan State Prison.
Birdsall, Baker & Co	281 Main			Wholesale Grocers.
Brown, D. H.	13 Mechanic			Keeper in Michigan State Prison.
Baker, E.	15 Lansing Av			Foreman in Michigan State Prison.
Bliss, A. A.	Fourth, near Griswold	1863	Conn.	Dealer in Crockery and Glassware.
Bennett, W. M.	4 N. Main	1847	N. Y.	Merchant.
Blair, G. B.	Waterloo Av	1873	Mich.	Keeper, State Prison.
Burdett, G.	Cor. Argyle & Waterloo Av	1869	Eng'd.	Mason. [Lightning Rods.
Barkalow, S.	175 Jackson	1867	N. J.	Manufacturer and Dealer in Eave Troughs and
Cook, C. W.	Whitney, near North	1868	N. Y.	Painter.
Cook, M. S.	Murphy Av., near Ganson			Civil Engineer.
Coats, O. P., & Co.	204 Main			Wholesale and Retail Furniture Dealers.
Camp, T. J. [werp.	59 Franklin			Dry Goods and Carpets (Camp, Morrell, & Camp,
Carlton & Van Ant-	Cor. Main and Jackson			Publishers Daily and Weekly Patriot. [272 Main).
Child, W. W.	276 Main ; res. 71 Wash'ton			Dealer in Watches, Jewelry, etc. (See View.)
Chapman, G. A.	106 Blackstone			Baker and Confectioner, Wholesale and Retail.
Cook, W. M.	Hurd House			Traveling Agent for Snow, Gilson & Co.
Cookingham, J. V.	222 Main ; res. 140 Jackson			Photographer.
Clement, C. E.	235 Main			Dealer in Groceries, etc. [Reaper.
Copps, C. W.	Park Place, near Hamlin			General Agent Wilber's Eureka Mower and
Chapin, E. W.	191 Main ; res. Blackstone			Tobacconist.

NAME.	BUSINESS PLACE AND RESIDENCE.	Date of Settlement.	NATIVITY	DESCRIPTION OF BUSINESS.
Frey, G. & C.	34, 36 and 38 Lansing Av.		Ger.	Brewers.
Griffith, H. D.	285 Main ; res. 141 Jackson.			Farmer and Grocer.
Gould, Jas.	258 Main ; res. 12 First.			Prosecuting Attorney.
Groom, O., Jr.	148 Mechanic			Insurance Agent.
Gregory, A. S.	198 Main			Physician and Surgeon. [win & Oberliesen).
Goodwin, C. P.	204 Main			Jewelers, & Ag'ts Grover & Baker S. M. Co. (Good-
Glasford & Bolton	241 Main			Millinery and Fancy Goods.
Gregg, L. P.	Van Buren			Grocer and Baker.
Gridley, G. T.	290 Main ; res. N. Main			Attorney-at-Law.
Grant, N. J.	111 Jackson			Dealer in Groceries, Provisions, etc.
Gross, B. S.	207 Milwaukee			Lightning Rod Solicitor.
Goodyear & Knapp	Hibbard House Block			Omnibus, Hack, and Baggage Transfer.
Galiup, Alonzo	141 E. Main			Saloon and Restaurant.
Grange, J.	101 Blackstone			Foreman Bennett's Engine Works.
Gould, A. J.	196 Main			General Agent Equitable Life Insurance Co.
Grosvenor, L. D.	127 Mechanic			Architect.
Holden, D. J.	245 Main ; res. 87 Ganson			Dealer in Hats and Caps.
Higby & Gibson	262 Main			Attorneys.
Halbert, John	Mechanic, opp. Post Office			Physician and Surgeon.
Hibbard, G. B.	205 Mechanic ; res. 88 Oak			Agent Singer Sewing Machine.
Hollister, R. O.				Farmer and Dealer in Sewing Machines. [etc.
Hobbs & Bliss	194 Main			Man's & Dlrs in Harness, Saddles, Robes, Trunks,
Hunt, E. L.	189 Jackson			Dealer in Paper, Paper Stock, and Old Metal.
Henderson, T. N.	109 Mason			Pattern Maker.
Hobart, C. D.	11 Third			Grocer (Hobart & De Lamater).
Halstead, G. W.	280 Main ; res. Mosher House			Dealer in Groceries and Provisions.
Hand, H. W.	113 Jackson ; res. 83 Franklin			Meat Market.
Hayne, E.	28 Francis			" "
Herrick, J. W.				Retired.
Hatch & Noyes	221 Main			Boots and Shoes.
Hunt, A. D.	Biddle, near Blackstone			Plasterer.
Haight, W. H.	46 Trail			Clerk in Kennedy's Mills.
Hall, A. K.	Summit, Jackson Co.			Machinist.
Huntington, H				" and Engineer.
Huntington, J. H.	43 Wesley			Foreman in Bennett's Foundry.
Hammill, Jas.	239 Main ; res. 148 Wilkins			Attorney-at-Law.
Haight, G. W.	8 Lansing Av.			City Sexton.
Hobart, A. J.	84 Cooper ; res. 86 Cooper			Miner, and Dealer in Groceries and Provisions.
Hickox, Rev. G. H.	84 Washington			Chaplain Michigan State Prison.
Hall, F.	205 Cooper			Assistant Engineer City Water Works.
Hollingsworth, C.	206 Main ; res. 206 Mechanic			Contractor, Michigan State Prison.
Hewitt, J. W.	36 Cortland	1849	N. Y.	Carriage Manufacturer.
Hibbard, D. B.	N. Main	1836	"	Retired.
Hills & Griffith	Cor. Mechanic & Wash'ton	1869	"	Marble Dealers.
Hyde, C. B.	Luther, near Blackstone			City Engineer.
Ismon, H. S.	306 Main	1846	N. Y.	Banker. President Jackson County Bank.
Jackson Co. Bank.	209 "			Banking.
Jackson, W.	252 "			Grocer.
Jackson F. & M. Co	34-38 Mechanic			Manufacturers Stationary and Portable Engines,
Johnson, W. F.	132 Blackstone			Salesman. [Mill Boilers, etc.
Jenkins, J. V.	38 Jackson			Pattern Maker, Jackson Foundry & Machine Co.
Johnson, B. G.	Clinton, near Jackson			General Contractor.
Jennings, G.	Cooper, near Argyle			Coal Mining and Farmer.
Kelly, John	Hibbard House Block			Dealer in Boots and Shoes. [(Kinsley & Stowell).
Kinsley, M.	48 Wesley			Wines, Liquors, and Cigars, Wholesale and Retail
Krumery, J. H.	26 Third			Baker and Confectioner.

Figure 4. Business directories gave subscribers a stake in the project. Source: Everts and Stewart, *Combination Atlas Map of Jackson County, Michigan* (Chicago: Everts and Stewart, 1874), 136.

Hunter or other established Philadelphia firms for printing. The time required to complete an atlas map seems to have varied considerably and apparently depended on the size of the crew fielded in any one county. For their Will County project, for example, the Thompson brothers noted that "ten men have been employed for the past eighteen months upon this work." In contrast, Everts and Stewart employed a much larger workforce in their southeastern Michigan canvass and subsequently accelerated the production schedule. In both Lenawee and Washtenaw Counties, workers took slightly less than a year to complete the projects, but often crews divided their time between the two counties. Production time in Jackson County ran just over five months.[25]

The identities of these work crews, the scale of their contribution to any one atlas map, their working relationships with the firm, and the quality of their lives are difficult to assess for several reasons. Histories and biographies were seldom signed, although a mention of the authors' names and qualifications sometimes appeared in a publisher's statement regarding the difficulty of their task and the accuracy of the final product. Illustrators occasionally signed or at least initialed their work, but often the lithographs bear no ascription. Credit for township and town or village maps was also limited and extremely variable. In the atlas maps for the counties of Jackson, Lenawee, and Washtenaw, mapmaker names are most likely to appear with city or town plat maps, but many township cadastral maps list no mapmaker. Other atlas-map companies sometimes named surveyors in an introductory portion of the book but gave no indication of the number of maps they actually produced.[26]

Despite the difficulty of reconstructing a comprehensive view of the workforce, Everts and Stewart's operations in Jackson, Lenawee, and Washtenaw Counties, coupled with additional experiences reported by Everts's employees, offer some clues about the industry. The *Jackson Weekly Citizen,* for instance, pointed out that Everts and Stewart had engaged Col. W. H. Chase to compile and write the history of the region and the biographies of citizens willing to pay for the privilege. Chase, the newspaper noted, was "eminently fitted for the work," for he had a "universal 'knowledge of men and things,' gained in varied experience as a war correspondent, an editor, the principal of a large school and an officer in the army."[27] Beyond the newspaper's recommendation, little is known of Chase, but the record of Samuel W. Durant, another writer who worked for Louis Everts both before and after the southeastern Michigan canvass, is more complete and helps to fill in the picture.

Like so many others involved in atlas-map production, Durant was born in the Northeast and moved with his family to Kane County in 1845. In search of a livelihood, Durant tried several occupations but eventually found work as a clerk in a St. Charles general store. With the outbreak of the Civil War, Durant, like Everts and Thompson, served in the Illinois Volunteer Infantry. After the war ended, Durant returned to St. Charles and once again cast about for a job to support his growing family. He turned first to insurance sales, worked briefly as the editor of a local newspaper, and then joined Thompson and Everts and, finally, Everts, Baskin, and Stewart, as they produced atlases for various Illinois and Wisconsin counties. In the years when Everts and Stewart's crews were working in Michigan and portions of Ohio, Durant partnered with O. L. Baskin on atlas-map projects in northern Indiana. He also worked for Andreas on several Ohio combination atlas maps produced in the mid-1870s.[28]

Returning to work for Everts in 1876, Durant seems to have been a versatile and capable employee. He frequently filled the often difficult role of project historian, but at least in his early association with atlas-map firms, he occasionally served as surveyor and mapmaker. Sometimes he was assisted in that capacity by his oldest son, Pliny A. Durant. Both Durant and his son listed themselves as civil engineers on map attributions, but whether this title reflected formal training or simply experience in the field is unclear. Durant's qualifications as a historian derived from "his mother's teaching, and his later pursuits of tastes and habits implanted and cherished as a natural consequence of such teaching." In the early 1880s, Durant once again left Everts and returned to St. Charles to establish the *Valley Chronicle,* a newspaper catering to the local community. He answered the call of large-scale publishing at least one more time when he agreed in 1883 to join Andreas's firm in the Dakota Territory as project historian, leaving a son at home to run the family newspaper business.[29]

Although a single writer such as Durant or Chase might compile historical or biographical texts no matter the project's size, the number of illustrators working in specific counties appears to have increased over time. In his early experiments in atlas-map publishing, Everts used only one or two illustrators on each project. In Johnson County, Iowa, for example, a single illustrator, J. D. Forgy, signed or initialed sixty of the sixty-six lithographs. By the time atlas-map crews moved into Jackson, Lenawee, and Washtenaw Counties in Michigan, the pace of the work had increased significantly, and a number of illustrators churned out hundreds of illustrations for each project. A survey of Jackson County lithographs bearing the name or initials of the illustrator indicates that at least seven illustrators worked within that county. The most prolific, G. W. Salisbury, completed at least forty-nine illustrations during about a four-month period. Others, such as C. H. Radcliff, signed thirty images; Joe K. French of Toledo, Ohio, completed thirteen images; and W. P. Whinnery produced at least six signed illustrations. All but two of the named illustrators also worked in Lenawee and Washtenaw Counties. Images attributed to particular illustrators were often clustered within each township, suggesting that the team divided the county and then worked a specific locale until demand was satisfied. Most illustrators continued to work for Everts as the crew moved eastward into Ohio counties.[30]

Although these illustrators left little record beyond their many images, the experiences of C. H. Radcliff offer at least some insight into their working lives. In 1870, eighteen-year-old Charles H. Radcliff and his sixteen-year-old brother, William M. Radcliff, lived with their parents and two younger siblings in Elgin, Illinois. Their father was a carpenter of very modest means, and both boys worked in the Elgin watch factory.[31] As the atlas-map trade gained prominence in the region, the brothers apparently recognized a career opportunity. In 1871, Charles Radcliff contributed a few illustrations to Thompson and Everts's Stephenson County atlas map, and he continued to work for Everts in the new partnership with Baskin and Stewart. Several years later, Charles's younger brother William began canvassing and sketching for the Thompson brothers, producing nearly sixty images included in their *Combination Atlas Map of Will County, Illinois,* and more than sixty-five illustrations for their DuPage County atlas map published in 1874. Charles Radcliff, in turn, followed Everts into Michigan and contributed illustrations to the atlas maps for both Lenawee and Washtenaw Counties. As crews moved into Jackson County, William Radcliff joined his brother Charles, producing a bird's-eye view of a small town and at least sixteen additional illustrations (fig. 5). When Everts moved into Ohio, both Radcliff brothers continued to work for the firm, contributing a large number of illustrations for Sandusky and Trumbull Counties in 1874 and for a cluster of counties in southwestern Ohio in 1874 and 1875.[32] It is unclear whether the Radcliff brothers had training as illustrators or simply parlayed their innate talent into a chance to get out of the watch factory and away from home.

Along with the illustrators, a crew of mapmakers worked simultaneously on the projects in Lenawee, Jackson, and Washtenaw Counties. In Jackson County, five men—B. A. Skeel, R. K. Lee, Cyrus Wheelock, H. R. Paige, and P. H. Dowling—all signed either township or village maps. Frank Krause and W. C. Jipson, along with P. H. Dowling, worked in Lenawee County, while Dowling, Skeel, Wheelock, and Krause signed some Washtenaw County maps. Several of these men had been with Everts from the beginning, and many continued to work with the firm after it moved into Ohio. Among Everts's mapmakers, the record for longevity may belong to Krause. Starting in Iowa, he worked for Thompson and Everts in the early days of map production; continued with Everts, Baskin, and Stewart, then Everts and Stewart; and finally worked for Everts when he shifted operations into northeastern Ohio.[33]

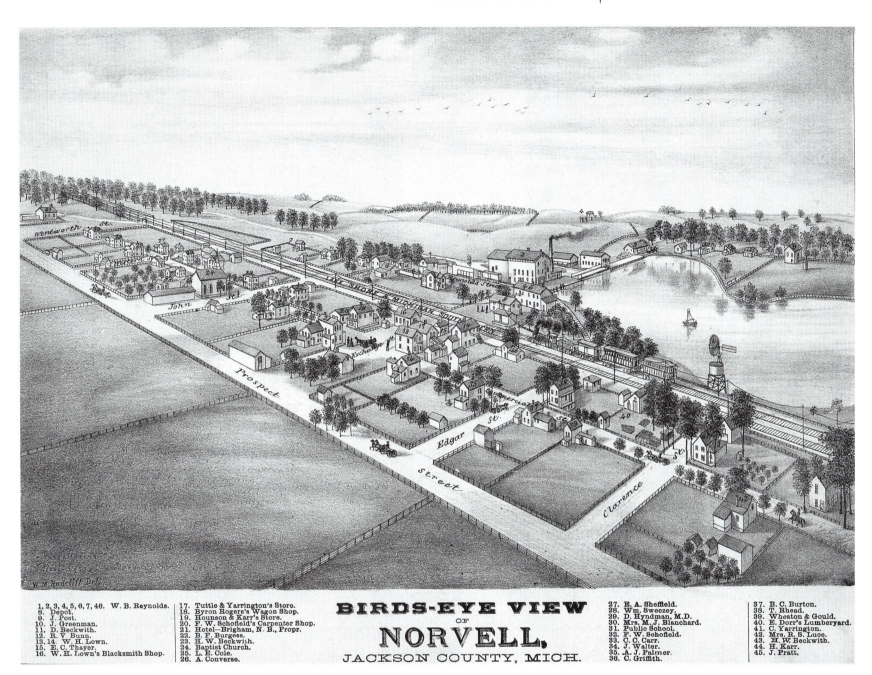

1, 2, 3, 4, 5, 6, 7, 46. W. B. Reynolds.
8. Depot.
9. J. Post.
10. J. Greenman.
11. D. Beckwith.
12. R. V. Bunn.
13, 14. W. H. Lown.
15. E. C. Thayer.
16. W. H. Lown's Blacksmith Shop.
17. Tuttle & Yarrington's Store.
18. Byron Rogers's Wagon Shop.
19. Hounson & Karr's Store.
20. F. W. Schofield's Carpenter Shop.
21. Hotel—Brigham, N. B., Propr.
22. B. F. Burgess.
23. H. W. Beckwith.
24. Baptist Church.
25. L. E. Cole.
26. A. Converse.
27. E. A. Sheffield.
28. Wm. Sweezey.
29. D. Hyndman, M.D.
30. Mrs. M. J. Blanchard.
31. Public School.
32. F. W. Schofield.
33. C. C. Carr.
34. J. Walter.
35. A. J. Palmer.
36. C. Griffith.
37. B. C. Burton.
38. T. Rhead.
39. Wheaton & Gould.
40. E. Dorr's Lumberyard.
41. C. Yarrington.
42. Mrs. R. S. Luce.
43. H. W. Beckwith.
44. H. Karr.
45. J. Pratt.

BIRDS-EYE VIEW
OF
NORVELL,
JACKSON COUNTY, MICH.

The training and background of the surveyors and mapmakers is just as elusive as that for atlas-map writers and illustrators. When mapmakers signed their work, they usually included their names, followed by the abbreviation "C.E.," for "civil engineer" or occasionally "city engineer." If the example of surveyor Adin Mann is any indication, these crews included at least some men with considerable map-making experience. Mann joined Everts's workforce in the mid-1870s, just as crews completed maps in southeastern Michigan. Another in the many links to Kane County, Mann came from a New Hampshire farm family that moved west to Elgin Township in 1838. Shortly after the move, Mann's father divided the claim among his three oldest sons, and Adin, still in his early twenties, began a pattern of farming

Figure 5. William Radcliff's bird's-eye view of Norvell, Michigan. Source: Eversts and Stewarts, *Combination Atlas Map of Jackson County, Michigan* (Chicago: Everts and Stewart, 1874), 41.

in summer and teaching school during the winter months. After marrying and starting a family, Mann increasingly took on additional roles within the local community, serving as justice of the peace, notary public, and eventually Kane County surveyor. While Mann was county treasurer, currency depreciation brought on by the Civil War devalued the funds he was holding, and he had to liquidate his family resources to make good on lost tax revenues. Perhaps to escape further financial embarrassment, Mann, then in his mid-forties, joined the 124th Illinois Volunteer Infantry and eventually served through the war along with four of his sons. After the war ended, Mann used his military pay to start a lumber business near Vicksburg, Mississippi, but the business failed, and he faced bankruptcy. Returning to Kane County "broken in health and penniless," he took up his old profession of surveying and began to work for Louis Everts as the firm moved atlas production into Ohio, Pennsylvania, New York, and eventually Kansas and Nebraska.[34] Mann's work record suggests he was a man of recognized ability and vast experience. An 1860 map of Kane County, produced while he served as county surveyor, indicated it was drawn "from original and recent surveys by, and under the direction of Adin Mann." During his military service, Mann acted as "chief engineer" for the Vicksburg district, and in that capacity he was responsible for rebuilding the railroad between Vicksburg and Jackson, Mississippi. While working for Everts, he also held the post of "city engineer" in several Kansas towns.[35] Mann's employment with Everts at such a difficult point in his life underscores the importance of his old Kane County links, as well as emphasizing how the atlas-map trade seems to have served many midwesterners as a bridge to new opportunity.

The experiences of Everts's crews varied tremendously in the atlas-map era, but there were some common attributes. Frequently, employees worked alone, carrying out their canvassing, illustrating, or mapmaking independently of other atlas-map employees. The purposeful clustering of counties for atlas-map production enhanced efficiency and meant that crews might easily move back and forth between assignments. Most workers were far from their homes, however, and for at least a portion of the year lived an itinerant life. Some, like Samuel Durant or James Everts, were established members of their home communities, and they probably returned there whenever a break in the workload offered the opportunity. Others appeared to relocate as job demands shifted. For example, while he was working on atlas maps in southeast Michigan, Frank Krause signed his maps "Frank Krause, C.E., Ann Arbor, Michigan." When the firm moved east, Krause appears to have moved, too, changing his address from Ann Arbor to Cleveland, Ohio. On earlier maps produced for Everts, Krause had cited both Anamosa, Iowa, and Janesville, Wisconsin, as his home base.[36] The constant movement involved in the atlas-map trade may have offered some men, such as Krause or the young Radcliff brothers, an opportunity to broaden their horizons. For others, however, the constant travel may have been a drawback. Samuel Durant never explained why he left the atlas business, but the strains of maintaining family life in Illinois while Everts's atlas projects continued to move eastward may simply have become too much for a middle-aged family man.

Whether itinerancy was a bane or a benefit, the atlas-map trade, at least under Louis Everts, did offer workers a chance to earn decent wages. According to Bates Harrington, most atlas work was done on commission, but if canvassers, illustrators, or mapmakers found consistent employment, they could expect good pay. Mapmakers, Harrington suggested, received as much as twenty-eight dollars for maps that actually required surveying and compilation. Illustrators were paid a 10 percent commission based on the cost of the lithograph, obviously profiting when atlas-map customers agreed to pay for large illustrations of their homes. Writers received a 30 percent commission for paid biographies, giving the atlas-map representative a real incentive toward wordiness. Harrington concluded that the "majority of men made between $25 and $60 per week" in the atlas-map trade.[37] Had workers chosen a more sedentary occupation requiring somewhat comparable skills, their wages might have been a bit lower. County surveyors, for example, could expect to receive between five and six dollars a day. If the Radcliff brothers had followed in their father's footsteps, they might have received between two and a half and three dollars a day as carpenters.[38]

When Louis Everts and David Stewart moved their varied workforce into southeastern Michigan in early 1873, they were pursuing a carefully orchestrated marketing strategy. At that point, their experience producing atlas maps had extended over several years, and they had learned that a profitable countywide canvass required a prosperous agricultural region with a substantial population base. By the 1870s, Jackson, Lenawee, and Washtenaw Counties easily met their criteria, with populations numbering between thirty-six thousand and forty-six thousand residents. These counties also offered three potentially profitable markets in close proximity, easing logistics for the firm and enhancing word-of-mouth advertising. Jackson, Lenawee, and Washtenaw Counties had, in fact, ranked among Michigan's most populous and productive regions since the early days of statehood. By the 1860s, the three counties were among the state's top livestock producers. Jackson County rated second among Michigan counties in wheat production, and Lenawee County led the state in corn production. Washtenaw produced more wool than any other county in the state, and Lenawee and Washtenaw Counties were centers for cheese and butter production. All three counties cultivated a variety of orchard products.[39]

Agriculture dominated the economy, but manufacturing and commercial enterprises flourished in the three-county area as well. In Lenawee County, for example, the railroad yards at Adrian and several companies that manufactured railroad cars and equipment employed many citizens. Jackson, in adjoining Jackson County, also became a manufacturing center for railroad equipment, agricultural tools, and wagons. In Washtenaw County, industries such as the Ypsilanti paper mills and carriage factories enhanced the general prosperity and increased population levels. In all three counties, millers, merchants, furniture manufacturers, and a host of other small businessmen met the needs of an expanding population.[40]

Residents of the three-county area were also willing participants in a marketplace of ideas and values that blended national trends with regional issues and concerns. Local newspapers along with agricultural journals such as the *Michigan Farmer* circulated widely and provided residents with a window on the world beyond their county's boundaries. Active agricultural and horticultural societies at the local, county, and state levels offered many families a forum for social exchange as well as access to the latest information on progressive horticultural or agricultural practices. The Patrons of Husbandry, an important nationwide reform organization founded in 1867, also drew county residents with its program of educational exchange, socializing, and political activism.[41]

Although, as historians Andrew Cayton and Peter Onuf have suggested, residents transformed the upper Midwest into "one of the most important centers of commercial agriculture in the world," the region was not immune to a darker side of rapid development. Contemporary commentators frequently warned that disruptive social change and declining values lurked just beneath the prosperous, progressive surface. Issues such as an increasingly mobile population, burgeoning materialism, the flight of rural youth from the farm to careers in the city, or the seemingly unending influx of new immigrants were familiar and very real concerns. Seeking a reasonable response to rapid social change, many midwest-erners adhered to an ideology that blended progressive attitudes with traditional values. Agricultural reformer and minister Henry Ward Beecher voiced this balanced view of rural life in his *Plain and Pleasant Talk about Fruits, Flowers, and Farming*. "We believe in small farms and thorough cultivation" and a "spirit of industry, enterprise, and intelligence," he told his readers. Evaluate progressive practices and select the best of the new ideas, Beecher urged, but at the same time "hold fast [to] that which is good."[42]

Appealing to the interests and concerns of regional residents was critical to a successful atlas-map canvass, and after evaluating their audience very carefully, Everts and Stewart set out to produce an atlas that would strike just such a reasoned balance between tradition and change. They indicated the volume's scope and purpose by the assemblage of artifacts portrayed on the atlas map's title page (fig. 6). In all three of southeastern Michigan's county atlases, the title page showed an open atlas, a globe, a sun-dial, a map, a compass, a protractor, a straight edge, a pantograph, and an engineer's transit. An artist's palette, quill pen, inkwell, and rolled parchment completed the arrangement. These easily recognized symbols both reassured customers and promoted the combination of elements that made the works so distinctive. Tools such as the compass and the transit implied that the maps' creators had employed scientific practices and were competent professionals. Inclusion of an artist's palette stressed the im-portance of lithographic illustrations to the overall value of the atlas. Finally, quill pens and parchment established the significance of local history in this regional portrayal. These combination atlas maps, the title pages suggested, would provide residents with a detailed, accurate portrait of the contemporary landscape that delineated its progressive attributes while affirming its historical roots.[43]

The title pages' emphasis on surveying and mapmaking tools underscored the importance of maps to the new genre. For decades, mapmakers and publishers had argued that maps, whether in atlas form or as wall maps, were essential to convey information and promote progress. Immigrants would find them useful, Henry Walling and Alexander Winchell suggested in their 1873 *Atlas of Michigan*, as they learned about their new home, while established residents might benefit from map depictions of topographical and cultural features as they contemplated new investment in the area or the best route for a proposed railroad.[44] In most regional wall maps, each township was clearly placed within the broader political boundaries of the county. Atlas maps, however, shifted the focus of mapping from the county as a whole to the individual townships. Atlas-map publishers argued that this change offered a more convenient and potentially more detailed portrait of the region, but it also marked a new emphasis. If they desired, users might view the broader world by consulting county, state, or national maps usually included at the beginning of the atlas, but township maps clearly promoted the local and the individual.

Township maps' portrayals of the region were also selective, placing particular emphasis on land-ownership (fig. 7). For many atlas-map subscribers, a glance through local township maps confirmed a landscape parceled out among friends and neighbors. For those less familiar with the locale, individual names on each tract plainly suggested a fully settled landscape and stable community. For both groups, maps also documented the distribution of resources among local families. The simple inclusion of a family's name on the map marked it as a stakeholder, while the size and quality of landholdings, access to markets, and proximity to cultural resources provided additional information about the owner's role and rank in the local community. These map portrayals favored farm families over town and village residents, for although atlas maps often included urban plat maps, they seldom distinguished property ownership. In addition to landownership, township maps documented a number of elements critical to

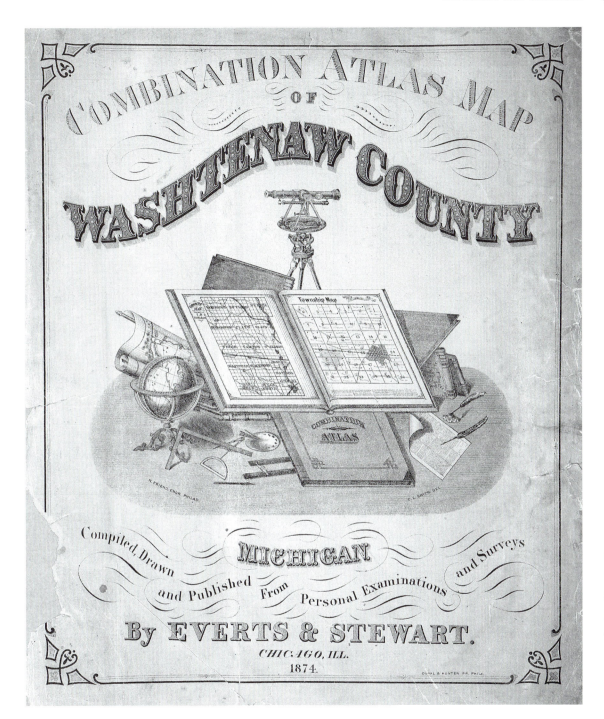

Figure 6. Title page artifacts emphasized atlas-map components. Source: Everts and Stewart, *Combination Atlas Map of Washtenaw County, Michigan* (Chicago: Everts and Stewart, 1874).

the smooth functioning of a market-oriented agricultural economy, including both extant and proposed rail lines and wagon roads, population centers, and blacksmith shops and mills. Maps also carefully documented natural resources such as water, timber, and quarries and routinely noted the distribution of churches, schools, and even cemeteries throughout the township.[45]

The emphasis on township cadastral maps marked a change in focus, but the real innovation in atlas-map content came with the inclusion of hundreds of lithographs of regional cultural institutions,

MAP OF CAMBRIDGE TOWNSHIP

TOWN 5 SOUTH   RANGE 2 EAST.

homes, and businesses. Although illustrations carried a price, atlas-map patrons often chose to have their homes or businesses pictured, and these decisions gave local residents considerable input into the image of their community that resulted. Illustrators normally included elements of interest to their clientele and on occasion conferred with customers about the most favorable perspective or which landscape components to feature as they sketched their homes or businesses.[46]

The atlas-map illustrations resulting from this essentially collaborative process reiterated some of the same themes favored in township maps. For example, many depictions of farmsteads or village scenes emphasized transportation links by featuring trains steaming across the landscape. A variety of conveyances drawn along roadways by prancing horses emphasized regional vitality and additional connections to markets and urban centers. Orderly farmyard layouts, well-constructed fences, agricultural implements, windmills, outbuilding construction and arrangement, ornamental plantings and gardens, varied livestock breeds, tree-lined country roads, and many other details of the rural landscape both documented the local scene and confirmed that residents had all the requirements of a widely touted progressive outlook (fig. 8). Frequent inclusion of schools, academies and seminaries, poorhouses and county farms, churches, courthouses, and other local institutions further underscored regional amenities and civic-mindedness. The collective number and quality of these illustrations, the *Jackson Daily Citizen* reminded residents, established a favorable impression of their county "in the eyes of the world."[47]

On the surface, both maps and lithographs documented the present and celebrated the up-to-date sensibilities of a self-selected group of local residents. There was another side to these "historical atlases," however. An illustration of a well-ordered landscape or the inclusion of a name on a township map implied stability and permanence, and historical narrative increasingly furthered that image, giving the contemporary portrayal of local landscapes not only a spatial permanency but also stability through time. In the brief evolution of atlas maps prior to their production in Jackson, Lenawee, and Washtenaw Counties, Everts and his partners had methodically added historical text. The first atlas map of Henry County, Iowa, included a one-page county history along with brief summaries of local history positioned below the much more prominent maps of each township. By the time the firm reached Kane County in 1872, the text had expanded to include a two-page county history, a list of county officers since settlement, and the histories of nine towns and villages, which encompassed five pages of atlas-map text. Several years later, residents of Jackson, Lenawee, and Washtenaw Counties could read even more local history, as well as an increasing number of biographies of local residents.[48]

The size of combination atlas maps also enhanced this impression of stability and permanence. In all three of these counties, the atlases were quite large, measuring fourteen inches by seventeen inches and including more than one hundred twenty pages of illustrations, maps, and text. In part, the need to make township cadastral-map detail legible dictated the grand proportions, but size had an additional purpose. Whether family members consulted atlas maps for local information or the book was simply displayed on a parlor table, its presence in the household was hard to miss. Coupled with the sturdy embossed cover, the book's size implied that it and its contents had real importance and, as the *Jackson Weekly Citizen* claimed, would be "handed down and passed around for generations."[49]

Although Everts and Stewart purposefully selected atlas-map components with the interests and concerns of their targeted audience in mind, the real measure of a project's success lay in the hands of local residents. Individuals who supported the atlas by commissioning a lithograph or subscribing to

Figure 7. Map of Cambridge Township, Lenawee County, Michigan. Maps detailed property ownership and selected cultural features. Source: Everts and Stewart, *Combination Atlas Map of Lenawee County, Michigan* (Chicago: Everts and Stewart, 1874), 35.

BURR OAK GROVE FARM . RES. OF M. L. RAY.
SEC 14 & 15 CONCORD TP. MICH.

Figure 8. Burr Oak Farm. Details of rural life were frequently depicted in atlas-map illustrations. Source: Everts and Stewart, *Combination Atlas Map of Jackson County, Michigan* (Chicago: Everts and Stewart, 1874), 47.

the work were a self-selected group, and that group's demographic composition has significance not only for the atlas map's finished appearance but also for the genre's usefulness in our understanding of mid-nineteenth-century midwestern rural culture. Two sometimes overlapping audiences held the key to a successful atlas-map project. The first, dubbed *patrons* in this chapter, were those individuals or families willing to commission a lithograph of their home or business. These atlas-map supporters made a serious commitment, as the price of a lithograph ranged from twenty-eight dollars for a four-inch image to one hundred forty-five dollars for a full-page illustration. In addition, some patrons commissioned biographies, paying two and a half cents per word to document their lives in atlas-map text. A few individuals even paid between one hundred and two hundred fifty dollars so that their portraits, or those of family members, would appear in the atlas maps. Finally, these patrons had to "subscribe" to the book if they wanted to see their names and homegrounds in print, which added nine dollars to their atlas-map bill.[50] Despite the costs, the patron sample in this study totaled 724 families. Nearly 4 percent of all Jackson County families, nearly 3 percent of families from Lenawee County, and almost 2.5 percent of Washtenaw County families purchased lithographs. The second and far larger audience needed for a profitable atlas-map canvass was composed of those individuals or families willing to subscribe to the project. In this three-county area, atlas-map canvassers were quite successful, inscribing nearly six thousand names, or slightly more than 26 percent of Jackson County families, 24 percent of all Lenawee County families, and almost 19 percent of Washtenaw County families on the roster of atlas-map subscribers.[51] To compare demographic information for these subscribers with that of atlas-map patrons and the broader population, a sample totaling 299 atlas-map subscribers was drawn from three townships, including Cambridge in Lenawee County, Saline in Washtenaw County, and Leoni in Jackson County. The portrait of atlas-map patrons and subscribers that emerges from this sample underscores both the diversity among supporters and some broad characteristics shared by many who were drawn to atlas-map projects.[52]

At the most basic level, farm families formed the core of regional atlas-map support. Among atlas-map patrons, 87 percent lived on farms scattered throughout the region. A similar pattern emerged from the subscriber sample, of whom an average of 79 percent lived on farms. Among both groups, a few supporters also lived in one of twenty-nine villages, towns, or cities in the three-county area. Most families in both samples obviously made their living as farmers, but in addition, doctors, businessmen, local officials, craftsmen, and many others supported the atlas-map projects.

Men headed the vast majority of households in the region and dominated both the patron and subscriber samples. In the three-county area, women made up about 10 percent of resident landowners but only 2 percent of the patron sample. Although not as pronounced, the same pattern emerged among subscribers. In the three targeted townships, women constituted nearly 6 percent of resident property owners but only a bit more than 3.3 percent of atlas-map subscribers. Saline Township had the highest proportion of female subscribers (5 percent), enhanced slightly by several businesswomen living in the town of Saline. Although other factors such as age or economic resources may have contributed to gender disparity in the samples, the underrepresentation of women among both patrons and subscribers suggests that atlas maps did not appeal to them as much as they did to their male counterparts.

The economic situations of patrons and subscribers varied considerably, but the majority of patrons in particular enjoyed above-average wealth. Among atlas-map patrons, the worth of combined real and personal property averaged $14,644, well above the $3,950 average for all families in the three-county area. A closer look at the income range reveals that not all atlas-map patrons were wealthy, however. In 1870, about 9 percent had a combined economic worth of less than $5,000, with several families having less than $1,000 in assets. Still, nearly 60 percent of the patron sample had a combined worth of real and personal property ranging from $5,000 to $15,000. An additional 21 percent of patron families had assets valued from $15,001 to $25,000. And nearly 10 percent of patrons reported combined assets of more than $25,000. Lawyers, mill owners, merchants, and even a few farmers were among the wealthiest residents in this group.[53]

Subscribers were on average better off than others in their townships, but the disparity was far less pronounced. In Saline Township, for example, subscribers averaged $7,565 in personal and real wealth, compared with $4,995 for all households in the township. The situation was similar in Leoni

Township, where subscribers' real and personal wealth averaged $5,867, in contrast to the township average of $4,465. In Cambridge Township, atlas-map subscribers' worth averaged $6,316, compared with a townshipwide average of $5,907.[54] A further breakdown of wealth distribution finds considerable diversity within the subscriber sample, however. About 45 percent owned resources ranging from $5,000 to $15,000; but compared with patrons, a far higher proportion of atlas-map subscribers (about 47 percent) had less than $5,000 in resources. In a number of instances, subscribers listed no economic assets in census records but were part of a household in which another member held the real and personal property.

At least a portion of this economic disparity between patrons and subscribers can be attributed to age differences. At the time of the 1870 census, the average age for all men in the three-county area was 26.7 years, but men in the patron sample were considerably older, averaging 48 years of age. Subscribers were older than the three-county average but somewhat younger than the patron sample. In Leoni Township, subscribers averaged 39 years of age; in Saline, 45; and in Cambridge Township, almost 41 years. Most striking, nearly 19 percent of subscribers were younger than thirty, compared with less than 4 percent of the patron sample. The fact that atlas-map patrons were somewhat older than subscribers suggests that these individuals were well established in their careers and had had time to accumulate financial resources. A far greater proportion of subscribers, in contrast, were young men, perhaps still working on the family farm or only beginning a trade or business.

One further demographic variable contributes to our understanding of the diverse support for atlas-map projects. In Jackson, Lenawee, and Washtenaw Counties, patrons came from many parts of the United States and Europe. The majority (86 percent) of the patron sample was born in the United States, and of those, 65 percent came from New York State. A few (11 percent) were native Michiganders, whose parents had been early settlers in the region. In addition, nearly 14 percent of the patron sample was foreign-born, a rate only slightly less than the overall 15 percent for nonnative residents in the three-county area. The English were the most numerous foreign-born patrons, followed closely by Germans. A few immigrants from Ireland, Canada, Holland, Scotland, and Wales were also among those patronizing atlas-map projects. Whether the ethnicity of this sample was pivotal or whether other factors such as age and economic rank mattered more is uncertain, but foreign-born residents were slightly underrepresented in the patron sample when compared with their overall presence in the population.

In the subscriber sample, numbers trend in the opposite direction. The foreign-born population represented nearly 20 percent of the subscribers, compared with slightly more than 12 percent of the total population in the three townships. The propensity of foreign-born citizens to support the project was particularly evident in Cambridge Township, where the predominately Irish nonnative population made up nearly 25 percent of atlas-map subscribers, compared with slightly more than 12 percent of the total township population. A similar pattern emerged in Leoni Township, where the foreign-born population, drawn mainly from England and Ireland, totaled more than 13 percent of the atlas-map sample but only 7 percent of the township population at large. The foreign-born population in the Saline Township subscriber sample, in contrast, was dominated by Germans, with only a few families from England and Ireland. These nonnative residents made up 21 percent of atlas-map subscribers, compared with 17 percent of the Saline Township population as a whole. Although Everts and Stewart clearly recognized the importance of this German clientele and continued to publish map "references" in both German and English, immigrants from Ireland and England appear to have been somewhat more enthusiastic supporters of the atlas-map project.

What did inclusion of a lithograph of their home mean to patrons? Although individual motivations varied, some patterns can be surmised. Most patrons were farmers who were well established in their careers. Not all were wealthy, but most had experienced at least some measure of success in the region's market-driven economy. For those patrons, an atlas-map portrayal offered a clear opportunity to document and validate lives of hard work centered among family, friends, and neighbors. For others with little status in the community or few resources, association with locally prominent individuals, if only in the self-selected world of atlas-map portrayal, may well have provided additional validation for their accomplishments.

Many atlas patrons also valued ties to their local communities, and for them, the decision to support the atlas-map project may have gone beyond personal aggrandizement. Some atlas-map patrons served as local officials, while others were strong supporters of agricultural societies or other organizations dedicated to promoting scientific agricultural practices and the enhancement of rural life. Many of these individuals attended county fairs, some entered their farms in regional competitions, and most read about progressive ideas in agricultural journals or their local newspapers.[55] These patrons undoubtedly believed that the promotion of progressive agricultural practices and the vitality and cohesiveness of their communities depended on the free exchange of information. As combination atlas maps detailed local material culture and provided a spatial overview of the region, they offered yet another opportunity for a comparative appraisal of progressive farm management and other up-to-date ideas. With the understanding that many learn best by example, some atlas-map patrons may have seen their support as a way to enhance a rich visual resource. By comparing images, they and their neighbors might learn from one another.

Although providing concrete information was an important function of atlas maps, they also offered patrons an opportunity to establish and support shared community values. The inclusion of cadastral maps, neatly ordered farmyards, well-tended orchards, ornamented village homegrounds, and other regional points of pride not only documented personal proclivities but also proclaimed those value-laden domestic landscapes as normative for the broader community. Depiction in these large, lavishly bound volumes lent the values of this self-selected community of patrons both permanency and legitimacy and in the process confirmed a lifestyle and an ideology that, even in the midst of booming prosperity, may have appeared to be threatened by the rapid changes that were sweeping the nation after the Civil War.

In the case of patrons who commissioned lithographs of their homes or businesses, the process of portraying and validating particular values was overt. For those whose names simply appeared on a list of subscribers, however, the motivation was far less clear. At least some of these subscribers were very much like atlas-map patrons. They owned land, had at least modest economic resources, and were comfortably established in their communities. This group's reasons for supporting atlas-map projects may have paralleled those of patrons: they, too, saw their values and their communities clearly depicted on atlas-map pages and may have hoped to confirm their support for the normative picture. But many subscribers were younger, had fewer economic resources, were slightly less likely to live on a farm, and were somewhat more likely to belong to one of the several ethnic groups present in the three-county area than were atlas-map patrons. The circumstances of these younger, less affluent subscribers varied considerably. Some supporters were young men in households where older family members may still have held the reins of economic power. In a few other instances, a wife purchased the atlas map, even though her husband appeared as the head of the household. In still other instances, two members of the same household subscribed to the atlas. Sometimes subscribers were father and son, sometimes siblings, and on at least one occasion, an elderly mother and her adult son both subscribed. In most cases, atlas-map subscribers were part of a household with at least some stake in the local community, but in several instances, subscribers were young farm laborers with no readily discernible family connection to the households in which they lived.[56]

What did atlas maps mean to these individuals with a far more tenuous link to the local community? It was not, after all, *their* property or *their* achievements that were documented on page after page. Once again, motivations certainly varied, but at least several benefits seem obvious. As they did for patrons, atlas-map depictions may have served as a visual resource to some subscribers, offering neighboring homes, farms, and businesses as examples worthy of emulation. For others, a lack of resources or settled occupation had no bearing on their sense of involvement in the local community. For these supporters, atlas maps portrayed possibility, and they understood the normative picture not as a barrier to their inclusion but as a community that they could and would proudly seek to join. Finally, for immigrants, for young men who had not yet established themselves, or for those with few economic resources, support of the atlas-map project offered entrance into a community of shared values. Although their homes might not appear among the pages of illustrations or their land on a township cadastral map, their names did appear among those listed in the "Patrons Directory," documenting for all to see their progressive sensibilities and their community spirit. Inclusion in the atlas map, in other words, provided opportunity for self-definition regardless of actual resources or status. Although proponents often worried about how their counties might appear "in the eyes of the world," it was the judgment of friends and neighbors that seems to have mattered and drawn such a diverse group into these projects.[57]

While atlas maps offered supporters eloquent validation of their lives or a chance to document a shared worldview, they also had real significance for those who produced and promoted them. Illustrators such as the Radcliff brothers found new careers in atlas-map production, and surveyors such as Adin Mann grasped the opportunity as a lifeline out of financial crisis. For Louis Everts and his competitors, the atlas-map bonanza generated considerable wealth and opened the door to even greater publishing opportunities and new business ventures.[58] Scrutiny of Everts's actions during the atlas-map phase and in subsequent publishing projects suggests, however, that county atlases and their audiences meant more to him than just a lucrative enterprise.

Louis Everts, after all, emerged from a background very similar to that of many families documented on the pages of his atlas maps, and he seems to have been in no hurry to divorce himself completely from that heritage. Through much of his career, Everts relied on family and friends from his early Kane County days to carry out his atlas-map projects. Partnerships with David Stewart, Dwight Ensign, and his brother James Everts and relationships with employees such as Adin Mann or Samuel Durant lasted many years and through various undertakings. James Everts eventually left publishing and established a dairy farm near his father's Kane County property, but the brothers continued to have a business relationship. In the early 1880s, they became partners in a stock farm in Richardson County, Nebraska, operated under James's supervision (fig. 9). Louis also continued business relations with his younger brother Edward. In the late 1880s, Edward returned to Chicago and assumed the position of secretary

"LOUILAND FARMS,"
PROPERTY OF LOUIS H. EVERTS.

and treasurer in Louis Everts's Cold Blast Feather Company, a firm "dealing extensively in wholesale bedding supplies." Although the publishing business seemingly removed Louis Everts from his farm roots, he turned the profits generated from depicting that life back into sustaining family ties and midwestern connections.[59]

Louis Everts also appears to have had a sincere belief in the importance of documenting local landscapes and history. After completing projects in southeastern Michigan, Everts (either alone or in various partnerships) continued to turn out atlas maps, historical atlases, and, finally, town and county histories that portrayed life in New Jersey, New York, Ohio, Pennsylvania, and a number of other states.

Figure 9. Louiland Farms. Source: Everts and Kirk, *The Official State Atlas of Nebraska* (Philadelphia: Everts and Kirk, 1885).

Perhaps most telling, Everts used historical atlases to memorialize the experiences of his own family, including a biographical portrait of his father in the *History of Cattaraugus Co., New York* and an illustration of the Everts's family farm in the *Combination Atlas Map of Kane County, Illinois*. Many years later, Everts's *The Official State Atlas of Nebraska* depicted "Louiland Farms," his Richardson County stock farm complete with elegant home, massive barns, and long stretches of the newly invented barbed-wire fencing.[60] All of these publications, as his firm's *History of Philadelphia* pointed out, "preserved in an enduring and concise form, the valuable records of many American cities and other political divisions."[61] Newspaper accounts suggest that efforts to compile atlas maps not only "preserved" regional history but also effectively stimulated further interest among local residents. As the *Jackson Weekly Citizen* reported in February 1874, "The more recent and more extensive efforts of several map publishing companies to gain information in regard to the early history of the several localities in which they have been laboring has had the effect to foster quite a salutary influence among old residents." Those "old residents," in turn, went on to establish "a society for the purpose of preserving the historical incidents of the early settlement of this county" that continued to meet long after Everts and his crews left the region.[62]

Unfortunately for Louis Everts and others in the atlas-map trade, the heady successes of the 1870s and 1880s could not be sustained. As it had before production began in southeastern Michigan, the atlas-map genre continued to evolve, with some features increasing and others declining. Local cadastral maps were the first to disappear. Many historical atlases published in the late 1870s and the 1880s contained national, state, and county maps, but they lacked the details about landownership and local items of interest typical of township cadastral maps. Eventually the number of lithographs also declined, and those that did appear tended to complement the historical narrative rather than serve as documentation in their own right. County histories that depended on text rather than illustrations emerged in the 1880s, becoming the new staple of the publication-by-subscription trade, and remained popular throughout the 1890s. The publishing career of Louis Everts also changed, and although historical atlases continued to be a mainstay of his business, he moved on to publish a number of institutional histories and a variety of other works.[63]

At the turn of the twentieth century, however, all of Everts's networks and partnerships fell apart and his prosperity vanished. Suffering severe financial embarrassment, Everts fell back on his Civil War experience, writing to the commissioner of Civil War pensions in July 1904 to describe his situation: "Up to 1898, I had accumulated a fortune slowly and by hard work, but the following three years swept every dollar of it away." He continued, "I am making another effort, but the years are somewhat against me." Although Everts had once parlayed his depictions of local landscapes into considerable wealth, times and interests had changed, and he was never again able to earn his livelihood from publishing. Until his death in 1924, Everts continued to ask for assistance. The records of the commissioner of Civil War pensions are full of his pleas for increased allotments. By 1918, his resources were so depleted that he admitted himself to the National Home for Disabled Volunteer Soldiers in Dayton, Ohio, so that his wife, Emma, might have the benefit of his entire pension. His presence there must have been a particularly painful reminder of his failures, for some forty years previously, Everts had carefully depicted the National Home in his *Combination Atlas Map of Montgomery County, Ohio*. Fortunately, Everts's stay was short-lived, and he returned to Philadelphia once Emma Everts had found a job that could support them both.[64]

The reasons for Louis Everts's financial debacle are unclear. His personal life took a turn for the worse in the 1890s, and this may have contributed to his decline. In 1890, Everts's wife of nearly twenty years filed for divorce, accusing her husband of "willful" desertion. In the divorce settlement, Everts lost custody of his only child, Louisa, and agreed to an alimony payment of two thousand dollars annually. Two years after the divorce, Everts married his third wife, Emma Montgomery of Philadelphia, a woman twenty years his junior.[65] In the days of historical-atlas success, Everts also may have overextended his resources; with the economic depression of the mid-1890s, he may have found his bedding company or the Nebraska stock farm difficult to sustain. Finally, in the late nineteenth and early twentieth centuries, large corporations came to dominate mapmaking and publishing, making it increasingly difficult for small enterprises to compete. The transformation of the industry may simply have left Louis Everts behind.[66] The experience of Everts's old friend and former competitor A. T. Andreas argues for the latter cause. Andreas made and lost several fortunes over the years, but, like Everts, he was unable to stage a comeback as the nineteenth century waned. At his death in 1900, the once wealthy and respected Andreas lived in a boarding house. He left behind a wife who, for lack of resources, immediately applied for a Civil War widow's pension.[67]

If we assess the atlas-map bonanza through the lens of Louis Everts's last years, the massive undertaking would seem to have been a dismal failure. But if we turn our appraisal to the atlas maps themselves and their significance in portraying a particular time and place, a different perspective emerges. As their commercial popularity proclaimed, the volumes' unique combination of spatial representation through maps, domestic landscapes detailed in lithographs, and historical perspective documented in text sold because it reflected the interests and concerns of local citizens. The validity of that portrayal as evidence of local values was strengthened by the number and diversity of residents who paid to be included in the projects. Whatever their motivation in putting themselves forward, residents understood the normative picture of midwestern rural life documented in atlas maps as a reasonable and meaningful depiction of their lives and their values. The atlas maps themselves, the landscapes they pictured, and the lives intertwined with their production, promotion, and purchase offer an unprecedented window on a post–Civil War culture eagerly embracing progress and change on the one hand while, on the other, clinging to traditional social values, the rootedness of home, and networks of family and friends. The ephemeral nature of the genre itself and the experience of promoters such as Louis Everts suggest that this balance was precarious.

NOTES

I would like to thank research associate Sally Warrick Morris for her valuable assistance in assembling demographic information for the atlas-map-subscriber sample and Robert Havira for his expertise in preparing illustrations for this chapter. Appreciation is also due Western Michigan University emeriti professors Charles Heller and John Houdek for helpful advice and the Department of History for providing resources, through the Macmillan Fund, to carry out this research project.

1. "The New County Atlas," *Jackson Daily Citizen*, December 18, 1873.
2. For listings of additional Jackson, Lenawee, and Washtenaw County maps, bird's-eye views, and city lithographs published prior to 1873, see John Cumming, comp., *A Preliminary Checklist of 19th Century Lithographs of Michigan Cities and Towns* (Mount

Pleasant: Central Michigan University, 1969), esp. iii–iv; John R. Hébert, comp., *Panoramic Maps of Anglo-American Cities: A Checklist of Maps in the Collections of the Library of Congress, Geography and Map Division* (Washington, D.C.: Library of Congress, 1974); Louis C. Karpinski and William C. Jenks, *Bibliography of the Printed Maps of Michigan, 1804–1880* (Lansing: Michigan Historical Commission, 1931); and Richard W. Stephenson, comp., *Land Ownership Maps: A Checklist of Nineteenth Century United States County Maps in the Library of Congress* (Washington, D.C.: Library of Congress, 1967).

3. "A County Atlas," *Dexter Leader*, April 25, 1873. For listings of subscribers, see *Combination Atlas Map of Jackson County, Michigan* (Chicago: Everts and Stewart, 1874), 136–44; *Combination Atlas Map of Lenawee County, Michigan* (Chicago: Everts and Stewart, 1874), 132–43; and *Combination Atlas Map of Washtenaw County, Michigan* (Chicago: Everts and Stewart, 1874), 113–24. For an estimate of atlas cost, see Bates Harrington, *How 'Tis Done: A Thorough Ventilation of the Numerous Schemes Conducted by Wandering Canvassers, together with the Various Advertising Dodges for the Swindling of the Public* (Chicago: Fidelity, 1879), 61–70.

4. For background on the county atlas industry, see Michael P. Conzen, ed., *Chicago Mapmakers: Essays on the Rise of the City's Map Trade* (Chicago: Chicago Historical Society, 1984); idem, "The County Landownership Map in America: Its Commercial Development and Social Transformation, 1814–1939," *Imago Mundi* 36 (1984): 9–31; idem, "Land Ownership Maps and County Atlases," *Agricultural History* 58 (Spring 1984): 118–22; John William Reps, *Views and Viewmakers of Urban America* (Columbia: University of Missouri Press, 1984); Walter William Ristow, *American Maps and Mapmakers: Commercial Cartography in the Nineteenth Century* (Detroit: Wayne State University Press, 1985); idem, "Nineteenth-Century Cadastral Maps in Ohio," *Papers of the Bibliographical Society of America* 59, no. 3 (1965): 306–15; and Norman J. W. Thrower, "The County Atlas in the United States," *Surveying and Mapping* 21 (1961): 365–73.

5. For example, see "County Atlas," *Jackson Daily Citizen*, February 7, 1874; and Harrington, *How 'Tis Done*, 42–43, 87–88.

6. *Combination Atlas Map of Will County, Illinois* (Elgin, Ill.: Thompson Bro's and Burr, 1873).

7. For examples of commentary on the accuracy of atlas-map illustrations, see Russell Swenson, "Illustrations of Material Culture in Nineteenth-Century County and State Atlases," *Pioneer America Society Transactions: P.A.S.T.* 5 (1982): 63–70; Karen D. Lux, "A Folkloric Approach to Nineteenth-century County Historians," *New York Folklore* 8 (Summer 1982): 25–34; Rodney O. Davis, "Coming to Terms with County Histories," *Western Illinois Regional Studies* 2, no. 2 (1979): 144–55; and Carolyn Baker Lewis, "Imperfect or Identical Images? An Investigation of the Accuracy of Nineteenth Century Subscription Property Illustrations of Clinton County, Michigan" (typescript, Clinton County Historical Commission, November 1987, Michigan Collection, Library of Michigan, Lansing, Mich.); and idem, "The Utility of Nineteenth Century Subscription Property Illustrations to Studies of the Relict Landscape," in *Historic Archaeology in Illinois: Papers from the Second Conference on Historic Archaeology in Illinois*, ed. and comp. Charles L. Rohrbaugh and Thomas E. Emerson (Normal: Illinois Historic Preservation Agency, 1988), 19–33.

8. "Samuel C. Everts," in *The Past and Present of Kane County, Illinois* (Chicago: W. Le Baron, Jr., 1878), 555; "Samuel C. Everts," in *History of Cattaraugus Co., New York* (Philadelphia: L. H. Everts, 1879), 305–6; "Samuel C. Everts," in *Commemorative Biographical and Historical Record of Kane County, Illinois* (Chicago: Beers, Leggett, 1888), 456–60. See also 1860 Federal Population Census, Kane County, Illinois, microfilm, roll 191, pp. 275, 741; 1870 Federal Population Census, Kane County, Illinois, microfilm, roll 237, pp. 372, 377R; and Lewis [sic] H. Everts, Civil War Pension File no. 1318.978, National Archives, Washington, D.C.

9. Peirce, Merrill, and Perrin, *Past and Present of Kane County*, 398; 1850 Federal Population Census, Kane County, Illinois, microfilm, roll 115A, p. 53; 1860 Federal Population Census, Kane County, Illinois, microfilm, roll 191, p. 1009; 1870 Federal Population Census, Kane County, Illinois, microfilm, roll 237, pp. 299, 390; "Moses H. Thompson," in *The Biographical Record of Kane County, Illinois* (Chicago: S. J. Clarke, 1898), 22–25; Ristow, *American Maps and Mapmakers*, 401–2; *Map of LaSalle County, Illinois* (Elgin, Ill.: Thompson Bro's, 1870).

10. Harrington, *How 'Tis Done*, 28–48.

11. *Map of Carroll County, Illinois* (Geneva, Ill.: Thompson and Everts, 1869); Harrington, *How 'Tis Done*, 74–75.

12. Harrington, *How 'Tis Done*, 55–59; Michael P. Conzen, "Maps for the Masses: Alfred T. Andreas and the Midwestern County Atlas Trade," in *Chicago Mapmakers*, ed. idem, 47–63.

13. Francis Amasa Walker, ed., *The Statistics of the Wealth and Industry of the United States . . . Ninth Census* (Washington, D.C.: Government Printing Office, 1872), 3: 26; Thompson and Everts, *Combination Atlas Map of Henry County, Iowa* (Geneva, Ill.: Thompson and Everts, 1870).

14. *Combination Atlas Map of Henry County.*

15. Conzen, "Maps for the Masses," 47–63; Clara Egli Le Gear, *United States Atlases: A List of National, State, County, City, and Regional Atlases in the Library of Congress* (Washington, D.C.: Library of Congress, 1950), 1: 324.

16. *Combination Atlas Map of Stephenson County, Illinois* (Geneva, Ill.: Thompson and Everts, 1871).

17. "Moses H. Thompson," 22; Harrington, *How 'Tis Done*, 71; 1870 Federal Population Census, Kane County, microfilm, roll 237, p. 377; *Map of LaSalle County.*

18. Harrington, *How 'Tis Done*, 80; 1880 Federal Population Census, Alameda County, California, microfilm, roll T 9–61, p. 137. See also Le Gear, *United States Atlases*, 1: 291.

19. J. Thomas Scharf and Thompson Westcott, *History of Philadelphia, 1609–1884* (Philadelphia: L. H. Everts and Co., 1884), 3: 2332.

20. Harrington, *How 'Tis Done*, 71; Le Gear, *United States Atlases*, 1: 237.

21. Le Gear, *United States Atlases*, 1: 236–37; Durant, Bradsby, and Durant, *Commemorative Biographical and Historical Record*, 460. See also James Gopsill, comp., *Gopsill's Philadelphia City Directory for 1876* (Philadelphia: James Gopsill, 1876), 482, 492.

22. "The New County Atlas," *Jackson Daily Citizen.*

23. W. W. Pasko, ed., *American Dictionary of Printing and Bookmaking* (New York: Lockwood, 1894), 3.

24. Henry Francis Walling and Alexander Winchell, *Atlas of the State of Michigan* (Detroit: R. M. and S. T. Tackabury, 1873), 6; Harrington, *How 'Tis Done*, 28–29.

25. "To Our Patrons," *Combination Atlas Map of Will County, Illinois* (Elgin, Ill.: Thompson Bro's and Burr, 1873). The approximate production time was derived from local newspapers. See "The County Atlas," *Adrian Times and Expositor*, April 1, 1873; "A County Atlas," *Dexter Leader*, April 25, 1873; "The County Atlas," *Jackson Daily Citizen*, January 15, 1874; and "An Historical Atlas," *Ypsilanti Commercial*, March 11, 1874.

26. For example, see *Atlas of Cass County, Michigan from Actual Survey by and under the Direction of D. J. Lake* (Philadelphia: C. O. Titus, 1872). The title page notes that Lake was "assisted" by four individuals.

27. "The County Atlas," *Jackson Weekly Citizen*, January 20, 1874, 5.

28. 1870 Federal Population Census, Kane County, microfilm, roll 237, p. 455; Durant, Bradby, and Durant, "Samuel Wilkins Durant," in *Commemorative Biographical and Historical Record*, 495–97.

29. Durant, Bradby, and Durant, "Samuel Wilkins Durant," 497.

30. *Combination Atlas Map of Johnson County, Iowa* (Geneva, Ill.: Thompson and Everts, 1870); *Combination Atlas Map of Jackson County; Combination Atlas Map of Lenawee County; Combination Atlas Map of Washtenaw County.*

31. 1870 Federal Population Census, Kane County, microfilm, roll 237, p. 309.

32. *Combination Atlas Map of Will County; Combination Atlas Map of Stephenson County; Historical Atlas of Sandusky County, Ohio* (Chicago: Everts, Stewart, and Co., 1874); *Combination Atlas Map of Trumbull County, Ohio* (Chicago: L. H. Everts, 1874).

33. Frank Krause and D. W. Ensign, comps., *Map of Blackhawk County, Iowa* (Geneva, Ill.: Thompson and Everts, 1869); *Combination Atlas Map of Trumbull County.*

34. *Combination Atlas Map of Greene County, Ohio* (Chicago: L. H. Everts, 1874); *Illustrated Historical Atlas of Clark County, Ohio* (Philadelphia.: L. H. Everts, 1875); *The Biographical Record of Kane County, Illinois* (Chicago: S. J. Clarke, 1898), 59 (quotation).

35. Durant, Bradsby, and Durant, "Adin Mann," in *Commemorative Biographical and Historical Record*, 56–60; *Map of Kane County, Illinois* (Philadelphia: Matthews, Crane and Co., 1860).

36. *Combination Atlas Map of Montgomery County, Ohio* (Evansville, Ind.: L. H. Everts, 1875); *Combination Atlas Map of Ogle County, Illinois* (Chicago: Everts, Baskin, and Stewart, 1872); *Combination Atlas Map of McHenry County, Illinois* (Chicago: Everts, Baskin, and Stewart, 1872).

37. Harrington, *How 'Tis Done*, 69–70, 81.

38. Peirce, Merrill, and Perrin, *Past and Present*, 161; "Rates of Surveying and Conveyancing," in *Proceedings, Constitution, By-Laws, List of Members &c., of the Surveyors' Association of West New Jersey*, ed. Leah Black (Camden, N.J.: S. Chew, 1880), unnumbered introductory page; Joseph D. Weeks, *Report on the Statistics of Wages in Manufacturing Industries* (Washington, D.C.: Government Printing Office, 1886), 176, 447, 475.

39. "Table I Showing the Total Population," *Statistics of the State of Michigan Collected for the Ninth Census of the United States, June 1, 1870* (Lansing: W. S. George, 1873), 4–6; "Statistics of the State of Michigan," *Michigan Farmer* 4 (February 22, 1862): 52.

40. Charles N. Lindquist, *Lenawee County, a Harvest of Pride and Promise: An Illustrated History* (Chatsworth, Calif.: Windsor Publications, 1990), 25–26; Brian Deming and Patricia McEnroe Koschik, *Jackson: An Illustrated History* (Woodland Hills, Calif.: Windsor Publications, 1984), 36, 39–42; *History of Jackson County, Michigan* (Chicago: Inter-state Publishing, 1881), 1: 551–60; Jonathan Marwil, *A History of Ann Arbor* (Ann Arbor, Mich.: Ann Arbor Observer, 1987), 49. See also Walker, ed., *Statistics of the Wealth and Industry*, 3: 532–33.

41. *Combination Atlas Map of Lenawee County*, 8–11; *Combination Atlas Map of Jackson County*, 18–19; *Combination Atlas Map of Washtenaw County*, 18–20.

42. Andrew R. L. Cayton and Peter S. Onuf, *The Midwest and the Nation: Rethinking the History of an American Region* (Bloomington: Indiana University Press, 1990), 34–35; Henry Ward Beecher, *Plain and Pleasant Talk about Fruits, Flowers, and Farming* (New York: Derby and Jackson, 1859), 10–11. A number of scholars have examined the stresses accompanying these changes from political, social, and cultural perspectives. For example, see Christopher Clark, *The Roots of Rural Capitalism: Western Massachusetts, 1760–1860* (Ithaca, N.Y.: Cornell University Press, 1986); John Higham, *From Boundlessness to Consolidation: The Transformation of American Culture, 1848–1860* (Ann Arbor, Mich.: William L. Clements Library, 1969), 24, 26; and Cheryl Lyon-Jenness, *For Shade and for Comfort: Democratizing Horticulture in the Nineteenth-Century Midwest* (West Lafayette, Ind.: Purdue University Press, 2004), esp. ch. 2.

43. Some atlas-map customers might have been unfamiliar with the illustrated tools' functions. The transit assisted surveyors in measuring both vertical and horizontal angles. The pantograph helped artists copy maps to the desired scale. For a thorough discussion of nineteenth-century surveying tools, see J. B. Johnson, *The Theory and Practice of Surveying: Designed for the Use of Surveyors and Engineers Generally, but Especially for the Use of Students in Engineering* (New York: John Wiley & Sons, 1904), esp. chs. 1–6.

44. Walling and Winchell, *Atlas of the State of Michigan*, 5–6.

45. For commentary on the selectivity of map portrayals, see Denis E. Cosgrove, "Introduction: Mapping Meaning," in *Mappings*, ed. idem (London: Reaktion Books, 1999), 1–23; James Corner, "The Agency of Mapping: Speculation, Critique, and Invention," in ibid., 213–52; and J. B. Harley, *The New Nature of Maps: Essays in the History of Cartography*, ed. Paul Laxton (Baltimore: Johns Hopkins University Press, 2001), 150–68.

46. Harrington, *How 'Tis Done*, 41–46.

47. "The New Atlas," *Jackson Daily Citizen*, February 21, 1874.

48. *Combination Atlas Map of Henry County, Iowa*; *Combination Atlas Map of Kane County, Illinois* (Geneva, Ill.: Thompson and Everts, 1872); *Combination Atlas Map of Washtenaw County*, 17–24.

49. "The New Atlas," *Jackson Weekly Citizen*, February 24, 1874, 5.

50. Atlas-map agents' success in selling biographies and portraits varied considerably in the three counties: Lenawee County's atlas map included eighty-one biographies, and Jackson County's had thirty-two, but Washtenaw County's atlas map con-

tained only seven biographies. In contrast, the Jackson County atlas map included forty-nine portraits, while the atlas maps for Washtenaw and Lenawee Counties had fewer than fifteen portraits each. In this chapter, individuals with biographies or portraits were included in the patron sample only if their homes also appeared among the lithographs. Harrington, *How 'Tis Done*, 61–70.

51. Totals were derived by counting the number of home lithographs and subscribers in each volume and comparing those figures to population statistics for each county. See *Census of the State of Michigan, 1874* (Lansing: W. S. George, 1875), 20, 26, 44; and *Statistics of the State of Michigan . . . Ninth Census*, 180–207.

52. These three townships were selected on the basis of their strong support for atlas-map projects. In each case, more individuals commissioned images of their homes than in any other township within the county. The townships themselves were also in the middle rank within their counties in terms of population and cash value of real estate. Demographic information for patrons and subscribers was extracted from the atlas maps and from the 1870 Federal Population Census for Lenawee, Washtenaw, and Jackson Counties. See 1870 Federal Population Census, Jackson County, Michigan, microfilm, rolls 678, 679; 1870 Federal Population Census, Lenawee County, Michigan, microfilm, rolls 685, 686; and 1870 Federal Population Census, Washtenaw County, Michigan, microfilm, rolls 707, 708. For comparative statistics from the counties or townships, see "Table I Showing the Total Population," *Statistics of the State of Michigan . . . Ninth Census*, 2–9; and "Table III, Population of Civil Divisions Less than Counties," in *Statistics of the Wealth and Industry*, ed. Walker, 3: 171, 172, 176.

53. The average for patron families was derived from combined personal and real property values listed in the 1870 population census.

54. Wealth was determined for the individual who actually purchased the atlas map. In Saline Township, this information was available for eighty-five residents; in Leoni Township, for eighty-three residents; and in Cambridge Township, for ninety-six residents. Subscribers were not necessarily heads of households. The average wealth for the entire township was calculated from the wealth attributed to heads of households. There were 225 households in Cambridge Township, 281 in Leoni, and 392 in Saline.

55. For an example of this kind of competition, see "Premium Farm," *Annual Report of the Secretary of the State Board of Agriculture of the State of Michigan for the Year 1866* (Lansing: John A. Kerr, 1866), 283–85.

56. For examples of these varied relationships, see 1870 Federal Population Census for Lenawee County, Michigan, microfilm, roll 685, pp. 161, 162; and 1870 Federal Population Census for Jackson County, Michigan, microfilm, roll 679, pp. 278R, 290R.

57. "The New Atlas," 5.

58. For comments about the profitability of atlas-map production, see Harrington, *How 'Tis Done*, 68–71; and Conzen, "Maps for the Masses," 54–58.

59. See Ellis and Nash, "Samuel C. Everts," 305–6; and Durant, Bradsby, and Durant, "Samuel C. Everts," 456–60.

60. Ellis and Nash, "Samuel C. Everts," 305–6; Durant, Bradsby, and Durant, "Samuel C. Everts," 456–60; *The Official State Atlas of Nebraska* (Philadelphia: Everts and Kirk, 1885), c. 136–37.

61. Scharf and Westcott, *History of Philadelphia*, 3: 2332.

62. "Historical Organizations," *Jackson Weekly Citizen*, February 17, 1874, 7.

63. For documentation of Everts's later publishing history, see Scharf and Westcott, *History of Philadelphia*, 3: 2332.

64. L. H. Everts to E. L Ware, Commissioner of Pensions, July 26, 1904, Miscellaneous Papers, Lewis [sic] H. Everts, Civil War Pension File No. 1318.978. See also *Combination Atlas Map of Montgomery County*, 20–21.

65. Miscellaneous Papers, Lewis [sic] H. Everts, Civil War Pension File No. 1318.978.

66. Michael P. Conzen, "Evolution of the Chicago Map Trade: An Introduction," in *Chicago Mapmakers*, ed. Conzen, 10.

67. Conzen, "Maps for the Masses," 60–61.

An Evaluation of Plat, Sanborn, and Panoramic Maps of Cities and Towns in Michigan

David K. Patton, Amy K. Lobben, and Bruce M. C. Pape

As nonindigenous settlement of Michigan expanded during the nineteenth century, the mapping needs of the area changed significantly. Land speculation, farming, logging, and construction of villages and towns began to dominate the area's geography, and the need for large-scale maps became critical. The common bond among all of these activities was local landownership and land use. These types of ventures could not and cannot be managed with small-scale maps, those less than 1:100,000 (1 inch equals 1.58 miles). In fact, many of these activities could not be effectively managed with the modern 1:24,000 (1 inch equals 2,000 feet) United States Geological Survey topographic maps. To adequately document parcel-level features generally requires a scale greater than 1:5,000. Although it is simple enough to declare that maps are needed at 1:4,800 (1 inch equals 400 feet), the cost and effort involved in creating large-scale maps are enormous. Even today, with the ever-expanding use of the Global Positioning System and geographic information systems, up-to-date parcel maps remain a significant challenge for local mapping agencies.

Three forms of cartographic products that specifically met the need for large-scale representation of cities and towns starting in the nineteenth century were plat maps, fire insurance maps, and panoramic views. Although these map types were similar in scale and were all often used to portray cities and towns, each was developed for quite different and specific reasons. Plat maps represented (as they still do today) the official government record for monitoring landownership and boundary locations. While the actual scale of plat maps varies, they are generally created on a scale larger than 1:2,000. Fire insurance maps evolved to provide insurance companies with accurate infrastructure inventories for the purpose of evaluating fire risk in urban areas. These maps are also very large-scale and include building footprints, building materials, and the type of activity carried on in each structure.[1] Finally, panoramic maps or views were created as artistic renderings for civic self-promotion. They generally depicted towns and cities at a slightly smaller scale than fire insurance maps, but they also showed individual buildings. Contrary to plats and fire insurance maps, panoramic views were drawn from an oblique angle and were far more artistic.

By the 1930s, changes in the insurance business precipitated a decline in the need for fire insurance maps, and changes in popular taste brought the era of panoramic views to an end. Despite their demise as commercially viable products, extant maps and views (along with plats) are enormously significant documents for students of urban places of the late nineteenth and early twentieth centuries. Because of the large scale employed in creating these maps and the corresponding detail they provide, these products have always been significant, but prior to the Internet they were fairly difficult to obtain. Large collections of original fire insurance maps are typically stored in one or two libraries within a given state, and even then the collections are generally limited to places within that state.[2] Large collections of panoramic views are even more difficult to locate.

Today, the Sanborn Map Company, in cooperation with the ProQuest Information and Learning Company, has made all of its fire insurance maps available on the World Wide Web.[3] The company's online catalogue includes more than twelve thousand cities, many mapped half a dozen times. Likewise, the Library of Congress (LC) has made its entire collection of panoramic views available on the Web.[4] The Library of Congress provides free access to its collection of panoramic views, and they can be downloaded without cost. Although the LC collection is not exhaustive, it is substantial. Even plat maps can be found on the Web. The State of Michigan has scanned more than sixty-six thousand plats and made them available on the Internet for free viewing.[5]

Given the increased accessibility of these historical documents, it is reasonable to assume that their use will also increase. The purpose of this chapter, therefore, is to examine each of these map types as tools for the modern researcher. Who created these maps? What is the extent of their coverage? What types of information can be found on these maps? What impressions of place do these maps give us? The objective, however, is not only to answer these questions but also to provide a context within which these important resources may be used in historic study. Early plat maps, fire insurance maps, and panoramic views are, respectively, repositories of property data, land-use data, and even the aesthetic sensibilities of citizens from an earlier time. As such, these maps have become invaluable to the historical researcher. It must be remembered, however, that these documents were not produced for the historian; they were created to meet contemporary needs, and they must be evaluated with a full understanding of their original purpose and the impact that purpose had on the representation of place that resulted.

This chapter has two main parts. The first supplies a historical context by discussing why, how, and by whom each type of map was produced. In the second part, we examine the different representations of place in the three map types. We also compare examples of each map type in terms of geographic and temporal coverage, scale, perspective, content, consistency, and character.

Plat Maps

Arguably, plat maps were the most significant of the large-scale map products to emerge in the region in the nineteenth century. Clearly, plats existed before the nineteenth century. It was, however, during

that time that the first plats of Michigan and the Great Lakes region were created. Plat maps stand apart in their importance for several reasons: they were the first large-scale maps to represent the region; as they were the basis for all land sales, their geographic coverage was the most complete; because the original plats were created before settlement (and, in fact, defined the shape of parcels to be sold and settled), the imprint of these plats can be seen throughout the landscape of the region; and plat maps are still important in land management today. The history of this map type, therefore, is continuous in the region from the early 1800s to the present.

The term *plat map* can mean different things to different people depending on their backgrounds and interests. Today, county plat maps show landholdings and ownership in rural areas. They may also show burial plots in a cemetery. To some people, the term *plat* means a subdivision-development proposal, while others use plats for genealogical research. By one definition, a plat is a precise and detailed plan showing the actual or proposed divisions, special features, or uses of a piece of land. A plat tends to be more restrictive in scope than other map types. As used by surveyors, a plat is a plan showing property lines and the interrelationship of property lines with dimensional data on the lines. On a plat, dimensional data may eliminate the necessity for scaling, and the value of the plat is not dependent upon the accuracy with which points are plotted.[6] These original plats or copies are still used by a wide variety of professional and lay people, from archaeologists and historians to surveyors and engineers to genealogists.

Unlike other maps, plat maps were required by state law to be developed for the establishment of communities. The first step in the platting process was to carry out a well-defined boundary survey of the land to be platted, with the corners carefully marked by permanent monuments. There could be no error in the placement of the original monument, and the plat needed to fit the land exactly. Within this boundary survey, a careful subdivision of the tract into streets, blocks, lots, and other designations had to be made.[7] Monuments must be placed at the corners of all blocks and stakes at the corners of all lots. Then the plat survey had to be committed to paper, showing in detail all blocks, lots, streets, alleys, parks, waters, and monuments and all other information pertinent to future transactions and surveys. Names of streets had to be on the document and all sites for parks, hospitals, amusement venues, churches, and other public uses indicated. Measurements of distance and angles of connecting lines were also necessary. The final plat had to be endorsed as correct by the surveyor, and the property owner had to acknowledge the survey by signing it. This step was necessary since the land titles of the various lots and blocks were involved.[8] If the landowner did not acknowledge the plat, then it had no legal standing and no purpose. The plat then had to be recorded in the registrar of deeds office of the county where the land was situated unless the state required that it be filed in another location. By recording the plat, the public acknowledged its authenticity and made it legal; it became a contract in which the public had vested rights. Thus, a finished plat represented an ocular view of the results of a legally registered survey.[9]

The need for plats in Michigan and the Great Lakes region stemmed from the desire to settle new lands and develop communities. In 1787, the Northwest Ordinance established a policy for governing the western lands, and townships were created and organized by counties. The surveying of the land into townships and ranges and permanent settlement by the European community made record keeping and the establishment of title to the land essential. English common law did not permit informal transfers of land; title to real estate could pass only in a manner approved by law. The settlers needed the

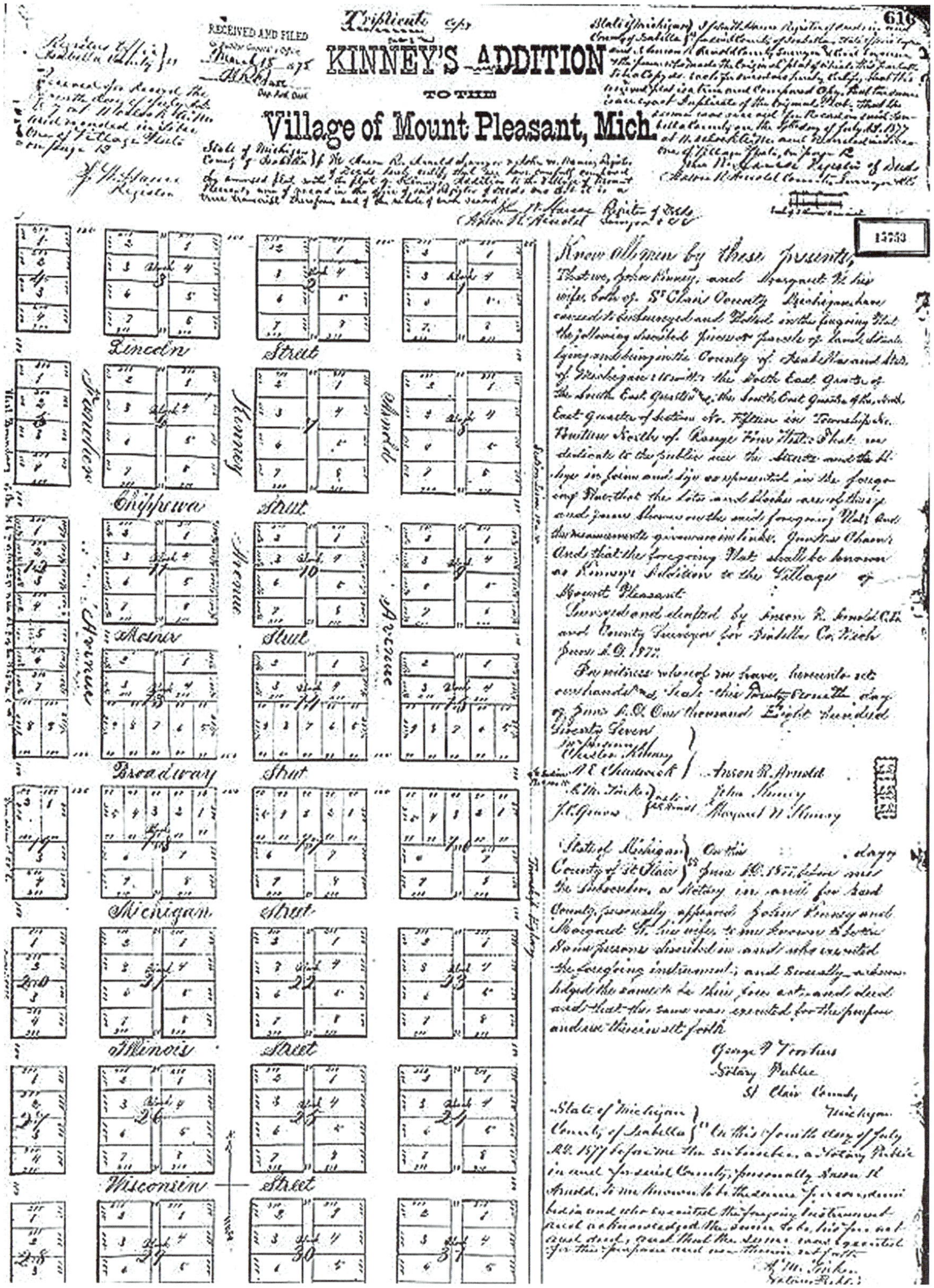

Figure 1. Plat map of "Kinney's Addition" to the village of Mount Pleasant, Michigan, 1875. Bureau of Construction Codes and Fire Safety, State of Michigan.

land, which the federal government owned, and the federal government needed money to run the country; thus, a record-keeping system and the bureaucracy to maintain these records were developed.[10]

Alongside or ahead of permanent settlers, speculators sought quick profits on the strength of rapid westward migration and developed many plats for communities that never made it past the planning stage. One example of the role of plats in land speculation in Michigan involved veterans of the War of 1812. For their military service, these men received bonuses in the form of land grants. More often than not, these land certificates were resold and used for speculation rather than turned in to claim land—a process that swelled the supply of available land and lowered prices.[11] The first plats were not governed by any state regulations and thus varied widely. They could be drawn on the back of a piece of buckskin with visual estimates for line placement and measurement, or they could be accurately surveyed with all the correct features expected at the time.

The first government surveys of land in Michigan began in 1815. Under the policies established by the Northwest Ordinance, Michigan was surveyed as a checkerboard of squares, one mile on a side. By 1825, most of the southern third of the Lower Peninsula was surveyed, but the entire state would not be platted until 1851. Land sales followed—the first in 1818 by auction at Detroit. The initial minimum price was $2.00 an acre, and the minimum parcel size was 160 acres (or one quarter-section), but lack of interest prompted a reduction to $1.25 an acre and a minimum parcel size of 80 acres. Gradually, the population of the state expanded, and land offices were added in Monroe, 1823; White Pigeon, 1831; Bronson (present-day Kalamazoo), 1834; and Ionia and Flint, 1836. By 1837, when Michigan became a state, thirty-eight counties were organized, with one city (Detroit) and fifteen incorporated villages.[12]

Ideally, a plat should be complete in and of itself and should present sufficient evidence so that any other surveyor can, without ambiguity, find the locative points and follow the reasoning of the original surveyor. On most plats, it is necessary to show record monuments and found physical monuments, along with a description of both. Other items that must be indicated include proof of the correctness of the found monuments, the basis of bearings, the expression of measurements on all lines including direction and distance, and coordinates. The number of each block and lot must also be shown. For parcels larger than one acre, a title, a date, and the names of the owner and surveyor are to be indicated. Oaths or witness evidence were also commonly included. The date of the survey and the client's name had to be on the plat map as well. A surveyor's certificate, which included a signature, a seal, a statement of accuracy, and a guarantee of location in accordance with a particular description, was supposed to be attached. All easements and encroachments also had to be noted.[13]

Needless to say, many plats, especially the early ones, were incomplete to one degree or another. Also, the majority of smaller cities that were platted, and many of the larger ones as well, were not correctly monumented. When cities were laid out with needle compasses, it was thought that one monument was sufficient to reproduce all lot and block locations. Quite often, however, this lone monument disappeared under the ravages of development. Thus, the resurveying of many original plats has been an ongoing chore and one that has ended in the courts many times as legal descriptions in these original plats are questioned.[14]

There are many variations in platting laws, but defining when a plat must be made and outlining the necessary steps to obtain the approval of governing agencies are essential elements. Platting laws in recent years have also created a review process to ensure that newly created lots have adequate provisions for roads, sewer lines, water, and other services before they can be sold. Other important items included

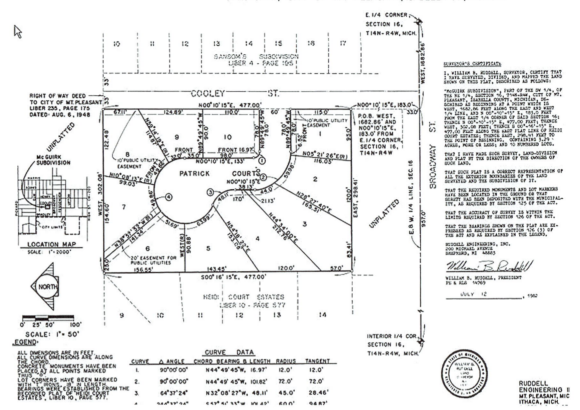

Figure 2. Plat map of the "McGuirk Subdivision," Mount Pleasant, Michigan, 1982. Bureau of Construction Codes and Fire Safety, State of Michigan.

in platting laws are a title guarantee statement, a provision for the issuance of performance bonds, and a definition of who may prepare maps. Additional items consist of preparations for dedications and street widths, monumentation, easements, the required measurement data, accuracies, and recordation.[15] There should also be a statement prohibiting lot sales prior to recording the plat.

Michigan began maintaining a file of all plats in the state in 1873. Copies of all plats prepared after that date had to be filed with the state. Beginning in 1909, copies were made of all pre-1873 plats on file with the eighty-three county registers of deeds and were incorporated into the state's files. This collection includes all plats in Michigan beginning with those created under the 1821 territorial act for recording town plats. This act was amended randomly, granting various authority to different municipalities until the 1929 Michigan Plat Act, which replaced the 1821 statute. Currently, there are more than sixty-six thousand plats on file with the State of Michigan.[16]

For many people, the term *plat* immediately brings to mind the commercially published county plat books. These show the ownership, shape, and approximate size of each major real property parcel of land within a county. Parcel maps do not adhere to a single standard of accuracy. The term *major* could mean different sizes to different plat-book publishers, but usually such a parcel is defined as one acre or more, which, when drawn, will provide enough paper space to include information on parcel size and ownership. Thus, in county plat books or atlases, city properties are generally not shown, and

the plat books are therefore only of interest concerning rural areas. County plat books have no legal significance; they just indicate who owned the land at some particular time. They rely on local records but are not the product of county government, having instead been produced by an outside entity intent on making a profit. The platting company will have based its new product on a previous map if there was one and then edited the document using title records and property tax assessments. Thus, a county plat map supplies the best information available for the time of publication but does not give a snapshot for any particular date prior to its publication. County plat books were published irregularly depending on the sale of advertising and the potential market in a particular area. Given the derivative nature of county plat books, this chapter concentrates on the official plats registered with local and state offices.

Fire Insurance Maps

If plat maps furnished exact descriptions of property boundaries, fire insurance maps provided insurers and communities with a detailed inventory of what was built on those properties. These highly detailed, large-scale maps supplied information on dwellings, commercial buildings, and factories, such as their size, shape, and interior details (firewalls, locations of windows and doors, and types of roofs). These maps also described building uses, the widths and names of streets, and the locations of hydrants and fire alarms.

The Sanborn Map Company was the leading producer of fire insurance maps in the United States and Canada for almost one hundred years. During the period from 1867 to the late 1960s, this company published large-scale maps for more than twelve thousand communities—many were mapped numerous times. In fact, the firm so dominated the fire insurance map business that this type of map is often simply referred to as a Sanborn map.[17]

Despite Sanborn's eventual dominance, an official history of the Aetna Insurance Company claims that Aetna was responsible for developing this style of insurance map during the 1860s: "An important step in the progress of scientific and intelligent underwriting was the invention by Aetna employees of the system of manuscript charts of cities and towns, known later as the Sanborn system. For many years this system of maps, enabling the home office to determine the character of risks, was in use in most of the large fire insurance offices, and paved the way for other systems."[18] It is likely, however, that Aetna did not invent the insurance map per se, since examples of such maps had been published fifty years earlier. Rather, Aetna developed the first systematic approach to fire insurance mapping.[19]

In 1710, Britain's first fire insurance firm, the Sun Company, was created in London, a city of disastrous fires. This company offered the first fire insurance coverage in the United States, and other firms soon followed.[20] However, these companies soon realized the difficulty of insuring structures that were located across the Atlantic Ocean. Before a company agrees to insure a building, several factors must be clarified. These include location of the structure, the type of activities occurring within it, the kinds of materials used in its construction, and the number of people who work or live in the building. In order to provide this information, English companies began to create maps and charts of the insured structures and their surrounding areas. The first such map is titled *The Ichnography of Charleston, South Carolina* and states that it was compiled "at the request of Adam Sunno, Esq. for the use of the Phoenix Fire-Company of London, Taken from Actual Survey, 2[d] August 1788 by Edmund Petrie. Published 1st

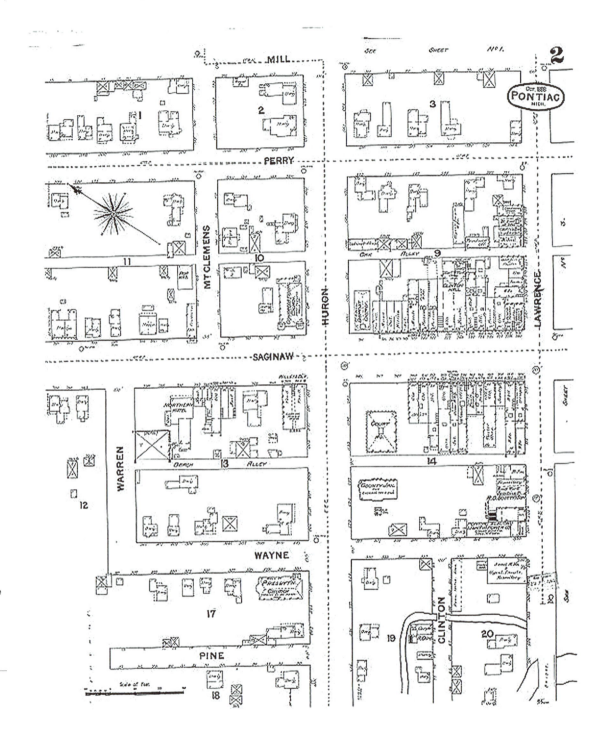

Figure 3. Portion of sheet 2 of the 1888 Sanborn fire insurance map set for Pontiac, Michigan. Image courtesy of the Sanborn Map Company in cooperation with the ProQuest Information and Learning Company, and Environmental Data Resources, Inc.

Jan. 1790 by E. Petrie No. 13 American Square."[21] This map includes a detailed, large-scale representation of the city's geography, including locations of public and private buildings, such as wharves and bridges, the transportation network, and the fire station.

English insurance companies did not maintain control over insurance practices in the United States for very long. Following the War of 1812, American insurance companies were established in the country's larger northeastern cities. Their creation meant that American companies would underwrite

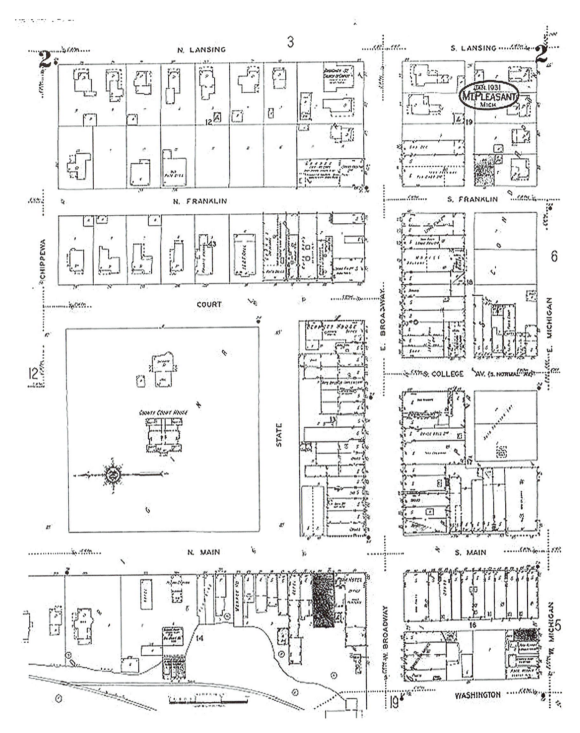

Figure 4. Portion of sheet 2 of the 1931 Sanborn fire insurance map set for Mount Pleasant, Michigan.

Image courtesy of the Sanborn Map Company in cooperation with the ProQuest Information and Learning Company, and Environmental Data Resources, Inc.

most of the insurance policies for properties in the United States. Proximity between insurance companies and the insured allowed agents to make personal visits to the actual properties.[22] As a result, there was less need for the detailed insurance maps drawn by English companies, but some were still created. These included *The Firemen's Guide, a Map of the City of New York Showing the Fire Districts, Fire Limits, Hydrants, Public Cisterns, Stations of Engines, Hooks & Ladders, Hose Carts, Etc.*, which was published in 1834 by Prosper Desobry.[23] Ironically, this map of New York City was drawn only one year before the disastrous 1835 fire. This fire caused more than twenty million dollars in damages, and consequently many small insurance companies went bankrupt. Reorganization of the insurance industry resulted in the formation of a few large insurance companies (as opposed to the many smaller neighborhood-style firms that existed before the 1835 fire). These newly formed larger insurance companies were, once again, somewhat removed from the structures they insured, and thus a new need for fire insurance maps arose. Mid-century, the Jefferson Insurance Company of New York City began creating detailed large-scale insurance maps that were even more thorough than those created previously by the English. The team of William Perris and Augustus Kurth produced many of these maps and eventually published the volume *Maps of the City of New York Surveyed under the Directions of Insurance Companies of Said City.*[24] Like the English maps, those included in this volume, as well as others created of New York City during the same time, provided detailed reproductions of the city's geography and included such features as public and private buildings, building construction materials, and building activities (such as residence, retail, manufacturing). However, new standards required even more detailed footprints of each building. Prior to the Civil War, similar volumes of maps were created for other large cities in the United States. Although mapping slowed considerably during the war, the changing political and economic climates and improved printing and production methods spurred expansion after the conflict.[25]

D. A. Sanborn began his career in fire insurance mapping in 1866, when he was employed for a short time by the Aetna Insurance Company. One year after he was hired, Sanborn published the *Insurance Map of Boston.*[26] That same year, he created the D. A. Sanborn National Insurance Diagram Bureau in New York City. The bureau focused mostly on making maps for clients in the United States. Then, in 1874, the firm was commissioned by several Canadian insurance companies to create a systematic approach to fire insurance mapping.[27]

Sanborn's was not the only firm making fire insurance maps; other such companies had been and would continue to be established. William A. Miller created fire insurance maps of New Jersey cities between 1872 and 1874, as did Spielman and Brush during the same period. Scarlett and Scarlett also made New Jersey maps between 1889 and 1891. In the Midwest, between 1885 and 1898, the Charles Rascher Insurance Map Publishing Company of Chicago and the Alphonso Whipple Company of St. Louis mapped cities in Illinois, Kansas, Michigan, Minnesota, and Missouri. By 1900, however, Sanborn had purchased all of these mapping companies. The only competition remaining was provided by Ernest Hexamer & Son (founded and operated by William Locher and Ernest Hexamer in Philadelphia), which created fire insurance maps primarily of Philadelphia. In 1915, it, too, was purchased by the renamed Sanborn Map Company, which then maintained a monopoly on the fire insurance mapping industry.[28]

As virtually the sole producer of fire insurance maps, the Sanborn Map Company set the industry standards. Its systematic authoring process was described in a company production manual. The surveyor gathered the field data, which was then inscribed in a map, which was sent to the examining and indexing department for quality control. Draftsmen added the standardized symbols found on all Sanborn maps. Then the map went to the proofreading department and thereafter to the coloring department. The print department produced the final map, and it was stored at the stock house until sold.[29]

The Sanborn Map Company continued to produce fire insurance maps, creating seven hundred thousand frequently updated maps of American towns and cities, until war once again caused a lull in the company's activity. Construction was scaled back during World War II, which meant there was less need for updated fire insurance maps. Prewar levels of production never resumed after 1945. Finally, in

1962 the National Bureau of Fire Underwriters' map committee reported that fire insurance maps were no longer needed. Production of fire insurance maps virtually stopped by 1967.[30] But the Sanborn Company continues to operate today, providing map-related services that include data acquisition, photogrammetric and traditional mapping, data conversion, and geographic information systems services.

The unparalleled success of the Sanborn Map Company may be partly a result of shrewd management. But the reliability of Sanborn maps kept its products in high demand. Today, the need for Sanborn maps continues but in a different way. No longer are the maps used specifically for insurance purposes; instead, they provide researchers and map enthusiasts with resources that reveal the geographic and cultural history of more than twelve thousand towns and cities across the United States.

Panoramic Views

Plat maps and fire insurance maps share two common elements of particular note. First, they both were, and in the case of plat maps still are, created primarily for utilitarian purposes. Attention to detail and accuracy were critical. Second, the maps that were produced had a high level of consistency. In the case of plat maps, legal statutes ensured that approaches used in their production were consistent. For fire insurance maps, the virtual monopoly enjoyed by the Sanborn Map Company ensured a consistent look and approach. For both of these types of maps, artistic license was not a part of the mapping process.

In contrast to these functional products, panoramic views are quite artistic. Panoramic views, also known as bird's-eye views and urban views, are detailed representations of cities and towns rendered as if the observer were viewing the area from an oblique overhead angle. Panoramic views were produced by many different limners and publishing companies—often for the purpose of showing cities and towns in a favorable light. Thus, it is not surprising that these views are often quite different from one another. Despite their artistic nature, panoramic views' popularity was based largely on the fact that they were detailed and generally depicted the local community accurately, even if it was through the lens of local boosterism.

According to John Reps, "artists, publishers, and their agents . . . employed nearly uniform methods for promoting and selling views."[31] They used local newspapers extensively to publicize these projects. The initial announcement would state that an artist was coming to create a view of the town. The article would stress the prestige that such an endeavor would bring to the area. A second article would announce that the artist was busy in the town sketching local buildings. During this phase, agents would begin to solicit advance orders for the views from businesses and individuals. Often, they would use existing views of other towns and the artist's preliminary sketches to entice potential subscribers. In a third announcement, the public would be notified that the drawing was complete. Citizens and businesses were again urged to place advance orders for the printed lithographs. The final announcement generally contained a warning that a sufficient number of subscriptions was required to justify the expense of printing. Reps states that two hundred to three hundred copies was the typical run for most small- to medium-sized places, and runs of more than one thousand were unusual.[32] These relatively small print runs explain why large collections of the original lithographs are so rare.

In many cases, the creators of panoramic views did not pay for newspaper coverage. They were often successful in convincing local newspapers to cover projects through a series of editorials. "Viewmakers

Figure 5. Bird's-eye view of Mount Pleasant, Michigan, 1884. Image courtesy of the Clarke Historical Library, Central Michigan University, Mount Pleasant.

sought and usually obtained free, continual, and favorable newspaper publicity. They found it easy to persuade editors that the publication of a view of their town would enhance its prestige, advertise its attractions, give pleasure and satisfaction to its residents, and promote its growth and prosperity."[33]

From a production standpoint, the process of creating a panoramic view was fairly straightforward. The field artists would often start with the layout of the town, and it was not uncommon for them to use local plats. Once a layout was obtained, the artist would determine the view angle that would allow him or her to portray the largest portion of the town with the greatest amount of detail. Balancing coverage and detail was critical to the operation because it could influence subscriptions. People and businesses would be less likely to subscribe if their businesses or residences were not clearly discernible on the final view. Once the orientation and perspective of the layout were determined, the artist would walk the streets, drawing each building in detail. The buildings were drawn from street level, but the limners' abilities permitted them to change the perspective to an overhead view. Upon completion, the field drawings would be sent to the print shop, where the lithographer would transfer them to stone for printing.

From 1825 to 1925, more than four thousand panoramic views were created of cities and towns in the United States and Canada. The popularity of this mapping form reached its zenith during the 1880s. Reps attributes the appeal of panoramic views to a general interest among Americans in images of their growing country, as well as to the commercial development of the lithographic process, which made all types of prints much more affordable than earlier printing methods.[34]

Of the 4,480 views catalogued in John Reps's *Views and Viewmakers of Urban America*, 3,199 were created by fifty-one different artists or publishers. Those who drew the remaining 1,281 views are unknown. Of the 3,199 views that can be attributed to a particular artist, just shy of two-thirds of them (1,993) are attributed to eight artists or publishers (T. M. Fowler, 426; O. H. Bailey, 374; J. J. Stoner, 314; Albert Ruger, 254; L. R. Burleigh, 228; Henry Wedge, 152; George Norris, 135; Augustus Koch, 110). Reps catalogues 195 views for 122 different places in Michigan. Most of the big names in panoramic views are represented in Michigan (O. H. Bailey, 6; T. M. Fowler, 2; George Norris, 4; Henry Wedge, 6). The most prolific artists or publishers of Michigan views, however, were J. J. Stoner, 51; Albert Ruger, 33; Clemens J. Pauli, 15; and E. S. Glover, 13.[35]

It is difficult to neatly categorize panoramic views by artist. First, the field was fairly inbred. Many prominent artists or publishers started as artists or sales agents for others in the same line of work. "Although each artist developed certain variations on the basic technique of depicting cities, their common or similar experiences in learning their craft made it almost inevitable that their products all bore a family resemblance."[36] Second, people playing a variety of roles often influenced the final product, which led to more uniformity than one would expect from a purely individualistic endeavor. Sales agents significantly influenced which cities would be portrayed and which buildings would be displayed prominently in each view. Artists, of course, had the important task of interpreting the towns and their buildings through their drawings in the field. Lithographers, in their turn, interpreted the artists' renderings and often altered them in the process. Reps described the impact of the lithographers as follows: "Some of this consistency of appearance also came from the printers where the drawings were put on stone by lithographers. The work of the artist in the field was thus filtered through a process that imposed a certain degree of standardization as house lithographic craftsmen endeavored to maintain a uniform product."[37] Finally, the publisher made decisions that had an impact on the final product, such as paper quality, print size, use of color, and so forth.

Although the process of promoting, creating, and selling panoramic views was fairly standardized, several significant variations remain from view to view that could have a serious impact on the use of a particular map for historical research. The two most critical variants are scale and view angle. Unlike Sanborn maps, panoramic views had no set scales. The views can generally be described as large-scale, but the exact scale varies from view to view. Additionally, the view angle has a huge impact on whether a view is suitable for reconstructing a town in a given time period. Finally, the interpretation of the city by the field artist and the lithographer has a significant influence on a view's appearance.

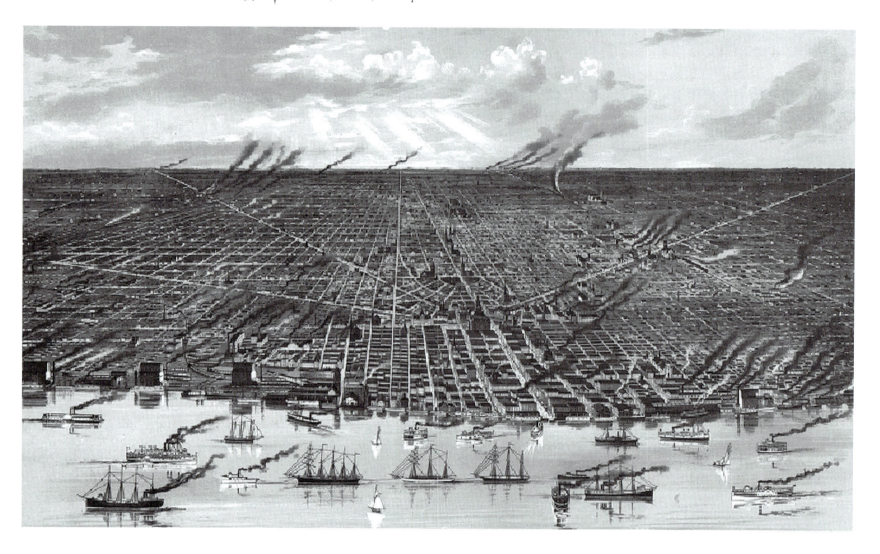

Figure 6. Bird's-eye view showing about three miles square of the central portion of the city of Detroit, Michigan, 1889. Image courtesy of the Library of Congress.

Two major factors must be considered when examining panoramic views in regard to scale: the variation of scale within a single view and the variation of scale from one view to the next. Because of the oblique perspective that is employed in these views, scale varies throughout the view. Features represented in the foreground will have a larger scale, whereas features in the back, toward the horizon, will appear much smaller. Although variations of scale exist in most maps (even supposedly orthographic maps), the scale variation within panoramic maps can often be extreme. In addition, because they are artistic renderings, the scale variation is not necessarily consistent or predictable.

Even if it were possible to assign an average scale to a particular view, the scales from one view to the next vary enormously. This is not surprising. Views were never created as "sets." The variation of scale does, however, present a challenge to the historical researcher. On one view, building types and architectural details may appear quite clear, while on another view, the majority of the buildings are indistinguishable. If there is any rule of thumb concerning scale, it might be that larger places tended to be drawn in a smaller scale so that more of the city could be portrayed. Even this is not, however, universally true. There are examples of small cities portrayed in a relatively small scale so that much of the surrounding natural landscape can be shown, and there are instances of large cities depicted at a relatively large scale and showing only a small area of the downtown.

The other great variable, the angle of view, is directly related to scale. Although virtually all panoramic views are drawn from an oblique angle, the degree of the angle often changes dramatically from one representation to another. There are examples of panoramic views that are drawn from a viewpoint that would appear to be no higher than the top of a tree. These examples tend to show much detail in the immediate foreground and relatively little in the background. Many other views are drawn from a perspective high above the town or city. These are able to portray the details of the city with much greater uniformity. As with scale, the choice of view angle was often related to the size of the city. Larger cities tended to be drawn from a low-angle perspective. This permitted more of the city to be portrayed (albeit much of it had to be drawn with relatively little detail). Smaller places tended to be drawn from a higher angle.

Comparing Map Types

Beyond summarizing the evolution of plat maps, fire insurance maps, and panoramic views, the purpose of this chapter is to evaluate these products as documents that can be used to educate people about cities and towns of the late nineteenth and early twentieth centuries. This evaluation involves a number of questions: What level of coverage is provided by each map type? What map scale is typical for each of the products, and how does map scale affect their usefulness? From what perspective are the maps rendered? What information is presented on each of the map types? Are the map types consistent in scale, perspective, and content? What can we learn about the character of a place from each of the map types? How might the original purpose of the maps influence our interpretation of a given place?

A fundamental difference among plats, fire insurance maps, and panoramic views is coverage. For the researcher, two aspects of coverage are critical: geographic and temporal. If one is to reconstruct an urban place from any of these three map types, it is necessary to consider their geographic completeness. From the macro perspective, the significant issue is *which* places are represented. From the micro perspective, the issue is the *extent* of coverage for a particular place. In other words, for which cities and towns do Sanborn maps exist, and what portion of a particular town does a particular Sanborn map portray? As will be discussed, given the varying purposes of the maps, the geographic coverage of each type varies. Of equal concern to the researcher is the temporal completeness provided by each product. Again, temporal completeness can be discussed in two ways. First, how frequently were the maps updated? Second, to what degree can the incremental changes that occurred between map updates be reconstructed? Does the particular map type limit the researcher to a handful of historical snapshots? If so, how accurately can the patterns of growth and change between snapshots be reconstructed?

From the standpoint of geographic coverage, plat maps are the qualified winners. Because of their role in the legal documentation of the subdivision of land parcels, the geographic coverage of plats should be complete. Plat maps exist for every city and town and for every part of every city and town. This is not true for either of the other map types. Plats are "qualified" winners, however, because the user may pay a high price in inconvenience for this completeness. Full coverage of a single city or town may involve many separate plat maps. For example, to obtain a complete view of the plats for the village of Mount Pleasant in 1890 would require one to gather the original plat map of the village of Mount Pleasant (1864), Smith's addition (1875), the Kinney addition (1877), C. Bennett's addition (1882), and so forth. It is true that the county plat books of the era often showed all of the existing plats for a town or city compiled together on a single map. However, the date that a particular plat was added was often missing, and the publication of plat books was not as regular as it has subsequently become. With enough effort, however, it is possible to compile an exact record of development for the complete geographic area of any city or town using plat maps.[38]

Unlike plat maps, macro-scale geographic coverage is incomplete for both fire insurance maps and panoramic views. Of the two, Sanborn maps come much closer to universal coverage. The checklist of Sanborn maps published by the Library of Congress lists 339 Michigan towns and cities.[39] A complete list of the incorporated places in Michigan for the year 1900 shows populations for 383 places.[40] Clearly, not all incorporated places were mapped by the Sanborn Map Company. However, if one examines all incorporated places in 1900 with a population greater than 500, only 15 were not mapped by the Sanborn Map Company, and all places with a 1900 population greater than 1,000 were mapped at least once.[41] The macro-level geographic coverage of panoramic views is much sparser. John Reps catalogued 195 views for 122 different places in Michigan.[42] Comparing this total with the number of incorporated places in 1890 (323) when panoramic-view production was at its peak, one finds just over one-third of the incorporated places represented. Coverage even of larger towns is also less predictable than in the case of Sanborn maps. Although very few places with an 1890 population of less than 1,000 were portrayed by panoramic views, numerous places with relatively substantial populations in 1890 were never portrayed, either, such as Sault Ste. Marie (population 5,760), Greenville (population 3,056), and Marine (population 3,268).[43]

As stated earlier, the micro-scale geography (i.e., spatial extent) of a particular city can be completely recreated using plat maps. This, once again, gives plat maps an edge as a research tool. Sanborn maps and panoramic views often do not capture the entire city or town. In particular, Sanborn maps tend to show a smaller area of a city or town than may actually have been developed at the time. Given the purpose of Sanborn maps, it is not surprising that their focus is on downtown business areas and more densely populated residential areas. Insurance companies (Sanborn's primary customers) had a greater need for accurate data for those areas. First, the business area tended to be the portion of town that had more mitigating factors that could have an impact on fire insurance premiums. Second, the cost of having a fire insurance map made for a city or town was dictated largely by the size of the area to be mapped. Therefore, strictly residential and low-density areas were often left off these maps. Panoramic views of smaller places often show the entire town. As with Sanborn maps, there is a commercial reason for this fact. It was easier to sell subscriptions for a view if more individual buildings were clearly visible. The problem of micro-scale coverage for panoramic views, however, becomes significant when dealing with larger places. As panoramic views were drawn from an oblique perspective with the representative scale decreasing as one looks toward the horizon, it was difficult or impossible to illustrate distant buildings with enough detail to make them recognizable.

Considering geographic coverage, therefore, plat maps represent the most reliable tool for recreating the extent of a historical city or town at both the micro and macro levels. At the macro level, because of their popularity, there is a very good chance that a Sanborn map would have been created for a particular city or town. Sanborn maps, however, often present less than the total area of an individual place. Far fewer panoramic views were created, so their macro-level coverage is sparser. For smaller places, the micro-level coverage of panoramic views can be quite good, but for larger places, space constraints typically prevented the artist from representing comprehensive detail.

Plat maps are unquestionably the best resource for tracing the succession of subdivision and land-ownership development in a particular place. The temporal coverage of plat maps can be thought of as continuous; there are no gaps in time. As individuals or municipalities decided to subdivide land parcels for development, plat maps were created. Reconstructing the sequence of development in this sense—but not that of the built environment—becomes a simple task of piecing together the plats by date. Although they do describe buildings, the temporal coverage of Sanborn maps and panoramic views is discontinuous; they can be considered snapshots in time. For example, both map forms might show a viewer what existed in 1884, but neither could elucidate the order of development that preceded that historical moment. Of course, it would be possible to compare the development that occurred from one Sanborn map or panoramic view to the next. Of the 339 Michigan towns mapped by the Sanborn Map Company, 296 were mapped in multiple years. Many of the cities and towns in Michigan were mapped more than seven times (for example, Cadillac was mapped in 1884, 1890, 1895, 1900, 1906, 1914, 1923, and 1950).[44] It may not be wise, however, to rely solely on Sanborn maps to document development. As stated earlier, not all development was portrayed on Sanborn maps because of their nature and cost. For example, it could be misleading to assume that development that was portrayed by the 1895 Cadillac map set but not the 1890 set must have been new development after 1890. The company could simply have mapped more of Cadillac in 1895 than in 1890.

Issues of scale can also mislead the unwary user. When creating a new map from existing maps, a fundamental rule of cartography is that one should work from larger to smaller scales.[45] The reason for this rule is simple: it is possible to throw detail away but not to add it. Therefore, when considering each map type, it is important to consider the scale at which the original documents were produced. If one is attempting to use all three map types to recreate the Mount Pleasant, Michigan, of 1884, then the scale of each map type should be comparable and large enough to incorporate necessary details.

Sanborn maps are the most consistent in scale. According to Ristow, Sanborn fire insurance maps were produced at a scale of 1:600 for larger cities and 1:1,200 for smaller ones.[46] Because a single company dominated the field of fire insurance mapping, map production was uniform, unlike plats or panoramic views. In the case of plats, the scale appears to vary depending on the size of the area being subdivided; for example, original Mount Pleasant plat, 1:1,584; Normal School addition, Mount Pleasant, 1:1,800; Bamber's addition, Mount Pleasant, 1:594.[47] This variation in scale need not present a significant problem to the researcher. Nonetheless, if one were piecing together a set of plat maps to recreate the Mount Pleasant that existed in 1884, it would be essential to recognize that the individual plats are not drawn at a common scale.

Panoramic views present the largest challenge in terms of scale. First, panoramic views tend to be slightly smaller-scale than plats or fire insurance maps. Foreground scales in the range of 1:3,000 to 1:4,000 are common. Maps with scales in this range would still be considered large-scale, but they are obviously smaller-scale than the other two map types. Of greater concern is the lack of internal consistency of scale within the panoramic views. The geographic size of the area being portrayed and the specific angle used in rendering a particular city appear to have had the greatest impact on scale variation. The foreground scales for panoramic views of the cities of Mount Pleasant, Lansing, and Detroit, respectively, are approximately 1:3,168, 1:3,600, and 1:3,600.[48] The scales for the same views toward the horizon, however, are approximately 1:3,461, 1:5,333, and 1:43,200, respectively. Detroit not only is the largest of the three cities but also is drawn from the lowest angle. The Detroit view exhibits a huge variation in scale such that very little detail can be discerned as one looks toward the horizon.

Directly related to scale is the issue of perspective. Plat maps and fire insurance maps are both drawn from an orthographic perspective; that is, the maps are created as if the observer were looking straight down on the area, and this perspective is maintained throughout the area of the map. Orthographic perspective's primary benefit is that it allows the mapmaker to maintain a consistent scale throughout the mapped area. Panoramic views were rendered from an oblique single perspective, as if looking down upon the city or town from a tall hilltop. The benefit of this perspective is that variations in the built environment and even the natural environment are easier to see. This may seem trivial, but it provides the viewer with significant benefits. Although both fire insurance maps and panoramic views portray buildings, it is only in the latter that the observer is able to see architectural differences and height differences and thus gain a greater understanding of a town's character. There are, however, problems: the scale is not consistent, large structures in the foreground will block smaller objects in the background, and it can be challenging to correlate the features in the perspective views with the same items in the orthographic plats and fire insurance maps.

Certainly, one of the most important factors to the researcher is the informational content of each map type. What can one find on plat maps, fire insurance maps, and panoramic views? Given the utilitarian nature of plat maps, it is not surprising that they are spare and to the point. Plat maps show divisions of land. Each new parcel is numbered, and a means of determining the dimension of the parcel is provided. Proposed street names are recorded, as well as the intended use of any special parcels, such as a courthouse or a high school. On some plat maps, small-scale inset maps are provided as a means of locating the map in a larger geographic context. To help put the plat map in both a historical and a geographic context, ancillary data are often provided. Geographically, the parcel to be subdivided is identified by name and by location. In Michigan, this generally means that the plat is identified by the name of the person or developer who is subdividing the land (e.g., Kinney addition) and by the parcel's identity as a specific portion of section x within township y. In addition to location information, the name of the surveyor, the dates that the plat was registered with the county and the state, and the scale of the original drawing are all recorded on a plat. In most cases, ownership data were not provided on original plat maps. This stands to reason, because the parcels could not be sold until the plat had been approved and registered. Counties and cities often add ownership data to plat maps after they have been registered, but this information was not part of the original plat.

Sanborn maps are also utilitarian in nature, but their use is very different from that of plat maps. Often, the base maps used for fire insurance maps were local plats, which insurance mappers then populated with the town's structures. Examination of a standard Sanborn map legend shows symbols for different building materials (concrete, wood, brick), types of fire protection (sprinklers, alarms, hydrants), the number of floors in a building, openings in walls (windows, doors), and land use (residential, manufacturing, commercial). In addition, the actual type of business is recorded for most commercial buildings, such as tannery, drugstore, church, hardware store. It is this final type of information that makes fire insurance maps so fascinating, as these records of specific activities carried on in particular structures allow researchers to recreate the business districts of nineteenth-century towns. No other single document makes this task so easy.

If fire insurance maps provide the substance of nineteenth-century towns, then panoramic views provide the feel of a particular place. Panoramic views portray the street scenes of towns in the late nineteenth and early twentieth centuries, complete with architecture, foliage, and street traffic. In many cases, there is little or no ancillary information; even street names are often absent. Because the artist was trying to capture the town's "look," panoramic views have the most varied content. Some views show street names; some views have elaborate legends that identify significant structures; some views provide enlarged illustrations of significant structures in the margin of the map; and some views include none of these features.

It is in the area of content that the benefit of viewing plats, fire insurance maps, and panoramic views as a group becomes evident. Each type of map provides researchers with part of the story. Plats provide a sequence of events, fire insurance maps provide an inventory of activities, and panoramic views provide the look and feel of a particular place in a particular time.

What was a place like? This qualitative question is often at the heart of research concerning historical places. Certainly, it is possible to tabulate quantitative data from all three map types. How many parcels were added to Muskegon in the 1890s? How many churches were in the downtown area of Marquette in 1892? How many styles of architecture were evident in Ypsilanti in 1865? The goal of a researcher, however, is often less concrete. What was the character of Ann Arbor in the 1880s? Was it a large city or a small town? Was it dominated by large industrial activities or smaller commercial businesses? Plat maps, unfortunately, do not add a great deal to our understanding of a particular place's character. They represent the land before it was built up. Granted, divisions of land are often made to facilitate a particular type of land use, such as residential or commercial, but future land use does not always follow suit.

Despite the utilitarian nature of Sanborn maps, it is possible to discern a great deal about the character of a town or city from examining them. The types of businesses, churches, and educational buildings these maps describe give an indication of the town's socioeconomic activities. The level of infrastructure (e.g., fire hydrants and water lines) tells researchers something about the place's prosperity and municipal administration. It is also possible to examine locational patterns, since groupings of businesses and residential areas are evident on fire insurance maps. The economic standing of particular neighborhoods might be inferred from the size of residential lots or the footprints of buildings, although a researcher should proceed with caution, because large size does not always translate into high value.

Panoramic views offer the greatest insight into the character of a town or city. Panoramic views were sold as attractive pieces of art that would capture the beauty and significance of a particular place. As such, great pains were taken to portray the details of the area. The architecture of prominent buildings was often shown in great detail. Trees and other vegetation that are absent from plats and fire insurance maps figure prominently in panoramic views. Bustling street scenes and industrial activities are also part of many views. If there is a concern about the portrayal of life in panoramic views, it is that artists overdid themselves to depict a thriving, active city. "Panoramic maps graphically depict the vibrant life of a city. Harbors are shown choked with ships, often to the extent of constituting hazards to navigation. Trains speed along railroad tracks, at times on the same roadbed with locomotives and cars headed in the opposite direction. People and horse-drawn carriages fill the street, and smoke belches from the stacks of industrial plants."[49] It is certainly possible that many panoramic views portrayed life more favorably than reality warranted.

How consistently do the preceding observations apply to each map type? Does a Sanborn map for Lansing in 1898 have the same look and feel as a Sanborn map for Grand Rapids in 1906? Obviously, they are different cities in different times, but are the data provided on each map equivalent? Of the three map types, the Sanborn fire insurance maps are the most consistent, which is not surprising given that a single company was responsible for their production. The Sanborn maps' consistency is one of their greatest assets. Once a researcher is familiar with their content and form, searching for similar information for a variety of cities on Sanborn maps becomes fairly simple. Next on the consistency continuum are plat maps. There is not a great deal of variation from one plat map to the next. As previously noted, there is some variation in scale, but the general content of the maps is consistent. When viewing plat maps over time, the most notable change is in relation to the surveying data that were recorded. Early plat maps provided a minimal amount of dimensional data. Modern plats provide extensive dimensional references for each parcel. As expected, the least consistent map type is the panoramic view. Variations in view angle, ancillary information, printing quality, artistic skills, and scale all affect the look of each view.

The large-scale depictions of cities and towns provided by plat maps, Sanborn fire insurance maps, and panoramic views represent an incredible resource for researchers interested in the historical development of places in Michigan. It seems reasonable that increased access to these maps through Internet sites will result in a rise in their use as research tools. Although each of these maps provides researchers with important clues about the history of places in Michigan, they must be examined with caution, as variations in coverage, scale, perspective, content, character, and consistency affect their usefulness for particular tasks. It is possible that these maps make their greatest contribution as a group. Despite variations in production methodology and purpose, these map types provide researchers with a more complete picture of the geography of towns and cities in the late nineteenth and early twentieth centuries.

NOTES

1. Walter W. Ristow, "U.S. Fire Insurance Maps, 1852–1968," *Surveying and Mapping* 30 (1970): 19–41. Fire insurance maps published by the Sanborn Map Company were produced at a scale of 1:600 (1 inch equals 50 feet) for large cities and 1:600 or 1:1,200 (1 inch equals 100 feet) for smaller towns.

2. Many large libraries have copies of the Library of Congress's collection of Sanborn maps on microfilm. The microfilm versions, however, are not in color, and the viewing area and quality are limited by the technology. The history and travel section of the Detroit Public Library holds the largest single collection of original Sanborn fire insurance maps in Michigan.

3. Http://sanborn.umi.com/.

4. Http://lcweb2.loc.gov/ammem/pmhtml/panhome.html.

5. Http://www.cis.state.mi.us/platmaps/sr_subs.asp.

6. Curtis M. Brown and Winfield H. Eldridge, *Evidence and Procedures for Boundary Location* (New York: John Wiley & Sons, 1962).

7. R. E. Davis et al., *Surveying: Theory and Practice,* 6th ed. (New York: McGraw-Hill, 1981).

8. Frank Emerson Clark, *A Treatise on the Law of Surveying and Boundaries,* 3d ed., ed. John S. Grimes (Indianapolis: Bobbs-Merrill, 1959).

9. Ibid.

10. Tom Huber, "A Location Guide to the General Land Office (GLO) Survey Plats," Springfield, Illinois State Library, http://www.lib.niu.edu/ipo/1999/il9904232.html.

11. Allan Wexler and Molly Braun, *Atlas of Westward Expansion* (New York: Facts on File, 1995).

12. Willis F. Dunbar and George S. May, *Michigan: A History of the Wolverine State,* 3d ed. (Grand Rapids, Mich.: W. B. Eerdmans, 1995), 155.

13. J. B. Johnson and Leonard S. Smith, *The Theory and Practice of Surveying* (New York: J. Wiley & Sons, 1914), 450–51.

14. Ibid., 812.

15. "Accuracies" refers to the positional accuracy of the surveyed locations with relation to established geodetic or planar coordinate systems. "Recordation" refers to an explicit description of when and where the plat was filed and by whom.

16. Http://www.cis.state.mi.us/platmaps/sr_subs.asp.

17. Walter. W. Ristow, *American Maps and Mapmakers: Commercial Cartography in the Nineteenth Century* (Detroit: Wayne State University Press, 1985), 260.

18. Henry R. Gall and William George Jordan, *One Hundred Years of Fire Insurance: Being a History of the Aetna Insurance Company, Hartford, Connecticut, 1819–1919* (Hartford, Conn.: Aetna Insurance Company, 1919), 98.

19. Walter W. Ristow, "United States Fire Insurance and Underwriters Maps, 1852–1968," *The Quarterly Journal of the Library of Congress* 26 (July 1969): 204.

20. Diane L. Oswald, *Fire Insurance Maps: Their History and Applications* (College Station, Tex.: Lacewing Press, 1997), 8.

21. Ristow, *American Maps and Mapmakers,* 247.

22. Oswald, *Fire Insurance Maps,* 24.

23. Ristow, *American Maps and Mapmakers,* 258.

24. Ibid, 238; Oswald, *Fire Insurance Maps,* 16.

25. Seymour Schwartz and Ralph E. Ehrenberg, *American Maps and Mapmakers* (New York: Harry N. Abrams, 1980), 279.

26. Ristow, *American Maps and Mapmakers,* 258; Ristow, "United States Fire Insurance and Underwriters Maps," 23.

27. Robert J. Hayward, *Fire Insurance Plans in the National Map Collection* (Ottawa: National Map Collection, 1977).

28. Ristow, *American Maps and Mapmakers,* 260; Oswald, *Fire Insurance Maps,* 23.

29. Oswald, *Fire Insurance Maps,* 35.

30. Ristow, *American Maps and Mapmakers,* 260.

31. John W. Reps, *Views and Viewmakers of Urban America: Lithographs of Towns and Cities in the United States and Canada, Notes on the Artists and Publishers, and a Union Catalog of Their Work, 1825–1925* (Columbia: University of Missouri Press, 1984), 8.

32. Ibid., 51–52.

33. Ibid., 8.

34. Ibid., 4.

35. Ibid., 159–217.

36. Ibid., 8.

37. Ibid.

38. Development in this instance refers only to the partitioning of land for future sale. Development as the "built" environment is not portrayed on plat maps.

39. *Fire Insurance Maps in the Library of Congress: Plans of North American Cities and Towns Produced by the Sanborn Map Company, A Checklist* (Washington, D.C.: Library of Congress, 1981).

40. Amos H. Hawley, *The Population of Michigan, 1840 to 1960: An Analysis of Growth, Distribution, and Composition* (Ann Arbor: University of Michigan Press, 1949), 96–111.

41. Checking the Library of Congress document against Amos Hawley's book reveals a total of twenty-five places that do not appear on the main listing for the Sanborn maps. Ten of those places, however, actually appear on maps under the heading of a larger place; e.g., Essexville appears on the 1912 Bay City map set.

42. Reps, *Views and Viewmakers*, 350–64.

43. Hawley, *Population of Michigan*. Sault Ste. Marie, Greenville, and Marine all had populations greater than one thousand in 1880.

44. *Fire Insurance Maps in the Library of Congress*, 278–305.

45. Arthur H. Robinson et al., *Elements of Cartography*, 6th ed. (New York: John Wiley and Sons, 1995), 426.

46. Ristow, "United States Fire Insurance and Underwriters Maps," 35.

47. Department of Labor and Economic Growth, State of Michigan, http://www.cis.state.mi.us/platmaps/sr_subs.asp. Plat maps of cities in the county plat books tended to be more uniform but also smaller in scale. For example, in the 1879 *County Plat Book* published by C. O. Titus, Mount Pleasant, Michigan, is rendered at a scale of 1:3,600.

48. *Mt. Pleasant, Michigan* (Boston: O. H. Bailey, 1884); A. Ruger, *Birds Eye View of the City of Lansing, Michigan 1866* (Chicago: Chicago Lithographing Co., 1866); *Birds Eye View—Showing about Three Miles Square—of the Central Portion of the City of Detroit, Michigan* (Detroit: Calvert Lithographing Co., 1889).

49. John R. Hébert and Patrick E. Dempsey, *Panoramic Maps of Cities in the United States and Canada: A Checklist of Maps in the Collections of the Library of Congress*, 2nd ed. (Washington, D.C.: Library of Congress, 1984), 4.

Tracing Euro-American Settlement Expansion in Southern Lower Michigan

Kenneth E. Lewis

DURING THE FIRST HALF OF THE NINETEENTH CENTURY, THOUSANDS OF EURO-American agricultural settlers immigrated to the southern portion of Michigan's Lower Peninsula, occupying the region and dramatically altering its appearance. These settlers transformed the aboriginal landscape as they established new farms and settlements and created an infrastructure of trade and communications capable of supporting an economy increasingly devoted to commercial production. The new landscape of Michigan reflected the nature of its colonization, a process that shaped the patterning of settlement and the distribution of population. Understanding why Michigan's colonization took the form it did demands that we ascertain the spatial history of its large-scale settlement.

One of the great shortcomings of past research is that it has produced no precise picture of population spread. Given the time during which these events occurred, it should be possible to base such an inquiry upon contemporary written documents and other graphic sources from the period. Certainly the evolution of Michigan's colonial landscape generated plentiful records that describe the placement of roads, rivers, and other features; identify the locations of pioneer land purchases; note the appearance and locations of nucleated settlements; plot the distribution of natural resources; and record the formation and growth of political subdivisions. Unfortunately, all of these records are silent regarding the actual arrangement of settlers on the land, and they provide no direct measure of population distribution on the frontier over time.

Although documentary sources do not permit us to observe the changing layout of settlement directly, they contain information that can serve as a basis for inferring this process. The written record can be employed to examine variables whose changing spatial distribution can help researchers discern the rate and direction of the state's settlement. These patterns can provide a historical basis for explaining how Michigan's landscape took on its present form and why its components developed the way they did. Tracing the distribution of pioneer settlement requires evidence capable of being presented in graphic form, and several types of data can be used to discover these patterns. Before examining the information contained in these sources, it is helpful to place them in historical perspective. What do we know about the course of agricultural colonization in antebellum Michigan and the variables that influenced this process?

The movement of agricultural settlers into southern lower Michigan was not an isolated or unprecedented event. It continued a process of expansion that began with the transplantation of European colonies to the eastern seaboard of North America. In the seventeenth century, France extended fur-trading activity in Canada westward along the St. Lawrence Valley, while British trade advanced inland from New York and New England. Participation in the trade drew Native peoples into political and economic alliances with European nations increasingly covetous of the resources of the American interior. The resulting competition precipitated the Iroquois wars that displaced aboriginal societies as far west as the Great Lakes and drew the British and the French into the region. By the early eighteenth century, France had established outposts along the Michigan shoreline, including a major post at Detroit, while the British had begun to move into the region via the Ohio Valley.

The scope of initial colonization in the Great Lakes affected the nature of the European presence in Michigan. The fur trade established exchange relationships that increased the economic dependency of Indian peoples and subjected their affairs to European influence, but the inability of any group to dominate encouraged an accommodation of one another's interests. Michigan became part of a "middle ground" in which the mutual dependence of the participating societies gave rise to interdependent arrangements that influenced the nature of the French and, later, the British presence in Michigan. European settlement remained confined to outposts on the region's periphery, a pattern that remained unchanged until the early nineteenth century, when the middle ground disappeared with the coming of the Americans to Michigan.[1]

The nature of British colonization on the eastern seaboard created a situation quite different from the middle ground. Instead of trade, a desire to resettle segments of its population became a principal incentive for British colonization. Waves of religious dissenters and those adversely affected by economic conditions began crossing the Atlantic, and by the mid-seventeenth century, British agricultural colonies occupied much of New England.[2] Colonies devoted to food production offered advantages over trading ventures in that they yielded a higher rate of return for a given amount of land and eliminated uncertainty over the control of production. Colonial agriculture justified the costs of gaining control over the land, and as the colonial population increased, British settlement soon expanded into the interior. In spite of attempts by the Crown to restrict growth, pioneer agriculture had reached and even extended beyond the Appalachian Mountains by 1770. American independence removed the political barriers to agricultural expansion, and by the close of the eighteenth century, American settlement had begun to encroach on the Great Lakes.[3]

The transfer of domain from Great Britain to the United States changed the nature of colonization in Michigan. Soon after the American Revolution, the United States began to consolidate its political authority over the Great Lakes. The Northwest Ordinance of 1787 created a mechanism for systematically occupying the region and incorporating its lands into the agricultural production base of the new nation. The first step in this process required that federal authorities extinguish native land claims through cessions. Between 1795 and 1836, the United States systematically acquired title to all Native lands in the Lower Peninsula by treaty. The location of these cessions and the order in which the federal government subsequently transferred the lands in them to immigrants influenced the shape of agricultural settlement in the region, but other factors helped determine the character of its occupation and how it would proceed. The order of settlement was not a foregone conclusion.[4]

In addition to the order in which land became available for Euro-American settlement, the immigrants' decisions about where to settle were affected by their perceptions of the new country, and these images helped shape the patterning of Michigan's colonization. With the end of the War of 1812, American agricultural colonization began in earnest. Although Americans were largely ignorant of the territory's interior in 1815, within a decade, they had acquired information sufficient to evaluate its potential for settlement. Assessing soil, vegetation, topography, wetness, and other characteristics they believed critical to establishing farms and growing crops, the newcomers ranked Michigan lands according to their relative suitability for agriculture. Pioneers chose lands selectively, and their choices affected the spread of settlement.[5]

The varied geography of Michigan's Lower Peninsula led settlers to recognize several environmental regions (fig. 1). The first area they encountered lay along the eastern shore bordering Lakes Erie and Huron and the Straits of Detroit. Here, low-lying, poorly drained shoreline lands discouraged settlement, and many pioneers avoided them in favor of higher land farther west. To the north, the wet pinelands of the Saginaw River drainage also presented a disheartening picture to prospective agricultural settlers. Settlement was further inhibited by reports of sickness among the unfortunate early settlers at Fort Saginaw and the proximity of numerous Saginaw-Chippewa reserves, whose inhabitants were perceived to be potentially hostile. In contrast, the drainages of the Kalamazoo and St. Joseph Rivers offered open landscapes of prairies and oak openings perceived to be fertile and easy to clear and inhabited by friendly Native peoples. Stretching across the western portion of the territory, these lands quickly attracted the attention of early settlers, whose favorable impression of their quality was reinforced by the amenability of the resident Potawatomis. In the center of the territory, the vast upper Grand River drainage presented a largely forested region of good soils but one that would require greater labor to put into agricultural production. Although the Thornapple Valley attracted colonists into the lower Grand River drainage from the south, the central timberlands deterred settlement. The resident Ottawas, like the Potawatomis to their south, were cooperative participants in the frontier economy, but they did not relinquish their lands north of the Grand River until 1836. The lateness of this cession, together with the effects of the economic depression of 1837, delayed northward expansion in southern Michigan. Farther west, initial unfavorable perceptions of the lands along the peninsula's Lake Michigan shore turned pioneer farmers away from this region. Only later did a better understanding of this distinctive environmental zone draw colonists there. Variations in Michigan's topography, soils, climate, and vegetation also helped Americans define the geographical boundaries of agriculture. In general, antebellum observers believed that farming could not be successfully practiced north of a line drawn westward from the southern tip of Saginaw Bay.[6]

Pioneer settlement in Michigan was not simply a matter of occupying the most desirable land in the order of its availability. The settlement strategies immigrants followed also influenced the distribution of newcomers on the land. Colonists coming to Michigan employed two broad approaches to establishing themselves in the new land. Most came as individuals or small groups and settled in "communities

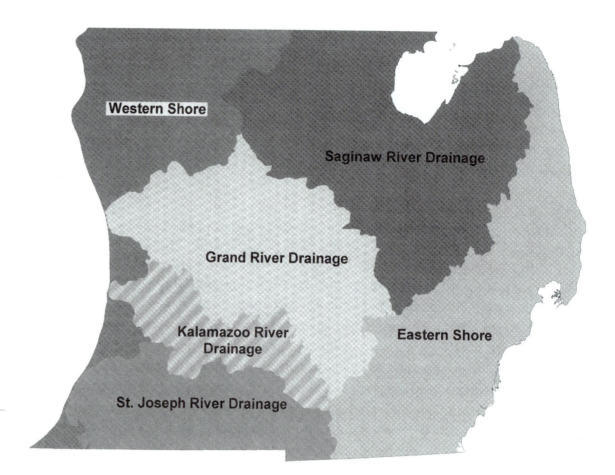

Figure 1. Perceived environmental regions in southern lower Michigan. Map by author.

of accretion." Here, in the absence of established social institutions, ties of kinship, religion, or common origin served to link these diverse frontier residents. Success depended on persistence and the difficulties of farm-making. Lack of support and perceptions of greater opportunity elsewhere caused many to move onward and resulted in a high rate of turnover among new residents. Those who made up communities of accretion generally based their selection of land on the quality of its resources, and the direction of their settlement reflected their perception of these variables.[7]

In contrast, "covenanted communities" provided more secure footholds for their members. Organized around a common set of rules or expectations that formed a basis for central institutions, covenanted communities provided the economic support and social benefits that ensured their members' success. The migration to Michigan included several large, formally organized communities of foreign immigrants bound by ties of ethnicity, language, and religion. In order to obtain contiguous space to accommodate all of their members, covenanted communities required substantial tracts. To obtain these, they often chose land bypassed by others and fostered successful colonization there. Large covenanted communities promoted late frontier settlement in the central timberlands of the upper Grand River drainage, the western shore, and the Saginaw River drainage.[8]

The variables that can be identified in historical narratives suggest some broad patterns that furnish a highly generalized description of the course of Michigan's antebellum colonization. These factors virtually ensured that settlement did not move uniformly across the Lower Peninsula. Prior to 1820, settlement had begun to spread inland from initial enclaves at Detroit and on the Lake Erie shoreline. Early in the following decade, immigrants swept rapidly across the peninsula as lands became available in the southwestern part of the territory. By 1830, they had occupied portions of the St. Joseph River and Kalamazoo River drainages and moved northward into the lower Grand Valley. Subsequent settlement began encroaching on the upper Grand River drainage, but substantial parts of this region remained unoccupied until the 1840s, when organized communities settled vacant lands there. By mid-century, similar covenanted communities also began successfully colonizing the lower Saginaw Valley and the western shore. In 1860, agricultural settlement remained confined largely to the area south of Saginaw Bay and the Thumb and did not progress northward until after the Civil War.[9] But how accurately do the patterns identified here predict the actual movement of settlement? Although the trends mentioned here describe the general sequence of settlement, they fail to provide the level of detail critical to estimate the intensity of activity and evaluate the economic importance of places people occupied. To obtain this kind of information, we must examine data that will give us a more precise picture of settlement spread during this critical period between 1815 and 1860.

The desirability of plotting the spread of frontier settlement in southern Michigan has long been recognized by scholars of the state's past. In order to document this phenomenon, they sought sources capable of providing direct, measurable evidence for the distribution of Michigan's population over time. The earliest attempts to examine the historical pattern and sequence of colonization employed a comparison of population figures derived from federal and state censuses. Researchers' analyses focused on counties, the smallest geographical units for which reliable and consistent numerical data were available. The appearance of counties and changes in the number of their inhabitants offered great promise for revealing the flow of settlement before 1860.[10]

County development shows that the colonial presence remained confined to Michigan Territory's eastern shore in 1820. In the following decade, administrative units expanded inland northward to Saginaw Bay and westward to the western shore (fig. 2). The most densely settled counties occupied the eastern portions of Michigan in 1830; however, the immense size of some early counties makes it difficult to estimate the actual spread of population. The 1830s witnessed a subdivision of counties that provides a somewhat clearer picture of settlement. During this time, a larger part of the southern portion of the peninsula appears to have been occupied, with the heaviest concentration of settlement still in the southeast. Counties on the western shore, the Grand River drainage, and the Saginaw River drainage remained poorly settled. A reduction in the size of several large early counties also reveals that the extent of American settlement was much more restricted than had heretofore been indicated (fig. 3). County formation in the 1840s and early 1850s implies marked growth in these regions and suggests that by 1854, settlement had advanced northward around Saginaw Bay and on the western shore as far north as the Straits of Mackinac (fig. 4). A general increase in county populations across southern lower Michigan signifies a filling in of less densely settled places as well as an intensification of agriculture in areas near developing urban centers.[11]

Although a comparison of county population figures provides a general picture of the spread of settlement and its changing density over time, reliance on counties as units of analysis limits our understanding in serious ways. Researchers can tabulate only the population residing within organized counties and must ignore the movement of settlement into unorganized territory. The state legislature created Michigan's counties in batches without regard to the actual extent of expansion or the degree of

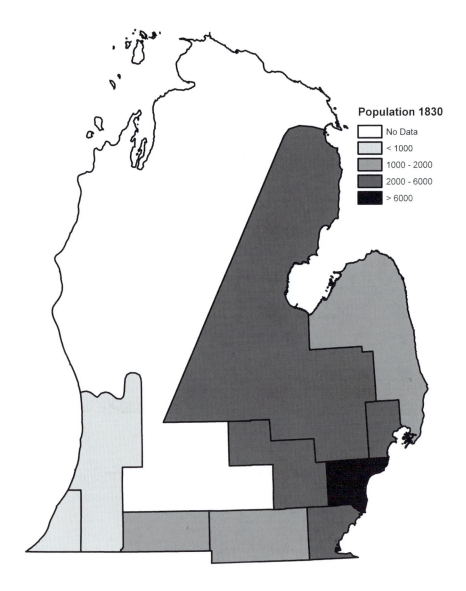

Figure 2 (left). Counties in lower Michigan in 1830.

Figure 3 (center). Counties in lower Michigan in 1840.

Figure 4 (right). Counties in lower Michigan in 1854. Maps by author.

development within each unit's boundaries. Well-settled counties were usually organized immediately, and their populations were recorded in the census returns. Poorly settled counties, on the other hand, were often administered by adjacent counties in complicated and changing arrangements that make it difficult to determine their populations accurately. As a result, county census figures are likely to reveal population distribution in areas of consolidated settlement while ignoring or obscuring the pattern of settlement on the outer edge of expansion. Furthermore, the large size of some counties masks internal variations that might be discernible using smaller units of analysis.[12]

The physical vastness of counties, their uneven size, and their varying size over time make it difficult to ascertain the distribution of population or measure its growth with any degree of accuracy. This is particularly true in areas experiencing rapid expansion, where county boundaries were extended to encompass large areas undergoing colonization. The extensive region administered by Ottawa County in 1854, for example, included not only the longer and more densely settled area around the mouth of the Grand River but also much of the newly opened western shore lands immediately to the north.

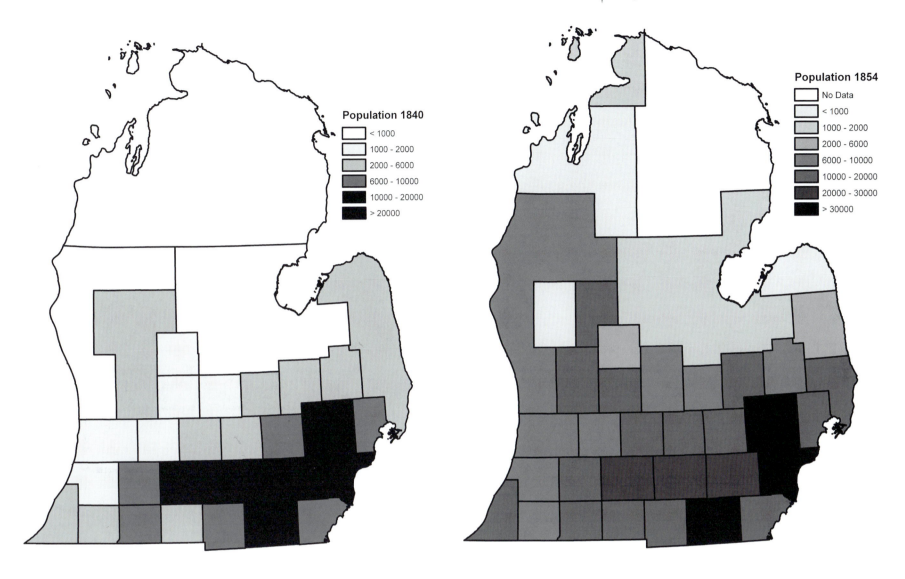

The county's geographical extent reveals nothing about the distribution of its residents or the nature of settlement spread within its extensive area. The inability of county population statistics to reveal the patterning of settlement over time makes it necessary to examine smaller units.

Observing the appearance and growth of townships seems to offer a more detailed picture of settlement density over time. Early in his career as a chronicler of Michigan's past, George N. Fuller recognized that the sequential appearance of townships might be used to measure the general direction and rate of pioneer settlement. Organized for the purpose of establishing local government, townships were founded to administer territories as they became settled. Although the boundaries of a township were laid out at the time it was surveyed, the township came into existence as an administrative unit only when its occupants required civil services. If this accompanied a certain population threshold, the order of township formation should be a measure of expansion over time.[13]

The use of township formation dates can be helpful in tracing population spread, but inconsistencies among these administrative units limit their ability to portray distribution accurately. Township

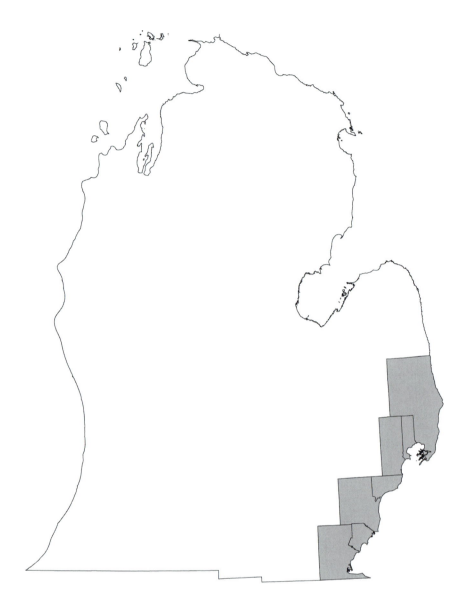

Figure 5 (left). Townships in lower Michigan in 1825.

Figure 6 (center). Townships in lower Michigan in 1832.

Figure 7 (right). Townships in lower Michigan in 1835. Maps by author.

creation usually preceded county organization and often involved the incorporation of large tracts of land, sometimes comprising entire counties.

The creation of township boundaries reveals the general trend and direction of settlement growth in antebellum Michigan.[14] Townships created in the decade following the War of 1812 were well suited to administer settlement that was largely confined to the areas along Lakes Erie and St. Clair and the intervening Detroit River (fig. 5). By 1827, the inland expansion of population prompted the Michigan legislature to authorize a general reorganization of townships to accommodate settlement growth.[15] The resulting restructuring of older boundaries and creation of new interior townships in Lenawee, Oakland, and Washtenaw Counties indicates the expansion of inland immigration as well as an increase in the density of populations around Detroit and Monroe. The early 1830s witnessed the appearance of townships in the southern tiers of counties and the subdivision of new townships, particularly in the lower St. Joseph and Saginaw Valleys (fig. 6). Notable gaps between townships imply that intervening

interior areas remained less densely occupied, as did the persistence of untypically large townships. Organized in 1830, Saginaw Township remained the administrative unit for a large area with a low population density.

The remainder of the decade saw an explosion of township creation across southern lower Michigan. By 1835, townships extended across the Lower Peninsula. In the southern two tiers of counties, all but one county contained multiple administrative units, and the older counties, especially those lying just inland from the eastern shore, were extensively subdivided. Large townships encompassed southern Ionia and Kent Counties and persisted in the Saginaw Valley and the Thumb (fig. 7), reflecting the beginnings of settlement in the forested lands of the lower Grand River Valley, where the land seemed less desirable and settlement was slow. As the 1830s drew to a close, most of the southern counties had been organized into smaller townships, including the newly established counties in the central timberlands along the upper Grand River drainage (fig. 8). Large townships remained in the counties along the

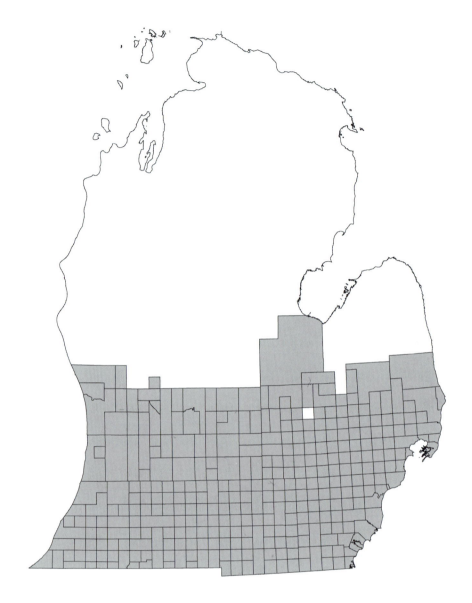

Figure 8 (left). Townships in lower Michigan in 1839.

Figure 9 (center). Townships in lower Michigan in 1850.

Figure 10 (right). Townships in lower Michigan in 1860. Maps by author.

western shore, in the Saginaw Valley, in the Thumb, and in the newly opened lands north of the Grand River. A number of larger townships also persisted along sparsely settled portions of the eastern shore. Despite that region's proximity to the point of entry for eastern immigrants, most pioneers apparently decided that better farmlands lay elsewhere and bypassed this wet, forested area.

The 1840s witnessed two trends in the development of Michigan's townships: a continued consolidation of townships in southern lower Michigan and a dramatic extension of administrative units northward. Township subdivision is most noticeable in the central timberlands and the lower Grand Valley. An increase in the number of townships in the lower Saginaw Valley and the western shore implies that population growth was not limited to more favorably perceived forests and open lands and that the colonization of environments previously seen as marginal had begun in earnest. The arrival of organized communities of immigrants provided the impetus for settling these disfavored lands. At the same time, the appearance of a number of large new townships anticipated expansion of settle-

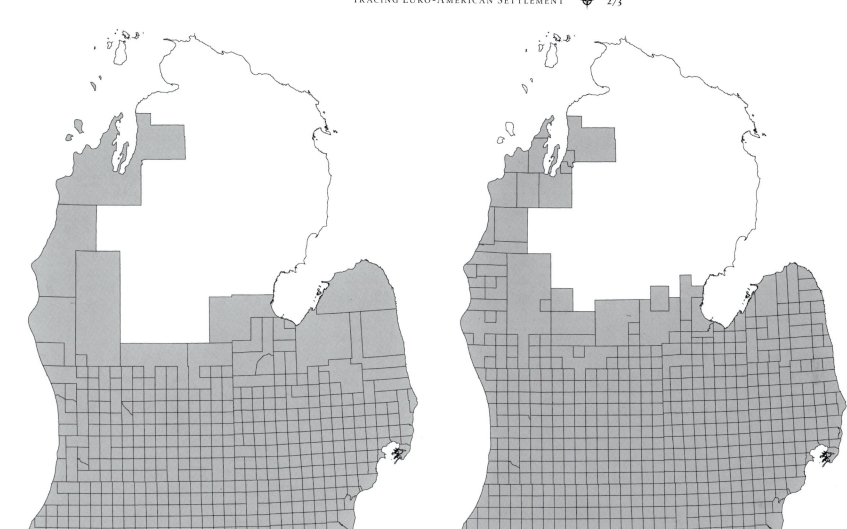

ment northward. By 1845, Tittabawassee Township included modern Gratiot, Midland, and a portion of Bay Counties, and Tuscola and Huron Townships included much of the Thumb region. The creation of Montcalm Township and Oceana Township on Lake Michigan's shore began the extension of political jurisdiction farther west, a trend that led to three more townships along Michigan's western shore as far north as Grand Traverse Bay by mid-century. The northern townships generally remained undivided during this decade, indicating that growth was slow in these newly settled areas (fig. 9).

During the closing years of the antebellum period, township formation trends of the previous decade continued. The subdivision of townships was nearly complete in the southern five rows of counties. In 1860, larger townships remained only in the more recently settled northern counties and those along the western shore. The emergence of new townships farther northward also accompanied the growth of commercial lumbering. An influx of settlers, presumably associated with covenanted communities, generated new townships in the Saginaw Valley and the Thumb. In the Thumb, townships quadrupled in number between 1850 and 1855 and more than doubled again in the next five years. But in 1860, the northern tier of counties remained unevenly settled. Several large townships between Saginaw Bay and the western shore organized the region that was perceived to be the northern limit for agriculture. The subdivision of larger townships along Lake Michigan attested to the growth of settlement there; however, their disproportionate size reflects an uneven distribution of population in a marginal area still undergoing colonization (fig. 10).

The sequence of township development in antebellum Michigan reveals a pattern of settlement spread similar to that indicated by county census data. Although townships lack census statistics, their organization implies a certain population threshold, and their subdivision suggests increasing density. The smaller scale of observation associated with township formation also gives us a much clearer picture of settlement patterning in Michigan. Despite these advantages, the formation of townships still affords only a general picture of initial population expansion. The varying sizes of initial townships make it difficult to measure and compare actual population densities among regions in Michigan. Large, often county-sized, townships frequently appeared at the edge of American settlement, followed by the creation of progressively smaller units as those areas became more thickly settled. Within such townships, the density of population was also likely to have varied considerably, making it difficult to ascertain population spread within their boundaries. Township boundaries based on arbitrary survey lines often left few clues with which to delimit actual settlement. To determine the patterning of immigrant settlement accurately, another source of information must be consulted.

How can researchers obtain a more reliable picture of settlement expansion? Tracking the movement of frontier settlement over time requires finding a set of markers that can be clearly linked to the placement of immigrant communities on the land. One of the best indicators of the presence of new settlers is the creation of post offices to serve their needs. The establishment of postal service by the federal government was central to integrating frontier regions into the social and economic fabric of the expanding United States. During the second quarter of the nineteenth century, the federal government worked actively to expand mail service and improve the efficiency of delivery. The result was a flexible postal system capable of growing rapidly as new areas were settled.[16]

The postal system played a key role in integrating society and the economy in antebellum America. Communication depended heavily on the mail. In addition to bringing individuals tidings from family and friends, the mail service offered agricultural and business enterprises vital communications and exchange services. Letters and printed matter carried news of politics, agricultural innovations, and marketing trends. Indeed, the marked increase in letters sent between 1800 and 1850 was largely a result of the growth in the use of the mail for conducting business affairs over long distances. The information and materials the mail carried linked the new country's settlements and maintained connections with older settled areas.[17] Accordingly, the federal government established offices in newly settled areas to handle mail prior to shipment and upon receipt.[18] Because they filled roles vital to the integration of frontier communities, post offices became central components of society in the newly colonized areas. The expansion of settlement and trade in the American West depended on the establishment of post offices, and their arrangement and placement reflected in turn the nature of the settlements they served.

The makeup of small-farm agricultural settlement determined the distribution of post offices in Michigan. This kind of colonization is a cumulative process, involving the occupation of an area by a growing permanent immigrant population that becomes progressively larger and denser over time. This brings about the eventual use of all suitable arable land and results in a settlement pattern characterized by a more or less even dispersal of households. Although the number of colonists may be substantial, the nature of small-farm agricultural production isolates individual households and requires institutions to integrate rural society and facilitate economic growth.[19] In antebellum America, post offices were established by the government to maintain regional communications and trade, and they became one of the most ubiquitous frontier institutions. The postmasters usually held respected positions in their communities and often played a central political role in these emerging areas. As key nodes in a growing network of information exchange, post offices became crucial elements in the occupation of new agricultural lands.[20]

The nature of mail service favored the central placement of post offices within areas of new settlement. Because mail in rural areas was not delivered to recipients directly, all incoming and outgoing mail had to pass through the post office, which was situated at a location convenient to the inhabitants of the areas it served. Rural post offices occupied space in stores, taverns, or the home of the local postmaster. In a time when most traffic was by foot or by animal-powered transportation, the radius of travel from such locations was limited and required that additional post offices be created or that older ones be moved to accommodate the expansion or changing geographical distribution of pioneer populations. Supported by a growing network of post roads that tied settlements together, post offices became the foci of rural communities.[21]

In southern lower Michigan, post offices proliferated as the expansion of agricultural settlement increased the density of the rural population. When immigrants arrived in new areas, access to postal service was one of their earliest concerns. Eager to maintain social and economic ties with correspondents in the East, pioneers petitioned their federal representatives for the creation of new mail routes. In response to these demands, the Post Office Department issued contracts to carry the mail and established post offices.[22] Early residents of Shiawassee County, for example, experienced considerable inconvenience in retrieving mail from the nearest post office, which was at Holly, in Oakland County. They petitioned for a closer site, which resulted in the creation of a more centrally located post office at Byron.[23] Similarly, Jackson County residents sought the regular delivery of mail from Ann Arbor and successfully petitioned for a post office at Jacksonburgh in 1830. Increasing business at the new county seat soon resulted in regular once-a-week delivery.[24] In the agricultural region of Michigan, frontier post offices usually occupied central locations that corresponded closely with the spread of the pioneer population they served.

In contrast to population patterns in the agricultural counties, settlement farther north centered around extractive industries such as lumbering and mining that tended to concentrate populations in a few settlements dispersed across wide areas. Social and administrative institutions congregated in a small number of regional foci, usually processing and transportation centers. In northern Michigan, this pattern dictated the placement of post offices. For example, when authorities established mail service to the forest industries along the vast Muskegon River drainage in 1837, they located one post office at Muskegon. This port at the river's mouth offered access to a wide region that depended on the river for commerce and communication. Although far removed from the timber camps and other settlements of the interior, the Muskegon post office sufficed to serve the scattered population tied closely to it.[25] Fewer post offices were opened in northern Michigan than in the south, and most were situated in ports along

Figure 11 (left). Post offices in lower Michigan in 1820.

Figure 12 (center). Post offices in lower Michigan in 1825.

Figure 13 (right). Post offices in lower Michigan in 1830. Maps by author.

the lakeshore or major rivers. The north region retained this distinctive pattern as long as extractive industries dominated settlement.

An examination of post office establishment and persistence should provide reliable and detailed evidence for the patterning of settlement in antebellum Michigan.[26] Fortunately, accurate lists of the opening dates of Michigan post offices and the periods of their operation, together with maps of their locations, are available in a recent volume titled *Michigan Postal History: The Post Offices, 1805–1986.*[27] This information has made it possible to construct accurate historical maps of the distribution of post offices over time. The earliest map reveals the arrangement of post offices immediately after interior lands in southern Michigan were opened to American settlement (fig. 11). In 1820, post offices were present only at Detroit and Monroe, implying that much of the immigrant population still remained concentrated around these two established areas of early settlement. The beginnings of expansion, however, are also evident. Two additional inland offices had opened shortly after the first interior lands were placed on the

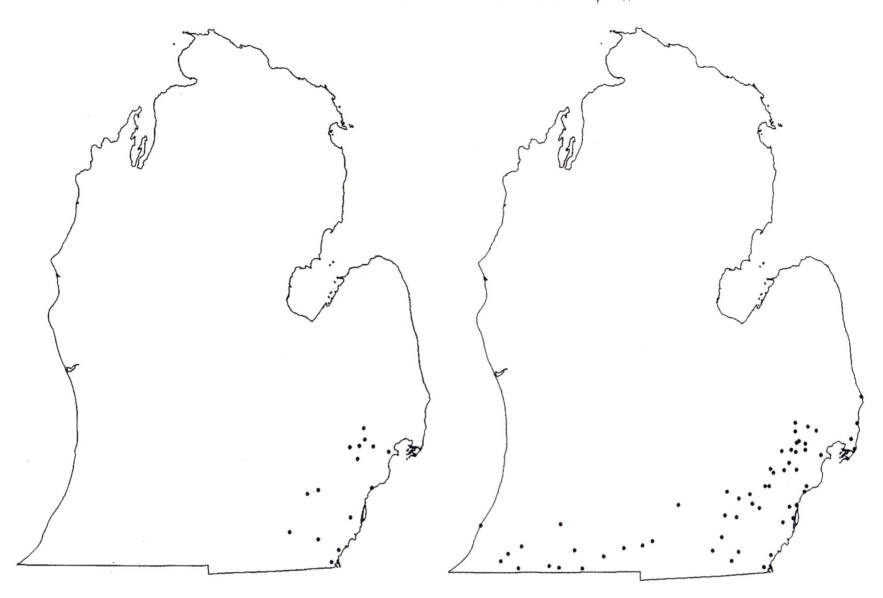

market. The post office at Flat Rock on the Huron River was the result of expansion along the eastern shore between Detroit and Monroe, while another office in Pontiac provides evidence for the early occupation of interior lands.

The spread of settlement into the interior during the following five years is apparent in the distribution of post offices in 1825 (fig. 12). It clearly shows a preference for lands beyond the low-lying eastern shore. In general, pioneer populations clustered in three areas: eastern Oakland and western Macomb Counties around Pontiac, the Ann Arbor vicinity, and western Monroe and eastern Lenawee Counties as far west as Tecumseh. New post offices in Macomb and Monroe Counties also indicate limited settlement along the lakeshore, although substantial portions of it still remained vacant.

The distribution of post offices in the last half of the 1820s reveals not only a consolidation of early inland settlement but also a dramatic expansion into the newly opened lands in southwestern Michigan (fig. 13). Much of the western expansion took place in the highly desirable open lands drained by the St.

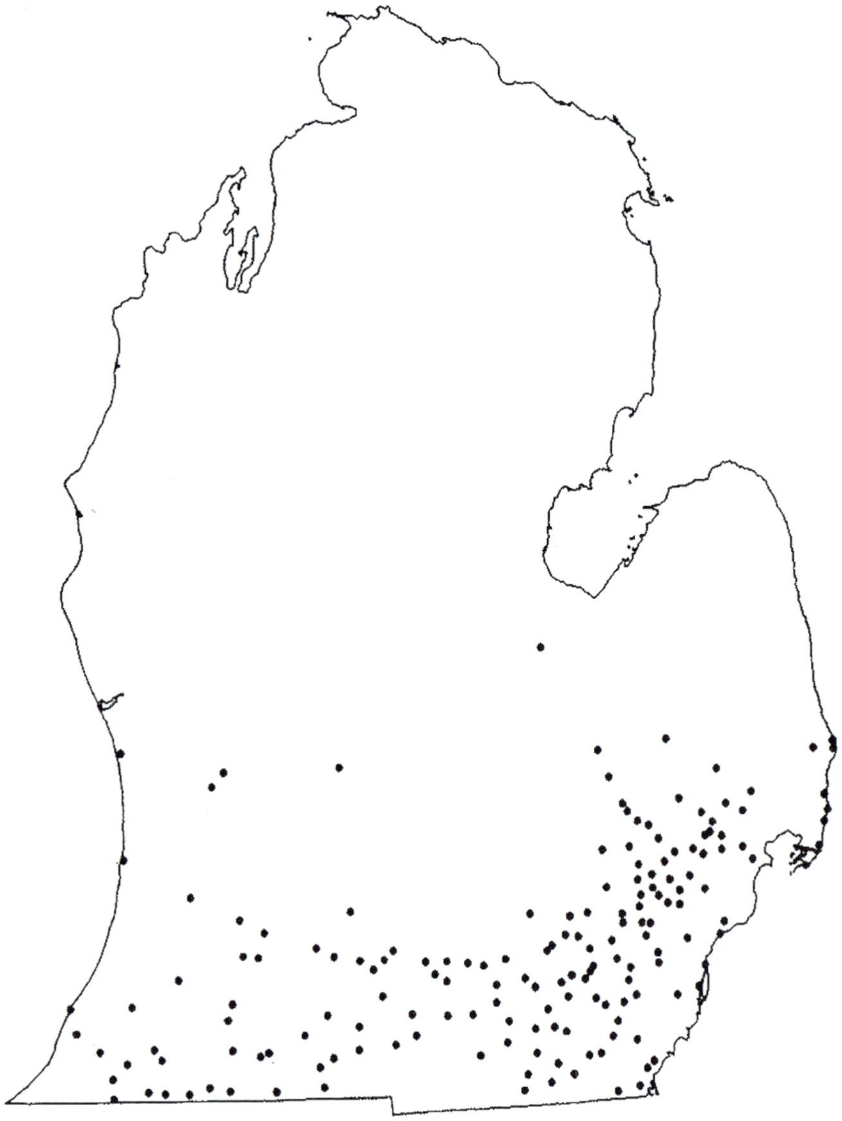

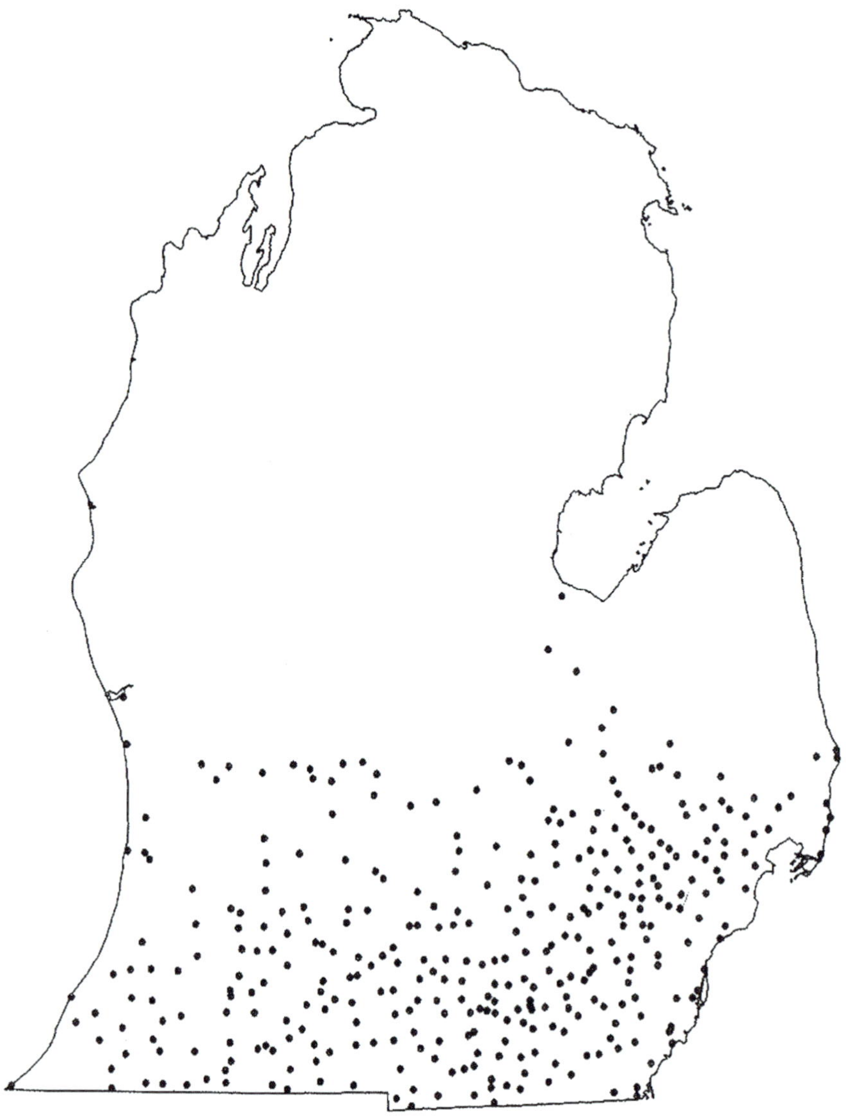

Figure 14 (left). Post offices in lower Michigan in 1835.

Figure 15 (right). Post offices in lower Michigan in 1840. Maps by author.

Joseph River, and settlements there tended to follow the course of the Chicago Road that provided access to them. Elsewhere, immigrants had not yet moved much farther inland, although increasing settlement density in Lenawee, Macomb, Oakland, and Washtenaw Counties indicates a continuous occupation across eastern Michigan. Despite the availability of lands in the Saginaw River drainage, intensive settlement had yet to penetrate this area; the post office at Grand Blanc marked the northward extent of settlement in the Saginaw River drainage at this time. The distribution of population shows a continued avoidance of the wet forests of the eastern lakeshore, where settlement remained concentrated near the mouths of major rivers. On the eve of the period of peak immigration, Michigan's population had only begun to venture into the region's interior.

This picture changed by 1835, as immigration spread across the southern interior (fig. 14). Post offices indicate expansion and settlement along the Territorial Road that led into the Kalamazoo River Valley and northward into the lower Grand River drainage. Postal facilities appeared at the Lake Michigan

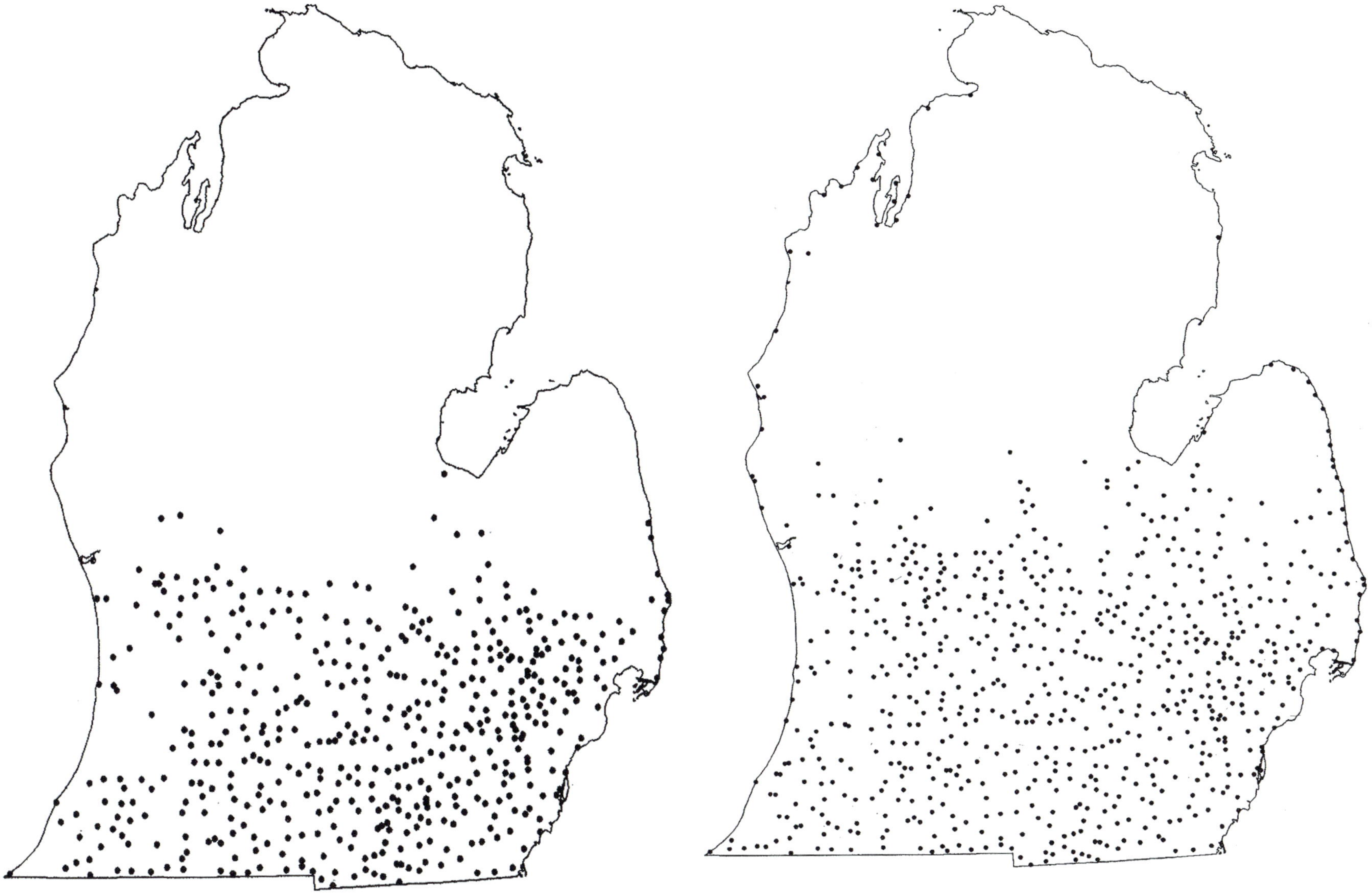

Figure 16 (left). Post offices in lower Michigan in 1845.

Figure 17 (right). Post offices in lower Michigan in 1860. Maps by author.

mouths of these two rivers in the early 1830s. Although settlement density increased broadly across the southern portion of the Lower Peninsula, settlers still avoided the central forested lands. In eastern Michigan, settlement grew more intensively north of Detroit and began to extend westward into Genesee, Lapeer, and Livingston Counties. A single isolated post office at Saginaw marked the beginnings of commercial lumbering in this region.

The late 1830s saw the height of Michigan's immigration boom and the acquisition of the last major tract of aboriginal territory. As the area of colonization expanded, new post offices appeared, and their locations signal noticeable changes in the distribution of population (fig. 15). These facilities show growth and a more even spacing of settlement in the eastern and southern counties, although portions of the eastern lakeshore still remained vacant. By 1840, settlement had moved north of the Kalamazoo River drainage, following the Thornapple River into the valley of the lower and middle Grand River. Although post offices were now concentrated along the Grand River in Ionia and Kent Counties, their absence farther north reveals that immigration had yet to expand into the newly acquired Ottawa lands. The number of post offices in the central timberlands increased as the area gained immigrant population from surrounding older settled areas. Scattered post offices along the Lake Michigan shore and the upper Saginaw River drainage attest to increased colonization there. The open lands that had attracted earlier pioneers were less available, and this undoubtedly led many settlers to occupy the forested regions; however, settlement on the western shore, in the Thumb, and in the lower Saginaw Valley was still deterred by perceptions that these were poor farming environments.

The area of American settlement in southern Michigan continued to expand over the next several decades. The extent of agricultural production grew more slowly during the 1840s as most new settlement filled in vacant portions of areas settled earlier (fig. 16). The trend toward more closely spaced post offices across the region indicates the increasingly dense pattern of rural population that accompanied the intensification of agriculture in an economy shifting toward export production. Expansion on the periphery of agricultural settlement occurred more gradually after 1845. In the north, the opening of post offices in Gratiot, Montcalm, and Muskegon Counties shows movement into the lands north of the Grand River, and the opening of additional offices in Genesee, Lapeer, Saginaw, Shiawassee, and Tuscola Counties indicates a similar growth in the Saginaw Valley. Farther north, scattered post offices along the Muskegon River in Newaygo County and along the Lake Huron shore in the Thumb reveal the beginning of industrial lumbering and other nonagricultural activities there.

In the last decade of the antebellum period, the distribution of post offices followed earlier trends (fig. 17). By 1860, northward expansion had brought the zone of agricultural settlement in lower Michigan to its perceived environmental limit. Farms now occupied southern Newaygo and Isabella Counties, encroached on Saginaw Bay, and advanced into the southern Thumb, particularly in St. Clair and Sanilac Counties. The 1850s also witnessed a continued movement by settlers into less densely populated portions of southern Michigan, including portions of the western shore and the lower Saginaw River drainage. Both areas received extensive immigration by well-organized ethnic communities. The creation of post offices attests to the substantial growth of the Dutch colonies in Ottawa and Allegan Counties and the large influx of German pioneers to the Franconian colonies in Saginaw and Tuscola Counties. Agricultural settlement expanded in the lower Kalamazoo River Valley, although portions of the western shore remained largely vacant. By the close of the 1850s, the extent and density of agricultural settlement formed a base for commercial production. Elsewhere, additional postal facilities affirmed the growth of nonagricultural activities in lower Michigan. Their appearance along the Lake Huron shore marked processing centers associated with the production of lumber, millstones, and other extractable resources. Similar settlements also spread northward along the Lake Michigan shore. Post offices on the Muskegon River accompanied the development of large-scale industrial lumbering, while those situated as far north as Little Traverse Bay also reflected a variety of activities. Although these areas still lay largely outside the zones of agricultural colonization in 1860, pioneer experiences here and in the Thumb began to alter perceptions of the environments of both regions and led to their eventual settlement as farming areas.

Changes in the distribution of Michigan post offices in 1860 also reveal the rise of commercial export centers in the state. Especially noticeable are concentrations in the vicinity of Adrian, Detroit, Grand Rapids, Kalamazoo, Pontiac, and other rapidly developing cities along the state's expanding rail network. Because growing settlement density usually accompanies more intensive agricultural land use, this change implies an alteration in the pattern of Michigan's production. Proximity to cities offered farmers important advantages, including substantial savings on shipping costs for farm produce and access to growing export and urban markets. Changes in the spatial organization of agriculture associated with this shift in southern Michigan's economy coincided with the close of colonization and the state's emergence as a component of the larger national economy.[28]

On the eve of the Civil War, the agricultural foundation of southern lower Michigan was nearly complete. The success of this development rested on the ability of immigrants to extend farm production across a substantial portion of the Lower Peninsula. In order to understand how colonization occurred and explain its changing form over time, I examined the distribution of population during this time using three sources of evidence: county population statistics, township formation, and post office establishment dates. Each source provided similar general information about the form and sequence of settlement spread. All three revealed initial colonization on the eastern shore, followed by sequential expansion immediately westward of Detroit and across the southern portion of the state, movement into the lower Grand Valley and into the central region, and later advancement across the Saginaw Valley, the western shore, and the lower Thumb. Although these observations are accurate, problems in using the first two sources have limited their usefulness in interpreting the form and sequence of settlement spread.

The key to examining the form of expansion is the ability to plot the appearance of settlement with great accuracy and recognize changes in its form as soon as they occur. In this regard, both county population statistics and township formation data have drawbacks. The size of counties limits the scale of analysis and makes it difficult to determine the distribution and density of population, especially in counties that temporarily encompassed large tracts of newly opened areas. The intervals between census enumerations also limit the number of points at which population levels can be observed. The sequence of township formation is somewhat more helpful. The arrangement of townships and how this pattern changed over time reveal the growth and spatial extent of political organization on a smaller scale but give few clues regarding the density of population or its distribution within a township's boundaries. Variation in township size further obscures these observations.

Mapping the appearance of post offices on the frontier avoids the pitfalls of the first two methods by addressing both the scale of observation and the problem of boundary recognition. Maps showing the locations of post offices as they opened provide a detailed picture of settlement spread in southern Michigan and clearly distinguish the portion of the state occupied by agricultural immigrants from that devoted to other purposes. Although a post office does not directly connote a given population, it does provide a relative measure of the population level and allows a comparison between areas. Thus, the pattern of post office locations indicates the recognition of relative densities of rural settlement. Post office locations also define the spatial extent of population movement. In short, by providing an accurate picture of the spread of colonization and its changing form, post office distributions help researchers discern initial expansion as well as subsequent intensification.

Initially served by a postal system that collected and circulated mail from central sites dispersed among the inhabitants of the countryside, antebellum immigrants to Michigan precipitated the creation of a postal network whose changing form reflects the developing patterning of settlement in this frontier region. The appearance and arrangement of post offices reveal settlement distributions produced by agricultural expansion and subsequent consolidation as the state's farmers became increasingly enmeshed in the national economy. The successful use of post office locations as a tool for examining settlement patterning in southern lower Michigan demonstrates its value as a source of information for investigating colonization in the United States, a process that occurred largely before the advent of rural free delivery in the late nineteenth century consolidated rural post offices and removed their operations to nucleated settlements. Only then did the distribution of post offices cease to mirror the pattern of American rural settlement.[29]

NOTES

This chapter benefited from the assistance of several individuals. LeRoy Barnett offered encouragement, and his expertise expedited the task of compiling the township maps. Mapping the distribution of Michigan's post offices would not have been possible without the statistical information compiled by David M. Ellis, who kindly gave me permission to use his data. Shaun M. Phillips produced the illustrations of the county and township maps, and Frank T. Krist created the post office maps. I would like to thank Margaret Holman, Carolyn Baker Lewis, Megan McCullen, and Keith Widder for their contributions to this research and acknowledge the assistance provided by the Peninsular State Philatelic Society and its members.

1. W. J. Eccles, *The Canadian Frontier, 1534–1760* (New York: Holt, Rinehart, and Winston, 1969), 19; Richard White, *The Middle Ground: Indians, Empires, and Republics in the Great Lakes Region, 1650–1815* (Cambridge: Cambridge University Press, 1991), x–xi, 51–53, 483–86; Helen Hornbeck Tanner, ed., *Atlas of Great Lakes Indian History* (Norman: University of Oklahoma Press, 1987), 29–37; David Beers Quinn, *England and the Discovery of America, 1481–1620* (New York: Knopf, 1974), 337–38.

2. Carl Bridenbaugh, *Vexed and Troubled Englishmen, 1590–1642* (New York: Oxford University Press, 1968), 396–97; Donald W. Meinig, *The Shaping of America: A Geographical Perspective on 500 Years of History,* vol. 1, *Atlantic America, 1492–1800* (New Haven: Yale University Press, 1993), 95–96.

3. James A. Henretta, *The Evolution of American Society, 1700–1815: An Interdisciplinary Analysis* (Lexington, Mass.: D. C. Heath, 1973), 8–11.

4. For a discussion of American territorial claims to the region, see Bernard W. Sheehan, "The Northwest Ordinance: An Annotated Text, Article the Third," in *The Northwest Ordinance, 1787: A Bicentennial Handbook,* ed. Robert M. Taylor, Jr. (Indianapolis: Indiana Historical Society, 1987), 62–63. For a history of federal land policy and the process of land transfer to immigrant settlers, see Roy M. Robbins, *Our Landed Heritage: The Public Domain, 1776–1970* (Lincoln: University of Nebraska Press, 1976), 5. Antebellum American Indian policy and its philosophical roots are discussed in Francis Paul Prucha, *The Great Father: The United States Government and the American Indians* (Lincoln: University of Nebraska Press, 1984), 64–77; and Bernard W. Sheehan, *Seeds of Extinction: Jeffersonian Philanthropy and the American Indian* (New York: W. W. Norton, 1974), 89–147. The cessions of Native lands in Michigan and the Great Lakes region are illustrated in Tanner, *Atlas,* 155–61; and Kenneth E. Lewis, *West to Far Michigan: Settling the Lower Peninsula, 1815–1860* (East Lansing: Michigan State University Press, 2002), 84–90. The order of land sales in Michigan has been presented graphically by LeRoy Barnett, "Mapping Michigan's First Land Sales," *Michigan Out-of-Doors* 53 (February 1999): 44–47; and Lewis, *West to Far Michigan,* 98–100.

5. George N. Fuller, *Michigan: A Centennial History of the State and Its People* (Chicago: Lewis Publishing, 1939), 1: 113–14; Lewis, *West to Far Michigan,* 51–54.

6. For discussions of Michigan's natural environment at the time of colonization, see Lawrence G. Brewer, Thomas W. Hodler,

and Henry A. Raup, "Presettlement Vegetation of Southwestern Michigan," *Michigan Botanist* 23 (October 1984): 153–56; Patrick J. Comer, Dennis A. Albert, and M. B. Austin, *Michigan's Native Landscape: As Interpreted from the General Land Office Surveys, 1816–1856* (Lansing: Michigan Natural Features Inventory, 1995); and Lewis, *West to Far Michigan*, 51–80. Discussions of Michigan's Native peoples and their impact on American immigration may be found in Margaret Mary Montfort, "Ethnic and Tribal Identity among the Saginaw Chippewa of Nineteenth-Century Michigan" (master's thesis, Michigan State University, 1990), 75–76; Margaret Wickens Pearce, "The Holes in the Grid: Reservation Surveys in Lower Michigan," *Michigan Historical Review* 30 (Fall 2004): 135–66; James A. Clifton, *The Pokagons, 1683–1983: Catholic Potawatomi Indians of the St. Joseph Valley* (Lanham, Md.: University Press of America, 1984), 17–19, 49; and James McClurken, "Ottawa Adaptive Strategies to Indian Removal," *Michigan Historical Review* 12 (Spring 1986): 36, 46–47.

7. For a discussion of community, see Conrad M. Arensburg, "The Community as Object and Sample," *American Anthropologist* 63 (1961): 248. For information on frontier communities of accretion, see John Mack Faragher, "Open-Country Community: Sugar Creek, Illinois, 1820–1850," in *The Countryside in the Age of Capitalist Transformation: Essays in the Social History of Rural America*, ed. Steven Hahn and Jonathan Prude (Chapel Hill: University of North Carolina Press, 1985), 236–37, 245–47; and Steven I. Thompson, *Pioneer Colonization: A Cross-Cultural View* (Reading, Mass.: Addison-Wesley, 1973), 8–9. Also see Lewis, *West to Far Michigan*, 133–41.

8. The concept of the covenanted community was introduced by Page Smith, *As a City upon a Hill: The Town in American History* (New York: Knopf, 1966), 17–21. For a discussion of these communities and their role in Michigan's settlement, see Lewis, *West to Far Michigan*, 141–49.

9. Lewis, *West to Far Michigan*, 179–84.

10. George J. Miller, "Some Geographic Influences in the Settlement of Michigan and in the Distribution of Its Population," *Bulletin of the American Geographical Society* 45 (May 1913): 321–48; Rolland H. Maybee, "Population Growth and Distribution in Lower Michigan: 1810–1940," *Papers of the Michigan Academy of Science and Letters* 31 (1945): 253–66.

11. *Fourth Census of the United States, 1820* (Washington, D.C.: Gales & Seaton, 1821); *Fifth Census, or, Enumeration of the Inhabitants of the United States, 1830* (Washington, D.C.: D. C. Green, 1832); *Sixth Census or Enumeration of the Inhabitants of the United States: As Corrected at the Department of State, in 1840* (New York: N. Ross, 1841); John T. Blois, *1838 Gazetteer of the State of Michigan* (1838; repr., Knightstown, Ind.: Bookmark, 1979), 151–52; *Census and Statistics of the State of Michigan, May 1854* (Lansing: G. W. Peck, 1854); *Census and Statistics of the State of Michigan, 1864* (Lansing: J. A. Kerr, 1865); "Michigan Map with Census Figures for 1840, 1845, and 1850," MS col. map 178 cm x 178 cm, no scale, n.d., State Archives of Michigan, Lansing.

12. For a discussion of the development of counties in Michigan and the difficulties involved in discerning the formation of unorganized counties, see William J. Hathaway, "County Organization in Michigan," *Michigan History* 2 (1918): 574–79. In southern lower Michigan, the first counties were organized in 1822. They included Wayne, Monroe, Macomb, Oakland, and St. Clair. The boundaries of Lapeer County were laid off the same year by proclamation. "Executive Acts of the State of Michigan, 1815–1822," in *Laws of the Territory of Michigan: Laws Adopted by the Governor and Judges, by Authority* (Lansing: W. S. George, 1871), 1: 323–36. The boundaries of Barry, Berrien, Branch, Calhoun, Cass, Eaton, Hillsdale, Ingham, Jackson, Kalamazoo, St. Joseph, Van Buren, and Washtenaw Counties were established seven years later by legislative act. Ibid., 2: 335–37. Those of Allegan, Clinton, Gratiot, Ionia, Isabella, Kent, Midland, Montcalm, Oceana, Ottawa, and Saginaw Counties were provided for in 1831, and Genesee County was set off four years later. Ibid., 3: 871–73, 1416–17. In 1840, the legislature redefined Oceana County's boundaries and established Huron, Mecosta, Newaygo, Sanilac, and Tuscola Counties. *Acts of the Legislature of the State of Michigan* (Lansing: W. S. George, 1840), 5: 119, 196–200.

13. George N. Fuller, "An Introduction to the Settlement of Southern Michigan from 1815 to 1835," *Historical Collections of the Michigan Pioneer and Historical Society* 38 (1912): 567, n. 158; Albert Baxter, *History of the City of Grand Rapids, Michigan* (New York: Munsell, 1891), 175–76.

14. Dates of township formation and boundary changes are based on information contained in Dennis E. Alward and Charles S. Pierce, comps., *Index to the Local and Special Acts of the State of Michigan, 1803 to 1927* (Lansing: Robert Smith, 1928).

15. *Laws of the Territory of Michigan,* 2: 479, 587.

16. The opening of western territories in the first half of the nineteenth century necessitated a dramatic expansion of postal service to incorporate these newly colonized lands. This growth involved both the creation of post roads linking western settlements and the establishment of post offices to extend mail service to their inhabitants. Between 1815 and 1828 alone, the number of western post offices increased nearly fivefold. The importance of the postal service was reflected in the elevation to cabinet-level status of the position of postmaster general in 1829. The following decades witnessed not only the continued growth of postal routes but also improvements in transportation of the mail. Organizational changes increased the efficiency of mail handling and the collection of revenues. D. D. T. Leech, *The Post Office Department of the United States of America* (1879; reprint, New York: Arno Press, 1976), 20–21; Wesley Everett Rich, *The History of the United States Post Office to the Year 1829* (Cambridge: Harvard University Press, 1924), 88–90.

17. Wayne E. Fuller, *The American Mail: Enlarger of the Common Life* (Chicago: University of Chicago Press, 1972), 88; Richard R. John, *Spreading the News: The American Postal System from Franklin to Morse* (Cambridge: Harvard University Press, 1995), 148.

18. Leech, *Post Office Department,* 19.

19. For a discussion of agricultural colonization as a process and its implications for settlement and the nature of pioneer economy and society, see Jerome O. Steffen, *Comparative Frontiers: A Proposal for Studying the American West* (Norman: University of Oklahoma Press, 1980), xvii–xviii, 23–24.

20. Ralph R. Tingley, "Postal Service in Michigan Territory," *Michigan History* 35 (1951): 447–60; Fuller, *American Mail,* 295.

21. The ubiquitous occurrence of post offices throughout the occupied portion of southern lower Michigan is indicated by their presence in nearly all of the settlements listed in Blois's *Gazetteer of the State of Michigan* (see note 11 above). Because access to older settled areas was crucial to maintaining post offices on the frontier, the establishment of a system of post roads accompanied the expansion of settlement. Furthermore, all railroads became post routes in 1838. The role of post roads in supporting the growth of colonial settlement in Michigan is discussed in Tingley, "Postal Service," 449–50, 456–57; and Fuller, *American Mail,* 86. For a map and chronological listing of post roads and routes authorized by federal legislation for Michigan, see Lewis, *West to Far Michigan,* 289, 429–34.

22. Fuller, *American Mail,* 45–46.

23. Franklin Ellis, *History of Shiawassee and Clinton Counties, Michigan* (Philadelphia: D. W. Ensign, 1880), 204.

24. *History of Jackson County, Michigan* (Chicago: Inter-State Publishing, 1881), 178.

25. Franklin Everett, *Memorials of the Grand River Valley* (1878; reprint, Grand Rapids, Mich.: Grand Rapids Historical Society, 1984), 448.

26. Several investigators have used the distribution of post office opening dates to plot the advance of agricultural settlement elsewhere in the United States. John A. Alwin, "Post Office Locations and the Historical Geographer: A Montana Example," *Professional Geographer* 26 (May 1974): 183–86; Morton B. Winsberg, "The Advance of Florida's Frontier as Determined from Post Office Openings," *Florida Historical Quarterly* 72 (October 1993): 189–99. The use of maps of post office locations to plot settlement spread in southern lower Michigan has also appeared in Lewis, *West to Far Michigan,* 186–93, 284.

27. The maps used in this analysis are based on statistical and graphic information contained in David M. Ellis, *Michigan Postal History: The Post Offices, 1805–1986* (Oak Grove, Ore.: The Depot, 1993). This book includes full listings of all Michigan post offices together with their locations and dates of operation.

28. Lewis, *West to Far Michigan,* 281–82, chapter 14; John Davis, "Transportation and American Settlement Patterns," in *The American Environment: Perceptions and Policies,* ed. J. Werford Watson and Timothy O'Riordan (New York: John Wiley & Sons, 1976), 174.

29. In 1896, the Post Office Department launched a limited experimental program to replace rural post offices with direct delivery to rural addresses. Its success prompted an avalanche of petitions that brought about the dramatic growth of the program. The number of routes steadily increased, and in 1902, rural free delivery became a permanent part of the postal service. Fuller, *American Mail*, 76–77. The expansion of rural free delivery displaced many rural post offices in Michigan at the close of the nineteenth century. In Gratiot County, for example, nine small hamlets lost their post offices, and at least twice that many rural post offices had closed by 1913. All of these offices' rural patrons were served directly from larger settlements. Willard D. Tucker, *Gratiot County, Michigan: Historical, Biographical, Statistical* (Saginaw, Mich.: Seeman and Peters, 1913), 1198–1205.

The Shifting Agendas of Midwestern Official State Highway Maps

James R. Akerman and Daniel Block

NOWHERE ARE THE MOTIVES FOR MAPPING MORE TRANSPARENT THAN IN THE HIStory of automobile highway cartography. Beginning in the mid-1910s, oil companies pioneered the practice of giving away maps to their customers as premiums, hoping that motorists would reward the company's generosity with regular patronage. By the early 1930s, oil-company cartography had evolved into a sophisticated advertising medium. Company logos were freely splashed about the maps and on their covers, while the accompanying text promoted specific products and services available at rapidly growing chains of service stations. Oil companies worked with their cartographic partners, chiefly Rand McNally, H. M. Gousha, and the General Drafting Company, to establish travel bureaus that distributed maps, literature, and advice to customers. They added information about points of interest to their maps, suggested itineraries, and included colorful cover illustrations of representative landscapes or well-known sites and landmarks—all in the interest of encouraging gasoline consumption and the growth of their customer base.[1] From a social and economic perspective, the complimentary oil-company road map was an entirely new kind of map—high in quality yet free to consumers because it was underwritten by its promotional value.

The success of oil-company maps has been well documented, but relatively little has been written about their cousins, the official state highway maps given away by state government agencies.[2] Denis Wood's brilliant deconstruction of the 1978–79 official North Carolina highway map in *The Power of Maps* reveals that the publication of official state highway maps is often deeply concerned with promoting state interests.[3] In much the same way that free oil-company maps were intended to reinforce corporate identities, inspire loyalty, and promote consumption, official state highway maps asserted the authority of state governments over road making and road travel within their territories, inspired the loyalty of their citizens, and persuaded noncitizens to visit and spend money.

In this chapter, we examine the evolution of the official state highway maps published in seven midwestern states: the six states west of Pennsylvania that border the Great Lakes and Iowa.[4] These maps were published and distributed primarily by state highway departments or commissions until the 1970s, when most states merged their highway agencies into unified departments of transportation. In some states, departments of conservation or natural resources, which administered state parks, forests, and recreational areas, contributed to these maps or produced their own maps. We have examined some early examples of these. However, we have generally excluded from our survey maps and cartographic publications of state departments of tourism, which in the past four decades have played a major role in the distribution of highway and travel information to tourists.[5] Although we acknowledge that the promotion of tourism has been a major factor in state highway mapping in the Midwest since the 1920s, our goal has been to clarify how this motive for mapping has competed with other agendas and practices within the confines of the somewhat narrower genre of maps issued by state highway departments.

Indeed, a recurrent theme in this chapter is the apparent tug-of-war between two broad promotional agendas during the roughly eighty years of official state highway map publication in the Midwest. The first of these agendas was the promotion of the geographical identity of the state. Targeted generally at tourists, this agenda drew upon the state's history, culture, economy, climate, topography, and geographical situation to form easily digestible images intended to stimulate motoring activity in the state. The second agenda was the promotion of the state government itself as a competent, active, and responsible force serving the needs of both state residents and visitors. Though they were closely intertwined in practice, we distinguish between these two approaches because they provide a useful framework for interpreting chronological and geographical patterns. What makes the development of the official state highway map in the Midwest most compelling is the way it reflects changing attitudes toward automobiles and highways, the role of state government in daily life, salient national events, and the Midwest's self-image.

The very idea of a state highway system is a product of the automobile era. When the first automobiles hit American roads in the late 1890s, responsibility for the construction and maintenance of streets and highways rested almost entirely on local governments. Streets were passable to cars in most urban areas, but rural roads, while suitable for horse and wagon traffic, were generally hostile to automobiles. No state could be said to have had a "system" of highways; the first state highway agency, the New Jersey Commission of Public Roads, was not established until 1894. But as automobile ownership increased, it became clear that government at both the state and federal levels would have to intervene to foster road improvements. In 1916, Congress finally passed the first federal aid road act. Though modest in scope—it allocated only $75 million among the states over five years to support the construction of roads chosen by the states—the law required states to pass their own road-aid laws establishing agencies to receive these federal funds.[6]

Like good automobile roads, published road maps developed specifically for motorists were uncommon until the second decade of the twentieth century. Maps claiming to be automobile road maps were often slightly modified versions of earlier maps made for stage or bicycle travel. Most motorists relied more heavily on route books that gave written directions and were published by motor clubs. Signs indicating routes between cities and towns were either nonexistent or placed informally on an

Figure 1. Detail of *State Highway System of Indiana* (Indianapolis: Indiana State Highway Commission, 1925). Courtesy of the Rand McNally Collection, The Newberry Library, Chicago.

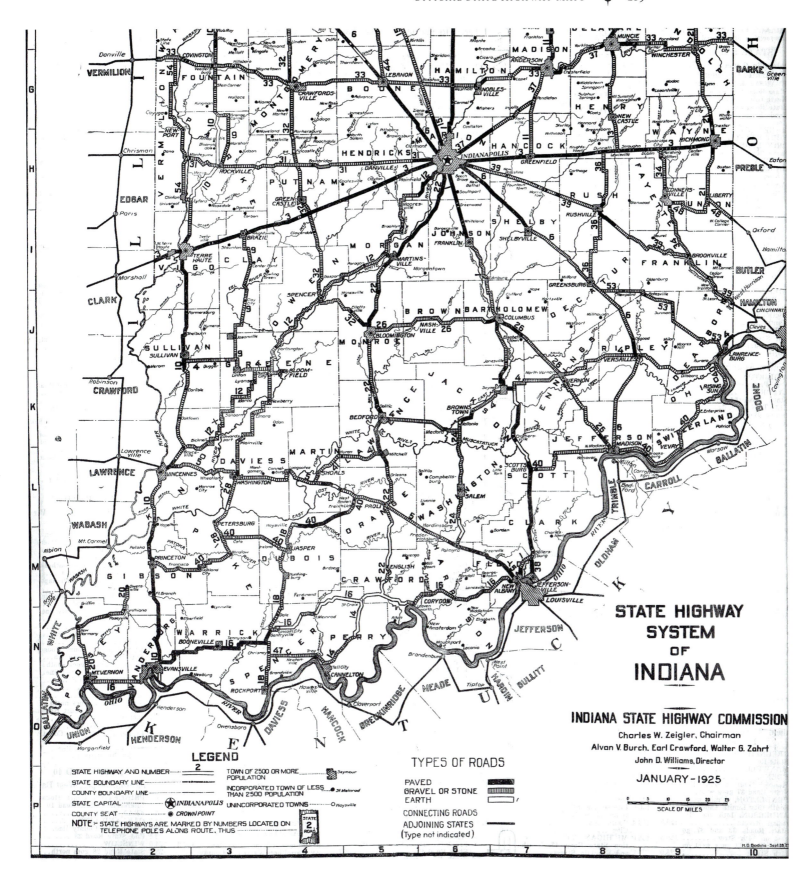

STATE HIGHWAY
SYSTEM
OF
INDIANA

INDIANA STATE HIGHWAY COMMISSION

Charles W. Zeigler, Chairman

Alvan V. Burch, Earl Crawford, Walter G. Zahrt

John D. Williams, Director

JANUARY - 1925

LEGEND

STATE HIGHWAY AND NUMBER········· 2
STATE BOUNDARY LINE···············
COUNTY BOUNDARY LINE·············
STATE CAPITAL·········· INDIANAPOLIS
COUNTY SEAT··········· Crown Point
NOTE - STATE HIGHWAYS ARE MARKED BY NUMBERS LOCATED ON
TELEPHONE POLES ALONG ROUTE, THUS

TOWN OF 2500 OR MORE
POPULATION ······· Seymour
INCORPORATED TOWN OF LESS
THAN 2500 POPULATION ···· St Meinrod
UNINCORPORATED TOWNS ···· Hoysville

STATE
2
ROAD

TYPES OF ROADS

PAVED
GRAVEL OR STONE
EARTH

CONNECTING ROADS
ADJOINING STATES
(Type not indicated)

SCALE OF MILES

ad hoc basis by local automobile clubs, by highway associations promoting specific routes such as the Lincoln Highway, or by private firms such as B. F. Goodrich as a promotional tool.[7] State involvement in route marking did not begin until states developed a system of trunk routes, an innovation that was eventually required by the Federal Aid Highway Act of 1921. Wisconsin was the first state actually to mark its roads with route numbers, in 1918, and by 1922, every midwestern state had followed suit.

The earliest official state highway maps were often cheaply printed documents that circulated internally among state highway authorities, engineers, and state legislators as parts of annual reports. These reports and maps laid out proposals for highway systems or documented progress on highway construction. Most of the seven states in our sample began to circulate versions of these internal maps publicly during the late 1910s or early 1920s. Michigan's Department of Transportation, for example, asserts that its first state highway map was published in 1919. Initially, these were revised every two weeks and sold for twenty-four cents. A free version of the map did not appear until 1928.[8]

These earliest publicly distributed official state highway maps bear the unmistakable influence of the internal reporting documents that spawned them. The 1925 Indiana edition is typical (fig. 1). Printed in a single color and issued without a cover, the map is simple in design, showing only the designated "state roads" and connecting roads in adjacent states against a background of cities and towns, county boundaries, and hydrography. It does not provide any explicit promotional information for tourists. An index of cities and towns occupies the left and bottom margins of the map. The right margin and all of the back of the map are devoted to logs of the various state roads, much in the manner of a railroad timetable, listing their termini, significant towns along the route, and the miles traveled to each town from either terminus.[9]

Because they were generally the product of state highway authorities, throughout their history, official state highway maps paid considerable attention to the character and quality of their highways; but this was especially true during the 1920s and early 1930s, when these authorities were busily overseeing the first paving of their road systems. The legend on Ohio's map from 1925 identifies five symbols for roads, ranging from "excellent condition—hard surfaced roads" to "poor condition—earth and badly worn gravel or stone."[10] The classification system used in Wisconsin maps of the late 1920s and early 1930s was similar; it recognized five surface grades for state and federal trunk highways and three grades for county highways. These were described in unusually chatty terms. The best state roads were "hard roads, surfaced with Portland cement concrete or bituminous surfacings; mudless, dustless and passable at all seasons." Next came "semi-hard roads, surfaced with crushed stone, gravel, etc., reasonably passable at all seasons but dusty when dry"; "all weather earth roads, normally good despite rains"; "heavy clay earth roads, slippery after rains and traveled with difficulty after prolonged wet spells and during spring break up"; and, finally, "sandy roads, traveled with difficulty during prolonged dry spells."[11]

Several midwestern states viewed the publication of the state highway map as an opportunity to brag about their diligence and energy in constructing highways. In Iowa, road improvement was particularly critical because the rich dark soil of Iowa turned into deep mud when wet. In 1931, even though an approximately two-hundred-fifty-square-mile area in the northwest quadrant of the state still had no paved roads, the designers of the state's official highway map felt compelled to declare that "Iowa Has Stepped Out of the Mud!" Text along the bottom of the map quantified the miles of pavement and gravel roads completed to date and the funds expended to achieve this. Such rhetoric was likely aimed at state residents as much as out-of-state travelers. Improved roads were considered essential to the improvement of rural lives, in terms of both bringing out harvested crops and bringing in American culture and products. Still, another caption on the map assured travelers that they could "plan [a] trip into and across Iowa with every assurance of keeping [their] schedule by the hour."[12] In the early 1930s, the Illinois Department of Public Works and Buildings, Division of Highways, also tracked the progress of highway construction on its publicly distributed maps. The 1930 edition included a chart showing road mileage financed by bond issues or state or federal aid from 1914 through 1929, plus tables breaking down the "total pavement available to traffic on January 1, 1930" and the additional miles under contract.[13]

Every state viewed the publication of an official highway map as an occasion for educating the motoring public about its system of highway markings, license fees, and traffic laws. This was particularly important in the early and mid-1920s, when there was relatively little coordination among the states in these areas and motorists were still unfamiliar with the emerging route systems. In 1923, the first year in which Ohio's state system was numbered, the designers of the state map felt obliged to inform their readers that the "numbers on this map correspond with the standard markers erected on each route."[14] Illustrations of the new markers were provided in the map's lower left corner. A reminder to "follow the numbers" remained on Ohio's official maps until 1937. In Indiana, as in Ohio, these features made modest intrusions into the margins of the main map. The left margin of the 1934 Indiana map, for example, depicted and briefly described the U.S. and Indiana state highway markers, a "night-sign . . . that serves . . . to prevent traffic from going over a steep bank," railroad crossing markers, and stop, curve, and school zone warning signs.[15] Large graphic explanations of traffic signs were also prominent features of Michigan and Wisconsin maps well into the 1930s.

Some of the driest prose ever written made its way onto midwestern official highway maps in the late 1920s and 1930s to explain state vehicle regulations, traffic laws, and rules of the road. The Automobile Department of the Illinois Secretary of State's office devoted large sections of the backs of its maps to a synopsis of all forty-six sections of the state's motor vehicle law. For example, one learns that an "application for [a] license must be accompanied by photographs of the applicant and statements of persons knowing him, showing that the applicant is a proper person to receive [the] license."[16] The single seven-by-four-inch panel devoted to "Important Motor Vehicle Laws of Wisconsin" on the 1933 Wisconsin map is perhaps more typical. Along with an explanation of passing and parking restrictions on state highways, it reminds motorists that "it is unlawful for any person to drive in a reckless manner or at such speed as to endanger the lives or property of others."[17] Later in the 1930s, Wisconsin maps added a feature informing motorists what to do in case of an accident, reminding them of their obligation to submit written reports of accidents involving injuries, deaths, or substantial property damage to the State Highway Commission's Safety Department. Similar features of this nature are found during this period on Indiana, Michigan, and Ohio maps. This early emphasis on state regulations, traffic rules and signs, and public safety reminds us that driving itself was still a relatively new phenomenon. Collectively, the motoring public was inexperienced, and the motoring environment of paved roads, highway numbers, and signs was still sorting itself out. The instructional features of early official state maps were no doubt useful to motorists, particularly as they traveled from state to state. Yet the presence of these features on early official maps may have had less to do with consumer demand for this information than with state officials' desire to assert their authority over motoring in their state.

Several other common features of early midwestern official state highway maps support this assertion. Emblems of state authority, such as state seals and images of state buildings, were prominent

Figure 2. Front cover illustrations: *1953 Wisconsin Highway Map* (Madison: Wisconsin State Highway Commission, 1953); *1937 Official State Highway Map Indiana* (Indianapolis: Indiana State Highway Commission, 1937). Private collection.

features on maps produced by several midwestern states during this period (fig. 2). From 1930 to 1935, the cover illustrations for the Wisconsin state map consisted entirely of the state seal; the same was true of Indiana from 1931 to 1936 and Ohio in 1928 to 1931. State seals also appeared on the covers of Illinois's two official state highway maps and were embedded in the pictorial covers Michigan adopted. The state capitol building achieved similar prominence in some states during the later 1930s and lasted through the early 1950s, appearing on Illinois's Secretary of State maps from 1946 through 1952, Indiana maps in 1937 to 1938, and Wisconsin maps in the years 1945 to 1947, 1949 to 1950, and 1952 to 1953. The names of governors, highway commissioners, and other state officials also appeared on map covers and as parts of map titles. Messages to map readers signed by the governor, often accompanied by his or her portrait

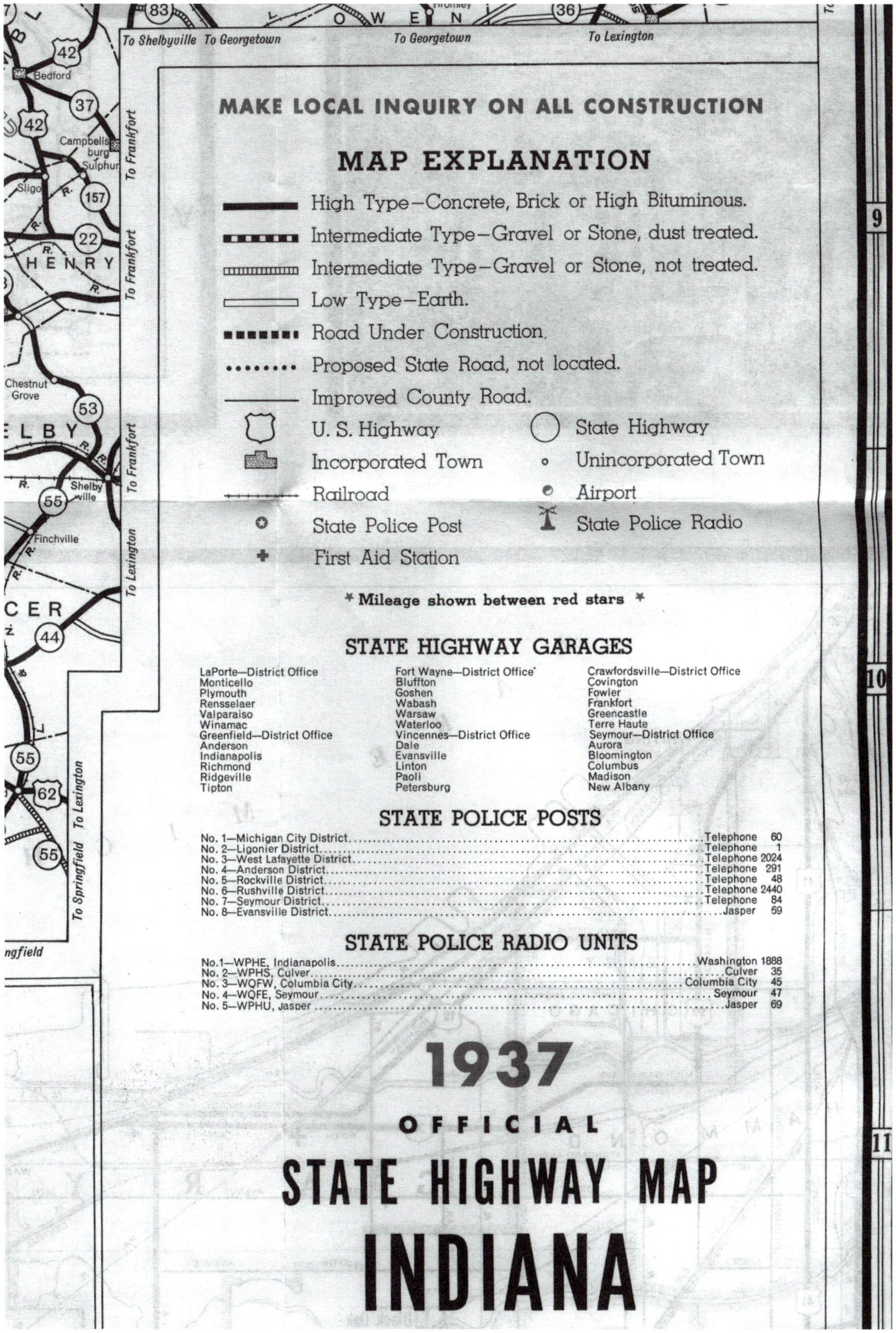

To Shelbyville To Georgetown   To Georgetown   To Lexington

MAKE LOCAL INQUIRY ON ALL CONSTRUCTION

MAP EXPLANATION

──────── High Type—Concrete, Brick or High Bituminous.

▪▪▪▪▪ Intermediate Type—Gravel or Stone, dust treated.

▥▥▥▥▥ Intermediate Type—Gravel or Stone, not treated.

▭▭▭▭ Low Type—Earth.

▪ ▪ ▪ ▪ Road Under Construction.

• • • • • Proposed State Road, not located.

──────── Improved County Road.

⬡ U. S. Highway   ◯ State Highway

▬ Incorporated Town   ∘ Unincorporated Town

┼┼┼┼ Railroad   ⊙ Airport

⊕ State Police Post   ⊥ State Police Radio

✚ First Aid Station

* Mileage shown between red stars *

STATE HIGHWAY GARAGES

LaPorte—District Office	Fort Wayne—District Office	Crawfordsville—District Office
Monticello	Bluffton	Covington
Plymouth	Goshen	Fowler
Rensselaer	Wabash	Frankfort
Valparaiso	Warsaw	Greencastle
Winamac	Waterloo	Terre Haute
Greenfield—District Office	Vincennes—District Office	Seymour—District Office
Anderson	Dale	Aurora
Indianapolis	Evansville	Bloomington
Richmond	Linton	Columbus
Ridgeville	Paoli	Madison
Tipton	Petersburg	New Albany

STATE POLICE POSTS

No. 1—Michigan City District	Telephone	60
No. 2—Ligonier District	Telephone	1
No. 3—West Lafayette District	Telephone	2024
No. 4—Anderson District	Telephone	291
No. 5—Rockville District	Telephone	48
No. 6—Rushville District	Telephone	2440
No. 7—Seymour District	Telephone	84
No. 8—Evansville District	Jasper	59

STATE POLICE RADIO UNITS

No.1—WPHE, Indianapolis	Washington	1888
No. 2—WPHS, Culver	Culver	35
No. 3—WQFW, Columbia City	Columbia City	45
No. 4—WQFE, Seymour	Seymour	47
No. 5—WPHU, Jasper	Jasper	69

1937
OFFICIAL
STATE HIGHWAY MAP
INDIANA

Figure 3. Detail of *1937 Indiana Official State Highway Map* (Indianapolis: Indiana State Highway Commission, 1937). Courtesy of the Rand McNally Collection, The Newberry Library, Chicago.

(sometimes with a spouse), are common features of official highways maps from virtually every state in every era.

The cult of official personality in Illinois is notoriously prominent, and this fact is reflected in the publication of two rival official state highway maps from the late 1920s to 1952. The editions published by the Division of Highways' Department of Public Works were signed by the governor. The name of the secretary of state, who had authority over the issuance of driver's licenses and automobile tags, was featured on the maps issued by that office's automobile department. After 1952, when the two agencies' efforts were combined, we find both of these state officers mentioned prominently on the cover of the state map.

Most subtly and powerfully, state authority was promoted by the map symbols referring to the geographical footprint of state institutions. It is not surprising to find state forests, parks, and recreational features on these maps. Symbols and listings for state game refuges, hunting grounds, and fish hatcheries were also commonly depicted features of obvious recreational interest, but there were also lists of and map symbols for state police posts, garages, first-aid stations, radio towers, and highway authority district offices (fig. 3). In time, the locations of other state institutions seemingly irrelevant to motorists were also added to many official state maps. Indiana maps in the 1930s adopted a generic areal symbol for state-owned property and a unique point symbol for Purdue University's experimental farm. Symbols for the extension centers of Purdue University and Indiana University were added after World War II.

The backdrop of driver education and official promotion was increasingly overlaid during the 1930s by a new promotional agenda targeting tourists. Gradually, the amount of map space devoted to state regulations was reduced in favor of descriptions of the state's landscapes, culture, history, economy, points of interest, and recreationally oriented state facilities. In several states, highway maps issued by state departments of conservation set the trend. Indiana appears to have published such a map as early as 1923.[18] A 1929 map entitled *Outdoor Illinois,* published by the Illinois Department of Conservation and printed in two colors, lists and locates 102 points of interest, including a variety of state institutions (hospitals and universities) and recreational facilities. Extensive text on the backs of the maps lauds the efforts of the state conservation movement and describes the state fish hatcheries and game refuges that generate revenue for this effort.[19] Michigan's 1930 map, *State Parks of Michigan,* offers a highway map identifying parks, forests, hatcheries, and game refuges and, on the map's back, an extensive illustrated inventory of state conservation lands, points of interest, and laws governing fishing and hunting.[20] This map appears to be the model for a 1931 map titled *Michigan Highways, Lakes, Streams, and Forests,* which was jointly issued by the state's department of conservation and its department of highways and was the forerunner of the more tourist-friendly maps published exclusively by the latter from 1932 onward.[21]

The glossier appearance of the maps published by several states by the mid-1930s can be compared favorably to promotional maps issued in the same period by oil companies. Printing in three and four colors was introduced, cover illustrations were added, and paper stock became noticeably thicker and sturdier. The states that were likely to gain the most from the promotion of tourism adapted their state highway maps to this purpose more quickly and more thoroughly. By 1934, Minnesota, Wisconsin, and Michigan had all added attractive promotional graphics to the backs of their maps. In Minnesota's case, this generally was a photomontage (fig. 4) depicting outdoor recreational activities and the scenic beauty of the state's lakes and forests. To these were added a few photos showing economic themes and usually

Figure 4. "Marvelous Minnesota," detail of *Minnesota 1938 Official Map* (St. Paul: McGill-Warner Co. for the Minnesota Department of Highways, 1938). Private collection.

U. S. Highways Leading to Minnesota

farther. The 1936 map's text emphasized the variety of vacation opportunities in Minnesota and invited visitors to think about buying a vacation home: "Vacation in the land of ten thousand lakes, where woods and waters make the outdoors a kingdom of happiness for everyone. Rent a comfortable family cabin, stay at luxurious resorts or set up your tent and camp out. Spend much or little, as you choose. After you enjoy a Minnesota vacation, you may do as hundreds of other Midwest residents have done and buy a piece of inexpensive lakeshore land for your summer cottage—a perpetual haven of content."[23]

The outdoor-oriented midwestern traveler was the apparent target of mid- and late-1930s promotions on the backs of Wisconsin's and Michigan's state maps as well. Michigan's 1934 map proudly observes: "As a state which each year entertains millions of visitors, Michigan has learned the art of true hospitality. Her people justly have a deep pride in the vacation wonders with which Nature has so generously blessed them. But Michigan people do not selfishly desire to hold these wonders for themselves to the exclusion of others. Their desire is to share these bounties."[24]

As in Minnesota's publications, photographs and illustrations on the backs of 1930s Michigan maps featured tourists engaged in a variety of outdoor activities, particularly fishing and boating amid a placid landscape of lakes and northern forests (fig. 6). Promotional material trumpeted the creation of a State Tourist and Resort Commission and the erection of tourist information lodges at New Buffalo and Menominee that served traffic entering the state from the metropolitan regions at the southern end of Lake Michigan. Michigan issued two or three editions of its maps each year until 1957 and began calling these winter, spring, or summer editions. Cover art and promotional material reflected seasonal recreational themes. The May 1938 edition tableau, titled "Michigan of the Blue Waters," emphasized water-based activities against an illustrated background of sunny yellow. The winter 1939 edition (issued in December 1938) focused on skiing, ice-skating, and other winter activities against an illustrated background of pale wintry blue. Three photographs and one drawing documented the highway department's efforts to keep the roads passable, noting that "it is Michigan State Highway Department policy to cater to tourists, and winter visitors are no exception. . . . Motor car transportation to the many areas where there are organized winter sports is simplified by highways that are always open."[25]

Official Wisconsin maps from this period also promoted the state's appeal to midwestern tourists who loved the outdoors. As early as 1926 (and possibly sooner), text on the map (and later on the map cover) proclaimed Wisconsin to be the "Playground of the Middle West." During the 1930s, Wisconsin "officials" bragged that the state was not only "economically and governmentally sound" but also blessed with "3,500 lakes," "60,000 acres of lakes and rivers," and "7,000 miles of dustless roads." Yet Wisconsin's message to tourists in the 1930s was slightly more complex than Minnesota's or Michigan's, and for many years thereafter, it also stressed the state's importance as an agricultural center. For several years in the 1930s, a large map printed on the back of the sheet titled "Pictorial History of Wisconsin," drawn by Laura R. Kremers of Madison, anchored the promotional content (fig. 7). Among the most prominent themes represented on this map are sites and events associated with the voyageurs, early American pioneers, the history of the lumber industry (including two references to Paul Bunyan), and lead mining. Some historic sites seem to have been selected as being particularly appealing to tourists. These include the Old Swiss Church at New Glarus and the Shot Tower near Blue Mound. There are modern tourist landmarks as well, such as the Wisconsin Dells, Holy Hill (a scenic Carmelite monastery), and several state parks. The map also identifies regions noted for specific agricultural products, including tobacco, cranberries, corn, potatoes, blueberries,

Figure 5. "U.S. Highways Leading to Minnesota," detail of *Minnesota 1938 Official Map.* Private collection.

A prize Rainbow.   A successful day.   Some prefer still fishing.

MAIN highways and wooded trails take you into the heart of Michigan's famous hunting and fishing grounds. With 1,624 miles of Great Lakes coast line, 5,000 inland lakes, and hundreds of miles of rivers and streams, Michigan provides an opportunity for every type of fishing.

There are vast public hunting grounds where large and small game is plentiful. In season the hunter can get his buck, or partridge as he may prefer. Wild life not only provides thrilling sport for hunters but adds to the beauty and interest of Michigan roadsides where it is frequently seen by tourists.

Wooded roads and trails lead to fishing and hunting grounds.

Figure 6. Detail of illustrations from the *1936 Official Michigan Highway Map* (Lansing: Michigan State Highway Department, 1936). Courtesy of the Rand McNally Collection, The Newberry Library, Chicago.

Figure 7 (opposite). Laura R. Kremers, "Pictorial History of Wisconsin," from *State of Wisconsin . . . 1935 Map Showing State and Federal Highway Routes* (Madison: State Highway Commission, 1935). Courtesy of the Rand McNally Collection, The Newberry Library, Chicago.

and cherries. By 1938, this historical map was replaced by a more conventional photographic tableau showing happy tourists engaged in the same outdoor activities shown on Minnesota and Michigan maps and by an inset regional map showing U.S. highways leading to Wisconsin similar to the inset discussed above found on contemporary Minnesota maps.

The more southerly midwestern states were perhaps less attractive as tourist destinations, but each dealt with this fact differently. Ohio's official maps introduced pictorial covers of motoring scenes in 1933, but the backs of the maps throughout the 1930s offered nothing more than indexes, descriptions of traffic laws, and traffic signs. The only nod in the direction of tourism promotion was a modest list of points of interest that were also indicated on the map itself next to a distinctive point symbol.

Important Motor Vehicle Laws of WISCONSIN

RULES OF THE ROAD

There is no speed limit on rural highways. Be reasonable and drive carefully. It is unlawful for any person to drive in a reckless manner or at such speed as to endanger the lives or property of others.

In overtaking a vehicle, pass to the left, but do so only where the left side is clearly visible and free from oncoming traffic for a sufficient distance to permit such movement in safety.

Do not overtake and pass another vehicle on the crest of a grade, on a curve, at railroad and highway intersections or where the operator's view is obstructed within a distance of 1000 feet.

Every vehicle must be equipped with rear view mirror, windshield wiper, horn, legal lights and efficient brakes.

Parking is prohibited on the main traveled portion of highways, also near the crest of hills or on curves and turns.

Restrictions as to size and gross weights of heavy vehicles are as follows:

On Class "A" (paved) Highways

4 wheel vehicles gross weight	24,000 lbs.
6 wheel—3 axle vehicles—gross weight	34,000 lbs.
Semi-trailer—2 axle, 4 wheels	18,000 lbs.
Semi-trailer—3 axle, 6 wheels	24,000 lbs.
Gross axle weight	16,000 lbs.
For inch of tire width	600 lbs.

On Class "B" (unpaved) Highways

4 wheel vehicles gross weight	13,000 lbs.
6 wheel—3 axle vehicles—gross weight	22,000 lbs.
Semi-trailer—2 axle, 4 wheels	12,000 lbs.
Gross axle weight	9,000 lbs.
For inch of tire width	400 lbs.

Maximum length of vehicle	35 feet
Maximum length of vehicle and trailers	85 feet
Width, of load	8 feet
Minimum distance between axles	40 in.
Snow bar or tire rope length	12 feet

SCENIC WISCONSIN

MOUNT TREMPEALEAU
PERROT STATE PARK

LEAD MINING DAYS

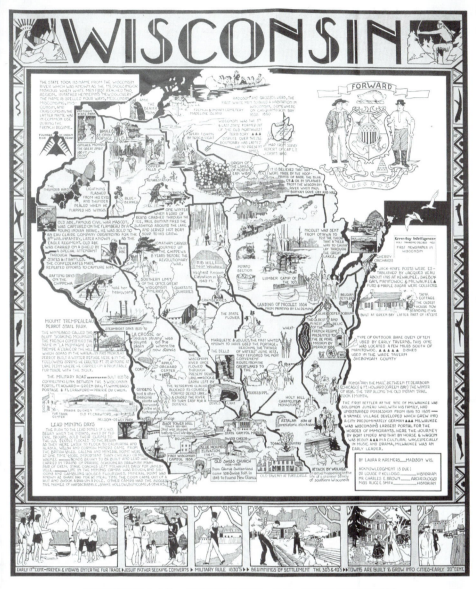

PICTORIAL HISTORY OF WISCONSIN

WISCONSIN STATE PARKS

INDEX TO INCORPORATED VILLAGES AND CITIES

WELCOME TO WISCONSIN

On behalf of the citizens of this state I welcome you to Wisconsin, to enjoy its great out-of-doors, visit its beautiful cities and partake of the hospitality and friendship of its people.

Its wooded hills and valleys, thousands of lakes and streams, spacious state parks, abundant game and fish, and rolling, diversified countryside have made this state a Mecca for tourists and visitors from every part of the continent. The Indian of yesterday picked his way on horseback through underbrush and wilderness to visit his favorite haunts in Wisconsin. Today a network of more than 80,000 miles of highways spreads through the state and makes its attractions and interests easily accessible to all.

Wisconsin's assets are not confined to its natural beauties. Its richest asset is its citizens—a sturdy, industrious people as intensely interested in good government as in their own personal welfare. I hope you will visit and get acquainted with them, for I am sure you will enjoy their warm friendship as much as the beauties with which God has blessed us.

PHILIP F LA FOLLETTE
GOVERNOR OF WISCONSIN

State of Wisconsin

State
Highway Commission
of Wisconsin
MADISON

1935
MAP SHOWING
State and Federal
Highway Routes
FOR FREE DISTRIBUTION ONLY

The PLAYGROUND
of the Middlewest

SCENIC VIEWS IN WISCONSIN

As we have noted, Indiana's Department of Conservation published an attractive map featuring state parks, recreational facilities, and other points of interest into the early 1930s. The official Indiana State Highway Commission map did not add a substantial promotional component until 1937, when the back of the map was given over to a two-color map of "Indiana Points of Interest" accompanied by seven monochrome photos of roads, bridges, and recreational scenes. This feature was replaced the following year by inset maps and a map showing road distances from major U.S. cities to Indianapolis. Photographs returned in 1940, but these showed highways in various settings with captions on highway design and maintenance.

The official highway maps published by the Illinois Secretary of State and the Division of Highways largely ignored tourist promotions before World War II. The latter's 1932 map was the first map produced by either agency that included photographs of points of interest—seven small images of sites connected to Abraham Lincoln and state parks. The publication also included a large inset of the grounds of the upcoming Century of Progress exhibition in Chicago. Another inset on the 1933 map shows officially designated "World's Fair Highways" leading to Chicago from surrounding states. The World's Fair prompted Illinois's Division of Highways to prepare a glossier publication than in the past; but the division abandoned this limited promotional effort after the fair. The Illinois Secretary of State maps added a modest promotional section to the 1936 version. This addition became more ambitious in 1939 and 1940, but it largely consisted of brief paragraphs on key points of interest, including major cities, state parks, and historical and archaeological sites.

Among the southern midwestern states, only Iowa was consistently committed from the early 1930s onward to the use of its state highway map for cultural and geographical promotions. The Iowa State Highway Commission abandoned its earlier emphasis on its efforts to improve the state's muddy roads; instead, the colorful Iowa maps published in the mid-1930s feature arguably the most attractive promotional tableaux found in any midwestern state map of this or any other time. The images and text chosen reflect a mixture of themes drawing on Iowa's pastoral landscape, pioneer history, and economy. On the cover of the 1934 map, a stereotypical Native American stands with a spear and looks out across a highway-laced landscape. Above him, a winged "1934" suggests the speed and modernity of Iowa's roads. The back of the map (fig. 8) presents the usual listing of towns, state parks, state facts, and the locations of state institutions, but it also includes photographs and drawings of recreational scenes surrounding an outline map of Iowa. The flowery text within the outline map asserts that while Iowa has had many tangible accomplishments, the real beauty of the state rests in its transformative pleasantness. The state's "intangible" beauty is of a sort that "only the poets can suitably enumerate and appraise" and which "inspires the meadowlark to purer floating." Travelers to Iowa should "go with [their souls] awake." The text also presents Iowa as the typical American state: "Iowa in outline . . . parallels the geographic pattern of the nation—the Mississippi River her Atlantic and the Missouri her Pacific coast, and even her Key West looks out over broad waters at Keokuk."[26]

The coming of World War II brought with it rationing of oil and rubber and official disapproval of nonessential automobile travel. But each midwestern state continued to issue official state highway maps in at least some of the war years, shifting the maps' promotional focus to the contributions that highways and highway authorities were making to the war effort. Anticipating the American entry into the war, the cover of the 1941 Indiana map proclaimed, "Unity for national defense. The nation and state will be prepared." The 1942 version's cover featured a photograph of the "Pro Patria" statue at the state's

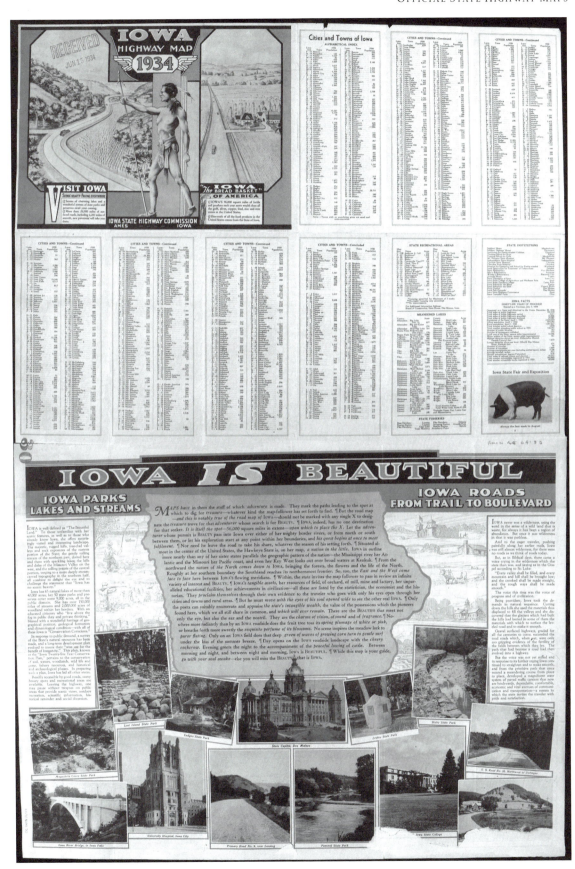

Figure 8. Detail of illustrations from the *Iowa Highway Map 1934* (Ames: Iowa State Highway Commission, 1934). Courtesy of the Rand McNally Collection, The Newberry Library, Chicago.

Figure 9. Detail of illustration from *The Official Summer Highway Map of Michigan, 1942* (Lansing: Michigan State Highway Department, 1942). Courtesy of the Rand McNally Collection, The Newberry Library, Chicago.

World War Memorial, while the back of the map included six photographs of military convoys with the highway commission's promise, "We will—keep 'em rolling."

A photographic tableau for the 1942 edition of Michigan's official map (fig. 9) illustrates the contributions the highway department was making to the war effort, including the construction of new access roads to military bases and an expressway for workers at "the greatest bomber plant in the world," Ford's Willow Run plant west of Detroit. Motorists are admonished to make their vehicles, "the first transportation link in the war materials supply system, . . . outlast the Nation's enemies." Although the caption for one photograph notes that "thin, orderly columns of grim looking Army gun carriers and trucks are replacing the helter skelter pattern of normal traffic on Michigan's highways for the duration," two photographs are targeted at tourists, presumably mostly in-state ones. One shows a family group at a roadside park under the caption "Saving Tires—Michigan's many roadside parks found 'just around the corner' from every community are expected to become more popular than ever this summer for a day of relaxation." Another caption, below a photograph of a lakeside picnic area, encourages motorists to maintain speeds of 40 miles per hour or less, observing that "beautiful shoreline views can be more fully appreciated" at slower speeds.[27]

Looking forward to a return to peacetime, the hopeful promotional tableau on the Michigan map of 1945 combines a renewed emphasis on tourism with the state's early leadership in superhighway construction. Two captioned pictures tout the war and peacetime benefits of the new expressways appearing in the Detroit area. Another discusses the traffic capacity of the locks at Sault Ste. Marie. Captions for photos of the skylines of Detroit and Lansing acknowledge the cities' roles in industrial production and political leadership, which were crucial to the war effort. The map cover features a large illustration of the Lumberman's Memorial in Iosco County with the caption: "The riverman, the timber cruiser, and the sawyer depicted by the sculptor were not Paul Bunyans. They were real men—alert, hard-working, craftsmen who created Michigan's first great industry and laid many of the foundations of the vast industrial development which implements today's mighty war effort. The world in which they worked—shady forests and sparkling waters beneath the open sky—is the land that will beckon the post-war tourists along our highways to havens of rest and relaxation."[28]

The end of the war brought renewed investment in and promotion of tourism. Michigan and Wisconsin returned to their emphasis on outdoor activities, with some modifications. Families and women (in Wisconsin represented mainly as bathing beauties) appear more frequently in the photographs of recreational scenes. And the dominance of boating and fishing images was somewhat diminished by the inclusion of dairy farms and football stadiums in Wisconsin and illustrations urging motorists to be good citizens and good drivers in Michigan.

On the other hand, Minnesota maps in the immediate postwar period, while still very handsomely presented, featured more inset maps and less promotional content. The single exception was the 1949 map, which commemorated the one-hundredth anniversary of the Minnesota Territory. Economic development and statistics played a larger role in Minnesota's self-presentation than before, particularly on the 1950 map, which attempted to cover a wide variety of interests in the small amount of space devoted to promotion: "Minnesota . . . with its farmlands, iron mines, and forest, takes pride in its growth as a State. . . . Minnesota is proud of its industries . . . but more proud of its cultural and scientific developments, its contributions to the advance of medicine, its civic centers, its schools, and colleges. . . . Last of all, but the most cherished gift of God, is the true beauty so generously manifested in its blue lakes, green trees, cool breezes, and fleecy white clouds. . . . This is Minnesota."[29]

Illinois, Indiana, and Ohio maps continued their prewar pattern of minimal promotional content, with the exception of the 1953 Ohio map, which commemorated the one-hundred-fiftieth anniversary of Ohio statehood. Iowa, however, renewed its publication of attractive maps promoting the state's agricultural might. On the back of the 1947 map, a feature titled "We call it Iowa" tells the story of a Martian who lands on Earth and searches for the best it has to offer. He is told to visit Iowa. Why? "Nature has favored it with a temperate climate, ample rainfall and productive soil; natural resources that attract thoughtful, industrious people who expect to work for a living and who have reason for confidence that their work will be rewarded."[30] In a similar vein, the 1949 Iowa map was titled "The Abundant Heart of the Nation" and included a poem that appeared on many maps titled "In This State Called Iowa," which contended that in creating Iowa, God was "building a garden." The backs of the 1950 and 1951 maps contained almost no writing at all but were devoted entirely to brightly colored agricultural scenes. Iowa abandoned its flowery agricultural promotions in 1952 in favor of a collection of inset maps and a modest list of points of interest.

Though the promotion of tourism had been a significant motivation for publishing official state highway maps in most midwestern states since the 1930s, the construction and maintenance work of state highway agencies was always in evidence. Wherever a pleasant landscape was depicted on map covers, there was usually a well-engineered highway winding through it (fig. 10). Generic messages of

Figure 10. Cover, *Minnesota 1938 Official Map* (St. Paul: McGill-Warner Co. for the Minnesota Department of Highways, 1938). Private collection.

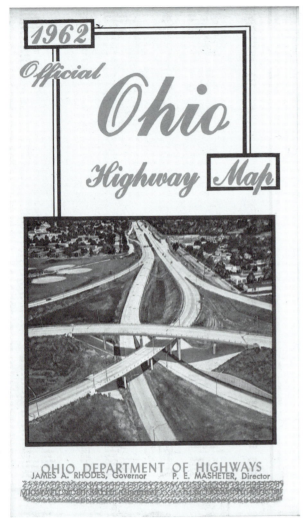

Figure 11 (above). Front covers, *1962 Official Ohio Highway Map* (Columbus: Ohio Department of Highways, 1962); *1963 Illinois Official Highway Map* (Springfield: State of Illinois, 1963); *Indiana Official Highway Map 1977* (Indianapolis: Indiana State Highway Commission, 1977). (From left to right). Courtesy of the Rand McNally Collection, The Newberry Library, Chicago; private collection (Illinois); courtesy of the Rand McNally Collection, The Newberry Library, Chicago.

Figure 12 (opposite). "Michigan Builds a Modern Highway System," from the *Michigan 1960 Official Highway Map* (Lansing: Michigan State Highway Department, 1960). Courtesy The Newberry Library, Chicago.

welcome that touted a state's scenic beauty, natural resources, friendly and industrious people, and illustrious history rarely failed to boast about the state's excellent highway system. As might be expected, the rhetorical interest in highway construction was intensified by passage of the 1956 federal act that created the national system of interstate superhighways.

The change in promotional tone is clearly marked by map cover illustrations (fig. 11). Iowa covers had featured two-lane highways winding through rolling rural landscapes in most years since 1939; these gave way during the years from 1957 through 1970 to landscapes dominated by four-lane limited-access highways. Ohio covers featured interstates from 1958 to 1962, and Indiana covers did the same from 1956 to 1964. Illinois's cover illustration featured its first limited-access highway (the Edens Expressway running north of Chicago) as early as 1954 and continued to feature interstates until 1966.

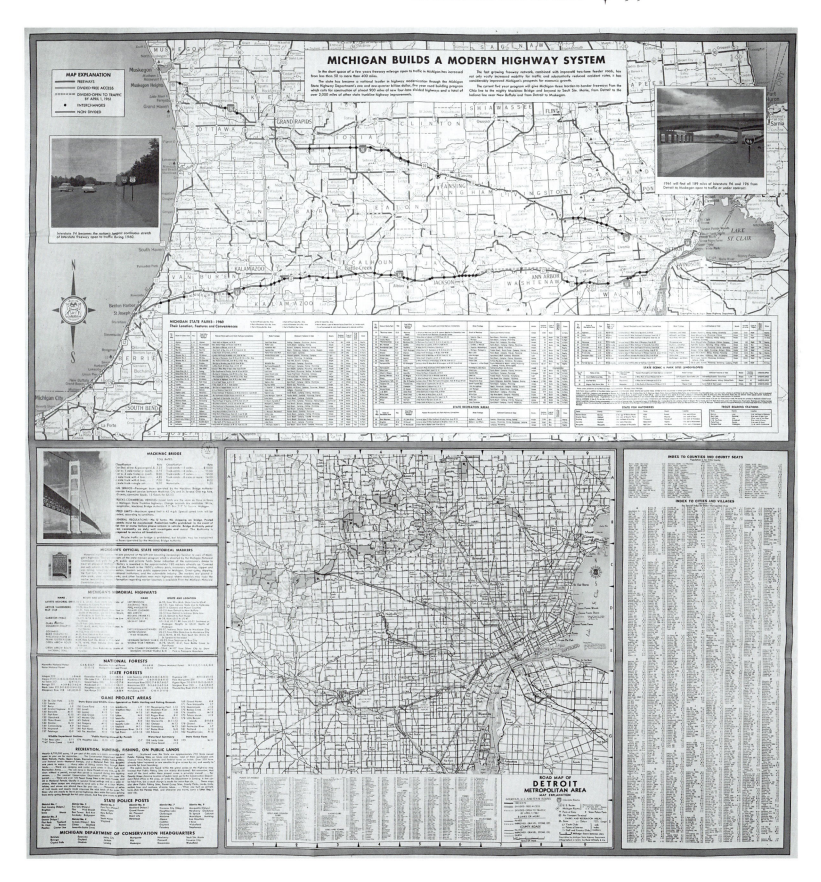

MICHIGAN BUILDS A MODERN HIGHWAY SYSTEM

Interstate 94 becomes the nation's longest continuous stretch of Interstate freeway open to traffic during 1960.

1961 will find an 189 miles of Interstate 96 and 196 from Detroit to Muskegon open to traffic or under contract.

MAP EXPLANATION

MICHIGAN STATE PARKS—1960
Their Location, Features and Conveniences

MACKINAC BRIDGE

MICHIGAN'S OFFICIAL STATE HISTORICAL MARKERS

MICHIGAN'S MEMORIAL HIGHWAYS

NATIONAL FORESTS

STATE FORESTS

GAME PROJECT AREAS

RECREATION, HUNTING, FISHING, ON PUBLIC LANDS

STATE POLICE POSTS

MICHIGAN DEPARTMENT OF CONSERVATION HEADQUARTERS

ROAD MAP OF
DETROIT
METROPOLITAN AREA
MAP EXPLANATION

INDEX TO COUNTIES AND COUNTY SEATS

INDEX TO CITIES AND VILLAGES

Even Minnesota's traditionally outdoor-themed covers followed the trend toward showing interstate highways for most of the 1960s.

Inside, tourist-promotional material was significantly reduced or modified to put new emphasis on highway construction. Not surprisingly, Michigan's rhetorical embrace of the new highway construction was particularly strong. Recreational promotions were virtually banished from the back sides of Michigan maps for nearly a decade (until 1968). The 1960 version instead includes a large inset map showing the progress in the construction of Interstates 94 and 96 in the urbanized southern part of the state, noting that in "the short space of a few years freeway mileage open to traffic in Michigan has increased from less than fifty to 400 miles"[31] (fig. 12). Modest albums of photographs of Iowa landscapes that had reappeared on Iowa's state maps in the early 1960s were supplanted in 1964 by photographs of highway construction and then (until 1978) by a map showing the progress of superhighway construction. The promotional content on the back sides of Ohio maps actually increased during the 1960s, but the designers included a small map showing the interstate highway system in the state. Minnesota maintained its focus on tourism promotion in the 1960s but added a map of the U.S. interstate highway system.

By the late 1960s, the frenzied promotion of highway construction was abating. Interstates were no longer novelties; in fact, critiques of their social and environmental consequences were beginning to surface. Michigan dropped the special interstate highway map from the back of its publication in 1968, replacing it with more conventional promotional features. In the early 1970s, state mapmakers returned to the old practice of educating the public about some aspect of highway operations: automobile safety tips were the subject in 1970, 1973's map described new highway signs, and the creation of the new Michigan Department of State Highways and Transportation was featured in 1974.

Following a national trend initiated by the creation of the U.S. Department of Transportation in 1967, every midwestern state except Indiana created its own department of transportation during the 1970s. These new agencies absorbed the former state highway departments or commissions and their responsibility for issuing official state highway maps, most of which were retitled "transportation maps." The new maps' cartography retained its essential focus on highways, but some new features reflected the broader governmental role in transportation policy. Railroads, which were usually omitted from highway maps, appeared in many of the new official maps. Michigan added Amtrak routes to its maps in 1975, along with new map symbols for international and domestic seaports and international rail interchange points. In 1973 trunk rail lines were included on Ohio's transportation map. Minnesota's first *Official Transportation Map,* issued in 1977–78, added a large inset "Minnesota Public Transportation Map" showing bus, airline, and Amtrak routes (fig. 13). A similar bus, air, and rail travel map appeared on Iowa's map in 1976–77, and railroads were added to the highway map in the same year.[32]

Perhaps more significantly, promotional material in several states acknowledged the change in institutional focus by promoting a more all-inclusive picture of transportation's role in the history and development of the state. Michigan's 1974 *Official Transportation Map* featured large photographs of six modes of transportation supported by state programs under the heading "Total Transportation": automobiles, airplanes, Amtrak service, bicycle paths, commercial shipping, and urban dial-a-ride services. Governor William Milliken's message proclaims that "Michigan, long the automotive capital of the world, is now mobilizing that expertise, technology and resources in the building of a total transportation system. The backbone of that system continues to be our excellent toll-free network of highways

Figure 13. "Minnesota Public Transportation Map," from *Minnesota, 1977–78 Transportation Map* (Minnesota: Department of Transportation, 1977). Courtesy of the Rand McNally Collection, The Newberry Library, Chicago.

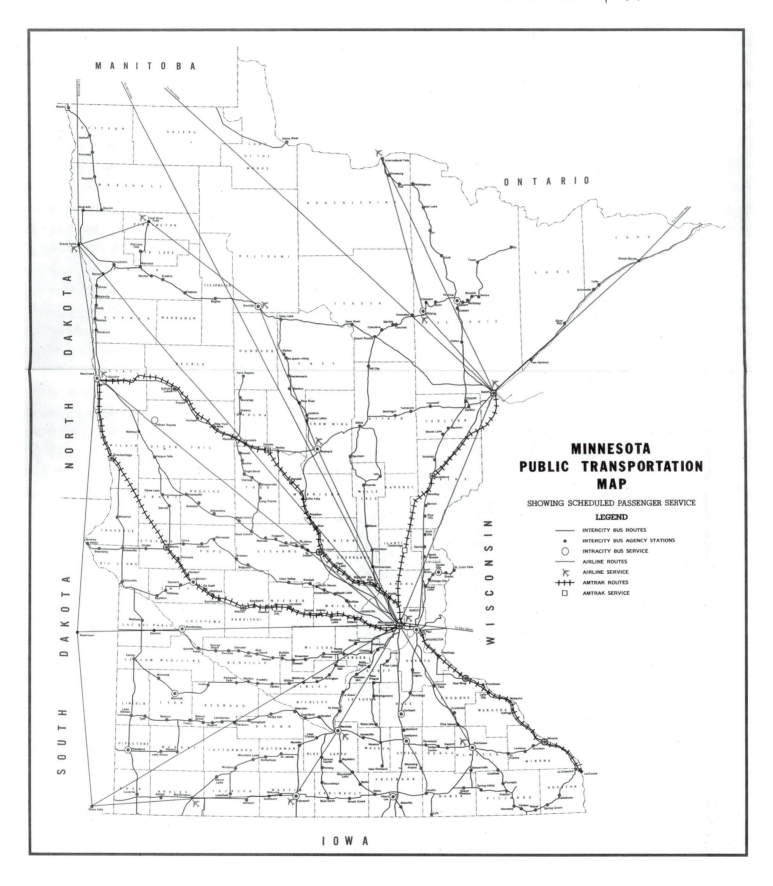

MINNESOTA
PUBLIC TRANSPORTATION
MAP

SHOWING SCHEDULED PASSENGER SERVICE

LEGEND

INTERCITY BUS ROUTES
INTERCITY BUS AGENCY STATIONS
INTRACITY BUS SERVICE
AIRLINE ROUTES
AIRLINE SERVICE
AMTRAK ROUTES
AMTRAK SERVICE

and freeways." Yet, the message continues, "Rails, bus lines, airports, lake ports and non-motorized facilities such as hard surface bicycle paths are growing in importance daily."[33]

The oil embargo of 1973 to 1974, the environmental movement, and simmering social justice issues motivated increased federal and state support for public transportation and inspired this rhetorical shift to an integrated transportation policy. Minnesota's 1977–78 map introduced the state's department of transportation logo, which featured a pine tree and the North Star within a circle. The accompanying text explained that "the circular design suggests the wheel as the basis for mechanized transportation. The colors blue and green reflect environmental concern for land, sky and water."[34]

A few editions of official maps from this period demonstrate an unusual concern for transportation's role in economic development as well. This was particularly true in Ohio. The full cover title of the state's 1969 map is the *1969 Official Ohio Highway Map and Economic Digest*. A huge promotional feature on the back of the map boasts that Ohio is the "Number '1' State" and offers a list of various social and economic achievements supporting this assertion.[35] Governor James Rhodes's attached "letter" explains that the "dramatic growth of the Wonderful World of Ohio during the past six years [Rhodes's term as governor] has rightfully earned the Buckeye State the rank of Number One among the nation's states. . . . This map has been produced for the pleasure of Ohioans and for the use of industry to show what Ohio offers, so that those who live here and those who will move here in the future will become proud of the 'Wonderful World of Ohio.'"[36]

Ohio's role in national transportation development dominated the promotional content of the state's maps from 1978 to 1982. The 1979 map surveyed the various modes of transportation available in Ohio, including air, bus, Amtrak, rapid transit, boat, and even the possibilities offered by high-speed rail. Another feature, titled "America's Transportation Future," discussed public transportation, and "America's Largest Marketplace" focused on the importance of the highway system to the Ohio economy, which "places Ohio closer to more people and places than any other state." The back of the 1982 map was devoted to "Ohio: Portraits of Progress," a focus on Ohio inventors with particular emphasis on the state's role in transportation innovation.[37]

Historical themes had occasionally made their way onto official highway maps in the past, especially for important state anniversaries. As early as 1938, Iowa's map commemorated the centennial of the creation of the Iowa Territory. State highway agencies celebrated their anniversaries as well. For example, in 1969, Indiana celebrated the fiftieth anniversary of the Indiana State Highway Commission with a photographic essay titled "Progress in Road Building," showing both old and new road-building methods. Historic Mackinac Island had been promoted on Michigan maps since the mid-1930s, as were Lincoln sites in Illinois. Wisconsin referred to its voyageurs, and Paul Bunyan made occasional appearances on both Wisconsin and Minnesota maps. The back of Ohio's 1962 map included two substantial inset maps showing sites associated with the War of 1812.[38]

The national bicentennial celebrations sharpened this focus on historical themes. Michigan's 1976–77 map featured a cover with British colonial soldiers in front of Fort Mackinac. Its promotional tableau proclaimed that "America's Transportation Heritage Thrives at Michigan's Greenfield Village," and cartographers added red, white, and blue symbols for featured "Revolutionary Era Sites" throughout the state (fig. 14). The Wisconsin map issued in 1976 offered an illustrated history of transportation in Wisconsin featuring specific transportation-related sites commemorated by roadside historical markers. Ohio's map celebrated the state's importance as a frontier "outpost of the American revolution." A

Figure 14. Detail, *1976–1977 Official Transportation Map, Michigan, Great Lake State* (Lansing: State Highway Commission, 1976). Courtesy of the Rand McNally Collection, The Newberry Library, Chicago.

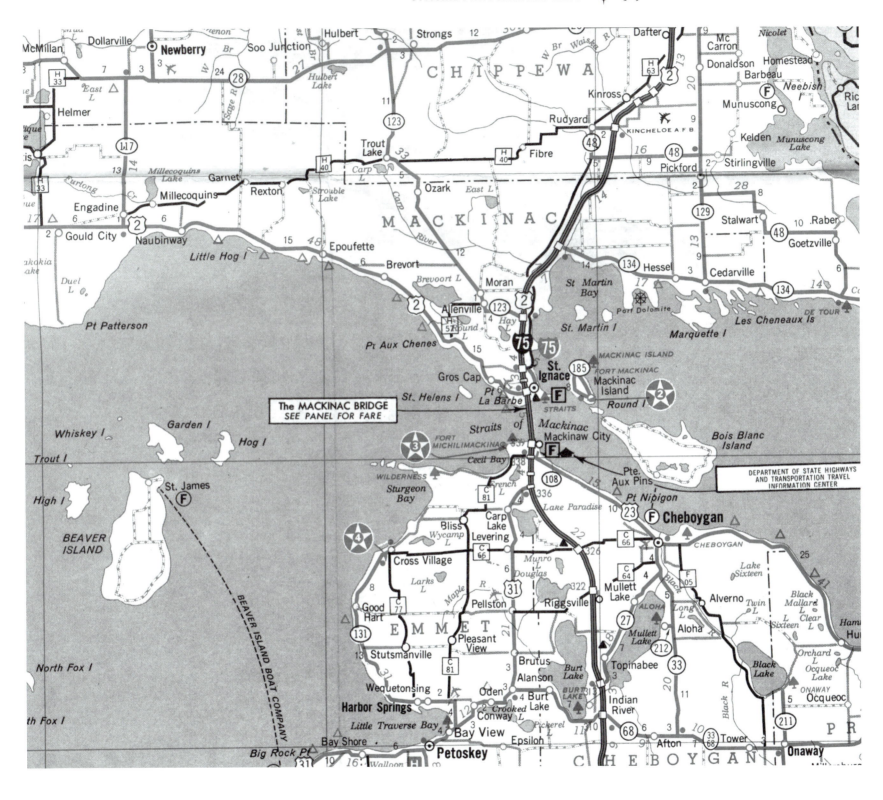

map on the back of the sheet was surrounded by pictures of important people from Ohio who figured in the Revolutionary War and traced the movements of military groups across the future state during the war. Indiana's 1976 map featured prize-winning photographs of historic sites submitted by citizens to a statewide "bicentennial map photo contest." The bicentennial edition of Minnesota's map featured a transportation-based history of the state, titled "Highway Heritage." Depictions included a voyageur canoe, a wagon on the Pembina Trail, construction methods then (with a horse) and now (heavy machinery), tourist travel of yesteryear (a car stuck in the mud), and a modern highway.[39]

From the 1970s onward, eclecticism ruled the day. In the mid-1980s, Ohio shifted to a more conventional promotion of a hodgepodge of tourist attractions. The back of the 1985–86 edition sported a particularly attractive map of points of interest, including sports facilities, historical attractions, amusement parks, nature and recreational attractions, Amish communities, and art centers. Indiana, whose maps had maintained a low promotional profile for a long time, began adding albums of promotional photographs to the backs of its maps in the late 1960s. Themes varied from year to year. The 1970–71 material focused on "Winter Recreation"; in the following year, the map commemorated the completion of the new Port of Indiana at Burns Harbor. In 1979 and for several years thereafter, photographs were supplanted by promotional text prepared by the Indiana Department of Natural Resources and the Department of Commerce, Division of Tourism. Indiana's 1986 map emphasized the history of higher education in the state. In 1987 Indiana hosted the Pan-American Games and the Special Olympics, which prompted a feature on the state as "America's amateur sports center." In 1991–92, Indiana commemorated its one-hundred-seventy-fifth anniversary with an illustrated historical timeline; and in 1993–94, it marked the seventy-fifth anniversary of the state highway system (1919 to 1994) with a photographic essay on the history of highway construction in Indiana.

Tourism became a popular theme in several states. In Iowa's maps during the 1980s and early 1990s, promotional material shifted to the description of tours designed to help travelers sample the scenic and cultural flavor of various parts of the state (fig. 15). Wisconsin and Michigan maps renewed their emphasis on outdoor recreation but focused less intensely and narrowly on it than earlier in the twentieth century. The 1986 Michigan map featured a familiar photographic tableau captioned "Michigan for the good life," which was dominated by people biking, boating, golfing, and skiing. From the late 1980s onward, however, Michigan's maps usually featured striking photographs and text about particular scenic wonders or cultural sites.

Wood paneling suggestive of backwoods cabins and hunting lodges adorned the cover and promotional back side of the Wisconsin maps from 1973 to 1975. But this evocative image still had to coexist with a clutter of other interests. For example, on the back of the 1973 map, the wood paneling provides the background for a familiar feature explaining the new nationally standardized highway signs (fig. 16). An attractive pictorial points-of-interest map reminiscent of those found on the backs of 1930s Wisconsin state maps is dominated by images of scenic spots, state parks, sportsmen in action, and wildlife, but these share space with such cultural attractions as the Green Bay Packers, the Milwaukee Bucks, the Milwaukee County Zoo, and the purported birthplace of the Republican Party. To the left is a small map showing the location of the offices of the state highway patrol and the division of highways. Above the map are other representations of state authority: the state seal and a reminder to drivers to fasten their seat belts. On the "paneled" back cover, Governor Patrick Lacey competes for visual prominence with other official symbols of the state, including the muskie, the badger, and the Holstein.[40]

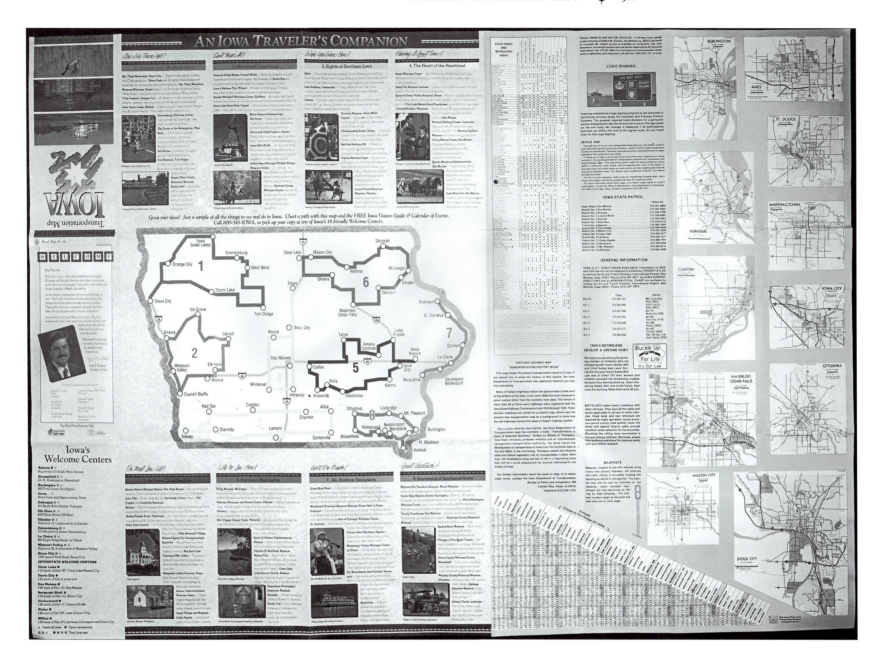

During much of the 1980s, Wisconsin state maps turned austere in their promotional content. Large arrangements of inset city maps dominated the backs of these sheets, interlaced with a few photographs of cultural sites, governmental messages, and a modest map and guide to state parks and recreational areas. In 1980–81, even Governor Lee Dreyfus's message urged restraint. He cautioned that "a map is especially important in the era of energy constraints. I urge you to use it in good health and with good sense. Pick your routes with care. Use the shortest and safest route to bring in your materials, ship out your products, and reach your recreational destination. Pick your times with care. Travel only as often as necessary so there may be fuel for all reasons in all seasons. And choose the most energy-efficient travel available to you."[41]

Figure 15. Back panel illustrations from *Transportation Map, Iowa* (Ames: Iowa Department of Transportation, 1991). Courtesy of The Newberry Library, Chicago.

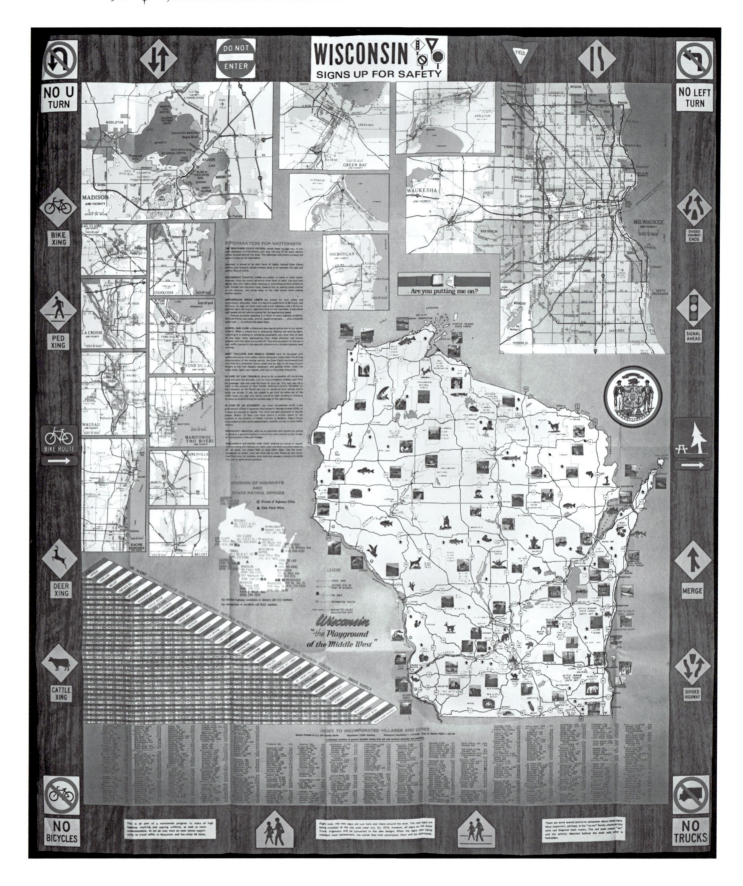

In the late 1980s and throughout the 1990s, the promotional content of Wisconsin's official maps substantially expanded once more. Inset maps on the back of the 1999 map, for example, were gathered in the bottom one-quarter, making room for an extensive promotional feature describing the state's attractions region by region and an unusually large and colorful table of state parks, forests, and recreation areas.

The promotional themes of Minnesota maps during this period were also eclectic. The northwoods image was still important after 1976, but references to economic development and cultural features were increasingly integrated into the state's promotion of itself. For example, the 1979–80 map included pictures of the St. Paul Chamber Orchestra and the Minnesota Zoo. The 1983–84 map returned to transportation themes tied to economic development. Its text included observations such as: "Serving industry and commerce, meeting the needs of personal and product movement, that is transportation—Minnesota's lifeline." The 1985–86 version was enlarged, allowing inset maps to be transferred to the front of the map. The entire back side of the sheet could then be devoted to information about travel throughout the state, including regional "Minnetours" with the theme "Explore Minnesota." The 1987–88 map returned to a historical theme and focused on transportation. A statement on this edition of the map reminds us that these documents had agendas beyond tourism promotion: "Consistently leading the nation in the rate of both high school graduation and voter turnout, Minnesota remains committed to preserving its reputation for good government and a high quality of life."[42] The 1989–90 map promoted the "Olympic Festival" being held in the state in 1990. The 1991–92 map highlighted state parks, while the 1993–94 version focused on historical sites, with a state map that pinpointed them and gave a description of each.

In the last three decades of the twentieth century, state agencies responsible for tourism promotion played an increasing role in map publication and distribution. From the late 1970s, notes on state official maps referring readers to other state agencies for information about attractions, parks, and accommodations were increasingly common—and by the late 1990s, such references could be found on almost every official midwestern state highway map.

During the 1990s, several state tourism agencies contracted with private cartographic publishers to produce what can only be described as semiofficial state highway maps. Though they essentially reproduced a version of the official state highway map, such maps were published and often marketed by these independent firms. They were (and are) splashed with advertisements for individual attractions and accommodations, which, of course, subsidize the maps' "free distribution." Northwood Map Designs, based in Boulder Junction, Wisconsin, currently publishes these kinds of maps for Wisconsin, Indiana, Ohio, and Michigan.[43] The attractive 1996 edition of the *Wisconsin Tour and Highway Map*, which was published by Northwood, features the standard state department of transportation highway map on one side and a simplified highway map on the other, which is flanked by pictures of wildlife, Native Americans paddling a canoe, a horse-drawn fire engine, and a farm. Pictures on the map itself show the locations of attractions that apparently have paid for the privilege, including the Paul Bunyan Lumberjack Cook Shanty, the Leinenkugel Brewery and Gift Shop, the Cedar Grove Cheese Company, and the Milwaukee County Zoo. More attractions are listed on the margins of this map, and color advertisements for hotel chains, casinos, and other attractions occupy entire panels on both the front and back of the map.[44]

In one sense, the introduction of these semiofficial and commercialized maps marks a new phase in state highway map production. In an era when state budgets are under increasing constraints, the authorization of these commercial editions apparently conforms to the broader trend toward

Figure 16. Back panel illustrations for the *1973 Wisconsin Highway Map* (Madison: Wisconsin Department of Transportation, Division of Highways, 1973). Courtesy of The Newberry Library, Chicago.

privatization of many state functions as a means of budgetary relief. The new semiofficial maps, like the postings by state highway agencies of lists of gas stations, restaurants, and attractions near interstate exits, seem to herald an era when the publication of all official state highway maps will be subsidized by advertisements. The editions of regular official maps published and distributed by state transportation and highway agencies persist. These continue to promote, if inconsistently, the broad tourist themes they have always emphasized, but by comparison to earlier maps and to contemporary semiofficial maps, this effort seems almost halfhearted. The energy of tourism promotion is now expended elsewhere, on other printed maps and on state tourism Web sites.

In the Midwest, as elsewhere, official state highway maps began life as internal documents reporting on the planning, creation, and early development of state highway systems. In the first decade or so after they went public, the maps' preoccupation with pavement quality, highway signage, and traffic regulations was understandable from a purely functional perspective. The character of much of the early promotional rhetoric of official state highway maps also reflected the pride that highway officials took in their work. The rhetorical emphasis on "highway progress" resurfaced occasionally in promotional material presented on state or agency anniversaries, during World War II, after the creation of the interstate highway system, and after the creation of state departments of transportation. Even in years when the promotional content of official maps shifted to other themes, we find depictions of highway signs, reminders to fasten seat belts, and subtle insertions of highways and bridges into landscapes ostensibly showing forests, lakes, beaches, and farmland. The weight of the state highway map as an institutional tradition may account for its continued support by state governments when other forms of free road maps—such as oil-company maps—have mostly disappeared.

Yet there is clearly much more to state highway maps than the extension and celebration of state authority. Since the 1930s, every midwestern state has recognized that the annual (or biennial) distribution of hundreds of thousands of official state highway maps presented an opportunity for the state to define itself. We began this study with the expectation that there might be some unity in the way the seven states presented themselves since the 1930s. We expected that some of this unity might come from the image of the Great Lakes themselves. But only Michigan, which is straddled by three Great Lakes, and, to a lesser extent, Wisconsin and Minnesota offer any consistent promotion of the Great Lakes as a tourist asset or as central to the history and economy of the region.[45]

If there is a clear regional image put forward by these midwestern states, it is centrality. For many years, Indiana's highway maps featured an inset map showing road distances from cities throughout the country to Indianapolis. Likewise, Ohio asserted its central location in the national transportation system. Both Minnesota and Wisconsin periodically published regional maps showing how well connected their tourist regions were to other states by highway. And Iowa consistently stressed its status as the agricultural heartland of the nation.

The absence of a readily promoted regional identity both reflected and reinforced the Midwest's lack of national recognition as a tourist destination. Midwesterners might appreciate Michigan's west coast, but most other Americans think of Maine and Florida when lighthouses and sandy beaches come to mind. The north-woods image of a sportsman's and recreational paradise promoted by Minnesota, Wisconsin, and Michigan has a lasting appeal, but primarily among tourists within the region.

Economically, agriculture has received more attention than industry. The Midwest's reputation as an agricultural region was embraced most enthusiastically and poetically by Iowa, although Wisconsin frequently counted its diverse agriculture and dairying among the many assets it promoted. Most states mentioned their industrial strength from time to time, but this was not a consistent theme.

In fact, cityscapes and metropolitan culture played only a very small role in the promotional content of official state highway maps, even in Illinois, where Chicago has long been the dominant tourist attraction. Chicago appeared only twice on the cover of the Illinois Department of Transportation map (1970 and 1999–2000) and Detroit only twice on Michigan maps. The explanation for this may rest partly on the fact that the scale of state highway maps is poorly suited for navigation of urban spaces. Map designers compensated by providing large-scale inset maps of urban areas, but the fact remains that even today, the predominant landscapes shown on highway maps are the small towns and empty spaces connected by two-lane state highways. We note also, however, that the headquarters of Illinois's Department of Transportation is in Springfield, Michigan's office is in Lansing, and Wisconsin's is in Madison, and it is structures in those cities that appear most often on their respective states' official highway maps. Iowa's emphasis on agriculture was partly influenced by the fact that the state highway commission and the modern department of transportation reside not in Des Moines but in Ames, home of the state's agriculture department and its historically agricultural university, Iowa State.

Finally, we have seen that there are broad subregional differences in the character of tourism promotion on official maps. Of these seven midwestern states, the three most northerly states were generally quicker than the four southern ones to use their official maps to appeal to tourists. The northern states' maps from the 1930s were lavishly illustrated and annotated with tourist information more consistently than their southern neighbors because they had a well-defined (if largely regional) tourist niche to promote. Over the course of the twentieth century, the outdoor world of the sportsman, the boater, and the skier was gradually diluted by other themes in these three states. This was partly a result of the fact that the tourism industry diversified to embrace historical and cultural themes more fully.

Because they had neither extensive forests nor lakes by the thousands, the four states in the southern tier struggled to find an enduring set of images that might appeal to out-of-state visitors. Indiana maps ignored historical or geographical themes for most of the century. Illinois highway officials gave up the effort entirely by the 1960s. Ohio's emphasis on transportation themes persisted in the 1970s and 1980s but afterward was largely abandoned. Only Iowa's promotion of itself as an agricultural center produced an attractive and consistent rival to the north's sportsman's paradise. Reflecting both the self-effacement and the pride in productivity characteristic of the region, a poem attached to the 1941 Iowa map transforms the very plainness of the state's landscape into a virtue:

> If you're seeking scenic grandeur—
> Mighty mountains capped with snow,
> I'm afraid we'll disappoint you
> For we haven't one to show.
> If you yearn for yawning chasms,
> If you seek a waterfall,
> Stranger, we just can't produce them—
> We don't have such things at all.
> When the Maker of Creation
> Fashioned out this Hawkeye Land,

Mountains sheer and painted deserts
Didn't fit the task at hand.
He was building us a garden
And for what He had in mind,
There must be abundant beauty,
But of quite a different kind.
Have you seen a field of clover
With its riot of red bloom?
You can duplicate those colors
Only with a magic loom.
Have you seen the silver ripples
Chase each other o'er the plain,
As the gentle summer breezes
Stir a field of ripening grain?
Have you seen a shimmering cornfield
Row on row in dress parade,
Dark green uniforms a-glitter,
Golden tassels for cockades?
Have you seen a herd of cattle
Grazing in some cool retreat,
Finding life quite to their liking,
Undisturbed by man's conceit?
In our peaceful land of plenty
Scenic grandeur won't be found,
But the beauty that we offer
Comes from deep within the ground.
Where the Greatest of all Chemists
Blending sunshine, soil and rain,
Through the ever changing seasons,
Makes the earth to bloom again.[46]

Lacking Grand Canyons and Great Smokies, our seven Midwest states produced official highway maps that were mostly inward-looking and understated. Targeted largely at in-state audiences and regional tourists, they promoted a mixture of governmental culture, outdoor leisure, and transportation in an unspectacular but productive landscape.

NOTES

1. On the history, rhetoric, and iconography of American oil-company maps, see James R. Akerman, "American Promotional Road Mapping in the Twentieth Century," *Cartography and Geographic Information Science* 29 (July 2002): 175–91; James R. Akerman, "Twentieth-Century American Road Maps and the Making of a National Motorized Space," in James R. Akerman, ed., *Cartographies of Travel and Navigation* (Chicago: University of Chicago Press, 2006), 151–206; Walter W. Ristow, "A Half-Century of Oil-Company Road Maps," *Surveying and Mapping* 24 (December 1964): 617–37; and Douglas A. Yorke, Jr., and John Margolies, *Hitting the Road: The Art of the American Road Map* (San Francisco: Chronicle Books, 1996).

2. Exceptions are Albert W. Ward, "The State of State Road Maps," *American Cartographer* 4 (January 1977): 5–9; Ron Peddicord, "The Evolution of the Illinois Official Highway Map, 1917 to 1992," *Illinois GIS & Mapnotes* 11 (Summer 1993): 2–12.

3. Denis Wood, *The Power of Maps* (New York: Guilford, 1992), 95–107.

4. We define official state highway maps as maps that depict on a single sheet the highway system of the entire state and that are published by a state agency for free distribution to the public.

5. Our survey is based primarily on an examination of copies of official state highway maps in The Newberry Library in Chicago and the Regenstein Library at the University of Chicago.

6. For a history of the good roads movement and the early history of state and federal involvement in highway development, see *America's Highways, 1776–1976: A History of the Federal-Aid Program* (Washington, D.C.: U.S. Department of Transportation, 1979); and P. J. Hugill, "Good Roads and the Automobile in the United States, 1880–1929," *Geographical Review* 72 (July 1982): 330–49. On the Federal Aid Road Act of 1916, see Richard F. Weingroff, "Federal Aid Road Act of 1916: Building the Foundation," at http://www.fhwa.dot.gov/infrastructure/rw96a.htm.

7. See James R. Akerman, "Blazing a Well-Worn Path: Cartographic Commercialism, Highway Promotion, and Automobile Tourism in the United States, 1880–1930," *Cartographica* 30 (1993): 10–20; and Roderick Clayton McKenzie, "The Development of Automobile Guides in the United States" (master's thesis, University of California–Los Angeles, 1963).

8. For a chronological listing of official state highway maps issued for the general public, see Mark Greaves's Web pages, "Official Maps Master List," at http://www.roadmaps.org/omml/index.html. We have also found useful the reproductions of official state highway map covers on "Mark's Highway Page," at http://www.geocities.com/mdo200. See also LeRoy Barnett, "Key Dates in Map History," at www.michigan.gov/mdot/0,1607,7-151-9615_11151-67883--,00.html.

9. Similar logs are also found on early maps issued by Minnesota and Ohio.

10. *Map of Ohio Showing State Routes . . . August 1, 1925* (Columbus: State of Ohio, Division of Highways, 1925). This map can be seen on the Web site developed by the Ohio State Department of Transportation, at http://www.dot.state.oh.us/techservsite/availpro/gis_mapping/mrsid/Sids/otm1925a.sid.

11. *State of Wisconsin Highway Commission, Madison, Map Showing State and Federal Highway Routes* (Madison: Wisconsin Highway Commission, 1933).

12. *Iowa Primary Road Map, State of Iowa* (Ames: Iowa State Highway Commission, 1931).

13. *Map of Illinois Showing State Highways* (Springfield: State of Illinois, Department of Public Works and Buildings, Division of Highways, 1930).

14. *Map of Ohio Showing State Routes* (Columbus: State of Ohio Division of Highways, 1923). This map can be seen at: http://www.dot.state.oh.us/techservsite/availpro/gis_mapping/mrsid/sids/otm1923a.sid.

15. *Map of the Indiana State Highway System . . . January 1934* (Indianapolis: State Highway Commission, 1934).

16. *Illinois Highway Guide Official 1928 Edition* (Chicago: H. M. Gousha for the Illinois Secretary of State Automobile Department, 1928).

17. *State of Wisconsin Highway Commission, 1933.*

18. We have not seen a 1923 map, but notations on the 1929 and 1932 editions tell us that they were the seventh and tenth revisions, respectively.

19. *Outdoor Illinois* (Springfield and Chicago: H. M. Gousha for the Illinois Department of Conservation, 1929).

20. *State Parks of Michigan* (Lansing: Michigan Department of Conservation, 1930).

21. In addition to the 1930 *State Parks* map, The Newberry Library possesses copies of these 1931 through 1933 editions, titled *Michigan Highways, Lakes, Streams, and Forests.*

22. *Minnesota 1938 Official Map* (St. Paul: McGill-Warner Co. for the Minnesota Department of Highways, 1938).

23. *1936 Map of Minnesota Showing Trunk Highway System* (St. Paul: McGill-Warner Co. for the Minnesota Highway Department, 1936).

24. *1934 Official Michigan Highway Map* (Lansing: State Highway Department, 1934).

25. *1939 Winter Michigan Highway Map* (Lansing: Michigan State Highway Department, 1938).

26. *Iowa Highway Map 1934* (Ames: Iowa State Highway Commission, 1934).

27. *The Official Summer Highway Map of Michigan, 1942* (Lansing: Michigan State Highway Department, 1942).

28. *Official Highway Map of Michigan, 1945* (Lansing: Michigan State Highway Department, 1945).

29. *Minnesota 1950 Official Highway Map* (St. Paul: Minnesota Department of Highways, 1950).

30. *Iowa 1947 Highway Map* (Ames: Iowa State Highway Commission, 1947).

31. *Michigan 1960 Official Highway Map* (Lansing: Michigan State Highway Department, 1960).

32. Railroads had been indicated on Wisconsin, Indiana, and Illinois official highway maps for several decades, and the transition to departments of transportation did not significantly affect the design of their maps or promotional features. Illinois, however, added a small inset map of Amtrak lines.

33. *Michigan Great Lake State Official Transportation Map . . . 1974* (Lansing: State Highway Commission and State Department of Highways and Transportation, 1974).

34. *Minnesota 1977–78 Official Transportation Map* (St. Paul: Minnesota Department of Transportation, 1977).

35. The achievement that apparently inspired this rhetoric, Ohio State University's national football championship for 1968, is not explicitly mentioned.

36. *1969 Official Ohio Highway Map and Economic Digest* (Columbus: Ohio Department of Highways, 1969).

37. *Ohio Portraits of Progress 1982 Official Transportation Map* (Columbus: Ohio Department of Transportation, 1982).

38. *Welcome to Iowa, Statewide Territorial Centennial 1838–1938, Iowa Highway Map* (Ames: Iowa State Highway Commission, 1938); *1969 Indiana Highway Map Official Highway Map 50th Anniversary 1919–1969 . . . State Highway Commission* (Indianapolis: Indiana State Highway Commission, 1969); *1962 Official Ohio Highway Map* (Columbus: Ohio Department of Highways, 1962).

39. *Minnesota, 1976 Official Highway Map* (St. Paul: Minnesota Department of Highways, 1976).

40. *1973 Wisconsin Highway Map* (Madison: Wisconsin Department of Transportation, 1973).

41. *1980–1981 Wisconsin Official State Highway Map* (Madison: Wisconsin Department of Transportation, 1980).

42. *Explore Minnesota Official State Highway Map* (St. Paul: Minnesota Department of Transportation, 1987).

43. See "Northwood Map Publishers, Inc.," at http://www.northwoodmap.com.

44. *Wisconsin Tour and Highway Map* (Boulder Junction, Wis.: Northwood Map Publishers, 1996).

45. There are occasional references to Lake Erie on Ohio's maps.

46. *1941 Iowa* (Ames: Iowa State Highway Commission, 1941).

Michigan: Cartographic Perspectives on the Great Lakes State

Gerald A. Danzer

SINCE THE BEGINNING OF AMERICAN STATEHOOD, A MAP OF THE COMMONWEALTH HAS been an important expression of sovereignty and civic identity. The United States, it was true, cemented together the separate states, a unity created out of many entities, *e pluribus unum*. In the federal vision, however, individual states, especially new ones carved out of the common domain, also needed ways and means to establish their specific identities. Thus, each of the original states desired a map of its territory as soon as one could be produced. Such a document would mark the state's boundaries and establish its jurisdiction. Beyond that, it would inventory its resources, towns, and cities, putting them in the context of natural features. Viewers of such a map would be able to find their specific location and place it in the geographic setting of statehood. A sense of attachment to a polity with a given geographic dimension encouraged a feeling of belonging to an expanded community, articulated connections to a wider place, and suggested obligations of a larger citizenship.[1]

Residents of Michigan, which was admitted to the Union in 1837, shared in this desire for an appropriate state map and a cartographic identity for the state's citizens. Although all of the states created from the Northwest Territory received separate maps in the process of attaining statehood, Michigan had a unique geographical situation to proclaim. Over the years, its citizens came to think of theirs as the "Great Lakes State," and indeed it was a special case, because it alone of the new states was surrounded by the Great Lakes, its boundaries defined mainly by the lakes rather than by narrower rivers or lines on a map. A fundamental fact of Michigan's geography is that the state lies entirely in the watershed of the Great Lakes. The exception to this statement is a few square miles of Gogebic County at the western edge of the Upper Peninsula. Michigan is the only state so situated, a geographical fact that sets it markedly apart from its sister states carved out of the Northwest Territory, each of which has the bulk of its territory in the Mississippi valley. This article explores a few aspects of Michigan's uniqueness by making a general survey of the maps of the Michigan region from the earliest mapmakers to the present.[2]

Much of the interest in the early history of Michigan maps centers on the gradual discovery of the Great Lakes by the French and the appearance of these shapes on the portrayals of North America.[3] Geographic information concerning the interior of North America was often guarded or misunderstood, filled with gaps that tempted imaginations and encouraged adventure. Yet out of the process came two fundamentally different ways to perceive the heartland of North America: an initial orientation by way of the St. Lawrence estuary and the Great Lakes basin, followed by a basic realignment of vision suggested by the dendritic pattern of streams and rivers that gradually defined the Mississippi valley. There was some tension between these two ways of comprehending the continent, and the French holdings eventually split into two parts, Canada and Louisiana, each positioned along a different geographic spine and each reflecting a different cartographic tradition.

Cartographically, the two angles of vision led to interesting results, especially as the mapmakers aligned the two watersheds, establishing their correct relationship to each other. Knowledge of these two approaches to visualizing America's heartland opens a door to understanding the history of Michigan maps and the state's developing conception of itself as the Great Lakes State. The actual lay of the land, of course, usually dictates the lines, shapes, and symbols on our maps. But each map uses this fund of knowledge selectively, addressing particular purposes and specific audiences, providing a center, an orientation, a set of icons, names, colors, and typefaces to present its message in the most convincing way.

Because the overriding objective of Europe's Age of Discovery was to reach the Orient by sailing westward, there was an initial inclination among European mapmakers to portray the intervening landmass as indented by deep bays and featuring long rivers and great lakes. In the best of all possible worlds, a convenient water route would facilitate seaborne commerce in the high middle latitudes, in other words, a Northwest Passage. In strict scientific honesty, the makers of the early maps of North America should have left the heartland blank, and some did or covered it with elaborate cartouches, illustrative drawings, or explanatory texts. But there were just enough early communications with Native peoples to justify recording their suggestions about large lakes and long rivers on the map, which lent a hopeful tone to the cartography.

The first separately published map devoted to the Americas, Sebastian Münster's celebrated woodcut of 1540, may have reflected a misleading observation by Giovanni da Verrazano in 1524. While viewing the North Carolina coast, the navigator peered over barrier islands to waters beyond, imagining a Western Sea that was, he hoped, connected to the Pacific. This "Sea of Verrazano" also appeared as a prominent feature on the world map in Münster's *Geographia Universalis,* which appeared in many versions over the next several decades.[4]

Meanwhile, as Jacques Cartier sailed up the St. Lawrence River in 1541, he received reports that led to a major revision of North American maps, essentially pushing Verrazano's "sea" northward to Hudson Bay. Reaching the site of Montreal, Cartier learned from the Indians how the long river was fed by a great lake that reached westward beyond their knowledge. Recognizable depictions of the St. Lawrence region soon appeared on European maps. These fell into three categories: the long-river tradition suggested by Gerhard Mercator, the "leave it blank" solution (because we do not know) employed by cartographers such as Henry Briggs, and the open-ended great-lake approach initiated by Nicolas Sanson.

Louis C. Karpinski started his discussion of the fundamental maps of Michigan with Mercator's map of the world issued at Duisburg in 1569. It featured a long St. Lawrence River reaching to the southwest corner of the continent. Flowing in a straight line, without benefit of a wellspring in a great lake, the stream suggested a transcontinental route heading toward Mexico. Mercator's son Rumold continued to use this template for the North American interior on his world map of 1587 and on the map of the Western Hemisphere in the various editions of the Mercator *Atlas,* which first appeared in 1595.[5] Earlier portrayals of North America on Italian maps had used a similar design featuring a great river of the interior flowing into the Gulf of St. Lawrence. Paolo Forlani's portrait of North America, published in Venice in 1565, is probably the earliest entry in this family of maps; but Tomaso Porcacchi's "New World" was more influential, appearing in six editions between 1572 and 1620.[6]

The long-river axis across North America also flourished in the maps of Abraham Ortelius. The world map in his great atlas, *Theatrum Orbis Terrarum,* followed Mercator, as did the map of the Americas in the same book.[7] These maps exerted an enormous influence as the Ortelius atlas appeared year after year in more than seventy editions. On both sheets, Ortelius split this continental axis into two sections, a great artery extending from New France westward and an incipient Colorado River reaching north and west from the Gulf of Lower California. The headwaters of these two streams nearly touched each other in the mountains of the Continental Divide.

The idea that the world's continents were spanned and dominated by great rivers became a popular way for Europeans to depict a world full of accessible, but unexplored, regions. These images, if they had endured, would have placed Michigan as a way station on a great corridor across North America. Then the state would have been one bead on the string, without a distinctive geography as a unique key to its identity.[8]

The map of "The North Part of America" that Henry Briggs prepared in conjunction with his *Treatise of the Northwest Passage* provides a good example of the "blank interior" approach to North American cartography. The map first appeared in 1625 in Samuel Purchas's *Hakluytus Posthumus,* attracting much subsequent attention because it was an early printed map that showed California as an island.[9] This map started a cartographic misconception that lasted, on some examples, for more than a century. Briggs tried to take a scientific approach and record only features about which he had some information. Unfortunately, he was either misinformed about California or he took his meager data much too far in the wrong direction. The region that became Michigan, like most of the continental interior, remained a blank space on Briggs's map.[10]

In the seventeenth century, a third approach to characterizing the interior of North America gradually supplanted the riverine-axis and blank-map approaches. In this case, great lakes dominated America's heartland. There were a few precedents in the previous century, starting with Paolo Forlani's map of the New World (Venice, 1565) and leading up to Edward Wright's map illustrating the *Principal Navigations . . . of the English Nation* (London, 1599).[11] But the gradual appearance of what are now known as the Great Lakes on printed maps actually reflected the exploration of the American interior by the French. The process of discovering these inland waters, of reporting the new knowledge back to Europe, and finally of translating these relations onto published maps has intrigued scholars and map collectors ever since the work of Francis Parkman.[12] The sequence of maps that gradually defined the Great Lakes was considered "fundamental" to understanding the mapping of Michigan by Louis C. Karpinski, and he devoted more pages to this background story than to the actual bibliography in his classic work.[13]

The dynamic between French exploration and North American cartography starts with Samuel de Champlain, the father of New France. He drew at least four comprehensive maps of New France, two of which illustrated his publications outlining the French explorations in the New World.[14] Champlain's 1612 map was part of an elaborate sheet that included botanical drawings and portrayals of Native peoples. Decorations and other features on the map suggested bountiful seas and lands of abundance supporting a colony covered with trees arranged in parklike fashion. Champlain took care to note that he had not visited much of the area portrayed on his map. Based largely on reports from the Indians, the map shows a broad St. Lawrence River leading to a pair of great lakes, the second of which is cut off by the map's border. Champlain set images of canoes and a great sturgeon on these waters, continuing the motifs of fecundity and accessibility evident throughout the map. This classic map, "the genesis of Great Lakes cartography,"[15] celebrated bountiful waters and verdant lands in the American interior as much as it suggested a passageway through them.

Champlain's second printed map appeared in Paris in 1632. By then, the great-lakes theme had been picked up by other cartographers. The rise of the great Dutch map-publishing firms occurred during these decades. A map of North America prepared by Johannes Jansson eventually reached nineteen editions, appearing in atlases published by Hendrick Hondius and eventually by Jansson himself. The original Jansson map (1636) followed the Briggs map of 1625. In the Northeast, however, Jansson used Champlain's 1612 map, drawing several lakes as the source of the St. Lawrence River. This map suggested two additional gateways to the American interior: from Button (Hudson) Bay to the north and by way of a miniature Mississippi River system draining into the Gulf of Mexico.[16]

Throughout the seventeenth century, as Jansson's maps kept appearing with a tentative great-lakes orientation, French exploration of the American interior advanced at a steady pace. In 1650, a map of North America by Nicolas Sanson became one of the first printed maps to show all five Great Lakes. His depiction of the Great Lakes illustrated Sanson's optimism about transcontinental travel, as the lakes were unbounded in their western reaches, hinting at a water route across North America.[17] His 1656 map of Canada or New France reinforced this hope. On this map, Lake Superior opened wide, reaching toward the northwestern coastline of the continent.[18]

The expanding French interest in Canada went hand in hand with the emergence of French map publishing, which soon challenged Dutch leadership in cartographic endeavors. Sanson's portrayal of the Great Lakes certainly benefited from the reports that explorers, especially the Jesuits, sent back to Europe. In the 1660s, at least ten different cartographers placed Sanson's view of the North American interior on their published maps. Nicolas Visscher's map of America, which may have been produced as early as 1658, suggested that one open-ended lake dominated the interior and named it "Lac contenant."[19]

The exploits of Louis Joliet and Father Jacques Marquette added another dimension to North American geography. In 1673, they left the Great Lakes basin to find the Great River of the American interior that the Native Americans had described to them. Although both Joliet and Marquette made maps of their adventure, it was not until La Salle followed their route while pursuing his dream of empire that a major concern emerged—how to relate the Great Lakes to the Mississippi valley—that affected published maps of the North American interior. It is upon this issue that the foundation for understanding Michigan maps must be laid.

Father Louis Hennepin's "Map of New France and Louisiana" appeared in Paris in 1683 along with an account of his adventures as part of the La Salle expedition of 1679. When La Salle was forced temporarily to stop his penetration of the American wilderness in the Illinois country and return to Canada for additional support, he sent Hennepin and a few companions to continue the expedition down the Illinois River. He asked them to turn upstream on the Mississippi River to explore its upper reaches. Hennepin's group was captured by hostile Indians and perhaps taken to the shores of Lake Superior. After some additional travel, they were freed and retraced their steps back to the Mississippi River. Then they used the Wisconsin River-Green Bay route to return to Canada and eventually to Paris.

Hennepin published the tale of his adventure in 1684. Accompanied by a map dated 1683, it became a best seller. Unfortunately, Hennepin's book often borrowed from the work of others, and its success led him to tell the story a second time in 1697. On this occasion, Hennepin made so many gross exaggerations that scholars have questioned the veracity of everything he reported.[20] Nevertheless, his map is very important as the first published attempt to relate the Great Lakes to the Great River. Its title, *Carte de la Nouvelle France et de la Louisiane,* balanced coverage of Louisiana with New France, signaling a new perspective. Hennepin's 1683 map featured the five Great Lakes in recognizable form but with Lake Erie reaching south all the way to Tennessee. The Great River played a prominent role in his portrayal of the area, starting in a different watershed west of Lake Superior and sending a great stream due south as far as the Illinois country. After that, in the 1683 version, the map is blank. However, Hennepin did point out many places where the two midcontinent drainage systems almost touched each other, suggesting ease of communication, if not across the continent, at least between the Gulfs of St. Lawrence and Mexico. Each drainage basin would soon support a major French colony. New France, in the Great Lakes basin, was already well mapped. Louisiana, the second domain, now became the land of cartographic opportunity.

After La Salle's death, Hennepin asserted that he had been the first European to descend the Mississippi River all the way to its mouth, and he produced two new maps to substantiate this claim. Both showed the "Newly Discovered Lands" and traced the entire course of the Great River but placed its mouth at the western edge of the Gulf of Mexico, the actual location of the Rio Grande. Hennepin's Mississippi River also lacked a delta, a second major clue that he had not actually descended the river. His larger-scale new map, dated 1697, clearly placed major tributaries of the Great River in close proximity to those of the Great Lakes (fig. 1). This map went through many editions extending well into the eighteenth century, often with the addition of place names and some alterations in the geographical features. Hennepin's maps exerted great influence on those issued in every center of cartographic production. In England, for example, Robert Morden developed "A New Map of the English Empire in America" to replace several small maps he had previously published in 1680 and 1687.[21] In his first effort, Morden's crude rendition of the Great Lakes pictured them as open-ended. The second version, for a pocket atlas, showed all five of the lakes in recognizable fashion, but they were pinched together beneath an enormous Hudson Bay. His "New Map" of 1695, which was more than four times as large, used the extra space to relate the English colonies to both the Mississippi River and the Great Lakes.

The most unusual feature that Morden placed on his 1695 map was a long mountain range extending, in our geography, from the Straits of Mackinac to the Everglades in Florida. It cut through the center of Michigan's Lower Peninsula and then slanted eastward to join the Appalachian spine. A note explained that the Michigan section of this cordillera featured a high plateau: "On top of these mountains is a plain like a terras [sic] walk above 200 miles in length." Thus, Morden furnished the future state with a wondrous topography as well as a unique situation. In 1719, the map was slightly revised by John Senex for inclusion in his *New General Atlas.*[22]

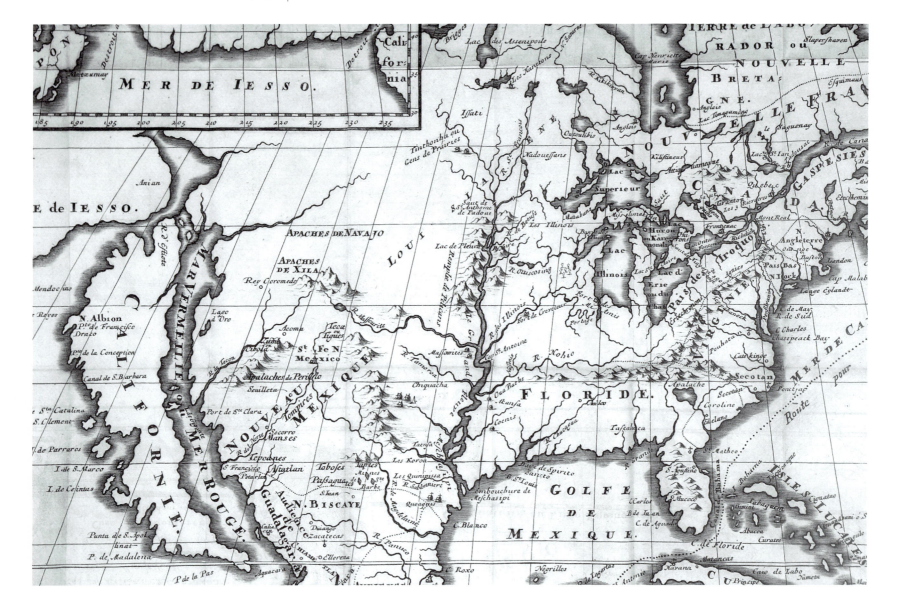

Figure 1. A portion of Father Louis Hennepin's map of North America from his *A New Discovery of a Vast Country in America.* The second of Hennepin's maps relating the Mississippi River to the Great Lakes, it was the first to show the entire course of the Great River. Justin Winsor, ed., *Narrative and Critical History of America* (Boston: J. R. Osgood, 1885), 4: 251.

After Hennepin's maps, or really after the reports of Joliet, Marquette, and La Salle, American cartography needed to portray a midcontinent balanced between great lakes and great rivers. Some maps by Sanson were updated to reflect this new perspective, but several of the most impressive maps in the new fashion came from Italian cartographers. This "Italian chapter" in North American maps started with Vincenzo Coronelli, a Franciscan priest with a great interest in the world picture emerging from the European discoveries that occurred during his lifetime. In 1688, he published a celebrated set of gores for making a terrestrial globe measuring about forty-two inches in diameter. The Great Lakes, shown in a remarkably accurate design, appeared above a great-river system whose branches fed a sturdy stem that flowed due south toward the western shore of the Gulf of Mexico.[23] For the present investigation, one of the most useful maps produced by Coronelli, featuring the western part of Canada, was engraved in Paris in 1688. Several later versions appeared in Venice, one with the title "La Louisiana."[24] It is noteworthy that the peninsulas later designated as Michigan lie entirely within the Great Lakes basin. In contrast, the southern and western reaches of the Great Lakes show tributaries of the "River Colbert" (Mississippi) reaching out to almost touch several short rivers belonging to the lakes. Coronelli has marked these connecting points as portages in several places. Scenes of Indian life take up blank spaces on the map, and trees are scattered across the landscape, reminders that this was a productive country, especially for the fur trade.

By 1700, enough knowledge of North America had been gathered in Paris to support a fundamental rethinking of the continent's maps. Following in Coronelli's footsteps, cartographers throughout Europe mounted a huge effort to map accurately not only the coastal outlines of the known world but also the lands in the interior. The ability to measure longitude, gained late in the eighteenth century, aided these efforts, but the endeavor started much earlier and centered around the maps produced by the Delisle family.

The Delisle map of North America (1700) has been called a foundation map because it repositioned the locations of places based on the best data available.[25] Thus, it moved the mouth of the Mississippi River to its proper location, provided a delta, and related it to the Great Lakes as accurately as possible. This repositioning reduced the extent of the Great Lakes and revealed vast unknown lands beyond the Mississippi. One might say that the concept of a "Great West" in North America was born with this map. Delisle followed Coronelli in drawing the shapes of the Great Lakes, but he dropped the idea of a mountain range stretching east and west across mid-America to separate the upper Mississippi valley of New France from the lower reaches of the Great River. In 1703, the Delisle firm published a map of Canada or New France that carefully positioned the Great Lakes in the graticule and distinguished the Hudson Bay drainage from the waters flowing into the Great Lakes–St. Lawrence system.[26] In these respects, this map also furnished a starting point for its successors throughout the century.

In 1718, when Guillaume Delisle published the first edition of his "Map of Louisiana and the Course of the Mississippi," his work suggested a new conception of the continent.[27] The stem of the Great River firmly centered the map. The long, narrow valley of the Rio Grande furnished a western border for the great valley of the interior, and the thin line of the Appalachian ridge provided an eastern frame, pushing Anglo-America to a marginal position along the Atlantic coast. Lake Superior was named, but its waters were cut off at the top of the map, thereby reducing the Great Lakes to a marginal feature. What remained on the map was a vast Mississippi River system draining the far reaches of the interior and suggesting the dynamic play between rivers and the land. An inset map set in the lower right-hand corner in the second state of the map emphasized the importance of the mouth of the Mississippi, and it located New Orleans, which had been established that very year.

Delisle employed mountains and hills to help shape the Mississippi valley. A prominent upland arc separated the Ohio valley from the Gulf coastal plain. A narrow, elongated plateau also sliced across the peninsula later known as Michigan's mitten. "Michigan" as a geographic name appears twice on the map, designating Lake Michigan as well as its sister, "Lake Huron of Michigan." But the main significance of this map for studying Michigan cartography does not lie in using names or setting out a geography for the state that would be formed later. Rather, the primary importance of Delisle's work was that it moved the Great Lakes from the center of the map to its northern margin. Then it defined the geography of the midcontinent by means of rivers, featuring New Orleans rather than Montreal as the city of destiny for the French empire in North America. The Gulf of Mexico then replaced the Gulf of St. Lawrence as the continent's major portal to the world ocean. Delisle's 1718 map suggested the later configuration of the American interior, pulling its commerce toward the Gulf of Mexico by way of the river systems. Only the peninsular regions set apart by the Great Lakes seem to have escaped this magnetic force. But the placement of prominent north-south uplands in the middle of the Lower Peninsula suggested that land routes in this region would necessarily take a north-south direction as well, aligning themselves to fit the geography of the Mississippi River valley. Delisle also pointed out several portages at the base of Michigan's Lower Peninsula to emphasize the linkages between the lands around the lakes and the Mississippi valley.

The publication of Delisle's maps of North America, especially the 1718 sheet, which emphasized the dominance of the Mississippi River valley, was part and parcel of the growing tensions among three rival empires active on the continent: the French, the Spanish, and the English. Publishers throughout Europe followed the Delisle example in developing their own maps, such as those of Johann Baptist Homann in Nuremberg (1714), Hermann Moll in London (1717), Nicolas de Fer in Paris (1718), Henry Chatelain and Zacherie Chatelain (1719) and Gerard van Keulen (1720) in Amsterdam, and Matthias Seutter (1730) in Augsburg.[28]

The work of a German cartographer, Heinrich Scherer, illustrates this imperial focus. His map of North America, dated 1700, showed a continent filled with mountains and hills that encircled the Great Lakes. He packed the surrounding seas and an elaborate cartouche with exotic animals, turning North America into a vast wilderness filled with strange creatures. In updating the map two decades later, however, Scherer kept the mountains but balanced the Great Lakes with the Great River, Hennepin-style.[29] Almost all of the unusual creatures disappeared, replaced by ships, Indians, and colonists. A large decoration at the lower right featured three panels, each one devoted to an imperial geographic image. The English owned the Atlantic coastal plain, and the Spanish received California, the Pacific Coast, and the Rio Grande. The French Empire was symbolized by the Great Lakes and the Great River.

In the eighteenth century, geopolitical themes began to replace an interest in the wonders of nature on many other maps portraying the North American interior. A pamphleteer in America, for example, reproduced the eastern portion of Delisle's 1718 map in his *Some Considerations on the Consequences of the French Settling Colonies on the Mississippi*. The title of the booklet exhibited English understatement, but the map sounded an alarm. And the text concluded: "Some time or other, the Mississippi will drown our Settlements on the Main[land] of America."[30] In many respects, this "New Map of Louisiana and the River Mississippi" was indebted to Delisle's concept of the North American interior. Like the French prototype, it cut off the upper Great Lakes to make the river system appear more dominant on the continent. The crest of the Appalachian Mountains still served as a boundary, but the southern fork of the Ohio (the Tennessee River) carried an ominous label: "the road the French take to go to Carolina."

Any road, of course, goes both ways. French activities in Louisiana were certainly stimulated by the persistent plans of Dr. Daniel Coxe, an Englishman, to establish a colony on the lower Mississippi. In 1699, he dispatched a ship to plant his colony of Carolana on the Mississippi River. Although a young French commander persuaded the new arrivals to turn back at a bend in the river that is still called English Turn today, Coxe kept up his campaign for an English presence on the lower Mississippi. In 1726, he published a description of his proposed colony along with an interesting map.[31] Based in general on Delisle's 1718 map, Coxe's work also added several important elements. He provided full coverage of the Great Lakes and the Gulf of St. Lawrence to give greater balance to the map. He also included the Long River popularized by Louis Armand Lahontan,[32] which provided a supposed route due west from the upper Mississippi valley to the Pacific Ocean. Coxe also turned the mountain range cutting across Michigan to point toward the Mississippi Delta, perhaps suggesting that the Lake of the Illinois (Lake Michigan) was tied geographically to the Great River as much as to the Great Lakes. Coxe even created another great lake to receive the waters of the Wabash, Ohio, Tennessee, and Kentucky rivers just before they entered the Mississippi. Rivers and lakes went hand in hand.

The influence of Delisle's map of Louisiana on popular cartography in the English-speaking world was also evident in the maps that accompanied the various printings of *The History of the Five Indian Nations* by Cadwallader Colden of New York. The purpose of the book, first issued in New York in 1727, was to show the great advantage of their trade and alliance to the British nation as well as to point out the intrigues of the French. Colden prepared two editions of the work, both published in London as well as New York. Although several maps were prepared for these editions, they were substantially the same, and the first one specifically announced in its title that it was "taken from the Map of the [sic] Louisiana done by Mr. DeLisle in 1718."[33]

Colden's map covered the region from Long Island north to Quebec City and west to Lake Michigan. The Great Lakes dominated an image that suggested three avenues of approach: the Gulf of St. Lawrence to the northeast, the Hudson River to the southeast, and the "Branches of the Mississippi" reaching up from the southwest at the base of the map. Each of these tentacles ended in a portage, labeled "carrying place" on the map. "The Country of the Five Nations" started at the headwaters of the Ohio River and centered on the Finger Lakes region. "The Countrys Conquered by the Five Nations" occupied all of the peninsula defined by Lakes Ontario, Erie, and Huron. The Michigan peninsula, divided by "A High Plain 70 Leagues Long," was left blank except for a cluster of villages around Detroit. Colden emphasized that the Native peoples actually controlled the heartland of America. He pictured an avenue of communication proceeding westward from Albany and continuing along the northern shore of Lake Erie to Detroit. He also pointed out that a route along the southern shore of Lake Erie would afford many opportunities for travelers to connect with the Mississippi valley.

Popular cartography—that is, small maps published in books, magazines, and pocket atlases—helped the British populace to comprehend the clash of empires in North America. In 1754, the *London Magazine* featured a series of three maps covering the whole of eastern North America. Part III, "A Map of the Five Great Lakes," which accompanied the September 1755 number, was filled with the names of Indian tribes and small rivers.[34] When *Gentleman's Magazine* reprinted the Royal Proclamation of October 7, 1763, at the end of the Great War for Empire, it included a simple map to illustrate the new governmental arrangements.[35] Its design emphasized the Atlantic coast from Newfoundland to Florida and included Bermuda in a large inset map. The Great Lakes received much more prominence than the Mississippi River, even though all five were in the "Lands Reserved for the Indians." For the first time, the Mississippi served as a border between British territory and Louisiana.

By then, British officials were employing large, elaborate maps of eastern North America to develop their imperial policies. In 1733, Henry Popple had used official records and surveys submitted by the colonial governors to produce an elaborate set of twenty maps.[36] These could be placed in an atlas or joined to form a wall map almost eight feet high and seven feet wide. Another sheet served as an index map for the larger effort. The Board of Trade quickly ordered copies of Popple's maps to be sent to each governor of an American colony. The set covered America from Darien to Hudson Bay, reaching the Rio Grande to the west. The two systems of the Great Lakes–St. Lawrence and of the Mississippi

River divided the interior between them, both outlined in French green rather than British red. But the ornamentation on Popple's map hid imperfections in its geography and a scarcity of detail unusual for a production of such size and scale.

Popple's map invited others to elaborate on his presentation by adding local knowledge from each colony. Dr. John Mitchell, a careful scholar and well-connected physician who had spent decades in America, took up the challenge. Upon returning to London, he published *A Map of the British and French Dominions in North America* (1755) in eight sheets.[37] Mitchell depended on French maps for the Great Lakes and the Mississippi River basin, but his connections gave him ready access to government files in London to help him depict the Atlantic coastal region. His map advanced English cartography to a position of leadership in picturing North America, and by 1791, it had appeared in more than twenty versions. Some of these iterations were in French and Italian, but Mitchell's map became known as the most important map in American history when it was used in the treaties ending both the Great War for Empire in 1763 and the American War of Independence two decades later. By setting the borders of his map to cut off both Hudson Bay and the Gulf of Mexico, Mitchell focused the viewer's attention on the seaboard settlements. At the same time, his conception of the continent's interior suggested that both the Great Lakes and the Great River could be appropriately employed as boundaries. Michigan's "Great Elevated Plain" continued on Mitchell's maps, but it was placed northward, assuming a much more natural shape and working visually to tilt the peninsula toward the Ohio valley.

When Mitchell worked in London in 1748, Jacques Nicolas Bellin's maps of North America had already set the standard for European cartographers.[38] In Bellin's map of the Great Lakes, developed in 1742, he picked up on the report of several large islands in Lake Superior and named these islands after officials in the hydrography office who sponsored his publications. It was natural for Mitchell to turn to this source for coverage of the French territories. He therefore included these islands on his map and the diplomats later followed suit. Thus, the red line boundary on George III's copy of Mitchell's map divided these mythical islands between the United States and British North America, which would pose problems in the future. Fortunately for Michigan, Isle Royale, the only real island of consequence appearing on Bellin's map, was specifically granted to the United States by the Treaty of Paris. The actual boundary between the United States and Canada took many years to work out. Negotiators on both sides preferred natural boundaries, possibly encouraged by the knowledge of American geography revealed so dramatically in the series of maps progressing from Hennepin through Delisle, Popple, and Bellin to Mitchell.

After the Great War for Empire, the context for reading maps of North America shifted to political designations rather than the physical geography of the American interior. The geography on these later maps generally followed the Bellin-Mitchell model or rival maps of North America by Jean Baptiste Bourguignon d'Anville, which left large blank spaces when the cartographer lacked data.[39] John Lodge's map of the Great Lakes, however, in William Russell's 1778 *History of America*, as well as the maps in contemporary accounts of the Revolutionary War, included Bellin's mythical islands.[40] It was not until maps of the Northwest Territory were drawn on the basis of actual surveys that the mythical islands finally disappeared.

There are two major elements in this new chapter of Great Lakes cartography. The first is the division of the region into American states and their subdivisions, counties and townships. The second, on which statehood and local governments often depended, was the system of land division which turned the region into parcels that were numbered, located, and measured so they could be bought and sold as commodities. Both of these fundamental components of later Michigan maps started under the Articles of Confederation, the Land Ordinance of 1785, and the Northwest Ordinance of 1787.

The earliest maps to label the United States as such were simply revised versions of readily available maps. These appeared first in Paris, then in London, but there was a widespread feeling in America that the new states and the new nation needed to produce their own maps.[41] Two individuals, one in Philadelphia and the other in New Haven, met this need for an American map of the new nation in 1784.

The first to appear was Abel Buell's wall map in four sheets: *A New and Correct Map of the United States of North America . . . Humbly Inscribed to His Excellency the Governor and Company of the State of Connecticut*.[42] The title, the elaborate cartouche topped by the new American flag, and the extension of the seaboard states west to the Mississippi River all followed traditional map design. In his depiction of Michigan, Buell retained the usual elevated plain in the center of Michigan's Lower Peninsula. Signs of hope, such as "around here is plenty of virgin copper," were qualified by an "extensive sandy desert" that reached from Grand Traverse Bay to Kalamazoo. Buell prominently labeled Detroit and included Fort St. Joseph next to the "Poutowatomi Town" to suggest a toehold for future settlement. The map designated the rest of Michigan's future territories as lands of the "Chipeways" and the "Ottowas."

William McMurray's wall map of the United States reflected the work of the cartographers serving in the Continental Army.[43] Their efforts did not reach the Great Lakes region, so the high plain remained on the map. McMurray added political subdivisions for the region northwest of the Ohio River according to the division of that area into ten new states set by a resolve of Congress. Thus, straight lines of latitude and longitude cut the Northwest Territory into unnamed blocks, suggesting a future union in which statehood would emerge from the work of surveyors rather than out of geographic circumstances or the processes of historical development. A year later, this region on McMurray's sheet would be featured on a separate *Map of the North West Parts of the United States of America* produced by John Fitch.[44]

The Northwest Ordinance of 1787 changed the number and alignment of states in the region, and the next wall map of the nation, issued in 1791 by Osgood Carleton, a Boston teacher and map publisher, simply omitted all suggestions about future states.[45] The early maps of the United States included in books and atlases produced in America also omitted political subdivisions for the Northwest Territory. Jedidiah Morse, "the father of American geography," folded two maps showing the northern and southern states into his 1789 volume, *The American Geography*.[46] John Stockdale prepared an additional "Map of the Back Settlements" for the 1794 edition of Morse's popular title. The 1796 edition carried a new "Map of the Western Territory" by Thomas C. Andrews of Boston. Neither map projected boundaries for the future states, but the second effort was pathbreaking in an important way. It was one of the earliest maps to show the lines of the congressional land survey.[47]

Also in 1796, Abraham Bradley, Jr., a post office official, published a map of the United States featuring post roads. Only a few details appeared in the Northwestern Territory, but Bradley included both the seven ranges of the original land survey and boundary lines for future states as prescribed by the Northwest Ordinance. A meridian boundary grouped both of Michigan's peninsulas into one state, adding a generous slice of territory on the western shore of Lake Michigan as well. Later, Bradley prepared a "Map of the Northern Parts of the United States" for the 1804 edition of Morse's *American Gazetteer* (fig. 2). Additional details on this sheet make an interesting State IV (Michigan), because its western boundary was placed on the Vincennes meridian a bit to the west of Lake Michigan, putting the Door Peninsula and Chicago in the same state as Detroit and the high plain.[48]

Most of these early maps provided two scales of longitude, one using London to mark the prime meridian and a second using Philadelphia, at the top and bottom of the sheets, respectively. This tradition started with the Buell map of 1784. Twenty years later, Bradley's map in Morse's *American Gazetteer* used only an American prime meridian, this time set in Washington, D.C. Thus, by 1805, when Congress established Michigan Territory, several cartographic fundamentals were in play to help readers interpret maps of this new entity. First, using the national capital to define the prime meridian was one way to pull a map of the nation together. Second, the straight lines of the land survey marked the imprint of the American style of government.

These "lines of civilization" not only divided the land into parcels for private ownership but also determined boundaries for the state's counties and townships. The publication of separate maps of Michigan seemed to wait for the surveyors and the arrival of American ways. The spread of township lines across the map, which would take a generation's work, would mark the progress of European-American settlement, creating a need for new maps year after year. In one way, these revised maps exhibited and celebrated the settlers' achievements. The lines laid down in Michigan by the government surveyors started in Ohio, specifically at the flagpole at Fort Defiance at the mouth of the Auglaize River. Michigan's principal meridian began there and ran due north, crossing the lakes just east of the Straits of Mackinac and just west of Sault Ste. Marie. It is noteworthy that in this respect, almost all the land in Michigan is still legally defined by a point that is within the Great Lakes basin but outside the state's boundaries.[49]

Indian claims to the lands in the southeastern portion of the future state were extinguished by the Treaty of Detroit in 1807, but surveying of the Michigan meridian that set the western edge of this cession did not begin until 1815, when the government needed land to provide a bonus for veterans of the late war. Discouraged in their initial efforts by swampy conditions and sandy barrens, a survey team headed by Edward Tiffin suggested delaying its work until the winter freeze would provide better footing. The authorities quickly decided that these Michigan lands were not fit for the veterans and suggested moving the military tract to the east bank of the Mississippi River in Illinois. Although surveyors continued to work in Michigan and soon encountered better land, it took a few years to overcome the discouraging impact of the initial report. Furthermore, potential settlers needed maps to get their bearings, but satisfactory ones of this area were slow in coming.

The first printed maps of Michigan Territory appeared in atlases issued by American publishers who continued the English practice of giving each county or state a separate sheet in the national atlas. In 1822, when Henry C. Carey and Isaac Lea published their work, *A Complete Historical Chronological and Geographical American Atlas,* they provided a double-page sheet on each territory to complete their set of maps. The Michigan map provided only a few bits of information. Detroit and five nearby counties were labeled, but no boundaries were shown.[50] Another atlas published the following year by Fielding Lucas, Jr., in Baltimore showed the full extent of Michigan Territory, extending its coverage all the way to the Mississippi River and the Lake of the Woods.[51] Although this map provided more information (fig. 3), the lack of internal boundaries suggested an open, empty land in the possession of various Indian tribes. Development could proceed only with the arrival of settlers, the establishment of local government, the creation of towns, and the stirring of commerce. Maps could be a big help in all these processes, and no one perceived this more clearly than John Farmer, a man who, along with his son, came to dominate the publication of Michigan maps through the rest of the nineteenth century.[52]

Figure 2. Detail of "Map of the Northern Parts of the United States," 1804, by Abraham Bradley, Jr., showing the fourth state to be created out of the Northwest Territory as encompassing all of Lake Michigan except for a portion of Green Bay. Private collection.

In the early 1820s, Farmer used his experience as a surveyor to produce several maps of the recently constructed military road from Detroit to the Maumee River. Subsequently, he prepared several other maps, including the "Map of the Surveyed Part of the Territory of Michigan," which Orange Risdon published in Albany in 1825.[53] This map had a north-south orientation, but Farmer thought that an east-west map would be more appropriate. He quickly took out several copyrights and sent a new version back to Utica, New York, for printing in the same year, 1825. The printed version of this map, covering only a portion of the territory, carried an 1826 date. Farmer's map quickly gained wide acceptance, including an accolade by Henry S. Tanner, who used it as a prime source for his "New Map of the United States" in 1829.[54] Farmer's success encouraged him to proceed with several other map projects. His *Map of Michigan* appeared in 1829, followed the next year by an *Emigrants' Guide* featuring a new edition of his map of southern Michigan. In 1830, Farmer issued his celebrated *Map of the Territories of Michigan and Ouisconsin,* which tilted the graticule so that it was oriented with northeast at the top. This enabled Farmer to extend his coverage westward. The realignment of the map not only created a dynamic image but also turned the Great Lakes into a benevolent canopy covering the grid of surveyors' townships that filled the Mississippi valley. The surveyed part of Michigan interlocked with this grid in northern Indiana and Ohio, cementing the territory into the American polity.[55] In 1844, Farmer issued a *New Map of Michigan* that went through many revised editions; indeed, it remained in print until the end of the nineteenth century. He turned to a larger format to publish a four-part map of Wisconsin, Iowa, and northern Illinois in 1848. A similar map of Michigan and Wisconsin in four sheets appeared six times after 1853, including an expanded version in six sheets in 1859, the year of Farmer's death.[56]

Farmer's wife and son continued the business, with Silas Farmer eventually controlling the firm. The 1862 revision of the well-known state map assumed a new title: *Farmer's Rail Road and Township Map of Michigan and Chart of the Lakes,* which indicates how important railroads and lake commerce had become to the state. After joining forces with a rival Michigan firm in the 1870s, Silas Farmer branched out into book publishing, but his standard Michigan map continued to appear even after his death, as the business was carried on by one of his sons.[57]

Meanwhile, maps of Michigan appeared in new atlases issued by American publishers. David Burr produced a map of the territory in 1831. Following the shape of the Great Lakes on Aaron Arrowsmith's map of the United States, published in London, 1802–1805, Burr introduced a thin, slanted Lake Michigan into American cartography.[58] The Burr-Arrowsmith portrayal of Lake Michigan found many imitators. For example, George Boynton of Boston prepared two versions of an interesting map, "Michigan and the Great Lakes," which appeared in several atlases issued by Edward R. Broaders and Thomas Gamaliel Bradford in 1835.[59] The maps served a double purpose, which was indicated by their common title. The sequence of names is interesting. Michigan as a territory came first, although neither version of the map specified where Michigan is located. The simpler version, a lithograph, labeled the mitten peninsula as "Territory." Given the full coverage of the Great Lakes, present-day Wisconsin was also included and designated as the "District of Huron attached to Michigan." The cartographer highlighted the southern half of the mitten by both dividing it into counties and supplying the names for a dozen towns. Located in the center of the map and framed by the Great Lakes, Michigan appeared to be on the verge of statehood, about to be ushered into the Union by the rigid rectangles of the land office survey. The Wisconsin region, in contrast, supported only a few towns set in huge counties that, by their vast extent, suggested administrative districts rather than communities. The other version of Boynton's "Michigan

Figure 3. Detail of "Michigan Ter.," 1823, by Fielding Lucas, Jr., showing the road leading from Ohio to Monroe, Detroit, and Mount Clemens. Fielding Lucas, Jr., *A General Atlas Containing Distinct Maps of All the Known Countries in the World* (Baltimore: by author, 1823).

New Settlement
Indian Line
Sagana
Huron District
M^c COMB Co.
F^t St Clair
Huron R.
Mt Clemens
Huron R.
Portage 3 Miles
Detroit
WAYNE Co.
Pontiac
DETROIT
District
L. St CLAIR
R. Thames
Sandwich
Huron R.
Erie
Browns T.
F^t Malden
Raisin R.
Amherstsburg
rie District
French T.
Monroe
MONROE Co.
N D O T S
Lawrenceville
ERIE
F^t Meigs
Maumee R.
O H I O
43
42
7°
6°
5°

and the Great Lakes," an engraving, appeared in Edward R. Broaders's *A New Universal Atlas,* as well as in later versions of Bradford's atlases.[60] In this case, the entire mitten was filled with rectangular counties that also covered the region south of the Green Bay–Fox River–Wisconsin River waterway west of Lake Michigan. Settlement, civilization, and progress seemed to follow the number of right angles on these maps.

Bradford's idea of combining maps of Michigan and Wisconsin on one sheet found imitators in other atlases, but the idea that an American atlas should include a map of the Great Lakes strikes the modern scholar as quite significant. "Michigan and the Great Lakes" occupied a position of transition in Bradford's atlases, appearing as the last map in a sequence of state and territorial titles starting with Maine. Both the 1835 and 1842 editions of the atlas placed maps of U.S. cities next, followed by a sheet of the "United States, exhibiting the railroads and canals," and a continental view to cover the far western territories.[61] In both atlases, the Great Lakes map started a progression away from state-centered maps to other types, ending with the larger focus of national, continental, and global coverage. Including the entire reach of the Great Lakes on the Michigan page turned it into the pivotal point of the atlas. After Bradford's publications and Michigan's statehood in 1837, however, a map devoted to the entire Great Lakes became a rare feature in general-reference atlases. Thus, Michigan's political gain seemingly led to a diminished geographical sensibility.

As Michigan approached and entered statehood, it attracted a flurry of cartographic attention. The atlases produced by publishers such as Carey and Lea, Lucas, Burr, Bradford, Tanner, and Mitchell between 1822 and 1840 all accorded the territory and then the new state a separate page, because they organized their contents on a state-by-state basis to facilitate their reference functions.[62] Maps featuring the Great Lakes disappeared.

Most of the separately published maps of early Michigan addressed the needs of people on the move, who were often looking for opportunities to acquire land and join emerging communities. The maps of Risdon, Farmer, and others such as Philu E. Judd (1824) and Oliver Gray Steele (1834) emphasized the division of land by surveyors from the General Land Office and the formation of counties based on their efforts.[63] John Farmer attached his map of the Michigan and Wisconsin Territories (1830) to an *Emigrant's Guide,* following a format set by earlier handbooks and tour manuals. Another example was Robert Baird's small volume, *View of the Valley of the Mississippi, or, the Emigrant's and Traveler's Guide to the West,* which appeared in several editions between 1832 and 1834. Each edition of this pocket-size book featured a variety of state, city, and regional maps. On the small folded sheet devoted to Michigan, which was about six inches square, the Lower Peninsula assumed a triangular shape because Lake Michigan was set on a sharp angle following the Arrowsmith example of 1802 to 1805. The map emphasized the lands west of the Great Lakes, because the angle of Lake Michigan's orientation pinched the Lower Peninsula, thereby extending the reach of what would become northern Wisconsin. The mapmaker reduced this western bias by including an inset of the "Environs of Detroit" in the lower left-hand corner. Both the main map and the inset emphasized the pioneer roads. Two major trunk lines connected the Great Lakes and the Mississippi River. One started at Detroit and swung around Lake Michigan to reach Chicago before proceeding to Galena and Prairie du Chien. The other road ran southwest from Green Bay to Galena. The inset map placed Detroit at the hub of roads that radiated out to pull the entire Lower Peninsula into the city's orbit, as well as to connect it to Upper Canada and Ohio.[64] But the Chicago Road was visually the principal artery on the sheet, suggesting that an east-west mind-set provided a better perspective when reading the map than a north-south orientation. As the major cultural feature on the map, the system of early roads underscored the east-to-west dynamic of pioneer activity.

Samuel Augustus Mitchell published a classic map of Michigan's formative years, *The Tourist's Pocket Map of Michigan Exhibiting Its Internal Improvements,* drawn by J. H. Young (fig. 4). This handy folded map first appeared in 1834, followed by additional printings over several years. The same map, but dated 1839, was included in James H. Lanman's *History of Michigan.* Young's map, used as a foldout frontispiece for the book, would help readers envision the new state as it entered "the age of agriculture, commerce and manufactures."[65] Later generations agreed that Young's map set the state on the course of progress. The state's "Official Highway Map" of 1953 reprinted the 1839 portrayal in full size alongside a smaller panel recounting the progress of transportation from Indian trails to Detroit's Industrial Expressway. Michigan's statehood stimulated an ambitious movement to support internal improvements, and the first legislature embarked on a massive program to construct canals and roads to facilitate east-west movement across the state. The cartographer's key to Young's map included symbols for canals and railroads as well as stage roads, but these features are almost entirely absent from the map itself. Young seems to have positioned and titled his map to record these improvements as they came into being.

Part of the later appeal of Young's map, however, was its quaint look, which was caused by the slant of a narrow Lake Michigan that followed the Arrowsmith model. As the surveyors laid out ranges of townships proceeding northward year by year, they gradually pushed the lake into its appropriate shape and reconfigured the triangular peninsula into a mitten. The rectangles of counties and townships, confined to the lower third of the 1834 map, gradually pushed northward to fill up the entire state.

For several reasons, notably the Panic of 1837, which curtailed both the pace and the scope of improvements, the surveyors' lines took precedence over transportation networks on many Michigan maps published in the first decades of statehood. The early railroads did not pull Michigan together as a state. Although they provided essential links between the developed part of the southern Lower Peninsula and the emerging commercial economy of the nation, these commercial ties further differentiated the various regions of the state. If a transportation system could pull Michigan together in the 1850s, it needed to be waterborne. A financial analyst stated the case in *Hunt's Merchants' Magazine and Commercial Review:* "The State of Michigan . . . is perhaps one of the most advantageously situated, in view of our vast future internal commerce. . . . Its southern base projects, as it were, 280 miles into the vast internal seas and is surrounded on its three sides by navigable waters."[66] The major atlas publishers of the mid-nineteenth century struggled to balance land and water in their presentation of Michigan, but in the end they emphasized the land.

The variety of atlases produced by the S. Augustus Mitchell firm furnished a good case in point.[67] *Mitchell's School Atlas* ran for almost a half-century between 1839 and 1886. Most editions did not contain maps of individual states, a regional approach using maps of the middle, southern, and western states being more suitable for a thin instructional aid. But the upper Great Lakes posed a problem. In the 1850 edition, the map of the western states included Michigan south of Saginaw Bay on a sheet extending from western Virginia to the Missouri River. In the 1850s, Mitchell added another map of Michigan and Wisconsin to cover the Great Lakes states. In the 1859 version of the atlas, "The Map of the States of Michigan and Wisconsin" took up a full page.[68] The counties, named and outlined in red, filled up the Lower Peninsula and southern Wisconsin with compact civil divisions. In addition, railroads generally traced east-west routes, and the map was adjusted to show these rail links proceeding around the south-

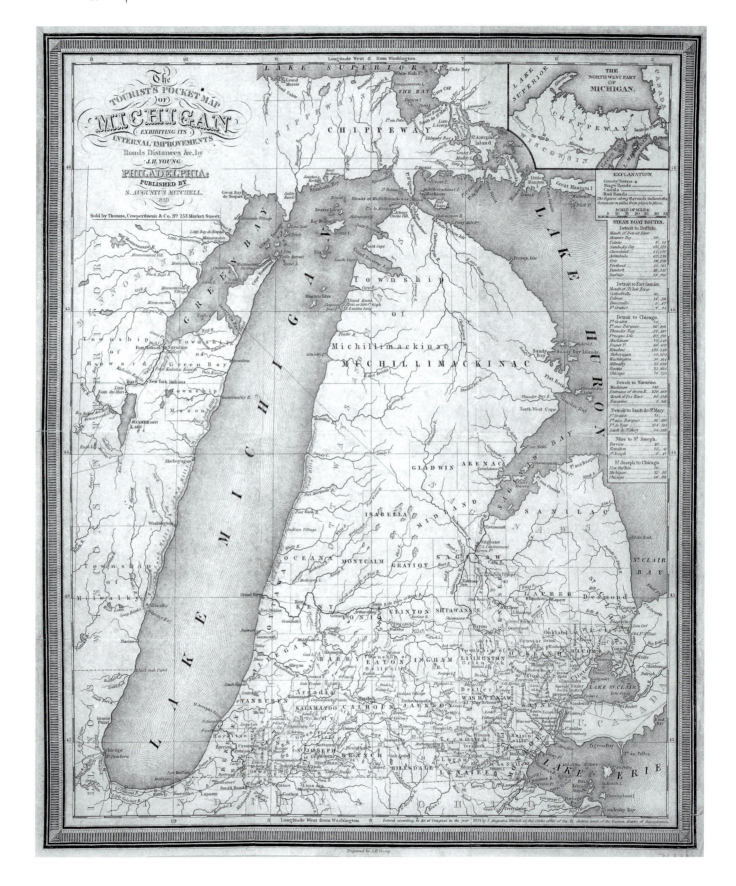

ern tip of Lake Michigan to Chicago. Since the cartographer included county names and boundaries only in the featured states, the railroad pattern showed up more forcefully in neighboring Illinois. The Great Lakes framed the image, but only Lake Michigan appeared in its entirety. The presentation of the lakes did not include sailing routes or harbors, but the international boundary crossed the peripheral waters and a broad wave pattern outlined each lake with a decorative flourish. The sheet showing Michigan and Wisconsin in the *New General Atlas* produced by the Mitchell firm in 1860 closely followed the *School Atlas* design, but it added a wide border with a floral pattern that took up much of the space given to the Great Lakes in the earlier map.[69] The floral frame also pinched off the railroad link to Chicago. Thus, the reference-atlas version seemed to increase Michigan's isolation.

The tendency of cartographic design to segregate a map's subject went even farther in Colton's deluxe *Atlas of the World,* a two-volume production that appeared in New York City in 1855–56.[70] In this work, Michigan received two full pages, the first picturing the mitten peninsula under the title "Michigan" and the second showing the remainder of the state in a map of "Lake Superior and the Northern Part of Michigan."[71] Splitting the state between two maps certainly did not use cartography as a way to develop a sense of community, and the design of each map showed no effort to relate Michigan's two peninsulas to each other.

Colton's General Atlas, which remained in print from 1857 until 1888, continued the two-map coverage for Michigan. However, another Colton production, which appeared in 1860 and endured well into the 1880s under the imprint of Johnson and Ward as *Johnson's New Illustrated Family Atlas,* was a more modest volume aimed at a wider audience. As such, *Johnson's New Illustrated Family Atlas* used a map similar to the one in *Mitchell's School Atlas* to present both Michigan and Wisconsin on one double-page sheet.[72] In the 1863 edition, a colorist set off each county only in the featured states, while the surveyor's townships that subdivided the counties covered almost the entire map, running into the neighboring states and even into Canada as well. The principal meridians and baselines appeared in bold markings and were numbered so that parcels of real estate could be precisely located on the atlas map. With both the major roads and railroads also pictured on the map, the atlas could meet the specific needs of immigrants, travelers, and investors as well as serving as a general reference tool. In contrast to all the activity pictured on land, the mapmaker supplied only the names of the Great Lakes and covered them with a subtle wave pattern. The only exception to this rule was the note between St. Joseph and Chicago: "Steam Boat, 60 Miles."

After the Civil War, every state desired its own atlas as well as readily available maps.[73] When the first atlas devoted exclusively to Michigan appeared in 1873, it provided an opportunity for a master of the craft to demonstrate the potential of such publications. Henry Francis Walling's *Atlas of the State of Michigan* combined a series of thematic essays and maps with county-by-county coverage of the entire state.[74]

No cartographer in the nineteenth century occupied a better position to reflect on the role of state and local maps in American culture. During his lifetime, Walling prepared maps for almost 20 states, 280 counties, and more than 100 towns and cities. Thus, his comments in the preface to this work, in many ways his masterpiece, are especially pertinent. "Maps of states," Walling informed his readers, "possess an intrinsic and a practical value far beyond . . . the mere pleasure they afford." Thus, Walling, who had begun his career as a civil engineer, started his section on the "Value of Maps" by acknowledging their aesthetic and entertaining qualities. But he hastened to emphasize "how closely and extensively

Figure 4. *The Tourist's Pocket Map of Michigan, 1839,* by J. H. Young. Note the exaggerated slant given to Lake Michigan, which turned the mitten peninsula into an arrowhead. Private collection.

the prosperity of a country depends on the existence of accurate maps of its domain with general facility of access to them." Walling then divided his remarks into four sections, each of which discussed a different type of practical use for state maps. The first, on "The Value of Maps in Promoting Immigration," pointed to a newcomer's need to compare the advantages of various sites and "thus to come to a satisfactory decision in locating his new home." Maps also played a role in internal improvements by promoting public discussion. "A careful determination of the most favorable routes" could then lead to the location, design, and construction of valuable public works. Discussing "General Uses," the engineer pointed to "persons in nearly every class of life" who needed to use maps in the course of their activities, from travelers and engineers to public officials and state legislators. Finally, under "Educational Uses," Walling emphasized a major civic benefit of producing American state maps: a citizen could use the map of his state to grasp "the relations, as to the position and magnitude, between his town . . . and the entire world."[75]

Alexander Winchell, formerly a professor of geology, zoology, and botany at the University of Michigan, followed up on these "Educational Uses" in a brief essay on topography and hydrology he contributed to Walling's atlas. He declared, "The State of Michigan occupies a position approximating the center of the continent of North America."[76] Winchell might have underscored this conclusion by pointing out how the American interior was balanced between the Great Lakes and the Great River. Instead, the professor seemed to have railroads on his mind. His map of "Michigan Showing Contour Lines," which portrayed only the Lower Peninsula, was really a railroad map. It pictured trackage in bold fashion but limited the contours of the land to a light red, making them quite difficult to read. The key map in the entire volume, which followed Winchell's essay, showed "counties, townships, railroads, stations, etc." But it omitted the western and northern parts of the Upper Peninsula so that the map could extend far to the south, all the way to Indianapolis. The volume's focal map thus emphasized Michigan's connections to the Mississippi valley. Railroads, in this case, provided the major linkages, and a chapter on "The Railroads of Michigan" by Ray Haddock, placed immediately after the key map, further emphasized rail transport.

After fifty pages of introductory essays, the atlas proper began, with detailed maps, county by county, arranged in geographical order, the Lower Peninsula first at a scale of three miles to the inch followed by the Upper Peninsula at six miles to the inch. The atlas section concluded with city maps of Detroit and Grand Rapids, general maps of the United States and Europe, four maps showing political districts in Michigan, a table of the "Population in the United States and Territories, by Counties," and a gazetteer. Almost fifty pages of "business cards" followed—a feature that helped finance this venture.

Walling's Michigan atlas received a second printing in 1884 but almost certainly exerted indirect influence as well. The editor's involvement with a host of similar ventures in other states between 1868 and 1876 led to many contacts with individuals in the map-publishing world who were, no doubt, inspired by Walling's enthusiasm for state and local maps. Henry S. Stebbins, who sponsored Walling's first book-length venture, an 1868 *Atlas of Ohio*, issued a "New Railroad and Township Map of Michigan" in 1870. In turn, O. W. Gray and Son, who had been involved in some way with most of Walling's state atlases, probably used Stebbins's map to develop a *Railroad Map of Michigan* for the state's Commissioner of Railroads.[77] It was then natural for the Gray firm to supply an attractive map for *The State of Michigan: Embracing Sketches of Its History, Position, Resources, and Industries,* a 136-page illustrated book that Michigan's Centennial Board of Managers conceived as a celebratory piece to distribute at the 1876 Exposition in

MICHIGAN

AND

ITS RESOURCES.

———◆———

SKETCHES OF THE GROWTH OF THE STATE, ITS INDUSTRIES, AGRICULTURAL PRODUCTIONS, INSTITUTIONS, AND MEANS OF TRANSPORTATION; DESCRIPTIONS OF ITS SOIL, CLIMATE, TIMBER, FINANCIAL CONDITION, AND THE SITUATION OF ITS UNOCCUPIED LANDS; AND A REVIEW OF ITS GENERAL CHARACTERISTICS AS A HOME.

———◆———

COMPILED UNDER AUTHORITY OF THE STATE BY THE COMMISSIONER OF IMMIGRATION.

———◆———

[THIRD EDITION.]

LANSING, MICH.:
W. S. GEORGE & CO., STATE PRINTERS AND BINDERS.
1883.

Figure 5. Title page of *Michigan and Its Resources,* a paperbound book addressed to prospective settlers in Michigan. Private collection.

Philadelphia.[78] The book was cast as a promotional tract to encourage emigration to and investment in Michigan, thereby making it possible to fund the work out of the governor's budget.

S. B. McCracken, the compiler, specifically acknowledged his indebtedness to the essays in Walling's 1873 *Atlas*, and in some ways the promotional book became the natural successor to the atlas. Reduced in size and scope for free distribution, it soon became a regular production of Michigan's Commissioner of Immigration. In 1881, much of the same material, plus a general description of each of the state's counties, appeared as *Michigan and Its Resources*. An updated version of the map from the centennial book, this time with Henry S. Stebbins of Chicago credited as the engraver and publisher, was folded inside the front cover of the third edition, which was published in 1883 (figs. 5 and 6). By 1885, probably sixty thousand copies of the book and the state map had been issued, including shortened versions in German and Dutch. The Columbian Exposition in 1893 demanded another edition, which was expanded to 287 pages.[79] By 1914, when the Public Domain Commission and the Immigration Commission jointly printed a similar "immigration publication," they omitted the foldout map and admitted that encouraging the settlement of newcomers was a secondary objective. The first goal was "to stimulate Michigan's own people to a deeper appreciation of the state in which they live . . . calling their attention to the opportunities and possibilities afforded by their home state."[80]

Between 1876 and 1893, Michigan produced several other attractive maps of the state to be distributed free of charge to residents and potential visitors. These were railroad maps, originally sponsored by the state's commissioner of railroads, but later also funded by the commissioner of immigration. In 1872, the office of Michigan Commissioner of Railroads was established, and in 1874, its second annual report included Ormando W. Gray's map that eventually received widespread distribution in the first version of the "immigration book" passed out at the Centennial Exposition in Philadelphia. Between 1881 and 1893, Henry S. Stebbins produced various official maps issued by the state of Michigan.[81] Occasionally, these early state maps were printed in large numbers to serve functions later assumed by the state highway maps.

In the meantime, several new publishers in Chicago used the new technology of wax engraving to supply a growing market for commercial and family atlases as well as inexpensive separately published state maps.[82] The latter were usually folded into cardboard covers or attached to small pamphlets. George F. Cram printed his first map of Michigan in 1874 with a title that emphasized its "sectional" character, in other words, its utility for locating parcels of real estate. The next year, the title changed to a "Railroad and Township Map of Michigan," and the sheet then found its way into Cram's *New Commercial Atlas*.[83] Rand McNally joined the competition for separately published maps of Michigan in 1879 with a folding map addressing a number of markets: *Rand McNally and Company's Township, County, and Railroad Map of Michigan and the Entire Upper Lakes Region*. Meanwhile, Silas Farmer continued to publish his map of the state, and George F. Cram hit the market that year (1879) with three separate issues: a *New Sectional Map of Michigan*, a *Railroad and Township Map*, and a very similar sheet titled *Smith's Railroad and Township Map of Michigan*.[84]

Although individual railroads issued a variety of maps to advertise their routes, few could be considered state maps. Most included several states to cover the entire region served by a particular line. In Michigan's case, many maps issued by the state's railroads were aimed at potential patrons in Chicago, New York, or Boston. For example, the title of a well-illustrated promotional book published by the Michigan Central Railroad, *From City to Surf*, referred to connections between Chicago and East Coast

Figure 6. Detail of "Michigan: Prepared for the Commissioner of Immigration," 1883, by Henry S. Stebbins. Note the hierarchy of towns described in the map's key. Private collection.

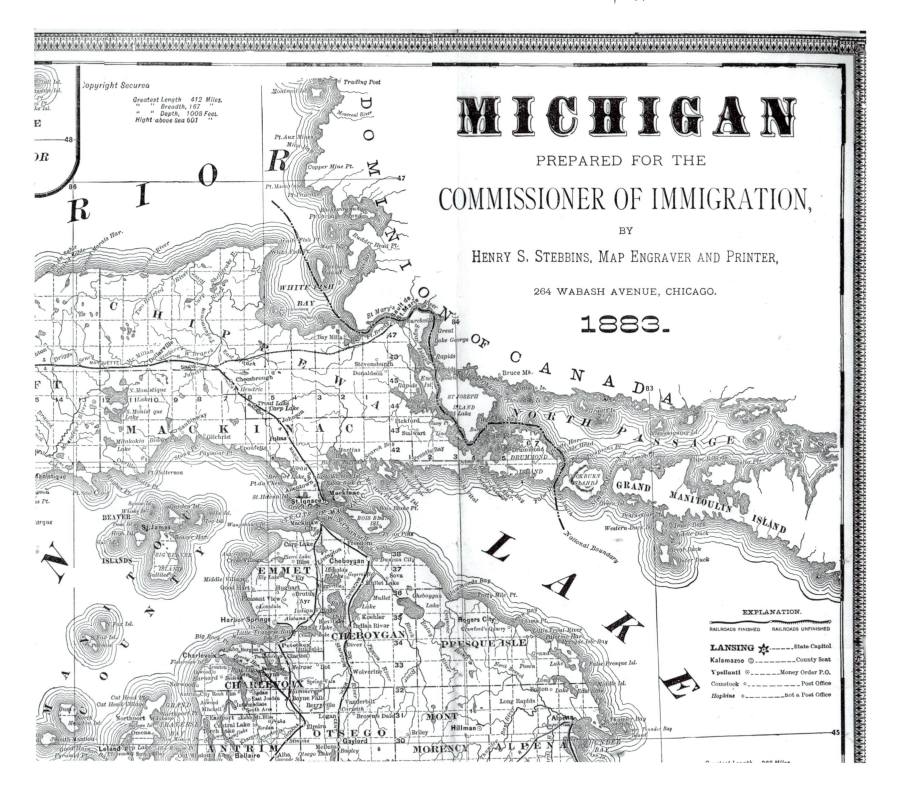

beaches. Even an 1888 pamphlet advertising the Michigan Central route between Detroit and "The Fairy Isle of Mackinac" included a map that qualified its state focus by extending prominent lines west to Chicago and east to Boston and New York City.[85]

Most of the state railroad maps issued between 1870 and 1920 were commercial ventures by firms such as Farmer, Cram, and Rand McNally. The state-by-state approach used by atlas publishers in the United States encouraged map readers to think of railroad networks in terms of state systems. As railroads spread across the landscape, state maps tended to drop coverage of the major stagecoach routes, a situation that would last until the bicycle craze of the 1890s again stimulated an interest in road improvement and highway maps.

As bicycles grew in popularity, they created an immediate reason for voters to support road improvements.[86] Horatio Earle, who served in the Michigan Senate, took over leadership of the national League of American Wheelmen in 1901. He soon headed a popular drive to amend Michigan's constitution to permit the improvement of the state's wagon roads. Michigan's voters approved the amendment in April 1905, and Earle became the first highway commissioner with a modest budget supported by vehicle license fees.[87] Meanwhile, in 1909, Wayne County laid down an experimental mile of concrete highway, the first in the nation. The success of such improvements soon led to a demand for highway maps that showed the status of a road's pavement, not simply the route the road followed.

Specialized road maps addressed to automobile tourists started to appear in the first years of the twentieth century, but most of these were either strip maps that showed only one particular itinerary or regional maps produced without regard for state boundaries.[88] Because most roads were not posted with names or numbers, the early maps had to be supplemented with written directions ("turn right after crossing the bridge") and/or photographs to help motorists find their way. Auto clubs erected directional signs for special events, and these probably led to a system of marks or signs to "blaze" certain routes or trails. Many of these named highways were interstate routes. The Dixie Highway, for example, started at the Straits of Mackinac and ended at the Gulf of Mexico. Others, like the Central Michigan Pike, marked intrastate routes. The *Goodrich Diagrammatic Road Map of Michigan*, published by the tire company in 1917, reported that eighty-five thousand "new galvanized armor-plate Goodrich Guide Posts" pointed out the directions to nearby towns "at every important turn" in the country. In addition, the Goodrich National Touring Bureau could furnish "State Maps showing the main highways or printed Tour Cards for main lines of travel." More than twenty-five hundred different road logs were printed on separate cards.[89] Before pushing the little strip maps on the "Tour Cards," Goodrich had published a *Michigan . . . Route Book* in 1916 (fig. 7) that had an "Index Map" of the state as page one followed by seventy-eight pages of strip maps, travel directions, and city plans.[90]

The idea of numbering highways is sometimes credited to John Brink, a young draftsman at the Rand McNally firm in 1916. His idea led to the "Auto-Trails" maps issued by his firm after 1917. Highway numbers made it easy to put up signs along these roads to coordinate with numbers on a map. The idea fit in well with the conception of a state highway system. Wisconsin was the first state to assign official numbers to its state routes in 1918, followed by Michigan in 1920. When a system of national highways was conceived in 1926, it also used a rational number system with odd numbers designating north-south routes and even numbers, such as the famous 66, marking those running east-west.

Numbered highways became the key to highway maps. This device simplified state highway maps and opened up space for additional information. The state highway map soon became much more than

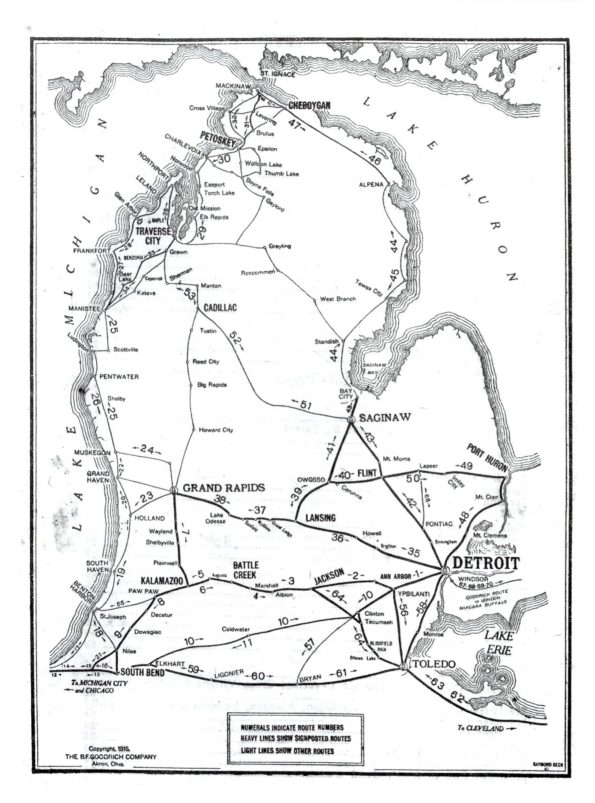

Figure 7. "Index Map," from *Michigan . . . Route Book, 1916.* The numbers on the highways refer to the detailed strip maps found in the pamphlet.

Private collection.

a way-finding aid, blossoming into a tourist guide and civic manual complete with calls to patriotism alongside brief history lessons. These elaborate state highway maps would find their fullest development in the late 1920s under the sponsorship of various oil companies. Soon, state highway departments and tourist-promotion agencies followed their example. Like the oil-company efforts, the state publications started as bare-bones maps outlining the road pattern but provided little in the way of geographic context. As these highway maps developed, however, they filled out in a way comparable to the state railroad maps of the late nineteenth century.

In 1920, the Kenyon Map Company of Des Moines published an interesting pocket map that marked the transformation from railroad maps to those of the automobile age. In size, design, and information presented, the *Map of Michigan Showing Distances between Railroad Stations* was very similar to the Stebbins map of 1881.[91] The original printing featured railroads, towns, stations, and surveyor's townships, then colored each of the counties in the state and filled the Great Lakes with steamship and ferry lines. A note under the title called attention to congressional districts and electric railway lines that were outlined in green. An index of towns on the reverse side of the map provided census data as well as indications about the railroads and express companies serving each community. Like the Stebbins map of 1881, this one identified county seats and places that had money-order post offices. The sheet was filled with useful information for the railroad age.

But the demand had shifted to maps for automobile drivers. Forty Michigan farm families out of one hundred had automobiles in 1920.[92] So when the *Successful Farming* magazine, also based in Des Moines, wanted to provide complimentary state maps for its subscribers, the Kenyon Company simply printed the state's major roads in red on top of the railroad map.[93] Lake Superior supplied space to repeat the title: "Successful Farming's Michigan Auto Road Map," and a strip at the bottom of the sheet identified the "official markings" of the major auto trails. These were then assigned numbers that were also printed in red on the map.

George F. Cram, the Chicago publisher who was always looking for new markets for his maps, issued a *Good Roads Atlas of the United States* about 1919.[94] It used the same solution as the Kenyon Company, overprinting the "Main Highways" in red on its current set of state railroad maps. After a merger with the National Map Company of Indianapolis, the successor to the *Good Roads Atlas* was published in Indianapolis, probably in 1921. It supplied two maps for each state. One was a railroad map; the other, using the identical railroad map as a base, featured the state highways in red. Titled *Auto Trails and Commercial Survey of the United States,* it looked to the future, not the past; a colorful initial page pictured forty-nine highway route markers that were numbered to correspond to the numbering system used on the maps.[95]

Rand McNally, Cram's major competitor, had grown to national leadership as a publisher for railroads, and its maps and atlases designed for a general audience were almost always conceived of as railroad maps. How would it make the transition to automobile maps?[96]

In contrast to the approach taken by Cram and the Kenyon Company, Rand McNally set out to rethink the whole idea of finding aids for motorists. The first solution, developed as early as 1908, combined photographs, text, and strip maps in a proposed series of "Photo-Auto Guides." The volume for Chicago to New York needed two hundred pages and three hundred fifty pictures. If a picture was worth a thousand words, a good map, in turn, might be worth hundreds of pictures. The key was to number the highways on the map and post signs along the right-of-way on the ground itself. Rand McNally agents soon posted some two hundred thousand painted signs across the nation.

Although Rand McNally pioneered the numbering of highways and the making of appropriate maps to support the system, it made the transition from railroad maps to automobile maps very gradually in Michigan. In 1918, *Rand McNally's Official Auto Trails Map, District No. 3: Southern Peninsula of Michigan* showed and named railroads and electric railways (interurbans) but omitted county names and boundaries in the interest of presenting a clear, simple transportation map. Moreover, the map took the form of a regional rather than a state map, since it omitted the state's other peninsula. At the lower left, an "Insert" continued coverage to the Chicago metropolitan area. The next year's version of this map provided an inset "Map of the Eastern Half, Northern Peninsula, Michigan" at a reduced scale. The 1920 *Auto Trails* map folder was titled "Michigan" rather than "District Three." The transition of the *Auto Trails* sequence from district maps to state maps was completed in the 1923 series when both of Michigan's peninsulas appeared on the same map at the same scale, using both sides of the sheet. In the process, the extension to Chicago disappeared. Finally, in some versions of the 1923 and 1924 *Auto Trails* maps, "Michigan" was boldly stamped on the southern peninsula side. The side with the Upper Peninsula was, in contrast, called "Cloverland and Vicinity," the name the region's tourist board used to describe the delights of the northland.[97]

When Rand McNally followed Cram's example and published an *Auto Road Atlas of the United States* in 1926, it also took the state-by-state approach but started with fresh maps, simplified and smaller versions of the Auto Trails series.[98] They were called "Junior Road Maps" and highlighted the paved roads with a broad red line. These maps included some rivers and lakes, but they omitted county names and boundaries. The highway maps therefore had limited utility as reference tools. Meanwhile, railroads continued to dominate Rand McNally's general maps. As late as the 1940s, the firm's offerings did not usually include highways on their "Popular Series of State Maps" or "Pocket Maps of the States." The firm's wall maps and atlas maps also featured railroads rather than highways until the interstate highway system finally forced its way onto general maps in the 1960s.[99] The usual practice was to keep railroad routes in black but to use red for highways, recalling the initial overprinted maps of decades earlier.

Generally, as oil-company sponsorship took over the development of state highway maps in the 1930s, railroads were not included on the maps. State and national parks, historical sites, landmarks, schools, and other attractions did appear as the oil companies promoted tourism. The upbeat messages provided by pictures and the accompanying text put automobile travel in the context of pleasure trips, vacations, and educational ventures.

Oil-company road maps were certainly on the side of progress and civic betterment, but some voices asked whether Michigan should turn the cartographic depiction of the state entirely over to private interests. In 1919, the legislature directed the highway commissioner to publish a road map of the state and to sell it to the general public. The first efforts were like blueprints showing the condition of trunk-line routes at a particular date. Each peninsula received a separate sheet indicating whether the roads were in good or fair condition, impassable, or under construction. Counties, state parks, and some connecting roads appeared on these maps, but they looked like working documents for road officials more than publications for a general audience. Michigan's two peninsulas would be put together onto a single highway map in 1924, probably because the state had set up its own car-ferry system to connect its two parts. Putting the entire state on a single sheet created ample blank space on the left-hand side to accommodate detailed insets showing the major streets in cities and larger towns.[100]

In 1928, the state road map became a free publication to promote tourism, and as a result, the steamship routes on Lake Michigan were included, but not railroads. Presumably, the rail network would visually complicate a map dedicated to highways. In 1931, the state road maps assumed a modern format and were printed in color on both sides of the sheet. By the last decade of the twentieth century, the "Official Michigan Highway Map" dominated the state's cartography. Commercial publishers such as Rand McNally and various automobile associations continued to publish maps of the state, but none of these came close to the two million printed copies of the official highway map. In the automobile age, our most common maps focus on the state, using the highway network to pull places together and give the state coherence. The nature of the document suggests that these are special people in a unique place, the "Great Lakes State" in Michigan's case. Moreover, this state map is the featured item on an interesting broadsheet, enjoying the support of pictorial and textual elements pointing to the good life, to patriotism, to community well-being, and even to personal fulfillment.[101] Maps of Michigan as rhetorical devices have addressed similar purposes from the very beginning. But the connections among civics, culture, and cartography are most clearly portrayed on our current state highway maps.

Previous maps that portrayed the land we call Michigan—and these reach back to the very beginning of European attempts to delineate the North American interior—focused on the dynamics of land and water. In the very nature of things, waters shape the land and often suggest its character. The Great Lakes and then a great-river system gradually defined the American interior on published maps. In the process, France and England stressed their territorial claims on these maps. Toward the end of the eighteenth century, the new United States joined the imperial struggles, dividing the western lands into states and territories. Maps of new states such as Michigan assumed a political character as they defined boundaries, recorded land divisions, nurtured communities, and guided prospective settlers in their quest for a better life.

After statehood, maps of Michigan focused on external boundaries and internal systems that employed straight lines to carve up the lands into countries, townships, sections, and individual farms. In the process, interest in the Great Lakes seemed to fade away, isolating the state from its larger geographical context. Cartographers concentrated on using networks of railroads and highways to pull the various parts of the state into a coherent whole, connecting each locality into a network of settlements, graphically suggesting a body politic surging with vital activities.

The growing importance of tourism to the economy in the age of the automobile seemed to revive an interest in water and to see in the Great Lakes a key to the character of the lands. Michigan called itself the "Great Lake State" or the "Great Lakes State," the appellation providing a mechanism for civic identity at the same time that it pointed out Michigan's appeal as a destination for fun and recreation (fig. 8). "Great Lakes" would lead to "Great Times." In the process, today's state maps have become more than way-finding aids, travel-planning documents, records of political jurisdictions, or devices to locate places. As they have elaborated their functions as tools of instruction and as civic emblems, they have encouraged residents and visitors alike to make positive connections between the people and the land. Putting our current map into the long procession of Michigan maps encourages us to see connections between land and water, past and present, and to think about the future as well.

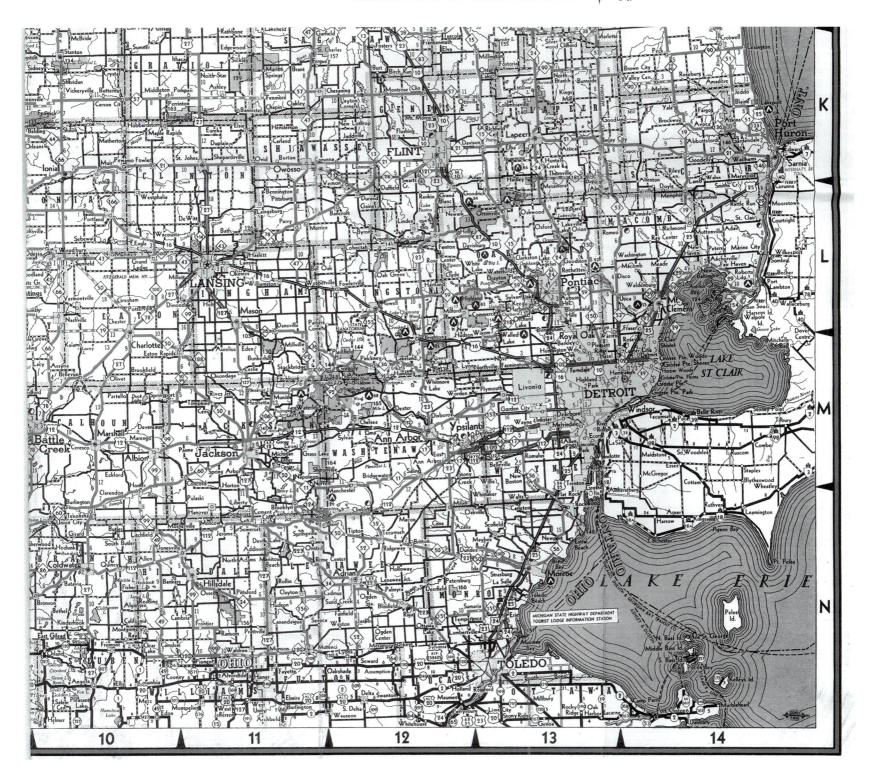

Figure 8. Detail of "Michigan: 1953 Official Highway Map," winter version, October 1, 1953. Private collection.

NOTES

1. On the social functions that maps generally serve, see Denis Wood, *The Power of Maps* (New York: Guilford, 1992). Martin Bruckner, *The Geographic Revolution in Early America: Maps, Literacy and National Identity* (Chapel Hill: University of North Carolina Press, 2006) is also very suggestive.

2. Those who study Michigan maps will always be indebted to Louis C. Karpinski's splendid *Bibliography of the Printed Maps of Michigan, 1804–1880* (Lansing: Michigan Historical Commission, 1931) and his accompanying *Historical Atlas of the Great Lakes and Michigan* (Lansing: Michigan Historical Commission, 1931). Although Karpinski's formal bibliography does not start until 1804, about half of the space in each work is devoted to the "fundamental maps" that antedated separate portrayals of Michigan. Extensive coverage is also provided in LeRoy Barnett, comp., *Checklist of Printed Maps of the Middle West to 1900: Michigan* (Boston: C. K. Hall, 1981), which is part of the series edited by Robert W. Karrow, Jr. Floyd Benjamin Streeter, *Michigan Bibliography* (Lansing: Michigan Historical Commission, 1921), includes a section on maps that is still valuable.

3. Several important collections and exhibits have given impetus to the study of Great Lakes cartography, e.g., Renville Wheat, *Maps of Michigan and the Great Lakes, 1545–1845* (Detroit: Detroit Public Library, Burton Historical Collection, 1967); Robert W. Karrow, Jr., *Mapping the Great Lakes Region: Motive and Method* (Chicago: Newberry Library, 1977); David Buisseret, *Mapping the French Empire in North America* (Chicago: Newberry Library, 1991); and Kevin Kaufman, *The Mapping of the Great Lakes in the Seventeenth Century* (Providence, R.I.: John Carter Brown Library, 1989), which is the most elaborate. See also Douglas W. Marshall, ed., *America and the Great Lakes: Discovery and Settlement* (New York: Richard B. Arkway, n.d.), which is a helpful dealer's catalogue.

4. Sebastian Münster's map of the Western Hemisphere is often reproduced, for example in John Goss, *The Mapping of North America: Three Centuries of Map-Making, 1500–1860* (Secaucus, N.J.: Wellfleet, 1990), 25. The world map of 1540 appears in Pierluigi Portinaro and Franco Knirsch, *The Cartography of North America, 1500–1800* (New York: Crescent Books, 1987), 60.

5. Gerhard Mercator, *Atlas Sive Cosmographicae Meditationes de Fabrica Mundi et Fabricati Figura* (Duisburg: n.p., 1595). See also Goss, *Mapping of North America*, 50–51.

6. Philip D. Burden, *The Mapping of North America: A List of Printed Maps, 1511–1670* (Rickmansworth, U.K: Raleigh, 1996), is the best source for the Italian maps. Another example, by Bolognini Zalterius, published in Rome about 1595, is featured in Emerson D. Fite and Archibald Freeman, *A Book of Old Maps: Delineating American History from the Earliest Days Down to the Close of the Revolutionary War* (Cambridge: Harvard University Press, 1926).

7. Abraham Ortelius, *Theatrum Orbis Terrarum* (Antwerp: N. Israel, 1570), is often called the first modern atlas. The *Theatrum* appeared in about forty editions up to 1612. Ortelius's world map is reproduced in Portinaro and Knirsch, *Cartography of North America*, 100. The 1570 map of the Americas is reproduced in Goss, *Mapping of North America*, 35.

8. It might be helpful to view several other maps of North America in this tradition. The most extreme example might be Hogenberg's North American map published in Cologne in 1589, in which an elongated St. Lawrence River almost crosses the continent. Franz Hogenberg, *Americae et Proximarum Regionum Orae Descriptio* (Köln: n.p., 1589). It is reproduced in Burden, *Mapping of North America*, map 90. The map of the north part of America by de Jode in his rare atlas of 1593 follows Ortelius, but he encloses the riverine corridor in solid walls of mountains. Cornelis de Jode, *Speculum Orbis Terrarum* (Antwerp: A. Coninx, 1593). This map is reproduced in color on the cover of Marshall, ed., *America and the Great Lakes.*

9. Samuel Purchas, *Hakluytus Posthumus, or, Purchas his Pilgrimes: Contayning a History of the World in Sea Voyages and Lande Travells by Englishmen and Others* (Glasgow: n.p., 1625).

10. The Briggs map is reproduced in Goss, *Mapping of North America*, 61.

11. Karrow, *Mapping the Great Lakes Region*, [1–2].

12. A recent example, accompanied by a stunning catalogue and a parcel of facsimile maps, is in Kaufman, *Mapping of the Great Lakes.*

13. Karpinski, *Bibliography.*

14. Marshall, ed., *America and the Great Lakes*, 10–11, 13–14, reproduced Champlain's maps of 1612 and 1632. For some reason, neither Goss, *Mapping of North America*, nor Portinaro and Knirsch, *Cartography of North America*, included any of the printed versions of Champlain's maps, although the latter did reproduce his 1607 manuscript, "La Nouvelle France," which is now in the Library of Congress. See also Buisseret, *Mapping the French Empire*; Seymour I. Schwartz, *This Land Is Your Land: The Geographic Evolution of the United States* (New York: Henry N. Abrams, 2000), 37–40. Fite and Freeman, *Book of Old Maps*, 104–7, 120–23, 132–34, presents three Champlain maps: the manuscript map of 1607 and both printed versions.

15. Marshall, ed., *America and the Great Lakes*, 10.

16. The Jansson-Hondius map of North America (1636), reproduced in Goss, *Mapping of North America*, 30, presents California as an island. Portinaro and Knirsch, *Cartography of North America*, reproduces a 1641 version of this map, where California is again attached to the mainland.

17. Nicolas Sanson's 1650 map "North America" appears in Marshall, ed., *America and the Great Lakes*, 15–16; Schwartz, *This Land Is Your Land*, 41; and Thomas H. Smith, *The Mapping of Ohio* (Kent, Ohio: Kent State University Press, 1977), 2. Buisseret, *Mapping the French Empire*, 14–15, uses a 1656 Sanson map.

18. See Goss, *Mapping of North America*, 78–79. Sanson's 1656 map is also reproduced, in part, in Charles O. Paullin, *Atlas of the Historical Geography of the United States* (Washington, D.C.: Carnegie Institution, 1932), plate 20b.

19. See Burden, *Mapping of North America*, 430–31, for examples for the years up to 1670. Several maps by Nicolas Visscher continued to show an open-ended great lake or lakes between 1660 and 1690. See Marshall, ed., *America and the Great Lakes*, 26–27.

20. Hennepin's 1683 map is reproduced with a commentary in Fite and Freeman, *Book of Old Maps*, 173–74. The two maps that accompanied Hennepin's 1697 publication are reproduced in later states by Goss, *Mapping of North America*. See also Schwartz, *This Land Is Your Land*, 77, 80.

21. All three of Morden's maps are reproduced in Marshall, ed., *America and the Great Lakes*, 22, 25, 29. This work also shows "A New Map of North America," by Edward Wells, dated 1700. This map was part of "A Set of Ancient Maps and Present Geography," designed for use in schools. It is also reproduced in Portinaro and Knirsch, *Cartography of North America*, 209.

22. John Senex, *A New General Atlas, Containing a Geographical and Historical Account of All the Empires, Kingdoms, and Other Dominions of the World: With the Natural History and Trade of Each Country* (London: D. Browne, 1721). The Senex version of Morden's map appears in Marshall, ed., *America and the Great Lakes*, 44; and Goss, *Mapping of North America*, 121.

23. Gores are flat, roughly triangular sections of mapping to be placed on a globe. For Coronelli's globe gores, see Rodney W. Shirley, *The Mapping of the World: Early Printed World Maps, 1462–1700* (Riverside, Conn.: Early World Press, 2001), entry 536.

24. See Marshall, ed., *America and the Great Lakes*, entries 59, 68, 70, 131. Goss called the 1696 Coronelli map of Louisiana "the best separate map of the five lakes published during the seventeenth century." Goss, *Mapping of North America*, 102. Although issued in Venice, this map contains a short note recognizing the 1673 expedition of Joliet and Marquette.

25. Delisle's 1700 map, "North America," is reproduced in Marshall, ed., *America and the Great Lakes*, 33–34, which also points out R. V. Tooley's designation of it as a foundation map (p. 33).

26. "The Map of Canada," dated 1703, is in Portinaro and Knirsch, *Cartography of North America*, 222. It marked the first appearance of Detroit on printed maps.

27. Delisle's 1718 map of "Louisiana" is in Portinaro and Knirsch, *Cartography of North America*, 223. A later edition, issued in Amsterdam about 1745, appears in Goss, *Mapping of North America*, 115. The English colonies always seem reduced on these maps because the Appalachian watershed was used to mark their western boundaries.

28. Goss, *Mapping of North America*, 111, reproduces Homann's magnificent map. See also Marshall, ed., *America and the Great Lakes*, passim.

29. The two maps by Heinrich Scherer can be found in Marshall, ed., *America and the Great Lakes*, 33; and Portinaro and Knirsch, *Cartography of North America*, 224, respectively.

30. *Some Considerations on the Consequences of the French Settling Colonies on the Mississippi* (London: J. Roberts, 1720), 45.

31. Coxe's map is reproduced in W. P. Cumming et al., *The Exploration of North America* (New York: Putnam, 1974), 153–55.

32. Baron Lahontan's 1703 map, part of which he claimed to have copied from one drawn for him on deerskin by the Gnacsitare, is reproduced and discussed in Buisseret, *Mapping the French Empire*, 22–23.

33. Cadwallader Colden, *The History of the Five Indian Nations Depending on the Province of New-York in America* (New York: William Bradford, 1727). The publication history of Colden's book and map is complex. Both versions of the map are reproduced and discussed in Lloyd Arnold Brown, *Early Maps of the Ohio Valley* (Pittsburgh: University of Pittsburgh Press, 1959), 84–87, plates 13, 15. London editions of Colden's book continued into the 1750s.

34. Marshall, ed., *America and the Great Lakes*, 56, shows the map and points out that the author was indebted to Jacques Nicolas Bellin for the map's configuration of the Great Lakes. A very similar map by John Lodge accompanied William Russell, *The History of America* (London: Fielding and Walker, 1778), 64.

35. Fite and Freeman, *Book of Old Maps*, 218–19.

36. Goss, *Mapping of North America*, 122–23, reproduces the index map in color.

37. Fite and Freeman, *Book of Old Maps*, 180–84, 290–93, reproduces both the first edition of the map and a later one with a "red line," which George III drew on his own copy of the map to mark the boundaries of the new United States in 1783. Fite and Freeman's work includes many of the notes as they were printed on the second edition of the map, the version owned by George III.

38. Marshall, ed., *America and the Great Lakes*, 50–60, covers a handful of relevant Bellin maps, some in several different editions, from 1742 to 1764. He also includes Bellin's 1764 map of Detroit, the city's earliest separately published map (p. 60). Goss, *Mapping of North America*, 124–25, features Bellin's 1744 Great Lakes map, which was reprinted up to the end of the eighteenth century. Buisseret, *Mapping the French Empire*, 48–51, contains versions of this map from 1750 and 1764.

39. British indebtedness to d'Anville's maps is emphasized by Susan Martha Reed, "British Cartography of the Mississippi Valley in the Eighteenth Century," *Mississippi Valley Historical Review* 2 (September 1915): 213–24.

40. Russell, *History of America*; Marshall, ed., *America and the Great Lakes*, 64, 72.

41. Walter W. Ristow, *American Maps and Mapmakers: Commercial Cartography in the Nineteenth Century* (Detroit: Wayne State University Press, 1985), 61–66; John Rennie Short, *Representing the Republic: Mapping the United States, 1600–1900* (London: Reaktion Books, 2001), 12–17.

42. The U.S. Geological Survey published a color reproduction of Abel Buell's *New and Correct Map of the United States of North America* (New Haven, Conn.: n.p., 1784), for the nation's celebration of the bicentennial of the Constitution in 1987. Information on Buell and his map is provided in John Warner Barber, *Connecticut Historical Collections* (New Haven, Conn.: Durrie & Peck, 1838), 531–32. See also Ristow, *American Maps and Mapmakers*, 66.

43. Ristow, *American Maps and Mapmakers*, 66–68.

44. The Fitch map is reproduced in Wayne C. Temple, *Indian Villages of the Illinois Country: Part I, Atlas Supplement*, comp. Sara Jones Tucker (Springfield: Illinois State Museum, 1975), plate 76; and in Karpinski, *Atlas*, 65.

45. On Carleton's map, see Ristow, *American Maps and Mapmakers*, 68–70.

46. Jedidiah Morse, *The American Geography* (Elizabeth Town, Md.: the author, 1789); Ralph H. Brown, "The American Geographies of Jedidiah Morse," *Annals of the Association of American Geographers* 31 (September 1941): 145–217; Short, *Representing the Republic*, 107–26.

47. Marshall, ed., *America and the Great Lakes*, 68–70, shows both of the Northwest Territory maps used in the early editions of Morse's geographies.

48. On Bradley, see Ristow, *American Maps and Mapmakers*, 70–71. Bradley's 1804 map appears in Jedidiah Morse, *The American Gazetteer* (Charlestown, Mass.: Samuel Etheridge, 1804); Karpinski, *Atlas*, 79.

49. The advance of the Government Land Office surveys across Michigan can be followed in various reports from that agency. Norman C. Caldwell, *Surveyors of the Public Lands in Michigan, 1808–2000* (Auburn Hills, Mich.: Data Reproduction Corporation, 2001), contains a brief history of the system in Michigan by Lane J. Bouman. See also Richard A. Santer, *Michigan: Heart of the Great Lakes* (Dubuque: Kendall/Hunt, 1977), 55–60; Barnett, comp., *Checklist*.

50. Marshall, ed., *America and the Great Lakes*, 76, shows the 1822 map by Carey and Lea, "Geographical, Statistical, and Historical Map of Michigan Territory," along with the side panels describing the "face of the country," its government, and its history.

51. Ibid.; Fielding Lucas, Jr., *A General Atlas Containing Distinct Maps of All the Known Countries in the World* (Baltimore: by author, 1823).

52. The story of the Farmer family and its maps is told by William L. Jenks in a supplementary note to Karpinski, *Bibliography*, 16–21; and in Ristow, *American Maps and Mapmakers*, 273–77.

53. Buisseret, *Mapping the French Empire*, 52, reproduces a detail from this map. The whole sheet appears in Karpinski, *Atlas*, 91.

54. Henry S. Tanner, *Memoir on the Recent Surveys, Observations, and Internal Improvements in the United States* (Philadelphia: the author, 1829), 87. Farmer's 1826 map appears in Karpinski, *Atlas*, 92. Ristow, *American Maps and Mapmakers*, 275, reproduces Farmer's 1830 "Improved Map of the Surveyed Parts of the Territory of Michigan."

55. Farmer might have taken the idea for the design of this map from an earlier (1824) Carey and Lea publication, "Map of the Country Embracing the Route of the Expedition of 1823 commanded by Major S. H. Long." Farmer's version, seemingly cut out of the center of the Carey and Lea sheet, is reproduced in Karpinski, *Bibliography*, xxx. Marshall, ed., *America and the Great Lakes*, 87, shows the 1836 edition of the map, its fourth version. The unusual portrayal later appeared in some railroad maps. See the advertisement for the Michigan Central Railroad from the 1850s reproduced in *Michigan History* 42 (January–February 2003): 42.

56. On the Farmer maps, see William L. Jenks, "A Michigan Family of Mapmakers," *Michigan History* 11 (April 1927): 242–50, which is substantially reprinted in Karpinski, *Bibliography*, 16–21. The entire corpus of the Farmer maps of Michigan is detailed in Barnett, comp., *Checklist*, passim.

57. Jenks, "Mapmakers."

58. On David Burr, see Ristow, *American Maps and Mapmakers*, 103–6; Short, *Representing the Republic*, 85–88; Karpinski, *Atlas*, 80, 94.

59. Marshall, ed., *America and the Great Lakes*, 81, shows both versions of the map. Bradford put together a variety of atlases between 1835 and 1842, often in association with other publishers. Boynton had an engraving firm in Boston and prepared a variety of maps for Bradford. Ristow, *American Maps and Mapmakers*, 270–71.

60. Edward R. Broaders, *A New Universal Atlas of Sixty Maps, Charts, and Plans, from the Latest Authorities* (Boston: by author, 1835); T. G. Bradford, *An Illustrated Atlas: Geographical, Statistical, and Historical of the United States and the Adjacent Countries* (Philadelphia: E. S. Grant, 1838).

61. T. G. Bradford, *A Comprehensive Atlas: Geographical, Historical, and Commercial* (Boston: William D. Ticknor, 1835), 57–60.

62. There is no systematic study of the atlases published in the United States in the nineteenth century. Ristow, *American Maps and Mapmakers*, 151–68, is the best source of information.

63. Judd died the year after the publication of his initial map of Michigan. Steele's effort lasted for only one edition. See George Newman Fuller, *Economic and Social Beginnings of Michigan: A Study of the Settlement of the Lower Peninsula during the Territorial*

Period, 1805–1837 (Lansing: Wynkoop Hallenbeck Crawford, 1916), passim. A photograph of Judd's 1824 map appears opposite p. 170. Steele's 1834 map is in Marshall, ed., *America and the Great Lakes,* 80.

64. The "Environs of Detroit," the inset map on "Michigan," in Robert Baird, *View of the Valley of the Mississippi* (Philadelphia: H. S. Tanner, 1834), 104, is a noteworthy early road map with some routes named "Indian Trail," "French Trail," and "Indian Path."

65. James H. Lanman, *History of Michigan, Civil and Topographical* (New York: E. French, 1839), vii.

66. Thomas Prentice Kettell, "Debts and Finances of the States of the Union . . . Michigan," *Hunt's Merchants' Magazine and Commercial Review* 22 (February 1850): 131.

67. On S. Augustus Mitchell and the firm he founded, see Ristow, *American Maps and Mapmakers,* 303–13; and Short, *Representing the Republic,* 155–59.

68. S. Augustus Mitchell, *Mitchell's School Atlas* (Philadelphia: E. H. Butler, 1859), map 15. The same map from *Mitchell's School Atlas* (Philadelphia: E. H. Butler, 1860), is reproduced in Karpinski, *Atlas,* 101.

69. S. Augustus Mitchell, *Mitchell's New General Atlas* (Philadelphia: S. Augustus Mitchell, 1860). Many editions of this atlas appeared up to the 1890s. The map is reproduced in Karpinski, *Atlas,* 99.

70. G. Woolworth Colton, *Colton's Atlas of the World,* 2 vols. (New York: J. H. Colton, 1856). On the Colton firm, see Ristow, *American Maps and Mapmakers,* 313–26, passim.

71. Karpinski, *Atlas,* 100, shows the pair of maps from Colton's 1855 *Atlas.* Marshall, ed., *America and the Great Lakes,* shows both maps in different printings: the Lake Superior region in 1855 and lower Michigan used as a pocket map in 1867.

72. Richard Swainson Fisher, *Johnson's New Illustrated Family Atlas* (New York: Johnson and Ward, 1863), 49, 50. The map on these two pages is pictured in Marshall, ed., *America and the Great Lakes,* 91.

73. On the importance of atlases and maps, see Susan Schulten, *The Geographical Imagination in America, 1880–1950* (Chicago: University of Chicago Press, 2001), passim; and Short, *Representing the Republic,* 201–33.

74. Henry Francis Walling, *Atlas of the State of Michigan* (Detroit: R. M. and S. T. Tackabury, 1873), 5. Walling's career is the subject of chapter twenty of Ristow, *American Maps and Mapmakers,* 327–38. On Walling's state atlases, see ibid., 427–31.

75. Walling, *Atlas,* preface, 5.

76. Ibid., 9.

77. The Stebbins map of Michigan, c. 1870, was published in Chicago. O. W. Gray & Son, *Railroad Map of Michigan* (Philadelphia: O. W. Gray & Son, 1874). Gray used Colton maps of Michigan for his atlases, which were issued in 1873 and 1874. See Barnett, comp., *Checklist,* passim.

78. S. B. McCracken, comp., *The State of Michigan: Embracing Sketches of Its History, Position, Resources, and Industries* (Lansing: W. S. George, 1876).

79. For the publication statistics, see *Michigan and Its Resources,* 3d ed. (Lansing: W. S. George, 1883), preface; and *Michigan and Its Resources,* 4th ed. (Lansing: R. Smith, 1893). The 1883 map was probably produced by George F. Cram in Chicago.

80. *Michigan: Agricultural, Horticultural, and Industrial Advantages* (Lansing: Michigan Public Domain Commission and Michigan Immigration Commission, 1914), preface. The cover title, which differed from the title page, was *Michigan: The Land of Plenty.* This was shorter than *Michigan and Its Resources,* omitting the county descriptions.

81. Stebbins appears as the printer or publisher of dozens of state official maps used in reports of the commissioner of railroads and similar publications. See Robert W. Karrow, Jr., *Checklist of the Printed Maps of the Middle West to 1900: Subject, Author, and Title Index* (Chicago: Newberry Library, 1983).

82. See David Woodward, *The All-American Map: Wax Engraving and Its Influence on Cartography* (Chicago: University of Chicago Press, 1977).

83. George F. Cram, *The New Commercial Atlas of the United States and Territories* (Chicago: George F. Cram, 1875). This was Cram's first atlas.

84. Cram's *New Sectional Map of Michigan* (1879) was part of a series titled "Cram's Indexed Rail Road and Township Pocket Maps," which enabled the reader to locate "every post office and the name and location of any place . . . at a moment's glance." Maps for twenty states were listed alongside an appeal for sales outlets: "Agents wanted. . . . All men out of employment will find it to their advantage to send for my circulars." Quotations are from the map's cover.

85. *From City to Surf: Compliments Passenger Department, Michigan Central Railroad, "The Niagara Falls Route"* (Chicago: Rand McNally, 1888); *The Fairy Isle of Mackinac* (Chicago: Rand McNally, 1888). The impetus for this publication was the opening of the Grand Hotel in July 1887.

86. The cartographic record can be found in *Mendenhall's Road Map of Michigan: Showing Through Bicycle Routes in the State* (Cincinnati: C. S. Mendenhall, c. 1900).

87. The story of the "Good Roads Movement" in Michigan is outlined in most general accounts of the state's history. See, e.g., Willis F. Dunbar, *Michigan: A History of the Wolverine State*, rev. ed. by George S. May (Grand Rapids, Mich.: Eerdman, 1980), 568–74.

88. There is as yet no single source to guide a study of early American automobile maps, but a good place to start is James R. Akerman, "American Promotional Road Mapping in the Twentieth Century," *Cartography and Geographic Information Science* 29 (July 2002): 175–92.

89. *Goodrich Diagrammatic Road Map of Michigan* (Akron, Ohio: B. F. Goodrich Touring Bureau, 1917). This was a folding map with promotional material and advice for travelers.

90. Michigan was one of six states to receive a comprehensive single-state route book in the Goodrich touring series in 1916. The Michigan title announced that thirty-six books were currently available, and three more were in preparation. Most focused on specific routes, such as "Kansas City to Denver." *Michigan . . . Route Book* (Akron, Ohio: B. F. Goodrich, 1916), 81.

91. *Map of Michigan Showing Distances between Railroad Stations* (Des Moines, Iowa: Kenyon Company, 1920).

92. Dunbar, *Michigan*, 574.

93. *Successful Farming's Michigan Auto Road Map* (Des Moines, Iowa: Kenyon Company, 1920).

94. The large atlas was similar in format to Cram's regular atlases, but it had soft covers. The National Highway Association provided the highway information. George F. Cram, *Good Roads Atlas of the United States* (Chicago: Cram Co., c. 1919).

95. *Auto Trails and Commercial Survey of the United States* (Indianapolis: National Map Company, c. 1921).

96. On Rand McNally's road maps, see Duncan M. Fitchet, "100 Years and Rand McNally," *Surveying and Mapping* 16 (April–June 1956): 128–29; and James R. Akerman, "Selling Maps, Selling Highways: Rand McNally's 'Blazed Trails' Program," *Imago Mundi* 45 (1993): 77–89. Fitchet's article should be supplemented by Andrew McNally III, *The World of Rand McNally* (New York: Newcomen Society, 1956). This is a pamphlet version of a speech delivered to the Newcomen Society in North America. Harland Manchester covered the same territory in "World of Rand McNally," *Saturday Review of Literature* 33 (January 21, 1950): 35–37.

97. A large file of Michigan *Auto Trails* maps can be found in the Rand McNally archive at The Newberry Library. On the name "Cloverland," see Aaron Shapiro, "Promoting Cloverland: Regional Associations, State Agencies, and the Creation of Michigan's Upper Peninsula Tourist Industry," *Michigan Historical Review* 29 (Spring 2003): 1–37.

98. See, for example, *Rand McNally Auto Road Atlas of the United States* (Chicago: Rand McNally, 1926).

99. See, for example, *Rand McNally Business and Reference Maps and Atlases, Catalog No. 149* (Chicago: Rand McNally and Co., 1947).

100. LeRoy Barnett, "Paper Trails: The Michigan Highway Map," *Michigan History* 83 (November–December 1999): 19–23.

101. The classic analysis of state highway maps as rhetorical documents is in Wood, *Power of Maps*, 95–107.

About the Contributors

JAMES R. AKERMAN is at The Newberry Library in Chicago.

DANIEL BLOCK is an associate professor of geography at Chicago State University.

DAVID BUISSERET was formerly Garrett Professor of History at the University of Texas at Arlington.

FRANCIS M. CARROLL is professor emeritus at St. John's College, University of Manitoba, Winnipeg.

GERALD A. DANZER is professor of history emeritus at the University of Illinois at Chicago.

J. P. D. DUNBABIN is an emeritus fellow of St. Edmund Hall, Oxford.

G. MALCOLM LEWIS is a retired reader in geography, the University of Sheffield, England.

KENNETH E. LEWIS is a professor in the Department of Anthropology at Michigan State University.

AMY K. LOBBEN is an assistant professor in the Department of Geography, University of Oregon.

CHERYL LYON-JENNESS is faculty specialist and director of undergraduate studies in history at Western Michigan University.

BRUCE M. C. PAPE is an emeritus professor in the Department of Geography, Central Michigan University.

DAVID K. PATTON is an associate professor in the Department of Geography, Central Michigan University.

MARGARET WICKENS PEARCE is an assistant professor of geography at Ohio University.

MARY SPONBERG PEDLEY is the adjunct assistant curator of maps at the William L. Clements Library at the University of Michigan.

HELEN HORNBECK TANNER is a senior research fellow at The Newberry Library, Chicago.

KEITH R. WIDDER is retired curator of history, Mackinac State Historic Parks.

Index

A

Adams, David P., 127

Adams, John, 124

Adams, John Quincy, 133, 134

Adams, Randolph G., 18

Aetna Insurance Company, 247, 250

Agosa, 183, 185, 195, 197, 202; buys land, 200; fears removal, 194; welcomes mission, 189–90. *See also* Akosa

agricultural reform, 223–24

Aishquagonabee, 55, 183, 185, 186, 188, 195, 197, 202; relocates, 190, 191, 202; welcomes Dougherty, 189

Akerman, James R., 9

Akosa, 55. *See also* Agosa

Algonkian speakers, 39, 43–44

Allegan County, 280

allotment of land under Treaty of Detroit (1855), 201

Alphonso Whipple Company, 250

American Fur Company, 136, 190; Indian debts to, 184; in treaty negotiations, 184, 185

American Gazeteer (1804), 329, 330, 331

American Geography, The (1789), 329

Amerique Septentrionale (map, 1685–86), 19, 20

Ames (Iowa), 315

Amherst, Jeffery, 67, 71, 85 n

Amherstburg, 133, 135, 141 n

Amtrak, 306, 307, 308

Andreas, Alfred T., 210, 219; career of, 211–12, 215, 235

Andrews, Thomas C., map by, 329

Angle Inlet (Lake of the Woods), as border marker, 137, 138

Anishinaabe. *See* Neshnabe

Ann Arbor East quadrant, USGS map of, 167, 169

annuity payments: late, 156, 159, 160, 201; use of, 200

Appalachian Mountains, 44, 45

Aranda, Count Pedro d', 124

Aroostook War, 139

Arrowsmith, Aaron, 26; map by, 32, 332

Ashburton, Lord, 138, 139

Ashkebe: negotiates reservation boundaries, 160; protests land surveys, 159–60

atlases: bibliography of, 22, 23; county, 7; general-reference, 334, 337; Michigan state, 337–38; for motorists, 344–45; school, 10, 30, 32, 335, 337; state-by-state contents, 334, 337

atlas maps, combination, 209–39; ages of supporters of, 230; biographies in, 223, 227, 228, 238 n; bird's-eye views in, 217, 221; birthplaces of supporters of, 230–31; business directories in, 209, 212, 217, 218; canvassers for, 217; contents of, 209, 212, 217; counties most receptive to, 223; critics of, 210; displaced by county histories, 234; emphasize farm land ownership, 224, 226; evolution of, 234; farmers as market for, 223–24, 225, 227, 229, 231; features documented in, 224–25, 227; format of invented, 211–12; gender and support for, 229; historical text in, 227, 234; illustrators for, 217, 220, 222, 227; itinerant workers for, 222; lithographs in, 209, 212, 214, 217, 225, 227, 228, 228, 229, 231; mapmakers for, 217, 220–21, 222; newspapers support, 209, 210, 227, 234; pay rates for work on, 222–23; plat maps in, 217, 224, 226; partnerships publishing, 210–17, 232; "patrons" who commissioned self-inclusion, 228–29, 230, 231; portraits in, 228, 239 n; prices of, 210, 229; prices to feature self or property in, 228; production process and times for, 217–18, 222; and progress-oriented values, 223–24, 227, 231, 232; publicity for, 209–10; size of, 227; and social anxieties, 223–24, 231; subscribers for (purchasers of), 209–10, 217, 227, 229–30, 231–32; surveyors for, 217, 221–22; title-page iconography of, 216, 224, 225; township maps in, 209, 211–12, 214, 224–25, 226; urban elements in, 224; values appealed to, 223–24, 227, 231; wealth of supporters of, 229–30; writers for, 217, 219, 223 See also Kane County

Atlas of the State of Michigan (1873), 224, 337–38

Auglaize River, 331

Auto Road Atlas of the United States (1926), 345

Auto Trails and Commercial Survey of the United States (1921), 344

B

Bagrow, Leo, 22, 37 n

Bailey, O. H., bird's-eye views by, 252, 253

Baird, Robert, immigrant guide and maps by, 334–35

Balfour, Henry, 65

Barnhart's Island, 138, 139, 142 n

Barclay, Anthony: as boundary commissioner, 127, 128, 133, 135, 137, 138, 139, 141 n; career of, 126–27

Baskin, Oliver L., 215, 219

Battle Creek, "battle" of, 160, 171 n

Baxter, Alexander, 82

Bay City quadrant, USGS map of, 164, 166

Bay County (Mich.), 273

Bayfield, Henry, 5; career of, 111, 121 n, 122 n; hardships, 111; surveys Lakes Erie, Huron, and Superior, 104, 111

Bayliss, Estelle M., and Joseph E., 131

Bay of Quinte, 103, 115 n

Beal, Junius, 18

Beaufait, Louis, 156, 159

Beecher, Henry Ward, 224

Bell, Robert, 53

Bellin, Jacques Nicholas, 4, 26; map by, 30, 328

bicycles, 342

Biddle, William, 194

Bigsby, John, 128, 131, 135

Bird, William A., 127

bird's-eye views, 7, 242, 251–55, 252, 254; access to, 242; angle of view in, 253, 255, 256, 258; artists for, 253; in atlas maps, 217, 221; completeness of, 256, 257; contents of, 259; coverage by, 256, 257; exaggerate urban activities, 259; and historical research, 242, 254, 256, 257, 259; lithography in, 253; press runs of, 251; production process of, 252–53; promotion of, 251–52; publishers of, 253; scale of, 253–55, 258; subscriptions for, 251, 252–53. See also lithographic views

Bishop, William Warner, 18

Blackbird, Andrew J., 180, 183, 193

Blackbird's Town, reservation at, 156; map of, 167

Block, Daniel, 9

Board of Trade, British, 67, 70, 75, 77, 78, 79, 82, 84, 327

Boardman, Horace, 199

Bois Blanc Island, 99, 133, 141 n, 183

borders: near Lake of the Woods, 95; from St. Marys River to Lake of the Woods, 105, 107; U.S.-Canadian, 5, 94–96, 104–5; U.S.-Mexican, 5–6. See also boundary commissions under Treaty of Ghent; Treaty of Paris; Webster-Ashburton Treaty

Bouchette, Joseph, 108; career of, 111; maps by, 109

boundary commissions under Treaty of Ghent, 94, 104–5, 111; agents for, and their duties, 127, 135; Article Six agreement, 135; Article Seven commission ends operations, 138; commissioners for, and their duties, 126–27, 135; and Detroit River islands dispute, 133–34; dividing rivers and allotting islands, 127, 133–34; Lake of the Woods issues debated and settled, 136, 137, 138; maps by, 129, 130, 133, 134; pay rates of, 126; procedures of,

127–28; St. Marys River issues unsettled by, 138; survey from St. Lawrence to Detroit Rivers by, 128; survey from Detroit River to Lake Huron by, 128, 131, 133; survey from Lake Huron to Sault Ste. Marie by, 131, 133; survey methods of, 105, 128, 131, 136, 137; surveyors for, and their duties, 127, 135; surveys from Lake Superior westward by, 134–83; travels around Lake Superior by, 136; and western border (from Lake Superior) disputes, 137–138; western issues unsettled by, 138. *See also* Webster-Ashburton Treaty

Boynton, George, maps by, 332

Bradford, Thomas Gamaliel, 332, 334

Bradley, Abraham, Jr., maps by, 329, 330, 331

Bradstreet, John, 71

Brady, Hugh, 193

Brant, Joseph, 95, 96, 97; criticizes Simcoe, 102

Brehm, Dietrich, map by, 67

Briggs, Henry, 320

Brink, John, 192

British Columbia, borders of, 5, 97

British regime in Great Lakes and Ohio country, 49–51, 63–65, 67, 70–75, 84, 84 n, 95, 97–98, 125

Broaders, Edward R., 332, 334

Brock, Isaac, map by, 103

Brookfield, William: plat map by, *162*; reservation survey by, 164

Brulc, Étienne, 51

Bryce, James, 107, 111

Buell, Abel, map by, 329, 331

Bureau of Indian Affairs, 199

Burleigh, L. R., 228

Burr, David, map by, 332, 334

Burr, G. S., 215

"Burr Oak Farm," 228

Butler, Walter, 95

C

Cadillac (Mich.), Sanborn maps of, 257

California, 321

Canada, 320. *See also* Upper Canada

Canada ou Nouvelle France (map), 28

Canadians (French), in fur trade, 70, 74–75, 77

Canning, Stratford, 133, 134, 135, 138

Cannon River, 53

canoes, 39, 50; counting, to record fur trade, 75; route maps for, 56, 91–94

Carey, Matthew, 26

Carey and Lea (map publishers), 173, 331, 334

Carleton, Guy, 97, 99, 101, 107, 109

Carleton, Osgood, map by, 329

Carnegie Institution, 18, 20

Carroll, Francis, 5

Carte Géographique de la Novvelle Franse, 42

Carte des Lacs du Canada, 30

Carte de la Louisiane et du Cours du Mississipi (map, 1718), 26, 31, 325

Carte de la Nouvelle France et de la Louisiane, 322, 323

Cartier, Jacques, 40–41, 320

cartography, study of history of, 4, 22, 41, 53, 55

Cartography of the Northwest Coast of America, 22

Cartwright, Richard, 101

Carver, Jonathan, 5, 49, 67, 78; diplomacy of, with Indians, 82–83; explorations of, 81–82; exploring instructions to, 68; maps by, 63, 66, 67, 82–84; *Travels*, 84, 89 n

Cass, Lewis, 128, 135, 136; and Indian removal, 164, 168; duplicity of, 156; as governor of Michigan Territory, 147, 168; initiates land cessions, 154, 159, 185; and reservation surveys, 147–50, 154, 159; misses annuity payments, 156, 160; as superintendent of Indian affairs, 147, 168

Cass River: maps showing reservations on, *155, 157, 158*; reservations along, 154, 155

Castlereagh, Lord, 133, 134

Cataraqui, 96

Catitugegwonhale, map by, 55

Cayton, Andrew, 223

celestial charts, 40

centennial (1876), Michigan book for, 338, 340

Central Michigan Pike, 342

Champlain, Samuel de, 4, 41–43; maps by, 41, 42, 44, 322

Charles Rascher Insurance Map Publishing Company, 250

Charlevoix, Father Pierre-François-Xavier de, 26, 94, 108

Chase, Col. H. W., 219

Chatelain, Henry, 326

Chatelain, Zacherie, 326

Chegeree "the Indian," map by, 50

Chemogobing, 183

Cherokees, 49

Chewett, William, 111; maps by, 101–2, 104, 109

Chicago, 315, 334

Chippewas. *See* Ojibwes

Chrzastowski, Michael, 9

Clements, William L., 18, 20–21

Cockburn Island, 131

Colden, Cadwalader, map by, 26, 327

Collins, John (surveyor), 96, 97, 109

Colton, J. H. (map publisher), 175, 337

Columbian Exposition (1893), 340

Comba, Rinaldo, 4

combination atlas maps. *See* atlas maps, combination

Combination Atlas Map of DuPage County, 216

Combination Atlas Map of Henry County, Iowa: contents of, 212; cover of, 213

Combination Atlas Map of Jackson County, Michigan: business directory in, 218; production of, 217, 219, 220; promotion of, 209

Combination Atlas Map of Stephenson County, Illinois, 212

Combination Atlas Map of Washtenaw County, Michigan (1874), 225

Commissioner of Immigration (Michigan) publications, 339, 340, 341

Complete Historical, Chronological and Geographical American Atlas, A, 331

conservation, maps by state departments of, 294

Conway, Henry Seymour, 78

Conzen, Michael, 210

Cook, Capt. James, 112

copperplates, 43

Copper River, 74, 75

Corne, Louis de la, 70

Coronelli, Vincenzo Maria, maps by, 4, 324–25

counties (lower Michigan): boundaries of, established, 283 n; as indicators of settler population, 267–70; organization of, 267–68; prominence of, in atlases, 335; maps of borders and population of, 268 (1830), 269 (1840), 269 (1854)

county atlases. *See* atlas maps, combination

county histories, 210, 234

county maps, 211–12; features of, 211, 243

county plat books. *See* plat books

Coxe, Daniel: colonization scheme of, 326; map by, 326–27

Cram, George F., maps by, 340, 342, 344

Crawford, T. Hartley, 191; on Indian land occupancy, 192

Crees, 69; maps by, 51, 52

Crooks, Ramsey, 184

Cumming, William P., 3, 22

Cuneo, John, 63, 64

D

Dablon, Claude, S.J., map published by, 29

d'Anville, Jean Baptiste Bourguignon, 328

Danzer, Gerald, 10

Delafield, Joseph, 127, 128, 131, 133, 135, 136, 139, 141 n

Delano-Smith, Catherine, 4

Deslisle, Guillaume, maps by, 26, 31, 325–26, 327

Detroit, 6, 180, 276, 280, 315, 327, 329, 334; besieged, 65, 70; bird's-eye view of (1889), 254, 257; ownership transfers of, 95, 97, 125–26; social life in (1820), 128

Detroit River: negotiation over islands in, 133–34, 141 n; described (1820), 128; maps of, 101, 129; settlement along, 270; ship channel in, 98–99; survey of, 128

Detroit River (map, 1820), 129

diplomacy: British-Indian, 71–74, 80, 82–83; French-Indian, 71–72; *See also* boundary commissions under Treaty of Ghent; Webster-Ashburton Treaty

distances, 50; problems estimating, 48–49, 137

Dixie Highway, 342

Dorchester, Lord. *See* Carleton, Guy

Dougherty, Peter, 6; arrival of, in Michigan, 173, 188; as

missionary, 188; buys land, 199–20; concern of, for Indian land tenure, 194–96; investigates possible mission sites, 188–89; establishes mission, 183, 184, 189; establishes new mission church, 200; maps by, 175, *181, 182* 190–91, *193*; establishes school, 190; starts new residential school, 200; moves mission, 197

Dowling, P. H., 220

Doysié, Abel, 20

Drew, John, 185, 194

Dreyfus, Lee, 311

Drummond Island, 131, 133, 135, 140–41 n, 184

Dunbabin, John P. D., 5

Dundas Street, 101, 102

Dundee (Mich.), 167, 169

Durant, Pliny A., 219

Durant, Samuel W., 219, 222, 232

E

Eames, Wilberforce, 36 n

Earle, Horatio, 342

Early Maps of Carolina, 22

Elk Rapids, 197

Ellicott, Andrew, 101, 117 n

Emigrants' Guide (1830), 332, 334

England, maps of, 4, 7, 22

Ensign, Dwight W., 216, 232

Eries, 49

Ernest Hexamer and Son, 250

errata slips, 8

Euro-American settlement in lower Michigan, 263–85; agricultural frontier of, 264–65; and agricultural potential of regions, 265, 280; census data and, 281; by communities of accretion, 265–66; counties and their populations as indicators of, 267–70, 281; by covenanted communities, 266, 272, 280; economic basis of, 280; in Grand Traverse area, 194–96; and Indian attitudes, 194, 265; limited, in fur trade era, 264; post office creation as indicator of, 274–82; regional pace of, 267, 281; in southern regions, 245; townships as

indicators of, 269–74, 281, 331

Evans, Lewis, 50

Everts & Stewart, 209, 210, 219, 224

Everts, Edward, 216, 232–33

Everts, Emma, 234, 235

Everts, James, 215–16, 232

Everts, Louis H., 209, 217, 222, 227; career of, 210–11, 215, 232–35; ends poor, 234–35; farm of, 232, 233, 234; promotes local history, 234

F

"Fairy Isle of Mackinac," 342

Fanon, Frantz, 168

Farmer, John, 21; career, 332; maps by, 175, 176, 177, 178, 331–32

Farmer, Silas, 332, 340, 342

farmers: and aerial maps, 7; and county atlases, 7; and road maps, 344; social and cultural resources of, 223; social anxieties of, 223–24. *See also* atlas maps, combination, farmers as market for

Farmer's Rail Road and Township Map of Michigan and Chart of the Lakes (1862), 332

farms, lithographs of, 214, 227, 228, 233

Farrer, John, 45

Federal Aid Highway Act (1921), 290

Felch, Alpheus, 201

Fer, Nicolas de, 326

Ferguson, James, 127, 135, 136, 137, 139

fevers (possibly malaria), 111, 126, 128, 132

Finlayson, J., map by, 27, 173, 174, 175

fire insurance maps, 8, 247–51, 248, 249, 253; access to, 242, 260 n; cost of making, 256; emphasize business district, 256; checklist of, 256; completeness of, 256, 257; consistency of, 260; contents of, 241, 247, 248, 250; coverage by, 256–57; few after 1967, 250; historical development of, 247–50; and historical research, 242, 251, 255, 257, 259; information on, 258–59; production process of, 250; scale of, 257, 260 n. *See also* Sanborn Map Company

Fireman's Guide: A Map of New York City (1834), 249

First Nations: cosmologies, 40, 43–44; economies of, 39, 180; on eighteenth-century maps, 83, 327, 329; intertribal hostilities among, 49, 71, 73, 180, 183, 200; land purchases from, 96, 184–85; as sovereign entities, 82–83, 84 n; territories of, 5, 39, 83; trading patterns, 39, 40, 180; travel by, 39–40, 180; treaties with, 96. *See also* First Nations geographical knowledge and mapmaking; Native Americans, *treaties by name; tribes by name*

First Nations geographical knowledge and mapmaking, 4, 39–57; acculturation of, to European perspectives, 51, 55, 57; and artifacts collected by nonnatives, 55; drainage networks central to, 40, 46, 50, 51–52, 56, 57; GIS use in, 57; linear or route, 43, 46, 47, 48, 51, 52, 53, 91, 113 n; modeling on floor or ground, 40–41, 46, 49, 51, 53; mythical elements in, 43–44, 52, 57; omission of Great Lakes in, 46, 47–48, 50, 57; purpose-focused, 47, 51; scale in, 41, 43, 55; as source for nonnative maps, 41–46, 48, 49–52, 56, 68, 83, 91; spatial awareness in, 39–42, 43; topological geometry in, 43, 47, 50

Fischer, Father Joseph, S.J., 17

Fitch, John, map by, 329

Flat Rock (Mich.), 277

Fletcher, Joseph, 150; plat map by, 153, 158

Florida, Spanish claims to, 124

Fond du Lac (near present Duluth), 136; as possible border marker, 137

Force, Peter, 49

Ford, Commander Henry, map by, 100

Fordham, Sir Herbert George, 22, 36–37 n

Forgy, J. D., 220

Forlani, Paolo, 321

Fort Brady, 135

Fort Defiance, 331

Fort Duquesne, 50

Fort Malden, 133, 135, 195

Fort William, 94, 108, 111, 136

Fowler, T. M., 253

Fox Island, 133, 134, 135

France, Joseph la, 51; map by, 51, 52

Franklin, Benjamin, 123

Franquelin, Jean-Baptiste-Louis, 24, 26; map by, 19, 20

French: diplomacy with Indians, 71–72, 80; penetration of North America, 10, 24, 40–43, 45, 69–70, 320, 322–23; settlers' removal advocated, 77

French and Indian War and maps, 327, 328

French, Joe K., 220

Friend, Norman, 212, 217

Frobisher, Benjamin, 74, 97

Frontiers: British-First Nations, 5; trans-Mississippi Franco-Spanish, 5;

Fry, Joshua, 94

Fuller, George N., 269

fur trade, 53, 56; at forts or by traders among Indians, 65, 68, 70, 77, 79–80; British merchants in, 74; imperial policies for, 65, 68, 70, 77, 79–80; interdependence during, 264; French-Canadian traders in, 70, 74–75, 77; French foundation of, 69–70; French system for, 80; Indian debts in spur land sales, 184; Montreal-based, 77; New Orleans-based, 77; route from Lake Ontario to Lake Huron, 97; route west from Montreal, 80–81, 97; routes west from Lake Superior, 91–95, 105, 106–8, 136; western French posts, 69–70, 80. *See also* American Fur Company; Hudson's Bay Company; North West Company

G

Gage, Thomas, 5, 46, 47, 49, 50, 64, 65, 66, 67, 70, 71, 72, 76, 77, 78, 81, 82, 88 n

Garry, Nicholas, 137

General Drafting Company, 287

General Land Office, 146

Genesee County (Mich.), 279, 280

Geneva Township (Kane Co., Ill.), map of, 214

Geographia Universalis, 320

Geographic Information Systems, 57

Geological Survey. *See* United States Geological Survey

George, Isaac, 193

George III, 67, 76, 328, 350 n

Georgian Bay, 40, 42, 45, 51, 56, 113 n; charting of, 5, 104

gifts, role of, in British- and French-Indian relations,

71–73, 76–77, 80, 81, 82, 89 n; until 1850s, 195

Gilbert, Henry C., 201

Glen, James, 49

Glover, E. S., 13

Goddard, James Stanley, 69, 81

Godfroy, James, 149, 150; expresses Indians' fear of expulsion, 160

Gogebic County (Mich.), 319

Good Roads Atlas of the United States (1919), 344

Goodrich, B. F., 290; maps by, 342, 343; signs by, 342

Goodrich Diagrammatic Road Map of Michigan (1917), 342

Goodrich National Touring Bureau, 342

Gousha, H. M. (mapmaking firm), 287

Graduation Act (1854), 201

Grand Blanc, 278

Grand Portage, 91, 94, 106, 136. *See also* Pigeon River

Grand Rapids (Mich.), 338

Grand River (Mich.), 6; drainage (map), 266; Euro-American settlers in basin of, 265, 267, 271, 272, 278, 279, 281; Ottawas of, 181, 185; reservation for bands of, surveyed, 192

Grand River (Ont.), 96, 97, 101

Grand Traverse Bay, 55; canoe routes bypassed, 180, 205 n; mapped by Dougherty, 175, 181, 182; mapped by Schoolcraft, 175, 179; Native settlements around mapped, 175, 181, 182; Native land purchases around, 196, 199–200; Ojibwe settlements around, 183, 197, 202; Ottawa communities around, 183, 197, 202

Grand Traverse Ojibwes and Ottawas reservation, 186; agriculture on, 196; Catholic school at, 190; Catholics leave, 199; choice and boundaries, 191; dispersion of population of, 199; government staff at, 193; insecure land tenure on, 196; land of sold, 202; not surveyed, 192–93; Presbyterian school at, 190, 193; withheld from public sale, 193

Grand Traverse region, 6; cherry growing in, 200; described by Dougherty, 188; early human occupancy of, 180; Euro-American settlement reaches, 196, 273; geography little known, 173–75; lumbering in, 199; Ottawa settlements in, 181, 183; resurvey of, 197, 198 (map)

Gratiot County (Mich.), 273, 280

Gray, Orlando W., and Son, 338, 340

Great Lakes, 39; absence from First Nations maps, 46, 47–48, 50, 57; accuracy of mapping of, 24, 26, 43, 94, 104, 325, 328; British hydrographic surveys of, 103–4, 118 n; early mapping of, 4, 5, 24, 26, 41, 42, 43, 44, 94, 321–22, 324–25; First Nations travel routes around, 40, 50, 51; in general atlases, 334, 337; maps of, 19, 20, 21, 22, 24, 26, 28, 30, 42, 44, 52, 66, 94, 104, 324, 332, 334; in school atlases, 335, 337; and states' senses of identity, 314, 318 n. *See also* lakes by name

Great War for Empire, 327, 328

Grosse Isle, 98, 133; map of (1820), 134

H

Haddock, Ray, 338

Hakluyt, Richard, 41

Hakluytus Posthumus, 321

Haldimand, Frederick, 95–97, 106

Hale, John, 127, 135, 137

Hamelin, Augustin, Jr., 194

*Hamilton, Henry, 97, 106

Harley, John Brian, 5, 68, 78

Harrington, Bates, 210, 211, 222, 223

Harris, R. Cole, 167

Harrison, William Henry, 126

Harrisse, Henry, 17

Hassler, John, 154

Hawkins, Samuel, 127

Hendrick, Hondius, 322

Hendricksen, Cornelis, map by, 45–46

Hennepin, Father Louis: maps by, 26, 323, 324; travels and claims of, 322–23

Hesse, District of, 92, 97, 105, 106, 108

Hexamer, Ernest, 250

H. H. Lloyd, 217

Higgins, Belden & Company, 210

highway maps: advertisements in, 313; agricultural themes in, 297–98, 303, 314–15; air routes added to, 306, 307; and bicentennial, 308, 309, 310; bus routes added to, 306, 307; celebrate highway building,

290–91, 302–6, 303–5, 308, 314; centrality of midwestern states emphasized by, 314; contracted to private publishers, 313; describe road surfaces, 289, 290, 293, 342, 345; different bureaucracies produce, 288; early commercial, 344–45; and economic development, 308, 313; explain signs, 291, 298, 306, 310, 312, 314; explain vehicle laws, 291, 298; for farmers, 344; highways departments' motives for producing, 287, 314; historical themes on, 297, 299, 308, 310, 313; and interstate highway boom, 303–6, 304, 305; mileage logs on, 290, 317 n; oil companies,' 287, 344, 345; origins of state, 290, 314, 345; outdoor recreation touted by, 294, 295, 297, 298, 298, 310, 315; rail lines added to, 306, 307, 318 n; preach safety, 298, 303, 306; seasonal editions of, 297, 302; and self-promotion by officials, 292, 294, 308, 310; and self-promotion by state governments, 288, 292, 294, 306, 314; and stagecoach or bicycle maps, 288; state capitols on, 292, 292; and states' identities, 288, 297, 300, 303, 310, 313, 314–16; show state institutions, 293, 294; state seals on, 291–92, 310; tourism promoted by, 288, 294–303, 306, 310, 311, 313–5, 346; urban themes in, 303, 310, 313, 315; World War II and, 300–2, 302. *See also* Illinois; Indiana; Iowa; Michigan; Minnesota; North Carolina; Ohio; route maps for motorists; Wisconsin

highways, national numbering of, 342. *See also* roads
History of the Five Indian Nations (1727), 327
History of Michigan (1839), 335
Holland, John, 112
Holland, Samuel, 95, 109, 112
Homann, Johann Baptist, 326
Howard, William, 65; diplomacy with Indians, 71; rebuilds fur trade, 70
Hubbard, Lucius L., 18
Hudson Bay, 320, 322, 323, 325
Hudson's Bay Company, 51, 53, 69, 107, 136, 137
Humber River (Ont.), 103
Huron River, reservation on, surveyed, 150
Huron Township (Mich.), 273
Hurons, 39, 42. *See also* Wyandots

Hutchins, Harry B., 18
Hutchins, Thomas, 21, 49; map by, 67
hydrographic surveys, British, 103–4, 118 n

I

Ichnography of Charleston, South Carolina, The (1788), 247–48
Illinois, 6, 9; format and contents of highway maps of, 291, 292, 294, 304; self-presentation of, in highway maps, 294, 300, 315
Illinois Official Highway Map, 1963, 304
Illinois River, 50
Imago Mundi, 22
immigrants and settlers, guides for, 334–35, 336, 337, 338–40, 339, 341
Improved Map of the Territories of Michigan and Ouisconsin, (1836), 177
Indian Affairs, U.S. Senate Committee on, 200
Indian Land Cessions in the United States, 193
"Indian Map of the Upper Missouri, 1801, An," 53
Indian removal. *See* removal
Indiana, 9; format and contents of highway maps of, 289, 290, 291, 292, 293, 294, 304, 308; self-presentation of, in highway maps, 294, 300, 310, 314, 315
Indiana Official Highway Map, 1977, 304
Indiana Official State Highway Map, 1937, 293
Indians. *See* First Nations; Native Americans
insurance industry, history of, 247–49
International Waterways Commission, 139
Internet, maps on, 242
interstate highways, 303–6, 304, 305; bring roads onto general maps, 345
Ionia County (Mich.), 271, 279
Ionia land office, 187, 196, 199, 200
Iowa: format and contents of highway maps of, 290–91, 304, 306, 308, 311; self-presentation of, in highway maps, 300, 301, 303, 306, 308, 310, 311, 314, 315–16; verse praising, 315–16
Iowa Highway Map, 1934, 301
"Iowa *Is* Beautiful" (1934), 301

Iroquois and Iroquoian peoples, 39, 40, 43, 46, 95, 96, 327; pressure other peoples, 49, 180

Isabella County (Mich.), 280

islands: apportioned by U.S.-British boundary commission, 104–5, 127, 133

Isle Phelipeaux, 125

Isle Royale, 124, 125, 136, 328

J

Jackson (Mich.), 223

Jackson, Andrew, 185

Jackson, Jack, 4

Jackson County (Mich.): combination atlas map of, 209, 217, 218, 219, 220; economy of, 223; post office for, 275

Jaillot, Alexis-Hubert, 26, 30

Jansson, Johannes, maps by, 322

Jay, John, 124

Jay-Grenville Treaty, 125

Jefferson, Peter, 94

Jefferson Insurance Company, 250

Jenks, William Lee, 21

Jesuit missionaries, 24, 322; map based on reconnaissance of, 29

Jesuit Relations, 26, 29

Jipson, W. C., 220

Johnson, John, 96

Johnson, William, 46, 47, 65, 66, 67, 70, 72, 76, 78, 81

Johnson's New Illustrated Family Atlas, 337

Johnston, George, 193, 194

Johnston, Jane, 184, 188

Johnston, John, 135, 175, 188, 193

Johnston, Susan, 135

Johnston, William, 200

Joliet, Louis, 26, 322, 324

Judd, Philu E., maps by, 334

K

Kagan, Richard, 8

Kain, Roger, 4

Kalamazoo River drainage: Euro-American settlers in, 265, 267, 278, 280; map, 266

Kaministiquia River: as canoe route, 94, 108, 136; as possible border marker, 138

Kane County (Ill.), 210–11, 212, 215, 219, 221, 222; atlas map of, 212, 214, 227, 234

Karpinski, Louis Charles, 3, 4, 10, 14–15, 16, 17, 33–34 n; on accuracy of Great Lakes maps, 24, 26, 94; *Bibliography of Mathematical Works Printed in America through 1850*, 13, 14; *Bibliography of the Printed Maps of Michigan, 1804–1880*, 13, 14, 21–33, 25, 321; career of, 14, 15, 16, 17–18, 34 n, 35 n; collections of, 13, 14, 20; on early mapping of Great Lakes, 24, 26, 321; *Early Military Books in the University of Michigan*, 13; and history of mathematics and science, 13, 14, 15; and mathematical education, 14, 15, 16, 30, 34 n; photostatic copying of maps by, 13, 19, 20, 20–21; portrait of, 14; slide lectures by, 17–18

Kelsey, Francis, 18

Kempenfeldt Bay, road to, 108, 110

Kendall, Henry P., 22

Kent County (Mich.), 271, 279

Kenyon Map Company, 344

Ketchewaundaugenink, reservation at, 155, 159; survey of, 159

Keulen, Gerard van, 326

Keweenaw Peninsula, 124

Kingston (Ont.), 97, 101

"Kinney's Addition," plat map of, 244

Kishkako, 156

Kishkawbawee, reservation at, 154, 155

Knaggs, William, 160

Koch, Augustus, 253

Koch, Theodore, 18

Kohl, Johann, 4, 53, 55

Kosheshawa, and reservation surveyors, 162

Kotté, Lewis, map by, 99, 101

Krause, Frank, 220, 222

Kremers, Laura R., 297, 299

Kurth, Augustus, 250

L

Lacey, Patrick, 310

La Chine Rapids, 40–41

la Croix, Jeronimus de, 46

la France, Joseph, 51; map by, 51, 52

La Galette, 46

La Salle, René-Robert Cavelier, Sieur de, 322–23, 324

La Vérendrye, Pierre Gaultier, Sieur de, 51–52, 69–70, 91

Lac la Pluie, 83, 136

Lac Superieur (map), 29

Laforce, René Hippolyte Pepin dit, 95; map by, 99, 101

Lahontan, Louis Armand, Baron de, 26, 326

Lake Athabasca, 112

Lake Erie, 40, 41, 43, 45, 46, 98; boundary survey of, 128; hydrographic survey of, 103, 104; maps of, 26, 42, 50, 92, 100, 108; uncertainty about location of, 26, 94, 323, 324

Lake Huron, 51; Bayfield's hydrographic survey of, 5, 104; boundary survey of, 131, 133; maps of, 42, 44, 98, 132; eastern shore of, 98

Lake Huron (map), 132

Lake Michigan, 40, 43; eastern shore and Euro-American settlers, 256, 267, 271–72, 273, 274, 280, 281; maps of, 26, 27, 32, 42; outline established, 191; shoreline erosion, 9; slanted in maps, 332, 335, 336, 337

Lake Nipigon, map of, 53, 54

Lake Nipissing, 45, 78, 79, 80, 81; as possible border marker, 124

Lake Ontario, 41, 43, 46; as barrier, 39, 47–48, 59 n; hydrographic survey of, 103; maps of, 47, 96, 99; shoreline of, traced, 95–96

Lake St. Clair, 50, 92, 114 n; described (1820), 131; map of, 130; maps of reservations on, 148, 150, 151, 168; settlement near, 270; survey of, 131, 133; temporary reservation on,167, 168

Lake St. Clair (map), 130

Lake Simcoe, 51; trade routes via, 97, 98, 103, 108, 110, 117 n

Lake Superior, 51; and boundary commission, 136; hydrographic survey of, 104; islands in, 26, 30, 94, 328; maps of, 26, 29, 30, 42, 44, 66, 74, 101, 108, 322

Lake Winnipeg, 51

Lake of the Woods, 5, 51, 91, 94, 95; as border marker, 105, 107, 108, 125, 136, 137, 138; northwesternmost point of, disputed, 136, 137, 138; surveys of, 105, 136, 137

lakes, delineation of shorelines of, 4, 5, 9, 26, 32, 47, 95, 104, 131, 136, 191

land cessions: and settlers, 192, 195; temporary use of, by Indians, 186

land offices in Michigan, 187, 196, 199, 200, 202, 208 n, 245

Land Ordinance (1785), 329

land sales: in Michigan, 245; legal process for, 245, 247

land for settlement by Indians: allotment of, 201; enfranchisement and buying, 199; Ottawas and Ojibwes buy, 196, 199–201; Ottawas and Ojibwes seek permanent, 186, 188, 193, 194; state of Michigan seeks more, 187

land speculation, in Michigan, 187, 195, 201, 245

Lanman, James H., 335

Lansing (Mich.), 315; bird's-eye view of, 257

Lapeer County (Mich.), 279, 280

L'Arbre Croche, Ottawas of, 71, 72–73, 181, 183, 184; seek to buy land, 194; write state governor, 194

latitude: 45th parallel of, 124, 125, 128; 49th parallel of, 120 n

League of American Wheelmen, 342

Lee, R. K., 220

Leelanau Peninsula: Indian settlements on, 188–89, 197, 198, 200, 201; resurveyed, 197

Legardeur de Saint-Pierre, Jacques, 70

Leland, Waldo G., 18, 20

Lenawee County, 270, 277, 278; atlas map for, 209, 218; economy of, 223

Léry, Gaspard-Joseph Chaussegros de, 24

Lewis, G. Malcolm, 4

Lewis, Kenneth, 8

Library of Congress, 20, 21–22, 49; checklist of Sanborn maps in, 256; panoramic views in, 242

Lincoln Highway, 290

List of Geographical Atlases in the Library of Congress, A, 22, 23

lithographic views, 253; in atlas-maps, 209, 214, 228, 233; as historical sources, 210, 236 n

Little Forks, reservation at, 155, 156

Little River, 74, 75

Livingston, Robert, 43

Livingston County (Mich.), 279

Lobben, Amy, 8

Locher, William, 250

Lodge, John, 328

London (Ont.), 101, 101

longitude, problems with, 45, 48–49, 325. *See also* meridians

Long Lake, as uncertain border marker, 114 n, 125, 137

long lots, 6, 149, 156

Long Point, 50

Long River (fictitious) across North America, 326, 348 n

"Louiland Farms," 233

Louisiana, 3, 6, 320, 323; map of, 31

Lower Peninsula of Michigan: Euro-American settlement of, 263–85; maps of, 6, 27, 28 174, 177, 336, 337; northern part little known, 173, 175, 191; perceived environmental regions of (map), 266; shape of, 10, 24, 26, 28, 32, 174, 175, 177, 178, 191, 334, 335. *See also* counties; Michigan, Mountains of; townships

Lowrie, Walter, 199

Loyalist refugees, 95, 96

Lucas, Fielding, Jr., atlas by, 331, 333

Lumberman's Memorial, 303

Lyon-Jenness, Cheryl, 7

Lyon, Lucius, 185, 187; as surveyor, 196–97

M

Macdonald, Craig, 56

Mackenzie, Alexander: contests St. Marys portage, 107; fame of, 111; reaches Arctic Ocean, 107, 122 n; reaches Pacific, 107, 108, 112

Mackenzie, Roderick, 94, 108

Mackinac, Straits of, 40, 71, 267

Mackinac Island, 183, 308

Macomb, Alexander, 128

Macomb County (Mich.), 277, 278

Madison (Wis.), 315

Manistee River, reservation on, 192, 193

Manitoulin Island, 131, 180, 184, 195

Mann, Adin, 221–22, 232

Mann, Gother: career, 111; report (1788) on Great Lakes by, 98–99

Manypenny, George, 201

Map of the American Lakes and the Adjoining Country, A (1813), 109

"Map of the Back Settlements" (1794), 329

Map of the British and French Dominions in North America (1755), 94, 95, 125, 328

"Map of Cambridge Township" (Lenawee County, 1874), 226

"Map of the Country about the Mississippi . . . Drawn by Chegeree (the Indian)," 50

Map of Michigan (1829), 331

Map of Michigan, Showing Distances between Railroad Stations, 344

Map of the Middle British Colonies in America, A, 50

Map of the North West Parts of the United States of America, 329

"Map of the North-West Territory of the Province of Canada," 94, 108, 111

"Map of the Northern Parts of the United States" (1804), 329, 330

"Map of Part of Canada from Bay de la Val and Island of Barnaby in the River St. Lawrence to the Lakes Huron and Erie" (1790), 92–93, 95

Map of the Province of Upper Canada, A (1800), 101–2

Map of the Surveyed Part of Michigan (1837), 178

Map of the Surveyed Part of the Territory of Michigan (1825), 176, 332

Map of the Territories of Michigan and Ouisconsin, (1830), 332

Map of United States of North America, A, 32

"Map of the Western Territory" (1796), 329

maps: aerial, 7, 9; bibliographies and lists of, 3, 4, 13, 14, 21–33, 23, 36–37 n; cadastral, 209, 211, 241–60; commercial, 7–8, 24, 26, 30, 43, 109, 209–60;

early publishing trade in, 26, 30, 43; electronic, 9; estate, 7; First Nations', 4, 39–57; and historical research, 242, 251, 255–60; inaccuracies in, 7, 8, 24, 26, 30, 30, 31, 32, 43, 94, 101, 101, 113 n, 115 n, 119 n, 173, 175, 210, 259, 322, 323; ignored by treaty makers, 96–97; manuscript and printed, 24, 26; perspective of, 255, 258; photostatic copies of, 3–4, 13, 19, 20, 20–21, 36 n; prices of, 17, 35 n, 104, 109; printing of, 7; route, 91–94; scale of, 41, 43, 55, 241, 253–55, 257–58; spatial perceptions in, 4, 39–42, 252–53; term for, absent in Indian languages, 40, 57–58 n; topographical, 145, 241. *See also* atlases; atlas maps, combination; bird's-eye views; cartography, study of history of; county maps; fire insurance maps; First Nations geographical knowledge and mapmaking; highway maps; maps, purposes of; plat maps; route maps for motorists; surveys
maps, purposes of: boundary marking, 5–6, 105, 126–43; civic education, 338; cosmological, 40, 43–45; delineating occupancy and reservations for Native Americans, 6, 55, 56, 57, 68, 82–85, 95–96, 145–72, 190, 327; delineating property, 6, 8, 55, 67, 75, 106, 107, 108, 209, 224, 241–60, 337, 340; delineating purchases and treaty cessions, 96, 175, 202 n; describing missions, 190; entrepreneurial profit, 7, 30, 43, 209–12, 251–56; expressing or exploiting local pride, 7, 209, 224, 242, 251–53, 288, 297, 300, 303, 308, 313–15, 319, 340; guiding and promoting Euro-American settlement, 7, 95–97, 101–2, 145–47, 175, 224, 334–35, 337, 338–41; guiding travelers, 9, 40–41, 43, 45–46, 51–53, 56, 91–94, 287–315, 340–46; imperial assertion, 10, 67, 69, 76, 94, 95, 323, 326–27; military, 46–47, 49–50, 98, 101–2, 108, 327; political control and planning, 5, 6, 48–49, 63–84, 94–95, 101–2, 106, 287–88, 293–4, 319, 327–28, 338; promoting specific businesses, 287; promoting trade and investment, 7, 45, 67–68, 69, 75, 106–8, 224, 308, 337, 338–40; promoting travel and tourism, 9, 56, 287–318, 344–46; recording new discoveries, 30, 42–43, 324; social and cultural research, 8, 53, 266–79;

Walling on, 337–38
Maps of the City of New York Surveyed under the Direction of Insurance Companies, 250
Marquette, Jacques, 322, 324
"Marvellous Minnesota," 294, 295
Mascoutins, 180, 183
Mason, Stevens T., and Indian land purchases, 194
Massey's Patent Log, 137
Matchebenashewish: reservation at, surveyed, 162, 164; map of reservation at, 163, 165
McCloskey, James, 164; instructions for surveys, 149–50; plat map by, 152; reservations surveyed by, 149, 150, 154, 167
McCracken, S. B., 340
McGillivray, William, 108, 111
McGregor Plan, 17, 35 n
"McGuirk Subdivision," plat map of, 246
McMurray, William, map by, 329
McNiff, Patrick, 111; maps by, 100, 101
Meigs, Josiah, 147, 148, 149
Menomonis, territories of, 83
Mercator, Gerhard, 320, 321
Mercator, Rumold, 321
meridians: as state boundaries, 329, 330; prime, 331; on state maps, 337; for survey of Michigan, 331
Métis, 6, 69; removal of, advocated, 77; role of, in fur trade, 77
Michigan, Mountains of (fictitious–also "elevated plain"), 26, 30, 31, 323, 325, 326, 328, 329
Michigan, State of: admission of, to Union, 187; bibliography of maps of, 3, 21–33, 25; bird's-eye views of places in, 253, 256; boundary with Upper Canada, 135; 1850 constitution of, 199; fire insurance maps of, 256; forests of, 187; format and contents of highway maps of, 291, 292, 294, 302, 305, 306, 309, 345, 347; French in, 10; as "Great Lakes State," 314, 319, 346; land hunger in, 187; maps of, 6, 27, 174, 176–79, 335–46, 336, 341, 343, 347; maps based on surveys of, 175, 176–78; meridian boundaries for, 329, 330; numbers highways, 342; and plat map access, 242, 246; resurvey of, 195, 196–99; self-presentation of, in

highway maps, 295, 297, 298, 302, 302–3, 308, 310, 314, 315, 346; survey of, 173, 191; township and range system in, 6, 8. *See also* Lower Peninsula of Michigan; Michigan, Territory of; Upper Peninsula

Michigan, Territory of: boundary of, 135; early estimates of resources of, 329, 331; Indian land cessions in, *146* (map), 265; land sales in, 245; land offices in, 187, 196, 199, 200, 202, 208 n, 245; maps of, 331–35; principal meridian of, 331; regional agricultural potential of, 265; survey of, 147, 245, 331. *See also* Lower Peninsula

"Michigan and the Great Lakes" (map, 1835), 332, 334

Michigan Bibliography (1921), 21, 22, 37 n

"Michigan of the Blue Waters" (1938), 297

"Michigan Builds a Modern Highway System" (1960), 305, 306

Michigan Central Railroad, 340, 342

Michigan Department of Transportation, 280, 306

Michigan Great Lake State Official Transportation Map (1974), 306, 308

Michigan Highways, Lakes, Streams, and Forests (1931), 294

Michigan Historical Commission, 21, 22

Michigan and Its Resources (1883), 338, 339

Michigan meridian, 203 n

Michigan 1960 Official Highway Map, 305, 306

Michigan Plat Act (1929), 246

Michigan Postal History, 276

Michigan: Prepared for the Commissioner of Immigration (1883), 341

Michigan . . . Route Book (1916), 342, 343

"Michigan Ter." (map, 1823), 333

Michigan Territory, 27, 173, 174, 175

Michilimackinac, 5, 51, 63, 64, 65, 67, 70, 98; Ottawas at, 180; proposed District of, 76–79, *79*, 84

Mickesawbe, 160, 162

Mickesawbe (reservation), 162; maps of, *161, 162*

Mide migration charts, 55

Midland County (Mich.), 273

Midland South quadrant, *167, 167*

Midwest, regional images of, 297, 300, 314–16

Miller, William A., 250

Milliken, William, 306, 308

Minnesota: early mapping of, 68, 82; format and contents of highway maps of, 306, *307*, 308; self-presentation of, in highway maps, *294, 295, 296, 297, 303, 310, 313, 314*

Minnesota, 1977–78 Transportation Map, 307, 308

Minnesota 1938 Official Map, 296, 303

Minnesota 1935 Official Map, 294, 295

"Minnesota Public Transportation Map" (1977), 306, *307*

missions, government support for, 187

Mississauga (Indians), 51, 73; land purchases from, 96, 97

Mississagi River, 131

Mississippi River, 6, 10, 50, 56, 95; as border marker, 107, 124, 125; English colonizing plans for, 326; maps of, 31, *66*; source of, sought, 136; as U.S. border, 124, 125; watershed of, mapped as central to penetrating North America, 320, 323, 324–27

Mitchell, John: creates map, 328; map by, used to negotiate Treaty of Paris, 94, 95, 125, 139

Mitchell, Samuel Augustus, 335

Mitchell's School Atlas, 335, 337

Mohawk River, 46

Mohawks, 95–96, 97

Moll, Hermann, 26, 326

Monroe (Mich.), 276; County, 277

Montcalm County (Mich.), 280; Township, 258

Montreal: British capture, 65, and fur trade, 77; trading center, 101

monuments (in surveying), 243, 245

Morden, Robert, maps by, 323

Morrison, James, 51

Morse, Jedidiah, 128, 329

mosquitoes, 112, 133, 189

Mount Pleasant (Mich.): bird's-eye view of (1884), 252, 258; fire insurance map of (1931), 248; plat maps of, 244, 246, 256, 257

Mullett, John: plat map by, 165; reservations surveyed by, 159, 160–61, 162, 163, 164, 187

Münster, Sebastian, 320

Muskegon: County, 280; post office at, 275

N

National Bureau of Fire Underwriters, 251

National Map Company, 344

Native Americans: dispossession of, 167–68; education of, 187, 189, 190, 200; limited enfranchisement of, by Michigan, 199; fears of public land sales among, 193–94, 196; buying land for settlement, 194, 196, 199–201; settlements of, omitted by most commercial mapmakers, 175; settlements of, mapped by Dougherty, 175, 181, 182; stereotyped, 300; temporary use of ceded lands by, 186; treaties alienate lands of, 145–47, 146, 159, 185–86, 187. *See also* First Nations; reservations; *treaties by name*; *tribes by name*

Native peoples. *See* First Nations; Native Americans

"Naudowessie Republic," 83

navigation, aids to, 104, 105

Neebish Rapids, 131, 136

Nelson, George, 53

Neshnabe: land losses of, by treaties, 145–46, 159; protests against land surveys by, 156, 159–60; temporary reservations of, taken by treaties, 164; responses to reservation surveys by, 168. *See also* Ojibwes; Ottawas; Potawatomis

New and Correct Map of United States of North America, A, 329

New Haven quadrant: USGS map of, *167*; temporary reservation in, *167*, 167

New Map of Michigan (1844), 331

"New Map of the English Empire in America, A," 323

"New Map of the United States" (1829), 332

New Orleans, 325; traders from, *77*

"New Railroad and Township Map of Michigan" (1870), 338

New Sectional Map of Michigan, A (1879), 340

New York City, fire insurance mapping in, 249–50

Newaygo County, 280

Niagara, Fort, 49, 50

Niagara Falls, 41; route around, 98, 106

Niagara-on-the-Lake, 101

Niagara River: border in, 133; maps of, 96, 101

1976–1977 Official Transportation Map, Michigan, Great Lake

State, 309

1969 Official Ohio Highway Map and Economic Digest, 308

1936 Official Michigan Highway Map, 298

Noble, Charles, 197

Norris, George, 253

North, Lord, 96

North America, early map portrayals of, 320–26, *324*

North Carolina, 320; highway map of, 287

North Channel (Lake Huron), 40, 51, 56; surveyed, 131, 133

North West Company, 51, 91, 94, 126, 135, 136; exploration and mapmaking by, 106–8, 111

Northwest Ordinance, 243, 245, 264; state boundaries proposed by, 329, 330

Northwest Passage, 63

Northwest Passage: dream of, distorts early maps, 320–21, 322, 326, 348 n; search for, 63, 64–66, 67, 68–69, 76, 78, 79–80, 82, 83, 84, 85 n, 107, 112, 320. *See also* western sea

Northwest Territory, 319, 329

Northwood Map Designs, 313

Norvell (Mich.), bird's-eye view of, 221

Nottawasepe, reservation at, 162, 164

Noyelles de Fleurimont, Nicolas-Joseph de, 70

O

Oakland County (Mich.), 270, 278

Oceana Township (Mich.), 273

Odawas. *See* Ottawas

Official Summer Highway Map of Michigan, 1942, 302

Ogilvy, John, 111, 126, 128

Ohio: format and contents of highway maps of, 290, 291, 292, 304, 306, 308; self-presentation of, in highway maps, 303, 308, 309, 310, 314, 315, 318 n

Ohio River, 40, 45, 48, 48, 49, 50

Ojibwes, 69, 71, 72, 73, 75, 329; buy forty-acre plots, 200; dispute with Cass, 135; efforts of, to keep lands in Michigan, 194–96, 199–202; and Euro-American settlers, 265; land grants by, 67–68, 75, 76; land cessions by, 187, 195; land purchased from, 96, 120 n; language, 40; maps by, 53, 54, 55–56;

major settlements of, 183; migration charts, 55; Mississauga division of, 203 n; settlement around Grand Traverse Bay, 183; territories of, 83, 183; and treaty of 1855, 201–2; U.S. government backs permanent residence of, in Michigan, 200–2; Upper Peninsula division of, 203 n. *See also* Grand Traverse Ojibwes and Ottawas reservation; Neshnabe; Treaty of Washington

Old Mission Peninsula, 183; after reservation ended, 202; map of, *197, 198;* selected as reservation, 191, 193; settlements on, 197; surveyed, 191

Old Ship Channel (Lake St. Clair), as border, 131

Olsen, Marilyn, 101, 104

Oneida Lake, 46

Oneidas, 46

Onomunese, 200

Ontonagon River, *74, 75*

Onuf, Peter, 223

Ortelius, Abraham, 41, 321

orthographic perspective, 258

Oshawan Epenaysee, 185

Oswego, 46

Otsego Lake, 46

Ottawa County (Mich.), 268, 280

Ottawa River, 45, 96, 97

Ottawas, 42, 55, 69, 71, 72, 73, 75, 329; divisions over land sales by, 185; efforts to retain lands in Michigan, 194–96, 199–202; land cessions by, 187; migrations of, 180–81; new settlements of, 200; offer to sell Drummond Island, 184; and smallpox, 183; territories of, 83, 180–81, 183; trading by, 180, 181; treaty of 1855 with, 201–2; U.S. government backs permanent residence of, in Michigan, 200–2. *See also* Grand Traverse Ojibwes and Ottawas reservation; Neshnabe; Treaty of Washington

"Ottigaumies, Kingdom of," 83

Outdoor Illinois (1929), 294

Owen, Edward, 103, 104

Owen, William, 103–4, 109, 111

P

Paige, H. R., 220

panoramic views. *See* bird's-eye views

Pape, Bruce, 8

Paris, archives in, 20, 21

Parkman, Francis, 321

Patrons of Husbandry, 223

Patton, David, 8

Pauli, Clemens J., 253

Pearce, Margaret Wickens, 6

Pedley, Mary Sponberg, 3

Pelee Island, 50

Penetanguishene, 108, *110*

Perris, William, 250

Perry, Oliver Hazard, 126

Peshawbe, 200

Phelippeaux, Jean Frederic, Count de Maurepas, island named for, 94

Phillips, Philip Lee, 21–22, 23

"Pictorial History of Wisconsin," 299

Pigeon River canoe route, 136; as border marker, 138, 139. *See also* Grand Portage

Pincier, Theodore de, 107, 120 n

"Plan by Actual Survey of the Street of Communication between Kempenfeldt Bay on Lake Simcoe and Penetangushene Harbour on Lake Huron" (1812), *110*

"Plan of the Province of Upper Canada" (1795), 101

plat books: contents of, 246; limitations of, 246–47, 256; omission of cities in, 246; unofficial status of, 247

plat maps, 8, 241, 242–47, 252; access to, 242; and atlas maps, 217, 224, 226; consistency of, 260; contents of, 245, 258; coverage by, 255–56; and historical research, 242, 243, 255–57, 259; illustrations of, *151, 152, 153, 158, 165, 166, 167, 244, 246;* scale of, 257

Plimpton, George A., 15, 17

Point Pelee, 133

Pond, Peter, 106, 107, 111, 112, 122 n

Pontiac (person), 65

Pontiac (Mich.), 277, 280; fire insurance map of (1888), *248*

Popple, Henry, maps by, 26, 327–28

Porcacchi, Tomaso, 321

Porter, Peter B., 101, 105, 126; as border commissioner, 126, 128, 133, 135, 137, 138

Port Huron, reservation at, maps of, 148, 149, 150

post offices in lower Michigan: and antebellum economy, 274, 280–81; central location of, in agricultural settlements, 274–75; consolidated with rural free delivery, 282, 285 n; establishment of, 8, 196; and growth of federal postal system, 284 n; maps showing, 276, 277, 278, 279; multiply near cities, 280–81; at ports in extractive regions, 275–76, 279; and post roads, 284 n; residents petition for, 275

Potawatomis, 75, 329; removal of, 193–94. See also Neshnabe

Power of Maps, The, 287

Powhatan, 44

Prairie Ronde, reservation at, surveyed, 164

Presbyterian Board of Foreign Missions, 173, 187–88, 196, 199, 201, 202

Presque Isle, 50

Preston, William: plat map by, 151; reservations surveyed by, 149

Price, Chase, 75

Principal Navigations . . . of the English Nation (1599), 321

ProQuest Information and Learning Company, 242

Public Domain Commission (Michigan), 340

public land sales, 193–94, 196. See also land offices

Public Land Survey, 145, 147, 195. See also surveys; township and range system

Purchas, Samuel, 321

Q

Quaife, Milo, 131

Quebec Act (1774) boundary line, 124–25

R

Radcliff, Charles H., 220

Radcliff, William M., bird's-eye view by, 221; career of, 220

Railroad Map of Michigan (1874), 338

"Railroad and Township Map of Michigan" (1875), 340

railroads: in atlases, 345; electric (interurban) on maps, 344, 345; on general maps, 345; maps issued by, 340, 342; maps of, changed to road maps, 344–45; on Michigan maps, 335, 337; official Michigan maps of, 340

Rainy Lake, 83, 136

Rand McNally, 217, 287, 340, 342, 344–45

Rand McNally and Company's Township, County, and Railroad Map of Michigan (1876), 340

Rand McNally's Official Auto Trails Map, District No. 3: Southern Peninsula of Michigan (1918), 345

Rat Portage canoe route, 105; as border marker, 136, 137

Raymond, Chevalier de, 71–72

Read, Molly E., 9

Reaume, Joseph, 69, 81

Rebert, Paula, 5

"Red Head, an Onondaga Indian," map by, 46, 47

removal, 189; fears of, 193–94; and Indian Removal Act (1830), 185; of Neshnabe, from Lower Michigan, 164; of Potawatomis, from Michigan, 193–94; proposed for northern Lower Michigan, 186; resisted by Indians, 186, 193–94; timing of, 192; U.S. Senate abandons idea of for Ojibwes and Ottawas, 200

Reps, John W., 7, 251, 253, 256

reservations, Indian, 55; mapped by Schoolcraft, 175. See also reservations, temporary Indian

reservations, temporary Indian, 6; chiefs' role in locating and surveying, 156, 159, 162, 164; and current villages, 149, 156; described in Treaty of Chicago, 159; described in Treaty of Detroit, 148; described in Treaty of Saginaw, 155; failure to survey or establish, 192, 193; grid-congruent shape for, 149–50, 154, 156, 159, 162, 164; as "holes" in township grid system, 147, 151, 153, 158, 164, 165, 168; maps showing, 148, 150–53, 155, 157–59, 161–63, 164, 165–69, 165, 166–69, 167; petition to extend term of, 195; resistance to survey of, 156, 160; survey instructions for, 148–50, 154, 159; surveying of,

145–72, 187, 192; surveyors of, 149, 154; temporary nature of, 154, 186, 192, 193; taken under treaties, 164; traces of, in physical landscape, 167, 167–69; under Treaty of Washington, 185, 186, 189, 191–93; and U.S. Senate, 186, 201–2; valuable sites excluded from, 149-50, 156

Reyneval, Joseph-Matthias Gérard de, 124

Rhodes, James, 308

Rice Lake (Minn.), 56

Rideau River, 96

Ridout, Thomas, 109, 111

Riel, Louis, 6

Rio Grande River, 5

Risdon, Orange, map published by, 176, 332; surveys by, 197

Ristow, Walter W., 257

River Raisin: maps of reservations on, 152, 153; reservations on, surveyed, 150; reservation boundary still visible, 167, 169

River Rouge, reservation on, surveyed, 150

rivers: channel use rights in, 139; estimating distances on, 49, 137; main channels of, used as boundaries, 127, 133; travel by, 40, 43, 48–49, 56

road maps. *See* highway maps

roads, 9; and bicycles, 342; condition of, 190; dropped from maps, 342; federal aid for constructing, 288; general maps show railroads instead of, 345; in Michigan, 187, 278, 284 n, 332, 333, 334, 342; military and trading, in Upper Canada, 101, 101, 108, 120 n; organized into trunk and numbered routes by states, 290, 291, 342; paving of, 342; pioneer, 333, 334–35, 351 n; signs along, 288, 290, 291, 314, 342, 344; state construction of, 288, 342. *See also* highway maps; interstate highways

Roberts, Benjamin, 72

Roberts, Kenneth, 63

Robinson, Rix, 185

Robinson Treaty (1850), 56

Robutel de la Noue, Zacharie, 69

Rockingham, Lord, 75

Rogers, Elizabeth Browne, 65

Rogers, Robert, 5; appointed commandant at Michilimackinac, 67, 78, 85 n; cedes land, 74, 75; conflict of, with Johnson and Roberts, 72; court martial of, 65, 82; disobeys orders, 78, 88 n; diplomacy of, with Indians, 71–74, 80; efforts to create colony centered at Mackinac, 64–65, 75–77, 78–79, 84; gifts of, to Indians, 72–73, 80; and grand council (1767), 73–74; granted land by Lake Superior Chippewa, 67–68, 82, 86 n; in literature and history, 63–64; instructs Carver and Tute, 68–69, 81; map for, 63–64, 64, 68, 78–81, 79; requests governorship, 65–67, 68, 70, 75, 77, 79; revives fur trade, 65, 68, 74–75. *See also* Northwest Passage, search for

route maps for motorists, 288, 342, 344–45

Royal Navy Hydrographic Office, 5, 103–4, 118 n

Royce, Charles C., 193

Ruger, Albert, 254

Rundstrom, Robert, 57

Rush, Richard, 133, 134

Rush-Bagot Agreement (1817), 133

Russell, William, 328

S

Sabin, Joseph, 21

Saginaw Bay, settlement around, 267, 280

Saginaw County (Mich.), 280

Saginaw River drainage region: and Euro-American settlers, 265, 267, 270, 271, 272, 273, 274, 278, 280, 281; map showing, 266

Saginaw Township, 271

St. Anthony, Falls of, 68, 69

St. Clair County (Mich.), 280

St. Clair River, 119 n; channels in, debated as national border, 131; map of land claims and reservations along, 150; surveyed, 131, 133

St. Croix River, 56, 97

St. Joseph Island, 131, 133, 141 n

St. Joseph River drainage: Euro-American settlers in, 265, 267, 270, 277–78; map shows, 266; surveying Neshnabe lands in, 159–64

St. Lawrence River, 5, 10, 40–41, 45, 96; border in,

133, 139; extended on early maps, 321; watershed mapped as central to penetrating North America, 320–22, 325; maps of, 46, 47, 119 n, 321–22; surveys of, 103, 128

St. Louis River, as possible border marker, 137, 138; surveyed, 137

St. Marys River, 135; described, 136; map of, 101; portage at rapids of, 107, 120 n; problems deciding border along, 136; surveyed, 131

Salisbury, G. W., 220

Salmon River, 46, 47

Sanborn, Daniel Alfred, 250

Sanborn Map Company, 8, 242, 247, 250–51; maps by, 248, 249, 253, 256, 257, 258, 260, 260 n

Sanilac County (Mich.), 280

Sanson, Nicolas, 26, 320; maps by, 28, 46, 322, 324

"Saugies, Kingdom of," 83

Sault Ste. Marie, 40, 98, 136; importance of, 135

Savoy, 4

Scherer, Heinrich, map by, 326

Scheybl, Johann, 16

Schoolcraft, Henry Rowe, 6, 55, 56, 135, 183; career of, 184, 195; dismissed as Michigan Indian Superintendent, 195; Michigan map by, 175, 179; and missions, 187–88, 189–90; nepotism by, 193; and reservations, 187, 191–92; suggests removal, 195; as treaty negotiator, 184–86

Schoolcraft, James, 191

Scotland, 3

Selkirk, Thomas, 109, 111

Senex, John, 323

Sereno, Paola, 4

Seutter, Matthias, 326

Shabwasson, 183, 197, 200

Shaw, Angus, 108, 110

Shawanaga Reserve, 56

Shiawassee County, 280; post office for, 275

Shiawassee River, reservation on, 155, 159

Simcoe, John Graves: as governor of Upper Canada, 101–2, 117 n; and exploration, 112; and land surveys, 105–6, 109; mocked by Brant, 101

Sioux, 71, 80, 81, 83

Skeel, B. A., 220

"Sketch of the Country from Fort Du Quesne to Niagara" (map), 48, 49

"Sketch of Grand Traverse Bay" (1839), 181; (1840), 182

"Sketch of the North Shore of Lake Superior, A" (1794), 102

"Sketch Plan of Lake Neepigon," 54

"Sketch of the River St. Lawrence from Lake Ontario to Montreal by an Onondaga Indian," 47

Slater, Leonard, 185

Smith, David (Canadian survey official), 106, 109; land speculation and career, 111

Smith, David Eugene, 15, 17

Smith, George N., 197, 200

Smith, John, 43–45; map by, 45, 52

Smith, Joseph (Indian agent), 156

Smithsonian Institution, 55

Some Considerations on the French Settling Colonies on the Mississippi, 326

South Carolina, 7, 22, 49

Southeast in Early Maps, 22

Spain, 3; and Indians (British view), 73; land claims in 1782, 124

Spiesmaker, Frederick, 82

Springfield (Ill.), 315

stagecoach routes, 9, 187, 342

State Highway System of Indiana (1925), 289

State of Michigan, The (1876), 338

State Parks of Michigan (1930), 294

State of Wisconsin, . . . 1935 Map Showing State and Federal Highway Routes, 299

Stebbins, Henry S., maps by, 338, 340, 341

Steele, Oliver Gray, maps by, 334

Stewart, David J., 209, 210, 215, 217, 232

Stevens, Henry N., 36 n

Stockdale, John, map by, 329

Stoner, J. J., 253

Stoney Island, 133, 134, 135

Streeter, Floyd Benjamin, 21, 22

Stuart, Robert, 185, 195

"Successful Farming's Michigan Auto Road Map" (1920), 344

Sugar Island (in Detroit River), 133, 134, 135

Sugar Island (in St. Marys River), 136; disputed, 138; to U.S., 139

"Superintendency of Michigan, Map of the Acting" (1837), 179

"Survey of Lake Ontario, A" (1783, 1789), 99

"Survey of the South Shore of Lake Erie, A" (1789), 100

surveyors: for atlas maps, 217, 221–22; careers and earnings of, 109, 111, 121 n, 127, 159, 196–97, 211, 219, 221–22, 223, 332; dangers and hardships of, 111–12, 114 n, 122 n, 128, 132, 133, 137, 190; for fire insurance maps, 250; instruments of, 109, 118 n, 121 n, 137, 146, 224, 238 n; land speculation by, 111, 122 n; methods of, 105, 128, 131, 136, 137, 146–47, 154; and plat maps, 243; qualifications of, 121 n; and Indian reservations, 146–49, 154. *See also* boundary commissions under Treaty of Ghent

surveys: by astronomical sightings, 137; eighteenth-century British, 49, 68–69, 95, 97, 98; of Grand Traverse region, 190, 191; of Indian reservations, 6, 145–72; menace temporary reservations, 195; in Michigan, 190, 195–96, 245; *precede* annuity payments, 156, 159–60; regulation of, 109; of road to Georgian Bay, 108; suggest progress on maps, 332, 334; of townships in Upper Canada, 105–6; by triangulation, 105, 128, 131, 136, 137; by U.S-British boundary commission, 5, 105; of U.S.-Mexican border, 5–6. *See also* hydrographic surveys, British; plat maps; township and range system

Susquehanna River, maps of, 45–46

Susquehannas, 45–46

T

Tanner, Helen Hornbeck, 6

Tanner, Henry S., map by, 331, 334

Tatausay, map by, 56

Tavernier, Gabriel, 43

Tecumseh (Mich.), 277

Texas, 3, 4, 5, 8, 10

Thames River (Ont.), 101, 101, 117 n

Theatrum Orbis Terrarum (1570–), 41, 321

Thessalon, 98

Thompson, David: career of, 107–8, 111, 112, 127; maps by, 94, 108, 111; surveying Lake Superior and westward, 107–8, 120 n; as surveyor for boundary commissions, 127, 131, 133, 135

Thompson and Everts, 211–12; headquarters of, 213

Thompson, Moses, 211, 215

Thompson, Samuel, 137

Thompson, Thomas Hinkley, 211, 215

Thornapple River valley, 265, 279

Thousand Islands, 46, 47; survey of, 128

Thumb (region of Michigan), Euro-American settlers in, 267, 271, 272, 273, 280, 281

Tiarks, Johann Ludwig, 108, 137

Tiffin, Edward, 149, 150, 164, 168, 331

Tittabawassee Township (Mich.), 273

Toledo (Ohio), 187

Topographical Description of the Province of Lower Canada, 109

Toronto, 51; becomes capital, 101; map of, 97; route from, 97, 98

Tourist's Pocket Map of Michigan (1834, 1839), 335, 336

Townshend, Charles, 67, 75–76, 77, 78

township-and-range system, 6, 8, 146–47, 243

townships: in atlas-maps, 209, 211–12, 214, 224–25, 226; formation and subdivision in lower Michigan, 269–74; in lower Michigan, maps of, 270, 271, 271, 272, 273, 273; on state maps in atlases, 337, 338; surveyed in Upper Canada, 105–6, 119 n; survey grid in Michigan, 150; resurveyed in Michigan, 195, 196–97

trails, travel by, 40, 200

transportation, state departments of, 280, 306, 308

Transportation Map, Iowa (1991), 311

treaties with Indians: Canadian, 56; in Michigan, 145–47, 146, 201–2; roles of maps in, 56. See *treaties by name*

Treatise of the Northwest Passage, 321

"Treaty boundaries of lower Michigan" (map), 146

Treaty of Brownstown, 149

Treaty of Chicago (1821), 146, 147; Indian removal under, 193–94; late annuity payments under, 160;

boundaries uncertain, 164; conflict over surveys under, 159–60; reservations named in, 159, *159*; surveys of reservations under, 159–64; temporary reservations taken by later treaties, 164

Treaty of Detroit (1807), *146*, 331; reservations in, 147, *148*, 150–53, 164

Treaty of Detroit (1855), 201–2

Treaty of Ghent, 5, 131; establishes boundary commissions, 104–5, 126; negotiation of, 126. *See also* boundary commissions under Treaty of Ghent

Treaty of Greenville (1795), 146, 147, 183

Treaty of Guadalupe Hidalgo, 5

Treaty of Paris, 91, 94, 104; geographical errors in, 95, 114 n, 139, 328; negotiation of, 122–26; border proposals for, 124–25; U.S.-British border provisions in, 125

Treaty of Saginaw (1819), *146*, 147; cessions inaccurately mapped; *174*, 202 n; maps of reservations named in, *155*, *157*, *167*; protest against late annuities under, 156; reservations in, 154, 156, *157*, 164

Treaty of St. Joseph (1827), 164

Treaty of Washington (1836): land cessions under, 187; negotiation of, 184–86; provisions of, 185–86, 187; reservations under, 191–93, 195

Trowbridge, Charles C., 185

Trygg, J. William, map by, *197*, *198*, *199*, 207 n

Tuscola County (Mich.), 280; Township, 273

Tute, James, 67, 78, 82; exploring instructions, 68–69, 81

Tyler, Moses Coit, 35 n

U

Umfreville, Edward, 91–94

United States Department of Transportation, 306

United States Geological Survey: maps by, 145, 242; temporary reservations visible on maps of, 164, 165–69, *167*

University of Michigan, 14, 15, 16, 18

Upper Canada, mapping of, 91–122

Upper Peninsula: acquisition of, by Michigan, 187; as "Cloverland," 345; mapping of, 68, 337, 338, 345; omission of, from map, 338

"U.S. Highways Leading to Minnesota" (1938), 296

Utah, 6

V

Van Tyne, Claude, 20, 21

Verrazano, Giovanni da, 320

Verrazano, Sea of, 320

View of the Valley of the Mississippi, or, the Emigrant's and Traveler's Guide (1832–34), 334–35

Views and Viewmakers of Urban America, 253

Vigneau, Henri, 18

Virginia, 3, 44–45, 94

Visscher, Nicolas, map by, 322

Voyages from Montreal . . . to the Frozen and Pacific Oceans, 111

W

Wabash River, 6, 49

Wagner, Henry, 22

Waldburg-Wolfegg, Prince Max, 17

Waldseemüller world map, 17, 35 n

Walk-in-the-Water (steamboat), 128, 131

Walling, Henry Francis, 224; and *Atlas of the State of Michigan*, 337–38; on maps' purposes, 337–38

Wampler, Joseph: maps of reservations surveyed by, *155*, *157*, *166*, *167*; reservations surveyed by, 154, 156

wampum belts, 55, 71, 72, 75; presented to Robert Rogers, *76*

War of 1812, 125–26, 133, 308; land grants from, 245; mapmaking in, 101–2, 108, 109; road building in, 108

Washington, D.C., as prime meridian, 331

Washtenaw County, 270, 278; atlas map for, *209*, *218*, *225*; economy of, 223

Waukazoo (chief), 200

Wayne County (Mich.), 342

Weber, Hans, 15

Webster-Ashburton Treaty (1842), 138–39

Webster, Daniel, 138, 139

Wedge, Henry, 253

Wendats. *See* Wyandots

western sea, hopes for route to, 44–45, 320

Wheat, Carl I., 3

Wheelock, Cyrus, 220

Whinnery, W. P., 220

Whistler, George W., 135

Whitcomb, James W., 191

Whitefield, George, 55

Widder, Keith, 5

Wieser, Franz von, 17

Wieser, Hans von, 17

Wilkinson, James, *Memoirs*, 103

William L. Clements Library, 17, 18

Williams, Glyn, 69

Wilmot, Samuel, map by, 108, 110

Winchell, Alexander, 224, 338

Winearls, Joan, 5

Winnebagos, territories of, 83

Wisconsin: early mapping of, 68, 82, 332; format and contents of highway maps of, 290, 291, 292, 292, 310, 311, 312; numbers roads, 290, 342; self-presentation of, in highway maps, 294, 297–98, 299, 308, 310, 313, 314–15

Wisconsin Highway Map, 1973, 312

Wisconsin Tour and Highway Map (1996), 313

Wood, Dennis, 287

World's Fair, Chicago (1933–34), 300

World War II war effort, 300, 301–2

World Wide Web. *See* Internet

Wolcott, Alexander, 159

Wright, Edward, 321

Wyandots: instructions to surveyor of reservation for, 149–50; land losses by treaties, 145; reservation surveyed, 150. See also Hurons

Wyatt, C. B., 109, 111

X

XY Company, 107

Y

Yale University, 17

Yonge Street, 101, 101, 108, 120 n

Young, J. H., map by, 335, 336

York (Upper Canada). *See* Toronto

York Factory, 51

York River, 43

Ypsilanti, 223

Z

Ziwet, Alexander, 15